Entrepreneurship
& Small Business Management

Student Resources

Log on to **entrepreneurship.glencoe.com**

Online Learning Center

- Interactive Practice Tests
- Vocabulary Puzzles and Games
- Software Application Activities
- Business Math Practice Tests
- Graphic Organizers

Business Plan Project Resources

- Business Plan Project Unit Labs
- Business Plan Project Appendix
- *Business Plan Project Workbook*
- Business Plan Project Template

Entrepreneurship
And Small Business Management

Kathleen R. Allen Ph.D.
Director, Center for Technology Commercialization
Professor, Entrepreneurship
Marshall School of Business
University of Southern California
Los Angeles, CA

Earl C. Meyer, Ph.D.
Professor Emeritus of Marketing Education
Department of Business and Technology Education
Eastern Michigan University
Ypsilanti, MI

New York, New York   Columbus, Ohio   Chicago, Illinois   Woodland Hills, California

Glencoe

The McGraw-Hill Companies

Printed in the United States of America

Send all inquiries to:
Glencoe/McGraw-Hill
21600 Oxnard Street Suite 500
Woodland Hills, CA 91367

ISBN 0-07-861303-5 (Student Edition)
ISBN 0-07-867759-9 (Teacher Annotated Edition)

8 9 079   09 08

Reviewers

GRACE M. BRADY

Marketing Teacher, DECA Advisor, Vocational Education Department Chair

Redmond High School

Redmond, WA

YVETTA CHURCHILL

Marketing Coordinator

Columbia High School

Decatur, GA

CHARLES CORNWELL

Marketing Teacher

Libbey High School

Toledo, OH

TERRY ELLIOT

Marketing Educator, DECA Advisor, Department Chair

Lakewood High School

Lakewood, CO

PATTY EVANS

Marketing Instructor

Taylor County High School

Campbellsville, KY

RICH GAARD

Decorah High School

Marketing Education Coordinator, DECA Advisor

Decorah, IA

BOB HICKEY

Business and Technology Department Chair

Brookwood High School

Snellville, GA

LAVONIA JOHNSON

Business Education Instructor

Floyd D. Johnson Technology Center

York, SC

TERESA JONES

Marketing Education Instructor

Santa Monica High School

Santa Monica, CA

HORACE C. ROBERTSON

CTE Regional Coordinator for Central Region

North Carolina Department of Public Instruction

Raleigh, NC

MICHAEL VIALPANDO

Business Marketing Department Chair

La Joya Community High School

Avondale, AZ

DARLENE WHITLOCK

Teacher

Fort Madison High School

Fort Madison, IA

About the Authors

DR. KATHLEEN R. ALLEN is a recognized authority on entrepreneurship and technology commercialization. Allen is the author of *Launching New Ventures* 4th Ed., *Bringing New Technology to Market,* and several trade books. She has also written for business magazines and newspapers and is called upon by the media for expert opinion on entrepreneurship.

As a professor of entrepreneurship at the nationally ranked Lloyd Greif Center for Entrepreneurial Studies in the Marshall School of Business at the University of Southern California, she has helped hundreds of young entrepreneurs start new ventures. She is also the director of the Center for Technology Commercialization at USC and leads an NSF-funded effort to create a national commercialization network. As an entrepreneur, Allen was involved in commercial real estate development for the past 15 years, having co-founded a development firm and a brokerage, which she sold. She is co-founder of two technology ventures and is a director of an NYSE company. Allen holds a bachelor's degree in music and foreign language, a master's degree in romance languages, an MBA, and a Ph.D. with a research emphasis in entrepreneurship.

DR. EARL C. MEYER has extensive experience in both business and education. Formerly a teacher of marketing and entrepreneurship at Eastern Michigan University, he has served as base coordinator and faculty member for Southern Illinois University and was also a high school marketing education teacher-coordinator. At the secondary level, he taught entrepreneurship for 8 years. For 16 years prior to moving into education, he was involved in advertising sales, retail, and financial services management. He has also owned and operated his own golf enterprise and quick serve restaurant.

Meyer has been the project director and principal writer for curriculum guides that address three stages of entrepreneurship education. He also authored articles, made state and national presentations, and held workshops on teaching entrepreneurship. In addition, he represented Michigan in the International Consortium for Entrepreneurship Education for which he has served as president and executive board member. He was also the co-founding chair of the Entrepreneurship Professional Interest Category of the national Marketing Education Association.

Meyer holds a bachelor's degree in marketing education from the University of South Florida. He has a master's degree and Ph.D. in vocational and career development (with an emphasis in marketing education) from Georgia State University.

Brief Table of Contents

Table of Contents

Table of Contents

Table of Contents

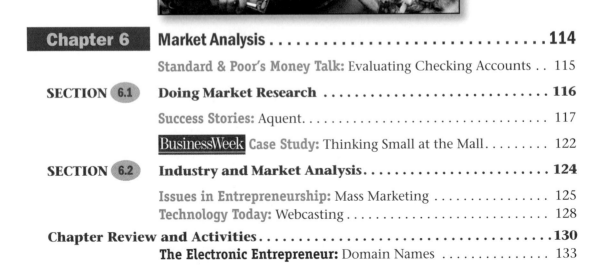

Table of Contents

Table of Contents

Table of Contents

Table of Contents

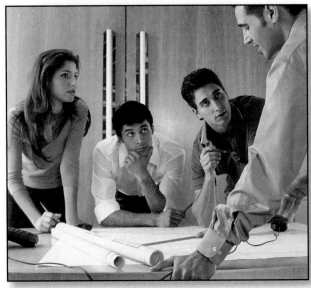

UNIT 4   MANAGING YOUR BUSINESS PROCESSES 302

Table of Contents

Table of Contents

Welcome to Entrepreneurship and Small Business Management

Do you dream of being your own boss? Do you have a great idea for a product or service? Have you always wanted to open up and run your own business? This book will provide you with the tools you will need to become a successful entrepreneur.

First you will learn about what it takes to go into business for yourself. You will learn what entrepreneurship is and about your potential to become an entrepreneur. You will find out how to recognize opportunities for business by understanding entrepreneurial trends, evaluating whether to start or buy a business, and by assessing global opportunities.

Once you decide on the kind of business you will launch, you will learn how to research and plan the venture. In this book you will learn about feasibility and business planning, market analysis, the different types of business ownership, the legal environment, and how to select a business site and plan its layout.

From there, you will learn about managing different aspects of your business. You will learn about managing marketing strategies. You will find out how to manage business processes, such as purchasing and inventory, production management and inventory, operations and staffing, and human resources. And, you will learn how to manage the finances of your business by taking a close look at options for financing, financial management, and accounting and record keeping procedures.

Finally, you will focus on the issues that must be addressed in order for your business to survive, grow, and profit. You will find out about risk management and learn how to identify and deal with business risks. You will learn how to make your business grow by managing growth and by examining the challenges of expansion. Then you will learn about the very important role that social and ethical responsibility have in making your business prosper.

Competitive Events and Entrepreneurship

It is likely that participation in competitive events and objective tests will be an important part of your learning experience in the Entrepreneurship course. Competitive events can help you to develop poise and presentation skills. They also help with learning and critical thinking skills.

Student Organizations

Competitive events and exams are sponsored by national student organizations that promote interest and excellence in business education for high school students. You will find that participation in these objective exams and competitive events are designed to test your skills, knowledge, and ability in specific business fields.

Developing Skills

Participating in competitive events offers you an opportunity to:

- Build self-esteem.
- Develop leadership and problem-solving skills.
- Understand the importance of making ethical decisions.
- Develop your public speaking and presentation skills.
- Enhance your entrepreneurial skills.
- Increase your self-confidence.
- Develop proper social and business etiquette.
- Develop your character.
- Analyze possible solutions to specific business problems.
- Develop business leadership skills.
- Increase your understanding of American business.
- Practice community service.

Individual and Team Events

There are competitive events for individuals and teams. Individual events often involve a written exam and role-play events. Team events often include writing a professional report or manual and then completing an interview with judges to discuss the report. You can compete on a local level and then may advance to state and national competition.

Role Playing

Role playing involves participants and observers in a real problem situation. The process enables you to gain insight into your own values, attitudes and perceptions.

In preparation for role playing, the problem must be clearly defined and the roles must be assigned. Following the enactment, discussion and evaluation take place. Role playing in entrepreneurship enables students to act upon, experience, and gain further insight into problem-solving situations and the problem-solving processes that are important components of the entrepreneurial process.

Previewing Your Textbook

Understanding the Chapter

Each chapter focuses on one specific area of entrepreneurship, such as market analysis or risk management.

Chapter Objectives

The **Chapter Objectives** list learning goals that are easy to understand and achieve. The objectives preview the chapter's key concepts, clearly explaining what you will accomplish.

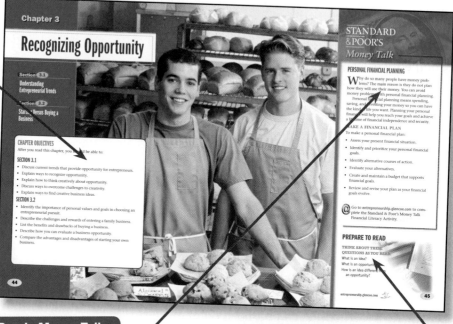

Standard & Poor's Money Talk

The **Standard and Poor's Money Talk** feature examines and promotes financial literacy, discusses the importance of financial goals, and teaches you how to integrate financial planning into your life.

Prepare to Read

Prepare to Read guides your reading by proposing questions to consider to help you prepare for the reading process. These questions correspond to the section topics.

Understanding the Chapter Review and Activities

Each **Chapter Review and Activities** is designed to help you recall, use, and expand on the concepts presented in the chapter.

- The **Chapter Summary** provides an overview of the main concepts in the chapter.
- The **Key Terms Review** is an activity that will help to reinforce your understanding of new vocabulary.
- The **Key Concept Review** asks you to respond to questions about the chapter's main ideas.
- **Critical Thinking** activities are designed to challenge you to use higher-level thinking.
- **Write About It** presents real-world writing assignments relevant to entrepreneurship.

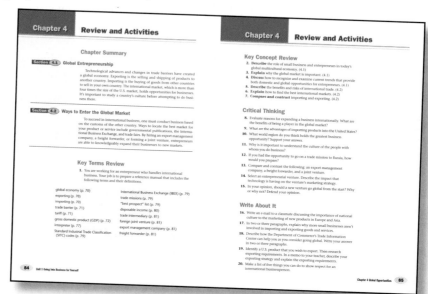

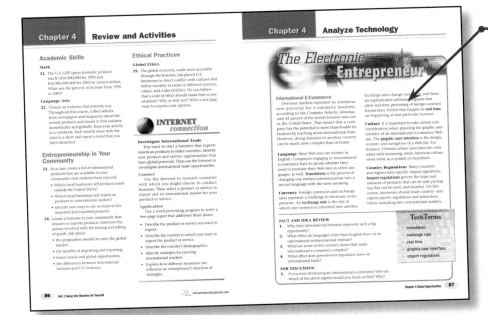

The Electronic Entrepreneur

The Electronic Entrepreneur feature presents a lesson about e-commerce issues relevant to entrepreneurs. It helps you to understand the complex relationship between technology and entrepreneurship. After the reading selection, there is a list of TechTerms, a Fact and Idea Review, and a question For Discussion. The reading and associated activities helps you prepare for the technologically advanced society of today and tomorrow.

Understanding the Section Opener

Each chapter is divided into two sections which introduce specific skills and knowledge. The section opens with Get Ready to Read which helps you understand the ideas and tasks you will encounter in your reading.

The Main Idea

The Main Idea summarizes the section's meaning and purpose.

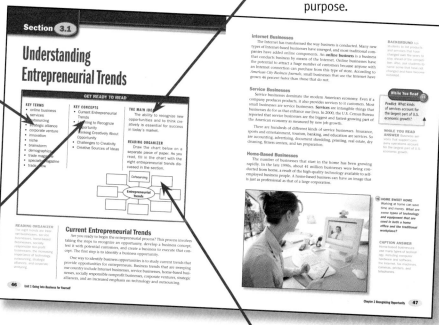

Key Terms

Key Terms lists the vocabulary terms in the section.

Key Concepts

Key Concepts is an outline of the section's significant topics.

Reading Organizer

The **Reading Organizer** provides a plan for organizing concepts visually.

Understanding the Section Review

Each section closes with **After You Read**, offering review questions and activities.

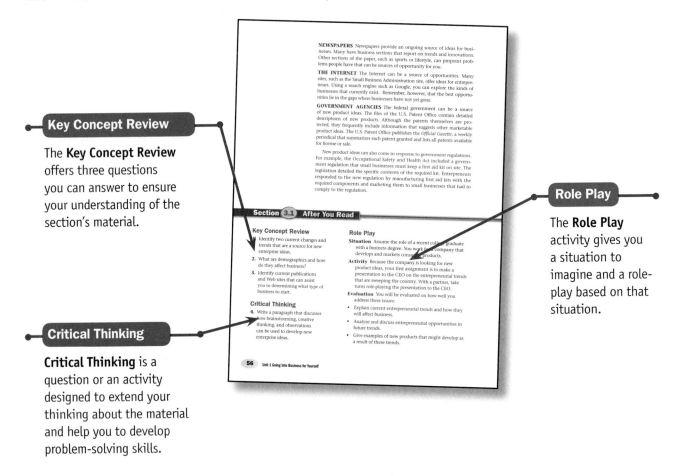

Key Concept Review

The **Key Concept Review** offers three questions you can answer to ensure your understanding of the section's material.

Role Play

The **Role Play** activity gives you a situation to imagine and a role-play based on that situation.

Critical Thinking

Critical Thinking is a question or an activity designed to extend your thinking about the material and help you to develop problem-solving skills.

Using the Reading Strategies

Each section offers a three-part reading strategy called **While You Read** that guides you in understanding and assimilating the new information as you read it.

PREDICT asks a question that you answer based on your personal experiences and past learning.

CONNECT poses a question or suggests an activity that will relate the text's material to your life.

QUESTION asks you a question that is answered in the text.

While You Read

Predict What kinds of services account for the largest part of U.S. economic growth?

While You Read

Connect Think of three types of businesses that offer outsourcing services to companies.

While You Read

Question How can you use your work experience as a source of business ideas?

The Unit

Each unit opens with a **Unit Overview** that describes what you will learn in the unit. The **Business Plan Project Preview** describes the components of the business plan you will begin to explore in the **Business Plan Project Unit Lab** at the end of the Unit.

The Business Plan Project Unit Lab

The **Business Plan Project Unit Lab** at the end of each unit introduces you to the components of the business plan, drawing on the material you will have learned in the chapters.

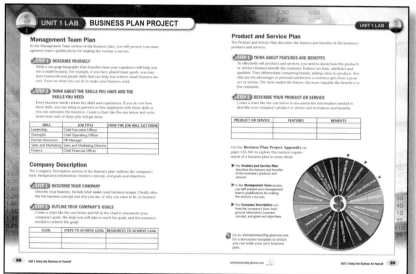

The Business Plan Project Appendix

The **Business Plan Project Appendix** expands upon the Unit Labs. It provides the content requirements of a business plan in detail.

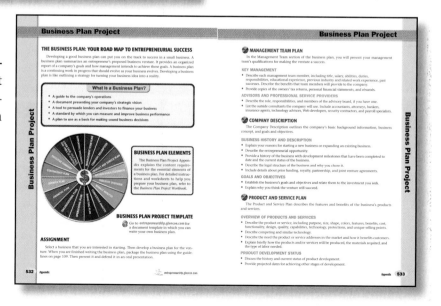

To the Student

Focus on the Features

Special features in each chapter are designed to stimulate your interest, promote your under-standing, and expand your exposure to real-world situations.

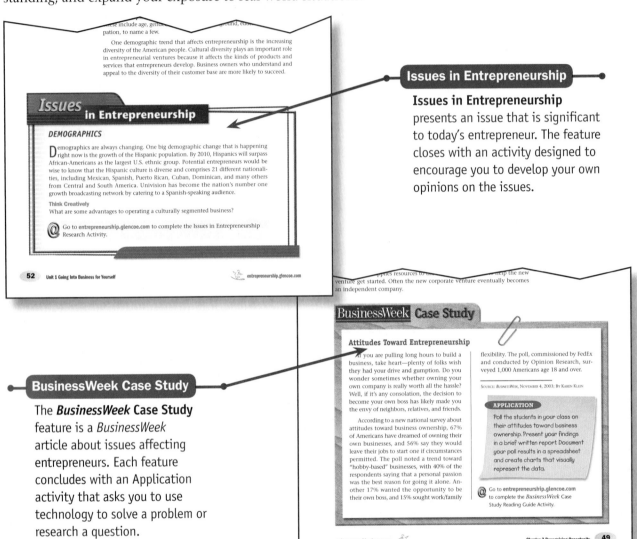

Issues in Entrepreneurship

Issues in Entrepreneurship presents an issue that is significant to today's entrepreneur. The feature closes with an activity designed to encourage you to develop your own opinions on the issues.

BusinessWeek Case Study

The *BusinessWeek* **Case Study** feature is a *BusinessWeek* article about issues affecting entrepreneurs. Each feature concludes with an Application activity that asks you to use technology to solve a problem or research a question.

Write About It

Practice your writing skills with **Write About It**. This features a thought-provoking writing exercise that requires critical thinking.

Success Stories

The **Success Stories** feature presents fascinating stories about the entrepreneurs who developed many successful and well-known businesses, starting small and using vision, creativity, and daring to become market leaders.

Success Stories

The First Franchise Empire

In 1954, Ray Kroc bought the rights to use the name of a popular California hamburger stand from the McDonald brothers. It was an exclusive 10-year franchise to license operators of McDonald's restaurants. Kroc proceeded to build a franchise empire, and in 1961 he bought out the McDonald brothers for $2.7 million. By 1966, there were 800 McDonald's restaurants; today there are over 30,000. The company serves an average of 38 million people each day and holds a whopping 42 percent of the $36 billion fast food market. Kroc's entrepreneurial venture redefined the food industry.

CRITICAL THINKING

Why do you suppose that Kroc chose to license someone else's name instead of starting from scratch? What are some of the advantages and disadvantages of owning a franchise?

Go to **entrepreneurship.glencoe.com** to complete the Success Stories Writing Activity.

Where to Find a Business

People find businesses in many ways. The simplest way is to look in the newspaper. Businesses that are for sale are listed in local papers as well as national business publications such as *The Wall Street Journal*. The most effective way to locate a business is to network with people in the community. accountants, attorneys, bankers, and local government administrators are ... let them know ... ness you are looking for ...

TECHNOLOGY Today

Solving Problems Using Technology

We live in the information age. Today, one of the most important skills is knowing how to use technology to come up with solutions for everyday problems. Technology and problem-solving skills are integral to small business success.

Cooperative Learning Activity

Your small business is growing rapidly but has a large inventory and limited storage space. In a small group, brainstorm technology-based solutions to the problem.

Go to **entrepreneurship.glencoe.com** to complete the Technology Today extension Vocabulary Practice Activity.

- What is the business's potential for growth? Once businesses are born, they go th... ...le of growth, maturity, and ...

Technology Today

Technology Today describes technology trends and topics that might affect an entrepreneur. The feature closes with an activity in which you analyze technology and its uses in business.

Quick Math

Practice your math skills with **Quick Math,** which poses a real-world math problem like those an entrepreneur might encounter.

The greatest advantage of a family business is the trust and togetherness that family members share. A family working as a team can often achieve more than its individual members can. At the same time, one of the greatest disadvantages of a family enterprise is that its owners can never get away from the business. Therefore, they may have difficulty viewing the venture and its problems objectively. Another common source of conflict is parents who are unable to see their child as a business person capable of making wise decisions and taking responsibility.

To minimize family conflicts and prevent some of the problems that family businesses face, it is important to establish clear lines of responsibility, be objective about family members' qualifications, keep decisions unaffected by personal emotions, and respect individual family members' needs.

Questions to Ask Yourself

Before entering a family business, ask yourself these questions:

- Do I have the ability to work for a member of my family?
- Do I get along well with the family members who will be involved in the business?
- Do we share the same goals for the business?

Quick Math

Of the 25 million businesses in the United States, 90 percent are family owned and managed. Given these statistics, calculate how many family-owned businesses there are in America.

UNIT 1

GOING INTO BUSINESS FOR YOURSELF

In This Unit...

UNIT OVERVIEW

Introduction

Chances are that at one time or another, you will consider going into business for yourself. It can be a challenging, exciting, and rewarding way to make a living. You can do what you enjoy, exercise your creativity, make the best use of your abilities, and be your own boss. Starting your own business puts you in charge.

BUSINESS PLAN PROJECT PREVIEW

When you complete Unit 1, you will begin to explore these sections of the business plan:

▶ In the **Management Team Plan** section, you will present your management team's qualifications for making the venture a success.

▶ The **Company Description** outlines the company's basic background information, business concept, and goals and objectives.

▶ The **Product and Service Plan** describes the features and benefits of the business's products and services.

What Is Entrepreneurship?

CHAPTER OBJECTIVES

When you have completed this chapter, you should be able to:

SECTION 1.1

- Discuss the role of small business and entrepreneurship in the economy.
- Describe economic systems.
- Explain how economics is about making choices.
- Discuss the role of economic indicators and business cycles.
- Describe what entrepreneurs contribute to the economy.

SECTION 1.2

- Describe entrepreneurship from a historical perspective.
- Discuss the five components of the entrepreneurial start-up process.
- Explain how to achieve business success.

Standard & Poor's provides the globally recognized S&P 500® financial-market index as well as a wide range of other products and services designed to help individuals and institutions make better-informed financial decisions with greater confidence. The S&P Money Talk feature examines the importance of financial planning and financial literacy to students' lives.

DEVELOPING PERSONAL FINANCIAL GOALS

How can you make sound financial decisions? You must know what your goals are. However, these will change as you go through life. The financial goals you set as a student will be different from the goals you'll have if you marry or have children.

Goals can be short-term (which you'll reach in a year or less—saving to buy a computer, for instance), intermediate (which will take two to five years, such as saving for a down payment on a car), or long-term (such as retirement planning).

When choosing your financial goals, follow these guidelines:

1. Your goals should be realistic.
2. Your goals should be specific.
3. Your goals should have a clear time frame.
4. Your goals should help you decide what type of action to take.

 Go to **entrepreneurship.glencoe.com** to complete the Standard & Poor's Money Talk Financial Literacy Activity.

PREPARE TO READ

THINK ABOUT THESE QUESTIONS AS YOU READ.

What is economics and how is it important to entrepreneurs?

What are the five key components of the entrepreneurial process?

Entrepreneurship and the Economy

GET READY TO READ

KEY TERMS
- entrepreneur
- venture
- entrepreneurship
- entrepreneurial
- economics
- free enterprise system
- profit
- market structure
- monopoly
- oligopoly
- goods
- services
- need
- want
- factors of production
- scarcity
- demand
- elastic demand
- inelastic demand
- diminishing marginal utility
- supply
- equilibrium
- Gross Domestic Product
- business cycle

KEY CONCEPTS
- Small Business and Entrepreneurship
- Economic Systems
- Basic Economic Concepts
- Economic Indicators and Business Cycles
- What Entrepreneurs Contribute

THE MAIN IDEA
Entrepreneurship is the primary catalyst for economic growth. To be a successful entrepreneur requires an understanding of how the economy works.

READING ORGANIZER
Draw the reading organizer on a separate piece of paper. As you read, fill in the chart with the four fundamental questions economic systems answer.

FOUR ECONOMIC QUESTIONS
1. <u>What goods and services should be produced?</u>
2. _____
3. _____
4. _____

Small Business and Entrepreneurship

Have you ever considered going into business for yourself? If so, you have thought about becoming an entrepreneur. An **entrepreneur** is an individual who undertakes the creation, organization, and ownership of a business. He or she accepts the risks and responsibilities of business ownership to gain profits and personal satisfaction.

Creating and running a business venture requires a variety of skills. A **venture** is a new business undertaking that involves risk. This book will help you understand what it takes to be a successful entrepreneur. Even if you don't become an entrepreneur, the lessons you learn will help you in any job. Knowing more about businesses will also benefit you as a consumer.

The terms *entrepreneurship* and *entrepreneurial* are used throughout this book. **Entrepreneurship** is the process of recognizing an opportunity, testing it in the market, and gathering resources necessary to go into business. Being **entrepreneurial** means acting like an entrepreneur or having an entrepreneurial mind-set.

Entrepreneurship Today

You might know someone who is an entrepreneur. About one in three households is involved with a new venture or small business, often a family business. More than 90 percent of all businesses are small businesses with fewer than 100 employees. Sixty-two percent of those are home-based businesses.

Owning and operating a business today is much different than it was in the past. The global marketplace has brought about new resources, markets, and ideas. Information technology allows people to communicate instantly and to keep records more efficiently. As a result, customers demand that business transactions and communication take place quickly. They expect innovative products to come out often. Therefore, businesses feel the pressure to provide better service and to make more options available.

To understand how entrepreneurs and customers interact in the economy, you need to start with economics and economic systems. **Economics** is the study of how people choose to allocate scarce resources to fulfill their unlimited wants. Economics has a profound influence on entrepreneurship.

While You Read

Predict How does economics influence entrepreneurship?

Economic Systems

An economic system includes a set of laws, institutions, and activities that guide economic decision making. All economic systems attempt to answer these four fundamental questions:

- What goods and services should be produced?
- What quantity of goods and services should be produced?
- How should goods and services be produced?
- For whom should goods and services be produced?

FOUR ECONOMIC QUESTIONS The way nations answer the four basic economic questions determines their economic system. *How does the government play a role in determining what is and what is not provided in a market economy?*

History has produced several different types of economic systems. The traditional economic system relies on farming and simple barter trade. The pure market system is based on supply and demand with little government control. Command economic systems are run by a strong centralized government. They tend to focus more on industrial goods than consumer goods. For example, the former Soviet Union had a command economy. Nearly all agricultural and industrial enterprises were controlled by the government. Mixed economies combine the principles of market and command economies. The United States and the European Union have mixed economies.

The Free Enterprise System

Most democratic nations have a free enterprise system. In a **free enterprise system**, people have an important right to make economic choices:

- People can choose what products to buy.
- People can choose to own private property.
- People can choose to start a business and compete with other businesses.

The free enterprise system is also called *capitalism* or a *market economy*. It is vital to entrepreneurship.

THE PROFIT MOTIVE Making a profit is a primary incentive of free enterprise. **Profit** is money that is left after all expenses of running a business have been deducted from the income. It is one way of measuring success in a free enterprise system.

However, there is also a risk of failure. Risk serves a positive function in a free enterprise system. It encourages the production of quality products that truly meet the needs of consumers.

THE ROLE OF COMPETITION Competition between similar businesses is one of the basic characteristics of a free enterprise system. It is good for consumers because it provides choices, it forces companies to improve quality and become more efficient, and it leads to a surplus, which brings prices down. For this reason, suppliers prefer to have as little competition as possible.

Businesses compete on the basis of price and nonprice factors. In a mature industry such as electronics, price is a factor, and the focus is on lowering prices. An established firm can usually lower prices because it benefits from lower costs and more experience. Lower costs come from producing in higher volume and having a more experienced workforce. On the other hand, a small firm setting up its first production line incurs much higher costs. In larger firms, revenues lost to lower prices can be made up through higher volume (more sales). This strategy accounts for the success of discount stores.

In younger industries, however, price is not as strong a factor. Other factors, such as quality, service, and reputation, are more important. Entrepreneurs typically avoid competing on price factors. Instead, they look for ways to create new value, thereby solving a need in the market. In that way, they can better differentiate themselves from the competition.

MARKET STRUCTURES The term **market structure** refers to the nature and degree of competition among businesses operating in the same industry. Market structure affects market price.

Economists group industries into four different market structures: perfect competition, monopolistic competition, monopoly, and oligopoly.

Perfect competition is a market structure in which there are numerous buyers and sellers, and no single buyer or seller can affect price. In a perfectly competitive market, the good or service being sold must be identical or nearly identical. Because there is no difference in quality, one seller's merchandise is just as good as another's. It is easy for sellers to enter the market. Perfect competition encourages economic efficiency by forcing prices down. Few, if any, perfectly competitive markets exist.

Monopolistic competition is a market structure in which many sellers produce similar but differentiated products. Through differentiation sellers have some power to control the price of their products. By making its product slightly different, the monopolistic competitor tries to dominate a small portion of the market.

A **monopoly** is a market structure in which a particular commodity has only one seller who has control over supply and can exert nearly total control over prices. Monopolies are discouraged in free market economies. However, sometimes monopolies are in the public's best interest. For example, the government grants a temporary monopoly to inventors in the form of patents and copyrights to encourage innovation.

An **oligopoly** is a market structure in which there are just a few competing firms. For example, several large companies have dominated the automobile industry for decades. They can sell automobiles at a lower price than small manufacturers, so they have some influence over price. Under antitrust laws, most forms of monopoly and some forms of oligopoly are illegal.

Figure 1.1 | Factors of Production

RESOURCES Resources are all of the things used in producing goods and services. The technical term for resources is *factors of production.* **If your school's student council decides to raise funds by selling smoothies at an upcoming basketball game, what specific factors of production would be involved?**

1. Land

In economic terms, land is all of the natural resources upon and beneath the earth's surface. Land includes not only geographic territory, but also air, water, trees, minerals, and crude oil.

2. Labor

The human effort used to produce goods and services is called *labor.* Labor is made up of full- and part-time workers as well as management.

3. Entrepreneurship

This factor consists of the ideas and decisions of the business owner, or entrepreneur. He or she is the initiator, the one who brings together the other factors of production to create value in the economy.

4. Capital

Capital consists of the equipment, factory, tools, and other goods needed to produce a product. It also includes money used to pay all of the expenses.

Basic Economic Concepts

To understand the entrepreneur's role in the economy, you need to know some basic economics. You may find that you are already familiar with many economic concepts from your everyday role as a consumer.

Goods and Services

Goods and services are the products our economic system produces to satisfy consumers' wants and needs. **Goods** are tangible (or physical) products. **Services** are intangible (nonphysical) products. A **need** is a basic requirement for survival, such as food and shelter. A **want** is something that you do not have to have for survival, but would like to have.

Factors of Production

Factors of production are the resources businesses use to produce the goods and services that people want. The factors of production include land, labor, capital, and entrepreneurship. These factors are explained in **Figure 1.1** on page 10.

Scarcity

Scarcity occurs when demand exceeds supply. The principle of scarcity says that resources are in limited supply. Therefore, to have one thing may mean giving up something else. A restaurant owner may forego a costly decor to have more money to put into kitchen equipment.

Supply and Demand Theory

In a free enterprise system, the price of a product is determined in the marketplace. Sellers want to sell at the highest possible price, and buyers want to buy at the lowest possible price. Customers decide what they are willing to pay for a product or service.

To understand how prices are determined, you have to look at both demand and supply. Supply and demand interact to determine the price customers are willing to pay for the number of products producers are willing to make. These are the basic tenets of supply and demand theory:

- If something is in heavy demand but in short supply, prices will go up. The rise in price will reduce demand and expand supply.
- If something is in heavy supply but in short demand, prices will go down. The fall in price will expand demand and contract supply.
- Prices tend to stabilize at the level where demand equals supply.

DEMAND **Demand** is the quantity of goods or services that consumers are willing and able to buy. According to the law of demand, as price goes up, the quantity demanded goes down. In this way, market prices ration goods and services among those who are willing to pay for them.

The demand curve in **Figure 1.2** on page 12 shows the number of CDs that would be purchased at specific prices. Notice that more CDs would be bought at $15 than at $25. This is because more people can afford the discs at the lower price.

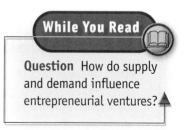

While You Read

Question How do supply and demand influence entrepreneurial ventures?

Figure 1.2 | **Demand Curve for CDs**

PRICE AFFECTS DEMAND
This curve shows that fewer items will be purchased at higher prices than at lower prices. *Which price increment reduces demand the most?*

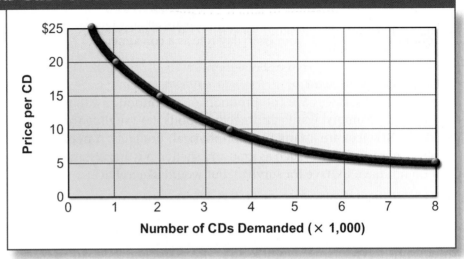

Figure 1.3 | **Supply Curve for CDs**

PRICE AFFECTS SUPPLY
This curve reveals a direct relationship between price and the number of items produced. *Describe the effect on supply of tripling the selling price from $5 to $15.*

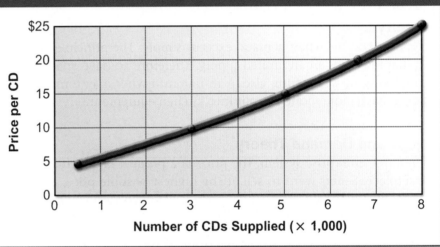

Figure 1.4 | **Demand and Supply Curves for CDs**

POINT OF EQUILIBRIUM
Merging the supply and demand curves into a single graph allows you to locate the equilibrium point or price. *What is the equilibrium price for CDs? At that price, approximately how many CDs will consumers demand?*

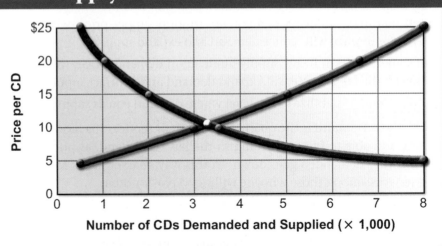

The degree to which demand for a product is affected by its price is *demand elasticity*. Products have either elastic demand or inelastic demand. **Elastic demand** refers to situations in which a change in price creates a change in demand. For example, demand for butter tends to be elastic because there are lower-priced substitutes. **Inelastic demand** refers to situations in which a change in price has very little effect on demand for products. There is no substitute for milk, so demand for milk tends to be inelastic.

In general, demand tends to be inelastic in these circumstances:

- No acceptable substitutes are available, and customers need the product.

- The price change is small relative to buyer income, so if customers want the product, they will buy it.

- The product is a necessity; customers need it.

Even when a product's price is low, people won't keep buying it indefinitely. For example, they will not buy more than they can reasonably use. This effect is known as the law of **diminishing marginal utility.** The law of diminishing marginal utility establishes that price alone does not determine demand. Other factors (income, taste, and the amount of product already owned) play a role as well.

SUPPLY The amount of a good or service that producers are willing to provide is called **supply**. Producers are more willing to supply products in greater amounts when prices are high. In this way, market prices provide an incentive to produce goods and services. They are less willing to do so when prices are low. **Figure 1.3** depicts a supply curve for CDs. Notice that as price goes up, the quantity supplied goes up, too.

SURPLUS, SHORTAGE, AND EQUILIBRIUM Supply and demand are dynamic in the marketplace. That is, they are continually shifting. This change creates surpluses (more supplies than needed), shortages (fewer supplies than needed), and equilibrium. **Equilibrium** is the point at which consumers buy all of a product that is supplied. At the point of equilibrium, there is neither a surplus nor a shortage.

Consider the CD example again. Upon the release of a new CD, fans flock to music stores. They buy every copy at the initial high price and still ask for more. A shortage develops. Stores have lists of customers waiting for the next shipment. Eventually the excitement passes. Soon the stores have more copies of the CD on hand than fans will buy at the marked price. In other words, the stores have a surplus. To solve this problem, they reduce the price. In a short time, a modest discount clears the excess inventory and brings about equilibrium. The principles underlying this situation are illustrated in **Figure 1.4.**

Supply and demand graphs can be a bit misleading, though. They seem to suggest that where demand exists, supply just follows. It's not that simple.

For businesses to respond to consumer demand, they must know about it. Information about supply and demand influences entrepreneurial activities. For consumers to make purchases, they must be aware of what is available. How do businesses learn what consumers want? How do consumers find out what businesses have to offer? The answer in both cases is the same: marketing. Marketing is discussed in Unit 3.

Quick Math

If a CD sells for $15, what will the price be when the record store drops the price by 20%?

While You Read

Connect Brainstorm a list of five products with elastic demand and five products with inelastic demand.

What's Missing from Those Economic Stats?

Plenty. So much of what small businesses do isn't measured by anyone. And that skews the picture for the overall economy.

As a small-business owner, if you have trouble reconciling your company's experience with the economic statistics in the headlines, it's not surprising.

A lot of what small companies do—doubling the size of the store, increasing profits, taking on debt, going out of business altogether—isn't reflected, at least initially, in the figures the government and others keep on, say, capital spending, earnings, and job creation or elimination.

Small companies are left out for a few reasons: It's simpler and cheaper to collect information from large, publicly held corporations because they have more stringent reporting requirements, for the sake of their shareholders. At the same time, small businesses are sometimes secretive—

about profits and spending, for example. It's a painstaking process for the numbers-crunchers to piece together revenue, hiring, capital spending, etc., from sales-tax payments and income-tax returns.

SOURCE: *BUSINESSWEEK*, JULY 16, 2001; BY THERESA FORSMAN

APPLICATION

Use software to create a presentation that assesses economic principles that influence entrepreneurship. In your presentation, identify the financial impact of changes in economic conditions.

 Go to **entrepreneurship.glencoe.com** to complete the *BusinessWeek* Case Study Reading Guide.

Economic Indicators and Business Cycles

The federal government publishes statistics that help entrepreneurs understand the state of the economy and predict possible changes. These statistics are called *economic indicators*. Examples include the employment rate, consumer confidence, and Gross Domestic Product (GDP). **Gross Domestic Product** is the total market values of goods and services produced by workers and capital within a nation during a given period.

The Federal Reserve (Fed) is a government agency that controls the economy and regulates the nation's money supply. The Fed controls the economy in several ways. It tells banks the percentage of their money they can lend. It controls interest rates, raising them to increase the cost of borrowing and reducing them to decrease the cost of borrowing. It also buys and sells government securities to increase or decrease the money supply. It constantly evaluates economic conditions and makes adjustments to monetary policies when needed.

History shows that sometimes an economy grows, and at other times it slows down. This is called a business cycle. A **business cycle** is the general pattern of expansion and contraction that the economy goes through. In terms of the national economy, business cycles mean that a period of growth and prosperity is usually followed by a recession, which can be followed by a recovery or a depression.

The Fed reacts to different economic conditions (or stages of the business cycle) in different ways. If the economy is growing too rapidly, inflation may occur. Inflation is an unhealthy jump in prices that slows consumer and business spending. When spending decreases, companies reduce their production levels and lay off workers. The result is higher unemployment rates. All of these factors can lead to a recession. If a recession occurs, the Fed will move to increase the supply of money. It does this by lowering interest rates to encourage people and businesses to borrow money and spend more. To avoid a recession when economic growth is too rapid, the Fed raises interest rates. An effective monetary policy balances the short-term goal of increasing output with the long-term goal of maintaining a low rate of inflation.

What Entrepreneurs Contribute

New companies are the driving force of economic growth. Business start-ups are beneficial because they generate employment and increase the production of goods and services. From what you have learned in this chapter, consider the role of entrepreneurship in the U.S. economy:

- Entrepreneurs are the mechanism by which the economy turns demand into supply. They recognize consumer wants and see the economic opportunities in satisfying them.

- Entrepreneurs are a principal source of venture capital. As part of the process of planning and setting up a new business, entrepreneurs gather resources. Money is one of the most important of these. Entrepreneurs usually start with their own funds, then seek contributions from private investors.

- Entrepreneurs provide jobs. To produce goods and services, they spend capital on setting up a place of business and hiring workers. In doing so, they provide for their own financial security and for the financial security of others.

- The most successful entrepreneurs change society. In 1976, Steven Jobs and Stephen Wozniak set out to create Apple, the first personal computer. In less than five years, they created an industry of hundreds of related businesses and thousands of new jobs. Today it is hard to imagine a workplace without personal computers.

- Entrepreneurs begin by responding to society's wants and end up changing society. As a result, they create even more wants to be satisfied. Entrepreneurs are not just one of many driving forces in the economy. They are the catalysts that make economic progress happen.

Small Businesses and Entrepreneurial Ventures

This book makes a clear distinction between small businesses and entrepreneurial ventures. While most businesses do start small, not all businesses stay small. There are many reasons for this. However, the principal reason is the intentions, motives, and goals of the founders of the business.

SMALL BUSINESSES Small business owners who start mom-and-pop businesses generally do so to create jobs for themselves. They want to create lifestyles that are satisfying and that meet their personal goals. A shoe repair shop in a shopping center near your home may be one such small business. An accountant or a lawyer may be another.

ENTREPRENEURIAL VENTURES Founders of entrepreneurial ventures have different motives for starting a business. Their principal goals are to innovate and grow the venture. Another goal is to create new value that can be harvested when they leave the business. The founder of an entrepreneurial venture has a plan to expand to a regional, national, or global level. Amazon.com, Dell, Outback Steakhouse, and Gap are examples of entrepreneurial ventures.

Section 1.1 After You Read

Key Concept Review

1. What roles do profit motive and competition play in the free enterprise system? What is their impact on business?

2. Describe price and nonprice competition and explain their impact on business.

3. Identify the difference between wants and needs.

Critical Thinking

4. Evaluate the relationship between cost and profit and supply and demand.

Role Play

Situation You and a classmate have been asked to work together to make a presentation to an elementary school class about economic systems.

Activity Work with a partner to create a game that will teach basic economic concepts in the simplest terms.

Evaluation You will be evaluated on how well you meet these performance indicators:

- Analyze the free enterprise system.
- Assess the importance of the free enterprise system in entrepreneurship.
- Compare and contrast other economic systems.
- Discuss the components of the laws of supply and demand in a free enterprise system and how they affect entrepreneurship.
- Compare the relationship of surplus and shortage to equilibrium.

The Entrepreneurial Process

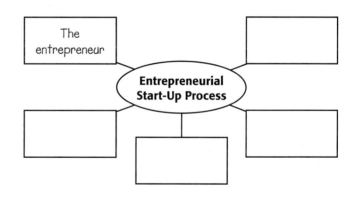

The History of Entrepreneurship

Entrepreneurship has been a distinct feature of American culture since the American Revolution. Enterprising colonists found innovative ways to bring new products and services to what would later become the United States of America, but it was not until the 1980s that entrepreneurship became a popular topic. **Figure 1.5** on page 18 depicts the evolution of entrepreneurship in the United States by decade since the 1960s. It also describes the economic environment at that time.

In the early years of the U.S. economy, small businesses were the norm. Early entrepreneurs supplied basic needs. The Industrial Revolution brought about the growth of large companies in steel, railroads, and manufacturing.

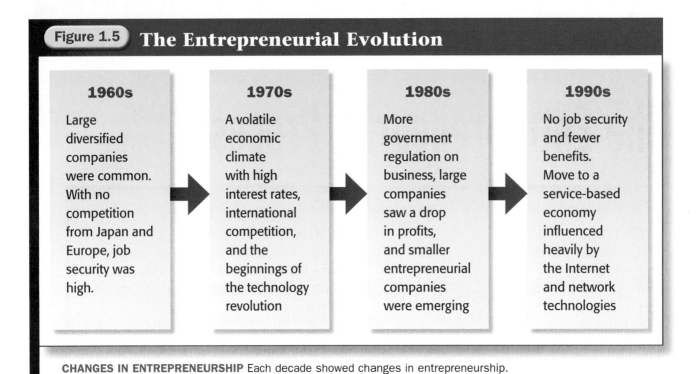

Figure 1.5 **The Entrepreneurial Evolution**

1960s

Large diversified companies were common. With no competition from Japan and Europe, job security was high.

1970s

A volatile economic climate with high interest rates, international competition, and the beginnings of the technology revolution

1980s

More government regulation on business, large companies saw a drop in profits, and smaller entrepreneurial companies were emerging

1990s

No job security and fewer benefits. Move to a service-based economy influenced heavily by the Internet and network technologies

CHANGES IN ENTREPRENEURSHIP Each decade showed changes in entrepreneurship. *What, in your opinion, was the biggest change in entrepreneurship over the years?*

By the 1960s, huge companies were common. With no international competition, U.S. companies were able to provide job security. This meant most workers spent their entire life with one company.

The 1970s brought about huge changes. High levels of inflation produced high prices and higher-than-normal interest rates. As a result, borrowing and spending slowed. Companies were facing competition from countries with lower labor costs. Finally, the informational society came into existence with the introduction of the microprocessor and the personal computer. Whole categories of products became obsolete. For example, adding machines and mechanical cash registers became outmoded.

By the early 1980s, large companies were suffering. New, smaller companies were responding to the changing market. They outsourced many of their activities to other companies. Service companies that handled those business needs began to emerge. As a result, many new jobs became available. The 1980s was known as the "Decade of Entrepreneurship."

Since the 1980s, entrepreneurship has had an increasing impact on the economy and economic growth. The advent of the Internet in the mid-1990s changed the way most businesses operate. It also spurred many new entrepreneurial ventures.

The Entrepreneurial Start-Up Process

The entrepreneurial start-up process includes five key components. These are the entrepreneur, the environment, the opportunity, start-up resources, and the new venture organization. These five components work together to create a new business.

Sliding Into Business

Not everybody can claim that they invented an entire sport, but Jake Burton Carpenter can do just that. An avid outdoorsman, Carpenter had grown tired of skiing, but found that he liked to go down hills on a board instead, combining skiing with the kinetic thrill of skateboarding. In 1977 he started Burton Snowboards, making the first commercially available snowboards. People laughed at first, but today snowboarding is the fastest growing sport in the country, with an estimated seven million enthusiasts. Carpenter's company controls about one-third of the market for boards and supplies.

CRITICAL THINKING

How did Carpenter transform a hobby into a career? What were some of the ways he used his creativity to establish his company?

 Go to **entrepreneurship.glencoe.com** to complete the Success Stories Writing Activity.

The Entrepreneur

The entrepreneur is the driving force of the start-up process. The entrepreneur recognizes opportunity. He or she pulls together the resources to exploit that opportunity. He or she then creates a company to execute the opportunity in the marketplace. The entrepreneur brings to the process all of his or her life experiences. The entrepreneur is the calculated risk taker. He or she has the passion and persistence to see the venture through from idea to market.

The Environment

A new business environment includes variables that affect the venture but are not controlled by the entrepreneur. In general, four categories of environmental variables affect a new venture's ability to start and grow:

While You Read

Predict What is the driving force of the entrepreneurial start-up process? Why?

1. The nature of the environment, whether it's uncertain, fast-changing, stable, or highly competitive

2. The availability of resources, such as skilled labor, start-up capital, and sources of assistance

3. Ways to realize value, such as favorable taxes, good markets, and supportive governmental policies

4. Incentives to create new businesses. **Enterprise zones** are specially designated areas of a community that provide tax benefits to new businesses locating there. They also provide grants for new product development.

The Opportunity

A good opportunity can be turned into a business. An **opportunity** is an idea that has commercial value. However, the idea has value only when customers are ready and willing to buy the product. An idea plus a market equals an opportunity. New businesses are founded on recognized opportunities in the environment. In Chapter 3, you will learn how to recognize opportunity and how to think creatively about opportunity.

Start-Up Resources

When an entrepreneur is ready to execute a concept for a new business, he or she must use his or her creative talent to pull together the necessary people and capital. The **start-up resources** include capital, skilled labor, management expertise, legal and financial advice, facility, equipment, and customers needed to start a business.

While You Read

Connect In your opinion, which category of start-up resources is the most important? Why?

The New Venture Organization

The fifth component of the new venture process is the execution of the new business concept. The **new venture organization** is the infrastructure of the business. It is the foundation that supports all of the products, processes, and services of the new business. Through it, the entrepreneur can create value to benefit himself or herself and the employees, customers, and economy.

New Business Success and Failure

There is a common myth that most new businesses fail. In fact, studies show that more businesses succeed than fail. Studies conducted by the Small Business Administration report that 66 percent of small businesses survive the first two years. That rate drops to about 40 percent by six years.

While You Read

Question What is the difference between a business failure and a discontinuance?

The Facts About Business Failure

A **business failure** is a business that has stopped operating with a loss to creditors. A business failure files Chapter 7 bankruptcy. It loses money for creditors, the people who lent it money, and for its investors. The business no longer appears on the tax rolls. Such businesses are rightfully counted as failures.

However, businesses that disappear from the tax rolls are not always failures. Some are discontinuances. A **discontinuance** may be a business that is operating under a new name. It also may be a business the owner has purposely discontinued to start a new one. These are not failures; their closings were planned and caused no harm to creditors.

How Entrepreneurs Can Succeed

The chances of a new business succeeding are good with effective planning and management. The key to entrepreneurial success is recognizing opportunity, testing that opportunity in the marketplace, and assembling a team with the necessary expertise to execute the business concept.

Section 1.2 After You Read

Key Concept Review

1. What are the five components of the process of new venture creation?

2. How does an enterprise zone encourage new businesses?

3. Why shouldn't discontinuances be counted as business failures?

Critical Thinking

4. Using all of the information and as many of the terms provided in this chapter as you can, describe an economic environment for entrepreneurship that would help ensure the success of a new venture.

Role Play

Situation You and a partner have been invited to speak to a group of high school students about the history of entrepreneurship in the United States.

Activity Prepare a 10-minute presentation that depicts the key points you want to make.

Evaluation You will be evaluated on how well you meet these performance indicators:

- Analyze entrepreneurship from a historical perspective.

- Analyze the role of entrepreneurs in America's development.

- Discuss the evolution of entrepreneurship, highlighting the 1980s, the entrepreneurial decade.

- Explain the impact of the shift from an industrial society to an informational society on entrepreneurial ventures.

- Identify contributions of entrepreneurs to the economic growth of the United States.

Chapter Summary

Section 1.1 Entrepreneurship and the Economy

To be able to compete and succeed in the free market system, entrepreneurs need to understand how the economy works. There are several types of economic systems. Most democratic nations have a free enterprise system. Fundamental to the free enterprise system is the right of economic choice. Factors of production are the resources businesses use to produce the goods and services people want. Supply and demand interact to determine the price customers are willing to pay for the number of products producers are willing to make. The federal government publishes statistics called economic indicators that help entrepreneurs understand the economy and predict possible changes. A business cycle is the pattern of contraction and expansion that the economy goes through. Entrepreneurs contribute to society in many ways.

Section 1.2 The Entrepreneurial Process

Throughout American history, entrepreneurship has fueled innovation, created new jobs, and satisfied wants and needs in the marketplace. Entrepreneurs start businesses through a process that includes five key components: the entrepreneur, the environment, the opportunity, the resources to start the business, and the new venture organization. Entrepreneurs can achieve business success by planning and managing effectively.

Key Terms Review

1. Working in teams of two or three, prepare an oral presentation explaining entrepreneurship and the role it plays in the free enterprise system. Use the following terms in your presentation.

entrepreneur (p. 6)	goods (p. 11)	supply (p. 13)
venture (p. 6)	services (p. 11)	equilibrium (p. 13)
entrepreneurship (p. 7)	need (p. 11)	Gross Domestic Product (p. 14)
entrepreneurial (p. 7)	want (p. 11)	business cycle (p. 15)
economics (p. 7)	factors of production (p. 11)	enterprise zones (p. 19)
free enterprise system (p. 8)	scarcity (p. 11)	opportunity (p. 20)
profit (p. 8)	demand (p. 11)	start-up resources (p. 20)
market structure (p. 9)	elastic demand (p. 13)	new venture organization (p. 20)
monopoly (p. 9)	inelastic demand (p. 13)	business failure (p. 21)
oligopoly (p. 9)	diminishing marginal utility (p. 13)	discontinuance (p. 21)

Key Concept Review

2. **Discuss** the role of small business and entrepreneurship in the economy. (1.1)
3. **Describe** economic systems. (1.1)
4. **Explain** how economics is about making choices. (1.1)
5. **Discuss** the role of economic indicators and business cycles. (1.1)
6. **Describe** what entrepreneurs contribute to the U.S. economy. (1.1)
7. **Describe** entrepreneurship from a historical perspective. (1.2)
8. **Discuss** the five components of the entrepreneurial start-up process. (1.2)
9. **Explain** how to achieve business success. (1.2)

Critical Thinking

10. How has the principle of diminishing marginal utility affected a product you have purchased?
11. How have environmental factors affected a small business in your community?
12. What are some methods entrepreneurs can use to help determine consumer wants?
13. Discuss the right to make choices in a free enterprise system or market economy.
14. Differentiate between goods and services. Describe the differences between a product-based business and a service-based business.

Write About It

15. Write a two-page report that assesses how market prices ration goods and services among those who want them. Explain how market prices provide an incentive to produce goods and services.
16. At the computer, define *land, labor, capital,* and *entrepreneurship* as factors of production.
17. In a letter to a classmate, describe the process of starting a small business.
18. Discuss the five components of the entrepreneurial start-up process.
19. In a couple of paragraphs, describe competition and its relationship to private enterprise and entrepreneurship.
20. Draw a Venn diagram and use it to compare and contrast the different types of market structures, competition, and monopoly. Include the effect of market structures on market price.

Academic Skills

Math

21. In the city of Orange, N.J., 187 new businesses opened in 2002. By 2003, 15 percent of these businesses were no longer in operation. How many were open in 2003? One year later another 12 percent were considered discontinued. How many businesses were still open in 2004?

Language Arts

22. You and a friend are starting a business repairing motorcycles. Create a list of technologies you need to run your business. Share the list with a classmate and make revisions.

Entrepreneurship in Your Community

23. Working with three or four students in your class, brainstorm a list of ten businesses the team might like to start. Consider the interests and skills of the group members to narrow down the list. Write a short description of one of the businesses. Include the product or service you will provide and the type of resources you need to begin.

24. Interview an entrepreneur or small business owner in your community. Ask what the factors of production are for that business. Then create a diagram illustrating the business's factors of production.

Ethical Practices

Employee Qualifications

25. You are hiring someone to handle the manufacturing operations of your new business. You receive a résumé from a promising candidate who claims to have graduated from the Wharton School of Business of the University of Pennsylvania. The candidate has a successful interview. You were impressed with her, and you extend an offer of employment. However, prior to the candidate's first day on the job, you learn that she did not graduate from the university. What do you do?

Virtual Business

Your friend wants to begin doing business on the Internet. He knows how to create a Web page. Now he has asked you to help him decide what kind of business to open. Using the Internet, research different virtual businesses.

Connect

Use a Web directory or search engine to find three examples of online businesses.

Application

Use a word processor to document the answers to the following questions about each business:

- Is the price of the product clearly defined?
- Are delivery dates mentioned?
- What process is used to place orders?
- How are the sites similar and different?

The Electronic Entrepreneur

The Digital Economy

Over the past century, the world's economy has undergone drastic changes. Individual economies used to be local; farmers and merchants met the needs of their communities, while occasional merchants would travel to other cities to sell their wares. A general store would sell to the people in its community.

Today, that same general store can sell its products around the world, thanks to the widespread use of information technology, or IT. **Information technology (IT)** refers to any technology that is used to communicate or exchange information, from telephones to the Internet. It is the driving force behind the information age. The **information age** is the era of history that began in the 1970s when computers became popular with the masses.

Infrastructure The backbone of the IT-driven economy is the technology infrastructure. **Technology infrastructure** includes all of the hardware and software used to support electronic communication.

E-Business When companies do business over an electronic network, they are conducting **e-business**. Examples include e-mail, videoconferencing, Web-based training, and using an **intranet**, an in-house network, to communicate with staff.

E-Commerce Today, many companies conduct **e-commerce**, selling their products and services over the Internet. Such e-commerce transactions include the sale of consumer goods, contracts between one business and another, and the sale of downloadable content (MP3s, e-books, etc.).

FACT AND IDEA REVIEW

1. What has been the major change in the world economy over the past century?
2. What is IT?
3. Look around your classroom. What are some examples of IT infrastructure that you see?
4. Explain the difference between e-business and e-commerce.

FOR DISCUSSION

5. What are some examples of businesses that benefit the most from the digital economy?

TechTerms

- information technology (IT)
- information age
- technology infrastructure
- e-business
- intranet
- e-commerce

Your Potential as an Entrepreneur

CHAPTER OBJECTIVES

When you have completed this chapter, you should be able to:

SECTION 2.1

- Describe the rewards of going into business for yourself.
- Describe the risks of going into business for yourself.

SECTION 2.2

- Identify the background, characteristics, and skills of successful entrepreneurs.
- Explain techniques that will improve your potential for becoming an entrepreneur.

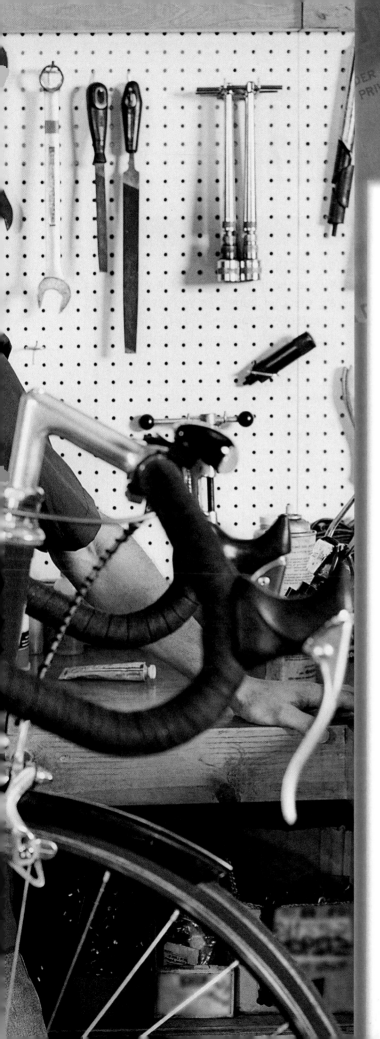

THE TIME VALUE OF MONEY

You make choices about money almost all the time. Will you buy the $100 pair of sneakers you saw at the mall or save that money? You can't do both.

Consider the time value of money, which is the increase of an amount of money as a result of interest or dividends earned. Future value is the amount your original deposit will be worth in the future based on earning a specific interest rate over a specific period of time. To calculate the future value of a single deposit over a one-year period, multiply the principal by the annual interest rate and add that interest amount to the principal. Each year, interest is earned on the original amount of your principal and on any previously earned interest.

Some savers like to make regular deposits into their accounts. Money can grow much faster this way because the principal gets larger every year, resulting in larger interest and dividend payments in future years.

 Go to **entrepreneurship.glencoe.com** to complete the Standard & Poor's Money Talk Financial Literacy Activity.

PREPARE TO READ

THINK ABOUT THESE QUESTIONS AS YOU READ.

What are the rewards of entrepreneurship?

What are the costs and risks of entrepreneurship?

Do the rewards of entrepreneurship outweigh the risks?

Why Be an Entrepreneur?

KEY TERMS
- competition
- investment
- capital

KEY CONCEPTS
- Rewards of Entrepreneurship
- Risks of Entrepreneurship

THE MAIN IDEA

When you are considering owning your own business, an important first step is to analyze the advantages and disadvantages of entrepreneurship.

READING ORGANIZER

Draw the reading organizer below on a separate piece of paper. As you read, list each reward of entrepreneurship on the left side and each risk of entrepreneurship on the right side.

REWARDS	RISKS
1. Being your own boss	1. Working long hours
2. _____	2. _____
3. _____	3. _____
4. _____	4. _____
5. _____	
6. _____	
7. _____	

Rewards of Entrepreneurship

What are the rewards of being an entrepreneur? You many think the rewards are owning a large house, driving a nice car, and leading a lavish lifestyle. However, having those things is not the primary motivation for most entrepreneurs. In fact, the greatest rewards are not material at all. For most entrepreneurs, the greatest rewards of owning a business are intangible. The rewards include such things as independence, personal satisfaction, and prestige.

Being Your Own Boss

Most entrepreneurs consider being their own boss as the biggest reward of owning a business. The reason is obvious—it gives them the freedom to make their own business decisions. They have the final word on all aspects of the operation. They can determine the hours of business, products offered, and direction for expansion.

Doing Something You Enjoy

A business venture typically starts with an activity the entrepreneur enjoys. Someone who takes pleasure in cooking for others might start a catering business. Someone who likes to in-line skate or skateboard might give lessons and sell equipment. The new business owner derives satisfaction from creating and developing the enterprise.

Having the Opportunity to Be Creative

Most people who work for others merely follow procedures; entrepreneurs make them. In other words, entrepreneurs are able to shape a business in ways employees cannot. This is especially true with daring or creative ideas. When a business owner has a creative idea, he or she has the power to act on it.

While You Read

Predict Why do entrepreneurs have more freedom than employees?

Having the Freedom to Set Your Own Schedule

Although entrepreneurs experience time demands, they have the flexibility to determine their own schedule. Also, they have the option of working at home, at the business, or at whatever location suits them.

Having Job Security

In today's world, employees are not guaranteed job security from their employers. Entrepreneurs, however, control their own destiny. As long as the business is successful, they are assured of a job.

Success Stories

A Television Pioneer

Robert Johnson might not be a household name, but the cable network that he started is. Johnson was working in the cable industry in 1980 when he saw the need for a network that tailored its programming to the African-American audience. With just a small personal loan and one investor, he created Black Entertainment Television (BET), which is now the country's largest minority television station. Johnson kept costs low in the early years by chiefly airing music videos and sitcom reruns. By 1991, BET was the first African-American-controlled company traded on the NYSE. Today, BET is a success, reaching over 60 million households.

CRITICAL THINKING
Why is it important to keep business costs low during the first few years?

 Go to **entrepreneurship.glencoe.com** to complete the Success Stories Writing Activity.

DIRTY WORK Business owners often work long hours to make sure everything is done. **Why?**

Making More Money

People who work for others are paid wages or a salary. When they work hard or when the company does well, they may get a raise. A business owner's earnings, however, are limited only by the potential of his or her business. If you want more control over your income, you may consider starting a business.

Being Recognized Within the Community

Business ownership carries with it a certain amount of prestige. Entrepreneurs, after all, have taken on a responsibility that involves hard work, daring, and know-how. In the process, entrepreneurs make an economic contribution to the community through their investment and creation of jobs.

Risks of Entrepreneurship

If being an entrepreneur is so great, why doesn't everyone do it? Because of intense competition, business ownership can be a difficult undertaking. **Competition** is the rivalry among businesses for consumer dollars. The prospective entrepreneur should consider the costs and risks. These include long hours, uncertain income, responsibility, and the potential of losing money.

Working Long Hours

Long hours are the norm for entrepreneurs, especially during the start-up period. During start-up, survival often depends on making wise decisions. A lot of entrepreneurs cannot afford paid help. Many entrepreneurs devote a lot of time to the business, often working seven days a week. Employees, on the other hand, do not usually have to work long hours.

While You Read

Connect Interview a local business owner. Ask which rewards are most important to him or her.

TECHNOLOGY Today

Global Positioning Systems

If you don't like asking for directions or dealing with cumbersome paper maps, global positioning systems (GPS) make finding your way easy. Using information from government satellites, GPS devices can tell you where you're located, anywhere on earth.

Cooperative Learning Activity

Why is GPS so useful? Who are some businesspeople that could benefit the most from GPS technology?

@ Go to **entrepreneurship.glencoe.com** to complete the Technology Today Vocabulary Practice Activity.

Having an Uncertain Income

Business owners make more money than employees—but only when business is good. When business is bad, earnings can be low or nonexistent. Most businesses do not make a profit right away. Even when a business makes a profit, the owner often has to put the money back into the business. Business owners do not get a regular paycheck. In addition, they may not have benefits such as health insurance and time off for vacations.

While You Read

Question Why can't entrepreneurs count on making a certain income?

Being Fully Responsible

The owner of a business is responsible for more than just decision making. He or she must see that everything gets done—sweeping the floors, paying the bills, and making repairs. Ultimately, there is no one else to take care of these tasks. An employee is only responsible for the tasks assigned to him or her. The business owner is ultimately responsible for all tasks. The success or failure of the venture rests entirely on the owner.

Risking One's Investment

The biggest risk of being in business is the possibility of losing one's investment. **Investment** is the amount of money a person puts into his or her business as capital. **Capital** includes the buildings, equipment, tools, and other goods needed to produce a product or the money used to buy these things. Employees, on the other hand, do not risk losing money. Before an entrepreneur can count on earnings, he or she must get the venture up and running.

Write About It

Do the rewards of entrepreneurship outweigh the risks? Write an essay explaining your position.

Section 2.1 After You Read

Key Concept Review

1. What do you consider to be the greatest reward of starting your own business? What do you consider to be the greatest risk of starting your own business? Explain your answer.

2. What is the difference between investment and capital?

3. Describe the responsibilities you take on when you start your own business.

Critical Thinking

4. Assess the advantages of owning a business versus working for someone.

Role Play

Situation You are an entrepreneur who is going to be interviewed by a student who is considering starting a business.

Activity Team up with a classmate. Assume the role of the entrepreneur. Have your classmate assume the role of the student. Work together to research and write a conversation that you will role-play for the class. In the conversation, discuss the risks and rewards of entrepreneurship and offer specific examples.

Evaluation You will be evaluated on how well you address these issues:

- Explain why individuals become entrepreneurs.
- Analyze the personal advantages and risks of owning a business.
- Differentiate between an entrepreneur and an employee.
- Compare the risks and rewards of entrepreneurship.

What Does It Take to Be an Entrepreneur?

GET READY TO READ

KEY TERMS
- role model
- foundation skills
- profile
- achiever

KEY CONCEPTS
- Who Are Entrepreneurs?
- Build Your Potential as an Entrepreneur

THE MAIN IDEA

Before going into business, you should determine the characteristics and skills needed to reach your goal of being successful.

CONCEPT ORGANIZER

Draw the chart below on a separate piece of paper. As you read the section, fill in the chart with the 12 characteristics of successful entrepreneurs.

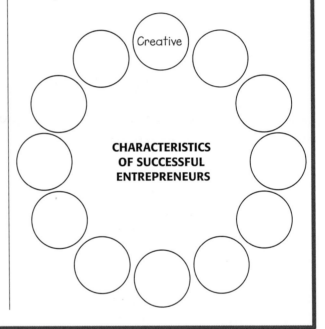

Creative

CHARACTERISTICS OF SUCCESSFUL ENTREPRENEURS

Who Are Entrepreneurs?

Entrepreneurs are important to the nation's economy. There is a great deal of interest in what makes them tick. They are featured in magazines and newspapers. Best sellers are written about them. Some entrepreneurs have become celebrities.

Research has been done to determine what, if any, traits, experiences, and skills entrepreneurs have in common. The object of these studies has been to learn whether entrepreneurs are born or made.

Background

Surprisingly, a variety of people become entrepreneurs. The research reveals a wide span of ages, educational backgrounds, and personal histories. It also reveals common life experiences and other factors that may lead people toward entrepreneurship.

- Nearly half (47 percent) of entrepreneurs were under age 35 when they started their business; 16 percent were under age 25.

- Forty percent of entrepreneurs had a high school diploma or less.

- Twenty-seven percent of entrepreneurs had some college; 33 percent had completed a college degree.

- Many entrepreneurs were independent from an early age.

- Many entrepreneurs worked when they were young (paper routes, yard-care services, babysitting, etc.).

- Sixty-two percent of entrepreneurs had parents or close relatives who owned a business.

- Many entrepreneurs were influenced early in life by a **role model**, a person whose attitudes and achievements they tried to emulate.

Issues in Entrepreneurship

THE ENTREPRENEUR OF THE FUTURE

Fifty years ago, the typical entrepreneur was a white male who owned a small shop or company that focused on local goods and services. The entrepreneur of the past knew most of his customers by name. Today, however, the face of the average American entrepreneur has changed dramatically. America's entrepreneurs are now more racially diverse, and there are many more female business owners.

According to a 2000 study by the Small Business Administration, the face of American entrepreneurship will continue to evolve in the coming years. The entrepreneurs of the future will be very different from even today's business owners. Not only will they continue to be more racially diverse and more likely to be female, they will also be older, better-educated, more committed to enjoying their personal lives, and more focused on global business and high-value services.

Think Critically

Why will entrepreneurs of the future be more educated?

 Go to **entrepreneurship.glencoe.com** to complete the Issues in Entrepreneurship Research Activity.

Twelve Characteristics of Successful Entrepreneurs

Successful entrepreneurs have certain personal characteristics and personality traits. Successful competitors possess the same characteristics as successful entrepreneurs. Successful entrepreneurs have these traits and qualities:

1. **Persistent.** Entrepreneurs are willing to work until a job is done, no matter how long it takes. They are tenacious in overcoming obstacles and pursuing their goals.

2. **Creative.** Entrepreneurs look for new ways to solve old problems.

3. **Responsible.** Entrepreneurs do not pass the buck. They take responsibility for their decisions and actions.

4. **Inquisitive.** Entrepreneurs want to know as much as possible about whatever affects their venture. They conduct research and ask questions to solve problems.

5. **Goal-oriented.** Entrepreneurs set and achieve goals.

6. **Independent.** Entrepreneurs want to make their own decisions.

7. **Self-demanding.** Entrepreneurs have high expectations.

8. **Self-confident.** Entrepreneurs believe in themselves.

9. **Risk-taking.** Entrepreneurs take risks, but they are not reckless.

10. **Restless.** Once entrepreneurs achieve their goals, they begin looking for new challenges.

11. **Action-oriented.** Entrepreneurs are doers as opposed to spectators. They set goals, make decisions, and act on their decisions.

12. **Enthusiastic.** Entrepreneurs are energetic and passionate about their pursuits.

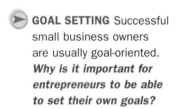

While You Read

Predict What are some things that you can do to build your potential as an entrepreneur?

GOAL SETTING Successful small business owners are usually goal-oriented. *Why is it important for entrepreneurs to be able to set their own goals?*

Ten Essential Entrepreneurial Skills

In addition to desire and characteristics, the research identifies foundation skills needed to be a successful entrepreneur. **Foundation skills** are skills that are used when setting up and running a business. They include:

1. **Communication skills.** Entrepreneurs need person-to-person, telephone, and written communication skills. They also need listening skills to build positive relationships and do accurate work.

2. **Math skills.** Entrepreneurs use basic math skills to budget, keep records, make decisions and calculations, and put together financial statements.

3. **Problem-solving skills.** Entrepreneurs need to be able to come up with logical ideas to solve problems. Solving problems requires creativity and thinking skills.

4. **Technology and computer skills.** Computer skills are essential in almost any business. The ability to understand and use technology is also essential because technology impacts all industries.

5. **Decision-making skills.** Entrepreneurs must be able to choose the best option from among many. Good decision makers know their values and are good at predicting the consequences of actions.

6. **Organizing and planning skills.** Entrepreneurs must be expert organizers and planners, which require logical thinking and good time management.

7. **Teamwork skills.** Entrepreneurs need teamwork skills to coordinate and manage work teams. This involves respecting others, being flexible, and knowing when to exercise leadership.

8. **Social skills.** Entrepreneurs need good social skills to interact well with employees, customers, and vendors. Social skills involve verbal and nonverbal behavior.

9. **Adaptability skills.** Entrepreneurs should be adaptable because the business and economic environment is constantly changing.

10. **Basic business skills.** Entrepreneurs should have a basic understanding of how the economy works and an understanding of fundamental concepts of finance, marketing, and management.

> **While You Read**
>
> **Connect** Choose one of the 10 entrepreneurial skills and develop a plan for improving the skill.

Build Your Potential as an Entrepreneur

As you have learned, the typical successful entrepreneur fits a certain profile. A **profile** is a set of characteristics or qualities that identifies a type or category of person.

What if you don't fit the profile? You shouldn't let that stop you from becoming an entrepreneur. Everyone has the potential to be an entrepreneur. What you really need are a can-do attitude and a genuine desire to go into business. There are many ways to build your potential as an entrepreneur.

Quick Math

If 8,400 new businesses are started each week, how many will be started this year? (8,400 x 52 = 436,800) If 1 in 4 fails, how many are still open?

Strengthen Your Entrepreneurial Characteristics

The personal characteristics described on page 34 are essential to people who want to set up and run their own business. The following steps can help you develop your entrepreneurial characteristics:

1. Determine the strength of your entrepreneurial characteristics. You can use the Entrepreneurial Characteristics Assessment shown in **Figure 2.1** to do a self-evaluation. This will help you to analyze the degree to which you possess the characteristics of an entrepreneur and assess your personal potential to become an entrepreneur.

2. Think of entrepreneurial characteristics as habits you can improve. It is within your control to improve your entrepreneurial traits.

3. Develop your weak characteristics by practicing and acting as though you have the traits you want to develop. After a while, you will find that the traits become part of you.

Figure 2.1 Entrepreneurial Characteristics Assessment

RATING YOUR CHARACTERISTICS By rating your entrepreneurial characteristics, you can assess your personal potential to become an entrepreneur. The circled numbers represent the strength of each characteristic. *If you had to use words instead of numbers to describe each level, what terms would you use?*

Each of the statements below represents a characteristic helpful to entrepreneurs. Read through the list and on a separate sheet of paper, record your reactions. If you think a particular statement describes you very accurately, write 5. If you think it doesn't describe you at all, write 1. If you think it only partially describes you, place yourself between the two extremes by writing a number from 2 to 4.

1. You stay with a task despite difficulties.   ❶ ❷ ❸ ❹ ❺

2. You're creative.   ❶ ❷ ❸ ❹ ❺

3. You take responsibility for your actions.   ❶ ❷ ❸ ❹ ❺

4. You want to know about things.   ❶ ❷ ❸ ❹ ❺

5. You set goals for yourself and work toward them. ❶ ❷ ❸ ❹ ❺

6. You like to work at your own schedule.   ❶ ❷ ❸ ❹ ❺

7. You set high standards for yourself.   ❶ ❷ ❸ ❹ ❺

8. You believe in yourself and in what you are doing. ❶ ❷ ❸ ❹ ❺

9. You like a challenge, but you're not a gambler.   ❶ ❷ ❸ ❹ ❺

10. You're rarely content.   ❶ ❷ ❸ ❹ ❺

BusinessWeek Case Study

Trade Associations' Broad Appeal

Entrepreneurs see many benefits in joining professional organizations, according to a new study. Nearly 60% of small-business owners belong to at least one trade organization, according to a new survey conducted by the National Federation of Independent Business (NFIB). "It appears that the information small-business owners get and the other benefits they receive from their associations are factors in successfully growing a business," notes NFIB Senior Research Fellow William J. Dennis, Jr. "Sometimes, these organizations are the only places where small businesses can find the current, industry-specific information they need."

Of trade-association members who responded to the questionnaire, 24% sought to keep abreast of new technologies. A similar number, 23%, said that specific industry news was the greatest incentive to join. A further 22% cited access to information about relevant laws and regulations as their chief reason for joining, and 18% were after the latest information on customers and market trends.

SOURCE: *BusinessWeek*, FEBRUARY 18, 2004; BY EDWARD POPPER

APPLICATION Poll owners of local businesses to find out if they are members of trade organizations, and if so, what benefits they receive. Present your findings in a written report. Use a spreadsheet program to create charts that visually represent the poll data.

 Go to **entrepreneurship.glencoe.com** to complete the *BusinessWeek* Case Study Reading Guide Activity.

Another way to strengthen your entrepreneurial potential is to think and act like an achiever. An **achiever** is a person with a record of successes. Entrepreneurs are motivated by a need for achievement—an inner feeling of personal accomplishment. To do this, you must think and act like an achiever.

- Set out to be the best at whatever you do.
- Set your sights on accomplishing the extraordinary.
- Write your goals down on paper.
- Pursue your goals with confidence and commitment.
- View difficulties as opportunities to learn and grow.

You can strengthen your entrepreneurial characteristics by reading, writing, observing, and solving. Examples are shown in **Figure 2.2** on page 38. Turning desirable traits and behaviors into habits takes time and practice, but these habits can become part of your makeup.

Figure 2.2   Strengthen Your Entrepreneurial Characteristics

You can strengthen your entrepreneurial characteristics by reading, writing, watching, and solving. *Which of these activities do you do regularly?*

1. Reading
Read articles and books about entrepreneurs and entrepreneurial activities.

2. Writing
Write brief stories about individuals who overcame obstacles to achieve success.

3. Watching
Watch films or videos about successful businesspeople, athletes, and others who are achievement-oriented.

4. Solving
Solve case problems that call for identification of goal-oriented behavior, creativity, and moderate risk taking.

Develop Your Entrepreneurial Skills

To be a successful entrepreneur, you need to develop the foundation skills discussed in this chapter: communication skills, math skills, problem-solving skills, computer and technical skills, decision-making skills, organizing and planning skills, teamwork skills, social skills, adaptability skills, and basic business skills. You do not have to be an expert. However, you must develop the skills necessary to set up and run a successful business.

While You Read

Connect How can you develop technical skills?

Follow this three-step process to gain competency in foundation skills:

1. Learn the techniques needed to use the skill.
2. Put the skill to work in real-world situations.
3. Ask yourself whether you get the results you want. If not, determine how you can improve and apply what you've learned.

You can develop technology skills and basic business skills, including computer skills, in school, through work experience, and by reading. When a proposed business's processes and technology are simple and straightforward, technical skills can be acquired quickly. In other instances, education and training are recommended for the prospective entrepreneur.

Obtaining employment in a similar or related business is a good way to develop technical skills. Another alternative is to take classes that pertain to the business. Still another option is to attend workshops. Workshops are often available through community colleges, economic development organizations, manufacturers, and suppliers.

Section 2.2 After You Read

Key Concept Review

1. What does the research on entrepreneurs' background mean to you personally?
2. What are 12 characteristics of successful entrepreneurs?
3. What are 10 skills entrepreneurs need to organize their business?

Critical Thinking

4. Analyze your class schedule to determine at least three ways that each course can strengthen your entrepreneurial characteristics or improve your entrepreneurial skills.

Role Play

Situation You are an entrepreneur who has agreed to meet with a local student to discuss how to gather information by telephone.

Activity Team up with a classmate and research communication skills and telephone techniques. Work together to write a telephone skills checklist. Then prepare and present a role play in which your classmate interviews you about telephone skills. In your role play, address all of the skills on your checklist.

Evaluation You will be evaluated on how well you:

- Describe and model appropriate telephone skills.
- Present the importance of telephone skills.
- Discuss the different situations in which telephone skills are used.

Chapter Summary

Section 2.1 **Why Be an Entrepreneur?**

People become entrepreneurs for many reasons. Prospective entrepreneurs need to weigh the advantages and disadvantages before deciding whether to start their own businesses. The rewards of going into business for yourself are being your own boss, doing something you enjoy, having the opportunity to be creative, having the freedom to set your own schedule, having job security, making more money, and being recognized within the community. The risks of self-employment are working long hours, having an uncertain income, being fully responsible, and risking one's investment.

Section 2.2 **What Does It Take to Be an Entrepreneur?**

Research shows that everyone has the potential to become an entrepreneur. Although certain background experiences may increase the likelihood of becoming an entrepreneur, a can-do attitude and desire are more important. Successful entrepreneurs are persistent, creative, responsible, inquisitive, goal-oriented, independent, self-demanding, self-confident, risk-taking, restless, action-oriented, and enthusiastic. The ten foundation skills entrepreneurs need to organize their businesses are communication skills, math skills, problem-solving skills, computer and technical skills, decision-making skills, organizing and planning skills, teamwork skills, social skills, adaptability skills, and basic business skills. Entrepreneurs should have a basic understanding of how the economy works and an understanding of fundamental concepts of finance, marketing, and management.

Key Terms Review

1. Using your own words, write a definition for each of the following terms. In addition, find a synonym for each term. Use context clues from the chapter or a thesaurus.

competition (p. 30)	foundation skills (p. 35)
investment (p. 31)	profile (p. 35)
capital (p. 31)	achiever (p. 37)
role model (p. 33)	

Key Concept Review

2. **Describe** the rewards of going into business for yourself. (2.1)
3. **Describe** the risks of going into business for yourself. (2.1)
4. **Identify** the background, characteristics, and skills of successful entrepreneurs. (2.2)
5. **Explain** techniques that will improve your potential for becoming an entrepreneur. (2.2)

Critical Thinking

6. Identify and describe the characteristics of a successful competitor. Contrast them with the characteristics of a successful entrepreneur.
7. Assess the advantages of owning a business versus working for someone.
8. Do you agree with the concept that everyone has the potential to become an entrepreneur? Why or why not?
9. Explain the relationship between entrepreneurial characteristics and achievement motivation.
10. What personality traits do you think would interfere with someone becoming an entrepreneur?
11. Why do you think some people become entrepreneurs while others do not?
12. How are role models important to entrepreneurial success?
13. Are the personal characteristics needed by entrepreneurs necessary for success in any career? Why or why not?

Write About It

14. Write a daily plan for strengthening your entrepreneurial characteristics.
15. Write a brief story about a fictional person who overcomes obstacles to reach a goal. Describe the character's feelings.
16. Write a checklist of things you can do to develop your entrepreneurial skills.
17. Draft a letter to your teacher explaining how to think and act like an achiever.
18. Use a Venn diagram to differentiate between entrepreneurial characteristics and entrepreneurial skills.
19. In a letter to your family, identify and explain foundation skills and describe how they can help you be a successful entrepreneur.
20. In a journal or diary entry, explain the top three rewards of entrepreneurship for you personally.

Academic Skills

Math

21. After calling the local chamber of commerce, Keela learned that there were 1,677 entrepreneurs in her town. Use the research summary on the background of entrepreneurs (page 33) to calculate the number of entrepreneurs under age 35 when they started their business, the number of entrepreneurs under age 25, and the number of entrepreneurs with a high school diploma or less.

Language Arts

22. Read a magazine article or book about a successful entrepreneur. As you read, note incidents or observations that illustrate entrepreneurial characteristics and skills. Prepare an oral report to the class that focuses on these traits. After presenting your report, have the class determine the traits that the successful entrepreneurs in your readings have in common.

Entrepreneurship in Your Community

23. Select a local company that has gone out of business recently. List some of the reasons the business might have failed and how the owner might have prevented the business from closing.

24. Interview the principal or another administrator at your school. Share the characteristics of successful entrepreneurs that you learned about in this chapter. Ask the administrator which traits he or she has. Ask about the skills and characteristics needed to be a successful administrator. Ask him or her to compare being a school administrator with an entrepreneur. Share your findings with the class.

Ethical Practices

Ethics in Changing Circumstances

25. Jon Horton was an entrepreneur who took great pride in his strong entrepreneurial characteristics. He thought of himself as a fair and honest person with high integrity. Jon's employees—most of whom had been with him for over 10 years—had a similar opinion of him. However, that opinion changed when Jon's lumber business burned down. Although he was heavily insured, he decided to let his workforce go and build an apartment complex on the property. Jon's employees charged that his actions were neither fair nor ethical. Do you agree or disagree with the employees? Write a three-paragraph paper stating your stand on the issue. Give both sides of the situation before stating your position.

Entrepreneurial Potential

You want to evaluate whether you have the characteristics and skills needed for success as an entrepreneur.

Connect

Use a search engine or Web directory to locate information about the characteristics, skills, aptitudes, abilities, and personality traits needed for entrepreneurial success. Then write a report that includes the following:

- List and explain the characteristics, skills, aptitudes, abilities, and personality traits needed for entrepreneurial success.

- Evaluate whether you possess each skill, aptitude, ability, and personality trait.

- Conclude whether you have your entrepreneurial potential based on your evaluation.

The Electronic Entrepreneur

Internet Basics

The Internet and the World Wide Web impact virtually every aspect of daily life. The **Internet** is a global computer network of computer networks that facilitates data transmission and exchange. The **World Wide Web (WWW)** is a vast global collection of Web pages that can be read, viewed, and interacted with via computers. The Internet is the system that supports the World Wide Web.

Web Browsers A **Web browser** is a software program used to view Web pages. Web browsers are applications that read **Hypertext Transfer Protocol (HTTP)**, a protocol used to request and transmit Web pages. **Hypertext Markup Language (HTML)** is the code used to structure Web pages and to set up hyperlinks between documents. Both HTTP and HTML depend on the use of **hypertext**, a system for writing and displaying text that can be linked to related documents. **Hyperlinks** are electronic links that provide direct access from one place in a hypertext document to another place in the same or a different hypertext document.

Internet Addresses An **IP address** is a unique numeric code that identifies a computer on the Internet. A **domain name** is the name that identifies a Web site, such as glencoe.com. The domain name identifies the numeric IP address. To find Web pages, you'll need to know the **uniform resource locator (URL)**, a series of letters and/or numbers specifying the precise location of a specific document on the Web. Each URL contains a **domain name extension** that tells the user what type of organization uses the address, such as a commercial (.com), educational (.edu), or governmental (.gov).

TechTerms

- Internet
- World Wide Web (WWW)
- Web browser
- hypertext transfer protocol (HTTP)
- hypertext markup language (HTML)
- hypertext
- hyperlinks
- IP address
- domain name
- uniform resource locator (URL)
- domain name extension

FACT AND IDEA REVIEW

1. What is the relationship between the Internet and the World Wide Web?
2. What are Web browsers, and why are they necessary?
3. What is HTML, and why is it important to Web browsers?
4. What can a domain name reveal about an organization?

FOR DISCUSSION

5. No one authority controls the Internet. As the use of the Internet continues to grow, should some organization, agency, or person take control? Why or why not?

Recognizing Opportunity

CHAPTER OBJECTIVES

After you read this chapter, you should be able to:

SECTION 3.1

- Discuss current trends that provide opportunity for entrepreneurs.
- Explain ways to recognize opportunity.
- Explain how to think creatively about opportunity.
- Discuss ways to overcome challenges to creativity.
- Explain ways to find creative business ideas.

SECTION 3.2

- Identify the importance of personal values and goals in choosing an entrepreneurial pursuit.
- Describe the challenges and rewards of entering a family business.
- List the benefits and drawbacks of buying a business.
- Describe how you can evaluate a business opportunity.
- Compare the advantages and disadvantages of starting your own business.

PERSONAL FINANCIAL PLANNING

Why do so many people have money problems? The main reason is they do not plan how they will use their money. You can avoid money problems with personal financial planning.

Personal financial planning means spending, saving, and investing your money so you can have the kind of life you want. Planning your personal finances will help you reach your goals and achieve a lifetime of financial independence and security.

MAKE A FINANCIAL PLAN

To make a personal financial plan:

- Assess your present financial situation.

- Identify and prioritize your personal financial goals.

- Identify alternative courses of action.

- Evaluate your alternatives.

- Create and maintain a budget that supports financial goals.

- Review and revise your plan as your financial goals evolve.

@ Go to **entrepreneurship.glencoe.com** to complete the Standard & Poor's Money Talk Financial Literacy Activity.

PREPARE TO READ

THINK ABOUT THESE QUESTIONS AS YOU READ.

What is an idea?

What is an opportunity?

How is an idea different from an opportunity?

Understanding Entrepreneurial Trends

GET READY TO READ

KEY TERMS
- online business
- services
- outsourcing
- strategic alliance
- corporate venture
- innovation
- niche
- brainstorm
- demographics
- trade magazine
- specialty magazine
- trade show

KEY CONCEPTS
- Current Entrepreneurial Trends
- Learning to Recognize Opportunity
- Thinking Creatively About Opportunity
- Challenges to Creativity
- Creative Sources of Ideas

THE MAIN IDEA
The abilities to recognize new opportunities and to think creatively are essential for success in today's market.

READING ORGANIZER
Draw the chart on a separate piece of paper. As you read, fill in the chart with the eight entrepreneurial trends discussed in the section.

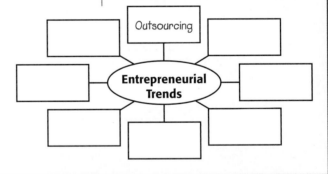

Current Entrepreneurial Trends

Are you ready to begin the entrepreneurial process? This process involves taking the steps to recognize an opportunity, develop a business concept, test it with potential customers, and create a business to execute that concept. The first step is to identify a business opportunity.

One way to identify business opportunities is to study current trends that provide opportunities for entrepreneurs. Business trends that are sweeping our country include Internet businesses, service businesses, home-based businesses, socially responsible nonprofit businesses, corporate ventures, strategic alliances, and an increased emphasis on technology and outsourcing.

Internet Businesses

The Internet has transformed the way business is conducted. Many new types of Internet-based businesses have emerged, and most traditional companies have added online components. An **online business** is a business that conducts business by means of the Internet. Online businesses have the potential to attract a huge number of customers because anyone with an Internet connection can purchase from this type of store. According to *American City Business Journals,* small businesses that use the Internet have grown 46 percent faster than those that do not.

Service Businesses

Service businesses dominate the modern American economy. Even if a company produces products, it also provides services to it customers. Most small businesses are service businesses. **Services** are intangible things that businesses do for us that enhance our lives. In 2000, the U.S. Census Bureau reported that service businesses are the biggest and fastest-growing part of the American economy as measured by new job growth.

There are hundreds of different kinds of service businesses. Insurance, sports and entertainment, tourism, banking, and education are services. So are accounting, advertising, document shredding, printing, real estate, dry cleaning, fitness centers, and tax preparation.

While You Read

Predict What kinds of services account for the largest part of U.S. economic growth?

Home-Based Businesses

The number of businesses that start in the home has been growing rapidly. In the late 1990s, about 41 million businesses were being conducted from home, a result of the high-quality technology available to self-employed business people. A home-based business can have an image that is just as professional as that of a large corporation.

HOME SWEET HOME
Working at home can save time and money. *What are some types of technology and equipment that are used in both a home office and the traditional workplace?*

Many people who lose their jobs or are laid off due to cutbacks choose to work from their home in the field where they were once employed instead of finding a job with another company. A few examples of home-based businesses include consultants, sales representatives, tradespeople, home and automobile inspectors, writers, graphic artists, and Web designers. Even companies that produce products can be operated from the entrepreneur's home if the manufacturing and distribution of products are outsourced to other companies.

Socially Responsible Nonprofit Businesses

Social entrepreneurs start their businesses to better society; they have a mission that is focused on doing good. Therefore, social entrepreneurs often form nonprofit organizations, which means that the business makes a profit, but the owner must keep the profits in the business. Some nonprofit businesses can also qualify to be tax-exempt. Some examples of socially responsible nonprofits are organizations to support a specific mission, such as feeding the hungry, a community theater company, or an education-focused business.

Focus on Technology

An increased reliance on technology is the main trend that affects businesses today. Entrepreneurs who know how to use technology to improve their business processes create a strong competitive advantage and enjoy a greater chance of success. Whether technology is a company's product or it is used to increase productivity, it is a critical component of any business strategy.

Outsourcing

In today's economy, you can outsource just about any business activity. **Outsourcing** is contracting with other companies for services. Running a small business is a complex task, and few entrepreneurs are experts at everything. Outsourcing allows a small business to focus on what it does best while tapping into outside expertise. For example, suppose you have invented a new video game. You can pay a software programmer to develop your game, contract with a packaging company to design the product packaging, and then contract with a distributor to find retail outlets for your game.

The most common type of outsourcing is business-process outsourcing, such as accounting, human resource management, benefits, payroll, and finance functions. These are some of the many benefits to outsourcing:

- Outsourcing allows greater efficiency, saving time and money.

- Outsourcing decreases overhead investment or debt.

- Outsourcing lowers regulatory compliance burdens.

- Outsourcing allows companies to start new projects quickly.

- Outsourcing makes companies more attractive to investors because it allows companies to direct more capital directly into money-making activities.

While You Read

Connect Think of three types of businesses that offer outsourcing services to companies.

Strategic Alliances

One step beyond outsourcing is forming a partnership with another company. This kind of partnership is known as a **strategic alliance**. Your small company may form an alliance with a larger company to supply it with a product or service that is not part of the larger company's core competency.

For example, 3M, the manufacturer of adhesive products such as Scotch™ brand tape, looks to small companies for complementary products such as tape dispensers. They form a strategic alliance. The small company provides 3M with all the tape dispensers it needs to package with its adhesive tape.

Corporate Ventures

A **corporate venture** is a new venture started inside a large corporation. Large companies are finding that they must act like entrepreneurs to remain competitive. It is difficult for a large company to behave like a small, flexible company, so starting a small company as a spin-off is a solution. The parent company supplies resources to the corporate venturers to help the new venture get started. Often the new corporate venture eventually becomes an independent company.

BusinessWeek Case Study

Attitudes Toward Entrepreneurship

If you are pulling long hours to build a business, take heart—plenty of folks wish they had your drive and gumption. Do you wonder sometimes whether owning your own company is really worth all the hassle? Well, if it's any consolation, the decision to become your own boss has likely made you the envy of neighbors, relatives, and friends.

According to a new national survey about attitudes toward business ownership, 67% of Americans have dreamed of owning their own businesses, and 56% say they would leave their jobs to start one if circumstances permitted. The poll noted a trend toward "hobby-based" businesses, with 40% of the respondents saying that a personal passion was the best reason for going it alone. Another 17% wanted the opportunity to be their own boss, and 15% sought work/family flexibility. The poll, commissioned by FedEx and conducted by Opinion Research, surveyed 1,000 Americans age 18 and over.

SOURCE: BUSINESSWEEK, NOVEMBER 4, 2003; BY KAREN KLEIN

APPLICATION

Poll the students in your class on their attitudes toward business ownership. Present your findings in a brief written report. Document your poll results in a spreadsheet and create charts that visually represent the data.

 Go to **entrepreneurship.glencoe.com** to complete the *BusinessWeek* Case Study Reading Guide Activity.

Learning to Recognize Opportunity

Entrepreneurial thinking is about generating ideas and recognizing opportunities. Entrepreneurial thinking involves training your mind to look at products and services in a different way and figuring out ways to improve upon them. To think like an entrepreneur, you need to continuously learn about and evaluate other types of businesses. If you learn to think like an entrepreneur, you can position yourself to recognize opportunities as they develop.

Creativity and Innovation

You may wonder where ideas originate. How do people come up with great ideas? Is creativity something that comes naturally? Not necessarily. Can you learn to be creative? Absolutely!

Creativity is the activity that results in **innovation**, which is finding new ways of doing things. While everyone approaches creativity slightly differently, there are some definite patterns to the process. In general, all creativity leading to the invention of something new involves connection, discovery, invention, and application.

You make a connection when you bring together things that are not usually connected. For example, Leonardo da Vinci, the great inventor and painter, connected his observations about tree branches to the engineering of a canal system to carry water to the sea. A connection often leads to a discovery that is turned into an invention. In da Vinci's case, the invention was a hydraulic system to control water levels so that boats could cross under a bridge in his canal system. Application is going beyond the original invention to other uses in new areas. Da Vinci's application was the idea of mills powered by wind and water. Starting with a simple connection can produce a wealth of new and innovative ideas.

Write About It

Brainstorm On a separate piece of paper, brainstorm several ways to think creatively about opportunities.

Idea Versus Opportunity

An idea is not the same thing as an opportunity. You generate ideas by thinking creatively. Opportunities are ideas that have commercial potential. A good opportunity can be turned into a business. Most good business opportunities result from the entrepreneur's alertness to unmet consumer needs and unique and unfilled market niches. A **niche** is a small specialized market.

Finding Opportunities by Understanding Industries

One way to identify opportunities is to understand industries. An industry is a grouping of businesses with a common purpose. In every industry, the marketplace continuously changes. Changes in industries create profitable niches for new businesses to fill. The development of new products and services in any industry creates the need for complementary types of businesses. If you know the inner workings of an industry, and you examine and analyze industry trends, you can identify opportunities that exist as a result of those trends. You can also understand where the problems are that customers experience.

Thinking Creatively About Opportunity

Creativity requires you to be aware of your surroundings. Use these strategies to activate your creativity and develop new enterprise ideas:

- **Practice brainstorming.** When you **brainstorm**, you think freely to generate ideas. During brainstorming, ideas are not judged as good or bad. Even those that seem silly should be given a fair hearing initially.

- **Look at ordinary items in new ways.** Find a simple item and figure out how many new products or uses you can find for it. With practice, you'll get better at seeing things in a different light.

- **Find creative solutions to common problems.** When you find yourself perplexed by a problem, think about how to find a solution. Have you ever used a flat-head screwdriver to pry something open? That's finding a creative solution to a problem.

- **Connect unrelated items.** Ask a friend to put together a tray of different items. Then try to come up with a new product from the items. This forces you to look at things in new ways.

Challenges to Creativity

Being creative presents many different challenges. These challenges include time pressures, the influence of unsupportive people, lack of confidence, and rigid thinking. The hardest challenges to overcome are the challenges you bring upon yourself. **Figure 3.1** outlines tips that will help you remove the roadblocks to creativity.

Figure 3.1 **Removing the Roadblocks to Creativity**

- Believe in yourself. Positive self-encouragement works.

- Use nonlogical thinking. Not everything has to make sense right away.

- Free your mind! Don't think of everything in practical terms.

- View problems as challenges that offer the opportunity to innovate.

- Entertain all ideas. There is no such thing as a frivolous idea.

- Relax! Relaxation is a key part of the creative process.

- Have a playful attitude. Don't worry about looking foolish.

- Look at failure as a learning experience that will lead to success.

- Model creative behavior. Anyone can learn to think creatively.

- Develop listening skills. You can learn a lot by listening to other people talk about their wants and needs.

ENHANCE YOUR CREATIVITY Entrepreneurs can stimulate and encourage creativity in many ways. *Can you think of any other techniques?*

Creative Sources of Ideas

Good business ideas involve popular trends such as those described in **Figure 3.2**. Ideas can come to you from anywhere, and sometimes in the strangest moments. Research has found that some of the greatest ideas have come to people when they're brushing their teeth, driving, or sleeping.

Observe the World Around You

Start watching people. Find places in your community where you'll be able to observe people. In a hotel lobby or a shopping mall, you can learn a lot about what people want and need. That's how Mary Naylor learned that people who work in office buildings wanted the same kind of concierge service offered in hotels. She formed Capitol Concierge to do just that. Her business handles special services such as arranging for theater tickets or making dinner reservations.

Watch for Demographic Changes

Demographics are personal characteristics that describe a population. These include age, gender, income, ethnic background, education, and occupation, to name a few.

One demographic trend that affects entrepreneurship is the increasing diversity of the American people. Cultural diversity plays an important role in entrepreneurial ventures because it affects the kinds of products and services that entrepreneurs develop. Business owners who understand and appeal to the diversity of their customer base are more likely to succeed.

Issues in Entrepreneurship

DEMOGRAPHICS

Demographics are always changing. One big demographic change that is happening right now is the growth of the Hispanic population. By 2010, Hispanics will surpass African-Americans as the largest U.S. ethnic group. Potential entrepreneurs would be wise to know that the Hispanic culture is diverse and comprises 21 different nationalities, including Mexican, Spanish, Puerto Rican, Cuban, Dominican, and many others from Central and South America. Univision has become the nation's number one growth broadcasting network by catering to a Spanish-speaking audience.

Think Creatively
What are some advantages to operating a culturally segmented business?

 Go to **entrepreneurship.glencoe.com** to complete the Issues in Entrepreneurship Research Activity.

Figure 3.2 Business Opportunities From Popular Trends

FINDING A GOOD BUSINESS OPPORTUNITY
You can find business opportunities in traditional industries as well as new industries that didn't exist five years ago. The secret to success is the ability to see these opportunities before anyone else does. *What are some other popular trends?*

Fitness and Health
Many people are interested in extending their life expectancy and improving their health and well-being. One major trend is that today people are concerned about healing both their bodies and their minds.

Ethnic Products
We are a multicultural nation. Entrepreneurs can find many opportunities to serve the special needs of particular ethnic groups with foods, hair-care products, cosmetics, and other products and services.

Indulgence Goods and Luxury Services
With the stresses of work, enjoying one's leisure time has become an important commodity. Many Americans indulge themselves with little luxuries, such as expensive chocolates, gourmet coffee, and other specialty products. Luxury services, such as errand services and day spas for people and their pets, abound.

Be an Avid Reader

Most successful entrepreneurs stay on top of what's going on in business and the world by reading newspapers, magazines, and books. Don't read just in your area of interest. Sometimes reading about an unrelated field will spark an idea that you can apply to your field.

Consider Your Own Experiences

Self-employment options within your own experiences are the easiest to identify and are excellent sources of opportunity. Look for opportunities in your interests, hobbies, and work.

INTERESTS Good business ideas often target problems observed in everyday life. Practice thinking about the problems you encounter each day as you pursue your interests. Then think about ways to solve the problems. Practicing these steps may help you think of great business ideas:

- List at least five of your interests.
- List at least one product or service you use while pursuing each of your interests.
- Identify one problem associated with each product or service.
- Describe ways you could improve each product or service.
- Evaluate whether any of your product or service improvements have business potential.

HOBBIES Many hobbies can be turned into successful ventures. Developing Web sites, restoring cars, playing a sport, making music—these are just a few pastimes that have potential. Try to evaluate your own favorite pastime in terms of its business potential. For example, suppose you play in a youth soccer league and you need a new type of protective gear that does not currently exist. You can use that experience as an idea source and turn that idea into an opportunity by designing and developing the gear you need.

WORK Your experiences in the world of work can be an excellent source of business ideas. When you work, you learn about the particular business you work in as well as the industry in which the business operates. You learn about the business's customers and suppliers and their wants and needs. You also learn about the technology used in the business and the industry and the government regulations that apply to the business and the industry. These insights can help you to recognize opportunities. If you work after school, ask yourself:

- Is there room in the market for a similar business, possibly in a different niche?
- Are there any gaps in the company's network of suppliers?
- Is the company in need of services that aren't being provided?
- Are the company's customers in need of products and services that are not provided?
- Has the evolution of technology altered business processes or created new business processes that provide new opportunities?

While You Read

Question How can you use your work experience as a source of business ideas?

WORK OR PLAY? Your interests and hobbies can help you choose an entrepreneurial pursuit. *What small businesses might be related to this young man's interest in cars?*

Consult Outside Sources

Look at people, places, and things in the business community for business ideas. Some outside sources to consult include trade magazines, specialty magazines, trade shows and exhibitions, newspapers, the Internet, and government agencies. As you explore these sources of information, routinely ask yourself, "What self-employment opportunities does this present to someone with my interests?"

TRADE MAGAZINES A **trade magazine** is a periodical published for specific types of businesses or industries. Trade magazines often contain articles and advertisements about new products, services, or business concepts. They offer current, industry-specific news and access to the latest information on customers and market trends. Some also offer continuing education programs and networking opportunities. Many trade magazines are available on the Internet.

SPECIALTY MAGAZINES A **specialty magazine** is a periodical that targets people with special interests in sports, camping, fashion, and a variety of other areas. A potential entrepreneur can use specialty magazines to identify the interests and needs of potential consumers. They can be a great source of ideas for new business ventures.

TRADE SHOWS AND EXHIBITIONS Nearly every field has national or regional trade shows. At a **trade show**, vendors and manufacturers introduce new items and promote established products and services. At a trade show, you can see exhibits and demonstrations of goods and services. These shows can be a source of spin-off ideas. Contact your local chamber of commerce or search the Internet for times and dates of shows and exhibitions.

NEWSPAPERS Newspapers provide an ongoing source of ideas for businesses. Many have business sections that report on trends and innovations. Other sections of the paper, such as sports or lifestyle, can pinpoint problems people have that can be sources of opportunity for you.

THE INTERNET The Internet can be a source of opportunities. Many sites, such as the Small Business Administration site, offer ideas for entrepreneurs. Using a search engine such as Google, you can explore the kinds of businesses that currently exist. Remember, however, that the best opportunities lie in the gaps where businesses have not yet gone.

GOVERNMENT AGENCIES The federal government can be a source of new product ideas. The files of the U.S. Patent Office contain detailed descriptions of new products. Although the patents themselves are protected, they frequently include information that suggests other marketable product ideas. The U.S. Patent Office publishes the *Official Gazette,* a weekly periodical that summarizes each patent granted and lists all patents available for license or sale.

New product ideas can also come in response to government regulations. For example, the Occupational Safety and Health Act included a government regulation that small businesses must keep a first aid kit on site. The legislation detailed the specific contents of the required kit. Entrepreneurs responded to the new regulation by manufacturing first aid kits with the required components and marketing them to small businesses that had to comply with the regulation.

Section 3.1 After You Read

Key Concept Review

1. Identify two current changes and trends that are a source for new enterprise ideas.

2. What are demographics and how do they affect business?

3. Identify current publications and Web sites that can assist you in determining what type of business to start.

Critical Thinking

4. Write a paragraph that discusses how brainstorming, creative thinking, and observations can be used to develop new enterprise ideas.

Role Play

Situation Assume the role of a recent college graduate with a business degree. You work for a company that develops and markets consumer products.

Activity Because the company is looking for new product ideas, your first assignment is to make a presentation to the CEO on the entrepreneurial trends that are sweeping the country. With a partner, take turns role-playing the presentation to the CEO.

Evaluation You will be evaluated on how well you address these issues:

• Explain current entrepreneurial trends and how they will affect business.

• Analyze and discuss entrepreneurial opportunities in future trends.

• Give examples of new products that might develop as a result of these trends.

Starting Versus Buying a Business

GET READY TO READ

KEY TERMS
- values
- goodwill
- franchise
- franchisee
- franchisor
- business broker

KEY CONCEPTS
- Personal Values and Goals
- Entering the Family Business
- Buying an Existing Business
- Evaluating a Business Opportunity
- Starting Your Own Business

THE MAIN IDEA

Whether you start a business from scratch or buy an existing business and make it better, owning a business that is compatible with your personal values and goals is critical.

READING ORGANIZER

Draw the Venn diagram on a separate piece of paper. As you read, write notes about franchisees in the left oval and notes about franchisors in the right oval. In the overlapping section, write notes that apply to both franchisees and franchisors.

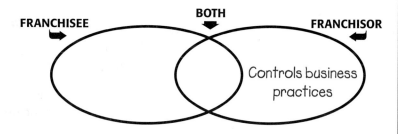

FRANCHISEE   BOTH   FRANCHISOR

Controls business practices

Personal Values and Goals

Owning a business is a huge responsibility and therefore a major decision to make. The job of deciding whether to buy or start a business is made easier if you consider your personal values and goals.

You should consider many things when choosing what type of business to start. One of the most important is your values. Your core values are the beliefs and principles you choose to live by. Your **values** define who you are, shape your attitudes and your choices, and help you identify your priorities. Values are usually influenced by family, religious beliefs, teachers, friends, society, and personal experiences. Many people share at least some of the basic values listed in **Figure 3.3** on page 58.

Figure 3.3 Values Inventory

CHOOSE YOUR VALUES
Choose ten values that matter to you most. *Who or what has been the greatest influence on your values?*

- Adventure
- Balance
- Commitment
- Community
- Compassion
- Competition
- Courage
- Creativity
- Environmentalism
- Fairness
- Financial security
- Fun
- Generosity
- Hard work
- Health
- Honesty

- Independence
- Integrity
- Kindness
- Knowledge
- Learning
- Loyalty
- Physical appearance
- Power
- Recognition
- Relationships
- Responsibility
- Security
- Social responsibility
- Solitude
- Spirituality
- Tolerance

Core values do not change in different situations, and they endure over time. Once you have identified your core values, you can use them to lay out goals for your future and guide your entrepreneurial pursuits. Other factors that will affect your choice of business include your personality, abilities, lifestyle needs, background, hobbies, interests, experience, and financial resources.

While You Read

Predict What can you do to minimize conflict in a family business?

Entering the Family Business

If your family owns a business, chances are you've had the opportunity to work there during the summers or after school. Perhaps you have thought about taking over the business one day. Joining a family business is one way to experience entrepreneurship. Family businesses are an important part of the U.S. economy. Although they are typically smaller enterprises, some, such as Mattel Toys and Marriott Corp., have become large, successful companies.

The Rewards and Challenges of Family Businesses

Although family businesses have great potential for success, only about one-third of them survive to the second generation. The reason so many family businesses fail lies in the dynamics of the family itself. Some families work well together and others do not.

The greatest advantage of a family business is the trust and togetherness that family members share. A family working as a team can often achieve more than its individual members can. At the same time, one of the greatest disadvantages of a family enterprise is that its owners can never get away from the business. Therefore, they may have difficulty viewing the venture and its problems objectively. Another common source of conflict is parents who are unable to see their child as a business person capable of making wise decisions and taking responsibility.

To minimize family conflicts and prevent some of the problems that family businesses face, it is important to establish clear lines of responsibility, be objective about family members' qualifications, keep decisions unaffected by personal emotions, and respect individual family members' needs.

Quick Math

Of the 25 million businesses in the United States, 90 percent are family owned and managed. Given these statistics, calculate how many family-owned businesses there are in America.

Questions to Ask Yourself

Before entering a family business, ask yourself these questions:

- Do I have the ability to work for a member of my family?

- Do I get along well with the family members who will be involved in the business?

- Do we share the same goals for the business?

- Do we share the same general goals for our personal lives?

- Can we be clear and specific about our expectations of each other?

- Can I leave business problems at work when I go home each night?

- Can we maintain a positive family relationship?

If you answered no to any one of these questions, you have identified a potential area of conflict. However, if the benefits to joining the family business outweigh the negatives, it will be worth your while to resolve the conflict.

Buying an Existing Business

Another way to acquire a business is to buy an existing one. In many respects, buying a business is less risky than starting one from scratch because the employees are already hired and trained, the equipment is already in place, and the company already has customers. Customers are especially important. Their continued business after you take over increases your chances of success. Such loyalty, called **goodwill**, is an extremely valuable business asset.

Acquiring an existing business has other advantages. An existing business usually has established procedures in place. There may be substantial inventory on hand and trade credit to facilitate future purchases. The owner may even offer his or her expertise during the transition period.

While You Read

Connect Think about your loyalty to a local business. What makes you return over and over again to a particular store or restaurant? What would keep you away?

Buying a Franchise

A franchise is another way to purchase a business opportunity. With a franchise, you can buy the right to set up a new business patterned on an existing model. A **franchise** is a legal agreement to begin a new business in the name of a recognized company. It gives the **franchisee** (buyer) the right to a product, process, or service; training and assistance in setting up the business; and ongoing marketing and quality support while the business is in operation. The most important advantage of buying a franchise is that the entrepreneur does not have to incur all of the risks associated with starting a new business. The franchisee usually buys into a business that has an accepted name, product, or service. Help-U-Sell, Dunkin' Donuts, and Meineke Car Care Centers are examples of franchises. The buyers of these franchises pay a fee and an annual royalty on sales, typically three to eight percent.

The seller is the **franchisor**. The franchisee is buying a way of operating a business and a product with name recognition. The franchisor is selling its planning and management expertise.

If you buy a McDonald's franchise, you will be trained in methods of operation, learn how to prepare McDonald's products, and be supplied through McDonald's distribution channels. You will also have the benefit of the company's national advertising efforts. All of these things reduce the risk of failure.

Before buying a franchise, however, make sure you understand all of the costs and limitations involved. For one thing, the franchisor can restrict how you run the business. Also, investigate the market saturation. The best locations may already be taken or another franchisee may have a location too close to yours, which will make it difficult to secure enough customers to succeed.

Evaluating a Business Opportunity

Whether you buy a regular business or a franchised business, it is important to evaluate whether the business is a good deal. Many businesses are put up for sale because they are not successful. They may be losing money or have a poor reputation, which can be impossible to repair. Inventory may be dated, and equipment or facilities may need repairs. Employees may lack the skills needed to keep the business competitive. The owner may simply be tired of running a business.

Every business has problems, but some problems are more critical than others. Take the following steps to prevent yourself from purchasing a business burdened with serious problems:

- Investigate the company and the industry carefully. Don't rely only on what the seller tells you. Talk to customers, employees, and suppliers.

- Hire an accountant to verify the value of the business's inventory, accounts receivable, and assets.

- Hire an attorney to advise you and to investigate the business for any legal liabilities.

The First Franchise Empire

In 1954, Ray Kroc bought the rights to use the name of a popular California hamburger stand from the McDonald brothers. It was an exclusive 10-year franchise to license operators of McDonald's restaurants. Kroc proceeded to build a franchise empire, and in 1961 he bought out the McDonald brothers for $2.7 million. By 1966, there were 800 McDonald's restaurants; today there are over 30,000. The company serves an average of 38 million people each day and holds a whopping 42 percent of the $36 billion fast food market. Kroc's entrepreneurial venture redefined the food industry.

CRITICAL THINKING

Why do you suppose that Kroc chose to license someone else's name instead of starting from scratch? What are some of the advantages and disadvantages of owning a franchise?

 Go to **entrepreneurship.glencoe.com** to complete the Success Stories Writing Activity.

Where to Find a Business

People find businesses in many ways. The simplest way is to look in the newspaper. Businesses that are for sale are listed in local papers as well as national business publications such as *The Wall Street Journal*. The most effective way to locate a business is to network with people in the community. Accountants, attorneys, bankers, and local government administrators are good sources. Let them know what kind of business you are looking for. Then keep in touch with them.

You can also hire a business broker. A **business broker** is someone whose job is to bring buyers and sellers together. You can find business brokers in the telephone book or online.

Questions to Ask

Before you purchase a business, ask these questions:

- Is the business interesting to me and to others? Make sure that you really enjoy it and that there are plenty of existing customers who are interested in the business.

- Why is the owner selling? Owners sell for many reasons—retirement, lack of interest, illness, and need for cash. You will want to know if the owner is selling for these more personal reasons or because the business is not doing well or the industry is in decline. Check the firm's financial statements against information from suppliers and competitors.

TECHNOLOGY Today

Solving Problems Using Technology

We live in the information age. Today, one of the most important skills is knowing how to use technology to come up with solutions for everyday problems. Technology and problem-solving skills are integral to small business success.

Cooperative Learning Activity

Your small business is growing rapidly but has a large inventory and limited storage space. In a small group, brainstorm technology-based solutions to the problem.

 Go to **entrepreneurship.glencoe.com** to complete the Technology Today extension Vocabulary Practice Activity.

While You Read

Question What are some additional ways you can find out why an owner is selling his or her business?

- What is the business's potential for growth? Once businesses are born, they go through a life cycle of growth, maturity, and eventually decline. Determine where the business you are considering is positioned in this life cycle. It is best to avoid a declining business or industry. Although it is possible to turn an enterprise around, you can't reverse an economic trend.

Starting Your Own Business

When you can't find an existing business that meets your needs, you will need to start from scratch. Starting a business has many advantages. You can do things your own way, and you can build the company with fresh ideas and enthusiasm.

Questions to Ask

Before you start your own business, ask yourself these questions:

- Do I have the motivation to start from nothing?

- Does the business align with my personality, abilities, values, and goals?

- Do I have sufficient knowledge of basic operations to undertake the business?

- Do I have the necessary managerial ability?

- Do I have the right partners to help me with the business?

- Do I have enough financial resources to start from scratch?

- Am I willing to accept the risk?

What You Must Do

The answers to the preceding questions are deceptively simple, but the actual process of starting a new business is very complex. It requires extensive planning and resource gathering. The following list is just a sampling of the many tasks involved in starting a business:

- Determine that your venture is feasible by testing your concept in the market to see if there are enough customers to make the effort worthwhile.

- Decide whether you want a traditional business with a physical location or an online business or a combination of both.

- Prepare a business plan to seek capital, partners, and employees.

- Secure professional advisors—accountant, lawyer, insurance broker, etc.

- Purchase equipment if required.

- Hire employees.

- Initiate relationships with suppliers.

- Set up distribution channels.

- Create awareness for the business.

Section 3.2 After You Read

Key Concept Review

1. What role do your values play in the decision to buy or start a business?

2. Why would you start your own business instead of buying an existing one?

3. What are three questions you should ask yourself before starting a business?

Critical Thinking

4. Describe the relationship between franchising and other forms of business ownership.

Role Play

Situation Assume the role of a consultant advising a young woman who must choose between going into her family's restaurant business or starting her own business in the apparel industry.

Activity Conduct research on the restaurant and apparel industries. Then pair up with a partner and take turns role-playing a conversation between the consultant and the entrepreneur.

Evaluation You will be evaluated on how well you address these issues:

- Assess and evaluate the various ways to start a business.

- Research, assess, and evaluate opportunities for business ventures in the restaurant and apparel industries.

- Distinguish the types of entrepreneurial ventures you find in these industries.

- Examine the challenges of entering a family business.

Chapter 3 | Review and Activities

Chapter Summary

Section 3.1 **Understanding Entrepreneurial Trends**

Some major entrepreneurial trends include Internet businesses, service businesses, home-based businesses, socially responsible nonprofits, strategic alliances, corporate ventures, and an increased emphasis on technology and outsourcing. The abilities to recognize new opportunities and to think creatively are essential for success in today's market. There are techniques to overcoming challenges to creativity and to finding creative business ideas.

Section 3.2 **Starting Versus Buying a Business**

Use personal values and goals to guide your entrepreneurial pursuits because they help you identify your priorities. Family businesses have great potential for success when family members work well together. When buying an existing business, carefully evaluate the opportunity. People find businesses by looking at ads, networking, or hiring business brokers. Starting your own business requires extensive planning and allows you to build your company with fresh ideas and enthusiasm.

Key Terms Review

1. Write a one-page article for your school newspaper describing how important it is to be creative when thinking about starting and running a business. Use the following key terms from the chapter:

online business (p. 47)	trade magazine (p. 55)
services (p. 47)	specialty magazine (p. 55)
outsourcing (p. 48)	trade show (p. 55)
strategic alliance (p. 49)	values (p. 57)
corporate venture (p. 49)	goodwill (p. 59)
innovation (p. 50)	franchise (p. 60)
niche (p. 50)	franchisee (p. 60)
brainstorm (p. 51)	franchisor (p. 60)
demographics (p. 52)	business broker (p. 61)

Key Concept Review

2. **Discuss** some current trends that provide opportunity for entrepreneurs. (3.1)
3. **Explain** some ways to recognize opportunity. (3.1)
4. **Explain** how to think creatively about opportunity. (3.1)
5. **Discuss** ways to overcome challenges to creativity. (3.1)
6. **Explain** ways to find creative business ideas. (3.1)
7. **Identify** the importance of personal values and goals in choosing an entrepreneurial pursuit. (3.2)
8. **Describe** the challenges and rewards of entering a family business. (3.2)
9. **List** the benefits and drawbacks of buying a business. (3.2)
10. **Describe** how you can evaluate a business opportunity. (3.2)
11. **Compare** the advantages and disadvantages of starting your own business. (3.2)

Critical Thinking

12. Describe and analyze sources for entrepreneurial opportunities for two trends not discussed in this chapter.
13. Discuss future prospects for entrepreneurship and its anticipated impact on the economy.
14. Summarize the influence of technology as it relates to small business. What will the use of technology enable businesses to do that they don't do now?
15. Explain how cultural diversity affects entrepreneurship and entrepreneurial ventures. Identify and analyze an entrepreneurial venture that has used cultural diversity to its advantage.
16. Discuss the importance of personality and ability when selecting what type of business to open. How can a potential entrepreneur overcome any incompatibilities in these areas?
17. Explain how demographic changes create entrepreneurial opportunities. Describe some of the current demographic changes that are under way and how they will affect the marketplace.

Write About It

18. Locate business opportunities and compare and contrast buying a business and starting a business. Put your answer in a paragraph or a Venn diagram.
19. Research the venture of a successful entrepreneur in an area of your choice. Write a descriptive paragraph outlining the person's success.

20. Compare and contrast the advantages and disadvantages of entering the family business, buying an existing business, starting an entirely new business, or purchasing a franchise. Present the information in a table.

Academic Skills

Math

21. After doing some research on the age demographics of the residents in his hometown, Antwoin learned the following:

years of age	number of residents
0–5	960
6–11	1,840
12–18	4,500
19–35	8,225
36–60	5,150
Over 60	2,960

Construct a bar graph to present this information. Use computer software if possible.

Language Arts

22. Write an essay on entrepreneurship as a personal goal. In your essay, explain how personal goals, lifestyle, background, hobbies, interests, experience, abilities, and financial resources will impact one's choice of business.

Entrepreneurship in Your Community

23. Consider the hobbies and activities that interest you. What types of businesses in your community have made an entrepreneurial pursuit out of these hobbies and activities? Prepare a list to share with the class.

24. Working in teams, prepare a list of franchises in your town. As a class, compile the lists and assign each team a different franchise to research. Be sure to find out the cost of the franchise, the planning, training and management expertise offered, and the national advertising available. Each team should present an oral presentation of the franchise to the class.

Ethical Practices

Unwanted E-Mail

25. Unwanted e-mail that advertises products and services can be a big nuisance for most Internet users. This e-mail, known as spam, costs people and companies time and productivity. Do you think it is ethical for companies to send mass e-mailings to people to sell their products and services? Write one or more paragraphs stating your position.

INTERNET *connection*

The Facts About Franchising

You are considering opening your own restaurant. Use the Internet to conduct research on franchising.

Connect

Use a Web directory or search engine to research and compile a list of ten questions a potential franchisee should ask when negotiating the purchase of a franchise business.

Application

Research franchise opportunities. Select one and research answers to the ten questions. Use a word processor to document the answers to the questions.

The Electronic Entrepreneur

E-Commerce Business Models

The Internet has revolutionized the way business is conducted. As the Internet has developed, new types of businesses have emerged that have transformed the way that consumers spend their money.

There are three principal business models that electronic entrepreneurs employ: business-to-business (B2B), business-to-consumer (B2C), and clicks and mortar.

B2B Many entrepreneurs are creating ventures that sell products and services to other businesses. This is called **B2B e-commerce**. Many B2B transactions are simple wholesaling transactions that are made over the Web. Other B2B transactions take place in **B2B exchanges**, electronic forums where businesses trade goods and services. B2B e-commerce racks up more sales than any other kind of e-commerce because of its potential to cut costs and increase productivity and profit.

B2C In **B2C e-commerce**, the business venture sells directly to the consumer. B2C is often called **e-tailing**, a word derived from retailing that means selling on the Internet. Selling directly to the consumer is the most common form of online business. There are many advantages for both consumers and businesses in the B2C marketplace. B2C markets offer consumers more choices and offer businesses access to a global customer base. The B2C market has the potential to generate $20 billion annually, and consumer businesses of all types want a share of this revenue.

Clicks and Mortar A clicks-and-mortar business is a business that operates both a traditional physical storefront and an online store. *Clicks* refers to the electronic aspect of the business and *mortar* refers to the physical aspect. This is a successful e-commerce business model because consumers have the choice to purchase online or in person at a physical store.

FACT AND IDEA REVIEW

1. What is the most common form of online business?
2. Which e-commerce business model has the most sales?
3. Which e-commerce business model offers consumers the most choices?
4. What is the difference between a B2C business and a clicks-and-mortar business?

FOR DISCUSSION

5. If you were to describe one Internet business model as "most likely to succeed," which would it be, and why?

TechTerms

- B2B e-commerce
- B2B exchanges
- B2C e-commerce
- e-tailing
- clicks and mortar

Chapter 4

Global Opportunities

CHAPTER OBJECTIVES

When you have completed this chapter, you should be able to:

SECTION 4.1

- Describe the role of small business and entrepreneurship in today's multicultural, global economy.
- Explain why the global market is important.
- Discuss how to recognize and examine current trends that provide both domestic and global opportunities for entrepreneurs.

SECTION 4.2

- Describe the benefits and risks of international trade.
- Explain how to find the best international markets.
- Compare and contrast importing and exporting.

BUDGETING TO ACHIEVE YOUR FINANCIAL GOALS

A budget is a plan for using your money in a way that best supports your financial goals. By using a budget, you'll learn how to live within your income and how to spend your money wisely.

Step 1 Set your goals. Make your financial goals as specific as possible. Prioritize them.

Step 2 Estimate your income. Record all of your estimated income for the next month, such as take-home pay and income on investments.

Step 3 Budget for unexpected events and savings.

Step 4 Budget for fixed expenses. List all your regular monthly expenses.

Step 5 Budget for variable expenses. List bills that vary from month to month.

Step 6 Record what you spend.

Step 7 Review your spending patterns. Revise your goals and adjust your progress. If you find yourself falling behind with bills, you may need to revise your budget.

@ Go to **entrepreneurship.glencoe.com** to complete the Standard & Poor's Money Talk Financial Literacy Activity.

PREPARE TO READ

THINK ABOUT THESE QUESTIONS AS YOU READ.

What global challenges and opportunities face entrepreneurs today?

How can you show respect and understanding for other cultures?

Global Entrepreneurship

GET READY TO READ

KEY TERMS
- global economy
- exporting
- importing
- trade barrier
- tariff
- gross domestic product (GDP)

KEY CONCEPTS
- Global Entrepreneurship
- The Global Economy
- Global Opportunities

THE MAIN IDEA

The countries of the world are linked in a global economy made possible by free trade agreements and advances in communications technology. International markets present opportunities in all regions of the world.

READING ORGANIZER

Draw the Venn diagram below on a separate piece of paper. As you read, define importing in the left circle and exporting in the right circle. In the overlapping section, write concepts that apply to both importing and exporting.

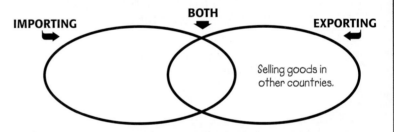

IMPORTING   BOTH   EXPORTING

Selling goods in other countries.

Global Entrepreneurship

Take a look at some of the things you own—your bike, your CD player, even your favorite pair of jeans. They may have an American brand name or label. However, chances are they were made in another country. Businesses sell and buy goods and services to and from other countries. In this section, you will learn about the global challenges and opportunities that face entrepreneurs today. You will also learn why international trade is so important to the U.S. economy.

The Global Economy

We live in a global economy. The **global economy** is the interconnected economies of the nations of the world. Entrepreneurship plays an important role in today's multicultural global society. **Exporting** is the selling and shipping of goods to another country. **Importing** is buying or bringing in goods from other countries to sell.

An Overnight Success

When 27-year-old Fred Smith started Federal Express in 1971, the idea of next-day delivery was a pipe dream. Computers were becoming crucial in business operations, and Smith saw potential: if an important component needed replacement, people might pay more to get the parts delivered right away. By modeling his new company on the way banks worked—with transactions passing through large central "hubs" rather than lots of individual locations—he was able to make overnight delivery affordable. Today, FedEx delivers much more than just computer parts and is one of the most successful businesses in the world—with annual revenues of $20 billion.

CRITICAL THINKING

Why has overnight delivery become so important, and what are some of the businesses that depend on it the most?

 Go to **entrepreneurship.glencoe.com** to complete the Success Stories Writing Activity.

When you purchase a CD player that was made in Japan and is sold in the United States, Japan benefits from a bigger market for its goods. The U.S. company that purchased the CD player from Japan and sold it to you benefits from being able to offer a wider variety of products to its customers. You benefit by buying high-quality equipment at a competitive price.

If you are a small business owner today, you may purchase and sell goods or services to other countries, manufacture in other countries, or have competitors in other countries. Two important factors that have brought about a global economy are a reduction in trade tariffs and advances in communications technology.

Trade Barriers Have Fallen

The World Trade Organization is a global coalition of governments that make the rules that govern international trade. It works to eliminate or lessen trade barriers and promote free trade. A **trade barrier** is a restriction on goods entering or leaving a country. The lowering of trade barriers has increased the flow of goods among countries. A **tariff** is a kind of trade barrier. Tariffs are taxes imposed by a government on imported or exported goods. In 1950, tariff rates were about 15 to 25 percent. Today, where tariffs exist, they are generally below 4 percent.

The North American Free Trade Agreement (NAFTA) is a trade agreement among the United States, Mexico, and Canada. NAFTA makes exporting and importing among these countries far more profitable. The European Union (EU) is Europe's trading bloc. The goal of the EU is to promote free trade and a shared currency among member nations.

The "Global Market"

Just a few decades ago, businesses were limited by their location—if you owned a retail store in a small town, your customers were probably just other people in the community. Today, technology allows companies to take their products around the world, wherever a potential customer may be.

Cooperative Learning

What are some of the key technologies that have made global business thrive? Why are each of them important?

 Go to **entrepreneurship.glencoe.com** to complete the Technology Today Vocabulary Practice Activity.

Technology Has Made the World Smaller

In recent years, there have been major advances in technology. Developments in communication, information processing, and transportation technology have transformed the way business is done. The Internet has dramatically affected trade between countries. Today it's easier than ever to communicate with people in other countries on the phone, through fax machines, with e-mail, and over the Internet. Even small businesses can reach customers anywhere in the world.

While You Read

Predict Which region is the top importer of U.S. goods?

Global Opportunities

The international market is several times the size of the U.S. market. It holds many opportunities for growing businesses. Cultural differences mean you have to study each country before attempting to do business there. Each year the U.S. Department of Commerce lists the top countries and regions for exporting U.S. goods. You will find them listed in **Figure 4.1.** Today these countries and regions make up more than 25 percent of the world's gross domestic product. **Gross domestic product (GDP)** is the total value of all goods produced during the year.

Asia

Asia is an enormous and diverse continent that includes many unique and sophisticated markets. Asia is also a growing source of products and services to the world. Many countries outsource their manufacturing to China, where wages are lower.

In China, the government controls business, and laws and regulations are strict; but the Chinese government is beginning to make it easier for U.S. companies to do business in China. China is the fastest-growing economy in the world. It is looking for new products and services from other countries that will help it grow.

Not all of Asia is the same. Japan has been called a "closed" society for marketers. This means it is hard to sell products that are not Japanese. Many Japanese, like the French, hold their culture in high regard. They do not want to be influenced by other countries. U.S. fast-food companies entered the Japanese market successfully by offering Japanese foods alongside the American favorites. In Japan, understanding the traditions, religion, and love for things Japanese is important to marketing success. Those companies that have found success marketing in Japan have learned to provide advertising and products that make use of five fundamental beliefs: humor, fantasy, harmony, collective material success, and things uniquely Japanese.

Latin America

Like Asia, Latin America is a diverse community of nations with many cultural differences. Latin America includes very traditional cultures as well as modern cultures. Latin America consists of the countries of South America and North America, including Central America and the islands of the Caribbean, whose inhabitants speak Spanish, Portuguese, or French.

Latin Americans tend to make buying decisions based on their family's needs rather than one person's individual needs so they tend to choose products that will benefit the family. Latin American consumers more often look at the merits of the products and do comparison shopping before they buy. In some countries, such as Mexico, consumers prefer U.S. goods. This presents a good opportunity for entrepreneurs.

Write About It

Write a profile of a foreign country to which you would like to export American goods. Include information about the culture, environment, political situation, economic system, government laws and regulations, and import requirements.

Figure 4.1 **Top Importers of U.S. Goods in 2002**

SOUTH AMERICA $28,899 million

MEXICO $97,531 million

EUROPEAN UNION $143,748 million

CANADA $160,830 million

ASIA $193,495 million

Source: International Trade Administration, U.S. Aggregate Foreign Trade Data: Table 6, U.S. Total Exports to Individual Countries 1996–02.

TOP IMPORTERS Finding out which countries and regions import American goods and services is a good start for your export business. ***Countries from which region import the most American goods?***

Europe

Only recently have Europeans begun to encourage entrepreneurship. In Europe, risk-taking and business failure are not as accepted as they are in other parts of the world. However, that outlook is changing.

Europe is a difficult market to define because there is no common European culture. The conversion of European currency to the euro made commerce easier, but there are still cultural differences. For example, Italy is very different from France.

In Europe, there are great cultural differences among certain countries. Products that do well in one country may not do well in another. Marketers attempt to seek out cultural information that will help them market across Europe. This information includes how people respond to uncertainty, the degree of individualism in the country, how individuals perceive power, the distribution of wealth, and masculinity. Some countries tend to be more masculine in nature. Marketers, knowing this, use ads displaying assertive, achievement-oriented behavior. By contrast, other countries are perceived as feminine countries, so ads there focus on concern for the environment, compassion, and championing of the underdog.

In summary, where cultural differences are small, marketing products across borders works well. Where cultural differences are great, products of one country may not sell well in the other. Marketers need to segment markets by cultural similarities rather than by national boundaries.

Regions in Transition

Developing countries, often with unstable governments, provide a risky form of opportunity for entrepreneurs. There are many barriers and little support for business owners. Some examples are Russia, the eastern European countries, Africa, and parts of the Middle East.

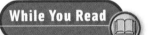

While You Read

Connect How does the global economy influence small business operations?

AN AMERICAN ICON
Certain American products are highly sought after in other countries. *What are some foreign goods that have gained good reputations in the United States?*

When doing business in unstable nations, research the culture and business practices carefully. Then consider partnering with a local company. Be sure you know your rights. In some countries, you may not be able to take your profits out of the business in U.S. dollars.

Entrepreneurship in the Global Marketplace

As the world shifts toward a truly integrated global economy, more and more businesses are getting involved in international business. Operating an international business is different than operating a domestic business for these reasons:

- Countries differ in their cultures, political systems, economic systems, legal systems, and levels of economic development.

- The management of an international business is more complicated than the management of a domestic business.

- Conducting business transactions across borders requires an in-depth understanding of the rules of international trade and the restrictions of foreign governments.

- An international business must have policies for dealing with movements in exchange rates.

While You Read

Question What is one approach to consider if you want to export to a nation or region that is politically unstable?

Section 4.1 After You Read

Key Concept Review

1. Discuss two reasons for the global economy today.

2. What are tariffs? How do they inhibit free trade?

3. Define *gross domestic product.*

Critical Thinking

4. Besides making it easier to communicate globally, how do you see technology playing a role in your ability to market products to other parts of the world?

Role Play

Situation Your employer has decided to expand its business from domestic to international. You will be transferred to Latin America for one year.

Activity Pair up with a classmate to write and present a role play on how to be a successful international businessperson. Take turns assuming the role of an international business consultant offering advice and answering questions.

Evaluation You will be evaluated on how well you address these issues:

- Explain the impact of the international economy on entrepreneurial ventures.

- Assess the impact of business expansion from domestic to international.

- Explain the challenges of selling to consumers in other countries.

- Describe the influences of other cultures on American business.

Ways to Enter the Global Market

KEY TERMS

- interpreter
- Standard Industrial Trade Classification (SITC) codes
- International Business Exchange (IBEX)
- trade missions
- "best prospect" list
- disposable income
- trade intermediary
- foreign joint venture
- export management company
- freight forwarder

KEY CONCEPTS

- Understanding International Business
- Strategies for Entering International Markets
- Importing and Exporting

THE MAIN IDEA

To conduct international business successfully, you must understand foreign customs and cultures. Whether you choose to import or export products, the international market presents many profitable business opportunities.

READING ORGANIZER

Make a list like the one below. As you read, write down five different ways to show respect for foreign cultures.

RESPECTING FOREIGN CULTURES
1. Be punctual.
2.
3.
4.
5.

Understanding International Business

Understanding how other countries conduct business is important to your success as an entrepreneur. In this section, you will learn about differences in business customs. You will also learn how to modify business practices to facilitate interaction in the global marketplace.

The Importance of Understanding Culture

When you travel abroad for business, you should prepare by studying the customs in the country you are visiting. Failing to do so may keep you from closing an important business deal. For example, American business owners often travel to Japan in a hurry to close a deal. They may allow themselves just a few days to negotiate an important business deal. The Japanese, by contrast, do not feel this same time pressure to complete a deal. They want to get to know the person they are dealing with before they strike a deal.

THE ART OF NEGOTIATION

Everyone negotiates something every day. Negotiating is the art of reaching agreements. Negotiating skills are critical to your success as an entrepreneur. To be a successful negotiator, you need to train, practice, have a game plan, and learn about the culture, etiquette, ethics, and attitudes of the people with whom you will be negotiating.

In a world increasingly dominated by the global economy, culture plays an important role in negotiation. Consider these cultural idiosyncrasies:

- In Japan, negotiators consider silence favorable and thoughtful.
- In Russia, compromise is seen as a sign of weakness.
- In South Korea, protocol and status are important.
- In China, negotiators seek agreement on general principles.
- In Great Britain, aggressiveness is viewed as a negative trait.

These differences have deep cultural origins. Entrepreneurs who understand cultural differences can develop profitable and satisfying business relationships.

Think Critically

Why is it important for businesspeople who negotiate outside their culture to learn how the other side negotiates? How would you describe a successful international negotiator?

 Go to **entrepreneurship.glencoe.com** to complete the Issues in Entrepreneurship Research Activity.

Tips for Showing Respect

It is important to show respect and understanding for the cultures of the people with whom you do business. Here are some tips. Other tips for showing respect are described in **Figure 4.2** on page 78.

- Dress conservatively in dark colors. In Asia, for example, white is a symbol of mourning.
- Do not correct the other person's English. Instead, make an effort to learn a few key words in his or her language. You will gain respect for your effort.
- Be prepared to remove your shoes in some situations. This shows respect.
- Do not comment on food except to praise it. Respect different tastes in food.
- Do your homework before the first meeting. You should know something about the country and its culture.
- Build a relationship before you do business. The goal is to build trust with your potential business partner.
- Bring your own **interpreter** to translate the other person's language into English.

Figure 4.2 **Conducting International Business**

RESPECTING CULTURE
Business is conducted differently in the United States than it is in other parts of the world. Here are some tips to help you become an internationally savvy businessperson. *How do you think American businesspeople are perceived in other countries?*

Currency
Speak in terms of the other person's currency, not U.S. dollars. Using the other person's currency is a sign of respect. Be clear about whose currency you refer to in negotiations.

Greetings
Americans tend to use first names from the moment they meet someone. This practice is not acceptable in most other countries. It is considered rude. Use formal greetings. Use a person's first name only after he or she asks you to. Accept business cards with respect. Look at it and put it carefully into a cardholder. Do not write on it! In Asia, that is considered an insult.

Time
Be punctual. Most cultures respect being on time. Do not be late to an important business meeting. Do not set time limits on business meetings. Remember that other countries are not as concerned about time as Americans are.

Strategies for Entering International Markets

The world market is huge. How do you find the best place to conduct business? This section will help you find the best international market for your product or service.

While You Read

Predict What are trade missions and how can they help U.S. businesses enter foreign markets?

Sources for Locating the Best Market

Many sources can help you locate the best market for your product or service. Start by consulting the U.S. Census Bureau's *Guide to Foreign Trade Statistics*. It can be found online. There you will find help in locating sources for various trade statistics.

Using **Standard Industrial Trade Classification (SITC) codes**, you can learn what kinds of products are traded in specific countries. You can also find information about how well your product or service does in different marketplaces. Suppose you are planning to export a toy. You can find out how many toys are sold in different countries every year. You would look for a country that imports more toys than the average. The country should also have a history of importing goods from the United States. Generally, about 5 percent of the country's total imports should be American goods. A country that meets those two criteria is a good export candidate.

Other Sources of Help

You might want to contact the International Trade Administration office and the Department of Commerce in Washington, D.C. The U.S. Chamber of Commerce has an electronic commerce system called the **International Business Exchange (IBEX)**. It lets you sell products and services online anywhere in the world. It is a good way to find trading partners, too.

The U.S. government and private agencies offer small businesses the opportunity to go on trade missions. **Trade missions** let small business owners meet and talk with foreign agents, distributors, or potential business partners. The participants make valuable contacts in other countries by traveling there. To participate in a trade mission, you need a product that is on the government's **"best prospect" list**. That means it is a product that other countries are looking to purchase. You also need to have a good business plan. It should show how you plan to market your product in the country you have chosen. You will learn about business plans in Chapter 5.

Importing and Exporting

What is the difference between importing and exporting products? How do you decide on a product? What are some things you should consider before attempting to import or export? As an entrepreneur, you will need to know the answers to these questions.

Exporting means selling and shipping goods to another country. For example, you may decide to export snack foods to Brazil. Importing means buying products from other countries to resell in your own country. For example, you might import custom bicycles from France to sell in your community.

Deciding on a Product to Export

The best products for exporting are paper products, electronic equipment, chemical products, apparel, industrial machinery, computers, and agricultural products. To be successful as an exporter, you must sell products that other countries want.

If you are going to export consumer products, you need to find a country where people have enough **disposable income**. Disposable income is money people have to spend after paying for necessary expenses. It is important because the products you export may not be necessities. Your products may even be luxuries, such as Coca-Cola® is in China.

Where to Find Import Opportunities

The United States imports a lot of goods from other countries. One reason is the low labor costs in other countries. With lower production costs, U.S. importers can sell products more cheaply. Some products are imported because they are found only in other countries. Coffee is an example.

To find opportunities in importing, attend trade shows. At these shows, representatives from other countries display their products and services. You can also read trade publications and catalogs. These show products available for importing and can give you an idea of what is available. However, they will not tell you if people want the products. To answer that question, you must research the market. Talk to potential customers to find out what they are looking for.

Where to Find Export Opportunities

Exporting is a way to expand your business to a new market. Exporting is more complicated than importing. You need to understand the countries with which you are doing business. It also takes longer to make a profit because of the time necessary to build relationships in those countries. Here are several ways to enter the global market:

- Establish an e-commerce Web site.

- Use a trade intermediary. A **trade intermediary** is an agency that serves as a distributor in a foreign country.

- Establish a foreign joint venture. A **foreign joint venture** is an alliance between an American small business and a company in another nation.

- License foreign businesses to sell your business's products or processes.

- Use an export management company. An **export management company** is a business that handles all the tasks related to exporting for a manufacturer. It usually receives a commission (a percentage of sales) for its efforts.

- Hire a **freight forwarder**, a business that handles overseas shipments.

The global market makes this an exciting time to be a business owner. Opportunities are plentiful and can be found in every country in the world. You can be successful if you take time to learn about potential markets.

Government Regulations on International Trade

Over 100 federal agencies are involved in the import and export process. For example, the Food and Drug Administration regulates the import and export of food and drugs.

The U.S. Customs Service is the primary federal agency with oversight over import requirements. General information on import requirements can be found at the U.S. Customs Service Web site. General information on export requirements can be found at the U.S. Census Bureau's Web site.

EXPORT ASSISTANCE PROGRAMS Exporting is a fairly complex process. A number of programs and forms of financial export assistance can help entrepreneurs export their goods. These types of programs are offered by U.S. government agencies and investment corporations.

The U.S. Department of Commerce International Trade Administration Trade Information Center (TIC) offers export assistance and export counseling programs. It employs trade specialists who guide businesses through the export process. You can find TIC's *Export Programs Guide to Federal Export Assistance* online. The U.S. Department of Commerce also has a Trade Development Office that offers information on world trade in specific industries.

The United States has 104 domestic Export Assistance Centers. These are operated in cooperation with the Small Business Administration and the Export-Import Bank of the United States. The centers provide marketing and trade finance support. Your local Export Assistance Center can direct you to your local District Export Council. These organizations are closely affiliated with the Export Assistance Centers. They offer advice and assistance to small-and medium-sized businesses that are interested in exporting.

Quick Math

In 2004, 400 U.S. companies were doing business in China. It was predicted that this number could be 600 by the year 2006. Determine the percent of increase.

While You Read

Connect Contact your local Small Business Administration office and find out the location of the nearest Export Assistance Center in your area.

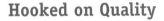

Hooked on Quality

All entrepreneurs can learn from Norway's Mustad family, the world's No. 1 maker of fish hooks: Consistency lands the biggest catches.

For six generations, Norway's Mustad clan has manufactured a small but crucial product: the fish hook. Since fishermen are scrupulous in their evaluation of each and every hook they use, production of the tiny pieces of metal is deceptively specialized.

To get it right, sales representatives from O. Mustad & Son travel the globe investigating the sorts of hooks favored by anglers from Alaska to Asia and then report back to the outfit's factories around the world. The globetrotting pays off: Family-owned Mustad has been the world's No. 1 maker of fish hooks for 125 years.

Mustad is one of the most innovative niche players in Europe. To stay ahead of the competition, Gjovik-based Mustad, the offshoot of a metal-wire manufacturer founded in 1832, consistently introduces new products. For instance, the company recently launched a range of fly hooks that are sharper than the models they replace. In all, Mustad markets more than 10,000 items, including fishing lines.

SOURCE: *BUSINESSWEEK*, JANUARY 21, 2004; BY LAURA COHN

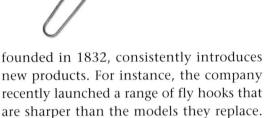

APPLICATION

Use a word-processing program to write your answer to this question: How does the Mustad family ensure that its products offer benefits sought throughout the world?

@ Go to **entrepreneurship.glencoe.com** to complete the *BusinessWeek* Case Study Reading Guide Activity.

Things to Consider Before Going Global

International entrepreneurs are concerned with many of the same issues as domestic entrepreneurs. When you think about going global, make sure you are ready for the challenge. Ask yourself these five questions:

1. **Do you have solutions?** Anyone can supply a product or a service. However, can you solve a problem that people in a particular country are facing? To do this, you need to study the country and its people.

2. **Do you have a new idea?** Ideas do not have to be completely new. They can also be improvements on something that already exists. However, the improvement must have value for the customer. The improvement must also stand out from the crowd.

3. **Is there a market for the product or service?** This is one of the most important questions to ask. Conduct market research to find the answer to this question. If you determine that there is a market for the product or service, the next step is to figure out whether modifications need to be made to the product or service to sell it in the foreign market.

4. **How good are you at handling risk and frustration?** Every country has different ways of doing business. Every group of customers has different needs and desires. You must be prepared to go through a process of trial and error.

5. **Do you have any good contacts in other countries?** You need to develop contacts with people who can help you. Talk to other students who have family from the country in which you are interested. Contact your local chamber of commerce or Small Business Administration (SBA) office. You can also contact the nearest Federal Trade Center. These offices often have international trade experts who can help you.

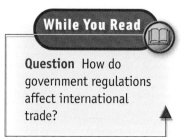

While You Read

Question How do government regulations affect international trade?

Section 4.2 After You Read

Key Concept Review

1. Why is it important to have your own interpreter with you when you do business in another county?

2. What is the difference between importing and exporting?

3. What are five questions you need to consider before going global?

Critical Thinking

4. Choose a product that you would like to export to another country. To which country would you choose to export this product and why? Justify your choice.

Role Play

Situation The success of your business leads you to consider expanding into the international market. From your research, you learn that in some countries, offering and taking bribes are acceptable ways of doing business.

Activity Team up with a classmate and present a role play. One can play the role of an American businessperson doing business in another country. The other can play the role of a foreign businessperson.

Evaluation You will be evaluated on how well you address these issues:

- Explain whether offering or accepting a bribe while doing business in another country is ethical when it is an acceptable way of doing business in that country.

- Describe whether American companies should have policies regarding bribes.

Chapter Summary

Section 4.1 **Global Entrepreneurship**

Technological advances and changes in trade barriers have created a global economy. Exporting is the selling and shipping of products to another country. Importing is the buying of goods from other countries to sell in your own country. The international market, which is more than four times the size of the U.S. market, holds opportunities for businesses. It's important to study a country's culture before attempting to do business there.

Section 4.2 **Ways to Enter the Global Market**

To succeed in international business, one must conduct business based on the customs of the other country. Ways to locate the best market for your product or service include governmental publications, the International Business Exchange, and trade fairs. By hiring an export management company, a freight forwarder, or forming a joint venture, entrepreneurs are able to knowledgeably expand their businesses to new markets.

Key Terms Review

1. You are working for an entrepreneur who handles international business. Your job is to prepare a reference manual that includes the following terms and their definitions.

global economy (p. 70)

exporting (p. 70)

importing (p. 70)

trade barrier (p. 71)

tariff (p. 71)

gross domestic product (GDP) (p. 72)

interpreter (p. 77)

Standard Industrial Trade Classification (SITC) codes (p. 79)

International Business Exchange (IBEX) (p. 79)

trade missions (p. 79)

"best prospect" list (p. 79)

disposable income (p. 80)

trade intermediary (p. 81)

foreign joint venture (p. 81)

export management company (p. 81)

freight forwarder (p. 81)

Key Concept Review

2. **Describe** the role of small business and entrepreneurs in today's global multicultural economy. (4.1)
3. **Explain** why the global market is important. (4.1)
4. **Discuss** how to recognize and examine current trends that provide both domestic and global opportunities for entrepreneurs. (4.1)
5. **Describe** the benefits and risks of international trade. (4.2)
6. **Explain** how to find the best international markets. (4.2)
7. **Compare and contrast** importing and exporting. (4.2)

Critical Thinking

8. Evaluate reasons for expanding a business internationally. What are the benefits of being a player in the global market?
9. What are the advantages of importing products into the United States?
10. What world region do you think holds the greatest business opportunity? Support your answer.
11. Why is it important to understand the culture of the people with whom you do business?
12. If you had the opportunity to go on a trade mission to Russia, how would you prepare?
13. Compare and contrast the following: an export management company, a freight forwarder, and a joint venture.
14. Select an entrepreneurial venture. Describe the impact that technology is having on the venture's marketing strategy.
15. In your opinion, should a new venture go global from the start? Why or why not? Defend your opinion.

Write About It

16. Write an e-mail to a classmate discussing the importance of national culture to the marketing of new products in Europe and Asia.
17. In two or three paragraphs, explain why more small businesses aren't involved in importing and exporting goods and services.
18. Describe how the Department of Commerce's Trade Information Center can help you as you consider going global. Write your answer in two or three paragraphs.
19. Identify a U.S. product that you wish to export. Then research exporting requirements. In a memo to your teacher, describe your exporting strategy and explain the exporting requirements.
20. Make a list of five things you can do to show respect for an international businessperson.

Academic Skills

Math

21. The U.S. GDP (gross domestic product) was $7,816,900,000 for 1996 and $10,983,900,000 for 2003 in current dollars. What was the percent of increase from 1996 to 2003?

Language Arts

22. Choose an industry that interests you. Throughout this course, collect articles from newspapers and magazines about the newest products and trends in that industry domestically and globally. Keep your articles in a notebook. Each month share with the class in a short oral report a trend that you have identified.

Entrepreneurship in Your Community

23. As a class, create a list of international products that are available in your community that students have enjoyed.

- Which local businesses sell products made outside the United States?
- Which local businesses sell American products to international markets?
- Identify new ways to use or improve the imported and exported products.

24. Locate a business in your community that imports or exports products. Interview the person involved with the buying and selling of goods. Ask about:

- the preparation needed to enter the global market.
- the benefits of importing and exporting.
- future trends and global opportunities.
- the differences between international business and U.S. business.

Ethical Practices

Global Ethics

25. The global economy, made more accessible through the Internet, has placed U.S. businesses in direct conflict with cultures that define morality in terms of different contexts, values, and codes of ethics. Do you believe that a code of ethics should stand firm in any situation? Why or why not? Write a one-page essay to express your opinion.

INTERNET *connection*

Investigate International Trade

You want to start a business that exports American products to other countries. Identify new product and service opportunities that have global potential. Then use the Internet to investigate international trade opportunities.

Connect

Use the Internet to research countries with which you might choose to conduct business. Then select a product or service to export and an international market for your product or service.

Application

Use a word-processing program to write a two-page report that addresses these issues:

- Describe the product or service you want to export.
- Describe the country to which you want to export the product or service.
- Describe the country's demographics.
- Identify strategies for entering international markets.
- Explain how different situations can influence an entrepreneur's selection of strategies.

The Electronic Entrepreneur

International E-Commerce

Overseas markets represent an enormous new potential for e-commerce business: according to the *Computer Industry Almanac,* only 43 percent of the world's Internet users are in the United States. That means that a company has the potential to more than double its business by reaching across international lines. However, doing business in another country can be much more complex than at home.

Language Most Web sites are written in English. Companies engaging in international e-commerce have to decide whether they need to translate their Web sites in other languages, as well. **Translation** is the process of changing one written communication into a second language with the same meaning.

Currency Foreign currencies and exchange rates represent a challenge to electronic entrepreneurs. An **exchange rate** is the rate at which one currency is converted into another.

Exchange rates change constantly, and there are sophisticated software programs that allow real-time processing of foreign currency transactions. Events that happen in **real time** are happening at that particular moment.

Culture It is important to take culture into consideration when planning the graphic user interface of an international e-commerce Web site. The **graphic user interface** is the design, content, and navigation of a Web site. For instance, Chinese culture associates the color white with mourning, while American culture views white as a symbol of cleanliness.

Country Regulations Many countries and regions have specific import regulations. **Import regulations** govern the types and amounts of products that can be sold, packaging that can be used, and taxation. For this reason, businesses should study country- and region-specific regulations and restrictions before launching into international markets.

FACT AND IDEA REVIEW

1. Why does international business represent such a big opportunity?
2. What effect do languages other than English have on an international entrepreneurial venture?
3. What are some of the currency issues that make international e-commerce complex?
4. What effect does government regulation have on international trade?

FOR DISCUSSION

5. If you were developing an international e-commerce Web site, which of the above aspects would you focus on first? Why?

TechTerms

- translation
- exchange rate
- real time
- graphic user interface
- import regulations

Management Team Plan

In the Management Team section of the business plan, you will present your management team's qualifications for making the venture a success.

✓ STEP 1   DESCRIBE YOURSELF

Write a one-page biography that describes how your experience will help you run a small business. For example, if you have played team sports, you may have teamwork and people skills that can help you achieve small business success. Focus on what you can do to make your business work.

✓ STEP 2   THINK ABOUT THE SKILLS YOU HAVE AND THE SKILLS YOU NEED

Every business needs certain key skills and experiences. If you do not have these skills, you can bring in partners or hire employees with these skills or you can outsource the function. Create a chart like the one below and write down how each of these jobs will get done.

SKILL	JOB TITLE	HOW THE JOB WILL GET DONE
Leadership	Chief Executive Officer	
Oversight	Chief Operating Officer	
Human Resources	HR Manager	
Sales and Marketing	Sales and Marketing Director	
Finance	Chief Financial Officer	

Company Description

The Company Description section of the business plan outlines the company's basic background information, business concept, and goals and objectives.

✓ STEP 1   DESCRIBE YOUR COMPANY

Describe your business. Include what makes your business unique. Clearly identify the business concept and why you are, or why you want to be, in business.

✓ STEP 2   OUTLINE YOUR COMPANY'S GOALS

Create a chart like the one below and fill in the chart to document your company's goals, the steps you will take to reach the goals, and the resources needed to achieve the goals.

GOAL	STEPS TO ACHIEVE GOAL	RESOURCES TO ACHIEVE GOAL

Product and Service Plan

The Product and Service Plan describes the features and benefits of the business's products and services.

✓ STEP 1 THINK ABOUT FEATURES AND BENEFITS

To effectively sell products and services, you need to know how the product or service's features benefit the customer. Features are basic attributes and qualities. They differentiate competing brands, adding value to products. Benefits are the advantages or personal satisfaction a customer gets from a product or service. The more useful the feature, the more valuable the benefit is to the consumer.

✓ STEP 2 DESCRIBE YOUR PRODUCT OR SERVICE

Create a chart like the one below to document the information needed to describe your company's product or service and its features and benefits.

PRODUCT OR SERVICE	FEATURES	BENEFITS

Use the **Business Plan Project Appendix** on pages 532–543 to explore the content requirements of a business plan in more detail.

▶ The **Product and Service Plan** describes the features and benefits of the business's products and services.

▶ In the **Management Team Plan** section, you will present your management team's qualifications for making the venture a success.

▶ The **Company Description** outlines the company's basic background information, business concept, and goals and objectives.

BUSINESS PLAN PROJECT TEMPLATE

@ Go to **entrepreneurship.glencoe.com** for a document template in which you can write your own business plan.

UNIT 2

RESEARCHING AND PLANNING YOUR VENTURE

In This Unit...

UNIT OVERVIEW

Introduction

Marketing, types of business ownership, legal requirements, and choosing a location are only a few of the issues that an entrepreneur must consider. Creating a business plan will help you address and organize your venture's concerns. It can also show your venture's worth to potential investors. A good business plan will help you turn your vision into reality.

BUSINESS PLAN PROJECT PREVIEW

When you complete Unit 2, you will begin to explore these sections of the business plan:

▶ The **Vision and Mission Statements** section of the business plan sets forth the guiding principles by which a company functions.

▶ The **Industry Overview** addresses the basic trends and growth within those companies providing similar, complementary, or supplementary products and services.

▶ The **Market Analysis** section of the business plan presents your market research and features a customer demographic profile that defines the traits of the company's target market.

Feasibility and Business Planning

CHAPTER OBJECTIVES

When you have completed this chapter, you should be able to:

SECTION 5.1

- Discuss the importance of defining a prospective business by writing a clear and concise business concept.
- Describe how a feasibility study can be used to test a concept in the marketplace.

SECTION 5.2

- Describe the importance of planning.
- Identify and describe the components and formats of a business plan.
- List two of the key mistakes that entrepreneurs make when writing a business plan.
- Identify and analyze various sources of information for a business plan.
- Describe how to professionally package and present a business plan.

TYPES OF SAVINGS PLANS

In order to achieve your financial goals, you'll need a savings program. Savings accounts pay interest. Here are some of your alternatives:

- **Regular Savings Accounts**—traditionally called passbook accounts, these are ideal if you plan to make frequent deposits and withdrawals.

- **Certificates of Deposit (CD)**—this type of savings account requires you to leave your money in a financial institution for a set amount of time (the term). The longer the term, the higher the interest rate.

- **Money Market Accounts**—a savings account in which the interest rate varies from month to month. They typically have a higher minimum balance than regular savings accounts but allow you to write checks.

- **U.S. Savings Bonds**—a government note that becomes worth its face value on a certain date. You buy the bond for half the face value. Although these bonds are guaranteed by the government, they lose value if cashed in too soon.

 Go to **entrepreneurship.glencoe.com** to complete the Standard & Poor's Money Talk Financial Literacy Activity.

PREPARE TO READ

THINK ABOUT THESE QUESTIONS AS YOU READ.

How can feasibility analysis help me test my business concept?

What are the advantages of a well-prepared business plan?

Feasibility Analysis: Testing an Opportunity

GET READY TO READ

KEY TERMS
- business concept
- feature
- benefit
- feasibility analysis
- industry
- target customers
- competitive grid
- prototype
- business model
- value chain

KEY CONCEPTS
- Developing a Business Concept
- Testing the Concept in the Market

THE MAIN IDEA
Business concepts need to be tested in the market. Once a concept is judged feasible, a business plan will help the entrepreneur develop a strategy for executing the concept.

READING ORGANIZER
Draw the reading organizer below on a separate piece of paper. As you read, write the seven categories of information you need to research when analyzing the feasibility of a new business venture.

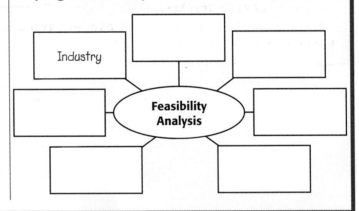

Developing a Business Concept

Once you have an idea for a new business, you need to turn it into a business concept. A **business concept** is a clear and concise description of an opportunity. It contains four elements: the product or service, the customer, the benefit, and the distribution. Its purpose is to focus your thinking.

Frank Almeda wanted to open a sporting goods store on the Lower East Side of Manhattan in New York City. It was a good idea, but he needed to develop it further to find out if it would work. To build his business concept statement, Frank answered four questions:

1. **What is the product or service being offered?** Frank wanted to offer sporting goods and clothing. He also planned to supply local teams with uniforms and supplies.

2. **Who is the customer?** The customer is the person who pays for the product or service. Frank's customers were the local sports teams and people who were interested in playing sports.

3. **What is the benefit that is being provided?** A feature is a distinctive aspect, quality, or characteristic of a product or service. For example, Frank will offer a neighborhood location. A **benefit** is something that promotes or enhances the value of the product or service to the customer. In this case, the benefit the customers will receive is convenience.

4. **How will the benefit be delivered to the customer?** Businesses have many ways to distribute the benefits of their products and services. Some of the choices are through a retail store, wholesalers, mail order, the Internet, or door-to-door delivery. Frank chose to deliver the product to the customer via a retail store.

Writing a Concept Statement

After answering the four questions, Frank could write the following concept statement:

Eastside Sports offers sporting equipment and apparel to local teams and to people who play sports. It provides the convenience of one-stop shopping at a retail outlet in the customer's own neighborhood.

Once you have a clear and concise concept statement, ask yourself "What is the compelling reason for this business to exist?" In Frank's case, many people in his neighborhood did not want to have to travel across town to find sports equipment. Having an outlet in the neighborhood solved a real problem and made Frank's business a success.

SELLING YOUR PRODUCT Some businesses specialize in selling to large, organized groups. *What are some advantages and disadvantages of this business approach?*

A Passion for Games

Childhood friends Alex Aguila and Nelson Gonzalez always loved playing games, but they grew tired of trying to get off-the-shelf computers to perform well on the latest games. So in 1996, they started Alienware, a company devoted to making computers specifically suited for gaming. Not only did they tweak what was inside the box, they changed the box itself—Alienware PCs boast distinctive bright colors and sleek designs, making them stand out from their competitors. The partners started the company on a very small budget, working out of their garage; today, Alienware enjoys annual sales of over $100 million.

CRITICAL THINKING

What are some of the ways Alienware made themselves stand out in the crowded field of PC manufacturers?

 Go to **entrepreneurship.glencoe.com** to complete the Success Stories Writing Activity.

Testing the Concept in the Market

The process used to test a business concept is called **feasibility analysis**. Feasibility analysis helps the entrepreneur decide whether a new business concept has potential.

A feasibility analysis can help you to decide if there is enough demand for your business's products or services. It also determines whether business conditions are appropriate for you to go forward with the business. A feasibility analysis includes questions related to the industry, customers, product and service requirements, the founding team, the competition, start-up resource needs, and the value chain.

Feasibility analysis will help you make a decision about your business concept. **Figure 5.1** provides a list of factors to consider in a feasibility analysis.

Testing the Industry

The broadest level of analysis looks at the industry in which the business will operate. An **industry** is a group of businesses with a common interest, such as telecommunications, computers, retail, and grocery. In the analysis, you look at factors such as the health of the industry, trends and patterns of change, and major players.

Talking to Customers

Testing the customer may be the most important part of the analysis. Talk with potential customers to measure the interest in your product and to better define the features and benefits. For Frank Almeda's business, local sports teams are the **target customers**, those most likely to buy his products and services. Frank will want to learn as much as he can about their needs.

While You Read

Predict How can you organize the research you conduct on your competitors?

Figure 5.1 Feasibility Analysis Considerations

INDUSTRY
demographics
trends
life cycle stage
barriers to entry
status of technology and R & D
typical profit margins

MARKET/CUSTOMER
target market demographics
customer profile
plan for speaking to customers
plan for speaking to competitors

FOUNDING TEAM
knowledge and skills
gaps and how to fill them

PRODUCT/SERVICE
features and benefits
product development tasks
product development timeline
intellectual property rights
product or service differentiation

FINANCE
business model
start-up capital requirements
positive cash flow
break-even point

VALUE CHAIN ANALYSIS
value chain description
distribution channel alternatives
distribution channel innovation

TESTING THE CONCEPT
The process used to test a business concept is called *feasibility analysis*. **How does feasibility analysis help an entrepreneur decide whether a new business concept has potential?**

Testing Product or Service Requirements

In this part of the analysis, you will consider what it will take to develop your product or service, to create a **prototype**, or a working model of a new product. Even businesses that do not manufacture products need to design prototypes. These kinds of prototypes are not physical, though. Instead, they will be designs, blueprints, or flowcharts that map out the business and the processes that will take place at the business. For example, if you plan to open a hair salon, you will create a blueprint of the layout of the salon, including the placement of equipment, workstations, and retail sales space, and the flow of customers and employees through the workspace. You will learn more about layout planning in Chapter 9.

When you develop a new product or service, you create an asset that must be protected. Your feasibility analysis must consider how you will protect your product or service. You can protect your intellectual property through patents, trademarks, copyrights, and trade secrets. You will learn more about intellectual property laws in Chapter 8.

Evaluating the Founding Team

Many successful businesses today are founded by teams—two or more people working together to launch a new venture. Teams bring together the knowledge and skills of the people involved. A founding team must gather the necessary resources to begin development.

An effective founding team can get a new business off the ground. A strong team is also attractive to investors. In general, investors look at the team first and the market second. So, it's important to have a team with a variety of knowledge and experience and access to people who can help you and give you advice.

Studying the Competition

An easy way to study the competition is to create a grid. A **competitive grid** is a tool for organizing important information about the competition. You can get this information by reading about your competitors, talking to them, visiting their businesses, and talking to their customers and suppliers.

THE COMPETITIVE GRID Create a five-column competitive grid. If you want to, you can add additional columns for marketing strategy, market share, and research and development. You can also add another row to fill in information about your own proposed business. This will help you to compare your proposed business to your competitors' businesses and identify your business's competitive advantage. Fill in your grid as shown in **Figure 5.2.**

1. **Competitor.** In the first column, list your direct and indirect competitors. Direct competitors are in the same or nearly the same business as you. Therefore, they compete for the same dollars. Indirect competitors include other ways your customers receive the same benefits. (For Frank Almeda, another sporting goods store in the neighborhood is a direct competitor. Mail-order catalogs and the Internet are indirect competitors.)

2. **Customer.** In the second column, list the primary target customer for each of your competitors. This list of customers may overlap.

3. **Benefits.** In the third column, list the benefits that customers receive from each of the competitors. Be sure to describe benefits, not features, of the product or service.

4. **Distribution.** In the fourth column, list the way the company distributes its product or service to the customer.

5. **Strengths/Weaknesses.** In the fifth column, list your opinion on the strengths and weaknesses of your competitors.

Figure 5.2 **Competitive Grid**

ORGANIZE YOUR RESEARCH Making a competitive grid can help you organize and understand the research on your competitors. *Where can you find the information to fill in your grid?*

Competitor	Customer	Benefits	Distribution	Strengths/ Weaknesses
Local sports store	Neighborhood teams and sports enthusiasts	Convenience of shopping locally; know the store owner	Retail store in the neighborhood	Owner knows the customers and understands their needs; not able to stock much variety
NikeTown	Sports enthusiasts and tours	Huge selection and exciting environment	Retail store in large commercial area	Huge selection; impersonal service
Catalog sales	Sports enthusiasts who don't like retail shopping	Quick and easy; don't have to leave home to order merchandise	Mail order	Lower costs bring lower prices; no personal contact with customers

Looking at Start-Up Resource Needs

A feasibility study will help you determine the potential profitability of a business idea. Jeffrey Bezos knew when he started Amazon.com that the Internet bookstore would not turn a profit for a long time. However, he was able to raise money to start the business because he could show strong financial projections and a business model that would work. A **business model** describes how you intend to make money with your business concept.

For a feasibility study, you need to calculate how much money is needed to do the following:

- Purchase or lease equipment, furnishings, and a facility
- Buy starting inventory and supplies
- Pay employees
- Finish product development
- Carry the company's expenses until you have enough sales for the business to generate a positive cash flow to operate on its own

Analyzing the Value Chain

There are many ways to deliver a benefit to your customers. The **value chain** is the distribution channel through which your product or service flows from the producer to the customer. The value chain includes manufacturers, distributors, and retailers. The goal is to deliver maximum value for the least possible total cost. Entrepreneurs can create a competitive advantage by looking at ways to make the value chain more efficient. Each link in the value chain adds value to the final product. They can bring products and services to customers in new ways. For example, the Internet created a new way to sell products and services.

While You Read

Question How does distribution add value to a product or service?

Section 5.1 After You Read

Key Concept Review

1. What is the purpose of a business concept?
2. List the four components of an effective business concept.
3. Discuss two things a feasibility analysis accomplishes.

Critical Thinking

4. Pick an idea you have for a new business. Develop a clear and concise business concept statement. Then write a one-page report that explains the importance of defining a planned business.

Role Play

Situation You plan to open a flower shop. Your concept statement reads, "Flower Power provides unique floral arrangements to people who buy flowers for hospital patients. It provides convenient shopping at the hospital."

Activity Team up with a classmate and role-play a debate on the feasibility of the business concept.

Evaluation You will be evaluated on how well you address these issues:

- Identify the customer.
- Describe the benefits to the customer.
- Describe the distribution channel.
- Describe the products and services that will be offered.
- Discuss the importance of determining what products and services will be offered by the business.

The Business Plan

KEY TERMS
- business plan
- executive summary
- vision statement
- mission statement
- distribution channel
- direct channel
- indirect channel
- Small Business Administration (SBA)
- trade association

KEY CONCEPTS
- The Business Plan: Your Road Map to Entrepreneurial Success
- The Parts of the Business Plan
- Common Mistakes in Preparing Business Plans
- Sources of Business Plan Information
- Packaging and Presenting the Business Plan

THE MAIN IDEA

A business plan presents a strategy for turning a feasible business concept into a successful business.

READING ORGANIZER

Draw the reading organizer below on a separate piece of paper. As you read, write the 18 components of a business plan.

Business Plan Components

1. _Executive Summary_	7. _____	13. _____
2. _____	8. _____	14. _____
3. _____	9. _____	15. _____
4. _____	10. _____	16. _____
5. _____	11. _____	17. _____
6. _____	12. _____	18. _____

The Business Plan: Your Road Map to Entrepreneurial Success

Once you have a feasible business concept, the next step is to develop a business plan. A **business plan** is a document that describes a new business and a strategy to launch that business. It shows the start-up and growth of a new venture. It is a complete and detailed picture of the business.

Planning is important to the success of any business. A business needs to plan in order to achieve its goals. Preparing a business plan will help you organize and analyze critical data. Researching costs and developing strategies about operations may reveal problems that you had not seen previously. You must work through those problems before actually going into business. A formal business plan helps ensure that you plan for all aspects of a business's operations.

Others will be interested in your business plan. These people include investors, bankers, potential management, and strategic partners. Each of them looks for different things in a business plan. For example, investors are interested in the track record of the founding team and the ability of the business to grow. They want to recover their initial investment plus a substantial return. By contrast, bankers are interested in the company's ability to repay its loans. They want to see the business generate a positive cash flow. Potential management will be interested in the company's ability to provide a stable work environment.

The Parts of the Business Plan

There is no right or wrong format for a business plan. However, you need to include the sections that investors, bankers, and others expect to see. Your aim is to emphasize the key points that will persuade the reader of the value of your business concept.

Formulating a business plan involves a lot of research in many different areas of the business. Therefore, it makes sense to divide the business plan into parts. A thorough business plan includes these sections: executive summary, management team plan, company description, product and service plan, mission and vision statements, industry overview, market analysis, competitive analysis, marketing plan, operational plan, organizational plan, financial plan, growth plan, and contingency plan. A business plan should also include a cover page, title page, table of contents, and supporting documents.

The components of the business plan are described here and covered in greater detail in later chapters. You can learn more about business plans using the Business Plan Unit Labs, the Business Plan Project Appendix, and the *Business Plan Project Workbook*.

> **While You Read**
>
> **Predict** What is the purpose of the executive summary section of the business plan?

TECHNOLOGY Today

Business Plan Software

A crucial aspect of any new business is its business plan. Writing a business plan is one of the most important steps in setting up a new business, especially for entrepreneurs looking to find venture capital. Special software can walk you through the creation of a business plan step-by-step. Business plan software helps by organizing all of the information needed and using a "question/answer" approach to help draft the document.

Cooperative Learning Activity

Why would business plan software be helpful?

 Go to **entrepreneurship.glencoe.com** to complete the Technology Today Vocabulary Practice Activity.

Executive Summary

The **executive summary** is a brief recounting of the key points contained in a business plan. Investors and lenders read many business plans every day. To save time, they rely on the executive summary to help them decide whether the concept interests them and is worth pursuing. Therefore, the executive summary should be no more than two pages and include the most important information from each section of the plan. It should open with a compelling story to persuade the reader that the business is going to be a success. Then it should support that statement by providing the evidence that was gathered through market research.

Management Team Plan

This section presents your qualifications and those of any partners. You must describe how your team has the capabilities to execute your business concept. Because you may be missing some expertise, you should discuss how you will fill the gaps. This may be done through partnerships or advisory board members.

Company Description

The company description outlines the company's background information and basic business concept. It helps investors understand the size, scope, and type of business. It describes the entrepreneurial opportunity and explains why you think the venture will succeed. It also provides a history of the business with development milestones that have been completed to date.

Product and Service Plan

In this section of the business plan, you present the product or service you are offering. The nature of your business should be clear to the reader. This can be accomplished by writing a clear and compelling concept statement. You should also note the unique features of the product/service and possible spin-offs. Spin-offs are additional products or services that you might do later, when the business is more established. Spin-offs alert the reader to the fact that this venture has growth possibilities.

Vision and Mission Statements

The vision and mission statements section of the business plan states the guiding principles by which a company functions. A **vision statement** establishes the scope and purpose of a company and reflects its values and beliefs. Walt Disney's vision for his company was "to bring happiness to millions." As you think about your company's vision, try to keep the vision broad so it will stand the test of time. Frank Almeda's vision statement might be "to open the world of sports to neighborhood residents." This broad vision lets you take your business in many directions.

A **mission statement** expresses the specific aspirations of a company, the major goals for which it will strive. Think about a mission statement to go along with Frank's vision statement for his sporting goods store. It might be "To provide equipment to 100 customers by the end of the first year."

Quick Math

An entrepreneur learns that the industry in which she is going to start her business is growing at a rate of 20% annually. If her new business can achieve an annual growth rate of 10% in the first year, 12% in the second year, and 14% in the third year, how long will it take before her business achieves the 20% industry rate of growth, assuming the pattern continues?

Will Your Plan Win a Prize?

Business plan competitions? Think of them as sporting events for MBA students. The stakes can be hundreds of thousands of dollars, and even taking third place is golden on a résumé. About 3,500 students entered some 70 regional, national, and worldwide contests last year, and several hundred more students are expected this year. Winners often get a big payoff: enough cash to start their own businesses. Indeed, some competitions backed by venture capitalists, such as the Carrot Capital VentureBowl in New York, provide upwards of $750,000 in equity funding to first-place finishers. Those sponsored by B-schools offer between a few thousand dollars and $100,000 in equity or cash.

Most contests start with 80 to 120 teams, each of which submits an executive summary of its plan. About half will be invited to the next round—submitting the full plan—and the judges then whittle that group down to 10 to 25 finalists. Along the way, students get valuable advice from successful entrepreneurs, a chance to hone presentation skills, and mentoring from professors and venture capitalists.

SOURCE: BUSINESSWEEK, MARCH 15, 2004; BY JENNIFER MERRITT

APPLICATION

Work as a class to identify the colleges and universities in your state that have business plan competitions. Find out how much the prizes are. Document your results in a spreadsheet, and create charts that visually represent the data.

 Go to **entrepreneurship.glencoe.com** for the *BusinessWeek* Case Study Reading Guide Activity.

Industry Overview

This section of the business plan presents your research into the industry. Think of your industry as those companies providing similar, complementary, or supplementary products and services. Every business operates within an industry. Your business plan must address the trends and growth within the industry. This will help you build a case for your company's success.

Market Analysis

The market analysis is important because the more you understand your customers, the better your chances of success. This section presents your research on the customer profile. This information should come from primary and secondary research resources. The results help you determine your overall marketing and sales strategies. In addition, this section analyzes your customers and the competition. The market analysis should also contain geographic, economic, and demographic data about the site for your business.

Competitive Analysis

The competitive analysis section should demonstrate that the proposed business has an advantage over its competitors. You can gather information on competitors by viewing their Web sites; by talking to their customers, vendors, suppliers, and employees; by attending trade shows; and by searching newspaper and magazine databases.

Marketing Plan

A marketing plan discusses how a company makes its customers aware of its products or services. It includes such features as the market niche, pricing, company image, marketing tactics, a media plan, and a marketing budget.

Operational Plan

The operational plan includes all of the processes in the business that result in production and delivery of the product or service. If you are manufacturing a product, you will want to discuss the status of product development. You will also want to explain the distribution of your product or service. A **distribution channel** is the means by which you deliver the product or service to the customer. If you are building Web sites, a service, you will probably have a **direct channel**. That is, you will be

Issues in Entrepreneurship

CAN YOU KEEP A SECRET?

Many potential entrepreneurs are reluctant to talk about their business ideas. Some fear rejection, while others fear that someone will steal their business concept.

Coming up with a brilliant idea is only a small part of what it takes to build a successful company. Successful entrepreneurs know they need to involve others to achieve success. The secret to sharing your idea while protecting yourself is simple: protect yourself legally. Signing nondisclosure or confidentiality agreements can help you protect yourself before you disclose any important secrets. Nondisclosure agreements, however, are often only as effective as your willingness to go to court.

Do not reveal everything, but do not be afraid to discuss your business. You will benefit from the ideas you receive. It is unlikely that people you share information with will have the drive, inspiration, and experience to make the idea a success.

Think Critically
Why are nondisclosure agreements only as effective as your willingness to go to court?

 Go to **entrepreneurship.glencoe.com** to complete the Issues in Entrepreneurship Research Activity.

uct or service. A **distribution channel** is the means by which you deliver the product or service to the customer. If you are building Web sites, a service, you will probably have a **direct channel**. That is, you will be delivering the service directly to the customer. On the other hand, if you are manufacturing a computer game, you may have an **indirect channel**. This means you will sell your game to a wholesaler. The wholesaler then finds retail stores and other types of outlets to carry your product.

Organizational Plan

The organizational plan looks at the people aspects and the legal form of the business. It discusses the management philosophy and whether the company will be a partnership, corporation, or limited liability company. The organizational plan also discusses the role and compensation of key management personnel and important employment policies.

While You Read

Connect Create a flow chart showing the organizational structure of a fictional exporting business with between 6 and 12 employees.

Financial Plan

The financial plan presents forecasts for the future of the business. It explains the assumptions made when the forecast figures were calculated. It is important to identify and examine the components of the new business financial plan. Usually, this information is in the form of financial statements. This part of the business plan is designed to show that all claims about the product, sales, marketing strategy, and operational strategy can create a successful business. In short, the information proves that the new business will be financially healthy.

Growth Plan

The growth plan looks at how the business will expand in the future. Investors and lenders like to know that a business has plans to grow and deal with growth in a controlled way.

Contingency Plan

The contingency plan looks at the probable risks for the business, such as changing economic conditions and lower-than-expected sales. It then suggests a way to minimize the risk.

Cover Page, Title Page, Table of Contents, and Supporting Documents

Every business plan should have a cover page that includes the company name, address, phone number, Web site address, e-mail address, and company logo. The page following the cover page is the title page. It includes the company name; the names, titles, and addresses of the owners; the date the business plan was issued; and the name of the person who prepared the business plan. The table of contents details the components of the business plan and the page numbers where they can be found within the business plan. The supporting documents section of the business plan includes items, exhibits, and documentation relevant to the business.

Figure 5.3 Developing a Business Plan

CREATING A BUSINESS PLAN There are several steps involved in creating a business plan. *Which of these steps do you think is most important in creating an effective business plan?*

1. Make a Research Plan and Gather Data
Start with a plan for the research by listing the questions you want answered. Then identify the type of data that will answer those questions. You will not find all of your data in the library. The information you find may be incomplete. It may need to be updated, supported, or clarified.

2. Set Up a Notebook to Organize Your Data
Setting up a business plan notebook is an effective way to gather and organize information. Write the source of each item on each item so that it will be easy to create footnotes or endnotes when you start writing the business plan. The notebook should have a separate section and at least one folder for each part of the business plan. As you conduct research, record your findings in the appropriate section.

3. Write a Draft
After you have finished your research, you are ready to compile a first draft of your business plan. Sort out the data in your various notebook sections. Set up a document with the headers you need, or use the business plan template document that can be found at **entrepreneurship.glencoe.com**. Begin to put the information you have collected into the appropriate sections. Once you have the information organized into sections, go through it again. Make sure your writing flows smoothly and presents a coherent and persuasive argument for your business.

Common Mistakes in Preparing Business Plans

When writing their business plans, entrepreneurs often make incorrect assumptions about investors. Consider these common mistakes.

Projecting Exaggerated Growth Levels

Entrepreneurs often believe that investors will be impressed with big sales figures. In fact, quite the opposite is true. Investors may think that the founding team cannot manage and control such rapid growth. Use conservative figures in your business plan, with the goal of exceeding your projections.

Trying to Be a Jack-of-All-Trades

Many entrepreneurs are proud of their ability to multitask. They claim to have expertise in all areas of the new venture. In fact, they may have a general knowledge of all aspects of the business and real expertise in only one area. For this reason, investors prefer a team to a solo entrepreneur.

Claiming Performance That Exceeds Industry Averages

A new venture does not usually outperform industry averages. Therefore, your business plan should project performance slightly below average. However, you should discuss how you plan to exceed industry averages at some time in the future.

Underestimating the Need for Capital

Your business plan should project enough capital to grow the company until there is sufficient internal cash flow. The business will then need additional capital to prepare itself for growth. If you underestimate the amount of money you need, investors may think you do not understand the business. When estimating capital needs, allow extra for the unexpected.

While You Read

Question Why is it not a good idea to project performance that exceeds industry averages even if you believe that it is true?

Sources of Business Plan Information

Where should you gather information for a business plan? There are local, state, and national organizations and government agencies that offer resources to help entrepreneurs develop business plans. The following agencies are great sources of information.

Small Business Administration (SBA)

To encourage entrepreneurship in our free enterprise system, the government runs the Small Business Administration. The **Small Business Administration (SBA)** is a federal agency that provides services to small businesses and new entrepreneurs. The agency offers publications for a minimal charge; gives special assistance to women, minorities, and the physically challenged; and offers financial assistance. You can find a link to the SBA Web site at **entrepreneurship.glencoe.com**.

Service Corps of Retired Executives (SCORE)

SCORE is dedicated to providing free, confidential face-to-face and e-mail business counseling to small businesses. SCORE has hundreds of satellite offices throughout the United States. You can find templates and guides for business planning on its Web site. You can find a link to the SCORE Web site at **entrepreneurship.glencoe.com**.

Small Business Development Centers (SBDCs)

The SBDC program is administered by the SBA. It provides management assistance to current and prospective small business owners. Its 63 centers offer a wide variety of information and guidance. You can find a link to the SBA's SBDC Web site at **entrepreneurship.glencoe.com**.

Chambers of Commerce

Local chamber offices provide information about the local economy, business trends, and business needs. In many cities, chambers of commerce operate small business development and assistance programs. You can find a link to the U.S. Chamber of Commerce Web site at **entrepreneurship.glencoe.com**.

Trade Associations

A **trade association** offers technical and general assistance to entrepreneurs in a specific profession or industry. Many trade associations publish publications like newsletters and magazines. Trade associations often supply information such as average start-up and operating costs and trend analysis. An association can also provide market research, technology news, and supplier contacts. You can find the representative trade association for any industry on the Internet.

> **BUSINESS PLAN INFORMATION** There are many different organizations that have resources to help entrepreneurs develop business plans. *What are some sources of assistance?*

Packaging and Presenting the Business Plan

The appearance of a business plan is as important as its contents. The appearance of the business plan is the first step in getting someone to read it. It must look professional without being distracting. To package your business plan effectively so that it appears professional, follow these guidelines.

Write About It

Create a brochure that shows how to package and present a professional looking business plan.

- Bind the plan so that it lies flat. A spiral binding works well.

- Use index tabs to separate sections so readers can find information easily.

- Use an easily readable 12-point type font, such as Times New Roman.

- Use bold subheadings and bullets to facilitate finding information.

- If you have a logo for your business, include it at the top of every page.

- Number each copy of the business plan and include a Statement of Confidentiality that the reader should sign. Keep track of who has a copy of the plan.

- Place a statement on the cover page prohibiting copying of the plan.

Section 5.2 After You Read

Review Key Terms

1. Why should you develop a business plan after you know you have a feasible concept?

2. In a business plan, what is the difference between the market analysis and the marketing plan?

3. What are two resources you can use to prepare your business plan?

Critical Thinking

4. Describe the importance of a vision/mission statement in identifying direction and objectives of a business.

Role Play

Situation You have an idea for a store selling school-spirit items and novelty gifts on your school campus. The athletic department, which already operates a store selling school supplies and snacks, opposes your idea. You have conducted a feasibility analysis and found that there is enough demand for a second store.

Activity Team up with a classmate and write a business concept statement. Then present your concept statement to the class.

Evaluation You will be evaluated on how well you meet these objectives.

- Present a business concept that describes the product or service being offered, the customer targeted, the benefit provided, and the manner of distribution of the product or service.

- Utilize effective oral presentation skills.

Chapter Summary

Feasibility Analysis: Testing an Opportunity

An idea for a business opportunity must be developed into a business concept. Then that concept must be tested in the market. A feasibility analysis will show if there is enough demand for your product or service to justify creating a business. By talking to potential customers and studying the competition, you should be able to determine if the industry will support your new business. Once the concept is judged feasible, a business plan will help the entrepreneur develop a strategy for executing the concept.

The Business Plan

The business plan presents the entrepreneur's strategy for executing the business concept. It explains to lenders and investors why a new business deserves financial support. Business plans also serve as living guides to the business and as start-up blueprints. Business plans have common features, including management team plan, company description, product and service plan, mission and vision statements, industry overview, market analysis, competitive analysis, marketing plan, operational plan, organizational plan, financial plan, growth plan, contingency plan, executive summary, supporting documents, cover page, title page, and table of contents. There are many sources of information for entrepreneurs creating business plans.

Key Terms Review

1. Select an entrepreneurial venture of interest to you. Write a short story about how you would develop such a venture. Use at least 12 of the key terms in your story.

business concept (p. 94)	competitive grid (p. 98)	distribution channel (p. 104)
feature (p. 95)	business model (p. 99)	direct channel (p. 104)
benefit (p. 95)	value chain (p. 99)	indirect channel (p. 105)
feasibility analysis (p. 96)	business plan (p. 100)	Small Business Administration (SBA) (p. 107)
industry (p. 96)	executive summary (p. 102)	trade association (p. 108)
target customers (p. 96)	vision statement (p. 102)	
prototype (p. 97)	mission statement (p. 102)	

Key Concept Review

2. **Discuss** the importance of defining a prospective business by writing a clear and concise business concept. (5.1)
3. **Describe** how a feasibility study can be used to test a concept in the marketplace. (5.1)
4. **Describe** the importance of planning. (5.2)
5. **Identify** and describe the components and formats of a business plan. (5.2)
6. **List** two of the key mistakes that entrepreneurs make when writing a business plan. (5.2)
7. **Identify** and analyze various sources of information for a business plan. (5.2)
8. **Describe** how to professionally package and present a business plan. (5.2)

Critical Thinking

9. Differentiate between a feasibility study and a business plan.
10. What information is needed to complete a target customer profile?
11. How can an entrepreneur use a competitive grid?
12. Select a product or service that interests you. What are its features? What are its benefits?
13. Which component of a business plan is the most important? Why?
14. If you had all of the money you needed to start your own business, would you develop a business plan? Why?
15. Access the Web site for SCORE. Identify five templates available for downloading. Would entrepreneurs find these templates useful? Why or why not?

Write About It

16. Write a two-sentence concept statement for a new restaurant.
17. You are preparing for your feasibility analysis. Write a plan for studying the industry and the market.
18. List the reasons for writing a business plan. Then write a paragraph explaining why business plans can be written for different reasons.
19. Locate and analyze vision statements from various businesses. Write two or more paragraphs to describe the similarities and differences among the vision statements. Describe how the vision statements address future trends.
20. Write a one-page critique of a real business plan. Analyze the company's use of the Internet and other technologies if appropriate.

Academic Skills

Math

21. While conducting a feasibility study for a new product in development, you interview 387 target customers at 15 different locations. Use these figures to compute the average number of target customers per location.

Language Arts

22. Contact a small business development center or another agency in your area that assists entrepreneurs in preparing business plans. Request a copy of an actual business plan. Evaluate and analyze the parts of the business plan. Does the plan have all of the basic features discussed in the chapter?

Entrepreneurship in Your Community

23. Identify a problem in your community that might be solved through a business you create. Develop a business concept statement for a product or service to solve the problem you have identified. Include the following:

- The product or service
- The customer
- The benefit you are providing
- The delivery method

24. As a class, divide into six groups. Work as a class to identify sources of assistance when planning a business, such as government agencies, a Small Business Development Center (SBDC), the Small Business Administration (SBA), chambers of commerce, or your local chapter of the Service Corp of Retired Executives (SCORE). Each group should select and research an agency. Find out about assistance available to entrepreneurs developing business plans. Request brochures, publications, and other materials. Report your findings to the class in a short presentation.

Ethical Practices

Management Decisions

25. One of your employees confides in you that another employee is planning to leave the company in three months to start her own company as a competitor. You are tempted to fire the employee immediately, but she is in the middle of a major project that is important to your company. This project will be finished in three weeks. What should you do?

Business Planning

You want to write a business plan for an Internet-based Web design company serving businesses in your community.

Connect

Use a Web directory or a search engine conduct research on the feasibility of the venture, the competitive climate, and business plans.

Application

Write a one-page report detailing the results of your research. Include this information in your report:

- Explain the purpose and importance of the business plan.
- Explain how a business plan can be used.
- Study competitors' Web sites, and analyze the competitive strengths and weaknesses of the entrepreneurial venture.
- Explain the feasibility of starting a home-based, Internet Web design company in your area.

The Electronic Entrepreneur

The E-Business Business Plan

A business plan is an essential tool, a roadmap that will guide the company as it grows and changes. A good plan is just as important for an e-business and it has some special needs of its own. In addition to the elements of a traditional business plan, an e-business business plan needs to include the following:

Timeline Detail the Web site development timeline and implementation schedule. Tell when the Web site will be launched. The **launch** is the first date on which the Web site is on the Internet.

Functionality Include a description of the Web site's functionalities. **Functionality** is how the Web site works. Explain if and when new features will be implemented.

Style Describe the Web site's visual "look and feel." Explain if the site's style will change or if it will remain consistent. Describe how the site's look and style will appeal to the target audience.

Metrics Describe how you plan to monitor activity on your Web site. The term **metrics** refers to methods used to measure activity and progress. Metrics software can measure number of visitors, what time of day is most active, and which products are receiving the most hits. Also, specify who will be responsible for monitoring the site's metrics.

Hardware Explain if the company will maintain its own Web server or if it will use a Web host. A **Web server** is a computer that delivers Web pages. A **Web host** is a business that provides server space and file maintenance services for Web sites controlled by businesses that do not have their own Web servers. Many Internet Service Providers (ISPs) offer Web host services.

International Markets Describe the countries the Web site is trying to target. Tell how your site will appeal to these markets. Tell if your Web site will be presented in languages other than English. If it will, describe how the translation will be done.

TechTerms

- launch
- functionality
- metrics
- Web server
- Web host

FACT AND IDEA REVIEW

1. What is the purpose of a timeline?
2. What are metrics? Why are they important?
3. Why does the "look and feel" of a Web site make a difference?
4. Why might it be important for an e-business site to offer information in languages other than English?

FOR DISCUSSION

5. What are some of the reasons why a company might want to host its own server? What are the benefits to using an ISP?

Market Analysis

CHAPTER OBJECTIVES

When you have completed this chapter, you should be able to:

SECTION 6.1

- Define areas of analysis for industry and market research.
- Discuss how to conduct effective market research.

SECTION 6.2

- Explain how to research an industry.
- Identify a customer profile and customer needs analysis.

EVALUATING CHECKING ACCOUNTS

How do you decide which type of checking account will meet your needs? You'll need to weigh several factors.

- **Restrictions.** The most common restriction is the requirement that you keep a minimum balance. Other restrictions include limits on the number of transactions allowed per month and the number of checks you may write in a month.

- **Fees and Charges.** Fees have increased in recent years—not only monthly fees but overdraft, check printing, and stop-payment charges.

- **Interest.** Interest rates, frequency of compounding, and the way interest is calculated all affect interest-bearing checking accounts.

- **Special Services.** Popular checking account services include ATMs, banking by phone, and online banking. Your bank may offer overdraft protection, an automatic loan made to you if you write a check for more money than you have in your account.

 Go to **entrepreneurship.glencoe.com** to complete the Standard & Poor's Money Talk Financial Literacy Activity.

PREPARE TO READ

THINK ABOUT THESE QUESTIONS AS YOU READ.

What are the five steps used in the marketing research process?

What industry forces affect your ability to do business?

Doing Market Research

KEY TERMS
- industry
- carrying capacity
- complexity
- market
- target market
- market segmentation
- market segments
- geographics
- psychographics
- industrial markets
- market research
- exploratory research
- focus group
- descriptive research
- historical research
- secondary data
- primary data

KEY CONCEPTS
- Defining Areas of Analysis
- Conducting Market Research

THE MAIN IDEA

To ensure success, the entrepreneur needs to understand the industry and the market. He or she should define areas of analysis and conduct effective industry and market research.

READING ORGANIZER

Draw the chart below on a separate piece of paper. As you read, fill in the chart with the five steps of the marketing research process.

| STEP 1 | STEP 2 | STEP 3 | STEP 4 | STEP 5 Analyze the data |

Defining Areas of Analysis

To succeed and make a profit, a business must satisfy the needs of its customers. However, you cannot satisfy current customers or attract new customers if you do not know who they are and what they want. To find out, you must conduct market analysis.

Markets for products and services are found within and across industries. An **industry** is a collection of businesses with a common line of products or services. It includes manufacturers, suppliers, distributors, and anyone else who deals with other businesses in the industry. A market, by contrast, is the customers for a particular product or service. Thorough market analysis requires that you examine your market from two different perspectives. You need to identify prospective customers and determine their buying habits. You also need to analyze your industry and assess your chances for success within it. This section will focus on how to conduct market research. The next section will discuss what to study about your industry and market.

Industry

Your industry represents the environment in which your business will operate. Therefore, you want to learn what the industry's current status is and where it is going. Ideas for new ventures frequently come from understanding and having experience with an industry. Knowledge of an industry can also help you find strategic partners and identify competitors.

Four broad factors are useful in understanding the nature of an industry. These are carrying capacity, uncertainty, complexity, and stage of life cycle.

CARRYING CAPACITY **Carrying capacity** is a way to understand the industry's ability to support new growth. You want to find an industry that can support expansion, thereby allowing your new venture to grow and prosper. Is there room for new businesses like yours?

UNCERTAINTY Uncertainty is the degree of stability or instability in an industry. An industry that is fast-changing presents a high degree of uncertainty and therefore more risk. Because of this, the rewards are typically higher, but you need to be prepared for a chaotic environment. Many high-tech ventures are in industries with uncertain climates.

COMPLEXITY **Complexity** is the number and diversity of contacts with which you must deal. Firms that operate in complex industries usually have more suppliers, customers, and competitors than firms in other industries. Highly complex industries, which are often global in nature, are very competitive and are costly to enter.

Success Stories

Creating Wealth From Creative Services

During the tech boom of the 1990s, John Chuang's firm MacTemps, which outsourced Web designers and computer experts to companies in need, was thriving. When the market took a turn for the worse and the Internet bubble burst, many such companies went under. However, Chuang changed the firm's focus, turning to marketing and creative services. Now called Aquent, the Boston-based company outsources entire teams of creative people to companies that need Web or print design, advertising, point-of-sale, or product design. Today, Aquent's annual sales are close to $300 million.

CRITICAL THINKING

Why is it important for a company to be flexible? Is there a downside to this idea—can a firm be "too flexible"?

 Go to **entrepreneurship.glencoe.com** to complete the Success Stories Writing Activity.

While You Read

Predict How does targeted marketing help businesses focus their marketing strategies?

STAGE OF LIFE CYCLE Like people, industries move through a life cycle. These stages include birth, growth, maturity, and then decline if research and development do not produce more growth. If you know the life cycle stage your industry is in, you can design a business strategy that is compatible with the life cycle.

Target Market and Customer

A **market** is a group of people or companies who have a demand for a product or service and are willing and able to buy it. The particular group of customers you are interested in is the **target market**. The target market will be the focus of your company's efforts. You want to know as much as you can about this market in as much detail as possible.

MARKET SEGMENTATION **Market segmentation** is the process of grouping a market into smaller subgroups defined by specific characteristics. When you study the characteristics of the total market, you can identify **market segments**, subgroups of buyers with similar characteristics. Once market segments are clearly identified, a business can customize its product offerings and marketing strategies to specific groups of potential customers. Consumer markets (customers who buy goods for personal use) are usually segmented in these ways:

- **Geographics** is the study of the market based on where customers live. This includes region, state, county, city, and/or area.

- Demographics are the personal characteristics of a population. This includes age, gender, family size, family life cycle, income, occupation, education, religion, race, nationality, and/or social class.

- **Psychographics** is the study of consumers based on social and psychological characteristics. These include personality, values, opinions, beliefs, motivations, attitudes, and lifestyle elements, including activities and interests.

- Buying characteristics are knowledge of and personal experiences with the actual goods or services.

Customers who buy goods or services for business use make up **industrial markets**. Industrial goods are goods or components produced for sale to manufacturers and used in the production of other goods. These markets are segmented differently. Variables include type of business, size, goods or services sold, geographic location, and products needed. Businesses that cater to industrial markets must consider customers' individual situations.

When you divide the total market, you create profiles of the customers you are considering. **Figure 6.1** shows an example of a market segment profile. Notice that only variables relevant to the business are included.

TARGET MARKETING After identifying all of the market segments, you are ready to select your target market. This is the specific market segment on which you will concentrate your efforts. Within this segment, you will find your first customer. This person has a problem that you can solve or recognizes an opportunity that you are offering.

Figure 6.1

Market Segment Profile

SITUATION: SPORTING GOODS STORE

Specializes in letter jackets and uniforms. Located in a large metropolitan area with several high schools and colleges.

PROFILE OF ONE MARKET SEGMENT

High school students, 15-to-18 year olds, male and female. Reside within city and nearby suburbs. Part-time annual income of $1,200–$2,000. Rarely buys expensive sports items. Dependent on parents for large purchases. Active in sports and gains feeling of importance from athletic recognition. Aware of current trends, and attitude toward where to buy influenced by peers.

MARKET SEGMENTATION Segmenting your market can make your customers' needs more clear. *What type of market is this company targeting?*

Here are some guidelines to use when segmenting the target market:

- The market segment should be measurable. You need to know how many potential buyers are in the market. Otherwise, how do you know if your venture is worth pursuing?

- The segment should be large enough to be potentially profitable. The segment you select must be big enough to enable you to recover your costs and make a profit.

- The segment should be reachable. First, you must be able to get information about your product and its availability to interested buyers. Second, you must be able to reach potential customers physically. You must be able to deliver your product to their homes or businesses or to the places where they shop.

- The market segment should be responsive. You should have some indication from your research that people in the segment are, in fact, interested in your product and willing to buy it.

A business can select and serve multiple market segments, but that does not usually happen in the start-up stage. If you have identified more than one target market, you need to decide which market will be easiest to enter first. In which market will you find it easiest to make sales? Those easy sales will give you the foundation needed to explore other markets as your company grows.

While You Read

Connect Think of a business that targets several market segments. How are the company's marketing strategies tailored to appeal to different markets?

Conducting Market Research

Once you know the areas of the market you need to analyze, you can begin investigating them. **Market research** is the collection and analysis of information aimed at understanding the behavior of consumers in a certain market. The marketing research process can be used to identify potential markets, analyze demand, forecast sales, and make other decisions. The market research process is the same whether you are doing research for an existing business or a new venture.

Identify the Focus of the Research

To begin market research, you need to focus your research so you do not waste time gathering useless information. For example, assume area high school students have never been able to buy healthy snacks from the vending machines. This situation may give you an opportunity to satisfy a need. To begin, you want to understand how the vending machine industry works. You need to know whether the market can support a healthy snack vending machine business. Finally, you should determine whether there is enough customer demand to make the business worthwhile.

Select the Type of Market Research

Once you have a research question, you can select a research approach. Ways to structure research are called *research designs*. The information you require will determine the design you use.

Exploratory research is used when you know very little about a subject. It forms the foundation for later research when you are focused on your area of interest. A good place to start exploratory research is government or industry publications. Most of these are available on the Internet. You can also talk to people who are knowledgeable about your field. You can organize a focus group. A **focus group** is a group of people whose opinions are studied to determine the opinions that can be expected from a larger population.

Descriptive research is done when you want to determine the status of something. For example, you may want to develop a customer profile. To do so, you need to learn the age, gender, occupation, income, and buying habits of potential customers. Such information can be collected through questionnaires, interviews, or observation.

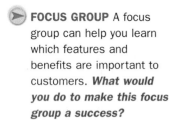

FOCUS GROUP A focus group can help you learn which features and benefits are important to customers. *What would you do to make this focus group a success?*

Historical research involves studying the past. Patterns from the past can then be used to explain present circumstances and predict future trends. Trade associations and trade publications are two sources of useful historical data. Owners in similar businesses can also provide you with historical information. You can use these findings to help predict your business's potential.

Start the Research Process

To successfully research your industry and market, you need a plan. An effective plan includes the following five steps:

STEP 1: IDENTIFY YOUR INFORMATION NEEDS Before you begin to collect data on your market, you should identify the kinds of information you need. For example, before opening a sporting goods store, you need to know who your first customer will be. You also should find out what that customer wants. You must gather information about the competition. Do you satisfy a need that your competitors cannot meet? Their deficiencies are your opportunities. Here are three questions to ask yourself when identifying your information needs:

1. How will the data be used?
2. What data needs to be collected?
3. What methods of analysis will be used?

STEP 2: OBTAIN SECONDARY RESOURCES Information that has already been collected by someone else is called **secondary data**. It is easily obtained and inexpensive. A good place to begin your search is the Internet. Consider the sources you find, particularly if you are not familiar with them. Just because information appears on a Web page does not mean it is true.

Government and community organizations are excellent sources of secondary data. The Web site of the U.S. Census Bureau provides current U.S. census data. This information is helpful in defining your market by a number of demographics. Community organizations such as the chamber of commerce keep statistics on local population trends and other economic issues. You can also consult trade associations, trade publications, and commercial research agencies.

Keep these questions in mind when collecting secondary data:

1. What are the demographics of the customer?
2. What are the psychographics of the customer?
3. How large is the market?
4. Is the market growing?
5. Is the market affected by geography?
6. How can you reach your market?
7. How do your competitors reach the market?
8. What market strategies have been successful with these customers?

While You Read

Question Why should you research secondary sources before researching primary sources?

BusinessWeek Case Study

Thinking Small at the Mall

To keep growing, chains have to keep chasing niches. Gymboree (GHMB), a 530-store chain based in Burlingame, Calif., serves a narrow niche: It sells kids' clothes aimed at parents making more than $65,000 a year. Since there are not enough of them to support more than another 120 stores or so, Lisa Harper, CEO of Gymboree Corp., opened Janie and Jack last year, a chain selling upscale baby gifts. "We thought we could spin off a separate design team and appeal to a different customer," she says. Since pricey baby gifts represent an even narrower niche, Harper already is working on the next idea. Eventually, she says, Gymboree could operate up to five niche chains.

From McDonald's (MCD) Corp. to Gap (GPS) Inc., one of the biggest conundrums in retailing is how to deal with the saturation problem. Once your store is in every mall, how do you get more growth—especially if the chain is narrowly focused to begin with? Increasingly, retailers like Harper are attempting to deal with the problem by launching

spin-offs that can cash in on an opportunity or a trend—even if they have only a three- or four-year run. Rather than managing a single chain for long-term growth, these retailers are managing an ever-shifting portfolio of store brands.

SOURCE: *BusinessWeek*, MAY 26, 2003; BY LOUISE LEE

APPLICATION

Imagine you are a consultant hired to help McDonalds gain more market growth. What type of spin-off business would you suggest? Create a short presentation describing the spin-off and the niche it could fill.

 Go to **entrepreneurship.glencoe.com** to complete the *BusinessWeek* Case Study Reading Guide.

STEP 3: COLLECT PRIMARY DATA Primary data is information you obtain for the first time and use specifically for your study. Primary data is important because it is current, and it relates directly to your objectives.

The most common methods of gathering primary data about customers are observation, interviews, and surveys. For your sporting goods store, you might go to a competitor's site and observe the kinds of equipment people buy. You might ask them questions and note how they make decisions about which products to buy. In surveys, individuals answer questions in person, by telephone, or through the mail. In-person interviews produce a higher response rate than other methods. Focus groups, which are more efficient than one-on-one interviews, can also be used. Whichever type of data you collect, use several reputable sources.

Keep these questions in mind when collecting primary data:

1. What are the demographics of your customer?
2. Would potential customers purchase your product or service? Why or why not?
3. How much would customers purchase?
4. When would customers purchase?
5. How would customers like to find the product or service?
6. What do customers like about your competitors' products and services?

STEP 4: ORGANIZE THE DATA Categorize data based on the research question it answers. Working on each question, note how many of your sources supported a particular conclusion and how many did not. Then create charts and graphs to depict your findings. If you decide to start your venture, you can refer to this information or add to it as needed. This data can help you refine your market analysis. It can also serve as the basis for a marketing plan.

STEP 5: ANALYZE THE DATA Now that your information has been organized, ask yourself these questions to help you judge your chances of having a successful business:

1. Is there a market for the product or service?
2. How big is the market?
3. Will the industry support such a business?
4. What do substitute products/services reveal about demand for the product/service?
5. What do customers, end users, and intermediaries predict the demand will be?

Write About It

Research Plan Write a question that you would like to answer through marketing research. Then write a plan for answering the question using all five steps of the market research process.

Section 6.1 After You Read

Key Concept Review

1. Why is it important to study your industry before developing a business concept?
2. What is the role of market research?
3. List and explain the types of market research and the steps in the market research process.

Critical Thinking

4. Using an idea you have for a business, explain how you will analyze the industry and the target market.

Role Play

Situation You are a marketing research consultant who has been hired by a flower shop owner to determine whether the flower shop should sell greeting cards.

Activity Assume the role of a marketing research consultant. Have a classmate assume the role of a flower shop owner. Prepare for and present a role play discussion about market research.

Evaluation You will be evaluated on how well you address these issues:

- Explain the steps of marketing research.
- Explain how the marketing research process can be used to identify potential markets, analyze demand, forecast sales, and make other decisions.
- Describe your research plan.

Industry and Market Analysis

KEY TERMS
- barriers to entry
- economies of scale
- brand loyalty
- mass marketing
- market share
- niche
- market positioning
- competitive advantage
- customer profile
- customer needs analysis

KEY CONCEPTS
- Researching the Industry
- Researching the Target Customer

THE MAIN IDEA

Studying a company's industry and market helps an entrepreneur create a product or service that people want. It also helps the entrepreneur develop a customer profile, estimate demand, and increase his or her chances for success.

READING ORGANIZER

Draw the chart below on a separate piece of paper. As you read, write the four questions to ask when creating a customer profile.

CUSTOMER PROFILE QUESTIONS

1. Who are my customers? _____

2. _____

3. _____

4. _____

Researching the Industry

In this section, you will look at industry trends and demographics and the competition. With this information, you can develop a profile of your first customer.

Trends and Patterns of Change

You can find opportunity in an industry by looking at trends and patterns of change. For example, is it becoming more difficult for new companies to enter the industry? Has the rate of sales growth slowed? Does the government heavily regulate the industry? How volatile is the industry? (Volatility refers to how quickly things change in the industry.)

Industry Forces That Affect Your Business

A number of forces will affect your ability to do business. They will also influence your business strategy. Understanding these competitive forces can help you plan a strategy to succeed.

1. BARRIERS TO ENTRY In established industries, the dominant businesses have advantages called *barriers to entry*. **Barriers to entry** are conditions or circumstances that make it difficult or costly for outside firms to enter a market to compete with the established firm or firms.

Established businesses have achieved economies of scale in production, marketing, and distribution. **Economies of scale** are situations where the cost of producing one unit of a good or service decreases as the volume of production increases. This means that production costs decline relative to the price of goods and services.

Brand loyalty is loyalty to or the tendency to buy a particular brand of a product. Customers who are brand loyal do not easily switch to a new company that enters the industry.

Existing businesses may bar new companies from certain distribution channels and may cooperate with other businesses to keep out new players. The government regulates many industries. Government regulation means higher costs. If you want to start a business that is subject to many government regulations, you may want to partner with an existing business in your industry to gain access to customers and distribution channels.

While You Read

Predict What does brand loyalty mean? Are you loyal to any brands?

Issues in Entrepreneurship

MASS MARKETING

In the past, products with universal appeal and few features to differentiate them from competitors were mass marketed. **Mass marketing** is trying to reach all customers with a single marketing plan. The advantage of mass marketing is that the costs are less because only one theme is used. The disadvantage is that the theme must be very general or it may not be understood by all potential customers.

Mass marketing is not as popular as it once was because markets for all products can be segmented. Even ads for products that use just one slogan, such as "Got Milk?," will use different models and themes to reach different markets. Market segmentation has advantages over mass marketing because products can be targeted more effectively.

For marketers, the evolution from mass marketing to targeted marketing is a fundamental change driven by necessity and opportunity. America today is a far more diverse society than it was in the past. The country has fragmented into countless market segments defined by demographics and product preferences.

Think Critically
What other factors may have influenced the evolution from mass marketing to targeted marketing?

 Go to **entrepreneurship.glencoe.com** to complete the Issues in Entrepreneurship Research Activity.

2. THREATS FROM SUBSTITUTE PRODUCTS In a competitive industry, your business competes with companies that produce products and services like yours. Your business also competes with companies that produce substitute products, those that offer an alternative to customers. For example, suppose you are planning to open a restaurant serving low-carbohydrate meals. You will be competing with other restaurants in your area, with grocery stores, and with specialty food stores. Most products have substitutes.

3. SOURCES OF SUPPLY Your suppliers will have an impact on sales. You must have access to affordable sources of inventory, raw materials, and goods. Otherwise, you will not be able to offer your product or service at prices that generate sales. You should also consider where your suppliers are located, the trade discounts they offer, and the availability of alternate sources. These can affect your costs, pricing, and sales.

4. BUYERS' ABILITY TO BARGAIN In industries where buyers have bargaining power, a new business may have difficulty gaining a foothold. Large discount buyers, such as Wal-Mart, Costco, and Toys "R" Us, have enormous bargaining power. This allows them to purchase their inventories at deep discounts. Small businesses don't generally have that power and must look for other ways to compete. Generally, they do this by offering personalized service and customized products.

5. TECHNOLOGY Technology allows companies to improve their business processes. Companies that use technology to operate effectively and efficiently are more likely to remain competitive.

Industry Demographics

Each industry has basic characteristics, or demographics. These include the number of companies, annual revenues, and average size of the companies by number of employees. These facts reveal whether the industry is growing, shrinking, or remaining stable.

The Competition

Outstanding sales potential for a product does not guarantee success. Usually, competing products are already established in the market. To succeed, you must be able to capture market share by differentiating your business. **Market share** is a portion of the total sales generated by all competing companies in a given market. Many entrepreneurial companies succeed by studying the competition to define a niche in the market. A **niche** is a small, specialized segment of the market, usually based on customer needs discovered in market research. **Market positioning** is the act of identifying a specific market niche for a product.

To succeed in the face of competition, you must do a thorough analysis of the competition. First, create a competitive grid (see Chapter 5, page 97). Use the information in the grid to identify what is unique about your business and define your competitive advantage. A **competitive advantage** is a feature that makes a product more desirable than its competitors' products. **Figure 6.2** shows ways to gather information about your competition.

While You Read

Connect Think of a company that has succeeded by focusing on a market niche.

Figure 6.2 **Competitive Intelligence**

COMPETITIVE ADVANTAGE Studying the competition is critical to finding your company's competitive advantage. *What kinds of data are helpful to understanding your competition?*

1. Visit competitors' outlets.
By visiting outlets where competitors' products are sold, you can evaluate appearance, number of customers coming and going, what they buy, how much they buy, and how often they buy.

2. Buy your competitors' products.
Purchasing competitors' products helps you understand the differences in features and benefits. You also learn a lot about how they treat their customers.

3. Search the Internet and your competitors' Web sites.
You begin your investigation by visiting your competitors' Web sites. The Internet can help you discover competitors and understand their competitive strategies.

Researching the Target Customer

No matter how large the target market, you must know your customer and have a market penetration strategy. A market penetration strategy is a plan to reach initial customers and increase market share. You must establish relationships with customers and target your marketing efforts.

Creating a Customer Profile

A **customer profile** is a complete picture of a venture's prospective customers. It includes geographic, demographic, and psychographic data, such as age, income level, education, buying habits (when, where, and how much), places customers typically shop, and method of purchase. This profile helps you make decisions about your product or service. It also helps you develop a marketing concept—how you will reach the customer. When you are creating your customer profile, ask yourself four questions:

While You Read

Question What kind of information does a customer profile include?

1. Who are my customers?
2. What do they generally buy, and how do they hear about the products and services they buy?
3. How often do they buy?
4. How can my business meet their needs?

Evaluating Customers' Needs

A **customer needs analysis** pinpoints the features and benefits of your goods or services that customers value. Suppose you are proposing to sell a new type of breakfast bar. You learn that more students like crunchy breakfast bars than soft breakfast bars. Because students are hungry before school, they want food that is easily accessible. Crunchiness is a feature of the product, while convenience is a benefit. You must provide the features and benefits the customers want. If you do, they will choose your product or service over the competition's.

TECHNOLOGY Today

Webcasting

Similar to a telecast, a webcast is the transmission of an event over the Internet. A webcast extends the audience from potential TV and radio news consumers to a targeted audience at their personal computers. Webcasts can be live or prerecorded and can range from entertainment to training films to corporate meetings. They can also be interactive, allowing the viewer to take part.

Critical Thinking

What are some practical business uses of webcasting?

 Go to **entrepreneurship.glencoe.com** to complete the Technology Today Vocabulary Practice Activity.

Forecasting Demand

It is difficult to determine with certainty how much of a product or service customers will buy. Several methods can be used to forecast a demand figure.

One way to forecast demand is to use historical analogy products. You may be able to predict the demand for your product or service based on demand for another one. For example, the demand for compact discs was a result of the historical demand for cassette tapes and records. You also may be able to forecast demand by considering demand for a similar product.

A second way to forecast demand is to interview prospective customers and intermediaries. No one knows the market better than the people who work in it. Talking with customers, distributors, wholesalers, and retailers can give you a good estimate of demand.

A third way to forecast demand is to go into limited production to test the market. The only way to test the reaction of potential customers may be to produce a small number of products. Then you can put them in the hands of people to test. Using a kiosk is a relatively inexpensive way to gauge demand for a product. A kiosk is an independent stand from which merchandise is sold, often placed in the common area of a shopping center.

Section 6.2   After You Read

Review Key Terms

1. Describe the importance of defining a target market and a market niche.

2. What is the role of competition in marketing?

3. What are four key questions you should ask about your target customer?

Critical Thinking

4. Pick an industry that interests you and research the trends and patterns of change. In a one-page report, project where the industry will be in ten years.

Role Play

Situation You and your friend work in a coffee house. You are thinking about opening your own coffee shop. Your friend has cautioned you to consider the competition and how you might differentiate yourself from them.

Activity With a partner, role-play a discussion you might have with your friend about the business concept and the competition.

Evaluation You will be evaluated on how well you address these issues:

- Describe your direct and indirect competitors.
- Discuss ways to differentiate your business from that of competitors.
- Forecast your chances of success.

Chapter Summary

Section 6.1 Doing Market Research

Understanding the industry and target market helps ensure that a new business is successful. A market analysis examines your prospective customers and the state of the industry before you enter it. Consumer market segmentation is based on geographics, demographics, psychographics, and buying characteristics. Industrial market segmentation involves business type, size, goods or services sold, geographic location, and products needed. The target market segment for your product or service should be measurable, profitable, reachable, and responsive. Market research is the process used to collect and evaluate market data. It involves defining the research question; selecting a research approach; and gathering, organizing, and analyzing information.

Section 6.2 Industry and Market Analysis

An entrepreneur must learn about the industry and study the market to create a product or service that people want. Industry research identifies your product's sales potential and your competition. Barriers to entry keep new business from either entering or succeeding in an industry. Research your competitors to determine your own competitive advantage and your ability to capture market share from other companies in the field. A customer profile increases an entrepreneur's chances for success.

Key Terms Review

1. Imagine you own a marketing research firm. Write a description of what your business does using at least 12 of the following key terms:

industry (p. 116)	industrial markets (p. 118)	economies of scale (p. 125)
carrying capacity (p. 117)	market research (p. 119)	brand loyalty (p. 125)
complexity (p. 117)	exploratory research (p. 120)	mass marketing (p. 125)
market (p. 118)	focus group (p. 120)	market share (p. 126)
target market (p. 118)	descriptive research (p. 120)	niche (p. 126)
market segmentation (p. 118)	historical research (p. 121)	market positioning (p. 126)
market segments (p. 118)	secondary data (p. 121)	competitive advantage (p. 126)
geographics (p. 118)	primary data (p. 122)	customer profile (p. 128)
psychographics (p. 118)	barriers to entry (p. 125)	customer needs analysis (p. 128)

Key Concept Review

2. **Define** some areas of analysis for industry and market research. (6.1)
3. **Discuss** how to conduct market research effectively. (6.1)
4. **Explain** how to research an industry. (6.2)
5. **Identify** a customer profile and customer needs analysis. (6.2)

Critical Thinking

6. Compare the sales potential of a company in the community to the trends in the industry.
7. Identify benefits and limitations of market research. Assess the need for conducting market research.
8. Can target market selection be done before market segmentation? Why or why not?
9. Give an example of a product you purchase based on the brand. Is brand loyalty important to you? Why or why not?
10. Design a plan to capture market share for a new breakfast bar you have developed.
11. Explain the marketing concept.
12. List and explain the competitive forces that can affect your business.
13. Choose a product or service. Explain the difference between a feature and a benefit of the product or service.
14. Why is it important to define a target market and market niche?

Write About It

15. In an e-mail to a classmate, explain market identification and what it means to you as an entrepreneur.
16. Choose a business concept you are interested in and in a one-page report, analyze barriers to entry for your new business that you can build to keep out competitors.
17. You are planning to open a specialty shop on campus. In a two-page report, discuss how you will determine the process for market analysis, which items to carry, and how to design the store.
18. Use a Venn diagram to describe differences between industrial and consumer goods.
19. Define and explain these terms: *market, market research, market positioning, market penetration strategy, market segmentation, market share, target market,* and *customer profile survey.*
20. In a memo to your teacher, identify the components of the market research process.

Academic Skills

Math

21. According to projections, total market sales for the health food industry should be $4 million in your first year of operation, $6 million in your second year, and $9 million in your third year. You have estimated that your healthy snack food shop will have total sales of $200,000 in your first year, $450,000 in your second year, and $900,000 in your third year. What is your market share percentage in each of the three years?

Language Arts

22. Locate a recent article about market research. Read the article and write a summary of its contents. Exchange summaries with a classmate. Critique each other's summary: What points are unclear? What points need more explanation? What errors do you find? After marking up the summary with your comments, return it to your classmate. Revise your summary based on your classmate's comments.

Entrepreneurship in Your Community

23. Working in teams of three or four, select a business concept you created from an earlier chapter or develop a new one. Survey and identify potential competitors.

    • List the competitor companies by name and location.

    • Determine (as closely as possible) the market share percentage for each company and estimate its sales.

    • Create a chart that summarizes the information you have gathered.

24. Invite a marketing specialist from a local company to speak to your class about the company's target market and competitive advantage. Find out how the company conducts its market research. Ask about the demographics of its target customers.

Ethical Practices

Researching the Competition

25. One of the aspects of market research that raises ethical questions is the practice of gathering intelligence on competitors. If you tell the competitors you are starting a competing business, you will not get the information you need. If you do not disclose the purpose of your research, are you being ethical? How can you conduct effective research and remain ethical?

Market Research

Laticia and Jorge are hoping to start a bicycle shop in your hometown. They have come to you for help on using the Internet to find demographic information. First, recognize and explain areas in which market analysis should be done. Then show them how to gather the data they need.

Connect

Use a search engine or Web directory to locate this information:

• Average age of target customers

• Number of men; number of women

• Average income and education

• Ethnicity

• Occupation information

Application

Use a spreadsheet program to compile the demographic information you locate about your potential customers. Then write a short paragraph summarizing who your customers are based on your research. Create charts and graphs that visually represent the data.

The Electronic Entrepreneur

Domain Names

A company's domain name is much more than the way customers can get to their Web site. Today, domain names have become a hot commodity, a crucial component of a marketing and branding plan.

Registering To get a domain name, a business makes a purchase from a **registrar**, a company that manages lists of domains and their owners. Popular registrars include VeriSign.com and Register.com. Registrars must first check to make sure the domain name has not been claimed by another registrar's customer, because each domain can only have one owner. The **Internet Corporation for Assigned Names and Numbers (ICANN)** is the nonprofit regulatory body that oversees domain registration.

Domain Types A top-level domain (TLD) is the most general part of the domain name in an Internet address. A TLD can be a **generic top-level domain (gTLD)** such as ".com" for commercial, ".edu" for educational, and ".org" for organization, ".gov" for government, ".mil" for military, and ".biz" for business. A TLD can also be a **country code top-level domain (ccTLD)**, such as ".us" for United States or ".fr" for France.

Branding No longer a luxury, today a domain name is an integral part of a company's brand. For large corporations such as Sears and Sony, their simple and intuitive domains are an enormous part of their marketing strategy. Also, for online-only companies such as eBay.com and Amazon.com, the domain name is the business name and is how customers identify them.

FACT AND IDEA REVIEW

1. What is a domain name?
2. What does a registrar do?
3. What is a top-level domain?
4. Why is having a particular domain name so important to a business?

FOR DISCUSSION

5. What are some Web sites that you think have effective domain names? What are some that you think are not effective?

TechTerms

- registrar
- Internet Corporation for Assigned Names and Numbers (ICANN)
- top-level domain (TLD)
- generic top-level domain (gTLD)
- country code top-level domain (ccTLD)

Chapter 7

Types of Business Ownership

Section 7.1

Sole Proprietorships and Partnerships

Section 7.2

Corporations

CHAPTER OBJECTIVES

When you have completed this chapter you should be able to:

SECTION 7.1

- Discuss the sole proprietorship legal form.
- Explain the partnership legal form.

SECTION 7.2

- Explain how the corporate form gives owners more protection from liability.
- Discuss the advantages and disadvantages of a C-corporation.
- Explain the purpose of a Subchapter S corporation.
- Compare nonprofit corporations to C-corporations.
- Explain the limited liability company.
- Discuss how to decide which legal form is best.

PROTECTING YOUR CREDIT

When you apply for a loan, the lender will review your credit report very closely. Since credit affects nearly every aspect of your life, protecting it is one of the most important things you will ever do. Some things to watch for:

- **Identity Theft.** Thieves might pick through your trash in hopes of finding personal information, so shred or tear any personal papers before throwing them out.

- **The Internet.** Make sure that any purchases online are done on a secure Web site from a trusted merchant. Keep records of your online transactions, and review all bank and credit card statements every month.

- **Cosigning Loans.** If you cosign a loan for a friend, you may be responsible for paying it back if the friend defaults. When you cosign a loan, you are taking a risk that a professional lender will not take. The lender would not require a cosigner if the borrower were considered a good risk. Be very cautious when cosigning, even with close friends or family.

 Go to **entrepreneurship.glencoe.com** to complete the Standard & Poor's Money Talk Financial Literacy Activity.

PREPARE TO READ

THINK ABOUT THESE QUESTIONS AS YOU READ:

What are the different types of legal business forms?

How do I decide what legal form is right for me?

Sole Proprietorships and Partnerships

GET READY TO READ

KEY TERMS
- sole proprietorship
- liability protection
- unlimited liability
- partnership
- general partner
- limited partner

KEY CONCEPTS
- Sole Proprietorship
- Partnerships

THE MAIN IDEA

Entrepreneurs need to understand the advantages and disadvantages of various forms of businesses so they can choose the most appropriate form for their business.

READING ORGANIZER

Draw the chart on a separate piece of paper. As you read, list facts about sole proprietorships and partnerships.

SOLE PROPRIETORSHIPS	PARTNERSHIPS
one owner	two or more owners

Sole Proprietorship

The easiest and most popular form of business to create is the sole proprietorship. A **sole proprietorship** is a business that is owned and operated by one person. Nearly 76 percent of all businesses in the United States are sole proprietorships.

The owner of a sole proprietorship receives the profits, incurs any losses, and is liable for the debts of the business. Most businesses begin as sole proprietorships because they are easy to create. However, entrepreneurs often switch to a form that provides more personal financial protection as the business grows.

Pick Your Partner — Carefully

You've got the business plan, the cash, and the energy to make a startup fly. But do you have a reliable sidekick?

Three months after their first meeting, a chef who aspired to own a gourmet store signed a partnership agreement with a woman whose business background guaranteed success—or so he thought. Then his real education began, not in the ways of running a small business but in the unseen consequences of forming a hasty partnership. "I didn't foresee the personality conflicts," says the older, wiser, and considerably less wealthy entrepreneur. Since the duo had neglected to take the possibility of personal friction into account when drawing up their agreement, the chef ended up minus his dream—and much of his savings.

That cautionary tale wouldn't surprise the experts at Service Corps of Retired Executives (SCORE), which cautions that an impressive résumé doesn't necessarily guarantee a good partner. What matters most, they say, is the dynamics between the two individuals involved.

SOURCE: *BusinessWeek*, March 12, 2003; By Alison Ogden

APPLICATION

What kind of person would be your ideal business partner? Use a word-processing application to write a short personality profile describing the ideal partner's work ethic, personality, and interests.

 Go to **entrepreneurship.glencoe.com** to complete the *BusinessWeek* Case Study Reading Guide Activity.

To decide whether a sole proprietorship is right for you, ask yourself the following questions:

1. How much **liability protection**, or insurance, do you need?

2. Do you need to seek investment capital?

3. What effect will the business have on your tax status?

Consider these questions as you examine the advantages and disadvantages of the sole proprietorship.

Advantages

The sole proprietorship is easy and inexpensive to create. It gives the owner complete authority over all business activities. It also allows the owner to receive all of the profits. It is the least regulated form of ownership. In addition, the business itself pays no taxes because it is not separate from the owner. Instead, the income from the business is taxed at the personal rate of the owner. The personal tax rate often is lower than the corporate tax rate.

OTHER TYPES OF PARTNERSHIPS

Joint ventures and strategic alliances are types of partnerships in which two companies come together to find ways to help each other.

A joint venture is a type of partnership where two companies join to complete a specific project. They act like partners for a specified period of time, and then the partnership ends. Many real estate developers make a joint venture with a financial source to design and build a project.

A strategic alliance is a partnership in which two businesses work together for mutual benefit. For example, you may form a strategic alliance with a manufacturer that agrees to produce your product. You do not have to set up a manufacturing plant, and the manufacturer gets your continued business.

Think Critically

How can forming a joint venture or strategic alliance give a firm a competitive advantage?

 Go to **entrepreneurship.glencoe.com** to complete the Issues in Entrepreneurship Research Activity.

Disadvantages

The biggest disadvantage of a sole proprietorship is financial. To start, the owner has **unlimited liability**, full responsibility for all debts and actions of the business. That means he or she is personally responsible for any and all debts of the business. The debts may have to be paid from the owner's personal assets. Thus, the owner's home, car, and bank account may be at risk. In addition, raising capital may be more difficult. The owner may not have enough assets to qualify for a loan or to satisfy investor requirements.

Other disadvantages center on the owner as a person. A sole proprietorship may be limited by its total reliance on the abilities and skills of the owner. These may not be sufficient. Finally, the death of the owner automatically dissolves the business unless there is a will to the contrary.

How to Set Up a Sole Proprietorship

Operating as a sole proprietor is as simple as deciding on the company name. When using a name other than your own, you must apply for a Certificate of Doing Business Under an Assumed Name. This is often called a DBA ("doing business as") or a fictitious business name statement. You can get a DBA from the government offices in the area where your business will operate. Filing a DBA ensures that the name you have chosen for your business is the only one in the area.

If you are going to hire employees, you need an Employer Identification Number (EIN). This number, which comes from the Internal Revenue Service, is used for tax purposes to track federal income tax withheld and federal income tax returns.

You need a sales tax identification number if you are a vendor or retailer. This number is assigned by a state's Department of Revenue. It is used for sales tax record keeping. The retailer acts as an agent for the state by collecting and remitting the required amount. You can apply for this number on the Internet.

Partnerships

A **partnership** is an unincorporated business with two or more owners. A partnership is the most common business organization involving more than one owner. Two or more people own a business and share the decisions, assets, liabilities, and profits. As a legal form of ownership, the partnership compensates for some of the shortcomings of a sole proprietorship. The partnership can draw on the skills, knowledge, and financial resources of more than one person. This is an advantage when seeking loans. A partnership requires a DBA when the last names of the partners are not used in naming the business. Professionals such as lawyers, doctors, and accountants are frequently set up as partnerships.

While You Read

Predict How does a partnership make up for the shortcomings of a sole proprietership?

General Versus Limited Partners

A partnership may be set up so all of the partners are general partners. A **general partner** is a participant in a partnership who has unlimited personal liability and takes full responsibility for managing the business. Anyone entering into a general partnership must remember that each general partner is liable for all the debts of the partnership. Furthermore, any partner alone can bind the partnership on contracts. The law requires that all partnerships have at least one general partner.

TECHNOLOGY Today

SBA Online

The Small Business Administration is a government agency founded in 1953 to provide services to small- and medium-sized companies. The SBA Web site offers a wealth of information on starting or buying a business, marketing, management, and much more, plus guides to state and federal regulations.

Critical Thinking

Visit the SBA Web site. Which features do you think might be most useful?

@ Go to **entrepreneurship.glencoe.com** to complete the Technology Today Vocabulary Practice Activity.

Partners do not have to share a business equally. They can assign the interest in the partnership according to the amount contributed at start-up. How the partnership interests are divided is spelled out in the partnership agreement. Sometimes businesses have limited partners. A **limited partner** is a partner whose liability is limited to his or her investment. If a limited partner invests $10,000 in a business, the most he or she can lose is $10,000. Limited partners cannot be actively involved in managing the business. If they become involved, they lose their limited liability status.

Advantages

The advantages of a partnership are similar to those of a sole proprietorship. This form of business is inexpensive to create, and the general partners have complete control. Partnerships have other benefits. They can share ideas and secure investment capital more easily and in greater amounts.

Disadvantages

Despite the advantages, a partnership may not be the preferred form of ownership. It is difficult to dissolve one partner's interest in the business without dissolving the partnership. In other words, if one partner wants out or dies, the partnership ends. The business is likely to survive only when specific provisions have been placed in the partnership agreement.

Personality conflicts among partners are why most partnerships end. Problems often start as disagreements over authority. Therefore, partners' roles must be clearly defined.

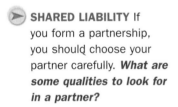

While You Read

Connect Think of an example of a partnership that operates in your community.

SHARED LIABILITY If you form a partnership, you should choose your partner carefully. *What are some qualities to look for in a partner?*

There are technical disadvantages, too. Partners are bound by the laws of agency. This means partners can be held liable for each other's actions. If one partner signs a contract with a supplier, the other partner is bound by the terms of the contract. Otherwise, the business may be sued for breach of contract.

While You Read

Question What are the benefits of a partnership agreement?

Making a Partnership Work

Partnerships start with the best of intentions. However, disagreements are bound to occur. Partners must consider each other's needs before committing to the partnership. Even more important is that they plan for disagreements.

In general, a partnership has the greatest chance of surviving when partners:

- Share business responsibilities.
- Put things in writing.
- Be honest about how the business is doing.

Partners also need to establish a partnership agreement in advance. The law does not require a partnership to be based on a written agreement. However, a partnership should still have one. Partnership agreements are usually drawn up by attorneys and are based on the Uniform Partnership Act. Agreements answer questions about profit sharing among partners and business responsibilities. They spell out what happens if one partner dies or quits. A well-constructed partnership agreement can solve many problems.

Section 7.1 After You Read

Key Concept Review

1. What is a sole proprietorship?
2. Explain why a partnership agreement is necessary.
3. What is the difference between general and limited partners?

Critical Thinking

4. Explain the procedure for registering a sole proprietorship and obtaining a sales tax identification number.

Role Play

Situation You are the sole proprietor of a bicycle shop. You sell a variety of bikes, accessories, clothing, and parts. Because you are a sole proprietor, you work seven days a week. A friend has approached you and has asked to become your partner.

Activity Team up with a classmate and research the advantages and disadvantages of sole proprietorships and partnerships. Then role-play a discussion between the business owner and the potential partner about forms of business ownership.

Evaluation You will be evaluated on how well you meet the following performance indicators:

- Identify factors that influence choice of ownership type.
- Compare and contrast these two types of business ownership.
- Select the most appropriate form of ownership for the business.

Corporations

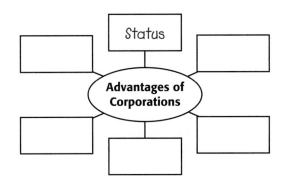
What Is a Corporation?

A **corporation** is a business that is registered by a state and operates apart from its owners. A corporation lives on after the owners have sold their interests or passed away. Ownership or equity in a corporation is represented by *shares of stock*. Corporations can purchase goods, sue and be sued, and conduct any type of business transaction.

Three major types of corporations are the C-corporation, Subchapter S corporation, and nonprofit corporation. **Figure 7.1** compares the types of business forms and identifies factors that influence the choice of ownership type.

C-Corporation

A **C-corporation** is an entity that pays taxes on earnings. Its shareholders pay taxes as well. It is the most common corporate form. It can protect the entrepreneur from being sued for the actions and debts of the corporation.

Figure 7.1 **Legal Forms of Ownership—A Comparison**

Issues	Sole Proprietorship	Partnership	Limited Liability Company	C-Corporation	Subchapter S Corporation
Number of Owners	One	No limit	No limit; most states require minimum of two	No limit on shareholders	75 shareholders or fewer
Start-up Costs	Filing fees for DBA and business license	Attorney fees for partnership agreement; filing fees for DBA	Attorney fees for organization, documents, filing fees	Attorney fees for incorporation documents; filing fees	Attorney fees for incorporation documents; filing fees
Liability	Owner liable for all claims against business; can overcome liability with insurance	General partners liable for all claims; limited partners liable only for amount of investment	Members liable as in partnerships	Shareholders liable to amount invested; officers may be personally liable	Shareholders liable to amount invested
Taxation	Pass-through taxation; the profits or losses of the business pass-through to the owner to be taxed at his or her individual tax rate	Pass-through taxation; the profits or losses of the business pass-through to the partners to be taxed at their individual tax rates	Pass-through taxation; the profits or losses of the business pass-through to the members to be taxed at their individual tax rates	Tax-paying entity; taxed on corporate income	Pass-through taxation; the profits or losses of the business pass-through to the shareholders to be taxed at their individual tax rates
Continuity of Life of Business	Dissolution upon death of owner	Dissolution upon death or separation of partner unless otherwise specified in the agreement; not so in the case of limited partners	Most states allow perpetual life; unless otherwise stated in Articles of Organization, existence terminates upon death or withdrawal of member	Perpetual life; the entity may live forever without interruption by death of shareholders, directors or officers	Perpetual life: the entity may live forever without interruption by death of shareholders, directors or officers
Transferability of Interest	Owner is free to sell; with valid will, assets transferred to estate upon death of owner	General partner requires consent of other generals to sell interest; limited partners' ability to transfer subject to agreement	Permission of majority of members to transfer interest	Shareholders free to sell unless restricted by agreement	Shareholders free to sell unless restricted by agreement
Distribution of Profits	Profits go to owner	Profits shared based on partnership agreement	Profits shared based on member agreement/articles of organization	Paid to shareholders as dividends according to agreement and shareholder status	Paid to shareholders according to percentage of ownership
Management Control	Owner has full control	Partners have equal voting rights unless there is an agreement	Management committee	Board of directors appointed by shareholders	Board of directors appointed by shareholders

ADVANTAGES AND DISADVANTAGES Each form of ownership has benefits and drawbacks. *Which form is best suited for your business?*

An attorney should guide the entrepreneur through the process of forming a corporation. This includes the filing of a Certificate of Incorporation with the state and the issuing of stock. **Shareholders** are the owners of the corporation. In smaller private corporations, the founders generally hold the majority of the stock. Therefore, they make the policy decisions. A corporation is also required to have a board of directors that makes decisions and selects officers to run the company.

Advantages

There are many benefits and advantages to incorporation. These include status, limited liability, the ability to raise investment money, perpetual existence, employee benefits, and tax advantages.

An officially incorporated business has a more professional appearance. Corporate status can help a business get loans. Corporations must hold certain types of meetings and appoint certain kinds of officers, which can help a business run more efficiently.

Corporate shareholders have **limited liability**; they are liable only up to the amount of their individual investment. However, some banks require corporate officers to personally guarantee the debts. The corporation can raise money by issuing stock.

Corporations have perpetual existence. They have a continuous life regardless of changes in ownership. Corporations are structured to accommodate employee benefits. Corporate owners can create pension and retirement funds and offer profit sharing plans. Corporations have tax advantages. They can deduct certain expenses from their reportable income. These deductions can include salaries and contributions to benefit plans, such as retirement and health plans.

Disadvantages

The corporate form is expensive to set up. It can cost between $500 and $2,500 to create a corporation. A corporation's income is more heavily taxed. The corporation is subject to double taxation on its earnings. The corporation pays taxes on profits; then stockholders pay taxes on dividends they receive from those earnings.

Subchapter S Corporation

An entrepreneur can avoid the double taxation of a C-corporation by setting up a Subchapter S corporation. The **Subchapter S corporation** is a corporation that is taxed like a partnership. Profits are taxed only once at the shareholder's personal tax rate. Therefore, unlike the corporation, the Subchapter S corporation is not a taxpaying entity. In general, Subchapter S corporations can have no more than 75 stockholders who must be U.S. citizens. Subchapter S corporations can have only one class of stock.

Cash businesses, such as restaurants, are often Subchapter S corporations. If the business produces enough cash, the form works. If the business shows a large taxable profit but has not generated enough cash to cover the taxes, the owners must pay the taxes out of their personal earnings.

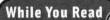

While You Read

Predict What are the disadvantages of the corporate form?

Quick Math

The Sharing Center, a nonprofit food bank, has a goal to raise 6% more in funds this year than it did last year. If last year's fund-raisers netted $175,000, what is this year's goal?

A Step in the Right Direction

In 1999, Nick Swinmurn tried to find a particular pair of shoes at a local mall. He was frustrated by the lack of choice—and decided to build the Internet's ultimate shoe store. What was originally dubbed ShoeSite is now Zappos.com, and today it claims to be "the Web's most popular shoe store." By focusing on exceptional customer service, as well as an enormous selection (the site offers thousands of brands and models), Zappos.com is a major success, with sales of over $70 million in 2003.

CRITICAL THINKING

How important is the size of a Web merchant's selection? Why?

 Go to **entrepreneurship.glencoe.com** to complete the Success Stories Writing Activity.

Nonprofit Corporation

Many entrepreneurs run businesses that benefit a certain cause in the community. A **nonprofit corporation** is a legal entity that makes money for reasons other than the owners' profit. The types of nonprofit corporations are shown in **Figure 7.2**. Nonprofit businesses can make a profit. However, the profit must remain within the company and not be distributed to shareholders.

Limited Liability Company

A **limited liability company (LLC)** is a company whose owners and managers enjoy limited liability and some tax benefits, but it avoids some restrictions associated with Subchapter S corporations. An LLC is similar in some aspects to a corporation and in other aspects to a limited partnership. There are many benefits to forming an LLC, including:

- An LLC is simpler to set up than a corporation.
- An LLC allows for the flexibility of a partnership structure.
- The LLC protects its owners with the limited liability of a corporation. Its members are not liable for the company's debts.
- An LLC is not subject to double taxation. The LLC provides the pass-through tax advantages of a partnership. Profits are taxed personally, and shareholders are taxed only once.
- Unlike a Subchapter S corporation, there are no limitations on the number of members or their status.

Many law and medical firms form LLCs to protect their partners. LLCs are also popular with foreign investors and family owners. Check with your state for its requirements on forming LLCs.

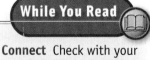

While You Read

Connect Check with your state for requirements on forming an LLC.

Figure 7.2 **Nonprofit Corporations**

NOT FOR PROFIT
Nonprofit corporations must fall within one of four categories: religion, charity, public benefit, and mutual benefit. *If you were starting an after-school program for elementary school children to help them experience entrepreneurship, into which category of nonprofit would this business fall?*

1. Charity
Charitable causes include feeding the hungry and providing job training for the unemployed.

2. Public Benefit
Many nonprofit foundations are created to advance science, education, and the arts.

3. Mutual Benefit
Trade associations, amateur sports leagues, and political groups are formed to benefit a specific group.

Making the Decision

It is very important that the entrepreneur carefully evaluate the pros and cons of the various legal forms before organizing a new venture. Consider your skills, access to capital, expenses, willingness to assume liability, desired degree of control, and the length of time you expect to own the business. With a good understanding of legal forms, you can make a wise decision about which form is best for you. Ask yourself these questions before making the final choice.

- Do you and your team have all of the skills needed to run this venture?

- Do you have the capital needed to start the business alone, or must you raise it through cash or credit?

- Will you be able to run the business and cover living expenses for the first year?

- Are you willing and able to assume personal liability for any claims against the business?

- Do you want complete control over the operation of the business?

- Do you expect to have initial losses, or will the business be profitable from the beginning?

- Do you expect to sell the business some day?

While You Read

Question Now that you have an understanding of legal forms, which do you find most desirable?

Section 7.2 After You Read

Key Concept Review

1. What are three reasons people choose the corporate form?

2. What is the difference between a C-corporation and a Subchapter S corporation?

3. Explain what a limited liability company is.

Critical Thinking

4. Ask the owner of a nonprofit company how he or she gives to the community. Describe how a nonprofit business can benefit both the owner and the community.

Role Play

Situation You are an attorney who specializes in advising business owners on legal forms of business ownership.

Activity Team up with a classmate who will assume the role of an entrepreneur who has hired you to give advice about the most appropriate form of business ownership for a fictional business opportunity. Then work together to research, write, and perform a role play in which you present a question and answer session about the various forms of business ownership.

Evaluation You will be evaluated on how well you address these issues:

- Identify factors that influence choice of ownership type.

- Describe legal implications and taxes for each type of business structure.

- Compare and contrast advantages and disadvantages of various forms of business organizations.

- Select the most appropriate forms of business ownership for a planned business.

Chapter Summary

Section 7.1 **Sole Proprietorships and Partnerships**

Entrepreneurs need to understand the advantages and disadvantages of the various forms of business available so they can choose the type that is most appropriate for them. The easiest businesses to form are sole proprietorships, where the owner is the only one responsible for the activities of the business, and partnerships, where two or more people own a business and share the assets, liabilities, and profits. These business forms also carry the greatest liability for their owners. Joint ventures and strategic alliances are two types of partnerships that form for a specific project or mutual benefit. A partnership agreement, which spells out specific information regarding business responsibilities and money issues, can prevent problems when disagreements occur.

Section 7.2 **Corporations**

In a corporation, the owners are protected from the actions of the company. Corporate forms include C-corporations, Subchapter S corporations, and nonprofit corporations. Because corporations can be complex to create and operate, an attorney should guide the entrepreneur through the process. This includes the filing of a Certificate of Incorporation with the state and the issuing of stock. In a limited liability company (LLC), the owners and managers enjoy limited liability and some tax benefits, but they avoid some restrictions associated with Subchapter S corporations. Before deciding on a legal form, you should ask yourself key questions about your skills, capital, expenses, and ability to assume liability, and about the level of control you want and the length of time you expect to own the business.

Key Terms Review

1. Assume you are a business attorney who is being consulted by a potential entrepreneur. In one or two paragraphs, categorize the forms and types of business ownership. Compare and contrast the forms. Include the following terms:

sole proprietorship (p. 136)

liability protection (p. 137)

unlimited liability (p. 138)

partnership (p. 139)

general partner (p. 139)

limited partner (p. 140)

corporation (p. 142)

C-corporation (p. 142)

shareholders (p. 144)

limited liability (p. 144)

Subchapter S corporation (p. 144)

nonprofit corporation (p. 145)

limited liability company (LLC) (p. 145)

Key Concept Review

2. **Discuss** the sole proprietorship legal form. (7.1)

3. **Explain** the partnership legal form. (7.1)

4. **Explain** how the corporate form gives owners more protection from liability. (7.2)

5. **Discuss** the advantages and disadvantages of a C-corporation. (7.2)

6. **Explain** the purpose of a Subchapter S corporation. (7.2)

7. **Compare** nonprofit corporations to C-corporations. (7.2)

8. **Explain** the limited liability company. (7.2)

9. **Discuss** how to decide which legal form is best. (7.2)

Critical Thinking

10. Which form of business would be best for a company with employees and a leased retail space?

11. Working as a team member is similar to being in a partnership. What are some advantages and disadvantages of working together?

12. Propose an example of a joint venture or strategic alliance that might be successful in today's global economy. Explain your proposal.

13. In which type of business structure would owners have the easiest time obtaining financing from a bank? Explain your answer.

14. Compare a limited liability company with a C-corporation.

15. What kinds of ventures might be more appropriate for a nonprofit structure than for a profit structure?

Write About It

16. Interview an entrepreneur involved in a partnership. In a two-page paper, report on your findings.

17. You have an idea for a consumer product—a new kind of backpack that has room for the storage of items that must be kept cold. You are going to develop the product in your garage, then find a manufacturing facility and hire employees after you have secured funding. In two paragraphs, describe your strategy for using the most appropriate legal form of business ownership at each stage.

18. In one paragraph, describe why a Subchapter S corporation is more effective for cash businesses than noncash businesses.

19. Write a two-page report detailing the circumstances for forming an LLC instead of a corporation.

20. Create a table that describes the legal forms of business ownership, and explains the implications and taxes for each form. Include an explanation of how to register each type of business.

Academic Skills

Math

21. You are the owner of a retail craft supply store. You pay your sales associate $7.50 per hour and 1.5 times the regular rate for every hour over 40 hours per week. Last week your associate worked 54 hours. How much did he earn?

Language Arts

22. Team up with a classmate. Choose a type of business ownership and explain it to your classmate. When you are finished, ask your classmate to summarize your explanation, telling what he or she heard you say. Discuss any discrepancies in what you said and what your classmate heard.

Entrepreneurship in Your Community

23. Volunteer to work or job-shadow in a nonprofit organization. Learn about the nonprofit's structure. As a class, share your experiences and compare your findings.

24. Invite local businesspersons representing sole proprietorships, partnerships, a variety of corporations (C-corporation, Subchapter S, and nonprofit), and LLCs to serve on a panel discussion in your class. Ask them to share:

- The pros and cons of each type of business ownership.

- Their story of how they got started.

- Qualities they believe are important for succeeding in the type of business ownership they represent.

Have questions ready when the panel members arrive. At the end of the discussion, thank them for their time.

Ethical Practices

Mixing Expenses

25. Good business practices suggest that you keep your business and personal expenses separate. Also, it is not legal to mix business and personal expenses. Why is this practice unethical, too?

INTERNET connection

Research Business Ownership

You and your business partner need to decide whether to create a partnership or a Subchapter S corporation. You decide to use the Internet to find background information before contacting a local attorney.

Connect

Use a search engine or Web directory to investigate the advantages and disadvantages of these legal forms of businesses. Find answers to the following questions:

- What legal issues do you face if you create a partnership?

- What legal issues do you face if you create a Subchapter S corporation?

- What types of legal information are available from the Internet?

Application

Summarize you findings in a one-page report. Your report should describe advantages and disadvantages of these forms of business ownership. It should also list and describe the legal information that is available on the Internet.

The Electronic Entrepreneur

Entry Level E-Commerce

Big companies can afford to spend millions of dollars developing their e-commerce sites. However, there are options that can allow small businesses to ease into e-commerce at a slower, less expensive pace.

Hosted Shopping A **hosted shopping cart** is a business that offers e-commerce services for a monthly fee; users can upload product information and have their store launched instantly. Yahoo! Stores is a prominent hosted cart service.

Online Auctions Many companies have found success by listing their products on on-line auction sites. Similar to a real-life auction in which property or merchandise is sold to the highest bidder, an **online auction** is an auction that takes place via a Web site, such as eBay. There are business-to-business (B2B) auctions, business-to-consumer (B2C) auctions, and consumer-to-consumer (C2C) auctions.

Open-Source Solutions A handful of e-commerce shopping cart programs are available as open-source software. **Open-source software** is software that is distributed free of charge. This type of software is not for novices; it does not include technical support, and setup and configuration can be complicated. If you have the technical background, open-source software can be a thrifty e-commerce solution. If you do not have it, you can hire a programmer to help you to install and maintain an open-source e-commerce application.

Virtual Stores Do you not have a product to sell? Virtual stores allow you to quickly set up an online storefront, with the orders going directly to the distributor. A **virtual store** is an online storefront that allows entrepreneurs to sell products they do not own. The Web site is maintained and provided by the distributor or manufacturer of the product. The entrepreneur works to bring traffic to the site; when orders are placed, they go directly to the manufacturer or distributor for fulfillment.

FACT AND IDEA REVIEW

1. What is a hosted shopping cart?
2. Why would a company want to sell products at an online auction?
3. What is open-source software? Why might a company want to use an open-source e-commerce application?
4. What is a virtual store?

FOR DISCUSSION

5. Which of these options do you think has the most potential—if you were in business, which of these would you choose to explore first? Why?

TechTerms

- hosted shopping cart
- online auction
- open-source software
- virtual store

The Legal Environment

CHAPTER OBJECTIVES

When you have completed this chapter, you should be able to:

SECTION 8.1

- Explain how to protect your intellectual property.
- Discuss the laws affecting the start-up of a business.

SECTION 8.2

- Explain the laws that affect employees.
- Identify the laws that regulate trade.
- Discuss the tax laws that apply to a new venture.

 STANDARD & POOR'S
Money Talk

TAX PLANNING STRATEGIES

If you do not want to be someone who has no money left after taxes and living expenses, the key is effective tax planning. First, find out how the current tax laws and regulations affect you. Second, make an effort to maintain complete and accurate tax records. Finally, learn how you can make decisions that can reduce your tax liability, the total amount of taxes you owe.

Throughout your life, you are probably going to pay taxes in four major categories:

- Taxes on purchases
- Taxes on property
- Taxes on wealth
- Taxes on earnings

You can pay your income taxes to the federal government in two ways: through payroll withholding or estimated payments. If you live in a state that has its own income tax, you will have to complete a state income tax return as well.

@ Go to **entrepreneurship.glencoe.com** to complete the Standard & Poor's Money Talk Financial Literacy Activity.

PREPARE TO READ

THINK ABOUT THESE QUESTIONS AS YOU READ.

What is intellectual property?

What laws and government agencies affect businesses?

Legal Issues Facing Start-Ups

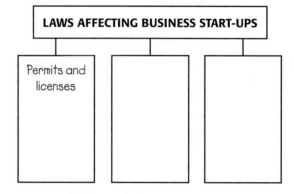
Protecting Ideas: Intellectual Property Law

When you develop a new product or service, you create an asset that must be protected. **Intellectual property law** is the group of laws that regulates the ownership and use of creative works. Protecting an invention falls under patent law. Protecting a logo for a business is a trademark issue. Writing music, software, or books involves copyright law. Trade secrets involve anything not covered under patents, trademarks, or copyrights. **Figure 8.1** on page 157 explains how intellectual property laws protect the inventions and new ideas of businesses.

Trade Secrets

The basis of all intellectual property is trade secrets. These may consist of a formula, device, idea, process, pattern, or compilation of information that gives the owner a competitive advantage. As a trade secret, theoretically, the design and proprietary information are not available to the public.

There are no legal means under patent and trademark law to protect trade secrets. However, companies can ask employees and others to sign agreements that detail what is considered a trade secret and not give all the components of a trade secret to any one individual.

Patents

A **patent** is a document that grants to an inventor the right to exclude others from making, using, or selling an invention or other intellectual property during the term of the patent. This means the inventor can defend the patent against anyone who attempts to manufacture and sell the invention. A patent lasts for a period of 21 years from the date of application. Then it is placed in public domain. The **public domain** comprises all intellectual property whose protection has expired. This means people can use any aspect of the device in their own invention free of charge. The invention must qualify under these four rules of the Patent and Trademark Office (PTO):

While You Read

Predict What does it mean for a patent to be in *pending* status?

1. **The invention must not contain prior art.** It should not be based on anything publicly available before the date of the invention.

2. **The invention must fit into one of five classes.** It must be a machine (e.g., a rocket, a fax), a process (e.g., chemical reactions), articles of manufacture (e.g., furniture), a composition (e.g., gasoline), or a new use for one of the four categories.

3. **The invention must be "unobvious."** The invention must not be obvious to someone with skills in the field. It should be new and unexpected.

4. **The invention must have utility.** This means it must be useful, not just whimsical or silly.

Many companies choose not to patent a new device. They know that once the patent is issued, the public can view it. Someone may then try to find a way around the patent.

TECHNOLOGY Today

Weblogs

A Weblog is a chronological record of messages and links posted on the Web. Sometimes shortened to blog, a Weblog uses a dated log format that is updated on a daily or very frequent basis with new information about a particular subject or range of subjects. Weblogs can be personal, family-oriented, or can be used to run an online business.

Cooperative Learning Activity

Work as a class to brainstorm some ways a small business can utilize a Weblog.

@ Go to **entrepreneurship.glencoe.com** to complete the Technology Today Vocabulary Practice Activity.

THE PROCESS To protect an invention, you should file a disclosure document with the PTO. In the application, you confirm that you are the inventor of the product and describe it in detail. Within two years, you must file a patent application with the PTO. Otherwise, the disclosure document will be abandoned.

PATENT APPLICATION Your first patent application may be for a provisional patent. It was designed to allow inventors to begin talking to manufacturers and strategic partners without risking their invention. The provisional patent lasts for 12 months, during which time you must do a formal patent application. How you word the claims of novelty, utility, and nonobviousness can determine whether you receive the patent. Therefore, you should use a qualified patent attorney when writing a patent application.

THE PATENT SEARCH After you apply for a patent, the PTO does a patent search. During this time, the patent is pending. **Patent pending** is the status of an invention between the time a patent application has been filed and when it is issued or rejected. If the PTO decides your claims are valid, it will issue you a patent. It may, as is typically the case, decide that some or all of your claims are not valid. Then, with the help of a qualified attorney, you may revise them and resubmit your application. Once the PTO declares that your claims are accepted, it will issue the patent. At that point, the public may see the patent. You can market your product during the patent pending phase. However, you must put the term *patent pending* and the patent number on the product or packaging.

PATENT INFRINGEMENT Patent infringement occurs when someone makes and sells a product that contains all elements of a patent claim. A patent is a powerful document. It gives the holder the right to enforce it in federal court. If he or she wins, the court will issue an injunction preventing the infringer from further use. The court will also award the patent holder a royalty from the infringer.

Copyrights

A **copyright** is a legal device that protects original works of authors. These works include books, movies, musical compositions, and computer software. A copyright lasts for the life of the author plus 70 years. After that, the work goes into the public domain.

If you plan to publish (or make public) your work, copyright law recommends doing two things. First, place a notice of copyright in a prominent location on the work. This notice must include the symbol © or the word *Copyright,* the year of first publication, and the name of the copyright holder. Second, register the work with the Copyright Office. The office is a branch of the Library of Congress.

Interestingly, a copyright protects only the form in which the idea is presented. It does not protect the idea itself. For example, you may compose a piece of music, but it is not protected until you convert it to a musical score on paper, compact disc, or another medium.

While You Read

Connect Locate the U.S. Patent Office Web site and review the most recent issue of the *Official Gazette,* a weekly periodical that summarizes patents granted and lists all patents available for license or sale.

Figure 8.1 **Protecting Your Ideas**

Patents

A patent is a grant to an inventor. It gives the inventor the right to exclude others from making, using, or selling the invention during the term of the patent.

LEGAL PROTECTION

Intellectual property laws protect the inventions and new ideas of businesses. Although there may be some similarities among patents, copyrights, and trademarks, they are different and serve different purposes. *What kind of intellectual property law protects an invention? A soft drink's logo? A film?*

Trademarks

A trademark is a word, symbol, design, or color that a business uses to identify itself or something it sells. For example, an apple with a bite taken out of it is the trademark of Apple Computer. Once a business registers its trademark with the PTO, a competitor cannot use the trademark.

Copyrights

A copyright is a legal device that protects original works of authors. These works include books, movies, musical compositions, and computer software.

Trademarks

A **trademark** is a word, symbol, design, or color that a business uses to identify itself or something it sells. Trademarks are followed by the registered trademark symbol ®. For example, an apple with a bite taken out of it is the trademark of Apple Computer. A logo, or a company's emblem, such as McDonald's double arches can be trademarked. Even container shapes, such as Coca-Cola's classic beverage bottle, can be trademarked. A word, symbol, design, or color that describes a service business is called a **service mark**.

Like a patent or a copyright, a trademark provides legal protection. If a business registers its trademark with the PTO, a competitor cannot use the trademark. However, a trademark cannot be registered until it is actually going to be used. A business seeking trademark status for its symbol must prove that the design is original and distinctive.

Unlike a patent, a trademark can be held indefinitely unless it becomes common usage in the English language. Words such as aspirin, yo-yo, and thermos were once registered trademarks. Today they are no longer used exclusively by the businesses that created them. They have become generic terms.

Laws That Affect Start-Up of a Business

Certain legal requirements are fundamental to your ability to do business. If you do not meet the requirements, you cannot start a company. There are three categories of laws you need to be aware of before you start a business.

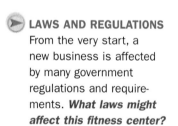 **LAWS AND REGULATIONS** From the very start, a new business is affected by many government regulations and requirements. *What laws might affect this fitness center?*

1. Permits and Licenses

Before you can officially open the doors of your business, you must get a business permit. A **permit** is a legal document giving official permission to run a business. You can obtain this from your local government office. You will probably have to renew it annually. In addition, you will be required to pay periodic fees over the life of your business. The amount is usually based on how much the business earns.

While You Read

Question What is the difference between a permit and a license?

Certain professions may require you to also get a license. A **license** is a certificate that shows you have the necessary education and training to do a job. For example, doctors, nurses, barbers, accountants, real estate brokers, and counselors all need special licenses. Such licenses protect consumers from unskilled or unqualified business operators. Licensing requirements vary from one state or locality to another. Therefore, you should check with the appropriate government agency for more information.

2. Contracts

A **contract** is a binding legal agreement between two or more persons or parties. As an entrepreneur, you will sign contracts to start and run your business. Some contracts will be with vendors or landlords, some with clients, and some with government agencies.

It is helpful to distinguish among various types of contracts. An oral contract is an unwritten contract that does not last for more than one year. A void contract is one that never existed in the first place. The parties did not have the capacity to enter into the contract. A valid contract is most common for businesses because it meets several important criteria. To be a valid and legally inferable contract, a document must contain the following components:

- **Agreement**—Agreement occurs when one party to a contract makes an offer or promises to do something or refrain from doing something, and the other party accepts. For example, suppose a vendor offers to sell your business a fax machine. There is no agreement until you send the vendor a purchase order or a check. Doing so signifies that you accept the offer. If you change any of the terms of the vendor's offer, you create a counteroffer. This is a new offer that requires the vendor's acceptance to form a new contract.

- **Consideration**—Consideration is what is exchanged for the promise. The money you pay the vendor for the fax machine is valuable consideration. It causes the contract to be binding. Money is not the only form of consideration. Being prevented from doing something by the terms of the contract is also consideration.

- **Capacity**—Capacity is the legal ability to enter into a binding agreement. By law, minors, intoxicated persons, and insane people cannot enter into valid contracts. If they do sign such a contract, the agreement can be considered void. This means the contract never existed.

- **Legality**—The final contract element is legality. For a contract to be valid, it must be legal. That is, it cannot have any provisions that are illegal or that would result in illegal activities.

Extreme Entrepreneur

While he might be best known for his incredible extreme sports maneuvers and the line of video games that bears his name, Tony Hawk has another claim to fame: along with his friend and fellow skater Per Welinder, he launched Birdhouse Projects Inc. in the early 1990s. The Birdhouse brand features boards, clothing and accessories, and is instantly recognized in extreme sports shops throughout the world. The friends started the business with only $80,000 in savings; today, Birdhouse Projects has annual sales of over $10 million.

CRITICAL THINKING

How does name recognition—in this case, a person's name—help a business stay successful? What are some other examples of this?

 Go to **entrepreneurship.glencoe.com** to complete the Success Stories Writing Activity.

Most people fulfill the requirements of the contracts they sign. If one of the parties fails to meet his or her obligations, the other party may be entitled to monetary damages. The right to these damages is usually determined in court. To avoid misunderstanding, the parties need to draw up a legally binding contract. The contract should clearly state the intentions of all parties.

3. Location

The law also affects where you locate the business; only certain types of real property are available to business owners.

ZONING LAWS AND BUILDING CODES If you build a new facility or locate your business in an existing building, you must conform to local zoning laws. Cities typically designate particular areas, or zones, for certain uses. Zones are usually specified as residential, commercial, industrial, or public. For example, you cannot locate a tire manufacturing plant in a residential neighborhood.

Zoning laws also address environmental issues. They may restrict disposal of toxic waste, noise and air pollution, and unsuitable building styles. For example, a residential neighborhood might permit office buildings but only those that fit in with the residential architecture. Zoning laws may define the type and style of signs that businesses can use and the appearance of buildings.

You also need to check the laws that relate to the actual construction of your facility. These are called *building codes*. Building codes set standards for construction or modification of buildings. These standards include such things as strength of concrete, amount of insulation, and other structural requirements.

Local governments employ inspectors to verify that building code requirements are met at each stage of construction. Licensed building contractors or architects should be familiar with local building codes. You can assure your facility is built to code by hiring such a person to supervise your project.

LEASING Most entrepreneurs start with few resources and little money. Therefore, prudent entrepreneurs usually lease buildings and equipment rather than buy them. A lease is a contract to use a facility or equipment for a specified period of time. The lessee (the person who is leasing the building or equipment) has no ownership rights. Those belong to the lessor (the person who owns the building or equipment).

Leasing usually does not require spending a large amount of money up front. The money saved can be used for purchasing inventory and supplies and hiring employees. This can be a definite advantage for a new business. Another advantage is that some lease expenses are tax-deductible. This can reduce the tax liability of the company.

Nevertheless, leasing may bring its own set of troubles. For example, the lease contract is a very complex document. It states the terms: length of the lease, monthly rent, penalty for failing to pay, and procedure for termination. Because a lease is a long-term contract, an entrepreneur should consult an attorney before signing.

Write About It

Research and write a checklist of things an entrepreneur should consider before signing a lease.

Section 8.1 After You Read

Key Concept Review

1. What is the first document you should file in the patent process? Why?

2. How can you protect the use of your business logo?

3. Define *license, permit, contract, patent, copyright, trademark,* and *logo.* Then identify the issuing agency for each.

Critical Thinking

4. Walk around a commercial area near your home. What kinds of businesses are located there? Call your city government offices and ask what the zoning is for that area. What kinds of businesses can locate there? If you wanted to start a new business in your neighborhood, what types of businesses could be opened given the zoning requirements?

Role Play

Situation You are about to start a landscaping business with a friend. The business will be a partnership of the two founders with no additional employees.

Activity Pair up with a classmate and present a role play in which you portray the two business owners. Explain the business concept. Present a flowchart of the workflow processes and operations of the business. Explain the laws and regulations that affect your business if you do not hire any employees.

Evaluation You will be evaluated on how well you:

- Identify relevant laws and regulations related to starting your business.

- Give examples of licenses a small business must obtain.

- Determine whether you need an occupational license.

- Discuss the importance of obtaining outside professional counsel to ensure compliance with government regulations and taxation.

Handling Government Regulations

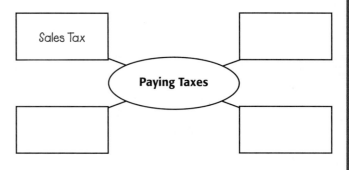
Laws That Affect Employees

Businesses large and small are affected daily by the laws of federal, state, and local governments. This section will touch on some of the more important laws that affect business. You will gain a better understanding of what you need to know before starting a business. **Figure 8.2** provides an overview of the areas covered.

When you start a business, you usually hire employees. Many laws affect the hiring, firing, and paying of employees. It is also important to identify regulations that protect employees.

Laws Against Discrimination in Hiring

The **Equal Employment Opportunity Commission (EEOC)** is the government agency charged with protecting the rights of employees. It ensures that employers do not discriminate against employees because of age, race, color or national origin, religion, gender, or physical challenge.

An employer cannot refuse to hire, promote, or give pay increases to an employee based on any of these characteristics. A company may give tests or use screening devices when hiring. However, the U.S. Department of Labor states that these tests or devices must be related directly to the job.

Child Labor Law

Federal child labor laws protect young workers. Employment cannot interfere with their education or be harmful to their health or well-being. Persons under the age of 18 can not work in jobs the government considers hazardous. Persons younger than 16 are restricted to hours and times they can work. Youths under 14 may work only in certain jobs. These jobs include delivering newspapers to consumers; performing in theatrical, motion picture, or broadcast productions; and working in a business owned by their parents, except in manufacturing or hazardous occupations.

Laws Against Wrongful Termination

Wrongful termination is the right of an employee to sue his or her employer for damages if he or she is terminated for an unacceptable reason. As a business owner, you should carefully document important events related to each employee. Keep records of all employee evaluations, disciplinary actions, and warnings. Notify in writing those employees who violate the rules. Then get a receipt from the employee, proving he or she was notified of the violation. Keeping good records helps if you are ever faced with a lawsuit for wrongful termination.

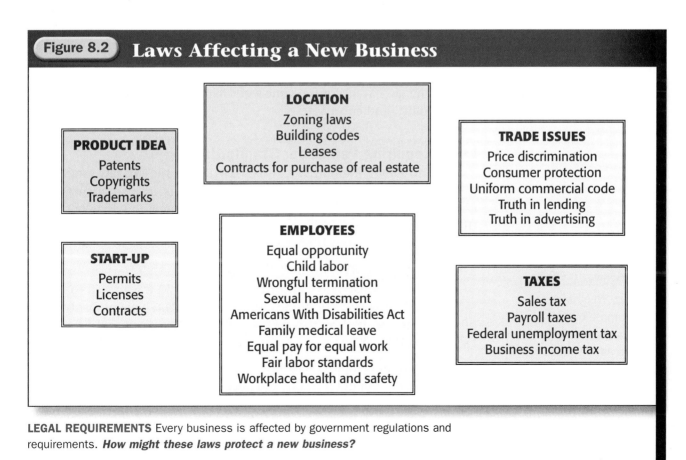

Figure 8.2 Laws Affecting a New Business

PRODUCT IDEA
Patents
Copyrights
Trademarks

LOCATION
Zoning laws
Building codes
Leases
Contracts for purchase of real estate

TRADE ISSUES
Price discrimination
Consumer protection
Uniform commercial code
Truth in lending
Truth in advertising

START-UP
Permits
Licenses
Contracts

EMPLOYEES
Equal opportunity
Child labor
Wrongful termination
Sexual harassment
Americans With Disabilities Act
Family medical leave
Equal pay for equal work
Fair labor standards
Workplace health and safety

TAXES
Sales tax
Payroll taxes
Federal unemployment tax
Business income tax

LEGAL REQUIREMENTS Every business is affected by government regulations and requirements. *How might these laws protect a new business?*

Sexual Harassment

Sexual harassment is any unwelcome sexual conduct on the job. It creates an intimidating, hostile, or offensive working environment. At the federal level, Title VII of the Civil Rights Act forbids harassment. In addition, most states have their own fair employment practices laws that prohibit sexual harassment.

Americans With Disabilities Act

The Americans With Disabilities Act requires employers to provide reasonable accommodation to the workplace that allows qualified employees to do the basic functions of their jobs. The act also restricts the questions business owners can ask job applicants about their disabilities before they make a job offer. Business owners can ask about people's abilities, but they can not ask about people's disabilities. Owners can ask how applicants plan to do the job, not what prevents them from doing the job.

Family Medical Leave Act

The Family Medical Leave Act (FMLA) impacts employers with 50 or more employees. The act provides employees with the right to an unpaid leave of absence for up to 12 weeks. The time off can be used to address family and medical issues. These issues include serious health conditions of the employee or his or her child, parent, or spouse. The time off can also be for the birth, adoption, or foster care placement of the employee's child. In most cases, the employer must reinstate the employee when he or she returns from leave.

Laws Requiring Equal Pay for Equal Work

The Equal Pay Act of 1963 says that all employers must pay men and women the same wage for the same work. Same work involves similar skills, responsibility, and effort.

Laws Requiring Fair Labor Standards

The Fair Labor Standards Act was passed in 1938. This law established a minimum wage and maximum working hours. It also ensured that children under the age of 16 could not be employed full-time except by their parents.

While You Read

Predict What is the purpose of the Occupational Safety and Health Administration?

Laws Requiring Workplace Safety and Health

The Occupational Safety and Health Act of 1970 was passed to ensure safe, healthful working conditions for employees. You have probably heard of the agency created by this Act—OSHA, the Occupational Safety and Health Administration.

OSHA requires employers to look for hazardous areas in their workplace. Employers must maintain health and safety records and provide safety training. They must also stay up-to-date on new OSHA standards and take care of violations promptly. The agency charges heavy fines on companies that do not follow its rules.

Laws That Regulate Trade

In general, the American government allows businesses to compete in the marketplace with relative freedom. However, since the early 1800s, many laws have been enacted that regulate and restrict business practices. These key trade laws were created to preserve competition and fairness in the marketplace.

Price Discrimination Laws

The Clayton Act of 1914 and the Robinson-Patman Act of 1936 are aimed at prohibiting price discrimination. **Price discrimination** is the charging of different prices for the same product or service in different markets or to different customers. Businesses must justify giving one customer a lower price than they gave another. They must show that the favored customer bought more, bought lower-quality goods, or benefited from the cost savings. This means entrepreneurs must be fair to all customers when setting prices.

BusinessWeek Case Study

What to Give to Get Your Take

Before suggesting an alliance with a larger outfit, look at things from the prospective partner's perspective: What can you do for them?

Q: I have an idea for a niche market-research company, and I'm looking for an alliance with an established market research firm to overcome my lack of credibility as a small startup. How do I decide what to ask for in terms of compensation? Should I ask for a percentage of the profits from each job I do with them, or a percentage of the revenue? How do I figure out an adequate percentage?—N.B., Detroit

A: Before you worry about compensation levels, you'd be advised to focus on interesting these larger companies in working with you, and making sure you have a pitch ready (with solid research behind it, not just optimistic speculation) that emphasizes what you are going to do for them—not the other way around. If you can't demonstrate

that your business will bring them more business, new customers, an expanded clientele, or something else that's beneficial, why would they bother getting involved with your company in the first place?

SOURCE: *BUSINESSWEEK*, AUGUST 7, 2002; BY KAREN E. KLEIN

APPLICATION

Think of a large outfit with which you would like your small company to partner. Create a presentation that lists five points you would use in a pitch to that company to demonstrate the benefits the alliance would bring to it.

@ Go to **entrepreneurship.glencoe.com** to complete the *BusinessWeek* Case Study Reading Guide Activity.

Consumer Protection Laws

If you are manufacturing products for the public, you must become familiar with consumer protection laws. That way you can avoid possible recalls of your product and potential lawsuits.

Most laws pertaining to trade are designed to protect the consumer. These laws protect against unscrupulous sellers, unreasonable credit terms, unsafe products, and mislabeling of products.

Many federal agencies are involved in regulating trade. Many of them function to protect the consumer as well. A list of some major federal trade regulators is shown in **Figure 8.3.**

THE FOOD AND DRUG ADMINISTRATION (FDA) One of the largest federal regulatory agencies monitoring product safety is the FDA. It researches and tests new products and inspects the operations of food and drug manufacturers. If your new product idea is a cosmetic, drug, or food item (or even suntan lotion), you need FDA approval to market it.

Figure 8.3 — Federal Trade Regulators

GOVERNMENT OVERSIGHT Many of the agencies that have the greatest impact on small businesses are part of the federal government. *Which ones will directly affect you when you start your business?*

Agency	Function
Consumer Product Safety Commission	Establishes product safety standards and recalls products
Environmental Protection Agency	Creates and enforces standards for the environment, regulating air, water, and noise pollution as well as toxic waste
Equal Employment Opportunity Commission	Establishes rules relating to discrimination in the workplace
Federal Communications Commission	Regulates all forms of interstate and international communication
Federal Trade Commission	Enforces antitrust, truth-in-lending, and labeling laws
Food and Drug Administration	Creates standards for foods and drugs and approves new drugs
Internal Revenue Service	Enforces tax statutes and resolves disputes
Interstate Commerce Commission	Determines trade practices, rates, and routes for interstate railroads, bus companies, and pipelines
Justice Department	Enforces laws to maintain free trade
National Labor Relations Board	Monitors and governs the relationship between employers and unions
Occupational Safety & Health Administration	Establishes and regulates safety and health standards for employees
Patent and Trademark Office	Issues patents and trademarks for new products

THE CONSUMER PRODUCT SAFETY COMMISSION (CPSC) This commission serves as a watchdog for consumers over products that may be hazardous. It also creates safety standards for products such as toys for children under the age of five.

THE FAIR PACKAGING AND LABELING ACT The act requires that manufacturer labels truthfully list all ingredients and raw materials used in production. Labels must include the name and place of business of the manufacturer, packer, or distributor. The act also requires that the size, weight, and contents of a product be on the label.

The Uniform Commercial Code

The **Uniform Commercial Code (UCC)** is a group of laws that regulates commercial business transactions. The UCC has been adopted by all states. Since it applies to sales transactions among merchants, its provisions will likely affect you as an entrepreneur.

FORMATION OF CONTRACTS When entering into an agreement to sell a product, you create a valid contract. This means you must abide by contract laws. However, as a merchant, you must also abide by the requirements of the UCC. In some cases, the two are not the same.

For example, in a valid contract, all terms of price, place, delivery date, and quantity should be present. Suppose you are a manufacturer. You have ordered parts from a supplier, but you have not asked the price. When the parts arrive, you find they cost more than you expected. Do you have a contract despite the confusion over price?

The UCC says yes, but assigns a price that is reasonable at the time of delivery. The code assumes the parties intended to form a contract and knew the consequences of any ambiguity. Why? Because both are merchants—professionals who understand the business. Different rules, the UCC rules, apply to merchants than nonmerchants.

WARRANTIES AND PRODUCT LIABILITY The law looks after the safety and economic interests of buyers. It also regulates sales warranties. Many of these laws and legal principles have been made part of the UCC.

Virtually everything you buy comes with an implied warranty of merchantability. A **warranty of merchantability** is a guarantee about the quality of goods or services purchased that is not written down or explicitly spoken. It is an assurance that a new item will work for its specified purpose. The item does not have to work wonderfully, and if you use it for something it was not designed for, say trimming shrubs with an electric carving knife, the warranty does not apply.

You have probably seen or heard news stories about product liability. This is the legal theory that manufacturers are responsible for injuries caused by their products. For example, automobiles can be recalled because of defects. Manufacturers can also be sued if their products cause injuries. The costs of product liability have boosted insurance costs for manufacturers. This raises prices for consumers. For example, about 25 percent of the cost of a football helmet pays for insurance.

While You Read

Connect Identify legal issues that face entrepreneurs who establish e-commerce sites.

If you are manufacturing a product to sell to consumers, you must be very careful. You must include clear instructions for the product's use. You must also give clear warnings of potential dangers involved. This protects you and your consumer.

While You Read

Question What is bait-and-switch advertising, and why is it illegal?

Truth in Lending

Those involved in retail businesses must familiarize themselves with the Consumer Credit Protection Act. This act requires those who give credit to reveal all terms and conditions of their credit agreements. As a result, it is called the Truth in Lending Act. Like price discrimination laws, it is enforced by the Federal Trade Commission. The Truth in Lending Act applies to anything purchased over a period of time greater than four months.

Truth in Advertising

The Federal Trade Commission is also concerned about protecting customers from false and misleading advertising. The laws that address this trade issue are sometimes called *truth-in-advertising laws*. Regardless of your business, when you advertise, you should be aware of the following rules:

- **Misleading ads.** Your advertising should not mislead customers about what your product can do. It should not claim that the product can do something it can not.

- **Sale prices.** You can not offer a reduced price on your product unless it has been offered to the public at the regular price for a period of time.

SAFETY INFORMATION It is important that all manufacturers include clear instructions for their products' use. *What are some instructions that might come with sporting goods?*

- **Price comparisons.** You cannot use list price as your comparison-selling price unless your product has sold for that amount. The list price is commonly the manufacturer's suggested retail price (MSRP). Also, when advertising that your prices are lower than your competitors', you must have proof.

- **Bait and switch.** Bait-and-switch advertising is an illegal way of selling that involves advertising a product at a very low price in order to attract customers who are then persuaded to switch to a more expensive product. It is illegal because it is a deceptive business practice.

Tax Laws

All business owners whose goal is to make a profit are responsible for certain taxes. These include sales tax, payroll taxes, unemployment tax, and income tax.

Sales Tax

Sales tax is a percentage of the price of an item that goes to a state or local government. The percentage varies from state to state. Retailers collect sales tax from their customers and send it to the appropriate government agency. Usually, this is the State Board of Equalization. Most retailers make payments every three months.

Payroll Taxes

When you hire employees, you need to deduct certain payroll taxes from their earnings. One such payroll tax is the **FICA**, or Social Security tax. (FICA stands for Federal Insurance Contributions Act.) The tax is figured as a percentage of an employee's income. You are required to contribute an amount equal to the amount deducted from each employee's paycheck. If you deducted $20.27 from an employee's paycheck for FICA, you would have to match that amount. You would send a total of $40.54 to the Internal Revenue Service. There is a ceiling on the amount of wages subject to the FICA tax. Wages above that ceiling are not taxed.

Withholding these taxes can be complex. You must be aware of changes in the FICA tax rate and in the amount of wages subject to it. You can obtain information on the current FICA tax rate and ceiling from the Social Security Administration.

You are also required to withhold certain income taxes from an employee's paycheck. These include federal and, usually, state income tax. These taxes are based on a percentage of gross pay. Contact your local and state governments and the Internal Revenue Service for information about these deductions.

Federal Unemployment Tax

As an employer, you are required to make contributions under the Federal Unemployment Tax Act (FUTA). The act was designed to help workers who are temporarily unemployed. You may also be responsible for state unemployment taxes. However, they are usually credited against the federal taxes paid.

Quick Math

You put $1,000 down on a car costing $10,000. You pay $537 per month for 24 months. What is the deferred payment price of the car? How much of this information must be disclosed?

AFFIRMATIVE ACTION

In addition to enforcing state and federal antidiscriminatory laws designed to ensure the fair treatment of every employee, the government also created affirmative action plans. Affirmative action aims to provide access to jobs for those who suffered discrimination in the past and to give everyone a fair chance to compete in the working world. These plans, which continue to be the subject of intense debate, sometimes set numerical goals for the hiring of groups such as ethnic minorities, females, or people with disabilities.

Companies that have both federal contracts worth more than $50,000 and more than 50 employees must provide an annual employee census to the U.S. Equal Employment Opportunity Commission. That report provides a census of employees, broken down by race, gender, and national origin. Those same companies must have written policies on affirmative action.

Think Critically

What are some pros and cons of affirmative action?

 Go to **entrepreneurship.glencoe.com** to complete the Issues in Entrepreneurship Research Activity.

Business Income Taxes

Your business is also responsible for paying federal and possibly state and local taxes on the income it earns. As a sole proprietor or a partner, the income your business earns is considered your personal income. As a result, the business income is taxed at your personal tax rate.

Imagine you are the sole owner of a catering business. Based on your income statement, your business's net income before taxes is $32,500. You use that amount as your personal income when paying taxes to your state and the Internal Revenue Service. As a self-employed business owner, you also pay a FICA tax. It is double what an employee pays because you are considered both employer and employee. The ceiling on the amount taxed is the same.

If your business is a corporation, the income tax situation is much different. The business must pay a corporate income tax. You pay personal income tax based on the salary you earn and other income derived from the business. In addition, the shareholders pay personal income tax on salaries or dividends.

There are severe penalties for failure to file and pay income taxes. Therefore, you should consult an accountant to help you plan for taxes.

Getting Legal Advice

Since all businesses are regulated by the law, you need to be aware of any regulations that may affect your new venture. At different stages of the start-up, you will need legal advice. A good working relationship with a lawyer will give you confidence and ease some of the risk of starting a new business.

You can research a great deal of legal information on your own. Many sources provide information for finding an attorney or getting up-to-date information on your legal obligations. They include the American Bar Association, the National Resource Center for Consumers of Legal Services, and the Commissioner of Patents and Trademarks. Also, the Internal Revenue Service can be of special help in tax matters. It often holds workshops and seminars to make business owners aware of their tax obligations.

If your business is involved in areas regulated by the government, you should consult the appropriate agencies. You can find contact information at your local library or on the Internet. You can also consult an attorney who specializes in regulatory matters.

Section 8.2 After You Read

Key Concept Review

1. What are the six main areas of business operations that the government regulates?
2. What is the purpose of OSHA?
3. What is the difference between general business contracts and contracts that fall under the Uniform Commercial Code?

Critical Thinking

4. Use the Web site of the Department of Revenue, the Internal Revenue Service, and your State Franchise Tax Board to determine the tax collection process. Find the current taxes and tax rates that business owners must pay at the federal, state, and local levels on the income they produce.

Role Play

Situation You manage a human resources department. A recently fired employee has filed a lawsuit against your company suggesting wrongful termination. The employee's supervisor reports that this employee was regularly late to work and consistently refused to make up the time. The ex-employee insists that he could not help the fact that his car was unreliable. You decide to seek advice from an attorney.

Activity With a partner, enact a dialogue between you and your attorney.

Evaluation You will be evaluated on how well you address these issues in your role play:

- Discuss the information the supervisor kept in the file regarding the employee's violations.
- Describe the procedure you used to fire the employee.
- Explain what you can do to prevent future lawsuits.

Chapter Summary

Section 8.1 **Legal Issues Facing Start-Ups**

When a new product or service is developed, it must be safeguarded through intellectual property protections. Depending on the type of asset, it may be protected through patents, copyrights, trademarks, or trade secrets. Before you start your business, you need to understand three categories of laws: permits and licenses, contracts, and laws relating to your location. To be a valid, legal contract, a document must contain four elements: parties who have the legal capacity to enter into a contract, agreement among those parties, consideration, and legality of provisions.

Section 8.2 **Handling Government Regulations**

Laws and regulations affect business owners' relationships with employees, with other businesses, and with customers. They are designed to protect these groups from unfair, unsafe, or unhealthy business practices. In hiring and compensating employees, a business may not discriminate on the basis of age, race, color, national origin, religion, gender, or physical challenge. Federal law protects consumers against price discrimination, unscrupulous sellers, unreasonable credit terms, and unsafe and mislabeled products. Businesses are responsible for collecting and paying sales taxes; payroll taxes; unemployment taxes; and federal, state, and local income taxes. It is important to research your legal obligations or seek legal advice at each stage of developing a business.

Key Terms Review

1. Prepare a presentation on today's legal environment and how the government affects the start-up of a new business. Use these key terms in your presentation:

intellectual property law (p. 154)	permit (p. 159)	wrongful termination (p. 163)
patent (p. 155)	license (p. 159)	price discrimination (p. 165)
public domain (p. 155)	contract (p. 159)	Uniform Commercial Code (UCC) (p. 167)
patent pending (p. 156)	consideration (p. 159)	
copyright (p. 156)	capacity (p. 159)	warranty of merchantability (p. 167)
trademark (p. 158)	Equal Opportunity Employment Commission (EEOC) (p. 162)	bait-and-switch advertising (p. 169)
service mark (p. 158)		FICA (p. 169)

Key Concept Review

2. **Explain** how to protect your intellectual property. (8.1)
3. **Discuss** the laws affecting the start-up of a business. (8.1)
4. **Explain** the laws that affect employees. (8.2)
5. **Identify** the laws that regulate trade. (8.2)
6. **Discuss** the tax laws that apply to a new venture. (8.2)

Critical Thinking

7. Suppose you have an idea for a new kind of applicator that takes the mess out of applying suntan lotion. What steps would you need to take to protect your invention?

8. If you owned a trademark for a product, how would you protect that trademark from becoming a generic term in the English language?

9. Compare leasing versus buying a building for your business. Include cost, ownership rights, need for an attorney, and contract terms.

10. How can you make sure you have complied with laws affecting the hiring, firing, and safety of your employees?

11. Should trade laws protect the buyer or the seller? Explain.

12. Why should the government oversee workplace health and safety?

13. You own a bookstore that sells to consumers. Under what circumstances can you charge different prices to different people?

Write About It

14. In a one-page report, describe the various forms of intellectual property protection.

15. Search the Internet for a case of patent infringement. In a two-page paper, report on the case and how it was settled.

16. Collect several examples of trademarks. Attach the examples to paper and write notes to identify the companies they represent.

17. Develop a checklist of important legal and regulatory items to consider when considering a specific location for your business.

18. Research and write a one-page report that analyzes the effect of government intervention on entrepreneurial incentives.

19. Design a pricing strategy for a business that sells customized office supplies to companies. Make notes on how you will design a strategy to avoid running afoul of price discrimination laws.

20. Study the warranty associated with a product. How is that warranty protecting you? How is it protecting the manufacturer? Report your findings in a one-page report.

Academic Skills

Math

21. Suppose one of your employees earns $1,500 this month. The current FICA deduction is 7.65%. How much in FICA contributions will you deposit with the Internal Revenue Service in the employee's name?

Language Arts

22. Compose an explanation of the role of government in the business activities of an entrepreneur and in dealing with customers and employees.

Entrepreneurship in Your Community

23. Choose a business you would like to launch. As part of the start-up process, research and determine the following:

- Necessary business permits and fees
- Sales, income, and employment taxes from the federal, state, and local levels that are the responsibilities of a business
- Required licenses
- Laws and regulations (including any major state laws) that affect the business
- Types of federal, state, and local taxes that are the responsibility of the entrepreneur (e.g. sales, income, self-employment)

Summarize your findings in a business report to the class.

24. Interview a member of the local zoning board or commission in your community.

- Ask about the differences among residential, commercial, industrial, and public zones in your town. Note these areas on a map.
- Find out about any restrictions regarding environmental issues.

Report to the class what you have learned.

Ethical Practices

Bait-and-Switch

25. You work as a customer care representative for a retail electronics store. Last Sunday a stereo system was advertised for only $89. This week you have received telephone calls from customers who tried to buy the system and found it unavailable. Salespeople pressured the customers to purchase a higher-priced stereo. The customers are complaining of bait-and-switch tactics. How do you handle this situation? What should you tell your boss? What do you think the store should do to satisfy the unhappy customers?

INTERNET connection

Understanding Copyrights

Puneeta has just written a trumpet solo that she will play in the National Youth Jazz Festival. Since she plans to publish the piece, she needs to protect it.

Connect

Use a search engine or Web directory to find out about copyrighting music.

- What is the procedure necessary to copyright a piece of music?
- How do you register your work with the Copyright Office?
- What specific laws protect the original works of authors?

Application

Use a word processor to write a memo advising Puneeta on how to protect her music. In the memo explain the steps she needs to take to copyright music. Also explain the laws that will protect her work once she has established a copyright.

The Electronic Entrepreneur

Steps to Conceiving a Web Site

In order to reach and sell to its intended customers, a Web site must target its audience and gear the site to that group. A clear plan to reach the targeted audience must be developed well before the Web site is even created.

Set Goals Plan exactly what you want your site to do. The plan offers you or another person a blueprint to follow during the design phase. The **site layout**, or the design of the site, can only come after you have outlined your site's mission and objectives.

Consider Your Audience Think about the customer, or target market, you are hoping to attract. You can identify your target market by common geographic characteristics, such as region, county size, size of community, density of population, and climate in the area. You can also categorize it by demographic characteristics, such as age, gender, martial status, family size, income, occupation, education, religion, and cultural background.

Organize Your Site Web sites display businesses' products with the use of text, photos, audio sounds, and video presentations. Make sure this content is appropriate for your audience. Think about how your site will be used when determining its layout and structure. The **content** is the text and graphic information contained in the Web site. Web sites are judged by their content and on their navigational flow. **Navigation** is the act of moving around a Web site by clicking on hypertext links.

FACT AND IDEA REVIEW

1. Why is it essential to plan your goals for a site before you begin building it?
2. How can a Web site identify its target market?
3. How can a Web site benefit from knowing a target audience's demographic information?
4. What considerations should be taken into account when choosing how to organize your Web site?

FOR DISCUSSION

5. Analyze the demographics of your classmates. Break your class down into different segments, and sort them by different characteristics—for instance, make a list of all the males in your class, then all the females; then make a separate list based on where people live. How might a business benefit from having this information?

TechTerms

- site layout
- content
- navigation

Chapter 9

Site Selection and Layout Planning

Section 9.1

Community and Site Selection

Section 9.2

Layout Planning

CHAPTER OBJECTIVES

When you have completed this chapter, you should be able to:

SECTION 9.1

- List the factors involved in deciding on a community in which to locate a business.
- Identify the factors to consider when selecting a business site.
- Describe the resources that can be used in finding potential business sites.
- Explain the steps involved in analyzing potential sites for a business and choosing between those sites.
- Describe the advantages of starting a business at home or in an incubator.

SECTION 9.2

- List the steps in layout planning that are common to all businesses.
- Describe the layout needs for each type of business.
- Discuss the final details of layout planning.

FINDING MONEY FOR COLLEGE

A college degree can be a great boost to your career, but it can also be expensive. Here are some ideas on how to find money for college:

1. Ask your school counselor about student loans, grants, and scholarships.

2. Search the Internet, using the keywords "college scholarships."

3. Ask for money for college instead of gifts at birthdays, Christmas, graduation, and other holidays.

4. Apply for scholarships offered by your parents' employers.

5. Get a part-time job and save as much as possible. Invest your earnings in accounts that will pay the highest possible interest.

Don't focus on any one single strategy—you might get a lot of small grants and scholarships rather than one or two big ones. Research as many options as you can.

 Go to **entrepreneurship.glencoe.com** to complete the Standard & Poor's Money Talk Financial Literacy Activity.

PREPARE TO READ

THINK ABOUT THESE QUESTIONS AS YOU READ.

What factors should be considered when selecting a business location?

Why is the physical layout of a business important?

Community and Site Selection

KEY TERMS
- economic base
- incentive
- census tract
- trade area
- industrial park
- incubator

KEY CONCEPTS
- Factors in Community Selection
- Criteria for Site Selection
- Locating Potential Sites
- Site Analysis and Decision Making
- Alternative Sites

THE MAIN IDEA

Selecting a community and a specific location in which to establish a business involves a systematic process.

READING ORGANIZER

Draw the reading organizer on a separate piece of paper. As you read, fill in the organizer with the major factors or steps to consider at each level. Focus on one type of business activity.

COMMUNITY SELECTION	SITE SELECTION
labor supply	accessibility

Factors in Community Selection

As an entrepreneur, the decision of where to put your new business is an important one. It is necessary to systematically examine the factors concerning community selection and site selection. A location can make or break certain kinds of ventures. It can determine who sees your business and how easily customers can get to it. In addition, your choice of location may be permanent. Once you invest in land, a building, fixtures, and equipment, it may be difficult, if not impossible, to move.

When selecting a location for a business, you need to consider your target market. First, you must select a community in which to do business. Second, you must select a specific site within the community. Both factors will be discussed in this section.

Your first thought may be to consider your community as the place to start a business. However, neighboring or distant communities may present a more favorable climate. You should ask certain questions about all possible localities.

Is the Economic Base Favorable?

First, you should determine the community's **economic base**—the major industries that provide jobs. Usually, the economic base is characterized as "primarily industrial" or "primarily service-oriented" or something similar. What you want to know, however, is whether that economic base is growing or shrinking.

If more money is coming into the community than leaving, the economic base is growing. A growing economic base is a favorable environment for a new business. A strong economy ensures more growth. Additional money creates additional demand, which translates into new business opportunities. Additional money also provides the capital that entrepreneurs can use to take advantage of those opportunities. Local government agencies regularly conduct economic analyses of the community. You can contact them for up-to-date information.

Are There Financial Incentives?

Many communities try to attract new businesses by offering special incentives. An **incentive** is a reward or advantage that helps businesses. Incentives include lower taxes, cheaper land, and employee training programs. At a community's request, states sometime establish enterprise zones that give tax-favored status to new businesses. Local economic development offices can tell you whether such programs are available.

What Is the Makeup of the Population?

Is the community's population aging as young people move away? Is it getting younger as families with children settle into the area? Such trends can affect a business. These trends determine who will spend. They also determine how much and on what types of products or services people will spend. Contact your local economic development office or chamber of commerce for information on population trends.

TECHNOLOGY Today

Utility Computing

An emerging idea in IT is utility computing, which sees computing power as a resource you use when you need it, such as electricity or telephone service. Currently, computer power has a fixed cost—the cost of the hardware and software you need. In the future, that might all change, as users pay only for the computing power they use.

Cooperative Learning Activity

Work as a class to brainstorm some benefits that might come from utility computing? Are there any downsides?

@ Go to **entrepreneurship.glencoe.com** for the Technology Today Vocabulary Practice Activity.

Every ten years, the Census Bureau conducts a survey to track changes in population size and demographics. Demographics include characteristics such as general age, education, gender, race, religion, and income. This information can tell you if a location matches your target market.

Access the Census Bureau's Census 2000 Web site for demographics that interest you. By following the links from *Summary File 3* to *Access to all Tables and Maps in American FactFinder* to *Detailed Tables,* you can narrow your search to census tracts. A **census tract** is a small geographic area into which a state or country is divided for the purpose of gathering and reporting census data. In the United States, the average tract contains 4,000 residents or approximately 1,200 households. Census tract outline maps are available from the U.S. Census Bureau. Several standard demographic tables are available for all census tracts. You can access additional tables by clicking on the "by keyword" tab. An example of census tract information is shown in **Figure 9.1.**

Does the Labor Supply Match Your Needs?

When considering a community, you must consider your labor needs. You also need to determine how well the local labor pool meets those needs. Ask yourself these questions: How many employees do I need? Is there a sufficient labor pool to meet my needs? Does the available pool have the appropriate skills to help my business? Do not rely on federal unemployment figures for this information. Rather, look to local workforce agencies. They can tell you skill levels and training needs of unemployed workers in the community.

Figure 9.1 **Demographic Data for Census Tract 6204***

POPULATION BY AGE NUMBER

13 and under	1,002
14-24	440
25-39	957
40-54	1,370
55-69	648
70 and over	605

HOUSEHOLD INCOME (1999)

Less than $10,000	112
$10,000-$19,999	62
$20,000-$34,999	149
$35,000-$49,999	178
$50,000-$74,999	360
$75,000 or more	1,215

EDUCATIONAL ATTAINMENT (PERSONS 25 AND OVER)

Less than 9th grade	29
High school graduate	454
Associate degree	214
Bachelor's degree	1,210
Graduate/professional degree	877

WORKERS PER HOUSEHOLD (1999)

None	196
1	463
2	621
3 or more	125

*CALIFORNIA, LOS ANGELES COUNTY
SOURCE: U.S. BUREAU OF THE CENSUS, 2000 CENSUS OF POPULATION AND HOUSING

THE VALUE OF DEMOGRAPHICS Here is a sample of the kind of data the Census Bureau makes available for every census tract in the nation. *If you were planning to open a day care center for pets, would this area be a promising location? Why or why not?*

VISUALIZE Using a map can help you visualize and organize your search for a business site. **What other tools can be used?**

Criteria for Site Selection

Once you determine that a community is suitable for your business, you can begin looking for sites. The factors to consider and the criteria used to judge sites vary with the type of business activity.

Retail Business Considerations

If you start a retail business, you will be selling directly to consumers. Therefore, you need to be accessible to your target market. You need to determine your **trade area**, the region or section of the community from which you expect to draw customers.

The type and size of your business determine the size of your trade area. If you offer a specialized line of merchandise, you may draw customers from a great distance. The only store in town that sells phonograph needles will attract record collectors from far away. A store that offers general merchandise solely for convenience will draw from a much smaller trade area; an example is a 7-Eleven store.

Once you pinpoint the area of the community you want to serve, you can begin locating potential sites. A city map is especially helpful. You can mark critical data on it as you investigate each site.

Begin by drawing a circle showing the trade area around each site you are considering. Then, within each trade area, you need to examine and note four additional features:

1. NUMBER AND SIZE OF COMPETING BUSINESSES You should mark all potential competitors. Then you can calculate the number, size, and location of stores that will compete directly or indirectly with you. This gives you a sense of where customers shop. It also tells you how large your trade area is. Look for clusters of stores and low vacancy rates. Vacancy rate can be determined by a simple walk-through, count, and calculation (vacancy rate = amount of vacant space/total space available).

Quick Math

What is the vacancy rate of a strip mall having six 300-square-foot stores and one 800-square-foot store if the largest store is empty?

2. NATURE OF THE COMPETITION What if your business is similar in size and merchandise to the competition? You may want to locate near them to encourage comparison shopping. That is why you often see an entire block of furniture shops, clothing stores, and auto dealers. However, your operation may be significantly larger, allowing you to offer a greater variety of products. Thus, you may generate your own drawing power, allowing you to locate away from your competitors.

3. CHARACTER OF THE AREA Look carefully at the character of the area. Is it attractive and inviting? Does it have the appearance of success? In general, consumers like to shop in attractive, safe, thriving environments. Individual businesses or blocks that counter this impression are potential problems. You should mark them on your map.

4. ACCESSIBILITY AND TRAFFIC Mark your map with the routes customers will use to reach your business. Identify the highways, streets, and public transportation routes that lead to the site. Make sure that they are convenient and accessible. The site should be easy to find.

Foot and car traffic are both important to a retail business. Entrepreneurs often stand at a potential site and count the cars and pedestrians passing by. If you use this technique, make sure you note variations in time of day and day of the week. Compare your results with data from different sites to help you make a more informed choice. Make sure your site has adequate parking. Customers appreciate convenient, safe, and free parking.

Service/Wholesale Business Considerations

In many ways, service and wholesale businesses have similar needs to those of retail businesses. This is especially true when they have customers who come to their place of business. Hair salons and wholesale outlets that sell to the public are good examples.

In contrast, many service and wholesale businesses do not have customers or clients coming to their business site. For example, exterminators and plumbers go to their customers' homes. Distributors are in a similar position. Their clients are manufacturers and retailers who do business primarily through sales representatives and with purchase orders. These businesses do not need expensive, high-profile locations.

Manufacturing/Extraction Business Considerations

If you start a manufacturing or extraction business, your location will be largely determined by the nature of your business. An extraction business must be near the product it is extracting—ore, fish, trees. A manufacturing firm can locate only where local zoning laws allow. Most communities set aside certain areas for industrial uses, sometimes called **industrial parks**.

Manufacturers and extractors are not concerned about access for pedestrians. Rather, they need access to sources of supply and major transportation routes. Being close to sources of supply can cut transportation costs and shipping times. They can quickly get products to buyers at a lower cost if they are close to transportation networks.

While You Read

Connect Conduct research to find out if your community has an industrial park. Find out what types of businesses are located there.

When Sales Meets Marketing

Too many businesses view sales and marketing as oil and water. It's a separation that hampers efficiency and undermines the bottom line.

Competitive success is often determined by one company's ability to overcome problems where others fail. So it's interesting to consider why some problems motivate businesses to rise above the crowd, while other problems settle into the fabric of a company's organization and culture. Some problems are so universal and so persistent that entire industries learn to accept them as the natural order of things when, in fact, solutions are readily available.

The breakdown between sales and marketing is one such problem. So many businesses and employees accept the Silo Effect between sales and marketing as operational reality, they no longer invest any confidence in efforts to correct it. But when the tension between sales and marketing becomes an accepted way of life, it is poisonous to business performance. Show me a company where one team rolls its eyes at the other, and I'll show you a company saddled with dead leads, grinding sales cycles, and endless channel conflicts—a trail of ruin that leads right to the bottom line.

SOURCE: *BusinessWeek*, FEBRUARY 19, 2004; BY CHRIS KENTON

APPLICATION

Use the Internet to conduct research on the meaning of "the Silo Effect." Then brainstorm solutions to solve the problems that occur when departments within a company do not work together.

 Go to **entrepreneurship.glencoe.com** to complete the *BusinessWeek* Case Study Reading Guide Activity.

E-Business Considerations

Electronic business sites are unique in that they can be located almost anywhere. In that respect, they are similar to service and wholesale businesses that do not have customer traffic. The difference is that e-businesses reach their customers through the Internet. In other respects, e-businesses are similar to retail operations.

The biggest factor in site selection for e-businesses is size of operation. For example, a Web site design service doesn't require a large facility. Work is done on a personal computer, and jobs can be sent or sampled via the Internet. A one-person e-business that sells a service or uses distributors to ship products does not need much space; one room may suffice. A larger operation needs more space for equipment and personnel. A retailer that stores and ships its own inventory may need an even larger facility. To get products out quickly, this type of e-business must be located near a post office or near shipping facilities.

Locating Potential Sites

Knowing what to look for is one thing. Finding it is another. A number of practical resources are available to you. When property owners want to rent or sell space, they often advertise in the classified section of newspapers. Realtors who specialize in business properties display ads in the Yellow Pages and list their offerings on the Internet. You can conduct visual surveys by driving through the community in which you plan to locate. This allows you to identify vacant facilities and get a sense of how suitable the property and the surroundings are. Personal or business contacts may have firsthand knowledge of available facilities.

Site Analysis and Decision Making

Once you identify possible sites for your business, you must consider three things before making a decision: the surrounding area; the building; and the costs of buying, building, or leasing.

Surrounding Area Analysis

The criteria outlined earlier in this section addressed site area considerations for your type of business. Each of the potential sites you identify should be evaluated on the basis of those criteria.

Building Evaluation

The building on your site must be big enough to take care of present needs and to allow for expansion. Most businesses need space for customers, storage, inventory, offices, work areas, and restrooms. It costs much less to pay for more room at the outset than to pay for a move later.

INTERIOR Check the building's interior. Look at the walls, floors, and ceilings in terms of how they meet the needs of your business. Are they functional, attractive, and easy to care for? Are there sufficient lighting fixtures and outlets? Is there access to enough power to run your equipment? How efficient are the heating and cooling units?

STRATEGIC LOCATION Some manufacturing plants are strategically located by train tracks. *What are other ways a manufacturing plant can save money on shipping?*

EXTERIOR Consider the building's construction. You may want to hire a professional building inspector to examine the building for structural soundness. Judge the building's appearance. Remember, customers get their first impression of your business from the front of the building. Check any signage on the building. Most communities have regulations that limit the number, type, and size of signs you can have on or in front of your building. Make sure your signs are easy to read, attractive, and correct. Evaluate the parking accommodations. Your community may have requirements on the number of parking spaces depending on the type of business.

Lease, Buy, or Build?

Another factor you must consider in your site analysis is whether to lease, buy, or build your facility. In most instances, for a new business, the advantages of leasing outweigh other options. Specifically:

1. **A large cash outlay is avoided.** The money saved by leasing can be used for inventory, supplies, and other expenses.

2. **Risk is reduced.** You can get an idea of how successful the business is going to be before you invest in buying or building.

3. **Lease expenses are tax deductible.** A reduction in your tax liability can increase profits.

While You Read

Question What are the benefits of leasing a business location?

If you decide to lease, obtain information about the terms for each property under consideration. Terms include monthly rent, length of the lease, and provisions for termination. Determine who is responsible for insuring against various risks, remodeling costs, and repairs. If you decide to buy or build, gather similar information. Buying and building usually require more time and effort. For example, you must apply for financing.

Whether you lease, buy, or build, study any lease or contract before signing. Have an attorney review the document. Remember that these types of agreements are negotiable. Before completing the deal, discuss the terms and agree to those that are best for you.

Making Your Decision

When your location analysis is complete, examine and compare the possible sites. For each, consider the three variables listed below. Then make your decision.

- **Cost comparison.** What is the initial outlay for each site? What is the monthly expense? What are the other expenses, such as utilities, water, and sewage?

- **Advantages and disadvantages.** What are the comparative advantages and disadvantages of each option? Consider the physical environment, the exterior, and the interior.

- **Desirability.** Besides the factual considerations, intangibles are often an issue. Atmosphere, character, convenience, and personal preferences all factor into the final decision.

Alternative Sites

Two sites that do not fit the traditional mold are home-based businesses and incubators. Both can be attractive choices for new entrepreneurs.

Home Business Option

Today, more than ever, new entrepreneurs are discovering the benefits of starting a business from home. The main advantage of working from home is financial. You do not have to pay rent, and you may be able to save on your taxes. This arrangement can work for businesses that do not have a large number of clients visiting the work site. In general, home-based enterprises involve little personal contact with customers.

Whether you decide to start your business at home depends on the type of business, space, and equipment you have; the effect on those with whom you live; and the laws of your community.

Incubator Option

An **incubator** is an enterprise that is set up to provide flexible and affordable leases, office space, equipment, management assistance, mentoring assistance, and access to financing for start-up businesses. Business incubators are set up by economic development agencies, nonprofit groups, and increasingly by venture capitalists, especially for new technology businesses.

Like home-based businesses, a major advantage of starting a business in an incubator is financial. Rent is less, and shared secretarial and administrative services mean reduced expenses. Other savings can come from on-site legal and accounting resources as well as group purchasing power. A second major benefit is the availability of business development services. These services may include financing, marketing, and management assistance.

Write About It

Interview a home-based business owner. Ask about the advantages and disadvantages of operating a business from home. Find out the characteristics that lead to home-business success. Then write a summary of the interview.

Section 9.1 After You Read

Key Concept Review

1. Identify three incentives a community might use to attract entrepreneurs.

2. Explain how information can be obtained to calculate a vacancy rate.

3. Describe three services that incubators typically provide to tenants.

Critical Thinking

4. Is surrounding area analysis equally important for all types of businesses? Explain.

Role Play

Situation You work in a restaurant. A coworker plans to establish a new quick-serve restaurant. She believes success will come easily regardless of location as long as the food is good. She asks for your input.

Activity Organize your thoughts so your advice focuses specifically on the restaurant business.

Evaluation You will be evaluated on how well you cover the following points in the role play:

- Explain the factors affecting the selection of the business location and site.

- Explain how to secure a location after researching the target market.

- List the elements to examine when selecting a building.

Layout Planning

GET READY TO READ

KEY TERMS
- layout
- workstation
- facade
- appointments

KEY CONCEPTS
- Physical Layout
- Layout Needs and Possibilities
- Finishing Touches

THE MAIN IDEA

The steps in layout planning apply to all types of businesses. However, development of a facility layout is based on the operational needs of the business.

READING ORGANIZER

Draw the reading organizer on a separate piece of paper. As you read, fill in the organizer. In the first column, list the key considerations for each type of business. In the second column, list the workable layouts for the type of business.

	CONSIDERATIONS	LAYOUTS
Manufacturing	production sequence	efficient placement of machinery
Retail		
Wholesale		
Service		
Extraction		

Physical Layout

Like site selection, proper layout planning is important to the success of a business. A well-planned layout can mean a more efficient operation, a more appealing sales floor, and greater customer convenience. A poorly planned layout can mean just the opposite.

A **layout** is a floor plan or map that shows the arrangement of a business. It shows how you intend to use the space in your site to conduct business. An interior layout might include display cases, lighting fixtures, and the traffic pattern for customers or production processes. An exterior layout might show landscaping, parking spaces, and the traffic pattern for pedestrians and vehicles.

In the planning of a layout, the business owner must follow regulations. All cities have standards that relate to safety and zoning, for example. Also, the Americans With Disabilities Act requires certain businesses to provide access for people with physical, hearing, or visual impairments.

Moms Want Fashion, Too!

When Liz Lange was working as a designer's assistant in 1996, fashion options for pregnant women were extremely limited—and stores were not looking to change that, because they thought expectant moms would not spend money on fashion. Lange proved them wrong when she introduced her line of high-fashion maternity clothes, selling them by appointment at first and then to select boutiques. In 2001 she landed an exclusive partnership with Nike, and a distribution deal with Target followed in 2002. Today, she offers not only maternity wear but evening and athletic wear; she is also the author of *Liz Lange Maternity Style*.

CRITICAL THINKING

Why do you think retailers were so resistant to Lange's ideas? How did she prove them wrong?

 Go to **entrepreneurship.glencoe.com** to complete the Success Stories Writing Activity.

There are six basic steps in layout planning:

1. Define the objectives of the facility.
2. Identify the primary and supporting activities that will take place in the facility.
3. Determine the interrelationships—access, arrangement, and flow—between the activities.
4. Determine the space requirements for all activities.
5. Design alternative layouts for the facility.
6. Evaluate the various layouts and choose one.

Layout Needs and Possibilities

Although the steps in layout planning are the same for all businesses, the options and considerations are not. Different types of businesses have different operational needs. A manufacturing business, for example, must be laid out differently than a retail operation.

This section will describe layout factors and plans needed for all types of businesses. As you read, focus on those considerations and layout options relevant to your type of business.

Manufacturing Businesses

If your proposed business involves manufacturing goods, your key layout concern will be the placement of machinery. You want an arrangement that maximizes the efficiency of your operation.

WHAT TO CONSIDER The following groups of questions will help you formulate your specific layout needs:

While You Read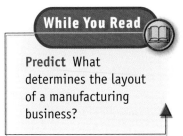

Predict What determines the layout of a manufacturing business?

- **Production processes.** What kind of manufacturing processes are you involved in? Are you breaking down raw materials into products? Are you assembling products from parts? Are you converting raw materials into products?

- **Production sequence.** Does your operation call for mass-producing standardized goods in assembly-line sequence? Do you manufacture your products one at a time or in batches? Do you use a combination of these two approaches?

- **Materials flow.** What is the most efficient flow of materials in your operation? **Figure 9.2** shows your options. Do materials come in one end of the building and finished goods leave the other? (That is an I flow.) Do materials enter and finished products leave from the same end? (That's a U flow.) What do you do when space is limited? (That is when you use an S flow.)

- **Control.** What is the best arrangement for managing your operation? What is best for inventory control?

- **Environmental needs.** Do you need to provide for chemical, water treatment, or other special processes? Are temperatures, noise, or fumes likely to be problems?

- **Space requirements.** How much space do you need for the placement and moving of equipment? What are your specific needs for machine maintenance, plant service, and storage? What is your anticipated production capacity?

Figure 9.2 **Flow Patterns for Production Materials**

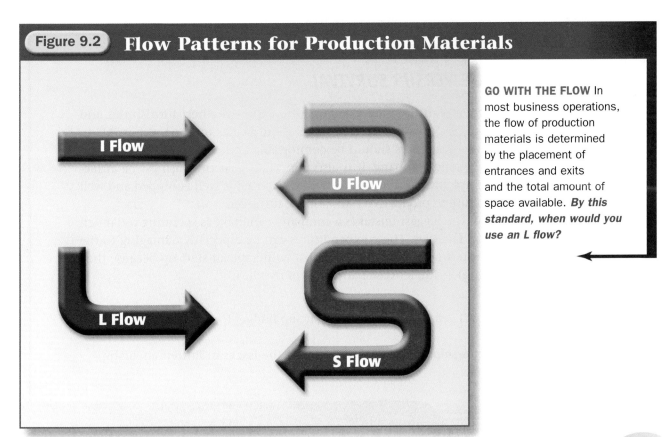

GO WITH THE FLOW In most business operations, the flow of production materials is determined by the placement of entrances and exits and the total amount of space available. *By this standard, when would you use an L flow?*

TYPES OF LAYOUTS The layout of a manufacturing business is influenced by the production process and sequence. There are three basic layouts. They can be modified to suit the needs of a particular operation or used in combination.

- **Product layout.** In this layout, all machines and supporting activities are arranged along a product flow line. As products come down the line, something is done to them at each workstation. A **workstation** is an area with equipment for a single worker. This layout is often used in an assembly-line sequence. It is useful for producing large quantities of a product.

- **Fixed-product layout.** This layout is used when the product is too heavy or bulky to be moved around the plant. An airplane is a good example. In fixed-product arrangements, parts are brought to the job and workers come to the product.

- **Process layout.** This type of layout involves the grouping of machines and equipment by function. For example, machines that perform welding functions are placed in one area and machines that do sanding are placed in another area. Products are then moved from one area to another, with a specific function being performed at each location. This setup is particularly efficient for producing small quantities of goods.

Secondary areas to map out include areas for shipping, receiving, storage, warehousing, maintenance services, and office space. Outside, they include storage yards, repair areas, loading docks, and parking.

Issues in Entrepreneurship

TOP-OF-THE-LINE VERSUS SURVIVAL

When planning their start-up, entrepreneurs often want the best furnishings and facilities. After all, they reason, their business should be as inviting as possible to customers and clients. Customers should be comfortable and confident that they are doing business with a solid company. It is also important that the business be attractive to prospective employees and hirees. A nice facility that is well equipped and well furnished can contribute to productivity and reduce turnover.

In contrast, one of the biggest mistakes a company can make is spending too much money on offices and facilities. These expenditures can be especially damaging to the financial health of a start-up. Companies are most vulnerable at start-up because they typically have lower sales, higher costs, and a lot of overhead.

Thinking Creatively
How can entrepreneurs get more out of their start-up budget for offices and facilities?

 Go to **entrepreneurship.glencoe.com** to complete the Issues in Entrepreneurship Research Activity.

Retail Businesses

The arrangement of a retail store has a major impact on sales and, hence, profits. The most important design consideration is the flow of customers through the operation. Merchandise and aisles should be laid out to "pull" customers through the store.

WHAT TO CONSIDER Two things enter the planning process for customer flow. One is selecting the most effective merchandise placement. Placement considerations are described below. The other is deciding on an appropriate layout. Those options are shown in **Figure 9.3.**

- **Products to be sold.** Does the merchandise require special care, such as refrigeration or extra security? Can the merchandise be shelved, or must it have standing space? Does it require space for trying out or trying on?

- **Projected clientele.** Will customers be concerned with atmosphere (including space and comfort)? Will they be concerned with getting in and out quickly?

- **Sales per square foot of selling space.** Is the store arranged to get the most sales out of each square foot of space? Is the opportunity for self-service maximized? Is the space for individual items of on-floor stock minimized?

- **Sales value of area within store.** Are the most salable goods placed in the area with the highest potential for sales (the middle and right)? Are staples in the low-sales-value area (the rear)? Are impulse and convenience items spread throughout?

- **Product coordination.** Is related merchandise placed in the same area to facilitate customer shopping? Are complementary groups (such as shorts and tops) placed together to encourage multiple sales?

- **Aisle exposure.** Does merchandise get maximum exposure? Do customers have ample time and space to examine it? Are there barriers to customer movement?

Wholesale Businesses

Wholesale operations can take a variety of forms. One common form is warehousing facilities that wholesalers who take possession of goods use. Two primary goals in planning a warehouse layout are to provide cost-effective storage and allow efficient movement of products in and out of the facility.

WHAT TO CONSIDER When planning the layout of a wholesale business, your most important considerations are storage and space utilization. When planning for storage, follow these guidelines:

- Store popular items near shipping points to minimize in-house travel distances.

- Store together those items that were received together and that will be shipped together.

- Provide for a variety of sizes of storage space.

- Assign storage space on the basis of ease of handling and popularity of items.

> **While You Read**
>
> **Connect** Identify a wholesale business in your area. Contact the business and ask if your class can tour the facilities.

Figure 9.3 **Types of Layouts**

RETAIL LAYOUTS
Retail layouts generally contain three types of floor space—selling space, storage space, and customer space. What distinguishes one plan from another is the way these spaces are configured. Different arrangements can produce different selling effects. Most store layouts fall into one of four categories. *How important is layout to a particular retail establishment?*

1. Right-Angle Grid
The pattern of crossing aisles in this supermarket provides a highly structured system for facilitating the flow of traffic. The layout reduces security concerns and lends itself to self-service operations.

2. Open Layout
The layout of this store consists of open sales space bounded by outside walls. It enhances visibility of merchandise, sales coverage, and security.

3. Enclosed Layout
The layout of this department store organizes types of merchandise into separate operations. Walls are placed between these units to create shopping environments.

4. Landscaped Layout
The landscaped layout of this store combines elements of the open and enclosed layouts. It improves customer and sales staff interaction and shows off creative displays.

There will be exceptions to these guidelines. For example, you may have to make special provisions for perishables, hazardous materials, valuable items, and items that can and cannot be stored together.

When planning how to use space, keep these guidelines in mind:

- Conserve space wherever possible.
- Observe limitations on space, such as ceilings, sprinklers, and safe stacking heights.
- Use adjustable racks and shelves where possible to accommodate changing needs.
- Plan entrances, exits, and aisles so products can be easily reached.

TYPES OF LAYOUTS Most modern wholesale operations are housed in single-story buildings. This makes controlling and moving stock easy.

Receiving, storage, order assembly, and shipping areas should be arranged so goods can be moved through them quickly and easily. This means working with and around certain key features. These include exterior access points (such as rail or truck sidings) and fixed interior obstacles (such as columns).

Interior layout plans should include office space and, if necessary, showroom areas. Exterior plans might show loading docks and vehicle storage areas.

Service Businesses

The physical layout of a service business depends largely on the specific service it provides. Consequently, there is no prescribed set of guidelines or layout patterns for these enterprises. However, service businesses can be categorized into general types. These types are identified in **Figure 9.4** on page 194.

Extraction Businesses

Like service businesses, extraction firms have unique layouts. They must adapt to the particular environment in which the extraction operation takes place. However, extraction businesses do have a few features in common. The businesses include an office area, storage areas for equipment and supplies, and the site itself.

The exterior physical operation of an extraction business may be spread out over a wide area. Consider a farm, for example. The operation may also be geographically separated from the business. Some mining ventures are headquartered in large cities far removed from the actual mining site. The business and extraction operations can be combined (as in a small fishing operation). All of these variations demand a different combination of layout plans.

E-Businesses

E-businesses require one or two areas. Layout of the operations area depends on how computers, phones, equipment, and storage are adapted to the workspace. If the e-business carries and ships products, a storage area is required. Wholesale storage principles apply to the layout of this area.

While You Read

Question Should the layout of an e-business be similar in any ways to the layout of a wholesale business?

Figure 9.4 Layout Considerations for Different Types of Service Businesses

LAYOUT CONSIDERATIONS
The service businesses listed in the top half of the table have customers who come to them. *Which types of businesses have fewer layout considerations?*

Business Type	Examples	Things to Consider
Customers come to the facility to use equipment	• Driving range • Laundromat • Car wash	• Customer appeal • Equipment • Space • Pay station • Safety
Customers come to the facility for assistance	• Copy shop • Car repair • Dry cleaner	• Customer appeal • Ease of access • Waiting area • Customer contact station • Equipment/service area • Supply storage
Customers come to the facility for care	• Day care center • Doctor's office • Beauty salon	• Customer appeal • Ease of access • Waiting area • Rest rooms • Service areas • Office space • Supply/equipment storage
Business operator goes to customer to provide service	• Exterminator • Painting contractor • Interior designer • Taxicab service	• Office space • Storage areas
Business operator brings customer and equipment together	• Car rental • Video rental	• Customer appeal • Display area • Storage area • Pay and return stations
Business operator brings customer and service together	• Employment agency • Real estate agency • Tax preparation	• Customer appeal • Private office space • Common office space • Conference room • Waiting area

Finishing Touches

Once you settle on a particular layout for your business, you can begin filling in the final details. You should consider, at the very least, the minimum office space you will need. You need to think about space for equipment, furnishings, and supplies. Finally, you should plan interior design features and alterations or improvements to the **facade**, or face of the building.

Planning for Office Space

Every business owner needs space to take care of paperwork and administrative tasks. In some cases, desk space in a back room is sufficient. In businesses where the office is the hub of activity, virtually all of the workspace is devoted to the office space function.

You have two options to consider when planning office space. If cost, space, employee supervision, or access to files and equipment are important, an open office layout may be best. This arrangement often uses partitions to divide workspace into cubicles. On the other hand, if privacy and noise reduction are primary concerns, a closed office layout is a better option.

If your operation requires multiple offices, they may be arranged in two ways. One way is to connect offices with corridors or aisles. The other, used with open workstations, defines the traffic patterns with appointments. **Appointments** are the furniture, equipment, and accessories, such as planters and fish tanks.

Charting Equipment, Furnishings, and Supplies

Planning your operation's layout involves more than just organizing floor space. You also need to plan for the placement of other components, including equipment, furnishings, supplies, and inventory. Your decisions should be based on your business's operational needs.

Detailing Interior and Exterior

Interior design details can help you create the atmosphere you want. Such details include lighting, wall and floor coverings, and decorative accessories.

Exterior design details include the facade of the building, signage, and entryways to your business. Outside design may be of little importance (home-based businesses) or of critical importance (most retail operations).

Section 9.2 After You Read

Key Concept Review

1. In your own words, explain the "determine the interrelationships" step in layout planning.
2. What are the different layout needs of retail and wholesale businesses?
3. What are the advantages of a closed office layout?

Critical Thinking

4. Analyze the components used to design a physical layout for a business.

Role Play

Situation Assume the role of an entrepreneur who just acquired a facility for a new business. You have decided to hire a commercial decorator to help you with the finishing touches.

Activity Pair up with a classmate. Have your classmate assume the role of the decorator. Work together to draw a floor plan for the business and a list of decorating ideas. Then role play a conversation between the entrepreneur and the decorator.

Evaluation You will be evaluated on how well you address these issues in your role play:

- Explain the importance of a proper layout plan for the success of your business.
- Describe the components of your business layout, including equipment, furnishings, and supplies.
- Explain what you see as your office needs and options.
- Discuss your ideas for detailing the interior and exterior of your location.

Chapter Summary

Section 9.1 **Community and Site Selection**

Selecting a business site requires the selection of a community and a specific location in the community. When selecting a community in which to start your business, examine the economic base, financial incentives, and relevant population data. When choosing a site for a retail business, consider the competing businesses, the character of the area, and the site's accessibility to customers. Wholesale and service firms base their site decisions on whether or not customers will be coming to their places of business. Manufacturing and extraction businesses look for sites with easy access to transportation, suppliers, and raw materials. The biggest factor e-businesses look at when selecting a site is the size and nature of their operations. A building should be chosen based on its suitability for the intended use, whether you will buy or lease, and costs. Starting your new business at home or in an incubator can reduce expenses.

Section 9.2 **Layout Planning**

Layout planning is necessary to turn a site into an effective, efficient, and desirable facility. The specific steps in layout planning are (1) define facility objectives, (2) define primary and supporting activities, (3) determine activity interrelationships, (4) determine space requirements, (5) design alternative layouts, and (6) select the final layout. Layout considerations and plans are different for each type of business. Details, such as the minimum office space needed; space for equipment, furnishings, and supplies; and interior design features and alterations to the facade, need consideration once a particular layout has been selected for a business.

Key Terms Review

1. Describe the ideal location for a business of your choice. Discuss the community, site, building, and layout. Use these terms:

economic base (p. 179)   incubator (p. 186)

incentive (p. 179)   layout (p. 187)

census tract (p. 180)   workstation (p. 190)

trade area (p. 181)   facade (p. 194)

industrial parks (p. 182)   appointments (p. 195)

Key Concept Review

2. **List** the factors involved in deciding on a community in which to locate a business. (9.1)
3. **Identify** the factors to consider when selecting a business site. (9.1)
4. **Describe** how to find potential business sites. (9.1)
5. **Explain** the steps involved in analyzing potential sites for a business and choosing between those sites. (9.1)
6. **Describe** the advantages of starting a business at home and in an incubator. (9.1)
7. **Describe** the steps in layout planning that are common to all businesses. (9.2)
8. **Describe** the layout needs for each type of business. (9.2)
9. **Explain** the final details of layout planning. (9.2)

Critical Thinking

10. Why is it important to know the demographics of the community in which you locate your business?
11. Describe how a clothing boutique owner might choose a location. Include community, site, and building considerations.
12. Are you the type of person who could locate a new business at home? Why or why not?
13. Review the basic steps in layout planning. Are these steps really useful for all types of businesses? Why or why not?
14. If you were starting an ice cream manufacturing business, what would be your primary site and layout considerations?
15. What is the ideal amount of office space for a business? Explain.
16. Think of a service business you might like to start. Discuss the finishing touches you want to include in your location and explain why you need them.

Write About It

17. Write a report that compares and contrasts the advantages and disadvantages of buying and building a business site. Explain how the options compare to leasing.
18. Research your equipment, furnishings, supply, and inventory needs for a start-up business. Compile a report describing those components, the quantities you need, and the space they require. Also indicate in your report where they will be placed in your facility.
19. Research incubators. Write a report on your findings.
20. Write a paragraph that explains how information can be obtained to calculate a vacancy rate. Include the specific calculation.

Academic Skills

Math

21. Suppose you are opening a 1,000-square-foot baseball card store. Your lease calls for a flat monthly rent of $1.75 per square foot plus 5 percent of your gross annual sales. What is the total rent you will pay in one year if you have sales of $85,000?

Language Arts

22. You just finished interviewing a successful entrepreneur for a school project. He told you that his site location happened by chance, that he did no research, and that research is a waste of time. How do you respond?

Entrepreneurship in Your Community

23. Choose a site for your business. Analyze the factors considered in the selection of the business location. As part of your decision-making process, do the following:

- Using population, demographic, and zoning data, select two or more potential sites.

- Visit each site. Note potential competitors and available buildings in the area.

- On a map, mark trade areas, potential competitors, and transportation routes for your sites.

- Compare your site possibilities. Summarize your findings in written or table form and make a final choice.

24. Interview two entrepreneurs.

- Ask them how they selected their sites.

- Find out what skills helped them in the process.

- Have them explain the pros and cons of the various sites they considered.

Report to the class about what you learned.

Ethical Practices

Property Problems

25. Most realtors, property managers, and other individuals who sell or lease property are fair and honest. However, not everyone with business property to offer has the same ethics. Some people believe the buyer is responsible for determining whether problems exist with a location. They avoid mentioning unsafe conditions—for example, faulty wiring or rotted floors or the likelihood of floods. Big problems can be costly to fix. Is this behavior unethical? How can you protect yourself from unethical people in your search for a business site?

Research Business Sites

You want to open a shoe business in your area, but you have not yet decided on a location.

Connect

Use a search engine or Web directory to find potential competitors in your area.

- Locate other shoe stores to determine your trade area.

- Determine what types of shoes are sold at the competitors' locations.

- Find out what other shoe-related services are offered.

Application

Use a spreadsheet program to organize the information you find. Present your data to the class and explain how you found the information.

The Electronic Entrepreneur

The Components of an Effective E-Commerce Site

While the Internet was originally designed as a communication tool, it has developed into an enormous consumer network. One of its key strengths is the sale of products and services online. E-commerce sites are extremely common today, some of them more successful than others. So what makes an e-commerce site successful?

Content and Design Nobody enjoys shopping in a store where things are hard to find and poorly labeled, and the same is true online. The most successful shopping sites are carefully categorized and offer easy-to-use links to get around. Successful sites have sticky content. **Sticky content** is the information and features on a Web site that gives users a compelling reason to visit it.

Credit Card Processing Using a credit or debit card online makes transactions quick and easy, as there is no need to mail a check. In order for this to work, the site should feature a **payment gateway**, software that automatically processes the credit card information so that it does not have to be typed in manually. When this gateway is properly connected to the company's bank, it can process a **real-time transaction**, meaning that the funds are transferred from buyer to seller instantly.

Security Certificate In order to help customers feel at ease, a site should have a **security certificate**, a credential that is issued by a third-party company that assures the user that all transactions are private and safe. There are several companies that sell and maintain these certificates for e-commerce Web sites.

FACT AND IDEA REVIEW

1. Why has the Internet become so successful as a consumer network?
2. Why is a site's design so important? Can you name e-commerce sites that you think are well designed?
3. What are the benefits to using a payment gateway and real-time transactions? How do they work together?
4. Why are security certificates important?

FOR DISCUSSION

5. What do you look for when choosing an e-commerce site to make a purchase? What things are most important to you?

TechTerms

- sticky content
- payment gateway
- real-time transaction
- security certificate

Vision and Mission Statements

The vision and mission statements set forth the guiding principles by which a company functions. They communicate what the business stands for, what its founders believe in, and what the company intends to achieve.

✓ STEP 1 THINK ABOUT YOUR COMPANY'S VISION

Write answers to the questions below. These issues need to be answered in your company's vision statement.

1. What is your company's scope and purpose?
2. How does your company's scope and purpose reflect the company's core values and beliefs?

✓ STEP 2 THINK ABOUT YOUR COMPANY'S MISSION

Write answers to the questions below. These issues need to be answered in your company's mission statement.

1. What are the specific aspirations of your company?
2. Are these aspirations measurable and achievable? Explain your answer.

Industry Overview

Your business plan must describe the industry and address the basic trends and growth within the industry. Think of your industry as those companies providing similar, complementary, or supplementary products and services.

✓ STEP 1 DESCRIBE THE INDUSTRY

Write a description of your proposed business's industry, including size by both revenue and number of firms. Describe the industry's distribution system, barriers of entry, failure rate, and typical profitability.

✓ STEP 2 RESEARCH INDUSTRY AND ECONOMIC TRENDS

Use industry publications and online resources to conduct research on trends. Create a chart like the one below to describe past, current, and future trends and the impacts of those trends on your business and the industry.

AREA OF ANALYSIS	TRENDS	IMPACT OF TRENDS
Government Regulations		
Industry Demographics		
Industry Growth or Decline		
Industry Standards		
Distribution Systems		
Regional Unemployment		
Regional Wages		

Market Analysis

The Market Analysis section of the business plan presents your market research and features a target market demographic profile.

✓ STEP 1 ORGANIZE RESEARCH ON CONSUMER MARKETS

Create a chart like the one below to research and organize information about your target market.

CONSUMER MARKET RESEARCH			
Ethnicities		Genders	
Occupations		Family Structures	
Level of Income		Geographics	
Social Status		Lifestyle	
Education		Leisure Activities	
Age Range		Motivations	

✓ STEP 2 ORGANIZE RESEARCH ON B2B MARKETS

If your product or service is marketed to businesses, research and organize information about your target market in terms of industry, product and/or service, geographic location, years in business, revenue, number of employees, and buying motivations. Create a chart to organize your research.

Use the **Business Plan Project Appendix** on pages 532–543 to explore the content requirements of a business plan in more detail.

▶ The **Vision and Mission Statements** section of the business plan sets forth the guiding principles by which a company functions.

▶ The **Industry Overview** addresses the basic trends and growth within those companies providing similar, complementary, or supplementary products and services.

▶ The **Market Analysis** presents your market research and features a customer demographic profile that defines the traits of the company's target market.

BUSINESS PLAN PROJECT TEMPLATE

@ Go to **entrepreneurship.glencoe.com** for a document template in which you can write your own business plan.

UNIT 3

MANAGING MARKET STRATEGIES

UNIT OVERVIEW

Introduction

Some of an entrepreneur's most important business decisions involve marketing. Marketing will determine whether or not your product or service sells. Successful marketing starts with research and planning. Objectives must be set, and factors must be considered. Pricing, promotion, and sales management are a few of the vital issues you will face. Understanding these will help you develop your strategies and adjust to and take advantage of changes as they occur in the marketplace.

BUSINESS PLAN PROJECT PREVIEW

When you complete Unit 3, you will begin to explore these sections of the business plan:

▶ The **Competitive Analysis** section of the business plan demonstrates how the proposed business has an advantage over its competitors.

▶ The **Marketing Plan** describes a company's marketing mix strategies or how it plans to market, promote, and sell its products or services.

Chapter 10

The Marketing Plan

CHAPTER OBJECTIVES

When you have completed this chapter, you should be able to:

SECTION 10.1

- Identify the role of marketing objectives in developing a marketing plan.
- Name the five marketing strategies that make up the marketing mix.
- Describe the part marketing tactics play in the marketing plan.

SECTION 10.2

- State the importance of ongoing market research.
- List the factors to consider for each strategy when reviewing the marketing mix.
- Describe how to update the marketing mix and marketing plan.

EVALUATING INVESTMENT OPPORTUNITIES

Because there is so much information available on investments, you have to be selective. The important thing is to be sure that your sources are accurate and reliable.

- **The Internet.** A search engine is a powerful tool for finding investment information online. Most investment firms have Web sites.

- **Newspapers and News Programs.** The financial pages of your metro newspaper or *The Wall Street Journal* are excellent sources of investment information.

- **Business and Government Periodicals.** You can find investment information in magazines, such as *Barron's*, *BusinessWeek*, and *Forbes*, or government publications, such as the *Federal Reserve Bulletin*.

- **Corporate Reports.** The federal government requires any corporation selling newly issued securities to provide a prospectus, a document that discloses important information about the company's earnings, assets, and liabilities.

 Go to entrepreneurship.glencoe.com to complete the Standard & Poor's Money Talk Financial Literacy Activity.

PREPARE TO READ

THINK ABOUT THESE QUESTIONS AS YOU READ.

What is a marketing plan?

What are the components of the marketing mix?

Devising a Marketing Plan

KEY TERMS
- marketing plan
- marketing objectives
- marketing mix
- brand
- package
- label
- product positioning
- product mix
- channel of distribution
- intermediaries
- intensive distribution
- selective distribution
- exclusive distribution
- marketing tactics

KEY CONCEPTS
- Forming Marketing Objectives
- Developing the Marketing Mix
- Marketing Tactics

THE MAIN IDEA

To succeed and grow, a business must have a marketing plan with realistic objectives, the proper mix of the five Ps, and an action plan for implementation.

READING ORGANIZER

Draw the reading organizer on a separate piece of paper. As you read, fill in the chart with the five strategies of a marketing mix.

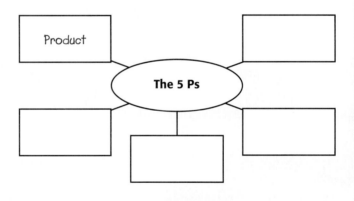

Forming Marketing Objectives

Marketing is important to every business. The success of a business is determined in the marketplace. Marketing is the process of developing, promoting, and distributing products to satisfy the objectives of customers and businesses. It brings the marketing concept—and its supporting concepts of customer orientation and customer satisfaction—to life.

A **marketing plan** is a plan used by a business to guide its marketing process to a desired conclusion. The plan is built on information obtained through market research and target market decisions. It includes a description of the target market, a profile of the primary customer, marketing objectives, marketing strategies and tactics, and a marketing budget. You must identify ways to reach the greatest number of potential customers. A convincing marketing plan includes a rationale for your selection of marketing strategies and tactics. When a business has multiple target markets, it needs to create variations of the plan to address differences in those markets.

Marketing objectives are what a business wants to accomplish through its marketing efforts. In a start-up marketing plan, the objectives should include such things as:

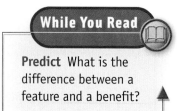

Predict What is the difference between a feature and a benefit?

- Product introduction or innovation
- Sales or market share
- Projected profitability
- Pricing
- Distribution
- Advertising
- Team organization

The objectives should be consistent with the overall goals of the business. They should be reasonable and consistent with the marketing situation and available resources. Objectives should be written in clear and simple language. In addition, they must be measurable. It is best to limit the number of objectives so they can be monitored and controlled.

Developing the Marketing Mix

Forming marketing objectives enables you to specify *what* you want to accomplish through your marketing initiatives. Developing the marketing mix enables you to map out *how* you are going to do it.

The **marketing mix** is made up of five marketing strategies you will use to reach your market. Historically, businesspeople have worked with four strategies. These strategies, commonly referred to as the four Ps, are product, place, price, and promotion. In recent years, a fifth P (the people strategy) has emerged and gained widespread acceptance.

The strategies of a marketing mix must be used together to ensure success. One strategy alone will not work. The strategies must be coordinated to influence the target market. They must be synchronized to result in company profits. The right combination used in the marketing mix will produce good results. The wrong combination will produce less than satisfactory results.

The following sections will discuss the product, place, and people strategies. Price and promotion will be discussed in separate chapters.

The Product Strategy

The product strategy deals with the goods or services your business will provide. The scope of products and services will vary based on the type of business. Product decisions are crucial to the success of your business. Products that do not satisfy customer needs or expectations will not sell. When you did your market analysis, you gathered product information and made preliminary decisions. This section will help you mold those efforts into a product strategy.

PRODUCT FEATURES AND BENEFITS A product is made up of all of the features and benefits it offers to consumers. When considering your product, you must think of a package of features and benefits your customers find desirable.

A "Neighborhood" Success

The first Applebee's restaurant opened in 1980 in Atlanta, Georgia. It focused on solid American food and a friendly, family-oriented environment. The company has grown by leaps and bounds in the past two decades, going public in 1989, and today is one of the most recognized names in casual dining. With over 1,600 locations and roughly 100 more opening each year, Applebee's is today "the world's largest casual dining concept."

CRITICAL THINKING

Aside from the food, what do you think are some of the reasons Applebee's has been so successful?

 Go to **entrepreneurship.glencoe.com** to complete the Success Stories Writing Activity.

Goods and services have physical features, such as style, distinctive characteristics, color, quality, and options. They also offer intangible features, such as warranties, service contracts, delivery, installation, and instructions. Both goods and services offer intangible benefits to improve the quality of customers' lives. Benefits include things such as convenience, improved health, a sense of well-being, saving time, and saving money. What will your product offer?

BRANDING, PACKAGING, AND LABELING Your product will be identified by its branding, packaging, and labeling. A **brand** is the name, symbol, or design used to identify a product. A **package** is the physical container or wrapper that holds the product. The **label** is the part of the package used to present information. All three, especially branding, serve as strategies for maintaining customer loyalty. For example, wearers of Puma® footwear may buy this brand repeatedly. They expect a certain quality of athletic shoe in a specific type of box with a clearly marked label.

PRODUCT SELECTION What products and/or services will your business offer? The answer depends on whether you are manufacturing or reselling your products.

Developing and manufacturing new products to sell adds value. You change raw materials into a form that satisfies customer needs. Manufacturing a product also involves several steps. First, you generate product ideas and sort out the good from the bad. Then you study the product's potential costs and revenues. You develop the product and test-market it. Finally, if everything looks promising, you introduce the product.

In contrast, choosing products for resale is largely a matter of gathering information. First, you study consumer demand and product availability. Then you make decisions to bring the two together. A second related concern is how well your new product fits in with other items you sell.

PRODUCT POSITIONING **Product positioning** refers to how consumers see your product compared to the competition's product. Do you want consumers to see your product as prestigious? Do you want them to see it as a good bargain? Do you want them to see it as equal in quality to other products? How you position your product relative to the competition depends on your marketing goals.

Positioning can be achieved through quality, availability, pricing, and uses. Branding, packaging, and labeling can also have a bearing on your product's image and, thus, on its positioning.

PRODUCT MIX Finally, you need to consider your **product mix**, all of the products a company makes or sells. If you plan to offer multiple products, you should think about how they relate to one another. That depends on the image you want to project and the market you are targeting. If you want to reach a single market, you may include only products that complement one another. If you are trying to reach multiple markets, you may decide on a more diversified mix.

QUESTIONS TO ASK ABOUT PRODUCT DECISIONS The following questions will help you develop a product strategy for your marketing plan. As you develop a strategy, keep your target market in mind.

- What products should I manufacture or sell?
- How will my products meet the needs of my target market?
- What level of quality should my goods or services have?
- How much inventory should I maintain?
- How will my products be different from or better than my competitors'?
- How will I position my products?
- What will my customer service policy be?

IMPACT OF TECHNOLOGY ON THE PRODUCT STRATEGY With the Internet, businesses can let customers participate in the design of products they are purchasing. Clothing, furniture, and automobiles are examples.

Technology has greatly affected the manufacture of products. Products function better, are more precise, and include more features. Production costs are cheaper. Packaging and labeling also benefit from technology.

Advances in technology have resulted in the emergence of new products and services. Examples include camera phones, plasma screen televisions, and online movie rentals. Other goods and services may spin off from new products. Some new products make existing products obsolete. For example, compact discs have replaced audiotapes. These situations open windows of opportunity for manufacturing or reselling new products.

The Place Strategy

The place strategy involves how you will deliver your goods and services to customers. It involves making sure your product is ready and available for sale, when and where your customers want it. Having your product available when and where customers want it adds to its value. Because place strategies involve movement of your product, this part of the marketing mix is also known as the *distribution strategy.*

You have probably already begun to plan some portions of this strategy. When you did your market analysis, you learned how your competitors operate. Do you want to copy them or go your own way? Likewise, when you investigated potential sites, you identified the options available to you. Examining the following areas will help you finalize your strategy.

CHANNELS OF DISTRIBUTION To formulate your place strategy, you need to understand the possible channels of distribution. A **channel of distribution** is the path a product takes from producer (or manufacturer) to final user (or consumer). As shown in **Figure 10.1** and **Figure 10.2,** consumer and industrial markets have different channel members. However, there are only two basic types of channels—direct and indirect.

A direct channel moves a product from producer to customer with no one in between. Service businesses are typical examples. When you give a tax preparer your financial records, he or she returns your finished taxes. No one else is involved.

In contrast, an indirect channel employs **intermediaries**. These are people or businesses that move products between producers and final users. They include wholesalers and retailers, who sell in the consumer market. They also include distributors, who sell in the industrial market, and agents, who arrange sales. For example, a clothing designer might use an agent to contact wholesalers and retailers. He or she can then reach a large market without worrying about maintaining a sales staff or store. This allows the designer to concentrate on what he or she does best—designing.

While You Read

Connect Think of a product or service that you have purchased in the past. Then map its channel of distribution.

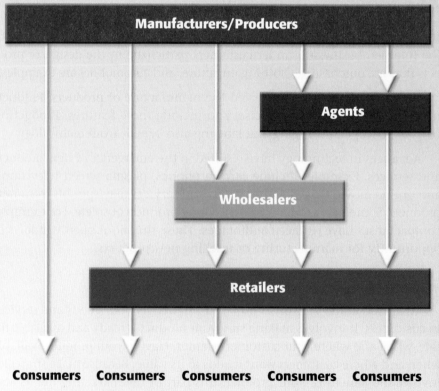

Figure 10.1 **Channels of Distribution—Consumer Market**

REACHING THE CONSUMER The path your product takes to reach the consumer can be either direct or indirect. *How many of the channels of distribution shown here are indirect?*

Manufacturers/Producers

Agents

Wholesalers

Retailers

Consumers Consumers Consumers Consumers Consumers

The type of business you have determines where you fit in your channel of distribution. If you are a producer, you send products through a channel. If you are a retailer, you receive them. If you are a wholesaler, you do both.

The channel of distribution you choose affects your product. It can raise or lower your product's cost. It can affect the potential for risk, such as the loss of or damage to your product while it is in transit. Most importantly, it can determine how quickly your product reaches customers. If you can find a highly efficient channel, you can gain a competitive edge.

INTENSITY OF DISTRIBUTION How broadly will you distribute your product? You have three choices. **Intensive distribution** involves placement of a product in all suitable sales outlets. For example, you can find best-selling paperbacks in bookstores, supermarkets, and magazine stands. **Selective distribution** limits the number of sales outlets in an area. For example, textbooks may be found only near schools. **Exclusive distribution** limits the number of outlets to one per area. For example, a museum might sell a special book for an exhibit.

TRANSPORTATION The physical movement of goods is part of your place decisions. How will your product be shipped? Your choices include by truck, train, airplane, ship, or pipeline. If you deal with information, you might be able to send your product via the Internet. The method of transportation you select affects how fast your product reaches consumers. It also determines your shipping costs. Generally, air transportation is most expensive, and waterway is least expensive.

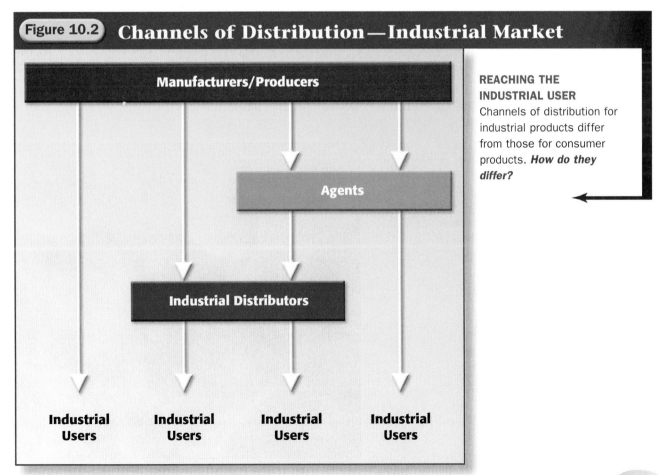

Figure 10.2 Channels of Distribution—Industrial Market

REACHING THE INDUSTRIAL USER
Channels of distribution for industrial products differ from those for consumer products. *How do they differ?*

LOCATION, LAYOUT, AND AVAILABILITY As you learned earlier, location, or site considerations, are also important to your place strategy. They are especially important to retail and service businesses that depend on customers to come to them. You can increase customer access and encourage sales by selecting a location near transportation routes. You might also lay out your site to have entries from the street and parking lot. You might favor evening over morning hours of operation. What do these options have in common? They are designed to match the needs and opportunities of potential customers. In other words, they are designed to make it easy for people to do business with you.

QUESTIONS TO ASK ABOUT PLACE DECISIONS When you make your place decisions, keep your target market in mind. Ask yourself the following questions:

- How will my product be sold and distributed?
- Will my product go directly from producer to user, or will it go through an intermediary?
- Can I use more efficient channels of distribution?
- What channel members will I use to obtain my products?
- What channel members will I use to distribute my products?
- How intensively will I distribute my products?
- Is my location appropriate for my target market(s)?
- Will the physical layout of my business encourage or discourage sales?
- Do my hours of operation match the times my target market prefers to do business?

IMPACT OF TECHNOLOGY ON THE PLACE STRATEGY In the place strategy, the Internet has had the biggest impact on channels of distribution. In particular, distributors have seen an increase in productivity. Their customers have benefited as a result.

GOODS AND SERVICES
A product can be a good or a service. *What goods are shown in this photo? What services?*

Use of the Internet by distributors has eliminated expensive guesswork related to customer needs. Suppliers can deliver what customers want in a timely manner and at lower costs. By doing so, suppliers can cut back on inventory. In addition, geography is no longer a problem. Distributors can connect easily with customers. Finally, the Internet can reduce the time customers spend searching for information. Many distributors have Web sites that provide prices, specifications, and third-party ratings of products. The Internet does not reduce the need for personal customer service. However, it does reduce the cost of that service.

The Internet and other technologies have affected suppliers and other channel members, too. For example, virtually all businesses can track shipments, both outgoing and incoming. Retailers, using bar codes and smart buttons, can determine changes in inventory each time a sale is made. In addition, software programs can be used to expedite layout design.

The People Strategy

The people strategy means assembling, preparing, and maintaining the people who will help you achieve success. Employees' actions, attitudes, and individual decisions impact business on a daily basis. Good employees are the ingredient in the mix that makes all of your other marketing mix strategies work.

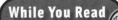

While You Read

Question Which of the five marketing mix strategies is most important to you as a consumer? Why?

In Chapters 17 and 18, you will learn specific techniques for hiring and motivating employees. The focus in this chapter is on the broader aspects of people strategy planning and decision making.

BASIC HIRING CRITERIA You must hire the right people. Qualifications for hiring are dictated by the needs of your business. If your business does not require unique skills, a good attitude and the ability to learn may be sufficient. If you need people with special skills, these special skills are an important part of the qualifications. You need employees who can help you reach your marketing objectives immediately.

DEVELOPING EMPLOYEES Employee development consists of two parts. The first is orientation. Orientation includes your vision for the company, plans to carry it out, and expectations of high performance. The second is providing training for the skills and knowledge employees need now and in the future. This process allows them to contribute to the performance and financial goals of the company.

ESTABLISHING A PRODUCTIVE ENVIRONMENT A productive environment is one with a healthy atmosphere. Employees are treated with respect and trust. They are empowered to do the right thing. In a productive environment, employees consider themselves members of a winning team. Team membership brings pride, cooperation, and team spirit. These factors set the stage for positive results.

REWARDING YOUR PEOPLE Recognize and reward employee contributions and achievements. If possible, share with them the financial rewards of the business. Investing in people is just as important as investing in other strategies. When people know their efforts are appreciated, they are more likely to stay for the long term. Committed, long-term employees will be more effective at implementing your marketing mix strategies.

Buzz Marketing

Frequent the right cafés in Sunset Plaza, Melrose, or the Third Street Promenade in and around Los Angeles this summer, and you're likely to encounter a gang of sleek, impossibly attractive motorbike riders who seem genuinely interested in getting to know you over an iced latte. Compliment them on their Vespa scooters glinting in the brilliant curbside sunlight, and they'll happily pull out a pad and scribble down an address and phone number—not theirs, but that of the local "boutique" where you can buy your own Vespa, just as (they'll confide) the rap artist Sisqó and the movie queen Sandra Bullock recently did. And that's when the truth hits you: This isn't any spontaneous encounter. Those scooter-riding models are on the Vespa payroll, and they've been hired to generate some favorable word of mouth for the recently reissued European bikes.

Welcome to the Summer of Buzz. This season, it seems, marketers are taking to the streets, as well as cafés, nightclubs, and the Internet, in record numbers. Vespa importer Piaggio USA has its biker gang. Hebrew National is dispatching "mom

squads" to grill up its hot dogs in backyard barbecues, while Hasbro Games has deputized hundreds of fourth- and fifth-graders as "secret agents" to tantalize their peers with Hasbro's new POX electronic game. Their goal: to seek out the trendsetters in each community and subtly push them into talking up their brand to their friends and admirers.

SOURCE: *BusinessWeek*, July 30, 2001; By Gerry Khermouch and Jeff Green

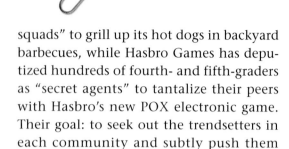

APPLICATION

Create a "buzz" marketing campaign for a product you would like to sell. In a one-page report, describe the product, the people you would hire to generate a buzz, and the method these people would use to create the buzz.

 Go to **entrepreneurship.glencoe.com** to complete the *BusinessWeek* Case Study Reading Guide Activity.

QUESTIONS TO ASK ABOUT PEOPLE DECISIONS As you consider your people strategy, ask yourself the following questions:

- What specific qualifications must my employees have?

- What training do I need to provide?

- Can I provide the training, or do I need to outsource it?

- What steps do I need to take to provide a productive environment?

- To what kind of reward system will my employees respond?

The Price and Promotion Strategies

The price strategy impacts business in two ways. First, it is a financial decision that ensures costs are covered and a profit is made. More importantly, it is a marketing strategy that affects the customer's motivation to buy. The price strategy is examined in detail in Chapter 11.

The promotion strategy is designed to tell potential customers about your products and their characteristics, benefits, and availability. It should also be used to enhance your company's image. The promotion strategy is addressed in detail in Chapters 12 and 13.

Marketing Tactics

To apply marketing strategies, you must develop an action plan to put the components of the mix into operation. The action plan consists of the **marketing tactics**, or activities that need to be taken to carry out the marketing plan. The action plan also includes a schedule. The primary activities in the action plan are the day-to-day marketing actions, also called *marketing functions*. They include financing, risk management, selling, promotion, pricing, purchasing, marketing-information management, product/service planning, and distribution.

Implementing the strategies also involves costs. When developing your action plan, you estimate and budget for costs. These costs will be used when preparing your financial plan.

In addition, you need to know how you will evaluate your marketing plan. The evaluation plans should include how you will (1) judge your business's performance, (2) evaluate your marketing plan, and (3) identify and solve problems. The information you obtain will help you make adjustments to your strategies and mix.

Section 10.1 After You Read

Key Concept Review

1. What is the difference between the marketing plan and the marketing mix?

2. Describe the five strategies of the marketing mix.

3. What questions should you ask yourself as you put together your product and place strategies?

Critical Thinking

4. Prepare preliminary drafts of the product, place, and people strategies for a proposed business.

Role Play

Situation You are a marketing consultant for a nationally franchised auto parts store.

Activity Give a presentation explaining the positioning of the store's product line in the local market. In addition to the presentation, you will be responding to questions from the audience, the employees of the store.

Evaluation You will be evaluated on how well you address these issues:

- Describe the store's marketing goals.
- Describe your customers.
- Describe quality and perceived quality.
- Describe the availability of your products.
- Describe how branding and labeling of the product affect the positioning.

Reviewing and Revising the Marketing Plan

GET READY TO READ

KEY TERMS
- private brand
- guarantee
- diversification

KEY CONCEPTS
- The Importance of Ongoing Market Research
- Reviewing Your Marketing Plan and Mix
- Revising Your Marketing Plan and Mix

THE MAIN IDEA
The target markets, customer demands, and competition of a business change over time. For a business to succeed, you must make timely adjustments in your marketing plan.

READING ORGANIZER
Draw the reading organizer on a separate piece of paper. As you read, fill in the second column with possible changes for each strategy.

THE 5 Ps	POSSIBLE CHANGES
Product	
Price	
Place	
Promotion	
People	

The Importance of Ongoing Market Research

Do not assume that target markets, customer demands, and competitors identified at start-up will remain the same. In business, change is constant. You must stay on top of any changes. If you do not, you may lose customers and miss promising opportunities.

How can you measure the ongoing changes in business? How can you predict changes and prepare for them? You need up-to-date information. Suppose you own and manage a CD store. The releases that are selling well this week may not be on the charts next month. To stay profitable, you must keep up with what is going on in the music scene. To do that, you must continue your market research. That process is shown in **Figure 10.3**.

Figure 10.3

Ongoing Marketing Research

Successful businesses make ongoing market research a priority. You can rely on informal research for much of your information, but at some point, you may want to consider hiring a professional researcher. *Why is it important to continue your market research?*

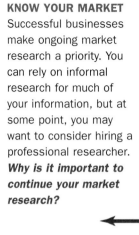

1. Gather primary data from your customers.

Gather information from current and former customers. Conduct surveys by mail, on the phone, over the Internet, in personal interviews, and through focus groups.

2. Gather secondary data from your business records.

Accounting records and sales receipts indicate your expenses. They also show which products are and are not moving.

3. Collect information that affects your operation.

Read newspapers, magazines, and trade publications. Save articles that pertain to your business and make a file.

Reviewing Your Marketing Plan and Mix

There are many benefits to ongoing market research. It provides information you need to make adjustments to your marketing plan. By being aware of what is happening in your market, you can revise your objectives and rework your marketing mix strategies.

Possible Changes to the Product Strategy

Concerns about product strategy are the same for both start-up and ongoing businesses. The only difference is that you will be making decisions about existing products rather than projected ones. What goods or services should you offer? How will your products be different from your competitors'? What can you do to make sure customers identify your products?

A change in any one of your products may affect other products. A change may stimulate sales through increased traffic. A change may also cause a loss of sales through negative consumer reaction. When Volkswagen reintroduced the Beetle in 1998, the increase in showroom traffic benefited all Volkswagen models. In contrast, if a car model gets a bad reputation, the entire image of a manufacturer may suffer.

ADDING PRODUCTS Before adding products to your line or adding lines, ask yourself these questions:

- Is there sufficient demand to add the new product? A few people may have expressed interest, but you have to sell enough products to break even.

- Is the product consistent with your current business? It may be a good idea for somebody's operation but not for yours.

- Will the new product compete with your current products? It may sell very well, but if it hurts current sales, what is the point?

- Is it the best use and application of your economic resources? Can money, labor, and facilities be put to better use in another product line? Can they be put to better use in another part of your marketing mix?

TECHNOLOGY Today

3-D Marketing

You might remember seeing pictures of audiences in the 1950s watching 3-D movies, wearing cardboard glasses that made the images on the screen seem lifelike. Today, 3-D is being used in serious marketing applications, such as hotels and other facilities offering "virtual walkthroughs" online and travel companies using 3-D films of exotic locations to entice prospective customers.

Cooperative Learning Activity

With a partner, list some other businesses that might benefit from 3-D marketing technology.

 Go to **entrepreneurship.glencoe.com** to complete the Technology Today Vocabulary Practice Activity.

ELIMINATING PRODUCTS One reason to eliminate a product is poor sales. Sometimes businesspeople are slow to take such action, thinking they can make the item sell. Not cutting a product can lead to a buildup of inventory and financial losses. By not cutting a poor seller, you may be using sales and/or production efforts unwisely.

Another reason for eliminating products is to simplify your line of goods or services. This allows you to focus on the things you do well. However, you should consider whether a broad range of products is necessary for you to compete.

CHANGING PRODUCTS Changing the style or design of your product can give you a competitive edge. Your changes must be consistent with customer demand. For example, you may decide to make changes to keep in step with current fashions. You may also improve your products by taking advantage of the latest technology. However, changing your product may affect your prices and distribution. Timing, too, must be considered. You want your offerings to be up-to-date, but you do not want to be ahead of the market.

IDENTIFYING NEW USES FOR PRODUCTS Identifying new uses for your product can expand its market or extend its life. One way to find new uses is to monitor how customers use the product. For example, sport utility vehicles, designed for rugged use, have gained acceptance as family vehicles. Sales are now aimed at families, a new market. Another way to find new uses is to conduct research. For example, the maker of Tums®, an antacid, increased sales by marketing the product as a calcium supplement.

CHANGING BRANDS, PACKAGING, OR LABELS If you manufacture products under different brand names, you may want to consolidate them all under one brand. This could help build a brand loyalty among customers. You may choose to sell your own private brand. A **private brand** is a brand that is owned and initiated by a wholesaler or retailer. Large supermarkets often offer a variety of products on their own label.

While You Read

Predict Why might a company choose to stop selling a product?

◄ **EXTREME MAKEOVER**
Changing the layout can improve sales for a business. *What are some of the costs?*

You may want to change packaging and labels to enhance the attractiveness, interest, and salability of your product. You may also change your packaging for environmental reasons. Budget Gourmet® dinners are packaged in molded paper containers. Because many consumers are concerned about the environment, this kind of change could make the product more appealing.

REVISING GUARANTEES AND SERVICE POLICIES To build customer confidence and increase sales, a business can improve or add service policies and guarantees. A **guarantee** is an assurance of the quality of a product. Guarantees and policies can make the difference in a sale, particularly with big-ticket items. Of course, you must be able to provide the additional guaranteed services.

Possible Changes to the Place Strategy

You are most likely to make changes in your ongoing place strategy with regard to location, layout, and availability. To some extent, you may also make changes in your channels of distribution.

IMPROVING LOCATION As your business grows, you may look for ways to improve your location. You may extend it by using kiosks, or stands, on street corners or in malls. With some businesses, you may decide to "take your location to the customer" through mobile units.

You may also want to consider more permanent and substantial changes. You might add outlets or branch operations. You might change your base location to be more accessible to customers. Because these are more permanent steps, they must be coordinated with your plans for growth.

REARRANGING LAYOUT You may also want to rearrange the physical layout of your operation. For retail and some service businesses, this change can enhance sales. Adding or expanding parking or access to your business can do the same. If you are a manufacturer, a wholesaler, or an extractor, you might reorganize how your goods are distributed. This could increase your ability to serve customers and, thus, increase sales.

INCREASING AVAILABILITY Availability is generally the easiest adjustment to make in your place strategy. It can also be the most effective because it allows customers to do business with you.

Assume you have a tutoring service. Presently it is open until 5 P.M. on weekdays. You can increase your availability and business by staying open evenings and Saturdays. Consider another example—you supply food to restaurants. You may change your delivery schedule to better meet the restaurants' needs. Both examples are ways to increase availability.

CHANGING CHANNELS OF DISTRIBUTION The type of business you have and where you are in the channel determine your choices. If you are in a manufacturing business, you have some control over channel decisions. You can look for ways to improve your channel choices. For example, you may decide to use a more direct channel with fewer intermediaries.

Businesses at other points in the channel have more limited options. If you are a retailer or wholesaler, you can look for different product sources. You may look for those sources that deliver more effectively and efficiently. You may also seek alternatives where you do have some control—channels between you and your customers.

While You Read

Connect Think of a local business that has made changes to its place strategy. What were the changes? Did they improve business?

COMPLEMENTARY MERCHANDISE Businesses can strengthen their appeal by offering complementary goods or services. *What are the risks of offering something unrelated?*

While You Read

Question Why are people so important to the success of a business?

Before you make any change in channels, you should look at the new channel, keeping in mind three questions:

- What effect will the new channel have on sales volume and stability?
- What effect will it have on gross profit?
- What effect will it have on operating costs?

Possible Changes to the People Strategy

Major changes in the people strategy may be necessary. Changes may be needed because of shifts in demand, changes in the nature of the business, or growth. If the demand for your goods or services goes down, you may need fewer people. If demand goes up, you may need more people. Your business may go from a people-intensive to a mechanized business. In this case, the size of your workforce will decrease. Qualifications of your workforce will change as well.

As your business grows, human resources responsibilities become more formalized and expand. Team-building responsibilities may shift to others in your organization. In addition, as times change, you must revisit your system of rewards.

Possible Changes to the Price and Promotion Strategies

Price strategy and price strategy revisions are discussed in Chapter 11. Price revision considerations include pricing for profit, reacting to market prices, and revising terms of sale.

Promotion strategy and promotion strategy revisions are discussed in Chapters 12 and 13. Promotion revision considerations include making the most of your advertising dollars, stimulating sales, and planning for the long term.

Revising Your Marketing Plan and Mix

You must consider possible changes in all marketing strategies before making revisions in the marketing plan. As you adjust each of your marketing strategies, you may need to make changes in other strategies. Here is an example:

- **Situation.** You are the owner of a no-frills golf driving range.
- **Change in Product Strategy.** You decide to upgrade your facility by covering the tee areas.
- **Change in Price Strategy.** You adjust your prices to pay for the improvements.
- **Change in Promotion Strategy.** You advertise more to let the golfing public know about your new-and-improved facilities.
- **Change in Place Strategy.** The increase in business that the improvements bring allows you to keep your business open all winter.
- **Change in People Strategy.** The increase in business requires that you hire more employees, including a professional golfing instructor.

Quick Math

A large manufacturer can save 28% by using a different trucking company. The cost of shipping projected for the coming year using the current service is $48,550. How much will the manufacturer save by using a different company?

Ideally, as you change one strategy, you adjust the others. However, in reality, it often does not work that way. Owners are busy with other business activities. As a result, they do not make the changes as quickly as they should. Therefore, they lose out on additional profits.

Reviewing and revising your marketing plan regularly can remedy this situation. You can identify and make strategy changes that should have been made but were not. You can make sure your strategies are consistent with your marketing objectives.

In addition, you should schedule an annual review of your marketing objectives and marketing plan. Such a review sets the stage for longer-term market planning. Once your business is under way, the result of this review may be expansion and revision. You may decide to add **diversification**. This is the process of investing in products or businesses with which you are not currently involved.

Section 10.2 After You Read

Key Concept Review

1. What are the factors to consider for possible changes in product strategy?

2. What are the factors to consider for possible changes in place strategy?

3. Why is it important to review and revise your marketing mix on a regular basis?

Critical Thinking

4. For each of the marketing strategies, develop a review checklist that is appropriate for your business.

Role Play

Situation You are the marketing manager of an auto parts store. Your marketing presentation was a huge success, and the owner of the auto parts store has asked you to meet with him and his partners. They are considering adding a well-known product line that, they believe, will reach a slightly different target market.

Activity Work with a partner to prepare a question-and-answer session on the key considerations for adding the product line. Your partner will play the role of the questioner. You will be responding to questions.

Evaluation You will be evaluated on how well you address these issues:

- Explain if the product is consistent with the store's current business.

- Explain whether the new product line will compete with your current products.

- Evaluate whether the store's resources can be better used in connection with another product line.

Chapter Summary

Section 10.1 Devising a Marketing Plan

A marketing plan gives direction to an entrepreneur's marketing efforts. A successful marketing plan contains objectives, the five Ps, and marketing tactics. The particular combination of the five Ps—product, price, place, promotion, and people—used to reach the target market is called the *marketing mix*. Product strategy deals with goods or services and how they match up with customer needs and expectations. The place, or distribution, strategy deals with how to deliver goods or services to customers. The people strategy deals with assembling, preparing, and maintaining the people who will help you achieve success. Price and promotion strategies are discussed in Chapters 11–13. Marketing tactics are the activities that put the components of the marketing mix into operation and thus carry out the marketing plan.

Section 10.2 Reviewing and Revising the Marketing Plan

A marketing plan must change along with the business environment. As a result, ongoing market research is necessary. Product changes, altering the style or design of a product, changing brands, or revising guarantees must be considered as markets change. When changes occur in place strategy, they often occur in the areas of location, layout, and availability. Shifts in demand, changes in the nature of the business, or growth may make major changes to the people strategy necessary. Reviewing and revising your marketing mix and plan regularly will help you identify and make necessary strategy changes.

Key Terms Review

1. Write a short-term marketing plan for a new product you want to sell. Use at least 15 of the following terms:

marketing plan (p. 206)	product positioning (p. 209)	exclusive distribution (p. 211)
marketing objectives (p. 207)	product mix (p. 209)	marketing tactics (p. 215)
marketing mix (p. 207)	channel of distribution (p. 210)	private brand (p. 220)
brand (p. 208)	intermediaries (p. 210)	guarantee (p. 220)
package (p. 208)	intensive distribution (p. 211)	diversification (p. 223)
label (p. 208)	selective distribution (p. 211)	

Key Concept Review

2. **Identify** the role of marketing objectives in developing a marketing plan. (10.1)
3. **Name** the five marketing strategies that make up the marketing mix. (10.1)
4. **Describe** the part marketing tactics play in the marketing plan. (10.1)
5. **State** the importance of ongoing market research. (10.2)
6. **List** the factors to consider for each strategy when reviewing your marketing mix. (10.2)
7. **Describe** how to update the marketing mix and marketing plan. (10.2)

Critical Thinking

8. Can you prepare a marketing plan before choosing a target market? Explain.
9. Explain the fundamental marketing concepts used by small businesses.
10. Consider the product you selected for the Key Terms Review question. Describe its marketing mix.
11. Research and define the nine marketing functions.
12. Explain how each component of the marketing mix contributes to successful entrepreneurial ventures.
13. There are five economic utilities: form, place, time, possession, and information. Which three were discussed in this chapter? Why were the other two not discussed here?
14. Draw a diagram of the channels of distribution. For each channel, analyze and discuss the different types of businesses in the channel.

Write About It

15. Which one of the five Ps is most critical to the success of your business? Which is the least important? Defend your answers in a paragraph.
16. Choose a product you recently purchased. Compose a memo to your teacher differentiating between its features and benefits.
17. Define the term *product mix* in your own words.
18. Write a one-page report describing how adding a new product might affect your other marketing mix strategies.
19. Outline the channels of distribution for consumer products, industrial products, and service businesses. Explain in two or more paragraphs why different channels are needed.
20. Do the strategies in the marketing mix apply to service businesses? If so, explain in a one-page report how they apply. If not, explain in your report how they should differ for service businesses.

Academic Skills

Math

21. Your boss has asked you to calculate the price of tennis shoes your company is planning to manufacture. Your cost to produce each pair of shoes is $40. Your related overhead and projected profits are $15. If the wholesaler's markup is 50 percent of the cost and the retailer's markup is 100 percent of its cost, what is:

- The manufacturer's price to the wholesaler?
- The wholesaler's price to the retailer?
- The retailer's price to the consumer?

Language Arts

22. Select a product that is marketed specifically to teens. Using a computer or other resources, create new packaging or labeling for the item so it will appeal to a broader market.

Entrepreneurship in Your Community

23. Interview a retail business owner, a wholesale business owner, and a service business owner.

- Ask about the products and services they offer.
- Ask about the distribution methods appropriate for the particular business.

Prepare a report that identifies how the scope of products and services varied based upon type of business.

24. Working in teams of three or four, conduct market research on a product or service sold at school to determine whether possible product or place changes are needed.

- Create and conduct the survey.
- Compile the results.
- Make recommendations in writing to the principal based on your findings.

Ethical Practices

Refusing to Do Business

25. Michelle James was attempting to open a pretzel stand in a small indoor mall. She had arranged to lease space and purchase used equipment. Unfortunately, she could not get the area's lone supplier of pretzel dough to do business with her. The company's position was that because Michelle was not an established business owner, affiliated with a franchise, or experienced, she might not succeed. The supplier further explained that its policy was to service only large orders, but it would not specify an amount. Do you think the supplier's position is unethical or just good business? Explain. As an entrepreneur, how would you deal with this situation? Explain your position.

INTERNET connection

Online Marketing Strategies

You own a wholesale nursery business. You want to add another channel of distribution to your business—direct-to-consumer sales via the Internet.

Connect

Use a search engine or Web directory to conduct research.

- Identify three direct and indirect competitors your online business will face.
- Evaluate online marketing strategies used by the competition.

Application

Use your research to create a one-page outline detailing your competition's Web sites and marketing strategies.

The Electronic Entrepreneur

E-Commerce Development Options

Once you have decided to take the plunge into an e-commerce business, it is time to figure out how your site will be developed. Will you do the coding work yourself, or hire a professional? Will you use an "off-the-shelf" shopping cart package? Many options are available for the e-commerce entrepreneur.

Web Development Services There are many companies that specialize in designing and implementing e-commerce sites. These companies employ Web designers and Web developers. A **Web designer** plans the aesthetic and navigational aspects of a Web site. A **Web developer** programs a Web site from a technical standpoint. Web development services take care of the technical and creative work, leaving you with the task of choosing your products, pricing them, and doing the marketing. However, Web development services can be expensive.

Hosted Services and Software Packages A number of hosted services offer **turnkey**, or preprogrammed and ready-to-operate, e-commerce sites—all you do is plug in your products and descriptions. These involve paying a monthly fee. You can also purchase an e-commerce software package for a one-time fee. In this case, you would need to install and configure the software on your own server or on a hosted domain from an ISP.

Templates Find out how many templates each solution offers. A **template** is a file that establishes the format and appearance of a Web page. Software packages that offer multiple templates offer more visual options for your Web site.

Evaluating Your Options When choosing your e-commerce solution, there are a number of things to keep in mind. Find out if the solution offers secure transactions. Find out if it offers real-time processing, which automatically sends the credit card information to your merchant account. Ease of use, flexibility, and ability to add new features are all important aspects to investigate before making a purchase.

FACT AND IDEA REVIEW

1. What is a web development service?
2. What is a turnkey service?
3. What is a template?
4. What is real-time processing? Why is it useful?

FOR DISCUSSION

5. Which features do you think are most important in developing and choosing an e-commerce solution?

TechTerms

- Web designer
- Web developer
- turnkey
- template

The Price Strategy

CHAPTER OBJECTIVES

When you have completed this chapter, you should be able to:

SECTION 11.1

- Identify factors that affect price strategy.
- Explain the marketing objectives related to pricing.
- Describe the components that go into making price strategy decisions.

SECTION 11.2

- Explain how to carry out a break-even analysis.
- Explain how to apply formulas used in calculating markup and markup percentages.
- Explain how to use markdown formulas to determine sale price.
- Explain how to employ formulas used to compute discounts.
- List considerations for updating the price strategy.

Money Talk

ESTABLISHING INVESTMENT GOALS

What do you hope for when you think about your future? To gather the funds you will need to make your dreams come true, you will have to plan carefully—and practice some discipline along the way.

An investment plan starts with a specific, measurable goal. For example, you may want to save $15,000 to make a down payment on a house within five years of graduating from school.

As you outline your financial goals, ask yourself:

- What will you use the money for?

- How much money do you need to satisfy your goals?

- How will you get the money?

- How long will it take to get the money?

- How much risk are you willing to take?

- Are you willing to make sacrifices to save?

- What will happen if you do not meet your goals?

 Go to **entrepreneurship.glencoe.com** to complete the Standard & Poor's Money Talk Financial Literacy Activity.

PREPARE TO READ

THINK ABOUT THESE QUESTIONS AS YOU READ.

How are prices determined?

What is price strategy?

Why are prices sometimes discounted?

Considering Price Strategy

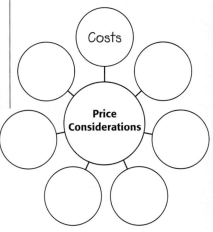
Factors Affecting Price

Setting a price for a good, a service, or an idea is not easy. You must consider costs, expenses, supply and demand, consumer perceptions, the competition, government regulations, and technological trends. Each of these factors can affect the market price.

Costs and Expenses

To stay in business, you must make a profit. That means your prices have to exceed your costs and expenses. Costs and expenses can be fixed or variable. **Fixed** costs and expenses are not subject to change depending on the number of units sold. **Variable** costs and expenses are subject to change depending on the number of units sold.

If you are selling goods, their costs are affected by the pricing structure in the channel of distribution. Each channel member has to make a profit to make handling the goods worthwhile. If you sell magazines, both the publisher and the distributor need to make money. Otherwise, you will not have magazines to sell. Their cost and profit together is your cost.

A business has many types of expenses. These include fixed expenses, such as rent, utilities, and insurance premiums. Examples of variable expenses include the cost of goods or services, sales commissions, delivery charges, and advertising.

Suppose you are selling services (pool cleaning, landscaping, financing) or ideas (self-improvement courses, weight-loss programs, counseling). Your channel and, thus, your pricing structure are much simpler. As Chapter 10 explained, these channels go directly from the producer—the service or idea provider—to the customer. In these cases, the cost is that of the resources that go into providing the service or idea.

Products that include a combination of goods, services, and/or ideas have the same price structure as goods. Products made up of ideas and services have the same direct channel price structure. The price structure of such combinations should reflect the total cost of the goods, services, and ideas that are included in the product.

Supply and Demand

The law of supply and demand also affects price. When the demand for your product is high and supply is low, you can command a high price. When the reverse is true (low demand and high supply), you must set lower prices.

Prices are not always affected by supply and demand. That is because prices reflect the sensitivity of market demand. When customers buy a product regardless of price (gasoline, for example), the demand is inelastic. In contrast, when prices are especially sensitive to demand (gourmet foods or other luxury items), the demand is elastic.

Success Stories

Having a Ball

You have probably seen those brightly colored balls on top of car antennas—everything from alien heads to smiley faces to the American flag. Jason Wall is responsible for many of those balls being there. In 1998 he started the company In-Concept, Inc. and the Web site Antennaballs.com, after seeing how successful the Jack in the Box chain had been at popularizing them. The site now offers dozens of designs, including officially licensed college football helmets, NASCAR helmets and Shrek heads. In-Concept manufactures more than half a million of the balls each month; and in addition to the Web site, it sells them through retail stores, such as AutoZone and Wal-Mart.

CRITICAL THINKING
How did Wall capitalize on an idea that had already been popularized by another company?

@ Go to **entrepreneurship.glencoe.com** to complete the Success Stories Writing Activity.

Consumer Perceptions

The price of your products helps create your image in the minds of customers. Prices set too low can lead customers to believe that your product lacks quality. Prices set too high may turn away customers. Prices set at the high end of a competitive range, however, convey quality and status. Consider the perceptions of your target market in particular. Different target markets have different perceptions and opinions about prices.

Competition

Competition also affects price. When the target market is price conscious, competitors' pricing may determine your pricing. Sometimes businesses choose to charge more than their competitors for a similar product. Businesses can charge higher prices by offering services that add value. Customers usually pay more for personal attention, credit, and warranties.

Government Regulations

Your price strategy may be affected by federal and state laws. The Clayton Act and the Robinson-Patman Act are two federal laws that impact pricing. Both make it illegal for businesses to sell the same product to different customers at different prices. For example, an auto dealer cannot charge a lower price to men than to women. Businesses that do must be able to show that certain conditions exist. For example, one customer may buy a higher volume or lesser quality of products.

To avoid problems, you should always be fair to customers. Familiarize yourself with federal and state laws that address pricing. Be mindful of laws involving price gouging, price fixing, resale price maintenance, unit pricing, and bait-and-switch advertising. **Price gouging** is pricing above the market when no alternative retailer is available. **Price fixing** is an illegal practice in which competing companies agree, formally or informally, to restrict prices within a specified range. **Resale price maintenance** is price fixing imposed by a manufacturer on wholesale or retail resellers of its products to deter price-based competition. **Unit pricing** is the required pricing of goods on the basis of cost per unit of measure, such as pound or ounce, in addition

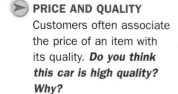

While You Read

Predict What is the best way to avoid legal problems regarding pricing?

PRICE AND QUALITY
Customers often associate the price of an item with its quality. *Do you think this car is high quality? Why?*

to the price per item. **Bait-and-switch** advertising is a deceptive method of selling in which customers, attracted to a store by sale-priced items, are told either that the advertised bargain item is out of stock or is inferior to a higher-priced item that is available.

Technological Trends

The Internet and technological trends affect price strategy. Big bookstores such as Barnes & Noble or Borders were competing with each other in the mid-1990s. At that same time, Amazon.com began changing the way people buy books. Through the Internet, Amazon.com provides customers with easy access to prices, product information, and services. Also, the company saves overhead by not running a store. These savings are passed on to the customer in the form of discount prices. Adapting to technological changes can give you a competitive edge. Not adapting can cause some businesses to become obsolete.

BusinessWeek Case Study

The Price Is Really Right

With a Web-savvy system, companies can figure out just what the market will bear.

It was a midsummer tradition, as enduring as roasting wieners and spitting watermelon seeds. Just after the Fourth of July, retailers all over the U.S., from the strip malls of Florida to the country stores of Maine, slashed prices on bathing suits. This wasn't scientific. But who had the smarts to figure out exactly when the demand for bathing suits would tail off in every region of the country? And who could calculate the exact date when the cost of carrying summer inventory outstripped the profits to be made from it?

It was mostly guesswork, and it bugged Steven Schwartz of clothing chain Casual Male Retail Group Inc. So, as senior vice-president for planning, he looked to Web-based pricing tools to eliminate it. After loading gobs of sales data into the system a year ago, he spotted enormous regional variation. Northeasterners slowed down on bathing suits in July, but Midwesterners kept buying until August. And Sunbelt shoppers

never stopped. While the previous sales system allowed only one chainwide price, Schwartz now had tools—and analysis—to slice and dice prices on all sorts of clothes. "We're doing much better than last year," he says. Gross margins for the chain rose 25% in the nine months ended November, 2002, thanks in part to the new pricing system.

SOURCE: *BUSINESSWEEK*, MARCH 31, 2003; BY FAITH KEENAN

APPLICATION

Use the Internet to conduct research on adaptive pricing. Then use a word-processing application to write a description of adaptive pricing. Describe its features and functionalities.

 Go to **entrepreneurship.glencoe.com** to complete the *BusinessWeek* Case Study Reading Guide Activity.

Pricing Objectives

Before setting prices, you must decide what you want to accomplish through pricing. For new companies, obtaining a return on investment and obtaining market share are the most important goals. Other objectives can be added as the company grows.

Obtaining a Target Return on Investment

A **return on investment** (ROI) is the amount earned as a result of that investment. Targeting a ROI is the practice of setting a price to achieve a specified return. Say you invest $20,000 in productive assets and you want a 20 percent return. The product should be priced to earn an expected profit of $4,000 ($20,000 x 0.20).

Obtaining Market Share

Market share is a business's portion of the total sales generated by all competing companies in a given market. **Figure 11.1** shows that Coffee Express has a 39 percent market share of local coffee shops. If your objective is to attract a percentage of customers who are doing business with competitors, you must set your prices accordingly. If your products are price-sensitive, offering lower prices may work, but remember customer perception. Lower prices may not be necessary or even desirable. You may be better off setting prices higher. You also may be able to gain market share through nonprice competition. Nonprice strategies include product quality, customer service, promotion, and packaging.

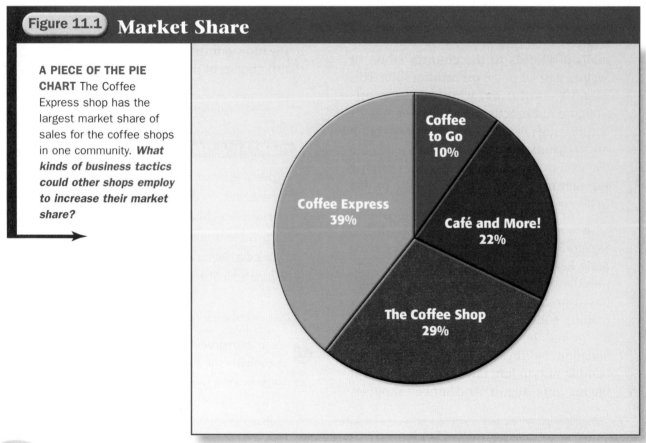

Figure 11.1 **Market Share**

A PIECE OF THE PIE CHART The Coffee Express shop has the largest market share of sales for the coffee shops in one community. *What kinds of business tactics could other shops employ to increase their market share?*

Coffee to Go 10%
Coffee Express 39%
Café and More! 22%
The Coffee Shop 29%

Other Objectives

Additional objectives can include social and ethical considerations. They can also include meeting the competition's prices and establishing an image. During difficult economic times, they might include survival. In industries that depend on price stability, they might include maintaining the status quo.

Pricing Strategy Decisions

To determine a pricing strategy, consider your target market and take these steps:

1. Select a basic approach to pricing (cost-based, demand-based, or competition-based).

2. Determine your pricing policy (flexible-price or one-price).

3. Set a price based on the stage of the product life cycle (introduction, growth, maturity, or decline) using an effective pricing technique (psychological pricing or discount pricing).

Setting a Basic Price

You can use three strategies when setting a basic price for your product. They are cost-based, demand-based, and competition-based pricing. In practice, you may employ a combination of these strategies. If you have a range of products, you may use all three. Regardless, the strategy or strategies you choose must be compatible with your target market and consistent with your pricing objectives.

1. COST-BASED PRICING With a cost-based strategy, you must consider your business costs and your profit objectives. To calculate price using this strategy, figure your cost to make or buy your product. Then figure the related cost of doing business. Finally, add your projected profit margin to arrive at a price. The amount added to your cost to cover expenses and ensure a profit is called your *markup.*

2. DEMAND-BASED PRICING This strategy requires you to find out what customers are willing to pay for your product. You then set the price accordingly. Demand-based pricing is useful only when certain conditions exist. One is when demand for your product is inelastic. Another is when customers believe your product is different from or has greater value than the competition's.

3. COMPETITION-BASED PRICING To determine prices using this strategy, you need to find out what your competitors charge. Then decide whether it is to your advantage to price below, in line with, or above the competition. This strategy does not involve cost or demand. It is only concerned with being competitive.

Pricing Policies

Establishing a pricing policy frees you from making the same pricing decisions over and over again. It also lets employees and customers know what to expect. Two types of pricing policies are flexible-price policy and one-price policy, as illustrated in **Figure 11.2** on page 236.

Figure 11.2　Pricing Policies

PICK A POLICY A basic pricing decision every business must make is to choose between a one-price policy and a flexible-price policy. That choice will determine the pricing decisions that are made. *What negative effects could a flexible pricing policy have on customer relations?*

Flexible-Price Policy

A flexible-price policy is one in which customers pay different prices for the same type or amount of merchandise. Allowing customers to haggle over price can bring customers into a business and may result in sales a business might otherwise lose. Flexible pricing takes into account market conditions, such as increased or decreased demand, and competitors' prices. It allows the business to react to these factors through its prices. Most car dealerships employ a flexible-price policy.

One-Price Policy

A one-price policy is one in which all customers are charged the same price for the goods and services offered for sale. Prices are quoted to customers by means of signs and price tags, and no deviations are permitted. A one-price policy tells customers they are all treated equally. The one-price policy is strongly recommended for service businesses. When customers are allowed to haggle over the value of a service, the price invariably goes down. Most of the retail stores that you are familiar with employ a one-price policy.

Product Life Cycle Pricing

All products move through a four-stage life cycle: introduction, growth, maturity, and decline. To maximize profit, these stages need to be considered when setting prices. Some products move through the stages very quickly. Others spend many years in one stage. For example, the automobile has been in the maturity stage for over 30 years.

STAGE 1: INTRODUCTION In the introduction stage, sales volume is relatively low, marketing costs are high, and profits are low or even negative. Two methods are commonly used when introducing a product—price skimming or penetration pricing. **Price skimming** involves charging a high price to recover costs and maximize profit as quickly as possible. Then the price is dropped when the product is no longer unique. **Penetration pricing** builds sales by charging a low initial price to keep unit costs to customers as low as possible. This approach may discourage competition. Pricing during the growth, maturity, and decline stages are determined by which introduction pricing method (skimming or penetration) was used.

STAGE 2: GROWTH In the growth stage, sales climb rapidly, unit costs are decreasing, the product begins to show a profit, and competitors come into the market. If you use price skimming during the introduction stage, you would lower prices to appeal to price-conscious customers in the growth stage. If you use penetration pricing during the introduction stage, you would make only minor price changes during the growth stage. Other promotions would be used to keep sales high.

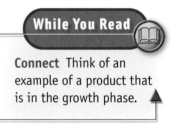

While You Read

Connect Think of an example of a product that is in the growth phase.

STAGE 3: MATURITY The principal goal of the maturity stage is to stretch the life cycle of the product. In this stage, sales begin to slow and profits peak, but profits fall off as competition increases. In order to maintain steady prices, businesses must identify new markets or make product improvements. If the effort is successful, the product will have an extended maturity stage. If not, the product will move into the decline stage.

STAGE 4: DECLINE In the decline stage, sales and profits continue to fall. At this stage, businesses should cut prices to generate sales or clear inventory. It is also helpful to try to reduce manufacturing and promotional costs during the decline stage. Once a product is no longer profitable, it is phased out.

Pricing Techniques

Once you have introduced your new product through penetration pricing or skimming, you need to arrive at a final, more permanent price. The goal is to adjust your prices so they are attractive to buyers. These techniques fall into two broad categories: *psychological pricing* and *discount pricing*.

1. PSYCHOLOGICAL PRICING Psychological pricing refers to pricing techniques that are based on the belief that customers' perceptions of a product are strongly influenced by price. This category of pricing techniques is most often used by retail businesses. It includes prestige pricing, odd/even pricing, price lining, promotional pricing, multiple-unit pricing, and bundle pricing.

Prestige pricing is a pricing technique in which higher-than-average prices are used to suggest status and prestige to the customer. Many customers associate higher prices with higher quality and are willing to pay more for certain goods and services. For example, a shirt that costs $100 suggests exclusiveness, status, and quality.

Odd/even pricing is a pricing technique in which odd numbers, such as $19.99, are employed to suggest bargains. The psychological principle on which the technique is based is that odd numbers convey a bargain image, and even prices, such as $20, suggest higher quality.

Price lining is a pricing technique in which items in a certain category are priced the same. For example, a store may price all of its jeans at $25, $50, and $75. When deciding on price lines, entrepreneurs must be careful to make the price differences great enough to represent low, middle, and high prices for the category of goods being offered for sale.

Promotional pricing is a pricing technique in which lower prices are offered for a limited period of time to stimulate sales. The main characteristic of promotional pricing is that it is temporary—after the promotion ends, prices go back to normal. A fast-food restaurant may promote its new "superburger" for 99 cents "for a limited time only."

Multiple-unit pricing is a pricing technique in which items are priced in multiples, such as 3 items for 99 cents. Pricing items in multiples suggests a bargain. This pricing technique can increase sales volume.

Bundle pricing is a pricing technique in which several complementary products are sold at a single price. The one price is lower than the price would be if the customer purchased each item separately. Computer companies use bundle pricing when they include software in the sale of a computer. Bundle pricing helps businesses sell items that they may not have sold otherwise, which increases their sales and revenue.

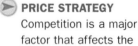 **PRICE STRATEGY**
Competition is a major factor that affects the prices you can charge. *If you were starting up a similar business near this one, where would you set your prices and why?*

M-Commerce

Although e-commerce continues to grow, the next big trend might be m-commerce, or "mobile commerce." The widespread use of high-end cellular phones and PDAs means that people can do their banking, pay bills, or purchase products—all of the crucial things that drive the e-commerce world—even when they are not sitting at their desk.

Cooperative Learning Activity

As a group, think of some potential applications for m-commerce. What are some business uses that will benefit from it?

Go to **entrepreneurship.glencoe.com** to complete the Technology Today Vocabulary Practice Activity.

2. DISCOUNT PRICING Discount pricing offers customers reductions from the regular price. These reductions may encourage customers to buy. Discounts are used by all types of businesses. In some instances, they are basic percentage-off price discounts. In other situations, they are specialized discounts. Specialized discounts include cash, quantity, trade, promotional, or seasonal discounts.

Cash discounts are given to customers for prompt payment. For example, you might see 2/10, n/30 on an invoice. This means the buyer can reduce the bill by 2 percent by paying within 10 days of the invoice. If the bill is not paid within 10 days, the full amount (net) is due within 30 days.

Quantity discounts encourage buyers to order larger quantities than they would ordinarily buy. The buyer gets a reduction in price. The seller reduces selling expenses and may shift part of the storing, shipping, and financing responsibilities to the buyer. Quantity discounts can be cumulative. For example, a buyer of more than $50,000 of materials during a year might be given a 10 percent discount.

Trade discounts are given to distribution-channel members who provide marketing functions for the manufacturer. These discounts are based on the manufacturer's suggested retail price (MSRP) and specify wholesaler and retailer discounts. As an example, a manufacturer might designate a discount relationship of 30–15 percent. This means the retailer takes 30 percent of the manufacturer's list price. The wholesaler keeps 15 percent for handling, storing, and delivering merchandise to the retailer.

Promotional discounts are used when manufacturers want to pay wholesalers or retailers for carrying out promotional activities. The discounts may be given in the price paid for promotional goods or made by a direct cash payment. They may even be in the form of promotional materials supplied by the manufacturer.

While You Read

Question What is a seasonal discount? Think of an example of a product that would be suitable for a seasonal discount.

Seasonal discounts are used for products that have a high seasonal demand. Heavy coats are not in demand in the middle of summer. Short-sleeve shirts are not in demand in the dead of winter. Manufacturers give seasonal discounts to customers who buy them in the off-season. This enables manufacturers to keep operations going throughout the year. It also enables them to shift storage costs to other points in the channel of distribution.

Questions to Ask About Price Decisions

The following questions serve as a guide for completing your price strategy. Keep your target market in mind as you make your decisions.

- What motivates customers who will buy my product? Are they price sensitive? Are they status conscious?
- How much will my customers be willing and able to buy at what prices?
- How will outside factors affect my price strategy?
- What will my price objectives be?
- What will my primary price strategy be for setting basic price? What will my secondary strategy be (if any)?
- Should I adopt a flexible or one-price policy?
- Where will my products be in the product life cycle?
- What pricing techniques are best for my type of business?

Section 11.1 After You Read

Key Concept Review

1. What are some factors that affect price?
2. What pricing objectives are most important to a new business?
3. Is it possible to have more than one basic pricing strategy?

Critical Thinking

4. Imagine you must draft a preliminary price strategy for your proposed business. What are the key objectives of your pricing strategies? Explain.

Role Play

Situation You and a friend run a house-cleaning service. You charge $45 per house. Recently, your client tried to haggle with you over the price, offering only $35.

Activity With a classmate, role-play a discussion between the entrepreneur and the customer.

Evaluation You will be evaluated on how well you role-play these tasks:

- Explain why you believe your price is a fair price.
- Defend your one-price policy.
- Describe what you can do to ensure your clients remain happy with both your service and your price.

Calculating and Revising Prices

Break-Even Analysis

The **break-even point** is the point at which the gain from an economic activity equals the costs incurred in pursuing it. It is reached when sales equal the costs and expenses of making or distributing a product. Break-even analysis does not tell you what price you should charge for a product. It does, however, give you an idea of the number of units you must sell at various prices to make a profit.

To calculate the break-even point, you divide fixed costs by the selling price minus your variable costs. Fixed costs, such as rent and insurance, do not change with the number of units produced or sold. Variable costs, such as the cost of goods or services and advertising, do change with the number of units sold. **Selling price** is the actual or projected price per unit.

$$\frac{\text{FIXED COST}}{\text{UNIT SELLING PRICE} - \text{VARIABLE COSTS}} = \text{BREAK-EVEN POINT (UNITS)}$$

For example, a board game manufacturer is considering selling a new product for $10 per unit. The cost per unit will be $6.50. To produce the game, the manufacturer must buy a new piece of equipment costing $7,000. How many units must be sold at $10 for the manufacturer to break even?

$$\frac{\$7,000}{\$10.00 - \$6.50} = \textbf{2,000 UNITS}$$

The manufacturer is also considering entering the market with a selling price of $12. She believes this would enable her to recover her costs quickly. 1167 units would have to be sold at $12 to break even. (Note: If your calculation includes a partial unit, round up to arrive at the break-even point.)

Break-even analysis has other applications. You can determine how many units it will take to break even and reach a profit target. You can determine how many dollars in sales it will take to break even. In addition, you can calculate how many units it will take to break even on an investment.

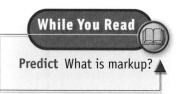

While You Read

Predict What is markup?

Markup

Businesses that purchase or manufacture goods for resale use markup pricing based on the cost of the item. **Markup** is the amount added to the cost of an item to cover expenses and ensure a profit. Businesses selling services or ideas use cost-plus pricing. Here markup consists of the costs and related expenses of the job plus a planned profit. In each case, the floor for estimating profit is the total of the costs and expenses. The ceiling is the highest price customers will pay. The business owner must decide what price point is best for his or her circumstances and target market. The difference between that point and the floor is the projected profit.

To illustrate a manufacturer's markup, suppose it costs $5 to make a fancy ballpoint pen ($3 for the casing and $2 for the ink refill). The manufacturer must charge more than $5 to make a profit. If the manufacturer marks up the cost by $2, the cost and markup are added to make a price of $7. The total of the cost and markup is the selling price.

COST	+	MARKUP	=	PRICE
$5	+	$2	=	$7

Once you understand the relationship among these items, you can compute any one figure if you know the other two. For example, if you know the price and the markup, you can figure the cost:

PRICE	−	MARKUP	=	COST
$7	−	$2	=	$5

If you know the price and the cost, you can determine the markup:

PRICE	−	COST	=	MARKUP
$7	−	$5	=	$2

◀ **LOW PRICES!** Suppose a bicycle shop has a sale in which $600 bikes are marked down 40 percent. *What is the sale price?*

To convert that figure to a percentage, use the following formula:

$$\frac{\text{MARKUP}}{\text{COST}} = \text{PERCENTAGE MARKUP ON COST}$$

$$\frac{\$2}{\$5} = 0.40 \text{ OR } 40 \text{ PERCENT}$$

The $2 markup represents a 40 percent markup on cost.

You can also calculate markups as a percentage of selling price. This is the approach used most frequently by retailers. The formula is the same except selling price is substituted for cost. The following example shows that the dollar markup on the pen is the same, but the percentage is different.

$$\frac{\text{MARKUP}}{\text{SELLING PRICE}} = \text{PERCENTAGE MARKUP ON SELLING PRICE}$$

$$\frac{\$2}{\$7} = 0.285 \text{ OR } 0.29 \text{ PERCENT}$$

As a rule, business owners do not figure markup on an item-by-item basis. Instead, they decide on a standard markup or percentage of markup. One way they do this is to use the average markup for their industry. Another way is to match their competitors' markup. They can also do individual calculations, such as those just shown, and apply them to all of their products.

Once a percentage has been determined, it can be applied to any cost figure to arrive at a price. Assume, for example, a jeweler marks up his merchandise 95 percent on cost. If the jeweler has a bracelet that cost $25, the markup would be found by multiplying $25 by 95 percent. The $23.75 markup would be added to the $25.00 cost to get a selling price of $48.75.

Service businesses that provide products (for example, food service) may also use a standard markup. Other businesses that provide the same service repeatedly (for example, physicians) can assume stable costs and a pre-set profit. However, businesses that offer contracted services or ideas do not have a standard cost and profit that applies to all situations. These companies often obtain their customers through competitive estimates, bids, or proposals. Consequently, they must stay abreast of changes in industry costs and rates. This information is then used to cost out individual jobs and projects.

Markdown

To reduce inventory, businesses sometimes mark down their merchandise. By lowering their prices a certain percentage, they tempt shoppers to buy. In other words, they have a sale.

Suppose a footwear store has a few pairs of $105 basketball shoes that are not selling. To encourage sales, the manager decides to mark them down by 30 percent. First, she determines the **markdown**, the amount of money taken from the original price:

PRICE	×	MARKDOWN PERCENTAGE	=	$ MARKDOWN
$105	×	0.30	=	$31.50

Then she computes the sale price:

PRICE	−	MARKDOWN	=	SALE PRICE
$105	−	$31.50	=	$73.50

Discounts

A discount is a reduction in price to the customer. Your customer might be another business in the channel of distribution, or it might be the final consumer. In all cases, the basic procedure requires two steps. First, you figure the dollar amount of the discount by multiplying the price by the discount percentage. Then you subtract the discount from the price to get the amount the customer actually pays.

Assume a golf pro shop is overstocked on starter sets of clubs. To move the $200 sets, a 20 percent discount is implemented. The discount price is calculated by applying the following steps:

1. PRICE	×	DISCOUNT PERCENTAGE	=	DISCOUNT DOLLARS
$200	×	0.20	=	$40

2. PRICE	−	DISCOUNT DOLLARS	=	DISCOUNTED PRICE
$200	−	$40	=	$160

Although the calculation is the same, some discounts involve additional steps. Cash discounts, described on page 239, are stated in terms. In the example 2/10, n/30, the only discount calculation is the first number (2 percent). The other numbers identify when payment is due—with and without the discount. Trade discounts are often quoted in a series. In the example on page 239, the discount was 30 percent and 15 percent for retailers and wholesalers, respectively. These series of discounts are calculated in sequence.

Thus, if the manufacturer's list price is $100, in the example, the calculation is as follows:

RETAILER'S DISCOUNT	$100	×	0.30	=	$30
COST TO RETAILER	$100	−	$30	=	$70
WHOLESALER'S DISCOUNT	$70	×	0.15	=	$10.50
COST TO WHOLESALER	$70	−	$10.50	=	$59.50

Note that in a series discount, the wholesaler's discount is based on the retailer's discount, not the list price.

Issues in Entrepreneurship

GENDER PRICING

Businesses commonly offer special pricing. Examples include ladies' nights at car washes and ballparks, discounts for single moms at children's clothing stores, discounts for men on Father's Day, and higher prices for women's clothing at dry cleaners. These pricing differences are accepted and expected by most customers and businesspeople.

Now these practices are being challenged as discriminatory pricing. Businesses using such discounts defend them as being an important tool in attracting customers. Businesses also say they do a lot of social good and cause no harm. Businesses charging higher prices based on gender say the difference is in the amount of extra service required.

Thinking Critically

What changes could be made in the above examples to eliminate possible gender discrimination?

 Go to **entrepreneurship.glencoe.com** to complete the Issues in Entrepreneurship Research Activity.

While You Read

Question What are three changes that can be made to a business's pricing strategy?

Possible Changes to Pricing Strategy

Developing a pricing strategy and establishing prices are complex processes. Nonetheless, changes in the business environment may require immediate action.

It is important to review your pricing objectives and strategy regularly. Your review should focus on price strategies, pricing policies, shifts in product life cycle, and pricing techniques. You should also consider the overall effectiveness of your price strategy. Where necessary, you should revise, add, and/or delete objectives. Adjustments to price strategy should reflect any changes in objectives. Changing your price strategy may affect other marketing objectives and strategies. If changes are made, you may need to adjust your marketing plan, too.

Adjusting Prices to Maximize Profit

Profit or loss is determined by the difference between your selling price and your costs. Eventually this fact will cause you to consider adjusting prices to increase profits. That could mean increasing prices. It could also mean lowering prices to increase sales volume. Before you do either, ask yourself two questions:

1. **Are your products' prices elastic or inelastic?** If the price is elastic, a small change in price may cause a significant change in demand. If the price is inelastic, changing the price will have little or no effect on demand.

2. **What are your competitors' prices?** Whether you raise or lower the price, you still want it to relate to the competition's price in a way that benefits you.

THE IMPORTANCE OF PRICING Companies spend a lot of time figuring out how to price their products and services. *Why is devising suitable pricing strategies the most critical decision a company can make?*

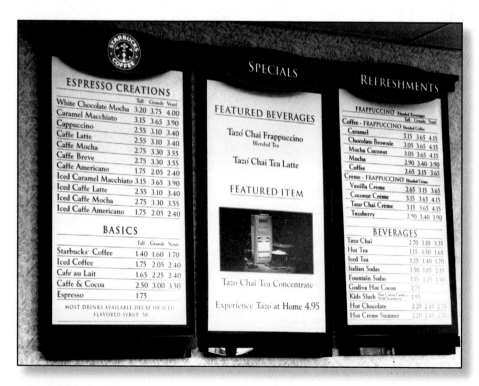

Reacting to Market Prices

As part of ongoing market research, keep an eye on current market prices for your products. If you are in a competitive market and prices fall, you can lose customers quickly if you do not lower prices. If prices are on the rise, raising prices is equally important to the financial health of your business.

Occasionally special market circumstances call for a temporary price increase. When a national convention comes to town, tourists arrive, spend money on souvenirs, and eat out. Natural disasters also increase demand for goods and services. During floods, hurricanes, and other emergencies, people buy provisions and pay for repair work. These cases require a balance between business responsibility and social responsibility.

Revising Terms of Sale

Another way to change your pricing strategy is to revise the terms of sale. You can change your credit policies or introduce trade, quantity, or cash discounts. You might offer leasing or arrange financing for customers with an outside lender. Whether any of these options is useful to you depends on the nature of your business.

Section 11.2 After You Read

Key Concept Review

1. What is the formula for calculating the break-even point?

2. What are the formulas for calculating markup and markdown?

3. What two factors should be considered when adjusting prices to maximize profit?

Critical Thinking

4. Describe the purpose of each of the steps when reviewing and revising pricing objectives and price strategy.

Role Play

Situation You and a partner co-own a popular retail sporting goods store. Yesterday your city's NFL team won the conference title, so it will be going to the Super Bowl. You carry a large supply of official team merchandise. In addition, you just special-ordered "Super Bowl Champion" merchandise.

Activity Role-play a conversation between you and your partner about the business's approach to setting prices for the special merchandise.

Evaluation You will be evaluated on how well you address these issues:

- Detail the pricing for team merchandise prior to the Super Bowl.

- Describe the immediate price changes you will make if your team wins.

- Describe how you will price the special-ordered merchandise if your team wins.

- Explain the duration of the price changes.

Chapter Summary

Section 11.1 Price Strategy Considerations

To develop an effective price strategy, you must consider costs, expenses, supply and demand, consumer perceptions, the competition, government regulations, and technological trends. Then, you must determine your pricing objectives. Marketing objectives related to pricing include obtaining a target return on investment and obtaining market share. Finally, you must make price strategy decisions. You must decide whether to use cost-based, demand-based, or competition-based pricing; choose a flexible-price policy or one-price policy; consider the stage of the product life cycle; and choose a pricing technique—psychological pricing or discount pricing.

Section 11.2 Calculating and Revising Prices

A break-even analysis provides the number of units that have to be sold in order to break even on the fixed costs at various prices. Markup is the amount added to the cost of an item to cover expenses and ensure a profit. To reduce inventory, businesses sometimes mark down their merchandise. Markdown is the amount of money taken from the original price. A discount is a reduction in price to the customer. You may adjust prices to maximize profit or react to market prices. Another way to change your pricing strategy is to revise the terms of sale. It is important to regularly review your pricing objectives, pricing strategies, pricing policies, shifts in product life cycle, and pricing techniques. Adjustments to price strategy should reflect any changes in pricing objectives. Changing your price strategy may affect other marketing objectives and strategies. If changes are made, you may need to adjust your marketing plan, too.

Key Terms Review

1. Define each of the terms and give real examples of each, such as products, advertisements, and news articles.

fixed (p. 230)

variable (p. 230)

price gouging (p. 232)

price fixing (p. 232)

resale price maintenance (p. 232)

unit pricing (p. 232)

bait-and-switch (p. 233)

return on investment (p. 234)

price skimming (p. 237)

penetration pricing (p. 237)

psychological pricing (p. 237)

prestige pricing (p. 238)

odd/even pricing(p. 238)

price lining (p. 238)

promotional pricing (p. 238)

multiple-unit pricing (p. 238)

bundle pricing (p. 238)

discount pricing (p. 239)

break-even point (p. 241)

selling price (p. 241)

markup (p. 242)

markdown (p. 244)

Key Concept Review

2. **Identify** factors that affect price strategy. (11.1)
3. **Explain** the marketing objectives related to pricing. (11.1)
4. **Describe** the components that go into making price strategy decisions. (11.1)
5. **Explain** how to carry out a break-even analysis. (11.2)
6. **Explain** how to apply formulas used in calculating markup and markup percentages. (11.2)
7. **Explain** how to use markdown formulas to determine sale price. (11.2)
8. **Explain** how to employ formulas used to compute discounts. (11.2)
9. **List** considerations for updating the price strategy. (11.2)

Critical Thinking

10. Which strategy for setting basic price is the best under what circumstances? Why?
11. Do you believe that a higher price suggests quality and prestige? Explain your answer and give examples.
12. Compare and contrast psychological pricing with discount pricing.
13. If you were going to introduce a new perfume into the market, would you use price skimming or penetration pricing as your strategy? Defend your answer.
14. How are pricing objectives related to marketing objectives?
15. Differentiate trade discounts from other discounts.

Write About It

16. In an e-mail or memo to your teacher, describe the importance of pricing strategy.
17. Explain how pricing policies and pricing strategies help businesses meet pricing objectives. Write your answer in a couple of paragraphs.
18. In a memo to a classmate, communicate the differences between pricing structures for goods, services, and ideas.
19. If you were operating in a system of pure competition, prices would be dictated entirely by supply and demand. You would have no control over the price of your products. If you charged higher prices, people would not buy your products. If you charged less, you would lose sales volume and profits. In a journal entry to yourself, write what you could do to command a higher price for your products in that situation.
20. Create a chart to compare and contrast pricing policies.

Academic Skills

Math

21. Otis pays $34 for a poodle he plans to sell in his pet store for $103. What is the percentage markup on the cost of this dog? Three months later Otis still has not sold the poodle. He decides to mark down the price 25 percent. What will the poodle sell for now?

Language Arts

22. Julia is a motivational speaker. Today she was asked to speak at a student organization's state conference. Her travel expense will be $80 each way. Lodging will be $120. Meals will add up to $40. In addition, she figures 20 hours at $20 an hour for her preparation. She will also spend $100 for visual aids. For conferences of this type and size, the typical fee is between $1,200 and $1,500.

Write one or more paragraphs about Julia's costs and expenses. Where should she set her price? What will be her planned profit?

Entrepreneurship in Your Community

23. Choose a product or service that you might like to sell. Develop a pricing strategy and include the basic price strategy you will use, the type of price policy you will implement, the pricing techniques you will employ, and the cost and break-even point. Justify your decisions.

24. If you are employed, choose a product sold by your company and determine the pricing structure at each point in the channel of distribution, the pricing strategy utilized by the company, the stage in the life cycle of the product, and any recent price changes and the reasons they were made. If you are not employed, interview a local businessperson to obtain the same information for a selected product.

Ethical Practices

Pricing Ethics

25. A Fortune 500 company markets contact lenses under three different brand names. Presumably the lenses are priced differently according to their use. Daily wear lenses cost about $250 a year. Frequent replacement lenses cost around $350; disposables, $400 to $500. According to a *BusinessWeek* report, the lenses are identical; only the packaging is different. The company admits the products are the same. It maintains, however, that eye specialists determine how long the lenses can be worn and what the price will be.

Is the company's practice ethical? Why or why not?

INTERNET *connection*

Research Pricing Strategies

You own a retail camera shop in your town. The market is very competitive.

Connect

Use a search engine or Web directory to find the following information:

- Competitors in your local market
- Internet competitors
- Industry trends that might affect your price strategy

Application

Use a pricing search engine to identify the range of prices for a particular type of camera. Use a spreadsheet program to document the retail and online places where the camera can be purchased and the price. Then write a report that explains the results of your pricing research. Include charts that illustrate your results. Conclude your report by setting a retail price and an online price for the camera.

The Electronic Entrepreneur

E-Commerce Payment Methods

After you have created an inviting environment for shoppers and they have selected an item they would like to buy, you will want to be sure they can easily and quickly pay for their purchase. The checkout process should be flexible, affordable, and secure for the buyer and the seller. E-tailers offer a variety of ways in which consumers can pay for their online purchases.

Credit Cards Approximately 95 percent of all purchases on the Internet are paid for using credit cards. To provide this service, you will need a merchant account. A **merchant account** is a bank account that enables a merchant to receive the proceeds of credit card purchases.

Debit Cards A **debit card** is a card issued by a financial institution that can be used as an alternative to cash. When purchases are made with a debit card, the funds are withdrawn directly from the purchaser's checking or savings account at a bank. Debit cards can only be used to spend the money in the bank.

E-Cash E-cash is a legal form of electronic money transfer used in e-commerce and transacted via the Internet. When you place an order on a merchant's Web site and use e-cash for the payment, the merchant securely transfers your order information over the Internet to your bank to request transaction authorization. One popular e-cash service is Paypal.

Smart Cards A **smart card** is an electronic prepaid cash card that includes a computer chip that can store data. E-cash can be stored on smart cards and used to make purchases or make financial transactions over the Internet. Smart cards are usually sold at banks and are exchanged at face value.

E-Wallet An **e-wallet** is a software application that stores a customer's data for easy retrieval during online purchases. The e-wallet encrypts your personal information so that it is secure. An e-wallet user can make purchases across a variety of Web sites without having to reenter information, such as name, address, and credit card number.

FACT AND IDEA REVIEW

1. Why is the selection of payment methods so important when designing an e-commerce site?
2. What is the chief difference between a credit and a debit card?
3. What is a merchant account, and why is it important?
4. Why are smart cards beneficial? Can you think of any downsides to using a smart card?

FOR DISCUSSION

5. Why do you think credit cards are the most widely used method of paying for purchases on the Internet?

TechTerms

- merchant account
- debit card
- e-cash
- smart card
- e-wallet

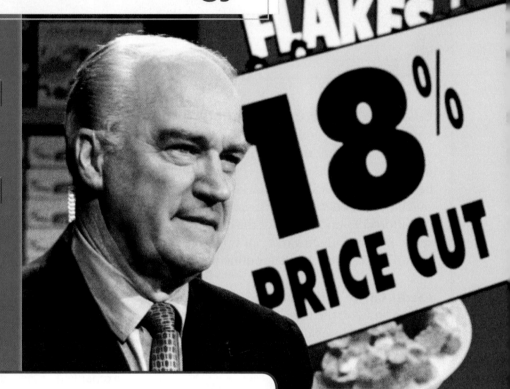

Chapter 12

The Promotion Strategy

CHAPTER OBJECTIVES

When you have completed this chapter, you should be able to:

SECTION 12.1

- Explain the role of the promotion strategy.
- Explain how to formulate promotional plans.
- Describe considerations for putting together a promotional mix.
- Describe the elements of a promotional mix.

SECTION 12.2

- Describe how to determine promotional costs for a start-up business.
- Describe approaches to implementing your promotion strategy.
- Discuss options for short-term changes in your promotion strategy.
- Name considerations for updating the promotion strategy.

THE VALUE OF LONG-TERM INVESTMENT PROGRAMS

Many people do not start investing because they have only a small amount of money. Others think that they are too young to start. Do not let your bank account balance or your age stop you.

Even small amounts add up because of the time value of money, that is the increase in an amount of money as a result of interest or dividends earned. Waiting just a year to begin your investment program can result in much lower returns in later years. The sooner you can begin your investment program, the better.

The higher the rate of return and the longer the time period, the more your money will grow. Also, to achieve the highest possible growth, you will need to continue to add money to your investments on a regular basis.

 Go to **entrepreneurship.glencoe.com** to complete the Standard & Poor's Money Talk Financial Literacy Activity.

PREPARE TO READ

THINK ABOUT THESE QUESTIONS AS YOU READ.

What is the role of promotion?

How do businesses design and carry out promotional plans?

Developing a Promotion Strategy

GET READY TO READ

KEY TERMS
- image
- preselling
- campaign
- promotional mix
- advertising
- specialty item
- publicity
- news release
- public relations
- premium
- rebate
- sweepstakes

KEY CONCEPTS
- The Role of Promotion Strategy
- Drawing Up Promotional Plans
- Selecting a Promotional Mix
- The Elements of the Promotional Mix

THE MAIN IDEA
The promotion strategy is the most visible marketing strategy. It is designed to get the attention of prospective customers and convince them to buy from you.

READING ORGANIZER
Draw the reading organizer on a separate piece of paper. As you read, fill in the chart with the four promotional elements.

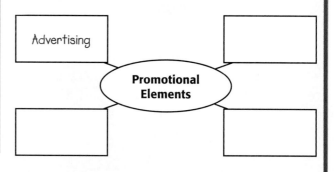

Advertising

Promotional Elements

The Role of Promotion Strategy

Promotion is communication intended to persuade, inform, or remind a target market about a business or its products. Businesses use product promotion to urge potential customers to buy from them instead of competitors. Businesses use institutional promotion to maintain positive relationships between themselves and various groups—including consumer and environmental groups.

The promotion strategy of a business coordinates all aspects of a product and institutional promotion. It involves planning, determining the right mix, and selecting specific activities.

Drawing Up Promotional Plans

As a new business owner, you need two kinds of promotional plans. To start, you need a plan to lay the groundwork for your opening. You need a second plan to support your operation once it is under way.

ENDORSEMENTS AND TESTIMONIALS

Advertisements built around endorsements and testimonials are effective attention getters. An endorsement is a statement of approval of a product, service or idea made by an individual or organization speaking on behalf of an advertiser. In these ads, the featured consumer, expert, or celebrity describes his or her positive experience with the product. Then the person suggests that you buy it. Despite skepticism about the honesty of the ads, they are effective in getting results.

Think Critically

As an entrepreneur, what steps can you take to make sure that endorsements and testimonials are believable?

 Go to **entrepreneurship.glencoe.com** to complete the Issues in Entrepreneurship Research Activity.

Preopening Plan

You need to ensure that money is coming in as soon as you open your doors. To do that, you must promote your business beforehand. This is called a *preopening plan*. Such a plan usually includes the following objectives:

- **Establish a positive image.** Your company's **image** is the impression people have of your company. It is, in effect, your company's personality. As such, it sets the tone for the implementation of your other objectives and your promotional plan.

- **Let potential customers know you are opening for business.** Timing is an important factor in your preopening plan. A good rule is to begin your promotion at least six weeks prior to opening. Promotional efforts should intensify as you near your opening date.

- **Bring in customers or have them contact your business.** In some types of businesses, preopening efforts should be capped off with a grand opening. In others, a party or reception for prospective customers is appropriate.

- **Interest customers in your new company and your products.** Make doing business with you an appealing option.

Ongoing Plan

Once your business has opened, what is the next step? You need an ongoing promotional plan to help you maintain and build sales. Some objectives for this plan parallel your preopening objectives. For example, you must maintain the positive image you have established. Other objectives, however, are new. They are added to help you presell your goods or services.

Preselling is influencing potential customers to buy before contact is actually made. Objectives for ongoing promotional plans usually include:

- Explaining major features and benefits of your products

- Communicating information about sales

- Clearing up customers' questions and concerns

- Introducing new goods or services

The length of your ongoing plan depends on your business. Promotional plans may be seasonal (every six months), quarterly, monthly, or weekly. When shorter plans (weekly or monthly) are used, they are usually based on quarterly or seasonal plans. Once the planning cycle is established, you should continually update promotional plans on that same basis.

For your new business, start with quarterly or seasonal plans. Then rough out monthly plans to estimate your promotional costs.

Promotional Plan Format

You can use the same format for your preopening and ongoing plans. Both can be organized around independent activities or a campaign of related activities or a combination of the two. A **campaign** is a series of related promotional activities with a similar theme. For each activity in your promotional plans, you should provide certain information. Include the following:

- Brief description

- Specific media placement

- Submit dates

- Scheduled date of run or release

- Number of runs, copies, or items

- Costs

- Rationale and other pertinent notes

SALE! On-site signage is an effective promotion technique. *What does this sign communicate?*

Selecting a Promotional Mix

A **promotional mix** is the combination of different promotional elements that a company uses to reach and influence potential customers. The exact mix varies considerably. One reason is because different types of businesses have different promotional needs. For example, a manufacturer of exercise equipment might use a television infomercial along with a call center. A produce store might use local newspapers to advertise specials and lighted signs to attract customers. A lawn service might use flyers and word of mouth to promote its work.

Even in the same type of business, promotional mixes vary greatly. Consider the cosmetics field. Revlon concentrates heavily on advertising, while Avon focuses on personal selling.

You do not need to use all of the major elements—advertising, sales promotion, publicity, and personal selling—in your promotional mix. You should, however, coordinate the promotional elements that you do use. Without coordination, your efforts at communicating to your target market may not be effective or efficient. When customers do not receive your message, they can not respond. When promoted items are not available or salespeople not informed, sales are lost and customers are dissatisfied. In addition, misused promotional dollars are lost.

The following considerations provide general guidelines for allocating promotional efforts and for spending among the elements.

- **Target market.** You must match your promotional option to your target market. For example, a manufacturer sells heavy equipment to the construction market. Its promotional mix must emphasize personal selling. Pull-up diapers, sold to parents, depend more on effective advertising.

- **Product value.** Most companies that sell low-value products, such as soap, soft drinks, and candy, cannot afford to emphasize personal selling. Instead, they use advertising and sales promotion. High-ticket items such as real estate and automobiles rely heavily on personal selling.

- **Promotional channels.** Products have established lines of communication the same way they have established channels of distribution. For example, when people want to know what is playing at the movie theater, where do they look? Most likely, in the newspaper. Finding new promotional channels for your products might provide an edge. However, existing channels are usually very effective in reaching the intended market.

- **Time frame.** Advertising is often needed in advance of new products, upcoming seasons, and sales. Advertising can highlight personal assistance. Postsale advertising can help customers confirm their decision to buy.

- **Cost.** You need to decide what combination of activities will give you the best results for your money. For most, but not all, businesses, you determine the advertising or personal selling budget first. After that decision is made, you determine the level of sales promotion and publicity efforts.

The Elements of the Promotional Mix

This section distinguishes between the elements of the promotional mix. It also describes the activities (or methods) within each of the elements and identifies their advantages and disadvantages. The breakdown helps you make decisions about promotion choices when you are putting together your promotional mix.

Advertising

Advertising is the paid nonpersonal presentation of ideas, goods, or services. It is directed toward a mass audience by an identified sponsor. There are two types of traditional advertising media—print and broadcast. Print media include newspapers, magazines, direct mail, outdoor advertising, directories, and transit advertising. Television, radio, and the Internet are examples of broadcast media.

NEWSPAPERS In the United States, most businesses spend about one-fourth of their advertising dollars on newspaper ads. Newspaper advertising can be tailored to the local community. Newspapers can reach nearly everyone in a target area. Also, ads can be placed on short notice. They generate immediate sales and cost relatively little.

Newspaper ads also have disadvantages. Not everyone who sees an ad is interested in the product. Newspaper ads also have a short life span.

You can offset some of the disadvantages. For example, you can advertise in newspapers with narrowly defined readerships. You can also choose to run your ads at specific times and in specific sections of newspapers.

MAGAZINES By advertising in general-interest magazines such as *People* and *Time,* a business can reach a large national audience. For a new business, this can be very costly. It can be less expensive to advertise in a regional edition. Specialty magazines, such as *Vogue, PC World,* and *Sports Illustrated,* can supply information that describes their readers. This simplifies your task of targeting a specific market. Trade magazines provide a similar opportunity for business-to-business advertisers.

Magazine ads are usually more expensive than newspaper ads because magazines have a longer life. An example of a rate sheet for a small magazine is shown in **Figure 12.1.** Ad files and artwork may be required six to eight weeks before publication.

DIRECT MAIL Direct mail advertisements are sent directly to the homes and businesses of potential customers. Direct mail includes announcements of grocery store specials, letters offering credit cards, and mail-order catalogs.

This promotional method allows you to cover a wide geographic territory and direct your mailings to a specific target market. A restaurant may send coupons to residents within a five-mile radius. A mail-order sports collectibles store may send catalogs to basketball fans across the country. You can purchase mailing lists of people with specific interests or backgrounds.

Direct mail does have limitations. Most significantly, these ads are often thrown away without being opened, let alone read. A second drawback is the cost of printing and postage.

Write About It

Make a list of your 5 favorite magazines. Then find out if the magazines provide information about their subscribers to their advertisers. Many magazines list this information on their Web sites. Write a description of each magazine's target market, then evaluate whether you fit the target market profile of each.

Figure 12.1 **2003/2004 Advertising Rates**

2003/2004 Advertising Rates

SOUTH AMERICAN EXPLORER

The quarterly magazine of the South American Explorers Club is circulated to club members in select retail outlets. The South American Explorer offers its advertisers a unique audience:

- ◆ Circulation, autumn 2003: 8,000 copies
- ◆ 79 percent of members earn more than $25,000 per year; 46 percent earn $50,000 or more per year
- ◆ 85 percent of members are college-educated; 42 percent have a master's or doctorate degree
- ◆ 82 percent of members purchase goods and services advertised in the *South American Explorer*
- ◆ 57 percent of readers are professionals

Display Ad Rates

Size	B&W	Color	Depth/Width
Full page	$850	$1,065	$9½″ × 7¼″
1/2	$430	$535	$4¾″ × 7¼″
1/3	$300	$380	$9½″ × 2¼″
1/4	$230	$290	$2¼″ × 7¼″
1/6	$160	N/A	$2¼″ × 4½″
1/8	$120	N/A	$3½″ × 2¼″
1/12	$90	N/A	$2¼″ × 2¼″
1/16	$70	N/A	$2¼″ × 1¾″
1/32	$45	N/A	$2¼″ × 1″

10% discount for multiple insertions
15% agency commission

THE PRICE OF ADVERTISING Newspapers, magazines, and other media prepare printed summaries of their advertising rates and mail them to prospective advertisers on request. *According to this chart, how much would it cost to run two quarter-page color ads?*

OUTDOOR ADVERTISING The advantage of outdoor displays is that they expose their message to large numbers of people. This category includes billboards, painted signs, and neon displays. It also includes small movable signs. On the sidewalk outside its entrance, a café may put up a sign listing its daily specials. Unfortunately, after the first few viewings, people often ignore outdoor displays. In addition, some communities restrict their use.

DIRECTORIES The yellow pages of the telephone directory are a relatively inexpensive form of advertising. Telephone books are also long-lasting because potential customers refer to them for a full year. The downside is that you can not update or make changes to your ad until the next printing.

TRANSIT ADVERTISING Advertising placed in public transportation has an obvious and unique advantage. It reaches a captive audience. Reading advertisements may be the only way for riders on a bus, subway, or train to pass time. Advertisements placed on the outside of buses serve as billboards that travel the streets of a city. Naturally, these forms of advertising are limited to areas that have public transportation.

While You Read

Connect Think of one example of outdoor advertising that you have seen in your community. What do you think was its target market? Did it influence you to purchase a product?

OTHER PRINT MEDIA A **specialty item** is a giveaway such as a pen, cap, or T-shirt printed with a business name or logo. Such items serve as a reminder of your business. Suppose your construction business hands out message pads that feature your company name, address, and phone number. If someone has a message pad, he or she can easily contact you about a possible job.

There is no guarantee, however, that your specialty items will fall into the hands of potential customers. Also, you probably will not be able to distribute the items to a wide area.

TELEVISION Television, a form of broadcast media, is the leader in national advertising. Its main advantage is that people can see your product as well as hear your message. It can also be used to reach audiences of various sizes. These include selected major market areas as well as national audiences. It can even be used to reach small local markets through cable channels.

Cost is the biggest obstacle to the use of television advertising. Large businesses may spend millions of dollars on major ad campaigns. Buying a spot of airtime can also be expensive. The prime-time hours of 7 P.M. to 11 P.M. are the most costly. A spot during the Super Bowl can cost millions.

RADIO Radio is an effective and economical way to reach a lot of customers. It allows advertisers to target a geographic area and an audience. Radio stations can tell you how their listener demographics match up with your target market.

As with television, rates for radio advertising vary according to the time of day. Prime-time hours for radio are usually during the early morning and the late afternoon. This is when most people are driving to and from work.

There are disadvantages to radio advertising. Radio advertisements have a short life-span. Also, the lack of visual involvement causes some listeners to become distracted and miss some or all of the message.

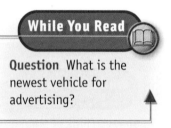

While You Read

Question What is the newest vehicle for advertising?

INTERNET The Internet is the newest and most rapidly growing vehicle for advertising. Companies can send advertising via e-mail, they can place ads on Web sites, or they can use pop-up ads. A pop-up ad is a window that presents an advertising message that appears on top of (over) the browser window of a Web site that a user has visited. Internet ads allow users to link to advertisers' Web sites. An enormous amount of product information is provided through the Internet. Customers can see what is available. If they want more information, they can contact sellers directly.

Computer users are increasingly comfortable with the Internet, and online transactions have become more secure. In addition, online advertising can be accessed by customers anytime day or night from anywhere in the world. Internet advertising is generating more sales. It is an inexpensive way to promote a business and its products and services.

Publicity

Publicity is placement in the media of newsworthy items about a company or product. Taking advantage of publicity means you must do more than just hope your efforts are noticed. There are ways to call attention to yourself and your enterprise.

1. **Write news releases.** A **news release**, also called a press release, is a brief newsworthy story that is sent to the media. **Figure 12.2** shows an example.

2. **Write feature articles.** Write articles on your area of business expertise. Submit articles to newspapers, magazines, or newsletters that reach your target market.

3. **Submit captioned photos.** Send photos and explanations of your company's new products, facilities, or employees to the media.

4. **Call a press conference.** Make major announcements about your company to the media.

5. **Seek interviews.** You might hold interviews with the media to discuss some newsworthy aspect of your business. You might also conduct interviews to offer your expert opinions.

Unsolicited publicity can also come from public relations. **Public relations** are activities designed to create goodwill toward a business. Such activities are often reported by the media. It can also control any damage done by negative publicity. News about an accident or unsafe product claim can hurt a company's image. Such incidents require a quick response with an apology, if warranted, and a pledge to monitor and/or correct any problems.

One advantage of publicity is that it is free. Also, because publicity is not company-sponsored, people often think it is more credible than advertising. There is a downside to publicity. You have no control over it. You do not know when, where, how, or even if it will be printed or aired.

Sales Promotion

Sales promotion involves the use of incentives or interest-building activities to stimulate traffic or sales. Examples of the most visible forms of sales promotion are shown in **Figure 12.3** on pages 262-263.

Figure 12.2 **News Release**

DATE: MARCH 12
TO: BUSINESS EDITORS
FROM: YIKES! BIKES! Bicycle Shop
RE: Grand Opening

At the grand opening of YIKES! BIKES!, disc jockey Bruno Reneaux from radio station WJX will be broadcasting live from noon until 4 P.M.

The store opens at 11 A.M., and there will be a free drawing every hour. The first 100 customers will be eligible to win a Nova 4000 mountain bike.

Our new store is located at 1331 Front Street in the newly restored River Front Warehouse. YIKES! BIKES! is a new concept in bicycle retail. In addition to state-of-the-art, currently manufactured bicycles, we also sell beautifully reconditioned classic bicycles. And we'll repair any bicycle in almost any condition.

Store hours will be Monday–Saturday from 10 A.M. until 6 P.M. and Sunday from noon to 5 P.M.

THE FIVE Ws A news release should answer these key questions: Who? What? Where? When? Why? *What is missing from this example?*

Figure 12.3 **Examples of Sales Promotion**

INCENTIVES Sales promotions are short-term incentives offered to stimulate sales. Displays, premiums, rebates, samples, and sweepstakes are examples of sales promotions. *Have you ever received a premium or a rebate? If so, describe the product you purchased and what you received in return.*

1. Displays
Window, showroom, point-of-purchase, and exterior displays all increase buyer awareness. While many displays are designed in-house, others are put together by manufacturers and wholesalers.

2. Premiums
A **premium** is anything of value that a customer receives in addition to the good or service purchased. Premiums include coupons and gifts. Premiums can be used to attract new customers or build loyalty among existing customers.

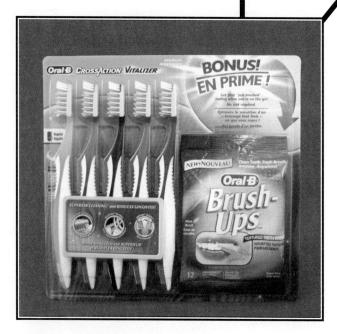

3. Rebates
Many companies give **rebates** (a return of part of the purchase price) as an incentive for customers to purchase their products. Rebates are available for software, computers, and many other types of goods.

4. Samples
Free trial-size and travel-size packages are particularly useful in introducing new products. Such samples can be distributed by mail, given out door to door, or handed out in retail stores.

5. Sweepstakes and Contests
Sweepstakes and contests are games used by businesses to get customers thinking and talking about what the company has to offer. **Sweepstakes** are simple games of chance. Contests require the customer to do something to win.

A specialized form of sales promotion is visual merchandising. This is the coordination of all physical elements in a business to create an inviting image and encourage purchases. It includes the business front, layout, interior, and displays.

Exhibits at trade shows and conventions are also a form of sales promotion. Exhibits at trade shows are excellent for introducing products. They draw customers who have a specific interest.

PERSONAL SELLING The intent of personal selling is to make a sale. It consists of oral presentations given to one or more potential buyers. Personal selling is often designed to close a sale after advertising, publicity, or sales promotions have attracted the customer.

Personal selling is the most adaptable of all of the promotional elements because the message can be modified to suit the individual buyer. However, personal selling is also the most expensive promotional method.

Two basic approaches can be used to incorporate personal selling into your mix. One is to hire and train your own sales force. The other is to contract with marketing intermediaries such as sales agents or manufacturers' agents. They can represent you and your products on a commission basis.

One variation of personal selling is telemarketing—selling over the telephone. This technique is less expensive than using salespeople, but it may not be well received by prospects. Another variation of personal selling is network, or multilevel, marketing. It involves the salesperson calling on his or her network of family and friends to sell products and to recruit them to sell. Distributors are paid commissions on the sales they generate as well as the sales generated by distributors they recruit into the business.

Section 12.1 After You Read

Key Concept Review

1. What objectives can be accomplished through preopening promotional plans? Through ongoing plans?

2. When should preopening promotion begin?

3. What are four options that can be used in a promotional mix?

Critical Thinking

4. Develop a preopening promotional plan for your proposed business. Then develop a promotional plan for your first six months of operation.

Role Play

Situation You and a classmate are getting ready to open a used CD shop where customers can buy and swap music CDs.

Activity Conduct research to determine the best way to reach your target market: local teens. Create a promotional mix. Role-play a discussion with your partner in which you present and defend your promotional mix. Your partner will present questions and challenges.

Evaluation You will be evaluated on how well you address these issues:

- Explain the concept of the promotional mix.

- Describe the elements of the promotional mix.

- Present and justify your ideas.

- Illustrate how each promotional activity and the coordinated activities address the target market.

Section 12.2

Budgeting and Implementing Promotional Plans

GET READY TO READ

KEY TERMS
- industry average
- cooperative advertising
- advertising agency
- consumer pretest

KEY CONCEPTS
- Budgeting for Promotion
- Carrying Out Your Plans
- Making Possible Promotion Changes
- Revising the Promotion Strategy

THE MAIN IDEA

Thorough planning and information gathering can help you arrive at a realistic promotional budget. That budget will have a direct effect on how you implement your promotional plans.

READING ORGANIZER

Draw the reading organizer on a separate sheet of paper. As you read this section, write the three most common adjustments to promotion strategies.

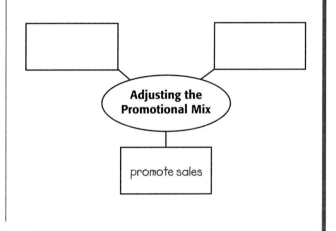

Budgeting for Promotion

In an established business, you have previous plans and sales figures to help you develop your promotional budget. With a new venture, you must gather information and estimate your expenditures.

Cost Out Promotional Activities

You can obtain advertising rates directly from radio stations, newspapers, and other media sources. Their sales representatives will quote you prices and supply you with rate charts. Another source is the Standard Rate and Data Service. It publishes rate cards for most major media.

Sales promotion items are unique. They have to be prepared specifically for the promotion. To determine their cost, you must contact whoever is going to produce the promotional pieces.

While You Read

Predict How should you carry out your promotional plans if you are on a tight budget?

Publicity your business gets from community or other events does not cost you anything. However, the event itself will. Grand openings, sneak previews, and press conferences can be expensive. If you are planning to use any of these options, include their costs.

Finally, you may hire an agency or a consultant to handle all or part of your promotion. In that case, you need to budget for those fees. Personal selling staff and sales training are not included in your promotional budget. These costs are part of your operating expenses.

Compare Industry Averages

After you know prices for all of the parts of your proposed mix, you can calculate the cost. Your next step, then, is to contact trade associations, business publications, the SBA, or business owners in the field. From them, you can find out the **industry average** (the standard used to compare costs) for promotional expenses. The figure is usually expressed as a percentage of sales.

Make Final Adjustments

The industry figures help you measure your estimate. If the difference between the two figures is large, you might want to reexamine and adjust your plan. If the difference is small, you probably have a realistic budget.

Carrying Out Your Plans

Now it is time to put your promotional plans into action. You or someone you hire must prepare and place ads, generate publicity, and create sales promotion pieces. If personal selling is part of your mix, you may need sales training.

A WALKING ADVERTISEMENT Many businesses sell T-shirts and baseball caps bearing their company name. *What are some advantages of doing this?*

Doing It Yourself

How big is your promotional budget? Do you have enough money to hire a professional *and* carry out the activities to reach your target market? Many new entrepreneurs do not. If your budget is limited, you may have to design your ads and other promotional items. This does not mean your promotional efforts will be ineffective or unprofessional. Many of the ads you hear on the radio and see in newspapers and on television are created by small business owners.

If you do design your own ads, you should use basic media formats as a starting point. For example:

- **Print.** Print advertisements should include certain elements: a headline, copy, illustrations, and a signature. The headline is the saying that gets the readers' attention. The copy is the selling message. It can vary from a few words to several paragraphs. The illustration is a photograph or drawing in the ad. It should relate to the headline and the copy. The signature is the identification for the business. It may include a symbol as well as the business's name, address, telephone number, and Web site address. These elements most often appear in the ad layout in that sequence.

- **Radio.** Radio spots require essentially the same elements as print ads. The main difference is that word pictures take the place of illustrations. Radio ads may also include music and/or sound effects. Scripts lay out the sequence and provide the wording as well as any instructional notes.

- **Television.** Television has the same elements, too, but it is more complex. It requires casting, set design, sound, and filming. Two-column scripts spell out the sequence. Audio (words, music, sound effects) appears on the right side of the script. Video (settings and action) is on the left. A storyboard (miniature sketches of scenes) is used to help visualize the sequence.

- **Internet.** Internet ads contain the same components as print ads, but they can also include audio, video, and animation. The most effective types of online advertising include text content and graphics designed to promote a product, service, or company. Users can click on a link that takes them to the company's Web site.

You can find detailed guidelines about the various media in advertising and marketing books and on the Internet.

Getting Help

Your other alternative is to hire professional help for some or all of your promotional activities. The cost can vary. It may be a no-fee arrangement or a sizable percentage of your promotional budget. The range depends on the services you receive. Professional help can come from the media, manufacturers and suppliers, as well as advertising agencies.

MEDIA All of the major advertising media—television, radio, newspapers, and magazines—have advertising departments. The people who work in these departments make their living by selling advertising. To encourage sales, they often help you prepare the ads or commercials that you run with them. In some instances, they even create the ads or commercials themselves.

Quick Math

You are evaluating your promotional budget. The industry average for your field is 20% of sales, and your projected monthly sales are $35,000. What figures should you be measuring your monthly promotional costs against?

BusinessWeek Case Study

More Tech, More Jobs, More Optimism

Entrepreneurs are making greater and better use of technology, according to a new study—and so will the additional workers they intend to hire

Reach out—and get some work done. That seems to be the new motto for Main Street businesses, which have been catching up with Corporate America in embracing telecommuting and remote work locations as key elements of their day-to-day operations. According to a newly released survey, 67% of 501 entrepreneurs and senior decision-makers at a nationwide sampling of small and midsize outfits either work outside the office or have key staff members who do.

The study, conducted in early May for Hewlett-Packard (HPQ), also points to the increasing savvy small businesses are displaying in choosing, purchasing, and setting up office technology, with 8 in 10 decision-makers endorsing the view that survival in today's economic conditions demands technology "on a par with, if not superior to, larger corporations."

On a broader note, the findings come as further confirmation that small-business owners are now convinced the economy is on a sustainable uptrend, and that it's time for their outfits to ride the wave. Of those questioned, 62% were optimistic that growth in 2004 would be good, with 49% saying they planned to expand payrolls in the months ahead. Given the other trends, the ranks of telecommuters are about to get a further boost.

SOURCE: *BUSINESSWEEK*, MAY 14, 2004; NO AUTHOR LISTED

APPLICATION

Use a word-processing application to describe the technology requirements for a start-up business. Explain whether the hardware and software is similar to that used by larger corporations.

 Go to **entrepreneurship.glencoe.com** to complete the *BusinessWeek* Case Study Reading Guide Activity.

MANUFACTURERS AND SUPPLIERS You may be able to get suppliers or manufacturers of goods you sell to share your advertising costs. **Cooperative advertising** is an arrangement in which advertising costs are divided between two or more parties. Usually, manufacturers offer such programs to their wholesalers or retailers as a means of encouraging those parties to advertise the product. For example, suppose you are a retailer who features a manufacturer's product in an ad. That manufacturer may be willing to pay all or part of the cost of the ad.

Some types of sales promotion can be done as a joint effort. If you are a manufacturer, you might provide retail outlets with displays. Your aim in this case is to set your product apart from the competition's.

AGENCIES An **advertising agency** is a company that acts as intermediary between a business and the media to communicate a message to the target market. Advertising agencies can handle all phases of your advertising. They write the copy, create the artwork, choose the media, and produce the ad or commercial. Nearly all television and national magazine ads are produced by professional agencies.

For their services, advertising agencies charge a substantial fee. Agencies typically charge a 15 percent fee. For example, if an agency creates and places a $200,000 ad, the agency bills the client for the full amount and retains $30,000 of the total as its fee. Because of such high costs, agencies tend to be used by large companies.

While You Read

Connect Contact a local advertising agency and find out how much their services cost.

Making Possible Promotion Changes

You may need to make changes in the promotion strategy if you are not getting the desired results. The three most common adjustments are described below.

Adjust Your Advertising

Advertising is expensive. When a campaign is not working, you should change it as quickly as possible. Most advertising problems result from using the wrong media or having bad timing.

One way to head off problems is to do a consumer pretest. A **consumer pretest** is a procedure in which a panel of consumers evaluate an ad before it runs. This involves getting reactions and perceptions from a panel of customers in advance of the ad's release.

TECHNOLOGY Today

Artificial Intelligence

Once just a dream of sci-fi writers, today artificial intelligence (AI) is becoming a real part of the computing world. Artificial intelligence is the branch of computer science that deals with writing computer programs that can solve problems creatively. By building computer systems that learn from their mistakes and from the behaviors of others, companies can use AI to make purchasing decisions, interact with customers, schedule employees, and even run a store.

Critical Thinking

Can you name some examples of artificial intelligence in a business setting? How effective were they?

 Go to **entrepreneurship.glencoe.com** to complete the Technology Today Vocabulary Practice Activity.

While You Read

Question What seven factors should be evaluated after an ad has run?

After the ad has run, specific factors should be evaluated. These include market, source, motive, message, media, budget, and overall results. Address these questions in a postevaluation:

- **Market.** How well did the ad succeed in reaching its target market?
- **Source.** Was the source of the ad the most effective source?
- **Motives.** What motivated the customer to buy?
- **Messages.** How appropriate was the message?
- **Media.** Did the selected media succeed in reaching the target market with the message?
- **Results.** How well did the ad accomplish its objectives?
- **Budget.** Was the budget acceptable?

You can use several techniques for getting information to measure. You can obtain feedback from customers and monitor sales to determine the direct effects of ads. You can conduct market research and hire professional advertising researchers. You can use the results of your information gathering and evaluation to make immediate and long-range changes.

Generate Publicity

As part of your promotional mix, you have planned activities that will result in favorable publicity. In addition, you can monitor community, school, athletic, and other events that might bring about positive exposure. These possibilities may take the form of sponsorships, leadership roles, or service roles.

Success Stories

One Smart Cookie

There is certainly nothing new about fortune cookies—after all, the crunchy treats have been an important part of Chinese takeout food for decades. Karen Belasco Staitman brought a new idea to the fortune cookie: let people put customized messages inside. Not only that, she introduced a huge variety of styles and flavors, dipping them in chocolate and decorating them with everything from golf tees to football helmets—she even created a "giant fortune cookie," about one foot around and weighing almost a pound. Her company, Good Fortunes, launched in 1995 and was an immediate success. Sales reached $8 million in 2003, and she expects them to hit $35 million within the next few years.

CRITICAL THINKING
Why do you think Good Fortunes' cookies became so successful?

 Go to **entrepreneurship.glencoe.com** to complete the Success Stories Writing Activity.

Promote Sales

No matter how well you plan your promotions, sales may not move at the pace you planned. To get sales rolling, you can use additional or new sales promotions. Displays, premiums, sweepstakes, contests, rebates, and samples provide people with an incentive to buy. These are often used to enhance other promotional tools and can be put into place quickly.

In other instances, adding salespeople or increasing productivity of the existing sales force may get results. Personal selling helps ensure that customers' needs are met. Chapter 13 will provide guidelines for recruiting, training, and overseeing your sales force, an essential part of the promotion strategy.

Revising the Promotion Strategy

Conduct a formal review of your promotion strategy on a regular basis—perhaps quarterly or semiannually. Apply evaluation strategies to determine the effectiveness of your promotional campaign.

Begin with your sales forecast for the upcoming period. You can then arrive at a promotional budget necessary to support that level of sales. Next, formulate a revised promotional mix. Like your original mix, you want the best combination of elements for reaching your target market. Be aware that the market may have shifted. You now have your market research, previous plans, and recent short-term decisions to draw on. In addition, past experience will give you an idea of what does and does not work.

Once you have determined your mix, you can prepare a new promotional plan. Any revisions in the promotional plan should be consistent with other marketing objectives and strategies. Any changes you make in the promotion strategy should become part of your new marketing plan.

Section 12.2 After You Read

Key Concept Review

1. What are the advantages and disadvantages of hiring an advertising agency?
2. List two ways to improve the results of a sales force.
3. Describe two techniques for determining whether your advertising is effective.

Critical Thinking

4. Develop a list of guidelines for reviewing and revising the promotional plan for your proposed business.

Role Play

Situation A local grocery store has hired you and a classmate to plan their promotions. The business has several outlets and draws primarily from low-income families.

Activity Team up with a classmate and plan a promotional campaign for the business. Then make a presentation to the class presenting your campaign.

Evaluation You will be evaluated on how well you address these issues:

- Describe the role of promotion as it relates to small business.
- Suggest and describe the promotional mix and explain how it will appeal to the target market.
- Explain how the business can apply evaluation strategies to determine the effectiveness of the promotional campaign.

Chapter Summary

Section 12.1 Developing a Promotion Strategy

The promotion strategy sets the course for promotional efforts to come together to reach potential customers and influence them to buy. Promotional plans, whether preopening or ongoing, should provide the following information: a brief description; specific media placement; submit dates; scheduled date of run or release; number of runs, copies, or items, costs, and rationale. Promotional strategies can vary, even in the same market. Consider your target market, promotional mix, and costs when creating your promotional strategy. Advertising is the paid nonpersonal presentation of ideas, goods, or services directed toward a mass audience by an identified sponsor. There are two types: print and broadcast. Publicity is the free placement of newsworthy items about your company or product in the media. Examples of sales promotions include displays, premiums, sweepstakes, contests, rebates, and sample giveaways. Personal selling consists of oral presentations to potential buyers.

Section 12.2 Budgeting and Implementing Promotional Plans

A realistic promotional budget has a direct effect on how you implement your promotional plans. Established businesses use previous plans and sales figures to determine a promotional budget. New ventures must determine a budget by costing out promotional activities and comparing them to industry averages. Many businesses with limited promotional budgets design and carry out their own ads. Others have major advertising media help prepare and create ads or engage in cooperative advertising with a supplier or manufacturer. Businesses with larger budgets hire advertising agencies to handle all phases of their advertising efforts. If your advertising is not generating results, you may need to change your promotional strategy by adjusting your advertising, generating publicity, employing sales promotions, or increasing the productivity of your sales force.

Key Terms Review

1. Create a promotion strategy for a new candy bar being introduced to the market. Be creative. Use the following terms in your plan.

image (p. 255)	publicity (p. 260)	industry average (p. 266)
preselling (p. 256)	news release (p. 261)	cooperative advertising (p. 268)
campaign (p. 256)	public relations (p. 261)	advertising agency (p. 269)
promotional mix (p. 257)	premium (p. 262)	consumer pretest (p. 269)
advertising (p. 258)	rebate (p. 263)	
specialty item (p. 260)	sweepstakes (p. 263)	

Key Concept Review

2. **Explain** the role of the promotion strategy. (12.1)
3. **Explain** how to formulate promotional plans. (12.1)
4. **Describe** considerations for putting together a promotional mix. (12.1)
5. **Describe** the elements of the promotional mix. (12.1)
6. **Describe** how to determine promotional costs for a start-up business. (12.2)
7. **Describe** approaches to implementing your promotion strategy. (12.2)
8. **Discuss** options for short-term changes in your promotion strategy. (12.2)
9. **Identify** considerations for updating the promotion strategy. (12.2)

Critical Thinking

10. Which type of promotional activity is most cost-effective? Why?
11. Is it possible to have more than one "best" promotional mix? Explain.
12. Compare and contrast print versus broadcast advertising.
13. As an entrepreneur, under what circumstances might you find yourself engaged in the promotion function rather than the planning and administering of your promotion strategy?
14. Distinguish between ongoing promotional plans and six-month promotional plans.
15. Describe the interrelationship of visual merchandising, public relations and publicity, personal selling, and sales promotion with advertising.

Write About It

16. Write a speech giving your views on whether promotion done by a small business owner can be as effective as promotion done by professionals. Defend your stand.
17. For one week, keep a log of television shows you watch and the ads that appear. Write a paper comparing the intended target markets with the probable audience. Explain whether the matches were good.
18. In a one-page paper, describe promotional media activities used by small businesses. Explain how these activities are different from those used by large businesses.
19. In Section 12.1 After You Read, number 4, you developed preopening and six-month promotional plans for your proposed business. In a one- to two-page paper, describe the specific steps you would take to implement each plan of action for that business.
20. Design and present a newspaper ad and a television ad to market your entrepreneurship class.

Academic Skills

Math

21. You have created a newspaper ad whose dimensions are 1 column by 12 inches (or 12 column inches). You want the ad to run every week during your first quarter of operation. The newspaper has given you three pricing options:

- A series of single runs at a rate of $19.69 per column inch

- A 13-week contract requiring you to run the ad 13 times in 13 weeks at a rate of $16.06 per column inch

- A "bulk rate" contract requiring you to purchase a minimum of 150 column inches a year at $15.16 per column inch

Which is your best option in terms of cost?

Language Arts

22. Write a news release about the grand opening activities of your new business. Make the news release about one page in length. Who would you send it to? Why?

Entrepreneurship in Your Community

23. If you are employed, interview the person who handles the advertising for your company to determine the company's:

- Promotional objectives
- Promotional planning cycle
- Promotional mix

If you are not employed, interview a local businessperson to obtain the same information.

24. Contact the media (at least three) you plan to use for advertising your proposed business. Obtain information about rates and services they provide. Write a summary of your results and compare your findings with those of your class.

Ethical Practices

Cause Advertising

25. In their advertising, many companies portray themselves as advocates for certain causes. This is called *cause advertising.* The message in these ads is that the business is engaged in protecting the environment, supporting cancer research, helping to rebuild a rundown neighborhood, or the like. As a result of supporting such causes, the company hopes to see increased sales.

Is cause advertising ethical? Why or why not? Does it have a positive effect on the company? As an entrepreneur, would you use cause advertising? Why or why not?

INTERNET connection

Advertising on the Internet

Your business's target market uses the Internet on a regular basis, so you want to create a new Internet ad to promote your business.

Connect

Research advertising on the Internet.

- Find a banner ad, a pop-up ad, and an e-mail ad.

- Evaluate their design and effectiveness.

Application

Use your research to help you to design your own Internet ad. Use a software application to create the ad.

The Electronic Entrepreneur

Using Web Site Personalization

Today, the technology exists for companies to make their Web sites come alive for each visitor. Tailoring a Web page for each visitor increases customer satisfaction.

Personalization Sometimes referred to as one-to-one marketing, **personalization** is the process of tailoring Web pages to individual users' characteristics or preferences. **Rules-based personalization** is a data analysis tool that is used to recommend products that go with products you have viewed or purchased. For instance, if you add a CD burner to your shopping cart, it will suggest you also purchase blank discs. **Inference-based personalization** is a data analysis tool that is used to suggest products that are similar to products you have viewed or purchased. For example, if you visit a book store online and look up a book, it might offer you other similar books.

Welcome, Visitor! Many Web sites today greet you by your name when you return, if you have registered with them in the past. This information is stored in a cookie. A **cookie** is a file sent to a Web browser by a Web server that is used to record and store information for later use. Cookies hold information that can allow a Web site to show you links to pages you have looked at recently. Many Web sites allow site visitors to use cookies to customize their home page to meet their personal preferences.

Privacy Concerns Privacy advocates find Web site personalization a cause for concern. The main concern is whether information is being used appropriately. The use of privacy policies is seen as a step in the right direction. A **privacy policy** is a statement on a Web site that explains how a company collects, uses, protects, and shares your personal information.

FACT AND IDEA REVIEW

1. Why would an e-commerce Web site want to personalize its content?
2. How do rules-based personalization and inference-based personalization differ? What are their strengths and weaknesses?
3. What is a cookie?
4. Why does Web site personalization raise privacy concerns?

FOR DISCUSSION

5. What are some Web sites that you visit often? Do any of them personalize the experience for you in any way?

TechTerms

- personalization
- rules-based personalization
- inference-based personalization
- cookie
- privacy policy

Chapter 13

The Promotion Strategy: Developing and Managing Sales

Section 13.1

Organizing and Preparing a Sales Force

Section 13.2

Planning, Directing, and Evaluating Sales

CHAPTER OBJECTIVES

When you have completed this chapter, you should be able to:

SECTION 13.1

- Explain the role of personal selling in businesses.
- Define the two types of selling situations.
- Describe the kinds of training needed by salespeople.

SECTION 13.2

- Identify the components of sales planning.
- List the elements that are involved in directing sales.
- Discuss the procedures used in evaluating sales performance.

DEVELOPING A PERSONAL INVESTMENT PLAN

To be a successful investor, you must develop a plan and put it into action. You may find these steps helpful:

1. Establish your investment goals.

2. Decide how much money you will need to reach those goals by a particular date.

3. Determine how much money you have to invest.

4. List all investments you want to evaluate.

5. Evaluate your risks and potential return for each investment.

6. Reduce the list of possible investments to a reasonable number.

7. For diversity, choose at least two investments. You might want to add to this number as your portfolio grows.

8. Recheck your investment program periodically.

Your plan will be unique, but the steps will be the same—just establish your goals, then follow through.

 Go to **entrepreneurship.glencoe.com** to complete the Standard & Poor's Money Talk Financial Literacy Activity.

PREPARE TO READ

THINK ABOUT THESE QUESTIONS AS YOU READ.

What is personal selling?

What kind of training do salespeople need?

Organizing and Preparing a Sales Force

GET READY TO READ

KEY TERMS
- personal selling
- prospect
- sales force
- order getting
- order taking
- rational buying motive
- emotional buying motive
- customer benefits
- buying process
- prospecting
- preapproach
- approach
- objections
- suggestion selling
- sales check

KEY CONCEPTS
- Personal Selling
- Staffing the Sales Force
- Providing Sales Training

THE MAIN IDEA
By thoroughly preparing the salespeople you hire, you can maximize their effectiveness. This is true no matter what background and experience they bring to the job.

READING ORGANIZER
Draw the reading organizer on a separate piece of paper. As you read, write the major areas of sales training.

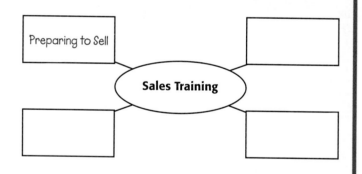

Personal Selling

Personal selling is selling conducted by direct communication with the prospect. A **prospect** is a potential customer. For many companies, personal selling is a key ingredient in their marketing mix. It is important because it involves the human aspect of promotion. Personal selling is particularly important to new entrepreneurial ventures and established small businesses. Both rely on direct contact to sell to their customers. Personal selling also is critical to companies whose customers need detailed information. For example, many people need assistance when buying large appliances, high-tech items, and real estate.

Staffing the Sales Force

Your **sales force** is the group of employees involved in the selling process. To put together your sales force, you must determine what kind of salesperson you need. The types of sales jobs and the necessary requirements vary with the nature of the business. A salesperson who calls on a group of retail stores has one kind of job. A manufacturer's rep who calls on wholesalers has another kind of job. Both of those jobs are different from a salesclerk's job in a retail or service business. You should define a position before you fill it.

Sales are classified into two groups: order getting and order taking. **Order getting** is seeking out buyers and giving them a well-organized presentation. It is sometimes called "creative selling." Order getting is necessary when customers may not be aware of their need for a product. Many people will go to a vacation resort or add home improvements after they discover what is available. Selling highly technical products and complex services also requires order getting.

Many order-getting positions involve calling on customers. Other positions can be found in retail stores where customers require a high level of sales assistance. For example, a family buying their first computer may seek help. They want to select the computer with the functions and features that are right for them.

In contrast, **order taking** is the completion of a sale to a customer who has sought out a product. Retail clerks who stand behind counters are an example of order-taking salespeople. Sales reps who call on retail stores are also typically order takers. They do little creative selling. Delivery people also take orders, but their primary function is to deliver products. Their selling responsibility is secondary.

ORDER TAKER OR ORDER GETTER? Flea markets offer a wide variety of selling opportunities for entrepreneurs. *Is the selling in a flea market order taking or order getting?*

Traits of Successful Salepeople

Besides determining the type of selling your people will do, you need to determine what traits you want in them. Some desirable sales traits identified by professional buyers include the following:

- Knowledge
- Organization
- Follow-through
- Punctuality
- Energy
- Empathy
- Promptness
- Ability to solve problems
- Willingness to work hard
- Honesty

Providing Sales Training

Whether you hire new or experienced salespeople, you must provide training. Your program must prepare them to sell your products. It must also teach (or reteach) the principles of selling—the buying and selling processes. In addition, training may also include the mechanics of selling.

Preparing to Sell

Before a salesperson is ready to sell your products, he or she must have the necessary knowledge base. Specifically, he or she should have company, product, and customer knowledge. In addition, a salesperson needs training in the foundational skills of selling.

TECHNOLOGY Today

Biometrics

Fingerprints can be used to uniquely identify a person, but they are only one form of biometrics, the science of identifying a person using some aspect of their biology. Other ways to biometrically identify a person include voice recognition, retinal patterns, the geometry of hands, and handwriting analysis.

Critical Thinking

What are some businesses that might benefit from biometric security systems?

 Go to **entrepreneurship.glencoe.com** to complete the Technology Today Vocabulary Practice Activity.

COMPANY KNOWLEDGE Sales trainees should understand your company's background, goals, organization, policy, and procedures. They also should understand your company's operating systems and values. With this knowledge, they will feel they are part of the company. The knowledge will also ensure that they represent your company's interests in their sales efforts.

PRODUCT KNOWLEDGE What does a salesperson need to know about your product? To be effective, he or she must be familiar with several things. These are listed in **Figure 13.1** on page 282.

CUSTOMER KNOWLEDGE Salespeople need three kinds of customer knowledge. They need an awareness of customer buying motives. They need to know how to handle different kinds of customers. They also need to be familiar with the company's customers.

Customers have either rational or emotional motives for making a purchase. A **rational buying motive** is a conscious, logical reason to make a purchase. Reasons may include:

- Product dependability
- Time or money savings
- Convenience
- Comfort
- Health or safety issues
- Recreational value
- Service
- Quality

An **emotional buying motive** is a feeling a buyer associates with a product. Feelings may include the following:

- Social approval
- Recognition
- Power
- Affection
- Prestige

Salespeople should be trained to read a customer's motivation in a selling situation. With that knowledge, they can match the product to the customer's motivation. Regardless of their motivation, customers can be at various stages of buying readiness when a salesperson makes contact. They may be decided customers—they know what they want. They also may be a casual looker or an information gatherer—they do not intend to buy now.

Customers may also exhibit different dispositions during the sales contact. They may be talkative or silent. They may be impulsive or procrastinating. In other cases, they may be disagreeable, opinionated, suspicious, shrewd, or decisive. Salespeople must be trained to recognize a customer's buying stage and mood. They must also be trained to handle a customer according to the situation and select appropriate methods to respond to customer concerns.

While You Read

Predict Why is it critical for a salesperson to understand a customer's buying motive?

Figure 13.1 Product Knowledge

INFORMATION IS POWER
Product knowledge is essential for success in selling. A salesperson must be knowledgeable about his or her product on at least three levels. *Why is it important for salespeople to know the competition?*

The Benefits to the Customer
Just knowing a product's features—its physical characteristics—is not enough. Feature/benefit selling requires being able to describe the features as benefits to the customer. **Customer benefits** are the advantages of personal satisfaction that a customer will get from the product. People buy products for their benefits.

The Details About the Company and Its Products
Sales trainees must be familiar with the goods or services they are selling. The more complex the product, the more training they need.

The Competition's Products
Salespeople must also be familiar with the competition. They should be able to tell customers the advantages of their products over the competition's.

FOUNDATIONAL SKILLS FOR SELLING Sales training must include several foundational skills. Time management is an important skill, especially for sales representatives on the road. Legal knowledge is important, especially for issues of product liability and false promotion. Depending on your business situation, salespeople may need additional foundational skills.

INTERNET SKILLS FOR SELLING Training might also include Internet skills for selling. In many companies, the sales staff can obtain information through their office and home computers. Additionally, many companies now equip their salespeople with laptops.

Laptops enable salespeople to access customer databases and prospect lists from the field. In addition, sales staff can exchange e-mail messages with clients, input orders, and update databases. They can also draft proposals and access information. Salespeople can use these tools to research prospective clients before making a sales call.

The Buying Process

In preparation for selling, the sales trainee also must understand the buying process. The **buying process** is a series of steps a customer goes through when making a purchase. All promotional activities, including selling, should be designed to take the customer through that process. These steps are often referred to as the stages of selling, or AIDA formula:

- **Attention.** Getting the prospective buyer's attention
- **Interest.** Developing an interest in the product
- **Desire.** Creating a desire to have the product
- **Action.** Getting the customer to take action to buy

WILL THAT BE ALL? Order takers close out sales when the customer is ready to buy. *What steps of the selling process can order takers carry out?*

The Selling Process

Salespeople can be more effective when they know all of the steps of the selling process. The complete selling process includes ten steps. In order getting, the salesperson usually carries out all of the steps. In order taking, many of the steps have already been completed before the customer and salesperson come together.

While You Read

Connect Interview a salesperson. Ask if the salesperson uses all ten steps of the selling process. Find out which steps are most challenging.

1. **Prospecting. Prospecting** is a systematic approach to developing new sales leads or customers. Prospects can be identified through referrals, public records, or surveys. They can also be found through cold canvassing, that is, making contacts without leads.

2. **Preapproach.** The **preapproach** is the marketing activities that precede a salesperson's approach to a prospective customer that are intended to help to achieve a successful sale. Prior to sales contact, the salesperson should gather information about prospective customers' needs and wants.

3. **Approach.** The **approach** is the salesperson's first contact with the customer. First, the salesperson should establish a friendly and professional relationship. Then, he or she should foster open communication and build credibility. These steps must be carefully planned to get the customer's attention and interest.

4. **Determining needs.** The salesperson must listen carefully and ask questions to determine the customer's wants and needs.

5. **Presentation.** In demonstration or presentation of the product to the customer, the salesperson explains the benefits of the product to the prospective customer. If possible, the customer should try using the product and learn how the product works.

6. **Overcoming objections.** Customers may voice objections during the presentation. **Objections** are concerns, hesitations, doubts, and other reasons a customer has for not making a purchase. A good salesperson selects appropriate methods to respond to customer concerns. He or she anticipates objections and uses them to provide clarification and additional information. Salespeople can often overcome objections by encouraging customers to talk about their concerns.

7. **Closing the sale.** The salesperson must ask for the sale to complete the process.

8. **Suggestion selling. Suggestion selling** is selling additional goods or services to the customer. The salesperson should suggest items that go with the products customers buy. For example, if a customer is buying a dress shirt, the retail salesperson may suggest a tie.

9. **Closing mechanics.** The mechanics of closing vary with the sales situation. They may involve writing up the order in an order-getting situation. In an order-taking situation, they may involve wrapping the merchandise and ringing up the sale.

10. **Follow-up.** The sale is not over until the salesperson is sure the customer is satisfied with the purchase. It might involve contacting the customer to make sure he or she is happy with the purchase. Follow-up contacts can lead to additional sales and long-term customer relationships.

Selling Mechanics

As part of the selling process, manual operations are sometimes necessary near the end of a sale. Some, such as wrapping or bagging merchandise, require minimal training. Others, particularly those requiring clear communication and math accuracy, demand more in-depth training. The basics of selling mechanics include order forms and proposals, cash register operation, sales checks, and sales tax.

ORDER FORMS AND PROPOSALS Outside sales representatives closing orders in the field must complete order forms. These forms show the quantity ordered, a description of the product(s), and costs. In some instances, special instructions are included. Outside sales reps, making a bid on a job, write up proposals. A proposal describes the job, the responsibilities of the company (materials and labor), and the proposed price. In both instances, the information may be transmitted back to the company manually or electronically.

CASH REGISTER OPERATION Most salespeople in retail and service operations use electronic cash registers to complete their sales transactions. These machines total purchases, figure sales tax, subtract refunds and returns, and calculate change due to customers.

The salesperson enters information in one of three ways. Manual entry using the register keys is the most common. Some businesses, such as department stores, use electronic wands to scan data from sales tags. Other businesses, such as supermarkets, use optical scanners.

Other basic cash register procedures include establishing an opening cash fund, making change, handling credit and debit card transactions, and balancing the cash drawer.

Selling Out, Staying On

So what if you're not the CEO anymore. The best way to make your business grow might be to sell it.

Like any other mountain biker at a crossroads, Steve Christini, 28, relies on experience to choose the best path. In deciding which way to go on selling his mountain bike company, he relied on something else: a cold calculation of the chances Christini Technologies Inc. could ever, on its own, become the big, successful bike manufacturer he dreamed of. The problem was not a lack of inspiration. Christini had devised an ingenious design for a two-wheel-drive bicycle—the biking equivalent of a sport-utility vehicle—while he was still a mechanical engineering student at Villanova University in 1994. Two years later, with help from his patent-attorney brother, he launched his Philadelphia-based company and set out on what would prove to be a long uphill journey. After raising about $500,000 from credit cards, family, and a state loan, he spent the first two years perfecting his design and patenting it. Over the next two, he built prototypes and cobbled together a distribution deal to sell bikes through a larger company. "We pulled a lot of all-nighters," he says. "I was sleeping on the office floor, running power tools

without sleeping for three days." The hard work paid off. Christini's prototypes, displayed at trade shows, started to build buzz among biking enthusiasts and manufacturers. However, by late 1999, Christini faced a choice: Seek additional financing to make the bikes himself as a high-priced premium product, or find a buyer for his company. In August, he agreed to sell his fledgling business in an all-cash deal to Stamford (Conn.) biking giant Derby Cycle Corp.

SOURCE: BUSINESSWEEK; NOVEMBER 6, 2000; BY ELLEN NEUBORNE AND MARC PERTON

APPLICATION

If you were faced with the prospect of selling your fledgling business or seeking additional financing to keep it going, which would you choose? Use a word-processing application to write a short essay explaining your choice.

 Go to **entrepreneurship.glencoe.com** to complete the *BusinessWeek* Case Study Reading Guide Activity.

At the start of each day, the owner or a designated employee must supply the cash register with currency and coins. This is called an *opening cash fund.* He or she should count it and write down the amount of each denomination. In addition, the person should verify the overall total against the total planned for the register.

When a cash sale is made, the salesperson should make change while announcing key amounts and counting aloud. This way, the customer can follow each step of the transaction. The exchange of funds begins with a statement of the purchase total, proceeds with the receipt of cash, and ends with making change, counting upward from the purchase total.

Credit and debit card sales are rung up on a register like cash sales. For credit sales, the salesperson accepts the card, checks identity, processes the card, and obtains the customer's signature. The salesperson places the signed credit slip in the cash drawer, giving the copy to the customer. Debit sales are handled in the same way, but they do not require a signature.

Most computerized cash registers secure authorization and print out the credit/debit slips. If a register does not have that capability, a separate electronic card reader or mechanical imprinter is used.

At the end of each business day, the designated employee should balance the cash register. Computerized cash registers keep a running tally of the day's sales. To balance, the employee simply compares the sales tape with the contents of the cash drawer.

SALES CHECKS A **sales check** is a written record of a sales transaction. It provides the customer with an itemized receipt. It also provides valuable information to the business. To complete a sales check form, the salesperson enters the date, items purchased, and purchase price. Many businesses use electronic cash registers that provide the same information.

SALES TAX To calculate sales tax, you must begin with the local rate. Sales tax varies from state to state, and sometimes county and city taxes are added. The sales tax is calculated on the total price of the items purchased. If, for example, you sell a CD for $20 and the tax rate is 7 percent, you would compute the tax as follows:

PURCHASE TOTAL	×	TAX RATE	=	SALES TAX
$20.00	×	0.07	=	$1.40

While You Read

Question You want to buy a pair of skates that cost $100. The tax rate is 7 percent. What is the total amount you will pay for the skates, including tax?

Section 13.1 After You Read

Key Concept Review

1. Which type of salespeople would be most appropriate for a bakery: order takers or order getters? Why?

2. What knowledge and skills do salespeople need to be able to sell?

3. What are the steps in the buying and selling processes?

Critical Thinking

4. Why is it important to have a training plan and schedule for the sales staff of your proposed business?

Role Play

Situation To gain experience for opening a similar sales-oriented business, you have taken a sales position in your uncle's used car dealership. During the next two weeks, you will be attending sales seminars on the buying and selling process.

Activity To practice your sales training, pair up with a classmate. Take turns playing the salesperson and customer in a variety of situations. The situations may involve customers' rational or emotional buying motives as well as different stages of buying readiness.

Evaluation You will be evaluated on how well you address these issues:

- Implement the steps in the selling process.
- Take customers through the buying process.
- Adjust to the customers' buying motives and readiness.
- Demonstrate product knowledge.

Planning, Directing, and Evaluating Sales

GET READY TO READ

KEY TERMS
- sales planning
- sales forecast
- sales territory
- sales quota
- salary
- commission
- sales call reports
- SWOT analysis
- morale

KEY CONCEPTS
- Planning Sales
- Directing Sales Operations
- Evaluating Sales Performance

THE MAIN IDEA
Effective sales operations are developed through careful planning, directing, and controlling.

READING ORGANIZER
Draw the reading organizer on a separate piece of paper. As you read, write the three key functions of managing sales.

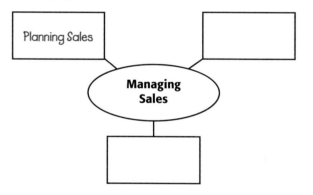

Planning Sales

Before you put your new sales force to work, you must complete your sales planning. Sales planning is tied to a company's marketing plan. **Sales planning** involves determining the goals and timing of sales efforts. It involves making sales forecasts, determining sales budgets, establishing territories where necessary, and setting sales quotas.

Forecasting Sales

Your **sales forecast** is an estimate of sales for a given period, such as the next quarter. In the market analysis for your marketing plan, you estimate the market share you think your business could obtain. Your sales forecast would be based on that estimate.

FORECASTING METHODS When you start a new business, you rely on your market analysis and industry information for forecasting. Established companies use more than one method to obtain a forecast range. After you are up and running, you have these other methods of forecasting available.

- **Surveys.** Surveys of executives, customers, and sales staff are used to arrive at a forecast. These surveys are based on individual or group opinions.

- **Data Analysis.** Mathematical methods are applied to company records or historical data to obtain a forecast. These methods may use sales for the last period or an average of sales in recent periods. They may also use projections based on sales trends as their base.

- **Operational Analysis.** The operation of the company is analyzed. One method of forecasting is based on sales volume needed to accomplish certain company goals. Another is based on capacity. If a company can sell everything it makes, its capacity is its sales forecast. Still another method is based on test market results.

Budgeting Sales

Three basic budgets are needed for your sales activities. In order of development, they are:

- **Sales budget.** The sales budget begins with the sales forecast. From that calculation, a detailed sales budget is developed. The sales budget includes expected sales of each item in the product line.

- **Selling expense budget.** This budget projects expenditures related to personal selling activities.

- **Administrative sales costs budget.** Administrative costs of managing the sales operation are budgeted separately.

When completed, these budgets, along with the sales forecast, give you criteria for judging performance. If sales are below budget, you can determine the cause and take steps to increase them. Similarly, if costs are above budget, you can look for ways to control them.

Establishing Territories

A **sales territory** is a geographical area in which existing and potential customers are grouped. Sales territories are not needed if you conduct only inside sales. Even with outside sales, territories may not be needed. Having just a few salespeople selling in a local market does not require sales territories. However, if your market covers a wide geographic area, setting territories ensures market coverage, reduces selling costs, and improves customer relations.

Establishing territories involves a three-step process. First, determine the probable areas—cities, counties, states, or other divisions. Next, determine the sales potential or time needed to cover the proposed territories. Then, make adjustments and decide on the boundaries. Once territories are established, you can assign salespeople.

While You Read

Predict Why would a company choose to establish sales territories?

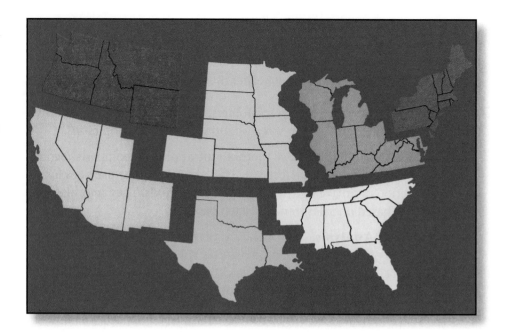

> **SALES REGIONS** Sales territories are beneficial when you have a wide geographic area to cover or areas with high customer density. *What are some common ways to divide markets into territories?*

While You Read

Connect Think of one way that a business can help to make sure that its salespeople can meet their sales quotas.

Setting Sales Quotas

A **sales quota** is a performance goal assigned to a salesperson for a specific period. These goals serve several purposes. They give you an indication of strong and weak areas in your sales operation. They provide incentives for your workforce. They improve the effectiveness of your compensation plans. They also control selling expenses.

There are three general approaches to setting quotas for a new business. One approach is to set quotas based on territorial sales potential. For example, some territories may have a higher population that better fits the target market profile. A second approach is to set quotas in relation to your company's total sales forecast. For example, each of four sales reps should make about one-quarter of the total sales. The third is to base quotas simply on your judgment. Using this approach, you must be able to provide a reason for giving different quotas to different salespeople.

After your business is in operation, there is a fourth approach. That approach is to use past sales as a guide.

Several advantages of sales quotas were already identified, but there are disadvantages as well. Salespeople may view quotas as a threat to their well-being. Thus, quotas may have a negative effect on their morale. Another disadvantage is that unrealistic quotas can put pressure on salespeople to perform. Therefore, you need to set sales quotas that are realistic, objective, fair, and attainable. They must also be easy to understand and to implement. As a first step, conduct a thorough overview of sales quotas and consider their advantages and design.

Directing Sales Operations

Once your sales staff and plans are in place, you must direct your sales activities. Doing so ensures that you reach your goals. You must provide motivation, incentives, a favorable environment, resources, and leadership to your salespeople. This enables them to do their job and reach their objectives.

Motivating Your Salespeople

Motivated salespeople are more effective at their job than unmotivated salespeople. Your responsibility is to determine the right combination of motivators.

Some motivational techniques are particularly useful when working with salespeople. For example, financial incentives such as bonuses are important to salespeople. Salespeople are achievement-oriented. Therefore, reaching a goal to get a bonus is as important as the bonus itself. Nonfinancial rewards such as plaques, pins, trophies, and certificates are also important. Motivational sales meetings, contests, and congratulatory communications can likewise be effective techniques.

Compensating Your Sales Staff

Your pay plan must be designed to attract and keep good salespeople. That means it should provide the opportunity for steady income and incentives. The pay plan should also be competitive with what similar companies are paying. Like sales quotas, it must be fair and easy to understand and implement.

Quick Math

You are paid a bonus if your sales exceed your quota by 15%. If your quota is $70,000, how much do your sales need to be for you to qualify for the bonus?

The right pay plan for your sales staff depends on your type of operation and your sales needs. The following options are often used as methods of payment for salespeople:

1. **Straight salary.** A **salary** is regular wages an employee receives from an employer. When a salesperson receives a salary, he or she is paid a specified amount. This amount is for a certain period of time—no matter how many sales the salesperson makes. This plan ensures a regular, stable income. It results in a low turnover rate. It also allows management to direct salespeople into sales-related activities. The major disadvantage is that it does not provide an incentive. It is also a fixed cost to the company.

2. **Straight commission.** A **commission** is a fee for services rendered based on a percentage of an amount sold. Payment is based on sales alone. The major advantage of this plan is the incentive it provides to salespeople. Usually, income opportunities are unlimited. It is the best way to weed out ineffective salespeople. It is a variable expense to the company—the expense occurs only when a sale is made. A major disadvantage is the difficulty in directing commission salespeople. In addition, sales reps tend to concentrate on easy-to-sell items and may overstock customers. Company interests are not their primary goal.

3. **A combination of salary and commission.** A salary is paid, and sales are rewarded. This plan uses the strong parts and overcomes the weaknesses of straight salary and straight commission plans. Most pay plans fall into this category.

Handling Expenses and Transportation

Typically, outside sales reps are reimbursed for their food, lodging, and travel expenses. They may also be reimbursed for personal expenses as a result of their travels.

CONGRATULATIONS!
Salespeople value recognition for their accomplishments. *What are some other nonfinancial ways to motivate salespeople?*

A good expense plan is fair, easy to understand, and easy to administer. To keep track of their expenditures, salespeople must keep receipts for business meals, hotel rooms, and airfare. They must also itemize (explain on paper) their expenses. This shows that the costs are reasonable. As expenses increase, more plans include limits on certain expenditures.

If travel expenses are high, you may want to consider alternatives. For example, leasing company cars may be less expensive than paying for mileage. Inside sales calls may be less expensive and just as effective as making outside contacts. These decisions depend on the size and nature of your operation.

Supervising Your Sales Force

The primary goal of sales force supervision is to increase sales while reducing costs. Reaching those goals requires training the sales staff, setting sales policies, and monitoring the activities of the sales force. Several techniques are useful in supervising a sales staff.

- **Personal contact.** Personal visits with inside and outside salespeople serve several purposes. They provide an opportunity to assist with sales problems and training. They also show support for the sales staff.

- **Sales reports.** A **sales call report** is an account of sales activities. It provides a way to monitor and evaluate outside sales activities. These reports include numbers of calls made, orders obtained, and miles traveled. They also include days worked, new prospects contacted, and new accounts sold. Salespeople who know they must account for their activities focus their efforts on those items.

- **Electronic communications.** Another way to maintain contact with salespeople is through electronic communications. The telephone, fax, voice mail, and e-mail provide those opportunities.

- **Meetings.** Motivational sales meetings can be used for training, providing information, and solving problems.

Write About It

For one week, practice keeping track of your expenses. Every time you spend money, write down how much money you spent and what you spent it on. At the end of the week, calculate how much money you spent. Then write a one-page report detailing how you spent your money. Determine whether you need to make any adjustments to your spending patterns.

Adjusting to Sales Environment Changes

You can stay on top of changes in the internal and external sales environment by conducting a periodic analysis. One such technique to use is a SWOT analysis. A **SWOT analysis** is a strategic planning technique that analyzes a company's internal strengths and weaknesses, and studies opportunities and threats in the external sales environment.

While You Read

Question What does the acronym SWOT represent?

Using SWOT analysis, you can assess your current situation on factors that influence selling. It also lets you identify strategies, thereby increasing strengths and opportunities and reducing weaknesses and threats.

Internal factors that may cause a difference in the performance of salespeople include:

- Changes in spending on other parts of the company's marketing and promotional mix
- Changes in what is happening in different territories or markets
- Changes in sales management practices
- Changes in number of salespeople supervised by one person

External factors that may vary from one territory or market to another include:

- Intensity of competition
- Total market potential
- Concentration of potential high-volume buyers
- Geographic distribution of customers

SWOT analysis can be used to plan beyond short-range adjustments. It can be used to assess the sales operation, then to revise promotional and marketing plans.

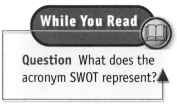

TRAVEL EXPENSES
Companies usually pay for their salespeople's travel costs and expenses. *What are some costs incurred when doing business out of the office?*

Maintaining Morale

A high level of morale is an important factor in a sales staff's success. **Morale** is a state of individual psychological well-being based upon a sense of confidence, usefulness, and purpose. To maintain high morale, foster a positive work climate and productive interaction among members of the sales force.

Evaluating Sales Performance

The final step in managing your sales operation is to evaluate sales performance. Sales performance evaluation involves evaluating company-wide sales and the sales of individual salespeople.

Evaluating the Company's Sales Performance

Evaluating the entire company's performance enables you to consider the effectiveness of your marketing plan and your operations. Two types of analysis are useful in this evaluation:

1. **Analysis of sales volume.** This analysis is a comparison of your company's actual sales volume with its budgeted sales goals. You look at total sales, but you also examine sales territory, products, customer groups, order size, and individual salespeople. Comparing these categories with industry figures indicates how your sales results stack up against the competition.

2. **Marketing cost analysis.** This is a study of marketing expenses to determine the profitability of various marketing endeavors. This analysis helps you identify misdirected marketing efforts and unprofitable segments.

Issues in Entrepreneurship

CUSTOMER APPRECIATION OR BRIBERY?

The practice of salespeople giving gifts to customers, especially during the holiday season, has been a time-honored business tradition. It is regarded as a way of thanking customers. Unfortunately, it also has been used to bribe customers to get their business. Often, it is unclear where one purpose stops and the other starts.

If you are ever asked for a bribe, explain that doing so would be a violation of your company's ethical guidelines. You can always agree to try to arrange some kind of authorized consideration.

Think Critically
Where should you draw the line when giving or accepting girfts?

 Go to **entrepreneurship.glencoe.com** to complete the Issues in Entrepreneurship Research Activity.

Evaluating Individual Sales Performance

Formally evaluating individual sales performance can benefit the company and the salesperson. Salespeople must know the process, guidelines, and standards beforehand. That way, they understand the purpose and value of the evaluation. When they know what to expect, they understand they are being evaluated objectively. They welcome the opportunity to improve their performance. A complete program for evaluating sales staff performance includes five steps:

1. **Establish guidelines.** The guidelines should include who will do the ratings, when and how often they will be done, the basis on which salespeople will be rated, and how the results will be used.

2. **Identify factors to be measured.** Include quantitative factors (calls per day, sales volume, number of orders, etc.) and qualitative factors (quality of sales presentation, product knowledge, customer relations, etc.).

3. **Set standards for performance.** Standards, or benchmarks, must be equitable and reasonable, tied to company goals, based on records, based on analysis of sales jobs, and evaluated using a rating form.

4. **Compare performance to standards.** Each salesperson's performance is compared to the standards.

5. **Discuss results with salespeople.** Individual conferences should be held with each salesperson. Achievements should be emphasized and recommendations made where improvement is needed. The conference should be a positive experience.

Section 13.2 After You Read

Key Concept Review

1. Where does the sales planning process begin?
2. What motivational techniques are especially appropriate for salespeople?
3. List the steps in establishing a procedure for evaluating salespeople.

Critical Thinking

4. Design an evaluation form for salespeople. Write one or more paragraphs explaining the form. Also explain what it is designed to evaluate.

Role Play

Situation You will be meeting with a new salesperson you hired for your business. The purpose of the meeting is to show her the sales performance evaluation and explain its purpose and value.

Activity To prepare for this meeting, make decisions about guidelines, factors to be measured, and standards. Design a qualitative evaluation form and prepare an outline. Pair up with a classmate, who will play the role of the salesperson.

Evaluation You will be evaluated on how well you address these issues:

• Develop fair and realistic guidelines, factors to measure, and standards.

• Explain the process, purpose, and value of the evaluation.

• Answer the salesperson's questions.

• Describe the performance evaluation as a benefit to the salesperson.

Chapter Summary

Organizing and Preparing a Sales Force

For many businesses, personal selling is the backbone of their marketing mix. Businesses use salespeople to help a customer make a buying decision. Sales are classified into two groups: order getting and order taking. Effective salespeople have common traits such as organization, punctuality, and follow-through. Salespeople must be trained. They need to know the company's products, customers, and selling mechanics. There are ten steps in the complete selling process. Knowledge of order forms and proposals, cash registers, sales checks, and sales taxes is often necessary near the end of a sale.

Planning, Directing, and Evaluating Sales

Managing sales involves three areas: (1) Sales planning must be completed before sales operations begin, (2) sales operations must be directed to ensure that company goals are reached, and (3) company and individual sales performance must be evaluated to determine their effectiveness. As a sales manager, you must be able to supervise and motivate your salespeople, compensate them adequately, handle sales expenses and transportation issues, and maintain high morale among your staff. Sales planning begins with determining the market potential and making sales forecasts. It is tied to a marketing plan. Evaluating the entire company's sales performance as well as the performance of individual salespeople is critical to the future success of the business.

Key Terms Review

1. Imagine that you are preparing an orientation workshop for your new sales force. Create a presentation using the following key terms:

personal selling (p. 278)	buying process (p. 283)	sales forecast (p. 288)
prospect (p. 278)	prospecting (p. 284)	sales territory (p. 289)
sales force (p. 279)	preapproach (p. 284)	sales quota (p. 290)
order getting (p. 279)	approach (p. 284)	salary (p. 291)
order taking (p. 279)	objections (p. 284)	commission (p. 291)
rational buying motive (p. 281)	suggestion selling (p. 284)	sales call report (p. 292)
emotional buying motive (p. 281)	sales check (p. 287)	SWOT analysis (p. 293)
customer benefits (p. 282)	sales planning (p. 288)	morale (p. 294)

Key Concept Review

2. **Explain** the role of personal selling in businesses. (13.1)
3. **Define** the two types of selling situations. (13.1)
4. **Describe** the kinds of training needed by salespeople. (13.1)
5. **Identify** the components of sales planning. (13.2)
6. **List** the elements that are involved in directing sales. (13.2)
7. **Discuss** the procedures used in evaluating sales performance. (13.2)

Critical Thinking

8. Compare the traits of a successful salesperson with the characteristics needed to be a successful entrepreneur presented in Chapter 2. What conclusions can you draw? Explain.
9. Explain the difference between rational buying motives and emotional buying motives. Give examples.
10. Choose a product you purchased recently from a retail store. Describe the steps that occurred in the selling process.
11. If you were a salesperson, which compensation method would you prefer? Explain your answer.
12. Compare the duties and responsibilities of a teacher with those of a sales manager.
13. Describe the evaluation process for individual sales performance.
14. Are Internet skills for selling as important to inside sales reps as they are to outside sales reps? Explain.

Write About It

15. Explain in two paragraphs how the buying process can also be the stages of selling.
16. How is selling in a small business different from and similar to selling in a large business? Explain your answer in two paragraphs.
17. Compare the advantages and disadvantages of sales quotas. Compose your answer at the computer in three paragraphs.
18. In an e-mail message to your teacher, explain the advantages of obtaining a range of both high and low forecasts for your sales.
19. Imagine you are a salesperson who is paid a salary plus commission. Your salary is $600 per month, and your commission rate is 2 percent of sales. Last month your sales were $14,763.52. How much money did you make last month? Explain in writing how you arrived at your answer.
20. Write a paper describing the cash register procedures used in your business.

Academic Skills

Math

21. You are planning to sell an item for $19.95. What is the total purchase price if sales tax in your state is 5.75 percent?

Language Arts

22. Working in teams of two, role-play a scenario between a salesperson and a customer. The salesperson should choose a product and describe its features as benefits to the customer. Change products and reverse roles. Decide if you would buy each other's product.

Entrepreneurship in Your Community

23. Choose a product you would like to sell. Prepare a sales presentation that includes the following:

- The benefits of the product
- How the product will meet prospective customers' needs
- Potential objections that might be raised about the product
- Follow-up activities you can use to ensure that your customers are satisfied

Share your presentation with the class.

24. Interview the owner of a sales-oriented business (for example, real estate agent, insurance agent, automobile dealer). Determine the internal and external environmental factors that affect sales. Ask how he or she would adjust sales plans as those factors changed.

Ethical Practices

Padding Expenses

25. Dale, a sales trainee, has been assigned to ride with Jack, an experienced salesperson, for his first week of training. As Jack is showing Dale how to complete an expense report, he points out that he routinely adds 10 percent to the miles he actually drives. He goes on to explain that in order to develop new contacts and service current clients, he often makes "off-the-clock" contacts on weekends, making calls from home. The additional 10 percent, according to Jack, helps to offset his out-of-pocket expenses and time invested. Is Jack's padding of expenses ethical? How would you control this practice in your sales force?

INTERNET *connection*

Research Mailing Lists

You are the sales manager for a company that sells framed photographs. You have thought about starting an electronic mailing list to boost sales. You want to conduct research first.

Connect

Use a Web directory or search engine to research:

- Electronic mailing lists.
- Software and hardware needed.
- Costs involved.
- Ideas for using e-mail to increase sales.

Application

Prepare a presentation slide show about mailing lists. Demonstrate how to create and maintain a mailing list.

The Electronic Entrepreneur

Using E-Mail for Selling

E-mail can be an effective tool for marketing. Many customers voluntarily sign up for e-mail mailing lists to receive updates on new products and services, special offerings, and sales. There are many laws that apply to e-mail marketing, so it is important that you understand the law before starting an e-mail marketing campaign.

Avoid Spam Although e-mail has become a crucial tool for business and personal communication, it has also brought about an enormous frustration because of **spam**, or unsolicited commercial e-mail. Sending spam is a serious violation of **netiquette**, the code of conduct that governs online behavior. Many states have banned unsolicited commercial e-mail messages, and violators can face high fines. Not all commercial e-mail is spam; businesses can still e-mail information to people who have requested it or to past customers.

Get Permission Make sure that you have permission from every e-mail recipient. An **opt-in list** is a mailing list made up of subscribers who have given permission to be sent e-mail by the mailing list owner. A **double opt-in list** is an opt-in list with a two-step confirmation process. Subscribers must confirm their registration by responding to an e-mail message. On the other hand, an **opt-out list** is a mailing list to which recipients do not choose to subscribe; recipients must complete an online form or send an e-mail if they do not want to receive mailings. Opt-out lists are closely associated with spam and are considered a bad practice.

Provide a Way Out State and federal law requires businesses to provide an opt-out mechanism in their marketing e-mails. Unsubscribe requests must be honored in as little as 10 days. If you rent an e-mail list, make sure that the list vendor has offered an opt-out option to subscribers.

FACT AND IDEA REVIEW

1. What is spam?
2. What are some of the reasons why someone would ask to receive commercial e-mail? Can you name some examples?
3. What are the differences between opt-in and opt-out lists? Which is preferred?
4. Why should you give e-mail subscribers the option to opt out?

FOR DISCUSSION

5. What are some commercial e-mail lists you have signed up for or might want to sign up for? Why?

TechTerms

- spam
- netiquette
- opt-in list
- double opt-in list
- opt-out list

Competitive Analysis

The competitive analysis section of the business plan should focus on demonstrating that the proposed business has an advantage over its competitors.

✔ STEP 1   **GATHER INFORMATION ABOUT YOUR COMPETITORS**

Conduct research on the top direct and indirect competitors of your proposed business. Prepare a competitive grid (see Chapter 5, page 98) to present highlights from your research.

✔ STEP 2   **DETERMINE YOUR COMPANY'S COMPETITIVE ADVANTAGE**

Create a chart like the one below. Use the information from your competitive grid to answer the four questions and determine your proposed business's competitive advantage.

COMPETITIVE ADVANTAGE	
Question	**Answer**
How are your company's products and services different from your competitors' products and services?	
How are your company's products and services better than your competitors' products and services?	
What key assets does your business have that your competitors do not have?	
How will your business strategies and marketing mix strategies help your business to attract and defend market share?	

Marketing Plan

A marketing plan describes a company's marketing mix strategies or how it plans to market, promote, and sell its products or services.

✔ STEP 1   **DESCRIBE YOUR MARKETING OBJECTIVES**

Write a description of your proposed business's marketing objectives. Explain your plan for finding the best market. Describe the message your marketing mix strategies are meant to convey, and explain how the marketing mix strategies will be implemented and evaluated for effectiveness.

✓ STEP 2 PLAN YOUR MARKETING MIX

Create a chart like the one below to organize information about the product, price, place, promotion, and people strategies your company will use to reach its target market. Evaluate the impact of each of the strategies on the other marketing mix strategies.

STRATEGIES	DESCRIPTION	IMPACT ON OTHER STRATEGIES
Product Strategy		
Price Strategy		
Place Strategy		
Promotion Strategy		
People Strategy		

Use the **Business Plan Project Appendix** on pages 532–543 to explore the content requirements of a business plan in more detail.

▶ The **Competitive Analysis** section of the business plan should focus on demonstrating that the proposed business has an advantage over its competitors.

▶ The **Marketing Plan** describes a company's marketing mix strategies or how it plans to market, promote, and sell its products or services.

BUSINESS PLAN PROJECT TEMPLATE

@ Go to **entrepreneurship.glencoe.com** for a document template in which you can write your own business plan.

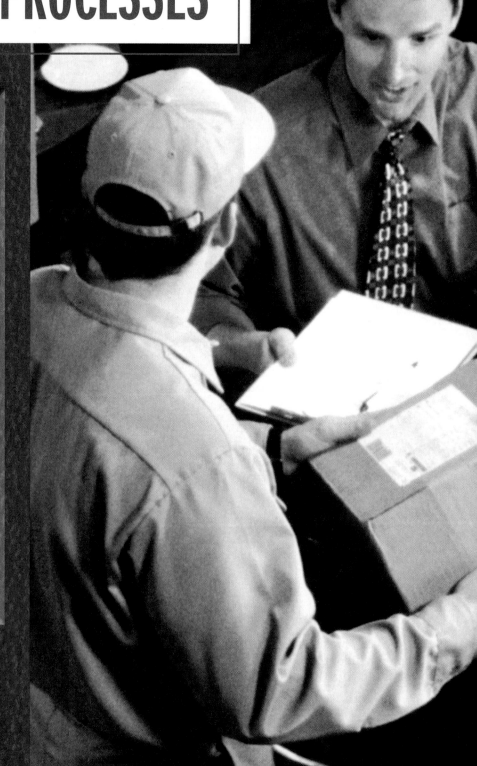

UNIT 4

MANAGING YOUR BUSINESS PROCESSES

UNIT OVERVIEW

Introduction

Do you have a great business plan? Have you developed an exciting marketing idea? Do you have ambitious long-term goals? To execute all your plans, you will need business management skills. Management activities include organizing, planning, and controlling resources. Entrepreneurs have to make many decisions about business processes, ranging from purchasing and production to operations and staffing. You need management skills to run your business smoothly and profitably.

BUSINESS PLAN PROJECT PREVIEW

When you complete Unit 4, you will begin to explore these sections of the business plan:

▶ The **Operational Plan** section of the business plan includes information about all the processes that take place in the business.

▶ The **Organizational Plan** offers information about the business's legal structure, methods of and responsibilities for record keeping, human resources, and legal and insurance issues.

303

Chapter 14

Preparing and Planning to Manage

Section 14.1
Entrepreneur or Manager?

Section 14.2
Management Styles and Skills

CHAPTER OBJECTIVES

When you have completed this chapter, you should be able to:

SECTION 14.1

- Describe the difference between the entrepreneurial role and the management role of a new business owner.
- Identify the management functions.
- List and explain the key elements in a positive business climate.

SECTION 14.2

- Name the three basic management styles.
- List the skills needed for managing.
- Explain the principles of management excellence.

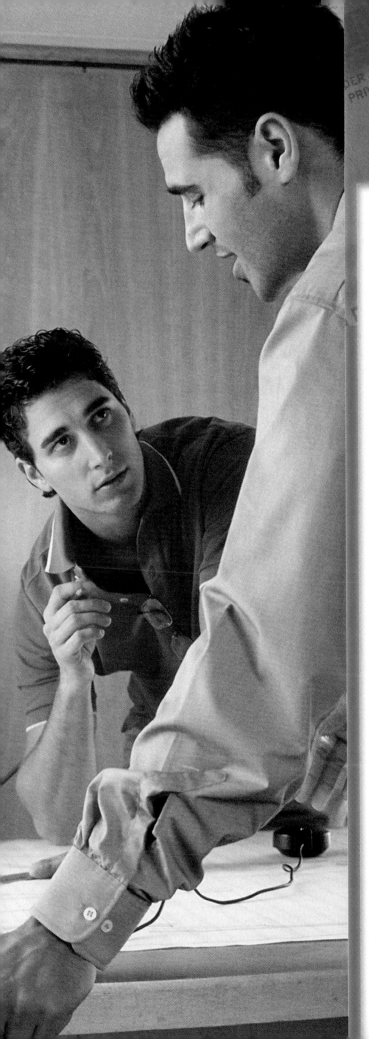

PAYROLL SYSTEMS

If you own a business, an important part of its accounting is payroll, a list of employees and the payments due to them for a specific time period. The period of time over which you pay your employees is a pay period.

A good payroll accounting system ensures that employees are paid on time and have the correct amounts on their paychecks. In addition to issuing checks, a payroll system maintains records needed for accounting purposes and for preparing reports to government agencies.

Every payroll system has some common tasks or steps. All are important and must be done carefully, accurately, and regularly. These include:

1. Calculating gross earnings

2. Calculating payroll deductions

3. Preparing payroll records

4. Preparing paychecks

5. Recording payroll information in your accounting records

6. Reporting payroll information to the government

 Go to **entrepreneurship.glencoe.com** to complete the Standard & Poor's Money Talk Financial Literacy Activity.

PREPARE TO READ

THINK ABOUT THESE QUESTIONS AS YOU READ.

How is the entrepreneurial role different from the management role?

What are the three basic management styles?

What skills are needed for managing?

Entrepreneur or Manager?

GET READY TO READ

KEY TERMS
- manager
- planning
- strategic plans
- tactical plans
- operational plans
- organizing
- directing
- controlling
- quality control program
- climate
- image
- team building
- communication

KEY CONCEPTS
- Managers, Leadership, and Teamwork
- Performing Management Functions
- Establishing a Positive Climate

THE MAIN IDEA

To be successful in a new business, an entrepreneur must perform management functions and establish a positive working climate.

READING ORGANIZER

Draw the reading organizer on a separate piece of paper. As you read, write the four management functions.

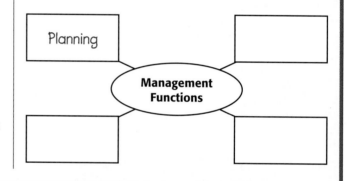

Managers, Leadership, and Teamwork

As a business owner, you must look to others for assistance. The saying "There's no *I* in *TEAM*" means that everyone in your organization is a valuable resource. Everyone works together toward a common goal. As a designer, you may rely on a salesperson to tell you that customers like short-sleeve shirts. You may rely on garment workers to create your fashions. Without an accountant, you may not know if you are making a profit.

This section will discuss how entrepreneurs organize their human resources and structure their businesses. You will also learn what it takes to be a responsible leader, an effective manager, and a team builder.

Entrepreneur and Manager

Once you open the doors of your business, you put on a second hat. You continue to wear the hat of the entrepreneur, but your focus shifts from starting your own business to growing and expanding it. Your second hat is that of a manager.

A **manager** is a person who is responsible for directing and controlling the work and personnel of a business or of a particular department within a business. Managers coordinate the people, processes, and resources of your operation on a daily basis.

You juggle those responsibilities to achieve your principal objectives—to survive and to make a profit. Even if you hire someone else to manage your business, you still must oversee the operation. For this reason, and because your operation will probably start out small, you may do your own managing.

Your Management Role

As a manager, you must deal with many situations, often at the same time. On any given day, you might send out orders, review sales figures, and attend a community meeting. You might also handle an employee dispute, interview a job applicant, and deal with a dissatisfied customer. You might spend an entire day negotiating a contract or revising short-term plans. To run a business effectively and provide good service, you must perform management functions and establish a positive climate.

Performing Management Functions

When managers are managing, they use a series of activities called *management functions* to achieve their objectives. These functions include the following:

- Planning
- Organizing
- Directing
- Controlling

While You Read

Predict How do managers achieve their objectives?

The four functions occur in that order. When managers are working, they often deal with multiple objectives—each at a different stage—in the same time frame.

MULTITASKING A manager must handle many different kinds of situations. *How can an entrepreneur prepare to handle so many tasks if it is his or her first business?*

While You Read

Connect Think of one business goal. Then write a list of the strategic plans, tactical plans, and operational plans that you would need to take to achieve the goal.

Planning

The first step in managing is planning. **Planning** is the act of setting goals, developing strategies, and outlining tasks and timelines to meet those goals. When you plan, you determine your business's objectives (desired results) and how you are going to reach them. Plans are on three levels—from the long range to the present.

- **Strategic plans** are long-range objectives based on long-term goals. They map out where you want your business to be in three to five years. Usually, they do not include a specific target date. For example, you may want your pet toy manufacturing company to grow into the largest in the industry.

- **Tactical plans** are midrange objectives that focus on a period of one year or less. They are built on specific objectives with target dates. Tactical objectives and plans help ensure that you accomplish strategic goals and plans. A major objective of your marketing plan for the year may be to increase market share.

- **Operational plans** are short-term objectives that help achieve tactical plans. They bring the tactical plans to life. These plans also include policies, rules and regulations, and budgets for the day-to-day operation of the business. Your operational plan may, in part, call for an ad campaign to roll out new pet toys.

Suppose a part of your strategic plan is to double your pet toy production capacity within the next four years. One tactical plan might be to complete a new pet toy factory by next March, increasing output 25 percent. Operational plans may include a request for bids to be sent to contractors for the proposed plant. **Figure 14.1** provides another example of how the three types of planning work together.

Planning is an ongoing process. Strategic and tactical plans must be reviewed at least once a year. Operational plans are done for much shorter periods—monthly, weekly, and daily.

Figure 14.1 **Strategic, Operational, and Tactical Plans**

PLANNING Strategic, tactical, and operational plans are great ways to zero in on your goals. *How might you use these plans to assist with your studies?*

STRATEGIC PLANS
- Double pet toy production capacity within four years.

OPERATIONAL PLANS
- Request bids from contractors.
- Contact Pet Toy Producers of America to get trade show dates.

TACTICAL PLANS
- Complete new factory with increased output.
- Travel to trade shows to see the latest technology in manufacturing equipment.

BusinessWeek Case Study

Brainpower on the Balance Sheet

Intangibles such as brands and intellectual property comprise well over half the market value of public companies. They should get toted up like other assets. The question is, where and how?

It may be a strange time to say this, just when the world is clamoring for truth in accounting. But what companies really need is greater tolerance of uncertainty. They should be allowed to assign dollar values to intangible assets such as patents, brands, and customer lists. With a better grasp of invisible assets, investors can make wiser decisions—though accounting authorities may not come around to this notion for another 20 years. This fictional balance sheet shows one possible approach, toting up intellectual property alongside plant and property.

As the embodiment of ideas, intangibles are what drive growth in an information economy. Baruch Lev, an accounting professor at New York University, reckons that in the late 1990s, businesses invested approximately $1 trillion per year in such assets. Taken together, intangibles comprise well

over half the market value of public companies. Yet, with statements prepared under U.S. generally accepted accounting principles (GAAP), investors can only guess at their value or makeup. Current reporting practices "fail to provide adequate guidance to managers, investors, or public policymakers," says Lev—though he does not expect a sea of change any time soon.

SOURCE: *BusinessWeek*, AUGUST 26, 2002; BY ADAM ASTON

APPLICATION

As a class, select a well-known business. Use a spreadsheet program to make a list of the "invisible" assets the business might have. Assign a dollar value to each asset listed.

 Go to **entrepreneurship.glencoe.com** to complete the *BusinessWeek* Case Study Reading Guide Activity.

Reasons why you may have to review your plans include the political climate, technological advances, and the economy. For example, a new law requiring expensive safety gear may dampen your company's expansion plans. Likewise, a weak economy may restrict your advertising campaign.

Organizing

To carry out your company's plans, you must organize people, equipment, materials, and other resources. **Organizing** is the grouping of resources in combinations that will help you reach your objectives. This means, among other things, deciding what jobs need to be done. You must set up an organizational chart that includes the jobs. You must then hire and train new employees to fill the positions. You also need to give your new hires authority and responsibility.

The Song Hunter

Music-lover Luke Eddins has a unique job—he's a "song bounty hunter" for movie and television producers. Movies and TV shows often need music for certain scenes, and they have to pay the bands whose music they use. For big-name acts, that can get pretty expensive—while smaller, less-established artists are happy to take less money because of the publicity they will receive. Enter Eddins, who finds unsigned and indie bands and puts their music in the hands of producers. He started his business, LukeHits LLC, in his apartment in 2002, and today he is well known and respected by both producers and musicians, having placed songs in films like *The Ring* and *Kangaroo Jack*.

CRITICAL THINKING

Why would a film or television producer want to use someone like Eddins? What are the benefits to the band?

 Go to **entrepreneurship.glencoe.com** to complete the Success Stories Writing Activity.

Directing

After organizing your people and resources, you direct their efforts to accomplish your planned objectives. **Directing** is the process of guiding and supervising employees, often one-on-one, while they work. Directing is carried out by communicating directions, assignments, and instructions to your employees. It also includes motivating employees to perform satisfactorily as well as providing effective leadership.

Controlling

The final step in managing is controlling. **Controlling** is the process of comparing your expected results (your objectives) with actual performance. If things are not working out as planned, you need to take corrective action.

How do you compare your plans with what is actually happening? You can use your budget to compare budgeted costs with actual costs. You can use personal observations and quality control programs. A **quality control program** is a set of measures built into the production process to make sure that products or services meet certain standards and performance requirements.

If you find significant differences between what you planned and what actually happened, you must take steps to correct the problem. Corrective action can take several forms. You may decide to replace input (people or other resources) or change the control process. You may put preventive measures in place to keep things from going wrong in the future. You may also decide to revise your objectives.

Establishing a Positive Climate

The climate that exists in a new business is linked to the tone the manager sets. **Climate** is the prevailing atmosphere or attitude. As the manager, you want to create a climate that provides for:

- Growth of employees as well as the business
- Creativity, innovation, and change
- Problem solving, goal development, and goal achievement
- Effective communication within the business

Three key elements in positive business climates include image, team building, and communication.

Image

To begin developing a positive business climate, strengthen your company's image with customers and the community. A business's **image** is the mental picture and feelings people have when thinking about the business. Employees want to be associated with a winner, and your company's image becomes part of their self-image.

Take image into consideration when you develop or revise marketing plans. Establish a program for improving company image by changing customer policies and improving customer service. Use a public relations approach to build your company's image. Identify a company spokesperson to develop and maintain media contacts, produce press releases, and handle media calls. Put together a fact sheet about your business that includes information about origin, location, number of employees, and accomplishments. Finally, share your successes whenever they occur.

While You Read

Question What are the three key elements in a positive business climate?

Issues in Entrepreneurship

CAMARADERIE VERSUS CLIQUE

When you have a close-knit group of long-time employees, you are likely to develop a good working relationship with them. You are also likely to place trust in them. They are good for teamwork and good for productivity.

However, if long-time employees make new hires feel excluded, both socially and professionally, you may lose new employees. In addition, it will have a negative effect on the company's climate and future growth.

Think Critically
As an owner/manager, how can you avoid this situation?

 Go to **entrepreneurship.glencoe.com** to complete the Issues in Entrepreneurship Research Activity.

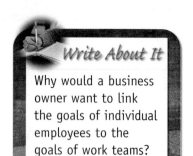
Team Building

Team building involves activities designed to encourage teamwork. Team building contributes to a positive climate in several ways. Most importantly, employees buy into common goals. As a result, work gets done. Team building also results in the development of respect, trust, cooperation, camaraderie, and communication among employees. These positive benefits spread throughout the entire business.

As the entrepreneurial leader in the team approach, you can take an active role in guiding the team by facilitating social interaction; encouraging participation; clarifying team roles, norms, and values; and facilitating task accomplishment.

Communication

Communication is the process of exchanging information. Effective staff communication is communication that takes place in an atmosphere of respect and trust. The traditional channels of communication among management and staff are interpersonal, departmental, interdepartmental, and company-wide. Interpersonal communication is communication with another person. Departmental communication is communication among members of a department. Interdepartmental communication is communication among members of two or more departments. Company-wide communication is communication among all members of a company.

Section 14.1 After You Read

Key Concept Review

1. What does a manager coordinate on a daily basis?

2. One strategic goal for your business is to improve your sales volume. List possible tactical and operational objectives to achieve that goal.

3. Describe effective staff communication and its uses: interpersonal, departmental, interdepartmental, and company-wide.

Critical Thinking

4. Why is it important to link the goals of the individual to the goals of the team?

Role Play

Situation Kathia manages a sales force of 200 people. The employees do not believe their problems are being heard, and Kathia does not think her employees understand the expectations she has of them. This leads to miscommunication.

Activity Pair up with a classmate and assume the role of a management consultant who has been hired to advise Kathia and devise a system of communication to improve the relations between her and her employees. Have your classmate assume the role of Kathia. In the role play, explain how Kathia can improve communication with her sales force.

Evaluation You will be evaluated on how well you address these issues:

- Describe the three key elements in positive business climates—image, team building, and communication.

- Explain how Kathia can improve communication with her sales force.

- Make recommendations for improving the overall business climate.

Management Styles and Skills

GET READY TO READ

KEY TERMS
- situational management
- human relations
- nonverbal communication
- networking
- time management
- conceptual skills

KEY CONCEPTS
- Adopting a Management Style
- Developing Management Skills
- Principles of Management Excellence

THE MAIN IDEA

To manage successfully and excel in leadership situations, you must establish a management style and draw on a specific set of skills.

CONCEPT ORGANIZER

Draw the reading organizer on a separate sheet of paper. As you read, list the three different leadership styles.

MANAGEMENT STYLES

1. power-oriented _____
2. _____
3. _____

Adopting a Management Style

Management style is the manner in which you approach your management responsibilities. It is a major factor in the directing function. Certain personal characteristics are needed in management situations. These include self-assuredness, decisiveness, and a desire to be the best. However, there are many differences in how managers with different styles go about managing. The question you must answer is which style is best for managing your business. The three styles are shown in **Figure 14.2** on page 314.

Generally, an achievement-oriented approach is most appropriate for small businesses. However, at times, you may have to adopt one of the other approaches, at least temporarily. You may have to take a power-oriented approach if you are at risk of losing a major customer. You may have to become routine-oriented to stabilize a part of your operation, perhaps daily office procedures.

Good managers are able to use **situational management**, adapting the management approach to particular circumstances. Making the adjustment from one style to another is not difficult. This is particularly true when you regard situational management as a supplement to your basic approach.

Figure 14.2 | Three Management Styles

MANAGERIAL APPROACH
Your choice of a management style can be a major factor in the success of your business. In general, you have three choices. *In your opinion, which management style(s) would be most effective? Explain.*

1. Power-Oriented Style
Managers who use a power-oriented style try to maintain total control over their whole operation. This style works in situations where employees are untrained, inexperienced, or involved in a crisis.

2. Routine-Oriented Style
Routine-oriented managers are concerned with keeping the operation running smoothly rather than accomplishing other goals. This style is most appropriate in middle management in large corporations.

3. Achievement-Oriented Style
Managers who are achievement-oriented are open to new ideas and seek out employee suggestions. Achievement-oriented management is most effective where a manager is dealing directly with employees who are turning out work.

Developing Management Skills

To manage activities successfully, you must draw on a specific set of skills. These skills can be gained through education and training and improved with practice and experience.

Human Relations

Human relations skills are considered the most important management skills. **Human relations** is the study of how people relate to each other. Human relations skills are interpersonal skills. They are tied closely to communication skills. Managers with good human relations skills are considerate, fair, and attentive when dealing with others. These skills are also a key ingredient in a manager's ability to interact with, lead, and motivate employees.

Communication

Communication is essential to your effectiveness whether you are planning, organizing, directing, or controlling. Communication skills include speaking, listening, writing, and negotiating. **Nonverbal communication** is communication not involving words. It is transmitted through actions and behaviors and includes facial expressions, gestures, posture, eye contact, personal space, and even clothing choices.

Networking

Networking is the process of building and maintaining informal relationships with people whose friendship could bring business opportunities. Networking skills can help you reach your goals. You can use business networking to discuss mutual opportunities, solve problems, and share or maximize resources.

Quick Math

Create a graph showing your organization's sales figures in dollars for the last five years:
Year 1 = $28,900;
Year 2 = 11% increase;
Year 3 = 15% increase;
Year 4 = 3% decrease;
Year 5 = 8% increase.

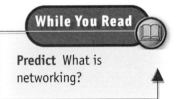

While You Read

Predict What is networking?

TECHNOLOGY Today

Electronic Workflow Applications

As companies do more of their work on the computer and less on paper, increasingly large amounts of data are being generated. Electronic workflow applications help keep that data under control. For example, a contract might once have been passed from person to person on paper—today, it might be moved electronically from one person to another. Workflow applications make sure the data goes to the right place, in the right order.

Critical Thinking

What business activities that were traditionally done on paper might be done electronically today?

 Go to **entrepreneurship.glencoe.com** to complete the Technology Today Vocabulary Practice Activity.

While You Read

Connect Which time management skill is most important? Explain your answer.

Math

The ability to perform math computations is another foundation skill that managers need. Math is necessary for overseeing daily operations, evaluating business performance, and making long-range projections.

Problem Solving and Decision Making

Managers use problem solving and decision-making skills for planning, carrying out plans, and handling situations that must be dealt with immediately. Before solving problems and making decisions, carefully assess the situation. By utilizing critical thinking and creative thinking skills in decision-making situations, you are more likely to attain your desired results.

Technical Skills

Technical skills involve the use of tools, equipment, procedures, and techniques that are critical to the business. These skills usually come from prior education and training. As your business grows, you may turn over management of technical aspects to supervisors you hire. However, in the early stages, you will need to know how things work.

Time Management

At any given time, managers may have several objectives to accomplish. The skill of time management can have a big impact on successful management. **Time management** is the process of allocating time effectively. **Figure 14.3** lists some useful time management techniques.

Conceptual Skills

Conceptual skills are skills that enable a person to understand concepts, ideas, and principles. In a managerial context, conceptual skills allow you to see and understand the relationship between the details and "the big picture." As a small business owner/manager, your conceptual skills enable you to appreciate how day-to-day decisions affect your business's future. Conceptual skills also help you make big decisions, such as when and how to expand your business.

Figure 14.3 · Time Management Suggestions

MANAGING TIME Study the time management techniques listed here. *Why do you think they would be especially valuable to a new business owner?*

1. Set and prioritize your goals.
2. Delegate work to others whenever possible.
3. Plan to spend blocks of time on specific activities that help you achieve your goals.
4. Schedule your activities on a planning calendar.
5. Schedule your most important work for times (mornings, evenings, etc.) when you do your best work.
6. Group your activities for the most efficient use of time.
7. Handle or eliminate interruptions so they take up as little time as possible.

Principles of Management Excellence

In the book *In Search of Excellence,* managerial researchers Thomas Peters and Robert Waterman list eight keys to management excellence.

While You Read

Question In your opinion, which of the principles of management excellence is most important? Why?

- Managers take action rather than overanalyze plans.
- They listen to their customers and put themselves in their customers' shoes.
- They encourage their employees to act independently, be innovative, and treat the business as if it were their own.
- They stress respect for the individual.
- They instill commitment to values and objectives by staying in touch with all employees.
- They keep the business focused on what it does best.
- They keep the organization simple, flexible, and efficient; and they do not overstaff.
- They keep operations under control, and they keep an eye on detail.

Section 14.2 After You Read

Key Concept Review

1. Will any of the management styles work in a new small business?
2. List and explain two key management skills.
3. List and explain two of the principles of management excellence.

Critical Thinking

4. How can the principles of management excellence help a business meet its goals?

Role Play

Situation You are the owner and manager of a retail store. One of your sales clerks is regularly late to work and often does not show up at all. Yet her monthly sales volume is two or three times higher than that of other salespeople. You do not want to fire this employee, but you need her to be at work every day on time.

Activity Pair up with a classmate and role-play a conversation between the store owner and the employee. Take turns assuming the role of the manager. Also employ any management skills you think would be effective.

Evaluation You will be evaluated on how well you address these issues:

- Utilize a management style that is effective in solving the problem.
- Use human relations skills to solve the problem.
- Use communication skills to solve the problem.
- Use problem-solving skills to solve the problem.

Chapter Summary

Entrepreneur or Manager?

When entrepreneurs open their business, they take on a second role—that of manager. To be effective managers, they must adopt their leadership style and develop the necessary skills. Managers plan, organize, direct, and control, usually in that order. A plan determines the objectives or desired results of a business. There are three types of plans—strategic or long range, tactical or mid-range, and operational or short-term.

Management Styles and Skills

Management styles include power-oriented, routine-oriented, and achievement-oriented. Good managers use them according to the situation at hand. The climate of a new business is set by the manager. Image, team-building, and communication are three key elements in a positive business climate. To manage a business successfully requires human relations, technical, time management, and conceptual skills, as well as foundational skills of communication, math, and problem solving. Excellent managers adhere to some common management principles that include taking action, listening to customers, and encouraging independence and innovation among employees.

Key Terms Review

1. Imagine you have just completed a seminar for new managers. Write a summary of what you learned. Use the following key terms in your summary:

manager (p. 307)

planning (p. 308)

strategic plans (p. 308)

tactical plans (p. 308)

operational plans (p. 308)

organizing (p. 309)

directing (p. 310)

controlling (p. 310)

quality control programs (p. 310)

climate (p. 311)

image (p. 311)

team building (p. 312)

communication (p. 312)

situational management (p. 313)

human relations (p. 315)

nonverbal communication (p. 315)

networking (p. 315)

time management (p. 316)

conceptual skills (p. 316)

Key Concept Review

2. **Describe** the difference between the entrepreneurial role and the management role of a new business owner. (14.1)
3. **Identify** the management functions. (14.1)
4. **List and explain** the key elements in a positive business climate. (14.1)
5. **Name** the three basic management styles. (14.2)
6. **List** the skills needed for managing. (14.2)
7. **Explain** the principles of management excellence. (14.2)

Critical Thinking

8. How can the management function of controlling be used to prevent problems?
9. Compare and contrast the three management styles.
10. Why should a manager encourage employees to treat the business as their own?
11. Why is image a component of a positive business climate?
12. Explain the value of leadership skills.
13. Determine the essentials of planning, organizing, staffing, and controlling.
14. What is the relationship between communication and nonverbal communication?
15. How do conceptual skills allow a manager to see and understand the relationship between the details and "the big picture"?

Write About It

16. Identify personal characteristics needed in leadership situations. Write a plan for developing those characteristics.
17. Establish goals and objectives for a planned business. Then outline strategic, tactical, and operational plans to meet your goals and objectives.
18. Create a schedule. Use time management principles in organizing your schedule to include school, work, social, and other activities.
19. Draft a one-page plan for creating a strong image for your proposed business.
20. Which of the skills needed to be a good manager do you think you possess? How can you improve or acquire those skills? How can you attain the skills you do not yet have? Write a journal entry answering those questions.

Academic Skills

Math

21. You decide to take corrective action only when an expense goes over budget by 10 percent. The amount you budget for long-distance telephone calls is $350. When you receive this month's phone bill, you find that long-distance expenses are actually $395. What is the difference between your budgeted and actual expenses in dollars and as a percentage? Would you take corrective action? Why or why not?

Language Arts

22. Armen, an entrepreneur and the manager of a print shop, arrives at work and writes up the following to-do list.

- Order paper and ink for next week's projects.
- Evaluate last week's sales figures.
- Attend luncheon at chamber of commerce.
- Check e-mail and voice mail.
- Review résumés for afternoon interviews.

Use time management principles to rank the tasks according to priority. Explain your reasoning.

Entrepreneurship in Your Community

23. If you are employed, observe the activities of your manager for a one-week period. If you are not employed, observe the activities of a particular teacher for one week.

- Record what he or she does at the end of each day.
- At the end of the week, make a chart categorizing each activity as planning, organizing, directing, or controlling.
- Make a separate category for those activities that were not related to management.

Language Arts

24. As a class, hold an "Entrepreneur of the Year" award ceremony. Identify successful entrepreneurs in your community who use the eight principles of management excellence. Invite them to a ceremony at your school and present them with certificates. Provide refreshments and seek publicity from school and local media.

Ethical Practices

Keeping Promises

25. Joe Stewart organized his start-up business with six employees. At the time of hiring, he promised that they would receive raises within the first three months. He also promised two weeks' vacation per year and group insurance. At the end of the first year, none of the things Joe promised happened. Are Joe's actions—or lack of actions—ethical? Explain. How would you handle the situation if you were Joe?

INTERNET *connection*

Time Management

Denise is a college student who owns and manages a children's bookstore. She has asked you for some time management tips.

Connect

Use a search engine or Web directory to find:

- Articles on time management
- Time management software or books

Application

Use a word processor to summarize your research in an e-mail to Denise. Include specific steps Denise can take to help manage her time. Also recommend a time management software program or a book she can use. Explain.

The Electronic Entrepreneur

Managing a Virtual Workforce

"A day at the office" has taken on a whole new meaning in recent years. Technology has made it easier for businesses to have workers who work out of the office. Having a virtual workforce can help a company to save a significant amount of money on travel and office expenses.

Telecommuting As businesses continually seek ways to cut costs and increase revenue, telecommuting is on the rise. Thanks to technology, many workers can **telecommute**, work outside the office on a computer linked to the workplace via a modem. When employees telecommute, they use tools that allow them to communicate and handle business affairs as if they were at the business location.

Technology To facilitate a virtual workforce, it is necessary to invest in technology. **Groupware** is software designed to be used by more than one person at more than one location. Company intranets often have employee log-in screens that can be accessed from any computer with Internet access; this allows telecommuting employees to log in and access company documents, post messages, and send e-mail.

E-Meetings Having a workforce that is distributed, or located in more than one place, has its challenges. Since face-to-face meetings are not practical for remote workers, you must adopt other ways to communicate. To face this challenge, companies use **e-meetings**, meetings that take place online or via telephone conference calls. There are software programs and Web-based applications that allow people to "meet" online.

Oversight Managers should focus on the output of their virtual workers rather than the actual hours on the clock. Managers of virtual workers should be available through instant messaging technology and hold regular conference calls and e-meetings. **Instant messaging** is a software application that allows real-time text communication between two or more people through a network.

FACT AND IDEA REVIEW
1. What is telecommuting?
2. What is groupware?
3. What are some ways e-meetings can be carried out?
4. Why is instant messaging an important component of managing a virtual workforce?

FOR DISCUSSION
5. Think about a business you hope to have someday. Would telecommuting be a good option for your workers?

TechTerms
- telecommute
- groupware
- e-meetings
- instant messaging

Managing Purchasing and Inventory

CHAPTER OBJECTIVES

When you have completed this chapter, you should be able to:

SECTION 15.1

- Describe the importance of planning purchases.
- Identify factors that affect purchasing.

SECTION 15.2

- Explain inventory procedures used by small businesses.
- Explain the importance and types of inventory control.

PAYROLL, INVENTORY, AND CASH FLOW

Blood flows through your body, keeping you healthy, active, and alive. Cash has a similar effect on a business. Cash flows through the business, giving it the financial resources it needs to operate in a healthy and profitable manner. If a business has a negative flow of cash, it might experience difficulty in daily operations. A negative cash flow experienced over a period of time often results in the death of many businesses.

Payroll and inventory are two financial areas that have great influence on your cash flow. If the inflow of cash is not enough to meet the needs of payroll and inventory, financial problems may result. A successful business carefully monitors its cash flow and constantly analyzes its payroll and inventory costs.

 Go to **entrepreneurship.glencoe.com** to complete the Standard & Poor's Money Talk Financial Literacy Activity.

PREPARE TO READ

THINK ABOUT THESE QUESTIONS AS YOU READ.

What factors affect purchasing?

What is inventory control and why is it important?

Purchase Planning and Management

KEY TERMS
- purchasing
- model inventory
- vendors
- trade discount
- quantity discount
- cash discount
- secured funds
- invoice

KEY CONCEPTS
- Planning Purchases
- Managing Purchases

THE MAIN IDEA

Businesses need to get the best possible products or materials for the price. Making smart spending decisions can result in better values for customers and larger profits for the business.

READING ORGANIZER

Draw the reading organizer on a separate piece of paper. As you read, write the six key factors that enter into purchasing decisions.

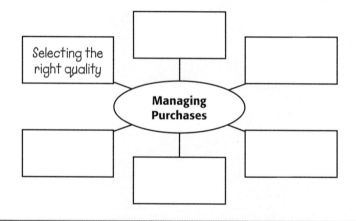

Planning Purchases

Planning your purchases means you can buy items at a low price and sell them at a profit. Planning involves reviewing your sales objectives, and then making purchasing decisions. What will you buy? How much inventory should you stock? How will you time your purchases so your money and storage space are not tied up any longer than necessary? Who will you buy from? How will you get the best price? How will you receive and follow up on your purchases? These questions are answered as you plan your purchases.

Purchasing, also known as procurement, is the buying of all the materials needed by the organization. In this chapter, purchasing refers to buying inventory. Inventory includes products for resale and the materials to create such products. It does not refer to the selection of goods and services for a business's operational needs, which was discussed in Chapter 9.

Developing a Model Inventory

A **model inventory** is a target inventory of what you think you will need to keep in stock. As a beginning entrepreneur, you already identified your inventory needs. You researched competitors and received input from suppliers as well as trade associations. Then you made your best estimate to arrive at a start-up inventory.

Once your business is under way, you can use sales records to guide your inventory decisions. In addition, you may be doing ongoing market research. By being in the business, you become aware of inventory trends and cycles. You also can rely on regular input from **vendors**, the businesses that sell you inventory.

While You Read

Predict Why is purchase planning especially important to wholesalers and retailers?

Managing Purchases

Purchasing management is a primary concern to retail, wholesale, and manufacturing businesses. It may also be a concern to service businesses. For example, a copier repair business needs to purchase copier parts. Only extraction businesses, such as mining and farming, have little concern with purchasing management.

Purchasing decisions may mean the difference between success and failure for an entrepreneur. If that seems extreme, consider how much money is invested in purchasing. Manufacturers spend up to 50 percent of every dollar they make on inventory. Wholesalers spend up to 85 percent. Retailers spend up to 70 percent. Service businesses spend up to 10 percent. Several key factors affect purchasing.

Success Stories

On the Auction Block

When Meg Whitman joined eBay as President and CEO in 1998, she had previously worked in marketing at companies like FTD and Walt Disney. She put those skills to work at eBay, transforming the site from a small auction house to a global marketplace, a consumer-to-consumer (C2C) market where individuals do business with one another rather than with a merchant. Today, eBay is a genuine success: in 2003, the site processed 971 million transactions, with the value of items sold hitting $24 billion.

CRITICAL THINKING

What are some things you (or someone you know) have purchased on eBay? Why were the items purchased there, rather than at a conventional store (online or not)?

 Go to **entrepreneurship.glencoe.com** to complete the Success Stories Writing Activity.

Selecting the Right Quality

To determine the quality of inventory to purchase, buy the products or materials that match your needs. For example, if you manufacture shelving, you should buy durable materials. If you are a retailer dealing in moderately priced footwear, stick to moderately priced product. If you buy high-priced products or budget footwear, your customers may go elsewhere to find what they want.

Buying the Right Quantity

How much inventory should you buy? Purchase enough to maintain your chosen inventory levels. The act of deciding on inventory levels is inventory management. This topic is discussed in Section 15.2.

Timing Your Purchases

Time your purchases so your money and storage space are not tied up any longer than necessary. Also take advantage of economic conditions. If prices are beginning to rise, stock up before they go even higher. If the economy is in a recession, keep purchases to a minimum. Making such timely buying decisions requires that you stay in touch with news.

Choosing the Right Vendors

Locating vendors is not a difficult process. However, several factors need to be considered when selecting vendors:

- **Reliability.** Is the vendor able to deliver enough products or materials when you need them? If deliveries are late or inadequate, you can lose sales and customers.

- **Distance.** How close is the vendor under consideration? The cost of transporting products or materials can be expensive. Local vendors often provide better service. In addition, coordination problems are easier to handle when the vendor is nearby.

- **Service.** What services does the vendor offer? You should inquire carefully. Do sales representatives call on a regular basis? Do they know the product line? Can they assist you with planning layouts, setting up displays, and solving production problems? If there is equipment involved, can they repair it? Do they make unscheduled deliveries in an emergency? What is the return policy? What other appropriate assistance can they provide?

NUMBER OF VENDORS Should you buy from one vendor or from several? When you buy from just one vendor, you may be able to get special treatment, including possible quantity discounts. However, you will be vulnerable if something goes wrong with the working relationship. To lessen your risk, work with more than one vendor. If the relationship with one vendor goes amiss, you will have other established vendors with which you can do business. For a good combination, consider using one vendor for 70 to 80 percent of your purchases. Divide the rest among several vendors.

While You Read

Connect Interview a local wholesale or retail business owner and ask about how the business times its purchasing. Share your findings with the class.

Quick Math

Assume you spend $70,000 a year on inventory. Using the suggested guideline, about how much of that would you purchase from one vendor?

VENDOR CONTRACTS

When dealing with vendors, some businesses prefer building partnerships instead of placing an emphasis on contracts. They believe both parties can best achieve their goals through open communication, information sharing, and working together. They see contracts as potential obstacles to working together to solve problems and develop opportunities. In contrast, other businesses want vendor contracts that spell out quantities, terms, lead times, shipping arrangements, product specifications, and vendor rights and responsibilities. They believe a contract is necessary to protect their interests.

Think Critically

If you were going to require a written sales contract, what rights and responsibilities of vendors would you include? What is your position on requiring vendor contracts? Explain.

 Go to **entrepreneurship.glencoe.com** to complete the Issues in Entrepreneurship Research Activity.

Getting the Right Price

Contact several vendors to find the best price. When orders are large, prices may be negotiable. However, the lowest price is not always the right price. You should factor quality and service into your decision. If quality is poor or delivery is undependable, you may lose more than you gain. The average dissatisfied customer tells ten people about poor products or services he or she received.

Purchase discounts can also affect prices. You may be able to take advantage of trade, quantity, or cash discounts. This depends on where you are in the channel of distribution.

A **trade discount** is a discount from the list price of an item allowed by a manufacturer or wholesaler to a merchant. For example, a manufacturer might give discounts of 50 percent to wholesalers and 40 percent to retailers to reward channel members for their role in getting the products to consumers. A **quantity discount** is a discount that a vendor gives to a buyer who places large orders. A **cash discount** is an amount deducted from the selling price for payment within a specified time period, such as 10 days. Cash discounts accelerate payments and improve cash flow for a business.

In addition to discounts, dating terms affect price. They specify when you must pay a bill and what discount you can take for paying early. Ordinary dating terms, such as 2/10, net 30, are based on the date of the invoice. In this case, the percent of discount for paying early is 2 percent. The number of days within which the discount can be taken is 10. The number of days in which you must pay in full is 30.

THE IMPORTANCE OF READING Entrepreneurs must handle numerous tasks at once. *Why is it worthwhile to set aside time to read about business news and events?*

Other dating terms are as follows:

- **Advance dating.** This occurs when manufacturers give a date other than the invoice date for the terms to take effect. For example, the invoice may be dated June 15 and read 2/10, net 30—as of August 1. August 1 is the date the billing terms go into effect.

- **Extra dating.** This gives additional days before the terms take effect. For example, the invoice terms may read 2/10, net 30, 60 extra. The 2/10, net 30 applies after the 60 days have passed. These terms can also be read as 2/70, net 90.

- **End-of-month (EOM) dating.** These terms change the date from which the terms take effect to the end of the month. For example, an invoice is dated June 15 with terms of 2/10, net 30, EOM. You can take the discount up to 10 days after June 30. The last day to pay the bill is July 30.

- **Receipt-of-goods (ROG) dating.** These terms begin when you receive the goods. Assume you receive an invoice dated June 15 with terms of 2/10, net 30, ROG. The goods are received on June 20. The last day for taking the discount is June 30. The last day for payment is July 20.

While You Read

Question What is the next step in purchasing management after an order is placed?

The price, discounts, and terms have been agreed upon. Now you usually prepare and submit a purchase order to the vendor. The purchase order includes the quantity, style, and number. It also includes the unit price of each item purchased along with extensions. Extensions are the result of multiplying the number of units by the cost per unit. Suppose you had several items on the same purchase order. You would total all of the extensions and enter them at the bottom of the Total column. Other entries on the purchase order might include shipping and delivery instructions.

PAYMENT METHODS Until you establish a good working relationship, your new vendor may request secured funds. **Secured funds** are a form of guaranteed payment. These include a credit card, a cashier's check, a wire transfer, or cash. As you establish credit, a vendor may be willing to accept a single-party check. A vendor may also allow you to deposit a series of post-dated checks into his or her account. It is important to pay your vendors on time. Then if you ever need to stretch your credit, they will allow you to do so.

Receiving and Following Up on Purchases

Purchasing management does not stop with placing your order. You or an employee must verify and record its arrival. If customers are unsatisfied with your goods or services, you should review quality issues with your vendors.

Retailers and wholesalers must mark size, cost, selling price, and other information on each unit. Manufacturing and service businesses may need to mark the grade or source of materials.

Effective managers follow up on how their purchased inventory performs. Retailers and wholesalers follow up on complaints and returns. Manufacturers and service businesses follow up on the performance of materials they use.

CHECKING INVOICES When you receive a shipment from a vendor, it should be accompanied by an invoice. An **invoice** is an itemized statement of money owed for goods shipped or services rendered. The invoice is based on and contains much of the same information as your purchase order. At the time of arrival, you should check the shipment against the invoice. This allows you to verify the correctness, quality, and condition of the order. You should match the invoice against the purchase order and check the accuracy of entries and extensions. If you find something wrong with the shipment or on the invoice, report it to the vendor immediately. Keeping a close eye on incoming shipments protects you from paying for somebody else's mistakes.

Section 15.1 After You Read

Key Concept Review

1. What factors should you consider when selecting a vendor?
2. List three types of discounts that apply to purchasing.
3. What should you or a designated employee do when inventory stock arrives?

Critical Thinking

4. Why do manufacturers and service providers spend different percentages of their income on inventories? Provide an example for each type of business.

Role Play

Situation Your school wants to sell helium balloons to raise money for computer equipment. You and a classmate are co-chairs of the committee in charge of the project.

Activity Team up with your co-chair to determine how many and what kind of balloons you need, to locate possible sources, and to negotiate delivery and price with several vendors. Also develop a plan to control inventory, sales receipts, and payment for the balloons. Put together and role-play a presentation to the general committee. Include steps you have taken, your recommendations for a vendor, and your plan for managing the inventory and finances.

Evaluation You will be evaluated on how well you:

- Explore sources of supply.
- Describe the process of selecting suppliers and sources.
- Perform calculations involving money and materials.
- Develop a system to keep track of inventory and cash transactions.

Inventory Management

Inventory Management

Inventory management is used to find and maintain inventory levels that are neither too small nor too large. Too little inventory may result in lost sales. It can mean losing customers. It can interrupt your operation. It also leads to frequent reordering. Time and energy on your part are required to place these additional orders.

However, too much inventory can add as much as 25 percent to the cost of inventory. Added costs may include the following:

- **Financing cost**: the cost of the interest you pay to borrow money to purchase inventory.

- **Opportunity cost**: the cost associated with giving up the use of money tied up in inventory.

- **Storage cost**: the cost associated with renting or buying the space needed to store the inventory.

- **Insurance cost**: the cost associated with insuring the inventory.
- **Shrinkage cost**: the cost associated with the loss of inventory items that are broken, damaged, spoiled, or stolen.
- **Obsolescence cost**: the cost associated with products or materials that become obsolete while in inventory.

Unfortunately, it is difficult to determine and maintain an ideal inventory level. Inventories constantly change, and the "right" amount of inventory shifts with changes in demand and season. However, by adopting sound inventory procedures, you can strike a profitable balance between too much and too little. Careful planning enables you to establish realistic inventory levels. Once you settle on these levels, you need to implement additional procedures to maintain them. These procedures help you do three things. First, they help you keep track of inventory. Second, they result in cost-effective storage. Third, they allow you to reorder the right amounts, keeping the levels where you want them.

While You Read

Predict What is an inventory turnover rate?

Planning Inventory

Planning inventories to achieve a balance between too much and too little requires that you answer two questions:

- How many months' supply should be on hand?
- How much of an investment would that represent?

CALCULATING THE SUPPLY YOU NEED Determining the amount of inventory you need is a two-step process. First, you must determine the inventory, or stock, turnover rate for your business. This is the average number of times the inventory is sold out during, say, a year. Once you know the turnover rate, you can find the number of months' supply to keep.

'TIS THE SEASON Certain businesses are seasonal. *How can a business adjust its purchasing strategy for the off-season?*

You can calculate inventory turnover rate for your business using several different ways. The one you decide to use depends on the information you have available and your type of business. Stores that keep records of the retail dollar value of their stock use this method:

$$\frac{\text{NET SALES (IN RETAIL DOLLARS)}}{\text{AVERAGE INVENTORY ON HAND (IN RETAIL DOLLARS)}}$$

While You Read

Connect Imagine that you are the owner of a produce market. Would you order inventory frequently or infrequently? Why?

Average inventory on hand is the total of the inventory amounts for each month divided by the time period. Net sales are retail sales minus returns and allowances.

For example, if the total inventory for a 12-month period was valued at $870,000, the average inventory would be $72,500. If the net sales during that time period were $344,000, the inventory turnover rate would be 4.74.

$$\frac{\$870,000}{12} = 72{,}500$$

$$\frac{\$344,000}{\$72,500} = 4.74$$

This calculation shows that, on average, the inventory was sold and replaced 4.74 times in a 12-month period.

You can use a second calculation to determine inventory turnover rate when you have only cost information. The formula for that method is as follows:

$$\frac{\text{COST OF GOODS SOLD}}{\text{AVERAGE INVENTORY ON HAND (AT COST)}}$$

You can calculate average inventory on hand (at cost or retail) even if you do not have monthly inventory figures. Simply add the beginning and ending inventories for the period and divide by two.

Another option is to use the industry average turnover rate for your type of business. For example, men's clothing stores have an average inventory turnover rate of 3; restaurants, 22. Some chemical manufacturers' rates are as high as 100. Contact trade associations in your field for the average turnover rate for your type of business.

In some situations, you may want to calculate unit inventory turnover rather than dollar inventory turnover. To do this, use this formula:

$$\frac{\text{NUMBER OF UNITS SOLD}}{\text{AVERAGE INVENTORY ON HAND IN UNITS}}$$

Once you know your inventory turnover rate, you can determine how many months' supply you should have on hand. Divide the number of months in a year by your average turnover rate.

If, for example, your average inventory turnover rate was 4, the calculation would be:

$$\frac{12}{4} = \textbf{3 MONTHS' SUPPLY}$$

Apply the calculation to the retail example with an average of 4.74. The retailer would need 2.53 (about 2½) month's supply. Applied to the restaurant average of 22, restaurants would need 0.54 (about ½) month's supply. Obviously, businesses that depend on a constant supply of fresh inventory must reorder frequently.

CALCULATING YOUR INVENTORY INVESTMENT You know how to estimate the amount of inventory to keep on hand. Now you need to figure out how much it will cost you. Divide the cost of goods sold for your forecasted annual sales by your average inventory turnover rate. Suppose you forecast sales for the coming year to be $100,000. Your cost of goods sold is 75 percent of sales. If you have an average inventory turnover rate of 4, you can determine your inventory investment as follows:

$$\frac{\$100,000 \times 0.75}{4} = \frac{\$75,000}{4} = \$18,750$$

For this situation, you should keep three months of inventory on hand at a cost of $18,750.

This example suggests that one set of calculations applies to the entire inventory. In many businesses, you must make calculations for different product lines or types of materials. For example, socks have a higher turnover rate than raincoats. Each requires separate calculations.

COMPARING WITH INDUSTRY AVERAGES The average inventory turnover rate for your industry can help you gauge your inventory management. Compare the number of turnovers you have in a year to the industry average. Of course, you want to try to turn your inventory over as fast as possible. However, if you are far ahead of the industry average, your prices may be too low. It may also mean you are not able to meet customer needs because you run out of inventory. A lower-than-industry average may indicate that your inventory is tied up in slow-moving merchandise or material.

Inventory Control

Keeping tabs on how much inventory you have in stock is the first step in controlling inventory levels. With a young business, you may be able to track inventory by looking at what you have. As your business grows, however, you will probably have to switch to more structured inventory control systems. To double-check any of the systems, you need to do a physical inventory count. **Figure 15.1** shows four systems used to keep track of inventories.

BusinessWeek Case Study

Bar Codes Better Watch Their Backs

New retail technologies have a way of lingering in dreamland until discount colossus Wal-Mart decides it's time for everyone to wake up. The alarm clock in Bentonville, Ark., just went off again, this time for a successor to bar codes called Radio Frequency Identification (RFID). The wireless technology aims for a world where shelves are always full, supply chains hum efficiently, and consumers are bombarded with promotions as they shop.

The wake-up call came from Wal-Mart Stores Inc.'s Chief Information Officer Linda Dillman. She recently announced that the megaretailer will require its 100 top suppliers to start using RFID for some applications by January, 2005. Given Wal-Mart's enormous size and influence, the technology could spread quickly: Not only will other retailers be forced to adopt it to remain competitive, the wider use will also bring down installment costs.

SOURCE: *BusinessWeek*, July 14, 2003; By Gerry Khermouch and Heather Green

APPLICATION

With a partner, research Radio Frequency Identification. Find out in which ways it is being used. Summarize your findings in a one-page report. Share your report with the class.

@ Go to **entrepreneurship.glencoe.com** to complete the *BusinessWeek* Case Study Reading Guide Activity.

Figure 15.1 **Inventory Systems**

KEEPING TRACK Here are four ways to keep track of your inventory. *Which inventory system might you use in your business? Why?*

1. Visual Inventory System

A small produce store might use this simple and quick visual inspection system: You look at how much inventory you have in stock and compare it to what you want to have on hand. This system usually works best where sales are steady, inventory is handled personally, and items can be obtained quickly.

2. Perpetual Inventory System

As inventory is sold, it is subtracted from the inventory list. As new inventory arrives, it is added. Computerized cash registers allow retail businesses to use this accurate and instantaneous system, which is also popular with warehouses and storage facilities.

3. Partial Inventory System

The partial inventory control system is a combination of systems. In this system, a perpetual inventory is maintained for only those items that account for a large share of the company's sales.

4. Just-in-time (JIT) Inventory System

The JIT system shifts most of the inventory chores to the vendor. By having suppliers deliver inventory just before it is used, stocks are kept at a minimum. For many manufacturers, this provides a very effective control.

Physical Inventory Count

No matter which inventory control system you use, you should conduct periodic physical inventory counts. Errors can occur when making visual estimates or when recording changes in inventory. Items can be removed from stock and not recorded. Merchandise or materials can be lost, be stolen, or go bad. Taking physical inventory gets your books in line with what you actually have in stock.

Taking a physical count also helps you evaluate your inventory control system. If your physical count is very different from your perpetual count, your perpetual system is not very accurate.

Physical inventory counts usually involve two employees. One counts and calls out the item and number. The other records the count on a tally sheet.

Physical counts can be done often or as infrequently as once a year. You can keep counting costs down by getting your inventories as low as possible before the inventory count. In retail, this is often done through special year-end sales.

While You Read

Question Why should a business that uses a perpetual inventory system also take a periodic physical inventory count?

Warehousing

Warehousing is the act of holding and handling goods in a warehouse. The warehouse can be an actual structure or an assigned space. When you plan your warehouse operations, plan these areas:

- **Receiving and shipping docks.** Vendors and transportation companies need easy access to and within your facility.
- **Bulk storage areas.** These are places where goods remain in their original crates, waiting to be broken down into more usable quantities.
- **Staging areas.** This is free space where inbound or outbound materials are sorted, organized, or temporarily stored.
- **Picking rows.** These are rows of small and large inventoried goods that may be placed in bins or on pallets. Here they can be gathered as needed for assembly and packing.
- **Assembly areas.** Here, goods are assembled individually or as kits.
- **Packing areas.** Boxing takes place in packing areas. Also, individual products ready for the consumer may need to be repacked in bulk units for shipping.
- **Management office and lockers.** Your employees need space to work and to keep their personal belongings.

Reordering

To maintain proper inventory levels, you need to decide when and how much to reorder. The type of inventory you keep determines which reordering system is best for you.

PERIODIC REORDERING Products or raw materials that are inexpensive, used often, and easy to get should be reordered periodically. They should be automatically reordered to keep inventory at the proper level. A manufacturer who uses nuts and bolts might restock such hardware every 60 days. A restaurateur might restock baked goods daily.

NONPERIODIC REORDERING Inventory that is not suited to periodic reordering must be reordered in another way. Needs must be projected. To do this, consider three key questions:

1. **What is the lead time?** **Lead time** is the gap in time between placing an order and receiving delivery.

2. **What is the usage rate?** **Usage rate** is how quickly the inventory will be used in a given period of time.

3. **How much safety stock will be needed?** **Safety stock** is a cushion of products or materials. It keeps you from running out of inventory while you are waiting for an order.

REORDERING PROCEDURES No matter what method of reordering is used, an entrepreneur should approach the matter systematically. He or she should plan inventory, order and reorder in accordance with the plan, check to see how well the plan has worked, and make any necessary adjustments.

Section 15.2 After You Read

Key Concept Review

1. Your industry's turnover rate is 11. Your sales are forecasted to be $90,000, and your annual cost of goods sold is 50 percent of sales. Find the number of months' supply to keep on hand and the cost for inventory.

2. You run a small mailbox rental business and sell paper goods on the side. What inventory system will work best for you?

3. You have noticed your inventory shrinking. Develop and list some controls you can put in place to stop this.

Critical Thinking

4. Draw the floor plan of a functioning warehouse for a business that sells kits of hair care products to individuals by mail order. Then write an explanation of the floor plan and how it meets the business's needs.

Role Play

Situation You are the owner of a busy landscaping business. Your business is expanding, and managing your inventory has become a priority. Your inventory includes mowing and edging equipment; gardening tools; sod, plants, and trees; and fertilizers and pesticides. You decide to hire an inventory systems consultant to help you identify a better inventory control system.

Activity Team up with a classmate. Assume the role of the business owner. Have your classmate assume the role of an inventory systems consultant. Then practice and present a role play in which you discuss inventory systems.

Evaluation You will be evaluated on how well you address these issues:

- Explain the importance of inventory control.
- Describe various inventory systems.
- Identify activities associated with product handling and inventory control.
- Select and explain the systems you will use to keep track of your inventory.
- Describe how often you will conduct a physical inventory count.

Chapter Summary

Section 15.1 Purchase Planning and Management

Managing the purchasing and inventory process effectively should be a high priority for entrepreneurs and can mean the difference between success and failure. Planning business purchases requires that you answer critical questions about inventory needs before committing financial resources. You want to get the right quality and quantity of inventory at the right time from the right vendor at the right price. Purchasing management also includes verifying and recording the inventory when it arrives, as well as marking the merchandise or materials.

Section 15.2 Inventory Management

The purpose of inventory management is to find and maintain inventory levels that are neither too small nor too large. To determine the proper amount of inventory, you must calculate how many months' supply you should have in stock and how much that stock will cost you. There are several systems to keep track of your inventory, including visual, perpetual, partial, and just-in-time (JIT). Warehousing involves the operations that are associated with inventoried goods, including receiving and shipping docks, bulk storage areas, staging areas, picking rows, assembly areas, packing areas, and management offices and lockers. Reordering procedures are necessary to maintain inventory at a proper level.

Key Terms Review

1. As a new entrepreneur, prepare a one-page document stating your purchasing and inventory policies. Use the following key terms in your document:

purchasing (p. 324)	opportunity cost (p. 330)
model inventory (p. 325)	storage cost (p. 330)
vendors (p. 325)	insurance cost (p. 331)
trade discounts (p. 327)	shrinkage cost (p. 331)
quantity discount (p. 327)	obsolescence cost (p. 331)
cash discount (p. 327)	warehousing (p. 336)
secured funds (p. 328)	lead time (p. 337)
invoice (p. 329)	usage rate (p. 337)
financing cost (p. 330)	safety stock (p. 337)

Key Concept Review

2. **Describe** the importance of planning purchases. (15.1)
3. **Identify** factors that affect purchasing. (15.1)
4. **Explain** inventory procedures used by small business. (15.2)
5. **Explain** the importance and types of inventory control. (15.2)

Critical Thinking

6. Is it better to buy from one vendor or several?

7. How do you use stock turnover rate to determine the success you have had in managing your inventory?

8. How can you use industry averages to determine how successful you have been in managing your inventory?

9. As your business grows, what inventory control system will be most useful? Why?

10. Compare periodic and nonperiodic ordering systems.

11. Identify the activities associated with storage of inventory in your proposed business.

12. Explain the difference between a visual inventory system and a physical inventory count.

13. Analyze and describe how you will receive, store, and handle inventory in your proposed business.

Write About It

14. In an e-mail message to a classmate, explain how entrepreneurs identify needs.

15. Develop a one-page chart for new business customers that explains trade, quantity, and cash discounts.

16. Imagine you are a vendor who supplies products to beauty supply stores. Create an invoice for a shipment to a store. Since the order was called in, you do not have a purchase order to go by. Calculate the invoice extensions and include invoice terms.

17. Write a letter to a trade association requesting information about average inventory turnover rates for the industry.

18. Describe the process you will use in selecting suppliers and sources for your proposed business. Write out the process in less than two pages.

19. Write a report describing the inventory you will need for your proposed business by categories and quantities.

20. For your proposed business, would the inventory turnover rate be the same for all products you carry? Explain your answer in a memo.

Academic Skills

Math

21. You own a business in a field with an average yearly inventory turnover rate of 6. You have forecasted sales of $240,000 for next year. The cost of your inventory is 70 percent of your selling price.

- How many months' supply of inventory should you keep on hand?
- What is the average dollar value of your inventory investment?

Language Arts

22. You and a friend work as shipping and receiving clerks in a warehouse. You have noticed that there are no procedures for receiving inventory when it arrives. With your friend, write a memo describing the procedures you think should be in place.

Entrepreneurship in Your Community

23. Investigate the possibility of choosing a product line to sell in a business. Talk with at least three local vendors. Be sure to:

- Evaluate them based on reliability, distance, and service.
- Determine what discounts they offer.
- Ask about payment methods they require.

Based on the information you obtain, choose the vendor or vendors for your business. Explain your decision.

24. Interview a manager of a local business regarding the following:

- Purchasing and inventory procedures
- Purchasing and inventory problems
- The handling or preventing of common purchasing and inventory problems

Report your findings to the class. Compile the results. With your classmates, try to determine the similarities or differences between businesses.

Ethical Practices

Ethics Problem or Opportunity?

25. You make custom parts. Over time, you have built up a strong relationship with your clients. On a recent visit, one of your customers confided in you about the design of a product she plans to bring to market. She believes it is a winner. Since the conversation, you have not been able to stop thinking about the product as something your company could make and sell. Although you would have to add some equipment, your operation could handle production. Would there be anything wrong with taking the idea and running with it? What should you do?

Research Purchasing Jobs

You plan to open your own business. To gain experience in purchasing and inventory management, you decide to search for a job in that field.

Connect

Use job-related Web sites to learn about the duties involved in careers in purchasing and inventory management.

- Use key words such as *inventory* and *purchasing*.
- Determine skills and experience necessary for a job in purchasing or inventory management.
- Determine the duties and responsibilities necessary for a job in purchasing or inventory management.

Apply

Write a description of one of the job ads you found in your search. Describe the skills and experiences required for the job.

The Electronic Entrepreneur

Internet Purchasing

While auction sites like eBay have tapped the Internet's potential to allow individuals to sell products to one another, the concepts behind online auctions have been adapted by the business world to change purchasing procedures. Online procurement, or **e-procurement**, is the business-to-business purchase and sale of supplies and services over the Internet.

Business-to-Business Increasingly, companies are turning to online business **B2B communities**, electronic marketplaces where companies can bid on products and services, or offer their services up for bid. These communities allow businesses to find the goods and services they need and negotiate for the best possible price. There is often a fee to join one of these communities, but many companies find them well worthwhile because of the exposure they offer.

Exchanges Companies using B2B networks are said to be using an exchange. A **public exchange** is a B2B network open to any company that wants to take part; there is often a fee to join the exchange. A **private exchange** is an exchange that is operated for exclusive use of a single company: for instance, a large company might have an internal exchange used to deal with vendors for all the parts and services used each day.

A Dual Approach Private exchanges are by far the more common of the two forms; they provide a company with complete control over the bidding and procurement process. Public exchanges are beginning to catch on, chiefly because they give businesses great potential to save large sums of money by dealing with an open marketplace. For many companies, the right approach is to use both methods.

FACT AND IDEA REVIEW

1. What is e-procurement?
2. What is a B2B community?
3. What is the difference between a public and private exchange?
4. Why would a company use both private and public exchanges?

FOR DISCUSSION

5. Give an example of both a private exchange and a public exchange.

TechTerms

- e-procurement
- B2B communities
- public exchange
- private exchange

Production Management and Distribution

CHAPTER OBJECTIVES

When you have completed this chapter, you should be able to:

SECTION 16.1

- Discuss how entrepreneurs develop new products.
- Explain the product development process.

SECTION 16.2

- Explain what is involved in production management.
- Describe the activities that are part of distribution management.

STANDARD &POOR'S
Money Talk

TYPES OF COSTS

It is important to distinguish between marginal costs and sunk costs. Marginal costs are the additional costs associated with creating one more item. For example, if a business can produce 150 widgets at a total cost of $5,000 and 151 widgets for $5,100, the marginal cost of the 151st widget is $100.

Sunk costs are costs that have already been incurred and that cannot be recovered. A common example of a sunk cost for a business is the promotion of a brand name. In contrast to fixed costs (land, equipment, etc.), sunk costs are completely "lost." With fixed costs, there is a possibility of resale to recover some of the cost; with sunk cost, recovery of costs is not possible.

Digital products typically have very low marginal costs, when compared with traditional goods. If a product is distributed via a Web site, then the marginal costs can be zero. Digital products also usually have significant sunk costs (when compared to other fixed costs), primarily in the form of research and product development.

 Go to **entrepreneurship.glencoe.com** to complete the Standard & Poor's Money Talk Financial Literacy Activity.

PREPARE TO READ

THINK ABOUT THESE QUESTIONS AS YOU READ.

How do entrepreneurs develop new products?

What is involved in production and distribution management?

From Idea to Product

GET READY TO READ

KEY TERMS
- product development
- outsourcing
- prototype

KEY CONCEPTS
- Product Development for Entrepreneurs
- The Product Development Process

THE MAIN IDEA

Entrepreneurs work with limited resources, so they must find creative ways to develop and manufacture their products, such as outsourcing. Product development is a repetitive process based on feedback from customers who test the product.

READING ORGANIZER

Draw the reading organizer on a separate piece of paper. As you read, write the four steps of product development.

THE FOUR STEPS OF PRODUCT DEVELOPMENT

STEP 1	STEP 2	STEP 3	STEP 4
Opportunity recognition			

Product Development for Entrepreneurs

The transformation from idea to marketable product is a lengthy process. In this section, you will learn how entrepreneurs develop new products with limited resources.

What Is Product Development?

Product development is the process of creating new or improved products. It involves taking an idea for a product, designing it, building a model, and testing it. Most large companies with big budgets have research and development departments that develop new products. They can afford to make mistakes and still succeed. The same cannot be said for small business owners who have limited resources.

Some consider product development of a new small business to be the riskiest part of start-up. Therefore, an entrepreneur may have difficulty raising money to develop a new product. However, through creative thinking, many entrepreneurs find the funds they need.

Radio Frequency Identification Tags

Theft and loss add up to big costs for manufacturers—every time a case of product gets stolen from shelves or lost on its way from the warehouse, revenue goes down. Savvy merchandisers are looking to radio frequency identification tags (RFID) to fight back. The technique involves implanting tiny microchips within product packages, so both the retailer and the manufacturer can know where the merchandise is at any time. Currently, the high cost of the microchips is a barrier, but prices are expected to go down over time.

Critical Thinking

What are some uses for radio frequency identification tags?

 Go to **entrepreneurship.glencoe.com** to complete the Technology Today Vocabulary Practice Activity.

Outsourcing Product Development

No matter what you are producing, you can use outsourcing to reduce the cost of product development. **Outsourcing** is hiring people and other companies to handle tasks that a business can not do or chooses not to do itself. Outsourcing provides a network of for-hire experts. Gregg Levin developed the PerfectCurve product. (This product prevented baseball caps from losing their shape after washing.) However, Levin did not have the knowledge, ability, or money to set up a complete manufacturing facility. So he outsourced it. He hired a plastics manufacturer to make the product. Then he had the finished product sent to a Boston rehabilitation program site. There, people with disabilities assembled and packaged it.

When outsourcing product development tasks, draw up contracts with all companies with which you do business. This will prevent misunderstandings about schedules, expectations, and tasks. During the process, always be available to answer questions. Some of the areas of product development that can be outsourced include:

- component design
- materials specifications
- machinery to process
- ergonomic design
- packaging design
- assembly drawings and specifications
- user guides and owner manuals

When your company begins to earn a healthy profit, you can bring some product development tasks in-house. Doing so allows you to better control quality and speed of production.

While You Read

Predict What is the first step of the product development process?

Quick Math

The total product development budget for a new toy is $289,000. The cost of the product design was $245,650. What percentage of the product's total budget was the product design cost?

While You Read

Connect What would you do if you learned that a competitor was planning to introduce a product similar to the one your company was planning? ▲

The Product Development Process

Product development for entrepreneurs is not a linear process. Although it appears to move forward in a step-by-step manner, it is actually a repetitive process. An entrepreneur may start developing a product. Along the way, he or she may discover something new that changes the direction of development. For example, suppose you are developing a new video game for children aged 6 to 10. Once you have a prototype, you decide to hold a focus group to see how children respond. Their comments and your observations send you back to the drawing board to do some redesign work. This process may repeat itself several times before you achieve the final product. The four steps of product development are:

1. **Opportunity recognition.** Entrepreneurs are opportunity seekers. For example, the inventor of Nerf foam toys knew parents wanted toys that children could throw indoors without damaging furniture.

2. **Concept investigation.** Study the market to make certain there is sufficient demand.

3. **Product design.** Design the product on paper or on a computer. Make sure the needs and wants of potential customers are incorporated. Also include input from the people involved in marketing, producing, and financing the product.

4. **Prototype building and testing.** A **prototype** is a working model of a product. Often you cannot gauge a product until you actually see, use, and handle it. Test the prototype or working model with actual customers.

Issues in Entrepreneurship

LEAN PRODUCT DEVELOPMENT

Lean product development, lean manufacturing, and lean production are musts for any manufacturing business. The goal of these initiatives is to produce top quality products in the most efficient and economical manner possible.

Lean manufacturing is a systematic plan to reduce waste. Engineers who develop products usually use materials and processes with which they are familiar. However, that does not necessarily mean that the materials and processes are the most efficient or inexpensive ones available. Throughout the product development and production process, a business can conduct a series of systematic evaluations that identify ways to reduce costs.

Critical Thinking

How can lean product development help a business to maximize and sustain a competitive advantage?

 Go to **entrepreneurship.glencoe.com** to complete the Issues in Entrepreneurship Research Activity.

Designing It Right the First Time

You should design your product right the first time. Three good reasons for doing so are:

1. **The cost of design.** Starting over or redesigning costs more than the original work. You can save a lot of money by designing carefully. In a dynamic market, delays caused by redesigning could cause you to miss a window of opportunity.

2. **The quality and marketability of the product.** How carefully you design your product determines quality, reliability, and success in the market. Getting customer input at the early stages of design helps ensure a successful launch.

3. **The time to launch.** If you design your product properly, you will not have to go back and make changes. Besides adding to production costs, making changes increases the time needed to release the final product.

While You Read

Question Why is it important to design a product right the first time?

Building a Prototype

The first prototype you build may not look like the final product. However, it should work like the final product. Gregg Levin built several prototypes of the PerfectCurve. He used clay, wood, and other materials before making a final decision. Throughout the process, he fine-tuned the product. With the prototype, he got better customer input because potential customers could actually see and use the product.

Section 16.1 After You Read

Key Concept Review

1. What product development tasks can entrepreneurs outsource?
2. What are the basic steps in the product development process?
3. Why is product design so important?

Critical Thinking

4. Interview an entrepreneur who has developed a new product. What steps did he or she take to move from idea to physical product?

Role Play

Situation You have an idea for a new product. You have decided to develop the product, and you are seeking investors.

Activity Pair up with a classmate. Assume the role of the entrepreneur. Have your classmate assume the role of an investor who is interested in the project. Role-play a question and answer session.

Evaluation You will be evaluated on how well you address these issues:

- Describe the four steps of the product development process.
- Identify quality initiatives you will implement.
- Describe stages of new-product planning.

Production and Distribution

Production Management

Once you have developed a prototype, you are ready to plan production. Outsourcing allows a new company to manufacture a product without having to invest in workplace costs. However, there are downsides to outsourcing. You have less control over the quality of the product and the speed of the process.

The principles of production management apply to all types of businesses, including service businesses. Production management has three functions:

1. Acquiring the resources needed to create a product.
2. Planning how to convert those resources into products.
3. Making sure the products meet the standards set for them.

Chapter 15 described the acquisition of resources needed to create a product. This section focuses on two other functions: scheduling and quality control.

Scheduling

Businesses plan their production by making schedules. These schedules describe each activity that must be completed to produce goods or services. Schedules include estimates of the amount of time each activity will take to complete. Schedules often include those activities that are critical to the completion of the project. There are two widely used graphic scheduling techniques: Gantt charts and PERT diagrams.

While You Read

Predict What is quality control?

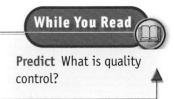

GANTT CHARTS A **Gantt chart** is a graphic schedule of a project's phases, activities, and tasks plotted against a time line. A Gantt chart is an effective way to depict basic information about a project. Using a Gantt chart can help you to keep track of tasks and manage the dependencies among tasks. Tasks are listed on the vertical axis. The time required for each task is shown on the horizontal axis. In **Figure 16.1,** individual orders (tasks) are listed vertically. Solid bars span the period over which each order is scheduled to be produced. Broken bars indicate actual production activity.

Gantt charts are simple and helpful. They force you to think through the steps of a job. You must estimate the time needed for each part of production. They also let you track actual progress against planned activities once the project is under way. You can immediately see what should have been achieved at a point in time. They also allow you to see how remedial action may bring the project back on course. They are also used to show the beginning and ending dates of several projects going on simultaneously. Gantt charts may be simple versions created on graph paper or more complex automated versions created using project management software applications.

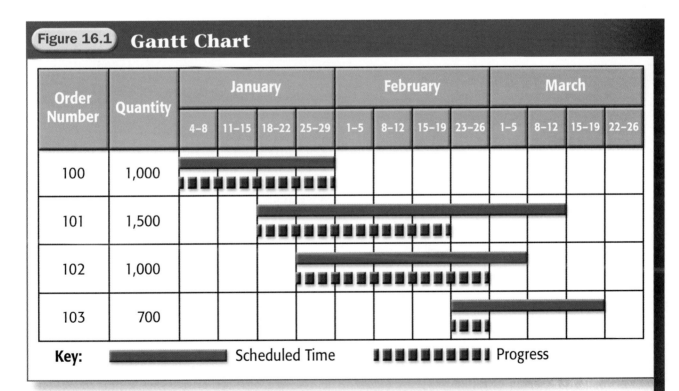

Figure 16.1 Gantt Chart

Order Number	Quantity	January				February				March		
		4–8	11–15	18–22	25–29	1–5	8–12	15–19	23–26	1–5	8–12	15–19	22–26
100	1,000												
101	1,500												
102	1,000												
103	700												

Key: ▬▬▬▬ Scheduled Time   ▮▮▮▮▮▮▮▮ Progress

PROJECT TRACKING TOOL Gantt charts make it easy to compare planned work (solid lines) with actual progress (broken lines). For example, if you were looking at this chart on February 26, Order 100 would be completed, and Order 102 would be $5/6$ completed and on schedule. *Where would Orders 101 and 103 be?*

PERT DIAGRAMS PERT stands for Program Evaluation and Review Technique. A **PERT diagram** is a project schedule that is arranged in a diagram. PERT diagrams are useful for scheduling more complex projects.

To use the PERT technique, identify the project's major activities. Then arrange the activities on the diagram in order. Connect with arrows those activities that must occur in a fixed sequence. Finally, estimate and indicate how much time is needed to complete each activity. An example of PERT scheduling is illustrated in **Figure 16.2.**

The longest path through the diagram is called the *critical path.* Activities on this path dictate the length of time needed to complete the project. By completing these activities on schedule, you can control the length of the project.

Controlling Quality

Quality control is the process of making sure the goods or services you produce meet certain standards. Standards can be set for appearance, performance, and consistency. In a frozen yogurt shop, customers expect the same quality and quantity every time they buy a cone.

The standards you set for your business reflect the market segment you are targeting. Customers who want high quality will pay more for it. Customers who want low prices will expect reasonable, but not particularly high, quality.

Quality control takes time and costs money, but it is a way to ensure customer satisfaction. How do you achieve quality control? Two common ways are quality circles and inspection.

While You Read

Connect Think of a circumstance in which setting up PERT diagrams or Gantt charts might cause problems.

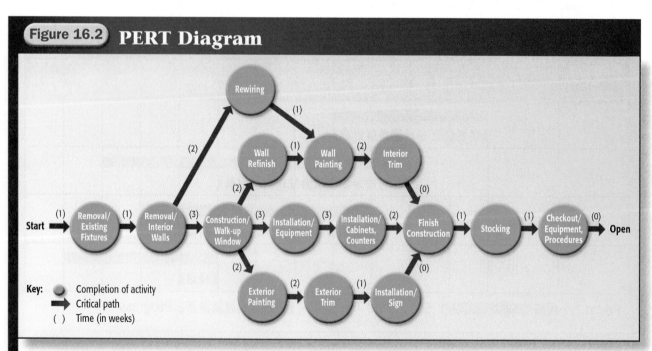

Figure 16.2 **PERT Diagram**

SCHEDULING TOOL This PERT diagram lays out the process of remodeling a building for use as a food carry-out business. *What is the least amount of time required for completion of the project?*

Google It!
Although the dictionary says a "googol" is a one with one-hundred zeroes after it, most people today use the similar sounding word to mean "searching on the Internet." Few company names enter the language as new verbs, but Google has done just that. Friends Sergey Brin and Larry Page were students in the doctoral program at Stanford in 1995 when their shared interests led them to tinkering with search technology. Today, Google is widely considered the best search engine on the Internet, indexing more than 4 billion Web pages and 800 million USENET messages.

CRITICAL THINKING
What are some other brands whose names have become common, even to the point of becoming general terms for similar products?

 Go to **entrepreneurship.glencoe.com** to complete the Success Stories Writing Activity.

QUALITY CIRCLES A **quality circle** is a small group of employees who do similar jobs and meet regularly to identify ways to improve the quality of what they do. They ultimately improve quality. This approach has been used successfully by large manufacturers such as Ford. However, the concept also works for small operations. Quality circles improve quality because they require employees to be responsible for their work. They give employees the power to make decisions about quality. Employees can stop production to correct defects before a product is completed. Quality circles are also a way to motivate employees. They give employees a vested interest in the success of the company.

INSPECTION Inspection is one way to control quality. If you use inspections, you must decide whether to perform them during or after the job. When you inspect your product depends on what you are selling.

If you manufacture complex equipment, you will probably inspect your product at several stages during production. That way, defects are caught and corrected before they end up in the final product.

If you provide a service such as dry cleaning, however, a final inspection is more appropriate. There are no points in the process where you could inspect the work.

You must also decide whether to inspect every product or just a sample of the product. Cost is the determining factor. For a mobile-home builder, inspection of each product would be relatively inexpensive. However, a chocolate chip cookie baker would check only selected batches. Any product that is used up when it is tested is normally sampled randomly for quality.

Managing Other Areas of Production

Productivity, automation, and preventive maintenance are additional areas of production that should be managed effectively. These areas are important to all types of businesses.

PRODUCTIVITY **Productivity** is a measure of how much a business produces in a given time. It also can be expressed in terms of the output of each worker per unit of time. Productivity ensures a strong economy by slowing inflation. Other benefits include greater profits, higher wages, greater product demand, low interest rates, improved market opportunities, and more jobs.

Businesses can use productivity rates to measure and improve employee performance. Machinists at a tool factory might have an average productivity rate of 35 units per day. A worker who produces only 25 units a day is not very productive. He or she may even hurt the business. Owners must find workers who contribute to increased sales by working productively.

BusinessWeek Case Study

Transport: More Business Than They Can Carry

Resurgent demand for shipping plus stripped-down capacity will push prices up. Small carriers will keep disappearing as big ones tighten their grip.

Thomas L. Finkbiner hasn't seen the trucking business look this good in five years. As president of Tampa-based Quality Distribution Inc., the nation's largest bulk trucking hauler, he's turning away 30 jobs a day. "It's a feeding frenzy out there," he says. Same story at United Parcel Service Inc. Compared to last year, "we're moving 200,000 more parcels a day," says CFO D. Scott Davis.

After years of consolidation and capacity reduction, haulers can finally raise prices and cherry-pick new customers. The result: The price to move goods in 2004 will jump by 3% to 4%, according to some industry analysts. "If you're one of the survivors, times will be good," says Robert P. Costello, chief economist for the American Trucking Association.

Revenue growth for the transport sector should inch up in 2004 following a disappointing couple of years. According to

Global Insight Inc., industry sales for 2004 should rise 1.7%, to $254.3 billion. Thanks to sustained cost-cutting and productivity gains, the consultant expects operating income for the sector to surge more dramatically, by 40%, to $125.1 billion, from 2003's $89 billion.

SOURCE: BUSINESSWEEK, JANUARY 12, 2004; BY CHARLES HADDAD

APPLICATION

Use the Internet to conduct research on current freight rates from three different trucking companies. Then use a spreadsheet application to list the rates. Share and compare your results with a partner.

 Go to **entrepreneurship.glencoe.com** to complete the *BusinessWeek* Case Study Reading Guide Activity.

AUTOMATION **Automation** is the use of machines to do the work of people. Automation can cut production time, reduce errors, and simplify procedures. However, automation also can be expensive. Manufacturing and clerical tasks often lend themselves to automation. New ventures that perform these tasks need to budget for technology to automate their systems. This ensures that they stay competitive.

MAINTENANCE Maintenance of machinery is a key factor in production management. There are three basic ways to manage maintenance:

1. **Organize your production process.** Arrange it so that when one machine is down, the work can be shifted to other machines.

2. **Build up inventories at each stage of the production process.** That way, other machines can continue to run while you are repairing a faulty machine.

3. **Conduct preventive maintenance.** Fix machines before they break down and check regularly for possible failure points.

Distribution Management

Distribution management includes transportation, shipping and receiving, storage and warehousing, materials handling, and specification of delivery terms. It controls the movement of a product from the manufacturer to customers.

Transportation

Part of distribution management is **logistics**, the planning, execution, and control of the movement and placement of people and/or goods. It involves figuring out how to move a product from the producer to the customer. Shipping a product by plane, truck, railroad, pipeline, or waterway is regulated by federal and state agencies. Transporters are classified into three categories: common carriers, contract carriers, and private carriers (see **Figure 16.3** on page 354).

You can handle the logistics yourself or outsource it. To decide, ask yourself three questions:

1. Is your competition using transportation as a competitive advantage?

2. Are you seeking markets in other countries?

3. Are you having problems with shipments you are handling yourself?

If you answer "yes" to any of these questions, you may need assistance from a logistics firm.

Shipping and Receiving

Shipping and receiving are important functions that require sound procedures. They ensure that you receive the correct supplies and inventory and make error-free deliveries. With shipping, you need to prepare shipping documents and mailing labels. You should check them for errors that could cause delays. You also need to record what has been taken from inventory. This allows you to replenish stock when inventories begin to run low.

Write About It

Identify and conduct research on a company that uses automation in its production processes. Then write a report on how automation affected the company's workflow processes and quality control efforts.

Figure 16.3 **Types of Carriers**

DELIVERING THE GOODS
Businesses that transport their products have different options from which to choose. They can use for-hire carriers, such as common carriers and contract carriers, or private carriers. *Why might some businesses use both for-hire and private carriers?*

Common Carriers

A **common carrier** is a firm that provides transportation services at uniform rates to the general public. Federal Express and United Parcel Service are common carriers.

Contract Carriers

A **contract carrier** is a shipping company that transports freight under contract with one or more shippers. A railroad is a contract carrier.

Private Carriers

A **private carrier** is a business that operates its own vehicles for the purpose of transporting its own products and materials.

With receiving, you should determine whether orders have been filled correctly. You do this by verifying incoming shipments against the original order and the accompanying invoice. Today many receiving clerks use handheld scanners to record bar codes on incoming products. Shipments are checked for discrepancies in quantity, price, and discounts.

Storage and Warehousing

Some manufacturers have warehouses for storing inventory for sale. Entrepreneurs with limited resources might not be able to afford their own storage facilities. They may have a wholesaler store and distribute their products. They may also store goods in a public warehouse.

Materials Handling

There is more to distribution than transportation and storage. You also need to handle the products without damaging them. Materials handling includes dealing with shipping containers and forklifts. It also includes other aids that help you move product within your facility and out to the customer.

Delivery Terms

All shipments have delivery terms. Delivery terms identify who is responsible for the various components of distribution. The most favorable delivery term for a small business owner is "free on board," or FOB. **Free on board (FOB)** is a delivery term that designates a shipment as delivered free of charge to a buyer. This means that the seller pays all freight costs. In addition, the title to the goods passes to the buyer when the goods leave the manufacturer.

While You Read

Question Can you think of products for which the preferred method of shipment would be by plane? truck? railroad? pipeline? waterway?

Section 16.2 After You Read

Key Concept Review

1. What is the difference between Gantt charts and PERT diagrams?
2. What are two ways to approach quality control?
3. What is productivity, and what are two ways to increase productivity in a business?

Think Critically

4. Investigate the various transportation modes a video game company could use to ship software from Atlanta to Singapore. Which mode seems best for this type of product?

Role Play

Situation Your entrepreneurship class has decided to run a food service on campus. You will be selling muffins and fruit to students. Every Friday you will prepare and serve a special lunch to the faculty.

Activity Since quality and consistency are important in food services, come up with a plan for quality control. Then role-play a discussion with your faculty advisor on your quality control plan.

Evaluation You will be evaluated on how well you address these issues in your role play:

- Discuss the importance of quality control.
- Create and describe a plan to achieve quality control of the food and the service.
- Explain how you will evaluate the effectiveness of the quality control program.

Chapter Summary

Section 16.1 **From Idea to Product**

Because they work with limited resources, entrepreneurs must find creative ways to develop and manufacture their products. Product development is considered the highest risk part of start-up for a small business. Small business owners can reduce the cost and risks involved with product development by hiring other people to do the work. The four steps in product development are: (1) opportunity recognition, (2) concept investigation, (3) product design, and (4) prototype building and testing.

Section 16.2 **Production and Distribution**

Production and distribution are two ways entrepreneurs bring new products to market. Production management has three functions: (1) acquiring the resources needed for production, (2) planning the steps to convert the resources into products, and (3) making sure the products meet the standards set for them. Businesses plan their production through schedules. Two commonly used graphic scheduling techniques are Gantt charts and PERT diagrams. Quality circles and inspections are two ways to ensure that the goods and services you produce meet the standards you set for them. Productivity, automation, and preventative maintenance must be managed effectively as part of the production process. Distribution management concerns the physical movement of the product from the manufacturer to the customer.

Key Terms Review

1. Describe the production management and distribution processes you might use for plastic key chains you plan to manufacture. Use the following terms in your description:

product development (p. 344)	productivity (p. 352)
outsourcing (p. 345)	automation (p. 353)
prototype (p. 346)	logistics (p. 353)
Gantt chart (p. 349)	common carrier (p. 354)
PERT diagram (p. 350)	contract carrier (p. 354)
quality control (p. 350)	private carrier (p. 354)
quality circles (p. 351)	free on board (FOB) (p. 355)

Key Concept Review

2. **Discuss** how entrepreneurs develop new products. (16.1)
3. **Explain** the product development process. (16.1)
4. **Explain** what is involved in production management. (16.2)
5. **Describe** the activities that are part of distribution management. (16.2)

Critical Thinking

6. Why is it essential to involve potential customers in the design and prototype process of a product?

7. Briefly describe how production management can be applied to each of the five types of businesses: retail, wholesale, service, manufacturing, and extraction.

8. When and how would Gantt charts or PERT diagrams be useful in your selected business?

9. Why is quality control important?

10. Explain why distribution can make or break a business.

11. How does the increased or decreased productivity of individual companies affect the economy?

12. What are the critical issues in the development of new products?

Write About It

13. In a one-page report, identify procedures to follow in shipping and receiving.

14. Use the Internet to learn more about quality initiatives. In a two-page paper, compare and contrast various quality initiatives.

15. Construct a diagram to describe stages of new product planning.

16. Write an outline on the advantages of automating the production process.

17. In a two-page paper, identify activities associated with transportation, storage, and product handling.

18. In a one-page paper, explain the role productivity plays in an economy.

19. In an e-mail or a memo to your teacher, explain whether outsourcing would be a viable option for your business.

20. Use the Internet to find three companies that use quality circles. In a one-page paper, list the companies and describe the effectiveness of quality circles.

Academic Skills

Math

21. Andrea works in a manufacturing plant and is paid a bonus at the rate of $3 per piece based on her productivity. Using the following information, determine how much money Andrea earned last month.

Base salary	$320 per week
Bonus, Week 1	6 pieces
Bonus, Week 2	4 pieces
Bonus, Week 3	10 pieces
Bonus, Week 4	9 pieces

Language Arts

22. Select a class or school project. Prepare a Gantt chart using a word-processing or spreadsheet program to schedule the tasks that make up your project. Estimate the time needed for each part of the project. Track the actual progress of your project against the planned activities. In creating your chart, what did you learn about your project that you did not know before?

Entrepreneurship in Your Community

23. Interview someone in your community who has created a new product or service. Find out how the product prototype was developed. Ask if the production process was outsourced. If not, why not? Determine what quality control methods were used during the production process. Find out how the product is distributed to customers.

24. Visit a manufacturing firm in your community. Identify activities associated with (1) transportation, (2) storage, (3) product handling, and (4) inventory control. During a class discussion, compare your findings with those of another group. How are the companies similar? How are they different?

Ethical Practices

Quality Control

25. A manufacturer of air bags for cars is trying to compete against companies that outsource their manufacturing to China, where labor costs are cheaper. The manufacturer knows he needs to cut costs somewhere. The easiest way is to use lower quality materials and parts. If he does this, his business will survive, but he faces an ethical dilemma. He could be risking the lives of people who drive cars with the inferior air bags installed. What should he do?

INTERNET connection

Research Distribution Options

You want to begin distributing a new line of watches. You plan to use a common carrier so that you can track the progress of shipments. You have decided to use the Internet to research your distribution options.

Connect

Use a search engine or Web directory to find information.

- Research the Web sites of three common carriers.
- Determine shipping costs on comparable weights.
- Compare tracking procedures.
- Find out if international services are available.

Application

Based on your research, select a carrier to use to distribute your watches. Write a report that summarizes the reasons why this carrier is the best option.

The Electronic Entrepreneur

Distribution in E-Commerce

In business, one of the important functions is delivering the right product or service in the right quantities in the right place at the right time. This is the goal of distribution activities, called *logistics*. Logistic activities involve managing the inbound movement of materials and supplies and the outbound movements of finished goods and services.

E-Commerce Channels Many online purchases are distributed through a direct channel of distribution. You receive the product directly from the manufacturer or producer of the product. This occurs when the goods and services are sold from the producer directly to the customer. This is a common method of distribution for many major e-tailers.

Intermediaries Most traditional retailing is indirectly distributed; the distribution channel involves one or more intermediaries.

An **intermediary** is a business that is involved in the process of moving a product from the manufacturer to the customer or user. The Internet has brought about a certain degree of disintermediation. **Disintermediation** is the removal of intermediaries, for example, wholesalers or retailers, from business transactions between producers and consumers.

Cybermediaries Intermediaries in the online world are called *cybermediaries*. A **cybermediary** is a business that acts as a broker or agent to facilitate transactions over the Internet. The cybermediary helps move products from the manufacturer to the consumer or industrial user. An example of a cybermediary is a **Web affiliate**, a company that aims to drive targeted traffic to a Web site, usually an e-commerce merchant. Web affiliates are usually paid a commission for the sales they generate on the merchant site.

FACT AND IDEA REVIEW

1. How are e-commerce channels of distribution different from traditional channels of distribution?
2. What does a cybermediary do?
3. What are logistics as they apply to distribution? What are some logistic activities?
4. What is a Web affiliate? How can a Web affiliate be helpful to an online business?

FOR DISCUSSION

5. How has the Internet affected channels of distribution?

TechTerms

- intermediary
- disintermediation
- cybermediary
- Web affiliate

Managing Operations and Staffing

CHAPTER OBJECTIVES

When you have completed this chapter, you should be able to:

SECTION 17.1

- Explain the significance of operational plans.
- Describe the purpose of operating policies, rules, and regulations.

SECTION 17.2

- Explain the staffing process.
- Determine the need for additional policies.

THE COST OF CREDIT

If you are thinking of taking out a loan or applying for credit, you should first figure out how much it will cost you and whether you can afford it—then shop around for the best credit terms. Two key factors will be the finance charge and the annual percentage rate (APR).

- **Finance charge** is the total dollar amount you pay to use credit. In most cases, you have to pay finance charges to a creditor on any unpaid balance.

- **APR** shows how much credit costs you on a yearly basis, expressed as a percentage. For example, an APR of 18 percent means that you pay $18 per year on each $100 you owe.

Every organization that extends credit must state its true APR to customers. This makes it easy to compare the cost of credit from several sources.

@ Go to entrepreneurship.glencoe.com to complete the Standard & Poor's Money Talk Financial Literacy Activity.

PREPARE TO READ

THINK ABOUT THESE QUESTIONS AS YOU READ.

Why are operational plans necessary?

What personnel policies need to be established for a business?

Managing Operations

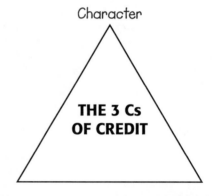

Character

THE 3 Cs OF CREDIT

Implementing Operational Plans

The goal of first-line management is to put operational plans into action. These plans govern the day-to-day business operations. They include productivity issues such as schedules and quotas. They also include the policies, rules, and staffing concerns that help keep a business going.

Operating Policies, Rules, and Regulations

When you start a business, you might manage the operation alone. However, as your business grows, you may have difficulty making all of the decisions yourself. You may eventually need to delegate your responsibilities to employees.

Policies simplify day-to-day management so you do not have to make the same decisions again and again. A **policy** is a statement of guiding principles and procedures that serves as a guideline for daily business operations. Policies should always support the company's goals and objectives.

Movies by Mail

The video rental store changed the way people watched movies—for the first time, people did not have to go to the theater to see movies. Reed Hastings, CEO and founder of Netflix.com, is trying to change the movie scene once again. Made possible by the light weight and small size of DVDs, Netflix offers unlimited rentals of DVDs by mail for a monthly fee. Users can keep a certain number of movies for as long as they want with no late fees. Movie buffs have latched on to the service: since its launch in 1998, Netflix.com has acquired more than 600,000 subscribers.

CRITICAL THINKING

How does Netflix.com's business model compare to other movie services, such as pay-per-view or downloading movies online? What are its relative strengths and weaknesses?

 Go to **entrepreneurship.glencoe.com** to complete the Success Stories Writing Activity.

A business may have a policy about working hours or overtime pay. Policies are meant to handle recurring situations, but they are flexible. They leave room for interpretation. Permitting an employee to come in late when he or she has a doctor's appointment is an example of policy flexibility.

In contrast, rules tell employees exactly what they should and should not do. A **rule** is a standard that is set forth to guide behavior or actions. Rules leave no room for interpretation. "Employees shall wear hard hats in all construction areas" and "All employees shall get two weeks of vacation after one year of service" are rules. At times, rules also impose restrictions on customers: "Smoking is not permitted in the building."

Not all policies apply to all types of businesses. Most policy statements include hours of operation, credit policies, return and rework policies, delivery policies, customer service policies, and employee and customer safety policies.

Hours of Operation

Hours of operation are an important part of a business's place strategy. When can your customers come to your location? When is it most convenient for you to contact them? Are you able to deliver your product to customers when they want it?

Hours should be set to suit customers. For example, a movie theater might be open between noon and midnight on weekdays. It would be open later on Fridays and weekends when most people want to see movies. In contrast, a wholesaler would likely have shorter hours. Office hours might be limited to 9 to 5 weekdays. Those are the hours when customers, typically businesses, could phone in orders. On the other hand, delivery hours might be longer to accommodate the varying business hours of customers.

CUSTOMER SERVICE SKILLS

The success of a business ultimately depends on identifying what customers want, then providing it. Companies need to understand their customers and respond quickly to their needs with customer service policies and practices.

Most businesspeople know the importance of customer service. Nearly all claim to provide it. Many even include it in their promotional messages. Unfortunately, the frequency of customer complaints about poor service indicates otherwise.

So what is the answer? Businesses must emphasize positive customer service skills.

Think Critically

What skills are needed to provide positive customer service? How would you ensure that your employees have those skills?

 Go to **entrepreneurship.glencoe.com** to complete the Issues in Entrepreneurship Research Activity.

Credit Policies

Pricing entails more than what you charge for your goods or services. It also addresses how much your customers can pay for them. One important part of your pricing strategy is credit. **Credit** is an arrangement for deferred payment for goods and services. Credit allows a business or an individual to obtain products in exchange for a promise to pay later.

Your first decision will be whether to offer credit and/or outside financing. Credit may encourage sales and give you an edge on the competition, but it also ties up your money. You can also lose money if a customer defaults. A no-credit policy suits businesses that sell low-priced items and consumable goods. That is why some convenience stores and fast-food restaurants do not offer credit. However, businesses that sell big-ticket items and companies who want to encourage customers to buy in large quantities should make their products easy to buy.

If you offer credit, you need to make a number of other decisions. You must select the form(s) of credit you will extend. You also have to decide to whom you will offer credit and in what amounts.

Several types of credit plans are available. Each has its own set of costs and advantages. Four major types (bank credit cards, charge accounts, installment plans, and financing) are described in **Figure 17.1.**

Other specialized credit card plans are offered by stores and gasoline companies just for their customers. Travel and entertainment cards, such as American Express and Diners Club, are also available. These require payment in full each month. Debit cards are variations of credit cards. Funds are withdrawn directly from a customer's checking account.

Figure 17.1 **Credit Plans**

1. Bank Credit Cards

Many businesses accept bank credit cards sponsored by Visa, MasterCard, and Discover Card. Since the bank that issues the card (not the customer) pays the bill, there is less risk for the merchant. However, bank card issuers take a percentage of each charged purchase as a collection fee.

Credit plans make it easy for a customer to make a purchase. However, each type has different costs and risks for the business. *Which form of credit, if any, would your business be least interested in offering customers. Why?*

Apply now. Save now.

Get instant approval when you apply at the register!

No annual fee SEARS

2. Charge Accounts

With this form of credit, the business gets the full purchase price plus a finance charge (a form of interest) if the balance is not paid within the established time limit. However, the business pays all costs associated with collecting on these accounts. It also assumes the risk of nonpayment.

3. Installment Plans

Businesses that sell costly goods or services might offer an installment plan. For example, some furniture stores allow customers to make a down payment and then make regular payments. Some offer incentives such as no interest for a year. The costs and risks of installment plans are similar to those of charge accounts.

4. Financing

Financing sales through a bank is usually reserved for expensive goods, such as new automobiles. With this form of credit, the business gets its money quickly. However, the customer can be inconvenienced by delays at the time of purchase. His or her credit history and situation must be checked and approved.

While You Read

Predict What are the three Cs of credit, and for what purpose are they used?

Other consumer credit accounts used by businesses are revolving accounts and budget accounts. Revolving accounts are open accounts to which purchases can be added on an ongoing basis. They usually require a minimum payment and have a balance limit. Revolving accounts charge interest on the balance. Budget accounts allow customers to pay over a certain time period with no finance charge.

Financing can be done through consumer finance companies as well as banks. Businesses also may have arrangements with lenders. An auto dealer may refer a customer because he or she needs a direct loan for a new car.

THE THREE Cs OF CREDIT Most businesses that offer credit have standards to determine who is eligible. One formula commonly used for financing consumer purchases is known as the three Cs of credit:

1. **Character.** Character is a borrower's reputation for honest dealings. Has the customer demonstrated responsibility in paying bills? You can find out by contacting a credit bureau. Credit bureaus give good credit ratings to people who pay their bills on time and poor credit ratings to people who pay their bills late.

2. **Capacity.** Capacity is a borrower's ability to repay a debt, as judged by the lenders. Based on the customer's income and expenses, does he or she have the ability to pay? You can ask applicants to report their income and monthly expenses on your credit application form.

3. **Capital.** Capital is the overall assets of an individual. What are the customer's physical and financial assets? You can request this information on your credit application form.

How much credit you extend to individual customers will depend on the three Cs. You will likely offer more credit to customers with higher incomes, good credit ratings, and substantial assets than you will to customers with modest means and people with bad credit ratings.

TECHNOLOGY Today

The Digital Divide

The digital divide is the division that exists between people who do and do not have access to modern technology. Several factors contribute to the digital divide: urban living, education level, economic class, and industrialization. People who do not have access to technology face limited opportunities for education and might have a tougher time finding good careers.

Critical Thinking

Why is access to new technology important to all people? What are some shortcomings of not having such access?

 Go to **entrepreneurship.glencoe.com** to complete the Technology Today Vocabulary Practice Activity.

Return and Rework Policies

You may choose to have a return or rework policy. This means your business guarantees the quality of the goods you sell or the services you provide.

A **return policy** establishes the conditions under which items that have been ordered, shipped, or delivered may be returned. A **rework policy** establishes the conditions under which items will be reworked. Reworking is the act of doing something again because it was not done right the first time. It can occur for a variety of reasons, including insufficient planning, failure of a customer to specify the needed input, and failure of a supplier to provide a consistently high quality output.

A fair policy for replacements, refunds, or repairs helps maintain customer goodwill. For example, "If we do not install it right, we will fix it free." Many businesses offer a more limited guarantee, such as free parts and labor for six months. Others offer a "money back guarantee, no questions asked" return policy. This policy may be costly, but you may need to adopt it to remain competitive.

Delivery Policies

Whether to deliver is another part of your place strategy. For some service businesses, a delivery policy can be the key to success. Domino's Pizza built a national reputation with its original delivery policy. It promised "Delivery in 30 minutes, or it's free."

Delivery policies can be crucial for other types of businesses as well. Retailers who sell big-ticket items such as refrigerators risk losing sales if they do not deliver. Wholesalers must guarantee on-time delivery to stay competitive.

There are other aspects of delivery to consider as well. Do you charge for the service? Do you limit delivery to a certain area? Your resources and the competition will determine your answers.

While You Read

Connect If you owned a local flower shop would you charge for delivery? Would you have a certain delivery area?

WE DELIVER Delivering your goods or services adds convenience to your business. *What are some locations that might be ideal for a restaurant that delivers food?*

While You Read

Question Have you ever been in a situation where you did not receive good customer service and complained about it? What happened?

Customer Service Policies

Other customer service policies that you should consider are the following:

- **Handling of complaints.** Most businesses use the policy "The customer is always right."
- **Servicing of your product.** If something you sell stops working within a certain time limit, will you fix it?
- **Courtesy to customers.** Some businesses require their clerks to ask departing customers, "Did you find everything you were looking for?"
- **Shopping climate.** Your business may have a policy of maintaining certain lighting or housekeeping standards.
- **Provision of restrooms.** Will these be open to the public or locked and usable by customers only upon request?
- **Response time.** Some businesses advertise "All orders filled within 48 hours of receipt."
- **Warranties.** Manufacturers usually guarantee the materials and workmanship that go into their products.

Employee and Customer Safety

The financial costs of an on-site accident can ruin a small business. However, you can take two basic precautions to reduce your liability. First, train your employees in safety practices and emergency procedures. Reinforce training with signs posted throughout the workplace.

You also need to protect your customers. A sign can keep customers away from potentially damaging equipment: "Authorized personnel only." A restaurant can let guests know when a section of the floor has been mopped. You should make it clear to customers not to use certain facilities, such as elevators, during emergencies.

Section 17.1 After You Read

Key Concept Review

1. What role do policies and rules play in managing operations?
2. Explain the difference between policies and rules.
3. Identify and list five common operating policies that apply to any business.

Critical Thinking

4. Describe how students who have jobs can employ the principles of safety in their work-based experiences.

Role Play

Situation You help out at your family's furniture store. Your parents have asked you to put together some credit policy recommendations for them.

Activity Review the credit policies described in this section. Outline a plan for what you think would work for the store. Practice the presentation by role-playing with two classmates in front of the class. One will play your mother; the other, your father.

Evaluation You will be evaluated on how well you address these issues:

- Discuss credit policies appropriate for a furniture store.
- Identify and recommend different types of consumer credit.
- Explain the advantages and disadvantages of offering credit.

Staffing and Company Policies

Staffing Your Operation

You make your staffing decisions based on how many and what kinds of employees you need. If you intend to run a one-person operation, your staffing plan will be simple. For most businesses, however, you probably will not be able to do all of the work yourself. Even when hiring only one or two employees, you should familiarize yourself with the process of staffing.

To determine your specific staffing needs, you need to assemble four types of documents. You must design an organization chart, write job descriptions, and list job specifications. You also need to have the résumés of yourself and others in key positions.

Types of Organization

Your first task in staffing is to design an organizational structure for your business. The easiest way to do this is to develop an organization chart. This diagram includes all of the jobs in your business and shows how they are related.

The structure of your organization chart should help you delegate responsibility, authority, and work. Consider the fact that each job may not require a full-time employee. Stay open to other possibilities. For example, some jobs (particularly staff positions) can be contracted out to consultants. Others may require only part-time employees.

The most common forms of business organization are the line organization, the line-and-staff organization, and project organizations.

Many new businesses use a **line organization**. Here managers are responsible for accomplishing the main objectives of the business. In addition, they are in the direct chain of command. Top management, such as an owner/manager, makes the decisions that affect the whole company. Middle management implements the decisions. Supervisory, or first-line, management supervises the activities of employees. Employees then carry out the plans made by top and middle management.

At start-up, you may have a line organization with only two levels of management. An example is shown in **Figure 17.2.** As the business grows, you may need to hire first-line managers for buying, warehousing, and sales. In the meantime, those responsibilities fall to your assistant manager.

Besides adding a layer of line managers as your organization grows, you must hire staff personnel. The term *staff* often refers to employees in general. Technically, **staff** refers to managers and others who provide support and advice for line managers. Accounting, legal services, and training and development, for example, are staff activities. When you add staff to your line organization, it becomes a **line-and-staff organization**. **Figure 17.3** illustrates that kind of organizational structure.

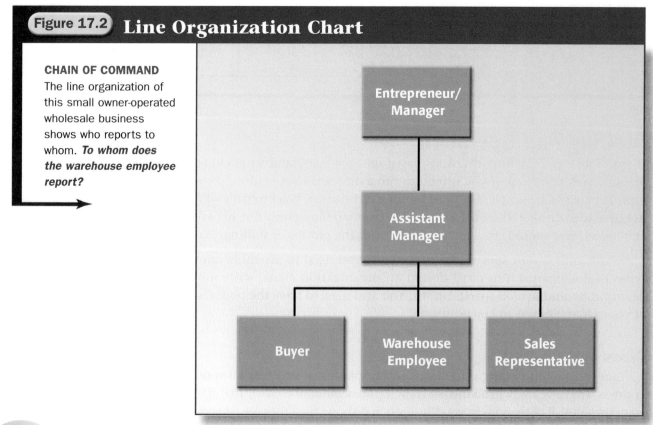

Figure 17.2 **Line Organization Chart**

CHAIN OF COMMAND
The line organization of this small owner-operated wholesale business shows who reports to whom. *To whom does the warehouse employee report?*

Entrepreneur/Manager

Assistant Manager

Buyer

Warehouse Employee

Sales Representative

Figure 17.3 **Line-and-Staff Organization Chart**

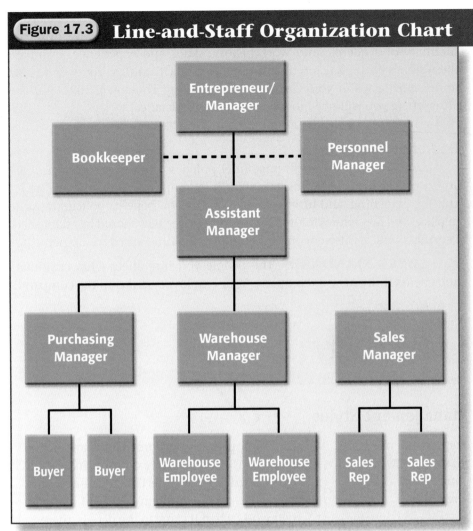

Project organizations supplement the line and line-and-staff structures. **Project organizations** are usually temporary organizations brought together from different parts of the business for special projects. For example, you might assemble experts from sales, purchasing, production, and shipping departments. Their goal may be to design a system for cutting delivery time by 50 percent. The project is carried out by teams or committees. The group may have responsibility to both a line manager and a staff manager. Employees assigned to these groups work on an as-needed basis or until the project is done. Then they return to their assignment in the formal organization. Matrix, task-team, and interdisciplinary setups are examples of project organizations.

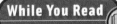
While You Read

Predict What is the difference between a job description and a job specification?

Job Descriptions and Job Specifications

For each position in your organization chart, you need to write a job description. A **job description** is a statement that describes the objectives of a job and its duties and responsibilities.

For each job description, you should then write a second statement—a job specification. A **job specification** is a document that details the abilities, skills, educational level, and experience needed by an employee to perform the job. Think of it as a kind of want ad.

IDENTIFYING STAFFING GAPS Examine the résumés of everyone involved in the start-up business to identify staffing needs. A **résumé** is a summary of academic and work history, skills, and experience. Compare the résumés with your job descriptions and specifications. You will be able to recognize gaps in your organization's staffing. These gaps highlight the areas where you will need to look for outside assistance.

Personnel Policies

Businesses must establish personnel policies that oversee the "people" aspect of the business. A business should set employee standards before recruiting, screening, and hiring employees. Pay and benefits policies must be in place, and procedures for maintaining employee files should be established. Personnel policies also encompass employee training and development.

EMPLOYEE STANDARDS The people you hire affect what customers and clients think of your company. Your employees make up the company's

---

BusinessWeek Case Study

Male and Female Management Styles

Male and female entrepreneurs manage differently, right? Not so, says a new study, which finds they have much more in common than either gender realizes.

When Jennifer Cliff interviewed 141 male and 88 female small-business owners in Vancouver in the spring of 1995, she heard a lot of what she calls standard-issue "gender stereotypic" talk. The men would tell her they want employees to see them as "The Boss," and that they expect workers "to do what I say." The women would emphasize teamwork, explaining that they did not want to be perceived as "above" their employees, but rather as working "alongside" them. None of this gave Cliff pause, since a popular theory in gender studies is that men and women have fundamentally different ways of approaching work relationships and, thus, business management.

Since what she was hearing fit that theory, Cliff fully expected these different "managerial archetypes" to show up in more objective measures—the hierarchical

structures, policies, and procedures in place at each business. But they did not. Instead, Cliff found that despite the difference in how these men and women talked about their work, when it came to the details, there were no differences in how men and women operated their respective businesses.

SOURCE: *BUSINESSWEEK*, NOVEMBER 4, 2003; BY LISA MILLER

APPLICATION

With a partner, interview a small-business owner about his or her managing style. What is his or her approach towards work relationships with employees? Is this approach "gender stereotypic"? Explain your findings in a short report to the class.

@ Go to **entrepreneurship.glencoe.com** to complete the *BusinessWeek* Case Study Reading Guide Activity.

---

face, voice, and reputation. That is why entrepreneurs establish hiring policies. All personnel decisions that you make will reflect this policy.

The type of people you hire depends on the type of business. For a retail operation, you may want social individuals. For a bookkeeping service, you probably want people who are detail-oriented. Under any circumstances, you want people who project a positive, professional image. You should set out these kinds of traits in your policy statement. Other personnel decisions you make will also reflect this policy.

RECRUITING AND SCREENING EMPLOYEES You can use classified ads and state-run and private employment agencies to **recruit**, or bring in, prospective employees. School and college placement offices, union hiring halls, and word of mouth are other sources. Each recruitment method reaches a different type of applicant. Listing a job opening on an Internet job board attracts computer-literate applicants. Use the recruiting method that best suits the position you want to fill.

When you begin to attract applicants, you must screen them. This usually involves having applicants submit an application form or a résumé. Either one helps you see how well an applicant matches up to your job specification. You can immediately eliminate those applicants who do not fit your requirements.

If you are impressed by someone's application or résumé, you should schedule an interview. It is illegal to ask the interviewee certain types of questions (age, religion, ethnicity, etc.). By meeting the applicant, you find out more about his or her qualifications. You can also learn about the person's interpersonal and communication skills. **Figure 17.4** lists guidelines for conducting effective interviews.

At the time of the interview, you may want to test the applicant. Tests evaluate an employee's intelligence, aptitude, achievement, interest, personality, and honesty. Be sure your tests relate to the job.

Finally, you can request character references. Former employers can tell you about a person's previous job performance. Teachers, coaches, and other references can help you learn about an applicant's reliability and work ethic.

While You Read

Connect Make a list of all of the different ways businesses use to recruit employees.

Figure 17.4 Rules for Effective Interviewing

1. Define what you are looking for before the interview.
2. Conduct interviews in private. Don't use panel interviews.
3. Put the interviewee at ease. Treat him or her with respect.
4. Ask general background questions first, more specific questions later.
5. Encourage the interviewee to talk. Be a good listener.
6. Confirm key observations several times during the interview.
7. Provide an opportunity for the interviewee to ask questions.
8. Look for how the interviewee conducts himself or herself, and note his or her attitude and enthusiasm.
9. Look for what the person will bring to the job.
10. Cover all of your planned areas in enough detail to allow you to make a sound decision.

HOW TO INTERVIEW
These rules provide general guidelines for conducting an interview. *What are some legal guidelines to consider during an interview?*

Quick Math

A business typically pays between 20 and 40% of an employee's salary for benefits. Suppose you paid an employee $940 per month. How much more would you pay for benefits?

PAY AND BENEFITS To attract and keep the kind of employees you want, you must do two things. First, you must pay a competitive wage or salary. **Wages** are an amount of money an employee receives for every hour the employee works. A **salary** is a fixed amount of pay an employee receives for each week, month, or year the employee works. Paying a competitive wage or salary means paying a rate similar to rates offered by other businesses with similar employee needs. Second, you need to offer competitive employee benefits. **Benefits** are extras that workers receive on a job.

Another way to pay is based on productivity. Productivity pay can be a **piece rate** (so much per unit produced) or a **commission** (a percentage of sales). For example, a person who makes teddy bears may get paid by the unit. The person who sells them may get a percentage of the sales. Sometimes employees receive a combination of productivity pay and salary. A person who sells cars may receive a salary and a commission. You will probably choose your pay plan based on the standard for your industry.

Some employee benefits are required by law. These include the employer's contribution to Social Security, unemployment compensation, and workers' compensation. Optional benefits include paid vacation days, paid sick days, health and life insurance, flextime, pensions, and child care. Companies offer benefits together with pay as a way to attract and keep good employees. Most full-time workers receive benefits. Most temporary and part-time workers do not receive benefits.

Keep cost in mind as you consider the benefits to offer your employees. Compensating your employees is a major business expense. Typically, benefits for an employee run between 20 and 40 percent of salary.

TRAINING AND DEVELOPMENT New employees work better and are more efficient when they receive immediate training. Unless your business is highly technical, you will provide this early on-the-job training.

As your operation grows, you may need to hire a specialist to handle employee training and long-term development. You can also contract with outside consultants to provide these services.

▶ **HEALTH BENEFITS** To compete with other employers, companies offer many forms of health care. *How does this benefit the employer and the employee?*

PERSONNEL RECORDS Staffing responsibilities include making decisions about establishing and maintaining personnel files.

For your own use, you need contact information and training and performance records. For government agencies, you must keep certain documents for a specified period.

An employee's records can all be kept in the same file or in separate file categories. Divisions for files may include personnel files, payroll records, medical records, and records of applicants not hired.

Policies must be established regarding security of the files, supervisor access, and employee access. Every document has the potential of becoming a legal exhibit. Therefore, you should consider a policy prohibiting personal notations on files.

Developing Additional Policies

You have many different policies and rules to consider for your operation. How can you make sure you will not miss any that are vitally important to your business? First, make a list of the operational rules and policies that apply to your business. Then, find out about your competitors' policies. Review their policy statements and find out which ones you are missing. Set up focus groups or survey potential customers to get feedback about policies they want.

Remember that the intent of a policy is to simplify day-to-day management. Too many can limit your flexibility. Make policies that eliminate having to make routine decisions. Use rules only when necessary. Use them in areas such as health and safety, fundamental fairness, and customer relations.

While You Read

Question What is the purpose of policies?

Section 17.2 After You Read

Key Concept Review

1. Differentiate between a line organization chart and a line-and-staff organization chart.

2. Write a sample job description and job specification for a position in your business.

3. What steps can you take to make sure that your business has a complete set of policy statements?

Critical Thinking

4. Develop a complete set of policy statements for your proposed business.

Role Play

Situation You and a friend co-own a retail exercise equipment store. Because your business has grown, you decide to hire a manager.

Activity Work with a classmate to design hiring procedures for the management job, ranging from the initial advertisement to the final interview. Work together to present the procedures to the class. Your role play should depict a discussion between you and your classmate as co-owners.

Evaluation You will be evaluated on how well you address these issues:

- Prepare a chart showing the organizational structure of the business, including the proposed position.

- Write a job description and job specification.

- Explain how you will recruit, screen, evaluate, and interview applicants.

Chapter Summary

Section 17.1 Managing Operations

Managing your business requires you to put operational plans into action. Establishing policies and rules allows your business to run smoothly. Operating policies include hours of operation, credit policies, procedures for returning/reworking a product, delivery policies, customer service policies, and employee and customer safety policies. When deciding whether to extend credit, businesses evaluate the character, capacity, and capital of credit applicants.

Section 17.2 Staffing and Company Policies

To determine your specific staffing needs, you must design an organization chart and write job descriptions and job specifications. An organization chart helps you delegate responsibility, authority, and work. Three of the most common types of organizational structures are line, line-and-staff, and project organizations. Job descriptions and job specifications help you determine the kind of employee you want. When trying to find prospective employees, use a recruiting method that best suits the position you want to fill. Try to avoid having so many policies, rules, and regulations that they limit your flexibility in managing your business.

Key Terms Review

1. Write a list of questions you could use when interviewing prospective employees. Use the following key terms in your questions:

policy (p. 362)	project organizations (p. 371)
rule (p. 363)	job description (p. 371)
credit (p. 364)	job specification (p. 371)
character (p. 366)	résumé (p. 372)
capacity (p. 366)	recruit (p. 373)
capital (p. 366)	wages (p. 374)
return policy (p. 367)	salary (p. 374)
rework policy (p. 367)	benefits (p. 374)
line organization (p. 370)	piece rate (p. 374)
staff (p. 370)	commission (p. 374)
line-and-staff organization (p. 370)	

Key Concept Review

2. **Explain** the significance of operational plans. (17.1)
3. **Describe** the purpose of operating policies, rules, and regulations. (17.1)
4. **Explain** the staffing process. (17.2)
5. **Determine** the need for additional policies. (17.2)

Critical Thinking

6. What policies, if any, should every business have?
7. What factors will help you decide whether to offer credit to your customers?
8. Create a list of customer service policies from businesses in your community. Are the policies similar to those listed in the chapter?
9. What is the best way to get information to prospective employees about job openings you have available? Defend your choice.
10. How does the structure of your organization chart help you to delegate responsibility?
11. What kind of organization chart would be most appropriate for your proposed business? Why?
12. When would you use all of the screening procedures described in the chapter? Explain.
13. When would "money back guarantee, no questions asked" be a good policy? Explain.

Write About It

14. Write a short story about a business. Include characters of different management levels. In the story, identify and describe the different levels of management.
15. Research the specialized forms and variations of credit cards. Present your research in a table.
16. Write two paragraphs explaining why customer service is or is not equally important in all businesses.
17. Interview the manager of a private employment agency. Identify types of companies that use recruiters and identify techniques recruiters use to market a company. Write a report on your findings.
18. In a memo to "new employees," describe how your business will provide training and development.
19. In a one-page paper, describe how you will organize the personnel records in your proposed business.
20. In an e-mail to your teacher, explain why policies should be flexible.

Academic Skills

Math

21. After screening all of the applicants, you hire the best candidate at a salary of $23,000 per year. Your benefits package normally amounts to about 25 percent of an employee's base salary. How much will your new employee's compensation add to your monthly operating expenses?

Language Arts

22. Contact a bank or the consumer credit counseling service in your area. Find out why good credit is important to a potential entrepreneur. Ask for an explanation of credit reports and the way reporting agencies collect credit information. Develop a plan for your own use of credit and how you will maintain good credit records. Write a report detailing the results of your research.

Entrepreneurship in Your Community

23. Working in teams of three or four, collect at least three examples of organization charts from local businesses. Determine their organizational structure. Analyze any similarities and differences. Then draw an organization chart of the administration of your school and compare it with those you collected. Share your team's findings with the class.

24. Choose a business you would like to own. Try to determine what the pay and benefits for potential employees would cost your business.

- Gather information on current salaries and wage rates for the kinds of positions you need to fill. As sources, use newspaper ads, occupational forecasting reports, state employment services, and personnel agencies.

- Contact the IRS, state tax office, and other appropriate agencies to obtain information about employer costs and withholding requirements.

Ethical Practices

A Tough Hiring Decision

25. You own a picture framing store. You need to hire someone to help with counter sales and routine framing jobs. After you ran an ad and interviewed several people, Kristen emerged as the top candidate. You offered her the job, and she agreed to start in one week. The day after you made the offer to Kristen, Stacy called and said she was looking for a job. You and Stacy had worked together in a similar business when you were in school. You know she would do an excellent job and could probably help you take the business to the next level. She is obviously the best person for the job. Should you hire the person to whom you made the commitment—Kristen? Or should you hire the person whom you know and who is best suited for the job—Stacy?

INTERNET *connection*

Customer Service 101

You are the proud owner of a record store. You believe that customer service is the key to a successful business. You are planning to provide specialized customer service training to your staff.

Connect

Use a search engine or Web directory to research customer service.

Application

- Prepare a slide show presentation that describes the importance of customer service.

- Discuss the importance of practicing positive customer service skills.

- Incorporate specific examples that will be helpful in your business.

The Electronic Entrepreneur

Web Design Basics

To do business on the Internet, you will need to build a Web site. Although you can pay someone to create your site for you, this can be expensive. The cost of designing and setting up an online store can easily run thousands of dollars. If you are just starting out, or if you are on a tight budget, you may need to design and build your own site. While this task might seem daunting at first, it can actually be a lot of fun.

WYSIWYG To build your own Web site, you will either need to learn how to code Web pages in HTML or use software that codes Web pages for you. Most beginning Web authors prefer to use WYSIWYG (pronounced "wizzy wig") software. **WYSIWYG** is an acronym that stands for "What You See Is What You Get." This kind of software enables you to design your page visually, without having to learn HTML.

Tables **Tables** are data structures that are used to organize Web page elements spatially. Tables make it possible to easily create complex page layouts. They can be used to present data that is best displayed in tabular form, such as lists or specifications. Tables can have any number of rows or columns, can be stretched or shrunk to a specified size, and can be made invisible. You can even nest one table inside another for precise control of where things appear on the screen.

Hyperlinks and Image Maps A hyperlink is an electronic link that provides direct access from one place in a hypertext document to another place in the same or different hypertext document. Hyperlinks can be placed in text or in images. An **image map** is a graphic image on a Web page that is used for navigation. Each image map is divided into multiple sections called "hot spots." A **hot spot** is a clickable hyperlink.

FACT AND IDEA REVIEW

1. Why is WYSIWYG software so helpful to novice Web page creators?
2. How are tables useful in Web page design?
3. What is a hyperlink?
4. What is an image map?

FOR DISCUSSION

5. What are some reasons why tables and image maps might cause problems, both for Web designers and Web users?

TechTerms

- WYSIWYG
- tables
- image map
- hot spot

Chapter 18

Managing Human Resources

CHAPTER OBJECTIVES

When you have completed this chapter, you should be able to:

SECTION 18.1

- Identify the components of human resource management.

SECTION 18.2

- Explain how managers influence motivation.

- Describe ways to maximize employee performance.

- Explain the importance of delegation.

- Explain how to assess motivational techniques used to increase performance levels.

PROFIT PLANNING

Business managers often use cost and profit data to maximize profits. Suppose you decide you want your business to earn a profit of $500 per month over a certain period of time. Assuming your selling price and costs remain constant, how much must you sell to achieve this target profit?

$$\textbf{PROFIT} \; + \; \begin{matrix}\textbf{VARIABLE}\\\textbf{COSTS}\end{matrix} \; + \; \begin{matrix}\textbf{FIXED}\\\textbf{COSTS}\end{matrix} \; = \; \begin{matrix}\textbf{TARGET}\\\textbf{PROFIT}\end{matrix}$$

Using this equation, you can figure how much business you must do to reach your target. When analyzing target sales and profits, consider what will happen if you do not reach your target. Your margin of safety is the target profit minus the break-even sales. A high margin of safety suggests a minimal risk that sales will fall below the break-even point.

 Go to **entrepreneurship.glencoe.com** to complete the Standard & Poor's Money Talk Financial Literacy Activity.

PREPARE TO READ

THINK ABOUT THESE QUESTIONS AS YOU READ.

What are human resources?

How can motivational techniques increase employee performance?

Developing and Keeping Human Resources

GET READY TO READ

KEY TERMS
- human resources
- human resource management
- labor union
- educational activities
- developmental activities
- cost effective
- employee complaint procedure
- Pregnancy Discrimination Act

KEY CONCEPT
- Human Resource Management

THE MAIN IDEA
People are the most important resource of a small business. Employees have a big effect on the company's performance.

READING ORGANIZER
Draw the reading organizer below on a separate piece of paper. As you read, write down the seven components of human resource management.

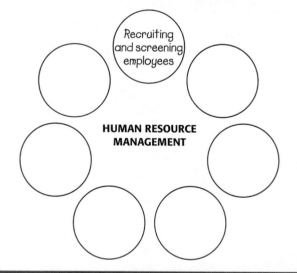

Human Resource Management

The human resources of a business represent one of its largest investments. **Human resources** are the people employed in a business, commonly referred to as *personnel*. People offer more than just labor to a business. They contribute character, ethics, creativity, intellectual energy, and social and business connections.

Human resource management is the part of business concerned with recruiting and managing employees. Its main goals are to facilitate performance and improve productivity. Several components make up human resource management:

- Recruiting and screening employees
- Managing dealings with unions
- Overseeing employee training and development
- Overseeing pay and benefits
- Resolving day-to-day problems
- Ensuring equal opportunity
- Handling employee termination

Recruiting and Screening Employees

As your business grows, you must add new employees. You must also replace employees.

As you learned in Chapter 17, you can use classified ads, Internet job boards, employment agencies, school and college job placement offices, union hiring halls, and word of mouth to recruit employees. Established businesses can recruit by asking for referrals from current and former employees and customers. They can also recruit walk-ins by hanging a help wanted sign at the place of business. Other sources are recruiting from within and recruiting from competitors.

Issues in Entrepreneurship

AN ENTREPRENEURIAL PREDICAMENT

Entrepreneurs sometimes have a need and/or an opportunity to hire a person from outside the company who can help move the company forward. The person may have proven turnaround skills, may bring in profitable clients, or may possess advanced skills. This kind of employee typically commands a high salary.

When such an employee is paid more than current employees, a difficult situation may arise. If employees find out how much money the new employee is being paid, it may cause morale problems or discrimination claims. To reduce the chance of encountering such a problem, keep salary information confidential and top secret.

Think Critically

As an entrepreneur, how can you bring in the exceptional person you need and still have your employees buy into the idea? Are there ethical issues related to this decision?

 Go to **entrepreneurship.glencoe.com** to complete the Issues in Entrepreneurship Research Activity.

RECRUITING FROM WITHIN Promoting someone who works for you has several advantages. You already know the employee's work habits. Recruiting and training costs are kept low. Disruption of your operation is minimized. Finally, other employees become motivated to work harder for promotions. One disadvantage is that employees who are not promoted sometimes feel resentful. Another is that hiring only from within limits opportunities for bringing "new thinking" into the company.

RECRUITING FROM COMPETITORS Hiring employees away from the competition also has advantages. The principal advantage is that the new hires already have the skills to do the job. They also can offer insight into competitors' operations. On the downside, recruiting from competitors can start a costly cycle of raiding each other's personnel. In some instances, it may cost less to train someone with no experience. An experienced worker may have to be untrained before being trained in your procedures.

SCREENING An established business owner uses the same screening methods that a new entrepreneur employs. Both review applications, conduct interviews, and check references. However, more people are included in the hiring process of an established business. For example, the prospective employee's immediate supervisor might be involved.

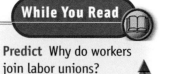

While You Read

Predict Why do workers join labor unions?

Managing Dealings With Unions

A **labor union** is an organization that represents workers in their dealings with employers. Workers join unions to strengthen their ability to bargain for wages, benefits, job security, working conditions, and other concerns.

As the manager of a small business, you may not like the idea of labor unions. They do represent some loss of control. Their demands can cause strains on financial resources. A business can not dismiss a union's demands without making a counteroffer.

THE SCREENING PROCESS An interview is an important part of the screening process. *Should you conduct an interview with both internal and external candidates?*

Workforce Management Software

An important part of a large business is its customer service call center—the place where a team of employees handles incoming calls and e-mail messages from customers. Customer service call center employees address customers' problems and ensure that customers are satisfied. The larger the call center, the trickier it can be to employ the right number of employees. Workforce management software helps businesses analyze the times and days when the call center is busiest and schedule accordingly.

Critical Thinking

What kinds of businesses would benefit most from workforce management software? Why is it important?

 Go to **entrepreneurship.glencoe.com** to complete the Technology Today Vocabulary Practice Activity.

How you deal with unions depends on the type of business you are in. Many small businesses are not affected by union activity. However, some industries, such as construction and textile manufacturing, are unionized. Whether your business is unionized or not, always be fair and open to communication.

Overseeing Training and Development

Training and developing employees becomes more complex as a business grows. You must provide initial training for new hires. In addition, you must offer ongoing training to improve the job performance of current employees.

Along with training, you should add education and development to your plans. **Educational activities** are actions that prepare employees for advancing in the organization. An example is a human relations workshop. **Developmental activities** are actions that prepare managers to lead the company into the future. An example is an industry conference. Here are the four steps in planning a training and development program:

1. DETERMINE YOUR NEEDS. Figure out your immediate, intermediate, and long-range training and development needs. Do you and other managers lack strategic planning skills? You may need developmental activities. Do you want key employees to be ready to move into management as you expand? They would need educational activities. Do too many customers leave without buying? Your employees may need training.

2. DESIGN YOUR PROGRAM. After you determine your needs, you must decide how to meet them. Will you create a program yourself? Will you designate someone else to do it? With the latter, you might need a full-time employee, a consultant, or a combination of the two. The local chapter of the American Society for Training and Development (ASTD) can help you find a consultant. **Figure 18.1** on page 386 describes some of the training and development techniques you can use.

> **While You Read**
>
> **Connect** Ask an employed adult to describe the training and development he or she has experienced during his or her career.

Figure 18.1 Training and Development Techniques

On-the-job training	Employees learn the job on the site under the direction of their manager or an experienced employee.
Vestibule training	Training takes place at a location away from the job that is equipped to simulate the actual work site.
Classroom teaching	Lecture, discussion, case studies, role playing and other traditional classroom techniques are used to provide knowledge and problem-solving skills needed to perform the work.
Coaching	Employees receive ongoing instruction and feedback regarding job performance from their manager.
Mentoring	Employees receive one-on-one assistance from an established employee to help them get oriented within the organization and develop their potential.
Job rotation	Employees are moved from one job situation to another to provide them with a variety of job experiences and/or an understanding of the total operation.
Conferences and seminars	Several trainees or employees meet with experts off the job to learn how to deal with specific concerns or to exchange ideas.

TRAINING AND DEVELOPING EMPLOYEES Many types of training and development techniques are available for managers. *Which techniques count as learning by experience?*

3. IMPLEMENT YOUR PROGRAM. If you want your program to make a difference, two things must occur. First you have to provide time and money for the program. Then you must follow up, making sure employees use what they learn.

4. EVALUATE YOUR PROGRAM. After your program is up and running, you should evaluate it. You want to know how effective it is. This means determining whether the program's objectives were achieved. For example, did sales improve?

You should also determine how cost effective the program was. **Cost effective** means economically worthwhile in terms of what is achieved for the amount of money spent. To find out if your program is cost effective, determine whether increased productivity exceeded the cost of training. In other words, did sales improve enough to pay for the training program? Evaluating developmental and educational activities is more difficult. They are long-term investments and not as easy to pinpoint. You should judge their effectiveness for yourself.

Overseeing Pay and Benefits

You should review your employees' compensation packages regularly. Make sure they include the latest benefits required by law. Also consider adding benefits you could not afford at start-up. For instance, you might offer pensions, profit sharing, or bonuses to be more competitive.

Expanding benefits costs more than money. It also adds to your responsibilities. For example, businesses that offer pensions are subject to the Employee Retirement Income Act. This act regulates pension plans. It makes sure eligible employees receive their pensions. This means you must manage the investment of pension fund moneys to meet the standards of the act. This, in turn, means more paperwork.

Resolving Day-to-Day Problems

You should encourage employees to resolve disputes using problem-solving techniques and human relations skills. However, some employee conflicts require formal procedures.

An **employee complaint procedure** is a formal procedure for handling employee complaints. It should be put in writing and distributed to employees. It is an effective form of staff communication. The first step may be the employee informing his or her supervisor of the concern. The second step may be an appeal to the next-level supervisor or an impartial committee. Although many problems have no clear-cut solutions, the manager or business owner must make a decision regarding every employee complaint.

Write About It

Make a list of additional problems that a business owner might face when dealing with employees.

Ensuring Equal Opportunity

As an employer and manager, you must ensure that employees are not discriminated against. It is illegal to discriminate on the basis of race, color, gender, religion, national origin, age, or physical impairment. You must set standards for your employees' behavior. You must inform them that discrimination is not acceptable.

Laws and regulations are designed to protect employees. They are enforced by the Equal Employment Opportunity Commission (EEOC). One law you may deal with is the **Pregnancy Discrimination Act**. The Pregnancy Discrimination Act is a federal law that requires that employers treat their pregnant employees like all other employees when determining benefits. The EEOC's sexual harassment guidelines are also important. Sexual harassment is any unwelcome behavior of a sexual nature. The EEOC forbids sexual harassment. Other laws affecting employees were discussed in Chapter 8.

DISCRIMINATION
A business cannot discriminate against people with disabilities. *What are some aids that a business can provide?*

Handling Problem Employees and Terminations

You make every effort to hire the right people and thoroughly train them. Unfortunately, some employees do not work out. They may perform below expectations. Their actions may be contrary to the company's goals.

When this happens, you can try to help them work out their problems. You may be able to guide them through finding a solution. Perhaps you come up with a mutually acceptable way to change their thinking or actions. In some cases, the solution may be professional counseling or assistance.

In the end, the only realistic way to deal with a problem may be through disciplinary action. This may include docking an employee's pay or terminating (firing) him or her. Neither situation is easy for those involved, and both should be handled tactfully.

Terminations, in particular, require special handling. It is important to have a document trail that proves that you have cause before firing. If possible, schedule a meeting for the end of the day. Give the employee exact reasons for the action. Explain severance pay and unemployment compensation. You may want to suggest other job options more suited to the person's skills. Keep in mind that the way you handle the situation can impact your relationship with other employees.

Not all of the problems you deal with are brought on by employees. Something may happen in or out of the job setting that is beyond anyone's control. For example, you may have to terminate an employee because of poor sales. This situation calls for special sensitivity on your part.

While You Read

Question Why should business owners be tactful when terminating employees?

Section 18.1 After You Read

Key Concept Review

1. Discuss the advantages and disadvantages of recruiting from competitors.

2. List the steps in setting up a procedure for handling employee complaints.

3. Summarize your responsibility for making sure your employees are not discriminated against.

Critical Thinking

4. Research and write an employee handbook on dispute resolution techniques. Include a written procedure for handling employee complaints.

Role Play

Situation You own a secret shopper service. Companies hire your company to send out employees as secret shoppers to evaluate the quality of customer service at their stores. Recently, you learned that one of your employees was not taking the time needed to shop each store. He filed his reports, but the information was inaccurate.

Activity Team up with a classmate. Have the classmate assume the role of the employee. Role play a conversation between owner and employee to solve the problem.

Evaluation You will be evaluated on how well you address these issues:

- Explain the importance to retailers of having accurate feedback about customer service.

- Describe the importance of providing good service and retaining the retailers as customers.

- Describe disciplinary action that will be taken due to the employee's haphazard handling of his duties.

Motivating Employees

How Managers Influence Motivation

Communication is a key factor that affects your employees' motivation. You must communicate goals and objectives clearly if employees are to meet them. Communicating clearly and providing feedback are important practices of an entrepreneurial leader.

How employees are regarded and treated also affects their motivation. There are many theories about how this works. Douglas McGregor and Frederick Herzberg provide two theories that apply to small businesses.

Assumptions Managers Make

In *The Human Side of Enterprise,* Douglas McGregor identifies two sets of assumptions, which he calls Theory X and Theory Y, that managers make about employees. **Theory X** is the belief that employees are basically lazy and need constant supervision. **Theory Y** is the belief that employees are responsible, like to work, and want intrinsic rewards. The theories are described in **Figure 18.2** on page 390.

Figure 18.2 Assumptions Managers Make

THEORY X AND THEORY Y Managers who believe in Theory X generally get poor results. Enlightened managers use Theory Y, which produces better performance and results and allows people to grow and develop. *Why would most small business situations benefit from the use of Theory Y?*

THEORY X ASSUMPTIONS

- People do not like work and try to avoid it.
- Managers have to push people, closely supervise them, or threaten them with punishment to get them to produce.
- People have little or no ambition and will try to avoid responsibility.

THEORY Y ASSUMPTIONS

- Work is natural to people and is actually an important part of their lives.
- People will work toward goals if they are committed to them.
- People become committed to goals when it is clear that achieving them will bring personal rewards.
- People usually accept and often seek responsibility.
- People have a high degree of imagination, ingenuity, and creativity, all of which can be used in solving an organization's problems.
- Employees have more potential than organizations actually use.

While You Read

Predict What are the benefits of having motivated employees?

As you might imagine, managers who make Theory X assumptions do not motivate employees very well. Still, those assumptions may be appropriate in certain cases. However, in most small businesses, Theory Y assumptions are most effective. Many companies combine elements of both theories of motivation. They allow employees freedom in some aspects of their professional lives and control their actions in others.

Hygiene Factors Versus Motivating Factors

Most people assume that money is a worker's principal motivator. According to the research of Frederick Herzberg and others, this is not so. According to his theory, people are influenced by two types of factors.

Herzberg concluded that compensation, working conditions, and fair company policies motivate only in the short run. Herzberg calls these factors hygiene factors. **Hygiene factors** are factors that do not improve situations, but they do keep situations from getting worse. Essentially, hygiene factors are needed to ensure that employees are not dissatisfied.

In contrast, Herzberg defined **motivating factors** as factors that motivate employees, such as achievement, recognition, responsibility, advancement, growth, and the reward from doing the work itself. Sound familiar? Many of these motivating factors are part of Theory Y's assumptions. Both McGregor and Herzberg emphasize the value of work, the importance of achievement, and the assumption of responsibility.

Maximizing Employee Performance

These motivational techniques can help you maximize employee performance:

While You Read

Connect Think of additional examples of job enrichment. How could a business owner enrich the job of a cashier?

- Provide meaningful work
- Allow scheduling flexibility
- Involve employees in decision making
- Give recognition
- Provide performance evaluations
- Reward performance

Provide Meaningful Work

Employees who are motivated by their work relate to it in a special way. They derive satisfaction from it. They take pride in it. To prompt such feelings, a job must be meaningful. It must offer a range of duties and responsibilities.

If your employees' jobs do not fit this description, consider redesigning them. You can do this through job enlargement or job enrichment. **Job enlargement** is the act of increasing the tasks, responsibilities, and scope of a job. For example, you might ask a production worker to perform an increased number of operations. **Job enrichment** is the act of making a job more rewarding and less monotonous for the worker by adding elements at a different or higher skill level. For example, you might give the accounts receivable clerk responsibility for following up on past-due accounts.

Success Stories

A Twenty-First-Century "Crystal Ball"

Everyone is besieged by information—all day, every day. Businesspeople are drowning in a sea of stock market reports, sales figures, forecasts, e-mail messages, instant messages, and countless other details. David Rose, founder and president of Ambient Devices, wants to see this information conveyed in a simpler fashion. His company makes the Orb, a small device that looks like a crystal ball. When you plug it into an electrical outlet, it taps into a nationwide network and downloads stock information. If the market is up, it glows green; if the market is down, it glows red.

CRITICAL THINKING

What are some existing technologies that work the same way the Orb does—conveying information at a glance? What are some possible uses for this idea?

 Go to **entrepreneurship.glencoe.com** to complete the Success Stories Writing Activity.

Allow Scheduling Flexibility

Allowing employees to plan and manage their own work schedule sends a clear message of trust. Flexible scheduling takes a variety of forms. Examples are shown in **Figure 18.3.** These techniques can lead to increased productivity, but they do not lend themselves to every work situation. An auto mechanic cannot work at home; neither can an electrician.

Involve Employees in Decision Making

Let employees make suggestions. Suggestions may be about where the organization is going and what their roles will be. This management approach has two positive outcomes. First, it gives employees a sense of purpose. Second, it allows employees to see their own ideas put to work. Both lead to extra motivation and a sense of ownership.

BusinessWeek Case Study

Tapping the Potential of Temporary Workers

When time and money are tight, entrepreneurs have a wealth of reasons for turning to placement agencies.

On a lean budget, you can't afford to recruit, train, and offer costly benefits to full-time employees who may or may not work out, and whom you might feel obliged to retain if business slowed—or let go, thus opening yourself to legal hassles. Fortunately, however, you have a solution: retain a temporary worker. The advantages are embedded in the way the business of bringing on a temp usually works, which is that the placement agency retained by the employer recruits and trains the worker, and also handles and covers the cost of administrative factors, such as benefits, payroll, and worker's compensation.

That's all of the stuff you don't have time for and can't afford to deal with. In addition, you'll never have to say you're sorry if things don't work out. Letting an ineffectual worker go is also the agency's responsibility. On the other hand, if things do work out, you'll have an inside look at a potential new hire.

Using a temp also allows you to avoid the risky strategy of farming out the work to consultants and contractors, who could, in turn, take the business away from you. Instead, you'll retain control of the work—and keep the client. The temp will be handling the duties in-house under your direction.

SOURCE: *BUSINESSWEEK*, APRIL 21, 2004; BY VALERIE FREEMAN

APPLICATION Interview the manager of a temp agency in your area. Find out what services the agency provides to businesses and what it charges for these services. Use a word-processing application to write a short report summarizing your findings.

@ Go to **entrepreneurship.glencoe.com** to complete the *BusinessWeek* Case Study Reading Guide Activity.

Figure 18.3 **Workplace Flexibility**

PEOPLE-FRIENDLY POLICIES Many businesses are offering a more flexible workplace as a convenience to employees and as a way to improve productivity. *Would you be willing to offer telecommuting and flextime in your business?*

Telecommuting

Telecommuting involves performing some or all of the job away from the business. The key is technology. Computers, cellular phones, fax machines, and overnight delivery services allow employees to work at home, on the road, or during business trips.

Family Leave

Family leave allows employees to take time off work to attend to significant personal events, such as births, deaths, and family illnesses, without fear of job loss. Large companies must offer family leave under federal law. Workers are entitled to up to 12 weeks of nonpaid family leave every two years.

Flextime

Flextime allows employees to choose the work hours and days that are most effective for their personal lives. It might result in four 10-hour days or afternoons and evenings or some other combination.

There are many ways to involve employees in decision making. One is quality circles, which were discussed in Chapter 16. Another is management-by-objectives. In **management-by-objectives**, employees are involved in setting their own objectives and gauging their own progress. A third is work teams. A **work team** is a group of employees assigned a task. They have no direct supervision and are responsible for their results.

You can increase the effectiveness of group decision making with training. **Figure 18.4** shows some group decision-making guidelines.

Give Recognition

Recognizing employees' contributions to the business increases employee morale and motivation. You can give informal recognition by praising employees for doing a good job or giving credit to someone for offering a useful idea or suggestion. You can give formal recognition by sending a letter of appreciation or presenting plaques or awards at meetings.

Provide Performance Evaluations

A **performance evaluation** is the process of judging how well an employee has performed the duties and responsibilities associated with a job. Formal evaluations are usually done once a year. In a private meeting with the employee, you evaluate the person's strengths and weaknesses. You can also give tips to help the employee become more productive. Informal evaluations may be given more often.

Evaluations can be very motivational. They often provide the basis for pay increases and future promotions. Even suggestions for improvement can be presented as something to strive for, a measure of future accomplishment.

Figure 18.4 **Group Decision-Making Guidelines**

LEADING A SMALL GROUP MEETING	**PARTICIPATING IN A SMALL GROUP MEETING**
1. Open the conference with a brief statement of the problem.	1. Keep your contributions brief and to the point.
2. Ask for contribution.	2. Take up only one topic at a time.
3. Make frequent summaries.	3. Support your contributions with statistics, examples, analogies, expert opinions, and other evidence.
4. Minimize your personal contributions.	
5. Keep the meeting moving and on track.	4. Listen attentively.
6. See that each person participates, but don't go around the table asking for each person's views.	5. Don't interrupt other participants.
	6. If you disagree with another individual, resolve the matter nonaggressively.

LEADER'S ROLE The leader of a small group meeting should not make personal contributions. *Why?*

Reward Performance

Systems for rewarding performance are used to acknowledge employee achievement. Usually, they rely on financial rewards. Many employees measure personal value and success with their salary and bonuses. Salespeople, for example, may look at their commissions as a way to "keep score." Reward systems can include things besides money. Other options are special assignments, job titles, and promotions. These, too, can represent acknowledgment and achievement.

Delegating Responsibility

Delegating responsibility is a useful management tool. When you delegate, you give an employee the authority to and responsibility for carrying out some of your work.

One advantage of delegation is that it allows you to work on other things. It also motivates the employee. It shows confidence in the employee and prepares him or her for more responsibilities.

Of course, certain conditions must exist before you decide to delegate responsibility. The employee must be capable and willing. You have to trust that he or she can handle the job. You also need to understand that the final responsibility rests with you.

While You Read

Question What conditions should exist before a manager delegates responsibility?

Evaluating Employee Motivational Techniques

You need to formally evaluate motivational techniques that require a large commitment of company time and resources. You should review flextime, quality circles, and awards banquets, for example, by asking yourself certain questions. Is it working as a motivator? Does it need revision? Is it worth the cost? Can it be done a better way?

Section 18.2 After You Read

Key Concept Review

1. What is the difference between hygiene factors and motivating factors?

2. List three ways to motivate employees.

3. What are four questions to ask about an employee motivation program?

Critical Thinking

4. Explain how money can be used as both a hygiene factor and a motivating factor.

Role Play

Situation A local company has hired you and a classmate to make a presentation to its management team about ways to maximize employee performance.

Activity Team up with a classmate and research, write, and perform a presentation on employee motivation in a question and answer format.

Evaluation You will be evaluated on how well you address these issues:

• Identify ways to maximize employee performance.

• Describe ways to motivate others.

• Assess motivational techniques used to increase performance levels.

Chapter Summary

Section 18.1 **Developing and Keeping Human Resources**

Staffing a business, whether ongoing or start-up, requires the same steps—recruiting, screening, setting pay and benefits, and providing training and development. The ongoing business, however, has more options and personnel to work with, making it much more complex. As a business manager, you will have to develop procedures to resolve disputes among employees, to ensure that employees are not discriminated against, and to deal with employees who are performing below expectations.

Section 18.2 **Motivating Employees**

Managers influence employees' motivation by making Theory X or Theory Y assumptions and using motivating factors. In order to get the most from their employees, managers can (1) provide meaningful work, (2) allow for schedule flexibility, (3) involve employees in decision making, (4) give recognition, (5) provide performance evaluations, and (6) reward performance. Delegating responsibility expands an owner's ability to manage in the workplace. In addition, it can be very motivating to employees.

Key Terms Review

1. Your boss has asked you to attend the local job fair and recruit new employees for your company. To prepare, write a summary of human resource issues that potential employees might want to know. Use these key terms:

human resources (p. 382)	hygiene factors (p. 390)
human resource management (p. 382)	motivating factors (p. 390)
labor union (p. 384)	job enlargement (p. 391)
educational activities (p. 385)	job enrichment (p. 391)
developmental activities (p. 385)	telecommuting (p. 393)
cost effective (p. 386)	family leave (p. 393)
employee complaint procedure (p. 387)	flextime (p. 393)
Pregnancy Discrimination Act (p. 387)	management-by-objectives (p. 394)
Theory X (p. 389)	work team (p. 394)
Theory Y (p. 389)	performance evaluation (p. 394)

Key Concept Review

2. **Identify** the components of human resource management. (18.1)
3. **Explain** how managers influence motivation. (18.2)
4. **Describe** ways to maximize employee performance. (18.2)
5. **Explain** the importance of delegation. (18.2)
6. **Explain** how to assess motivational techniques used to increase performance levels. (18.2)

Critical Thinking

7. How can business owners benefit by hiring employees who belong to labor unions?

8. Would you provide employee training that was worthwhile but not cost effective? Why or why not?

9. Are most employees like those described by Theory X or Theory Y? Why? If you work, what type of employee are you?

10. Identify three businesses in your community where you think:
    - Flextime would be an acceptable option.
    - Telecommuting would not be feasible.

11. What do you think motivates employees most? Defend your answer.

12. When you delegate responsibility to an employee, who has the final responsibility? Why?

13. Explain why you might not expand benefits to employees.

Write About It

14. At the computer, list two motivating factors and two hygiene factors. Briefly explain your answer.

15. In one paragraph, describe ways managers can motivate others.

16. In a memo to your manager, explain the advantages of recruiting from within.

17. Prepare an e-mail message to your teacher explaining the purpose of developmental activities.

18. What are Theory X assumptions? Theory Y assumptions? Write your answer in one paragraph.

19. How does involving employees in the decision-making process motivate them? Compose your answer at the computer.

20. In a memo to employees, explain the value of formal performance evaluations.

Academic Skills

Math

21. Errors by your telephone sales staff are costing you $12,000 per year. You would like to send four telephone salespeople to a three-day training seminar to correct the situation. The expenses will be as follows:

- Registration costs: $500 per employee
- Travel and lodging: $625 per employee
- Salary and benefits: $125 per day per employee
- Temporary replacement staff for three days: $1,500

Will the training be cost effective? How many years will it take for the training to pay for itself?

Language Arts

22. Forrest pays his employees a salary that is slightly under the industry standard. Consequently, employees often work for him to get experience but then leave to earn more money. What can he do to retain employees besides raising salaries?

Entrepreneurship in Your Community

23. Choose a business you would like to open. As you consider the training and development of your employees, prepare a plan that will include the following:

- Immediate, intermediate, and long-range training and development needs
- Type of programs you will offer
- Implementation procedures
- Evaluation procedures

24. Interview an entrepreneur or small business manager in your community about the techniques used to motivate employees.

As a class, compile your results. Are there similarities between companies? Which techniques would motivate you?

Ethical Practices

Keeping a Motivator Motivating

25. Two years ago Rosa established an Employee-of-the-Month Award for the 24-hour printing and copy center she owns. The award has worked well as a motivational tool. Rosa, however, is concerned because the same few employees keep winning the award. She is considering "spreading it out" so all employees eventually win. That would be easy to do because she selects the winner each month. Is Rosa's idea ethical? What results would be likely? What should she do?

Research Telecommuting

One of your employees has requested permission to telecommute from home. You know telecommuting is becoming popular, but you need more information.

Connect

Use a search engine or Web directory to research telecommuting. Find out the answers to these questions:

- What types of jobs are appropriate for telecommuters?
- What are the benefits of allowing employees to telecommute?
- What are the appropriate ways to supervise an employee who telecommutes?
- What methods can be used to evaluate an employee who telecommutes?

Application

Use your research to prepare an addendum about telecommuting for your company's employee handbook. Explain which jobs are eligible for telecommuting, why it is beneficial, how telecommuters will be supervised, and the methods used to evaluate telecommuters.

The Electronic Entrepreneur

Positioning a Web Site

When someone does an Internet search, they will likely receive pages and pages of results, containing links to hundreds (or thousands) of sites. Most viewers give their primary attention to the first few Web pages listed, so businesses strive to be among those at the top.

Search Engine Basics A **search engine** is an online software application that creates indexes of Internet sites based on the titles of files, keywords, or the full text of files. The search engine has an interface that allows the user to type keywords into a blank field. A **keyword** is a word or phrase you type in order to begin an online search. It then gives you a list of the results of the search.

Position When a user conducts a Web search, the order of the results is significant. Securing a good search engine position can mean the difference between being seen and not being seen. **Position** refers to where a search engine result falls on the result list.

Meta Tags To boost search engine positioning, use **meta tags**, information coded within the HTML programming of a Web page. This text—a description, a list of keywords, or the name of the author, for instance—can not be seen by the viewer, but can be read by a search engine **crawler**, a program used to compile search engine databases. A Web page author can use meta tags to control how a site is indexed by search engines.

Paying for Results Some search engines sell the best positions in their search result listings. **Pay-for-performance** is a search engine payment model in which companies pay a fee to be listed at the top of the search results page. A similar arrangement is **pay-per-click**, in which companies only pay for clicks to the destination site through the search engine site based on a prearranged rate.

TechTerms

- search engine
- keyword
- position
- meta tags
- crawler
- pay-per-performance
- pay-per-click

FACT AND IDEA REVIEW

1. What are meta tags, and why are they so important?
2. What is a crawler-based search engine?
3. What is a pay-for-performance search result?
4. What is pay-per-click? How does it affect Web-site placement on a listing?

FOR DISCUSSION

5. Why is positioning of a Web site on search result pages so important? Give several reasons.

Operational Plan

The Operational Plan section of the business plan includes information about the business's location and zoning, property ownership or lease terms, equipment needed, manufacturing processes, channels of distribution, key suppliers, purchasing processes, storage needs, inventory control procedures, and quality control measures.

✔ STEP 1 PLAN YOUR EQUIPMENT NEEDS

Every new business needs equipment and machinery. Create a chart like the one below to document the equipment your proposed business will need.

TYPE OF EQUIPMENT	PURPOSE	TECHNOLOGY REQUIREMENTS	PURCHASE OR LEASE	COST

✔ STEP 2 DESCRIBE HOW YOU WILL CONTROL QUALITY

Write a brief description of your proposed business's quality assurance policies. Include an explanation of the quality control measures that will be taken. Describe how you will evaluate the effectiveness of your quality control program.

Organizational Plan

The Organizational Plan offers information about the business's legal structure, methods of and responsibilities for record keeping, and legal and insurance issues. It also covers the people aspects of the business, including staffing and training of personnel and the organizational structure of the planned business.

✔ STEP 1 PLAN YOUR HUMAN RESOURCES

Diagram and describe the organizational structure of the business. Develop a job description for each position on the organizational flowchart, including skill sets needed and salaries offered. Develop charts or graphs that classify employees by function, skill set, hourly pay, and part-time or full-time status.

| 2.05 | 2.30 | 0.00 | 0.00 |
| 2.60 | 2.85 | 0.00 | 0.00 |

✓ STEP 2 CONSIDER LEGAL ISSUES

Create a chart like the one below to organize information about legal issues that may affect your proposed business.

ISSUE	DESCRIPTION	IMPLICATIONS
Type of Legal Business Form		
Advantages of Legal Type		
Legal Agreements		
Legal Liability Issues		
Government Regulations		
Environmental Regulations		
Zoning Matters		
Licensing Requirements		

Use the **Business Plan Project Appendix** on pages 532–543 to explore the content requirements of a business plan in more detail.

▶ The **Operational Plan** section of the business plan includes information about all the processes that take place in the business.

▶ The **Organizational Plan** offers information about the business's legal structure, methods of and responsibilities for record keeping, human resources, and legal and insurance issues.

BUSINESS PLAN PROJECT TEMPLATE

 Go to **entrepreneurship.glencoe.com** for a document template in which you can write your own business plan.

UNIT 5

MANAGING THE FINANCES OF YOUR BUSINESS

UNIT OVERVIEW

Introduction

Money fuels your business from start-up to growth to maturity. How well you manage your finances will determine whether or not your venture opens its doors, stays in business, and grows. As an entrepreneur, you will need to analyze finances, prepare statements, keep accurate records, and create budgets. Keeping control of your finances will take time and effort. It is necessary to make the best use of your resources and maximize your profits.

BUSINESS PLAN PROJECT PREVIEW

When you complete Unit 5, you will begin to explore these sections of the business plan:

▶ The **Financial Plan** section of a business plan presents past and current finances and financial forecasts and explains the assumptions made when calculating forecast figures.

▶ The **Growth Plan** looks at how the business will expand in the future.

Financing Your Business

CHAPTER OBJECTIVES

When you have completed this chapter, you should be able to:

SECTION 19.1

- Describe the resources available to entrepreneurs to start their business.
- Compare and contrast sources of financing for start-up ventures.
- Describe the importance of financial planning.

SECTION 19.2

- Describe the information needed to obtain financing.
- Explain the types of growth financing available to entrepreneurs.
- Describe how to calculate start-up capital requirements.

 STANDARD &POOR'S
Money Talk

THE ROLE OF THE FINANCIAL PLANNER

When making your investment decisions, you may want to consult a financial planner, a specialist who is trained to offer specific financial help and advice.

A financial planner should provide these basic services:

- Help you assess your current financial situation

- Offer a clearly written plan, including investment recommendations, and discuss the features of the plan with you

- Help you keep track of your progress

- Guide you to other financial experts and services as needed

A financial planner may have credentials, such as Certified Financial Planner (CFP) or Chartered Financial Consultant (ChFC). Not all planners are licensed, however. It is up to you to be cautious and investigate thoroughly any financial planner you are thinking of hiring.

@ Go to **entrepreneurship.glencoe.com** to complete the Standard & Poor's Money Talk Financial Literacy Activity.

PREPARE TO READ

THINK ABOUT THESE QUESTIONS AS YOU READ.

Where can entrepreneurs find resources to help launch their ventures?

What sources of financing are available to help entrepreneurs grow their ventures?

Financing the Small Business Start-Up

GET READY TO READ

KEY TERMS

- bootstrapping
- factor
- equity capital
- equity
- risk capital
- angel
- venture capital
- venture capitalists
- dept capital
- operating capital
- line of credit
- trade credit

KEY CONCEPTS

- Entrepreneurial Resources
- Financing the Start-Up
- Financial Planning for your Business

THE MAIN IDEA

Entrepreneurs use their creative talents to secure necessary resources to start their business. Most start-up funds come from an entrepreneur's personal resources; however, there are other common sources of funding.

READING ORGANIZER

Draw the reading organizer on a separate piece of paper. As you read, write notes about debt financing in the left circle and notes about equity financing in the right circle. In the overlapping portion, write notes that apply to both equity financing and debt financing.

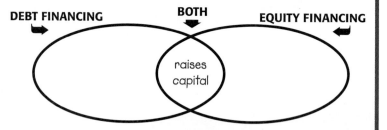

DEBT FINANCING **BOTH** **EQUITY FINANCING**

raises capital

Entrepreneurial Resources

Finding the resources to launch a business is a creative process. It is one of the unique talents of entrepreneurs. It requires understanding the differences between short-term and long-term capital needs. Short-term needs are associated with activities that are not part of normal operations. An example is a seasonal increase in sales that requires purchasing more inventory than normal. Long-term needs generally relate to preparation for future growth. An example is acquiring a larger facility or purchasing additional equipment. Financial planning has an important impact on entrepreneurial decisions. In this section, you will learn how to identify, research, and locate the finances to meet your needs. You also will learn how to make a plan for your business's financial future.

Bootstrapping

Most entrepreneurs get their businesses off the ground by bootstrapping. **Bootstrapping** involves operating as frugally as possible and cutting all unnecessary expenses. It involves borrowing, leasing, and partnering to acquire resources. Bootstrapping involves:

- **Hiring as few employees as possible.** Employees generally are the greatest single business expense. Entrepreneurs often get by as long as they can without hiring employees. They do this by leasing temporary workers and hiring independent contractors. Independent contractors are individuals who have their own businesses and offer specialized services to other businesses. The temporary service or independent contractor handles its own taxes and insurance.

- **Leasing anything you can.** Do not tie up your money in equipment or a building. If you lease, you usually have no down payment, and costs are spread out over a long period of time.

- **Being creative.** When Marianne Szymanski started her toy research company in Milwaukee, she knew she could not afford a test center. Instead, she asked a friend at Marquette University to let her use the basement of the child-care center. The children at the center tested her toys, and student interns provided free help.

Entrepreneurs can ask suppliers to allow longer payment terms. They can require customers to pay in advance or pay half up front and half upon delivery. They can also sell their accounts receivable to a factor. A **factor** is an agent who handles an entrepreneur's accounts receivable for a fee.

Success Stories

Speaking Their Language

Elizabeth Elting was a student at New York University in 1992 when she decided to start a company that would help other companies translate and publish materials in various languages, which is always a challenge for firms looking to market their products in other countries. Borrowing $5,000 from her credit cards, she formed TransPerfect Translations, Inc., and set a series of small goals—to move into an office, then expand. She revised those goals every year, aiming a little bit higher each time. Today, TransPerfect has offices in 21 cities on three continents, is considered one of the leaders of the translation industry, and has more than 160 employees.

CRITICAL THINKING

What are the risks involved with how Elting started her company? Why is setting goals so important?

 Go to **entrepreneurship.glencoe.com** to complete the Success Stories Writing Activity.

While You Read

Predict What is the difference between equity financing and debt financing?

The factor pays the entrepreneur cash for the receivables. He or she charges a fee of 1 or 2 percent on each account, plus interest on the cash advance. The factor then assumes the responsibility of collecting the accounts receivable from the customer. Using a factor gives a business immediate cash from credit transactions.

Start-Up Money

A new business has no track record to prove that it will survive. For that reason, it may have a hard time attracting investors. Therefore, the main source of start-up money for entrepreneurs is personal resources—friends, family, and others. These resources can include savings, credit cards, loans, and investments. If you plan to start a business, you should begin saving now. Then you will want to identify people and other resources you can approach in the future.

Financing the Start-Up

To finance a new business, entrepreneurs can use banks, finance companies, investment companies, and government grants. Two broad types of financing for new ventures are equity and debt financing.

Sources of Equity Financing

Equity capital is cash raised for a business in exchange for an ownership stake in the business. **Equity** is an ownership in a business. For example, an investor might invest $50,000 in your business in exchange for a 25 percent ownership stake. Equity funding is sometimes called risk capital. **Risk capital** is money invested in companies where there is financial risk. An individual who invests in a business risks his or her money. If the business is successful, the investor makes a return on the investment. However, if the business fails, he or she may lose the entire investment.

MONETARY INVESTMENT The entrepreneur's own savings is the number one source of business start-up income. *Why would an entrepreneur's own investment be important to an outside investor?*

There are many forms of equity financing:

- **Personal savings.** The number one source of start-up capital is the entrepreneur's personal savings. The U.S. Department of Commerce reports that 67 percent of new businesses started without borrowing any money. When a business does borrow money, the entrepreneur should contribute more than half of the start-up capital. This allows him or her to keep control of the business.

- **Friends and family.** Entrepreneurs often borrow money from friends and relatives. You need to weigh the advantages of this option. What happens to the relationship if the business fails and the investment is lost?

- **Private investors.** An **angel** is a private investor who funds start-up companies. Angels are nonprofessional financing sources. They are often friends, relatives, and business associates who invest because of their belief in a business concept and founding team. The most common way to find an angel is through networking.

- **Partners.** By finding a partner with similar goals, you can share the costs of a business and divide the responsibilities as well. Your business can also form a strategic alliance with another business that has special skills you need. When entering a partnership, put the partnership agreement in writing and have it reviewed by an attorney.

- **Venture capitalists.** **Venture capital** is a source of equity financing for small businesses with exceptional growth potential and experienced senior management. **Venture capitalists** are individual investors or investment firms that invest venture capital professionally. They often also provide managerial and technical expertise. The primary goal of the venture capitalist is to make money for the investors. Venture capitalists fund less than 1 percent of all ventures, and those are typically in high-tech areas. An existing business can use venture capital financing to raise $50 million, $100 million, or larger amounts of money to achieve its goals.

- **State-sponsored venture capital funds.** Some states use their own funds to encourage the start-up of new businesses and to create jobs. Because they are not as focused on making a profit, these funds are more likely to support a small business. Check with your local economic development corporation for help in locating such funds.

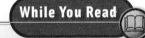

While You Read

Connect Ask a local small business owner how he or she financed his or her business.

Sources of Debt Financing

Sources of debt capital are far more numerous than sources of equity capital. **Debt capital** is the money raised by taking out loans. With debt financing, an entrepreneur borrows money and must repay it with interest. When an entrepreneur raises capital by borrowing, he or she retains full ownership of the business. However, the loan must be carried as a liability on the business's balance sheet. You must be certain that your business can generate enough cash flow to repay the loan. Many companies have found themselves in trouble by taking on more debt than they could repay. Therefore, you must consider the impact of interest rates (the cost of borrowing) on short- and long-term financing. Short-term rates are typically higher, but in either case, you need to calculate the total cost of using debt sources. This includes the principal amount borrowed and the total interest you must pay on the loan.

➤ **MESBICS** The SBA has established MESBICs to support female, minority, and disabled entrepreneurs. *How do MESBICs function?*

BANKS Banks were once the primary source of operating capital. **Operating capital** is the money a business uses to support its operations in the short term. Today, however, banks are conservative in their lending practices. They are likely to lend only to well-established businesses. Therefore, start-up companies generally cannot obtain bank loans unless the entrepreneur personally guarantees the loan. After your business is up and running, banks may make some types of financing available.

An established business can usually get a line of credit (a loan) from a bank. A **line of credit** is an arrangement whereby a lender agrees to lend up to a specific amount of money at a certain interest rate for a specific period of time. The company can then borrow against that credit line and pay back the money on a regular basis. For example, you may be able to borrow money using your business assets or real estate as security. If you do not pay back the loan, the bank can take those pledged assets.

Applying for a loan involves three things. First, you prepare a comprehensive business plan. Second, you prepare a loan proposal (sometimes in the form of a loan application). Third, you make an appointment to speak with a loan officer. You supply any additional information the officer requires. If you are granted the loan, you will be asked to sign loan documents. These spell out your obligations as well as the bank's. You will also learn the total amount of the loan. This includes the total interest for the life of the loan.

TRADE CREDIT **Trade credit** is credit one business grants to another business for the purchase of goods or services. It is a source of short-term financing provided by companies within your industry or trade. Suppose you purchase goods from a supplier on 60 days of credit, interest free. This means you must pay the supplier within 60 days of receiving the goods. If your customers pay promptly, you can use that money to pay your bill.

MINORITY ENTERPRISE DEVELOPMENT PROGRAMS Funded by the private sector and the Small Business Administration, MESBICs (Minority Enterprise Small Business Investment Companies) provide funding to businesses whose owners are at least 51 percent ethnic minority, female, or disabled. The SBA also helps minority-owned businesses secure government contracts and find strategic partners.

COMMERCIAL FINANCE COMPANIES Commercial finance companies provide a more expensive alternative to commercial banks. Finance companies are less conservative than banks, and they typically are willing to take more risks. Consequently, they also charge more. Some form of security is usually required for a loan (for example, the entrepreneur's home).

SBA LOAN If the Small Business Administration approves your request for a loan, it will use a commercial bank to process and release the money. It will also guarantee repayment to the lender of up to 90 percent of the loan should your business fail. The SBA assures the bank that it can lose only the portion of the loan that is not guaranteed. You and anyone with more than 20 percent ownership also must guarantee the loan with your personal assets. The SBA lends public funds to qualified veterans and people with disabilities. You can learn more at the Small Business Administration Web site.

SMALL BUSINESS INVESTMENT COMPANIES (SBICs) SBICs are privately managed venture capital companies. They are licensed by the SBA to provide equity and debt financing to young businesses. The government provides funding at favorable rates to the SBIC. The SBIC then matches the funding with its own capital. SBICs invest about twice as often in start-up ventures as venture capitalists.

Issues in Entrepreneurship

ALL IN THE FAMILY

Investments by family and friends account for about 70 percent of the funds that start-up businesses raise. Entrepreneurs who turn their loved ones into creditors need to take steps to ensure that their relationships remain harmonious as their businesses grow. Do not ask friends and family for money before a formal business plan is in place. Be as rigorous as you would be if you were trying to get financing from a bank.

Before you ask for money, think about how to structure the arrangement. Are you willing to give up equity? Would you rather pay interest on a loan? The answers to these questions have major implications. Most entrepreneurs prefer debt financing because there is no loss of control. However, if you think that the business will have a low cash flow for the first few years, equity financing can help your balance sheet look stronger.

Think Creatively
Interview an adult friend or family member who has invested in a start-up company owned by a family member. Ask whether the investment was worthwhile. In an e-mail memo to your teacher, write a brief summary of the interview.

 Go to **entrepreneurship.glencoe.com** to complete the Issues in Entrepreneurship Research Activity.

Financial Planning for Your Business

Financial planning means finding the right kind of financial resources at the right time in the right amount. Financial planning provides you with a better chance of securing the money you need when you need it.

Financial planning starts with identifying the stages of growth in your business. Then you must identify critical milestones that require more resources than your business can supply. One milestone may be hiring your first employee. Another may be moving to a larger facility.

Another financial planning consideration is identifying business advisers who can introduce you to funding sources. Experienced advisers will help you locate "smart" money, that is, investors who bring money, expertise, guidance, and contacts.

Financial planning includes hiring the best management expertise you can. The founding team may have worked for an equity stake. However, you must pay the management personnel you hire at market rates.

Section 19.1 After You Read

Key Concept Review

1. What is bootstrapping, and how can it help entrepreneurs start their business?

2. What is the difference between debt and equity financing?

3. What is the most common source of start-up capital for entrepreneurs? Why?

Critical Thinking

4. Visit a bank or commercial finance company and inquire about the requirements for a loan for a new business. Identify sources of credit and list steps in applying for a loan. How difficult is it to meet the loan requirements? What are some personal risks you would face in financing this business?

Role Play

Situation You have developed a new business idea: a small retail outlet on campus to sell goods made by students. You have already filed for permission from the school system. All you need now is funding. Your aunt owns a retail business and plans to advise you.

Activity Pair up with a classmate. Have your classmate assume the role of your aunt, who will offer advice and information. Role-play a question and answer session.

Evaluation You will be evaluated on how well you address these issues:

- Discuss personal risks involved in financing a business.
- Identify the major sources of funding for a business.
- Identify sources of credit and list steps in applying for a loan.
- Discuss the impact of interest rates on short- and long-term financing.
- Describe differences between short-term and long-term capital needs.

Obtaining Financing and Growth Capital

GET READY TO READ

KEY TERMS
- pro forma
- character
- capacity
- capital
- collateral
- conditions
- due diligence
- private placement
- initial public offering (IPO)
- stock
- working capital
- contingency fund

KEY CONCEPTS
- How to Obtain Financing
- Types of Growth Financing
- Calculating Your Start-Up Capital Needs

THE MAIN IDEA
Additional sources of funding become available when entrepreneurs are ready to grow their business. Entrepreneurs must calculate their start-up needs so they can communicate this information to potential funders.

READING ORGANIZER
Draw the reading organizer on a separate piece of paper. As you read, write the five Cs that bankers rely on to determine the acceptability of a loan applicant.

THE 5 Cs

C haracter _____

C _____

C _____

C _____

C _____

How to Obtain Financing

Once you have identified potential sources of financing, you must create pro forma financial statements to include in your business plan to support the financing request. **Pro forma** refers to proposed or estimated financial statements based on predictions of how the actual operations of the business will turn out. Your plan must include income statements, cash flow statements, and balance sheets. All of these statements provide a financial road map for the business. They give potential investors and other sources of funds a sense of confidence that you know what you are doing. Chapter 21 will discuss these financial statements in more detail. In this section, you will discover what investors and others look for in a new business.

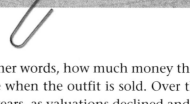

VCs: More Than You Bargained For

Eager to secure the financing their start-ups need, many entrepreneurs pay too little attention to the fine print. That can be a very costly mistake

When entrepreneurs begin negotiating with venture capitalists, they are invariably preoccupied with making sure they maintain at least 51% ownership of their companies. That way, they figure, they will keep control of important corporate decisions about strategy and growth. In the process of focusing on ownership, however, entrepreneurs often gloss over the fine print that spells out who will get what when the start-up eventually achieves success. Based on how ownership is divided, those unnoticed elements in a deal can pack quite a surprise, since venture capitalists may well be entitled to a much more lucrative payday than entrepreneurs in their innocence ever imagined.

While founders tend to focus on ownership, venture capitalists' sights are set on the pot of gold at the end of the rainbow—in other words, how much money they will make when the outfit is sold. Over the last few years, as valuations declined and investors became harder to find, venture capitalists have moved the pendulum ever further in their favor when it comes to negotiating ownership rights.

SOURCE: *BusinessWeek*; JANUARY 6, 2004; BY GABOR GARAI

APPLICATION Imagine that you are seeking funding from a venture capital company for your proposed business. Use a word-processing application to write a one-page report. Explain the terms you would agree to in exchange for funding and what you would offer the venture capital company in return.

 Go to **entrepreneurship.glencoe.com** to complete the *BusinessWeek* Case Study Reading Guide.

What Venture Capitalists Expect

As an entrepreneur, your primary goal is to build a business that survives and grows. The goal of the venture capitalist is to achieve a large capital gain in a short period of time. At the outset, you and the venture capitalist do not have the same goals.

Venture capitalists rarely invest in start-up companies. When they do, however, they look for high-growth technology firms with huge market potential. What is "high growth"? Venture capitalists want a 30 to 70 percent return on their investment for a growing company and a return of 50 percent or more for an early stage venture because of the high level of risk. Here is a simple example: Suppose venture capitalists give your business $2 million for five years. At the end of that period, they want to receive their investment plus an additional $600,000 to $1 million. That means your business must generate enough increase in value to pay off the investors.

Above all, venture capitalists look for a business with a good management team. They believe a good team is the key to success.

The process of obtaining funding from venture capitalists is a slow one. They examine every facet of your business, often taking months. Therefore, you should not go to a venture capitalist when you are desperate for money. You should go to them long before you really need money.

What Private Investors Expect

Private investors, often called angels, are often former entrepreneurs who want to take a different role in venture start-up. Unlike many venture capital firms, angels enjoy getting involved in the business. They typically invest in businesses they understand or in businesses where they know the entrepreneur. Today many angel investors network with like-minded investors, pooling their funds to invest in larger opportunities. In general, these bands of angels fill the gap between individual investors and larger venture capital firms.

Most private investors put between $10,000 and $500,000 into a new business. In the technology arena, though, a single investor may put up as much as a million dollars. Private investors typically find opportunities in their local metropolitan area through friends and business associates. On average, these investors aim to get ten times their investment at the end of five years. Like bankers and venture capitalists, private investors look for a strong management team.

What Bankers Expect

Bankers have different needs than venture capitalists. They must invest conservatively and follow strict rules about how to invest the bank's money. Therefore, they are most interested in a company's ability to repay the loan. That means they will examine a company's cash flow. They want to determine whether the company has enough cash flow to pay monthly expenses *and* the loan payment.

Quick Math

A venture capitalist gives your business $100,000 for two years. In return the venture capitalist seeks a return of 30 to 50 percent. At minimum, how much will you owe at the end of the two years?

FINANCING GROWTH
After a business has established a track record, financing growth can be easier to secure. *What are some sources of growth capital?*

Bankers rely on five Cs to determine the acceptability of a loan applicant. The bankers' five Cs are:

- **Character.** A bank must believe in the character of the entrepreneur. **Character** is a borrower's reputation for fair and ethical business practices. They will consider your business experience and your dealings with other local businesses. Your reputation in the community and among creditors is important. Like venture capitalists, bankers recognize the value of a good management team.

- **Capacity.** **Capacity** refers to the ability of a business to pay a loan in view of its income and obligations. Banks look for businesses with sufficient cash flow to repay the loan.

- **Capital.** Banks place a strong emphasis on whether a business has a financially stable capital structure. **Capital** is the net worth of a business, the amount by which its assets exceed its liabilities. Capital is used to operate a business. Banks prefer businesses that do not have too much debt.

- **Collateral.** Banks are more likely to lend to businesses with valuable assets, or collateral. **Collateral** is security in the form of assets that a company pledges to a lender. The banks can claim these assets if a business does not repay its loan.

- **Conditions.** Banks consider all of the conditions of the environment in which the business will operate. **Conditions** are the circumstances at the time of the loan request. Business conditions include potential for growth, amount of competition, location, and form of ownership. Banks even check insurance coverage. They may demand certain types of insurance, depending on the risk involved in the business.

To be considered for a commercial bank loan, you and your business must score high on all five Cs. Therefore, it is important for you and your business to maintain a favorable credit rating. It is also important to establish a relationship with your banker before you ask for money. Let the banker see your business plan. Keep him or her up to date on major happenings with your business. Then when you do need a loan, the banker already knows the business and you.

While You Read

Predict What might a banker look for when screening an application for a business loan besides the five Cs of credit?

RISK MANAGEMENT In addition to the five Cs of credit, many bankers look at insurance coverage when screening business loan applications. *Why is this?*

Autonomic Computing

Computer problems are a fact of life, but some researchers and businesses are working on making them less common. An evolving field of study is autonomic computing, which means "automatic responses"—that is, computer systems detect when something has gone wrong and can repair themselves. Autonomic systems also reconfigure their settings when changes are needed, so that employees do not have to spend much time endlessly adjusting and repairing them.

Critical Thinking

What are some examples of autonomic computing that you have encountered? Can you think of any potential business uses?

@ Go to **entrepreneurship.glencoe.com** to complete the Technology Today Vocabulary Practice Activity.

Types of Growth Financing

When your business is ready to grow, you may find more financing options than you had at start-up. If your company has established a successful track record, some of the risk for investors is reduced. You have proven your concept, so more people are interested in it. In this section, you will learn about some of the types of financing available to grow your business.

Venture Capital (VC) Companies

Venture capital (VC) companies are unlikely sources of start-up funding for most businesses. With a proven concept and huge potential for growth, however, your business may attract venture capital. As discussed previously, most VC companies expect returns that range between 30 and 70 percent depending on the stage of the company. They also may require significant ownership interest and a seat on the board of directors. However, the older and more established your business, the less risk there is for the VC company. As a result, it will want less in return for its investment. VCs also look for intellectual property (patents and copyrights) and a strong market.

The best way to find a VC company is through an introduction by someone close to it. You will probably be asked to supply a business plan and present it to the partners in the VC firm. If the firm decides that your company has a sound plan, it will begin due diligence. **Due diligence** is the investigation and analysis a prudent investor does before making business decisions. This means that the VC will run background checks on you, your team, and your business. If the experts like what they see, the terms of the agreement will be negotiated and an agreement made. Do not expect the money to show up quickly. Venture capitalists often do not contact their investors until the deal with you is complete. They want to make sure you are represented in the best possible manner.

> **While You Read**
>
> **Connect** Interview the owner of a local business that has recently expanded or opened a new location. Find out how the expansion was funded.

Private Placements

Private placement is a way to raise capital by selling ownership interests in your private corporation or partnership. **Private placement** is a private offering or sale of securities directly to a limited number of institutional investors who meet certain suitability standards. These ownership interests are called *securities*.

If you raise capital this way, follow Securities and Exchange Commission Regulation D. Regulation D states that your investors meet certain suitability standards, such as they must be "sophisticated." That means they invest on a regular basis and have a net worth of at least a million dollars. That may sound like a lot of money, but the investors' homes, cars, bank accounts, insurance policies, and other properties do add up. You should use a qualified attorney to set up the private placement memorandum. If your business fails, this memorandum details what investors can and cannot expect from you.

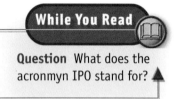

While You Read

Question What does the acronmyn IPO stand for?

Initial Public Offerings (IPOs)

The **initial public offering (IPO)** is the sale of stock in a company on a public stock exchange. A **stock** is a type of security that signifies ownership in a corporation and represents a claim on part of the corporation's assets and earnings. An IPO is a popular way to raise a lot of money for growth. All proceeds of the IPO go to the company. However, once you have made an IPO, your company is no longer private. It is public. Public companies are regulated heavily by the SEC and the federal government. All of the company's information must be made available to the public. The CEO is now responsible primarily to the people who own the company stock. In effect, the entrepreneur no longer owns the company. The shareholders, of which the entrepreneur is one, now own it. The IPO process is expensive and lengthy. Entrepreneurs spend up to a year preparing for the date of a public offering.

There are five steps to becoming a public company with stock for sale on a public stock exchange.

1. **Choose an underwriter or investment banker.** These professionals sell securities and help you through the initial public offering process, much like a tour guide.

2. **Draw up a letter of intent.** This letter outlines the terms and conditions between you and the underwriter and gives the price range for the stock.

3. **File a registration statement with the SEC.** This document is called a "red herring" or prospectus. It spells out the potential risks of investing in the initial public offering. You also need to choose the stock exchange where your stock will sell.

4. **Announce the offering in the financial press.** The advertisement you place in the financial paper is called a "tombstone."

5. **Do a road show.** This is a whirlwind tour of all major institutional investors (insurance companies, pension plans, etc.) to market the offering. This is done so the offering can be sold in one day, the "coming out" day.

Calculating Your Start-Up Capital Needs

You already know you can acquire money to start or grow your business. Now you need to calculate exactly how much money. This requires estimating start-up costs, which include capital expenditures, working capital (operating costs), and contingency funds.

Start-Up Costs

Start-up costs are those costs you incur before you start the business. To figure start-up costs, you need to talk to suppliers, vendors, manufacturers, distributors, and others in your industry. They can help you determine what you need and how much it will cost.

Suppose you are starting a simple service business that provides temporary workers to the restaurant industry. Your list of start-up costs might look like those found in **Figure 19.1** on page 420.

You need to calculate what it will cost to purchase equipment and facilities. These are called *capital expenditures.* They are usually one-time expenses. Figure 19.1 shows that equipment, furniture, and fixtures are included as capital expenditures. They should be included in your start-up costs. You can reduce the amount of start-up capital by cutting capital expenditures.

Operating Costs

Operating costs, often referred to as **working capital**, is the amount of cash needed to carry out the daily business operations. It ensures that the business has a positive cash flow after covering all of its operating expenses. Working capital covers the time between selling your product or service and receiving payment from the customer.

START-UP COSTS A business must invest in many different types of equipment and supplies before it can open for business. *What other expenses would be involved in keeping this copy machine running?*

Figure 19.1 **Start-Up Costs**

COSTS AND EXPENSES
Start-up costs are those costs you incur before you start the business. You may need to rent space, lease equipment, purchase phones, and train employees. All of these expenses occur before you ever make a sale to a customer. *Which of the start-up costs depicted will also become operating expenses?*

Lease and security deposit
When you sign a lease, you are entering into a long-term contract. Most leases require the advance payment of a security deposit to the landlord. The landlord holds the deposit as security in case you damage the property or fail to fulfill the lease terms.

Furniture, fixtures, and equipment
Funds are needed to pay for equipment, including desks, chairs, phone systems, counters, display cases, shelving, and other fixtures. Your business may also need computer hardware, software, and peripherals like fax machines and scanners.

Promotion expenses and office supplies
Initial advertising and promotion expenses include signs, business cards, and brochures. You will also need to buy office supplies, such as business cards, stationery, and various business forms, such as sales checks, invoices forms, and purchase order forms.

THIS CERTIFICATE MUST BE POSTED AT PLACE OF BUSINESS

CITY OF LOS ANGELES TAX REGISTRATION CERTIFICATE
THIS CERTIFICATE IS GOOD UNTIL SUSPENDED OR CANCELLED
BUSINESS LICENSE   ISSUED: 05-04-05   V

ACCOUNT NO.	FUND	CLASS	DESCRIPTION	STARTED
123456-78	L	167	RETAIL SALES	04-16-05

LUNA GRAPHICS
5 WILLOW AV #3
N HOLLYWOOD CA 91607-1199

ISSUED BY:

DIRECTOR OF FINANCE

NOTIFY THE OFFICE OF FINANCE IN WRITING OF ANY CHANGE IN OWNERSHIP OR ADDRESS — 201 N. MAIN ST, RM 101, LOS ANGELES CA. 90012
FORM 2000 (rev. 6/01)   IMPORTANT - READ REVERSE SIDE

Fees and licenses
Most start-up businesses need to have funds to pay for accounting and legal fees. Some businesses also need to pay for permits and licenses.

You will learn how to do a cash flow statement in the next chapter. This will help you decide how much working capital you need to maintain a positive cash position.

Contingency Funds

No one can predict the future. That is why you should include extra funds, called contingency funds, when you calculate start-up needs. A **contingency fund** is an extra amount of money that is saved and used only when absolutely necessary. These funds are used if you are not paid on time. They also are used to cover unforeseen business expenses.

How much to allow for contingencies depends on several factors, which include type of business and dependability of customers. Some business owners keep enough money in reserve to cover two or more months of fixed costs. (That includes salaries, rent, and other items that must be paid regardless of sales.) Those in seasonal industries, such as snowmobile dealers, might put 6 to 12 months of capital in reserve.

Section 19.2 After You Read

Key Concept Review

1. What do private investors look for when they invest in a new business?
2. Why is venture capital not a good source of start-up capital?
3. What are the three categories of funds you need to estimate to determine your start-up needs?

Critical Thinking

4. Describe a start-up business that would attract venture capital. Consider the needs of venture capitalists and do some research on the Internet to support your business description.

Role Play

Situation Tomorrow the board of directors at the bank will be voting whether to lend you $30,000 for your new business. One of the bank's board members is a friend. She tells you that if the loan is approved, she will invest an additional $10,000 of her own money in return for a 10 percent interest in the business.

Activity Pair up with a classmate and role-play a conversation. Have your classmate pretend to be the member of the board of directors who is willing to provide additional investment capital.

Evaluation You will be evaluated on how well you address these issues:

- Discuss the importance of maintaining a favorable credit rating.
- Your classmate's ability to ask appropriate due diligence questions to determine whether your business is a worthy investment.
- Your ability to arrive at a conclusion that is a win-win situation for both parties.

Chapter Summary

Financing the Small Business Start-Up

Entrepreneurs must find resources to help launch their business. Many entrepreneurs start up their business very frugally by hiring as few employees as possible, leasing rather than buying, and being creative. Equity and debt sources are two options for finance. Equity sources of financing involve giving up some ownership in the company. Debt sources of financing involves borrowing money and paying it back with interest. A financial plan provides an entrepreneur a better chance of securing money when it is needed.

Obtaining Financing and Growth Capital

Once you have identified potential financial sources, you need to make sure that your business plan meets their criteria. Banks look for evidence of the five Cs: character, capacity, capital, collateral, and conditions. Venture capitalists and private investors look for a strong management team and a good return on investment. When entrepreneurs are ready to expand their operations, other sources of financing become available. These sources include venture capital companies, private placements, and initial public offerings. To determine how much money you will need for start-up or for growth, estimate your start-up costs, which include capital expenditures, working capital (operating costs), and contingency funds.

Key Terms Review

1. For each of the following terms, write a sentence that describes its role in financing your start-up and/or growing business.

bootstrapping (p. 407)	debt capital (p. 409)	collateral (p. 416)
factor (p. 407)	operating capital (p. 410)	conditions (p. 416)
equity capital (p. 408)	line of credit (p. 410)	due diligence (p. 417)
equity (p. 408)	trade credit (p. 410)	private placement (p. 418)
risk capital (p. 408)	pro forma (p. 413)	initial public offering (IPO) (p. 418)
angel (p. 409)	character (p. 416)	stock (p. 418)
venture capital (p. 409)	capacity (p. 416)	working capital (p. 419)
venture capitalists (p. 409)	capital (p. 416)	contingency fund (p. 421)

Key Concept Review

2. **Describe** the resources available to entrepreneurs to start their business. (19.1)
3. **Compare and contrast** sources of financing for start-up ventures. (19.1)
4. **Describe** the importance of financial planning. (19.1)
5. **Describe** the information needed to obtain financing. (19.2)
6. **Explain** the types of growth financing available to entrepreneurs. (19.2)
7. **Describe** how to calculate start-up capital requirements. (19.2)

Critical Thinking

8. How might you use bootstrapping to help your new business get off the ground?
9. If you wanted to retain as much control of your business as possible, what sources of financing would you consider? Why?
10. What advantages does equity financing have over debt financing?
11. How would you go about developing a financial plan for the first ten years of your business?
12. Describe the differences between private placements and initial public offerings.
13. In what circumstances would an entrepreneur want to give equity (instead of a salary) to an employee?
14. Why would you choose to do a private placement rather than bring in equity stakeholders from among your friends?

Write About It

15. Write out definitions to these terms: *equity capital, debt capital, line of credit, collateral,* and *factoring.*
16. In a one-page report, summarize three forms of equity financing and their advantages and disadvantages.
17. In a paragraph, describe reasons why trade credit would be preferable to a bank line of credit.
18. In a couple of paragraphs, compare and contrast funding growth through internal cash flow with funding growth through bank financing.
19. Describe the trade-offs between debt and equity financing. Compose your answer at the computer.
20. Use the computer to describe types of funding within each funding source (e.g., mortgage, short-term loan, long-term loan, and credit line).

Academic Skills

Math

21. Roberto has estimated start-up costs for his new business to be $6,500. He projects that for the first six months, his ongoing operating costs will be $4,300 and personal expenses will total $8,200. Roberto has saved $12,780 to put toward the new business. How much money must he borrow? What percentage of his total costs must he borrow?

Language Arts

22. You are selling a product for which there are no readily available substitutes. Therefore demand is constant or inelastic relative to price. Write a short paragraph explaining how this will affect your company's financial strategy.

Entrepreneurship in Your Community

23. Research and identify three sources of financing for your new business. Evaluate each type of financing based on these questions:

- What is the risk to the business of using that type of financing?

- If you borrow money, how will the loans be repaid?

- If you finance through an equity source, how will the investors be paid?

Based on your research, which funding source is best for your business?

24. Obtain a loan application from a local bank.

- Fill it out to the best of your ability.

- Make a list of questions about the things you do not understand.

- Go back to the bank and get the answers.

If possible, invite a banker to your class to answer questions about loans to small business owners.

Ethical Practices

Financing Ethics

25. Your friend has a brilliant business idea and wants to start a new business right away. However, he does not have experience or a proven track record. He is desperate to find capital to launch his venture, and he is tempted to do whatever it takes to secure the needed capital. Prepare a script for offering advice regarding the ethical issues that surround the financing of new ventures.

INTERNET *connection*

Research IPOs

Your corporation has been in business for five years. It has had great success and sound financial performance. You want to begin selling stock to the public to raise growth capital.

Connect

Use a search engine or Web directory to research three companies that have recently sold stock on a public stock exchange for the first time. Research these issues:

- The advantages and disadvantages of selling shares of ownership in a corporation.

- The Securities and Exchange Commission rules and regulations for IPOs.

- Ways the companies managed their offering.

- Ways the companies marketed their offering.

Application

Use a spreadsheet application to present the results of your research in a table. Then use a word-processing application to write a one-page report that discusses the circumstances in which "going public" is right for a business. Import your spreadsheet table into your word-processed report.

The Electronic Entrepreneur

Technology Enabled Marketing

In the past, business departments such as sales, production, and marketing kept their information separate. Technology enabled marketing (TEM) ties all of the departments together, so that all departments can work from the same pool of data. TEM can take a number of shapes and forms.

Sales Force Automation Salespeople drive a company. Keeping them organized and in touch with customers enables them to work more efficiently and generate more revenue. **Sales force automation** are tools that automate the business tasks of sales. This includes order processing, contact management, lead tracking, information sharing, inventory monitoring and control, order tracking, customer management, sales forecast analysis, and employee performance evaluation. SAF allows salespeople to keep track of customers, check stock on items, record customer preferences, or ship samples to potential buyers.

Online Customer Service Keeping customers happy is crucial, and company Web sites can help customers get the answers they need quickly. **Online customer service** is the service businesses provide to customers via the Internet. Many companies allow customers to sign up to be registered users of a Web site. Then customers can manage their accounts and access information on their own.

Marketing Information New technologies enable businesses to gather useful information about their customers. This information can be shared among all company departments to improve customer service and increase sales. If you opened your own online book store, you could create a "frequent reader" discount card, for example. Customers would sign up to be members in exchange for discounts. By doing this, you can gather valuable information about your customer base. You can use this information as a basis for market research.

FACT AND IDEA REVIEW

1. How would you define technology enabled marketing?
2. In addition to the examples mentioned, what are some other ways technology tools might aid a sales force?
3. Why is online customer service becoming so popular? What are some other uses of it?
4. Why does it benefit a business to keep track of a customer's purchases?

FOR DISCUSSION

5. What are some other examples of how companies use technologies to gather information on your spending? What are some ways they might use this information?

TechTerms

- sales force automation
- online customer service

Chapter 20

Accounting and Financial Reporting

CHAPTER OBJECTIVES

When you have completed this chapter, you should be able to:

SECTION 20.1

- Explain the important role accounting plays in business.
- Explain the accounting system for a small business.
- Describe the importance of daily sales and cash receipts reports.

SECTION 20.2

- Describe the items of information included on each financial statement.
- Identify ongoing accounting activities.
- Explain how technology helps business owners with all the accounting functions.

STANDARD &POOR'S
Money Talk

FINANCIAL ACCOUNTING

Whether you are keeping financial records for a rock band, a bike shop, or a major corporation, accounting principles and procedures are universal. All businesses follow "generally accepted accounting principles," or GAAP.

Businesses make financial reports in specific blocks of time, called *accounting periods*. This may be a month or a quarter (three months), but the most common period is one year. By using a set period of time, you can compare financial reports from one period to those from another period.

During this period, you record all financial transactions for your business and report the results. You will engage in activities that maintain your accounting records in an orderly manner. The activities, or steps, that help a business keep its accounting records in an orderly manner make up the accounting cycle.

 Go to **entrepreneurship.glencoe.com** to complete the Standard & Poor's Money Talk Financial Literacy Activity.

PREPARE TO READ

THINK ABOUT THESE QUESTIONS AS YOU READ.

Why do all business operations use the same system?

Why are financial statements prepared?

Financial Record Keeping

GET READY TO READ

KEY TERMS
- GAAP
- financial reports
- accounting period
- calendar year
- fiscal year
- assets
- current assets
- accounts receivable
- fixed assets
- liabilities
- accounts payable
- owner's equity
- chart of accounts
- debits
- credits
- cash basis
- accrual basis
- journal
- journalizing
- general journal
- posting

KEY CONCEPTS
- Accounting for Business
- The Accounting System
- Using Sales and Cash Receipts Report

THE MAIN IDEA

All businesses must record and report all financial activities using established concepts and procedures.

READING ORGANIZER

Draw the reading organizer on a separate piece of paper. As you read, write the numbers 1 through 5 on the lines to list the accounting procedures in the order they are completed.

ACCOUNTING PROCEDURES

_____ Post amounts to the general ledger

_____ Analyze business transactions

_____ Prepare the balance sheet

_____ Enter amounts in a general journal

_____ Prepare an income statement

Accounting for Business

One of the most important operations in running any business is the maintaining of accurate, up-to-date financial records. Accounting plays a vital role in the day-to-day activities of your business—and of every business. Accounting records and reports help you run your business efficiently and profitably by keeping track of how much is earned and how much is spent. If you are keeping your records by hand or using a computerized accounting program, the system will be the same.

Whether you are keeping financial records for a delivery service, a small bike shop, or a major corporation, accounting principles and procedures are universal. All U.S. businesses use the same system, which follows established accounting guidelines called "generally accepted accounting principles," or **GAAP**. If all businesses use the same system of recording and reporting financial information, anyone interested in examining the records of a business will be able to understand its financial reports.

Success Stories

Premier Snowskate

When he was 25 years old, Andy Wolf moved to Salt Lake City to become a professional snowboarder. Andy was a passionate skateboarder, too, and found that his new home was too snowy for good skating. In 1999, with just a small amount of money loaned from a friend of his father, Andy invented the snowskate, which combined the best elements of both sports. He hoped to sell 1,000 of them as a hobby—but when 5,000 of them flew off the shelves, he knew he had come upon something special. His company, Premier Snowskate, is a leading supplier of skates for this new sport that Wolf invented.

CRITICAL THINKING
What are the benefits of creating a career out of a hobby?

 Go to **entrepreneurship.glencoe.com** to complete the Success Stories Writing Activity.

The accounting system is designed to collect, record, and report financial transactions that affect your business. **Financial reports** or statements are documents that summarize the results of your business operation and provide a picture of its financial position. These reports indicate to banks, financial institutions, potential buyers, government agencies, and consumers how well your business is doing. They also provide you with the financial information needed to make sound business decisions.

Accounting Assumptions

When you are creating the accounting books for your business, you will make two assumptions about your business. The first is that your business will operate as a separate entity. This means that the records and reports of your business must be kept completely separate from your personal finances.

The second assumption is that your financial reports always cover a specific period of time. A block of time covered by an accounting report is called an **accounting period**. The accounting period can be a month or a quarter (three months), but the most common period is one year.

If your one-year period begins on January 1 and ends on December 31, it is called a **calendar year**. However, you can choose to have your year begin and end in months other than the calendar year. This is referred to as a **fiscal year**. If you run your business on a fiscal year, it must be the same 12-month period year after year. For example, a ski shop would not want to end its year on December 31—its busiest time. Instead it might operate on a fiscal year from July 1 to June 30. However, a convenience store probably does not have a busy time period and might choose to use the calendar year. Whether a business runs on a calendar year or a fiscal year, taxes will be paid on that period of time.

TECHNOLOGY Today

Open-Book Financial Management

Traditionally, a company's financial information is available to just a small handful of people—the accountants and bookkeepers, the CFO, and the high-level executives. Open-book financial management turns that idea on its head. Using high-tech applications such as Intranets and groupware, open-book financial management makes this information available to all employees. Proponents of the method say it cuts costs, as employees begin to take responsibility for budgeting and spending.

Critical Thinking

What are some of the pros and cons of open-book financial management?

@ Go to **entrepreneurship.glencoe.com** to complete the Technology Today Vocabulary Practice Activity.

The Accounting Equation

The accounting equation is the basis for keeping financial records. The equation is as follows:

ASSETS = LIABILITIES + OWNER'S EQUITY

Quick Math

If your business has assets that total $320,000 and liabilities that total $200,000, what is your equity?

Assets are anything of value that the business owns. They include items such as cash, equipment, or buildings. Assets are further broken down to include current assets and fixed assets. **Current assets** are cash or other items that can be converted to cash fairly quickly and are used by the business within a year. Cash, supplies, merchandise, and accounts receivable are all examples of current assets. **Accounts receivable** is the amount customers owe your business. **Fixed assets** are items that will be held for more than one year. These could include equipment, trucks, and buildings.

Liabilities are the debts of the business. The most common account used in this classification is **accounts payable**. This is the amount your business owes to creditors. The total amount of assets minus total liabilities will give you the worth of the business or the **owner's equity**.

As an example, if Jenny had a fabric store that had total assets of $64,000 and total liabilities of $21,000, Jenny's equity in the business is $43,000. Jenny could say that the worth of her business is $43,000.

ASSETS	=	LIABILITIES	+	OWNER'S EQUITY
$64,000	=	$21,000	+	$43,000

Notice that the value or worth of a business is not the amount of assets it owns.

 entrepreneurship.glencoe.com

The Accounting System

All businesses use the same accounting system, but each business must create its own set of accounts. Each business will have different accounts, but all will use the same concepts and procedures for recording, summarizing, and reporting the financial information.

Creating Accounts

When you create the books of your business, you create accounts for each of the three categories in the accounting equation. An account shows the balance for a specific category such as cash or equipment. The accounts for a small delivery business could be as follows:

ASSETS	=	LIABILITIES	+	OWNER'S EQUITY
CASH IN BANK		ACCOUNTS PAYABLE		MATT HOYT, CAPITAL
ACCOUNTS RECEIVABLE				
OFFICE EQUIPMENT				
DELIVERY EQUIPMENT				

The list of accounts a business uses in its operation is called the **chart of accounts**. The chart of accounts for Jenny's Window Shop will be somewhat different than the chart of accounts used in Luis's Plumbing Store.

Issues in Entrepreneurship

CORRECTING ERRORS IN GENERAL JOURNAL ENTRIES

Occasionally, errors occur when journalizing transactions. When an error is discovered, it must be corrected.

In a manual system, an error should never be erased. An erasure looks suspicious. It might be seen as an attempt to cover up a mistake or, worse, to change the accounting records illegally. To correct errors, use a pen and a ruler to draw a horizontal line through the entire incorrect item and write the correct information above the crossed-out error. To correct an error for an erroneous account name, cross out the incorrect information and write the correct names above.

Think Creatively

What is the purpose of leaving a record of corrected entries? When might this trail be needed?

 Go to **entrepreneurship.glencoe.com** to complete the Issues in Entrepreneurship Research Activity.

Double-Entry Accounting

Most businesses use a double-entry accounting system. This means that when a business transaction occurs, it affects two or more accounts. The accounts may increase or decrease, and these changes are identified by entering debits or credits. **Debits** are the left side of an account. **Credits** are the right side of an account. The rules of accounting regarding debits and credits are as follows:

> **FOR ALL ASSETS AND EXPENSES ACCOUNTS**
> - Debits *increase* the balance.
> - Credits *decrease* the balance.
>
> **FOR ALL LIABILITY AND REVENUE ACCOUNTS**
> - Debits *decrease* the balance.
> - Credits *increase* the balance.

For example a debit increases the balance in the Cash in Bank (an asset) account, and a credit decreases the balance. A credit increases the balance in Accounts Payable (a liability), and a debit decreases the balance.

Cash or Accrual Basis

Income and payments may be recorded in two ways. If you use a **cash basis**, you record your income when it is received and your expenses when they are paid. If you use the **accrual basis**, you record income when it is earned and expenses when they are incurred. Most businesses operate under the accrual basis. This means they record unpaid bills and expenses as Accounts Payable and money owed to the business from sales as Accounts Receivable.

Journalizing Business Transactions

A **journal** is like a financial diary of the business. If you keep a diary or a personal journal, each day you write down important events that may occur. A business does the same thing with a journal. The process of recording business transactions in a journal is called **journalizing**. In journalizing you record the business transactions as they occur, usually on a daily basis. The most common journal is the **general journal**. This is an all-purpose journal that records any business transaction. **Figure 20.1** shows how two business transactions are entered in a general journal.

Figure 20.1 **General Journal Entries**

DAILY RECORD KEEPING
Suppose you sold $500 in office equipment for cash. *What account would be debited?*

GENERAL JOURNAL   PAGE ___36___

	DATE		DESCRIPTION	DEBIT	CREDIT	
1	*May*	*4*	*Office Equipment*	3 000 00		1
2			*Cash in Bank*		3 000 00	2
3						3
4		*6*	*Delivery Equipment*	9 000 00		4
5			*Accounts Payable/Wilton Auto*		9 000 00	5
6						6

In the first journal entry, the business paid cash for some office equipment. Office Equipment is an asset account. The Office Equipment account is increasing and is debited. Cash in Bank is an asset account and is decreasing and therefore credited. In the second entry, delivery equipment was purchased on account (on credit). The account Delivery Equipment is an asset and is debited, and Accounts Payable is a liability and is credited.

If a business gets larger, it may find that using one journal is not sufficient to keep track of all its transactions. The business can then set up separate journals, called *special journals,* which record specific types of transactions. Commonly used special journals include the following:

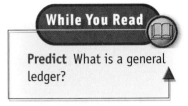
- A *cash receipts journal* is a special journal in which cash and checks received are posted.

- A *cash disbursements journal* is a special journal in which payments made in cash or check form are posted.

- A *sales journal* is a special journal in which sales on account are posted.

- A *purchases journal* is a special journal in which purchases on account are posted.

Posting to the General Ledger

A general ledger is a collection of all accounts created for your business. Examples of general ledger accounts are Cash in Bank, Supplies, Accounts Payable, and Sales. The general ledger account for Cash in Bank is illustrated in **Figure 20.2.**

Write About It

Interview a local business owner. Ask how the business handles its accounting. Write a brief report on your findings.

By looking at the general journal, you cannot easily determine the balance in each of your accounts. You may want to know how much cash you have, how much your business owes in Accounts Payable, or what your sales have been for the fiscal period.

In order to find the balance of each account, you must transfer the amounts recorded in the general journal to the general ledger accounts. The process of transferring amounts from the general journal to accounts in the general ledger is called **posting**. After you have posted all the journal entries, the final balance in each account will appear in the balance column. You can now easily determine what the balance is for Cash in Bank, Supplies, Sales, or Accounts Payable.

Figure 20.2 **General Ledger Account**

ACCOUNT _Cash in Bank_

DATE		EXPLANATION	DEBIT	CREDIT	BALANCE	
					DEBIT	CREDIT
June	10		6 0 0 00		2 7 0 0 00	
	12		8 0 0 00		3 5 0 0 00	
	13			4 0 0 00	3 1 0 0 00	
	14		5 0 0 00		3 6 0 0 00	

THE GENERAL LEDGER
Suppose another credit entry was entered for $200. *What is the new balance in the account?*

While You Read

Connect If you owned your own business, how often would you post your journal entries to the general ledger?

Figure 20.3 illustrates a business transaction that has been recorded in the general journal and posted to the two accounts in the general ledger. Notice both of the general ledger accounts, Supplies and Cash in Bank, have current balances. The balance in Supplies is $740 and the balance in Cash in Bank is $2,295.

Cash in Bank is an asset account. On the general ledger, debits increase the balance, and credits decrease the balance. However, because it is an asset account, the balance is always in the debit balance column.

Post your journal entries to the general ledger as often as necessary to keep your accounts current. However, posting weekly is probably sufficient to give you a good idea of how your business is doing.

Figure 20.3 **Posting to the General Ledger**

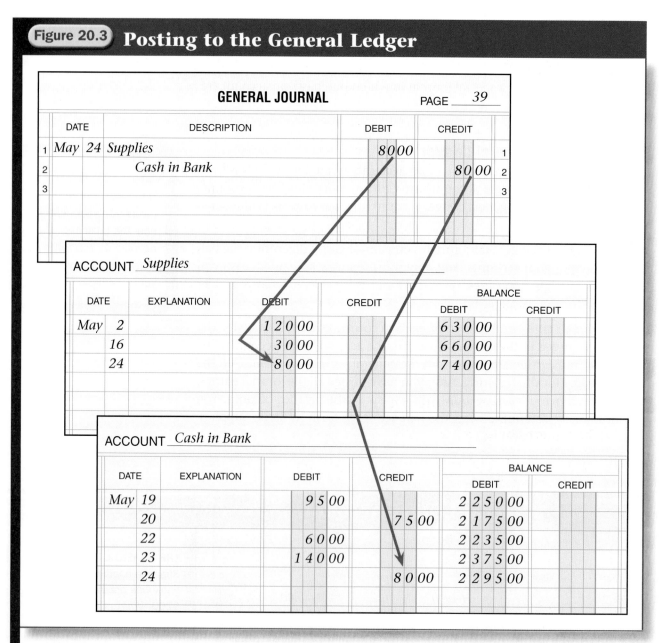

GENERAL JOURNAL PAGE _39_

	DATE		DESCRIPTION	DEBIT	CREDIT	
1	May	24	Supplies	80 00		1
2			Cash in Bank		80 00	2
3						3

ACCOUNT _Supplies_

DATE		EXPLANATION	DEBIT	CREDIT	BALANCE DEBIT	BALANCE CREDIT
May	2		1 20 00		6 30 00	
	16		3 0 00		6 60 00	
	24		8 0 00		7 40 00	

ACCOUNT _Cash in Bank_

DATE		EXPLANATION	DEBIT	CREDIT	BALANCE DEBIT	BALANCE CREDIT
May	19		9 5 00		2 2 5 0 00	
	20			7 5 00	2 1 7 5 00	
	22		6 0 00		2 2 3 5 00	
	23		1 4 0 00		2 3 7 5 00	
	24			8 0 00	2 2 9 5 00	

THE GENERAL LEDGER Suppose the entry on the 16th for Supplies was credited in error.
Would the incorrect balance be higher or lower than the one shown?

Using Sales and Cash Receipts Report

Businesses that have regular daily sales should prepare a daily report of sales and cash receipts. This report allows the business owner to examine the total daily sales and verifies the total of the cash received. An example of a daily sales and cash receipts report is given in **Figure 20.4.** There are three main headings: *Cash Receipts, Cash on Hand,* and *Sales.*

Calculating Cash Receipts

The Cash Receipts section lists cash sales, collections on account, and miscellaneous receipts. Miscellaneous receipts are items that you do not normally receive during a day's business. An example would be if you sold a phone owned by the business to an employee.

Figure 20.4 **Summary of Sales and Cash Receipts**

January 20, _ _ _ _

TOTAL DAILY SALES A summary tells the total daily sales. *How and where?*

Cash Receipts		
Cash sales		$2,160.85
Collections on account		160.35
Miscellaneous receipts		69.77
Total Cash Receipts		$2,390.97
Cash on Hand		
Cash in the register		
Coins	$ 75.31	
Bills	780.00	
Checks	1,635.66	
Total Cash on Hand		$2,490.97
Less opening cash/petty cash fund		
Petty cash slips	$ 20.55	
Coins and bills	79.45	
Petty Cash Fund		100.00
Total Cash Deposit		$2,390.97
Sales		
Cash sales		$2,160.85
Credit sales		465.39
Total Sales		$2,626.24

While You Read

Question What can you learn from analyzing your total daily sales?

Calculating Cash on Hand

The Cash on Hand section of the report shows the amount in the register broken down into bills, coins, and checks. It also includes the opening cash balance, which must remain in the register.

At the end of the Cash on Hand section, calculate how much cash to deposit in the bank for the day. To do this, subtract the opening cash balance from the amount in the register. The amount for Total Cash Deposit must agree with the amount for Total Cash Receipts. If the amounts are not equal, you should check the following:

- Did you record all cash transactions?
- Did you record a transaction for the wrong amount?
- Did you give a customer an incorrect amount of change?

Recording Sales

The final section of the report tells you the total daily sales. This includes the cash sales and the sales on account. This information is vital to analyze sales trends and to maintain a positive cash flow.

Section 20.1   After You Read

Key Concept Review

1. Describe why businesses must follow a set of standards and procedures in keeping accounting information.
2. Identify five general ledger accounts that might be found in a small business.
3. What problems might an owner encounter if a sales and cash receipts report was not completed daily?

Critical Thinking

4. What is the difference between accounts receivable and accounts payable?

Role Play

Situation Paul manages the College Corner, a store that sells books and supplies for the local community college. At the end of each working day, he prepares a summary of sales using figures supplied by his sales clerks. Over the past two months, his summaries have not balanced with the sales reports generated by the computerized cash registers.

Activity Research different ways of accounting and preparing a summary. Then pair up with a partner and take turns role-playing a conversation between Paul and a consultant.

Evaluation You will be evaluated on how well you address these issues:

- Advise Paul on a better way to balance his reports.
- Explain the procedures he could put in place to ensure customers were charged the right amount and were given the correct change.

Preparing Financial Statements

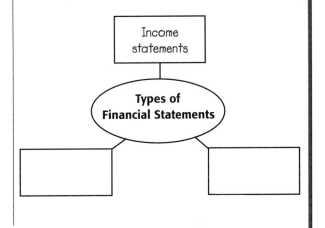
Types of Financial Statements

To operate a business profitably, you will need to have up-to-date financial information. You cannot make sound business decisions if you do not have current figures. Financial statements provide this vital information.

The primary financial statements are the income statement, also called the *statement of operations and earnings,* and the balance sheet. A third statement, called the *statement of cash flows,* is also often used.

Income Statement

At the end of an accounting period, you want to know how much money your business made or lost. You will want to know how much was made in sales and where the money went. This information is reported on the income statement. An **income statement** is a report of the revenue, expenses, and net income or loss for the accounting period. Remember, the revenue coming in minus the expenses going out results in the net income or net loss for the period.

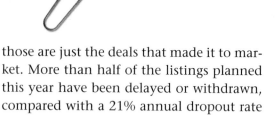

IPOs: Look Out Below

Sure, the number of offerings has risen—but a lot of them have crashed. For years, investors lucky enough or plugged-in enough to get allocations of initial public offerings had a license to print money. At the height of the NASDAQ market boom, the "first-day pop" became notorious as issues such as VA Linux Systems (LNUX) soared as much as 700% overnight. Investment bankers made fortunes as they handed out favors to their friends, leaving retail investors who couldn't get shares fuming and companies angry that so much of their money was being left on the table.

No longer. After the scandals—and reforms—of the past two years, the IPO market is a very different place. These days, the first-day jump averages 12%, barely a fifth of the typical 68% pop back in the heady times of 1999. More than 40% of the 21 IPOs launched in the four weeks through Nov. 25 are now trading below their offering prices, as opposed to the 28% that typically suffered such a fate over the past decade. And those are just the deals that made it to market. More than half of the listings planned this year have been delayed or withdrawn, compared with a 21% annual dropout rate over the past decade, according to Thomson Financial Corp.

SOURCE: *BUSINESSWEEK*, DECEMBER 8, 2003; BY EMILY THORNTON, DAVID HENRY, AND ARLENE WEINTRAUB

APPLICATION

Research a recent IPO. Find out the IPO price and the first day closing price for the stock. Did the stock jump or decrease on the first day? By what percent?

 Go to **entrepreneurship.glencoe.com** to complete the *BusinessWeek* Case Study Reading Guide Activity.

The income statement for different types of business operations vary in content. A service business would have sales, expenses, and net income as illustrated in **Figure 20.5**. A merchandising business would also include the cost of merchandise purchased for resale. This is illustrated in **Figure 20.6**.

Balance Sheet

The other primary financial statement is a balance sheet. A **balance sheet** is a report of the final balances of all asset, liability, and owner's equity accounts at the end of an accounting period. The main purpose of the balance sheet is to present your business's financial position on a specific date. It reports what a business owns, owes, and is worth. This is your present financial situation. It is like taking a financial photo of your business on the last day of the period. An example of a balance sheet is illustrated in **Figure 20.7** on page 440.

Figure 20.5 **Service Business Income Statement**

Bug Runner Delivery Service Income Statement
Year Ended December 31, 20—

Revenue

Sales	$74,400

Operating Expenses

Advertising Expense	6,000
Interest Expense	2,400
Insurance Expense	4,300
Miscellaneous Expense	800
Rent Expense	12,000
Utilities Expense	3,800
Total Expenses	29,300
Net Income	45,100

INCOME STATEMENT An income statement for a service business often has one account under revenue. *Why does this business need only one revenue account?*

Figure 20.6 **Merchandising Business Income Statement**

Swim World Income Statement
Year Ended December 31, 20—

Revenue

Sales	$450,000
Costs of Merchandise Sold	250,000
Gross Profit on Sales	200,000

Operating Expenses

Advertising Expense	35,000
Interest Expense	3,200
Insurance Expense	2,300
Miscellaneous Expense	2,700
Rent Expense	41,000
Salary Expense	16,400
Utilities Expense	3,900
Total Expenses	104,500
Net Income	95,500

INCOME STATEMENT A merchandising business has goods to buy, markup, and sell. *What is another term for gross profit?*

Figure 20.7 **Balance Sheet**

NET WORTH A balance sheet shows how much a business is worth. *How much equity does the owner have in this business?*

Balance Sheet
December 31, 20—

Assets

Cash in Bank	$6,800	
Accounts Receivable	2,700	
Computer Equipment	7,300	
Office Equipment	8,100	
Supplies	1,100	
Total Assets		26,000

Liabilities

Accounts Payable	3,400	
Notes Payable	7,200	
Total Liabilities		10,600

Owner's Equity

Jenny Aguilar, Capital		15,400
Total Liabilities & Owner's Equity		26,000

Notice that the balance sheet consists of three sections: assets, liabilities, and owner's equity. The balance sheet represents the basic accounting equation.

$$\text{ASSETS} = \text{LIABILITIES} + \text{OWNER'S EQUITY}$$

Statement of Cash Flows

Both the income statement and balance sheets provide vital financial information, but neither document shows how the cash position of the business changed during the period. For a business, **cash flow** is the amount of cash that is available at any given time. The **statement of cash flows** reports how much cash your business took in and where the cash went. It also explains why the Cash in Bank account either increased or decreased during the accounting period. **Figure 20.8** is an example of a statement of cash flows.

While You Read

Predict What are the consequences of having a negative cash flow?

When your business has a negative cash flow, you will often experience a lack of available cash. You may not be able to pay your bills or buy more merchandise for resale.

Your statement of cash flows is often a major consideration when you want to borrow money for your business. Potential investors and lenders want to see cash flowing into your business in a constant, positive manner.

Figure 20.8 **Cash Flow Statement**

	March 31, ____	
Cash Receipts		$23,000
Disbursements		
Equipment	$12,000	
Cost of goods	2,500	
Selling expense	200	
Salaries	700	
Advertising	130	
Office supplies	20	
Rent	200	
Utilities	90	
Insurance	170	
Taxes	70	
Loan principal and interest	240	
Total Disbursements		16,320
Net Cash Flow		$ 6,680

RECEIPTS AND EXPENDITURES If a business has more money coming in than going out, it has a positive cash flow. If more money goes out than comes in, it has a negative cash flow. *Which situation does this statement illustrate?*

Ongoing Accounting Activities

In order to have accurate, up-to-date financial information, accounting procedures and activities must be done on a continuing basis.

While You Read

Connect Contact the school bookkeeper and find out about the daily, weekly, and monthly record-keeping systems that are in place.

Weekly Accounting Activities

In order to properly have financial information when it is needed, some accounting activities should be done each week.

POSTING TO THE GENERAL LEDGER Posting on a weekly basis will help keep your account balances accurate. Vital financial information is available if business decisions need to be made.

KEEPING TRACK OF PAYMENTS Keeping track of your business bills is important so that you are not late on payments. By reviewing which bills are due on a weekly basis, you can pay your bills on time.

KEEPING PAYROLL RECORDS If your business has employees, you need to keep accurate and complete payroll records. These include amounts earned by employees (gross pay), deductions for taxes and other items, and the amount paid to employees each week (net pay). This information must be up-to-date in order to pay your payroll taxes to local, state, and federal governments.

KEEPING TAX RECORDS In addition to payroll taxes, businesses also owe taxes for sales tax, state and federal unemployment tax, and other local, state, and federal business taxes. Examining these taxes on a weekly basis will assure that you will meet all your tax obligations on time.

FILING OF RECORDS Properly filing all business documents ensures easy reference. These include purchase orders, invoices received with purchases, bills, receipts, contracts, and any business correspondence.

While You Read

Question Which accounting activities should be done on a monthly basis?

Monthly Accounting Activities

Some accounting activities should be done on a monthly basis.

PREPARING FINANCIAL STATEMENTS Financial statements report the financial position of your business. In order to make sound business decisions, this information must be available.

PAYING PAYROLL TAX DEPOSITS You must be sure all payroll taxes are paid in a timely manner. These include all local, state, and federal tax deposits for payroll withholding. Records of the payments of all taxes and bills and cancelled checks should be filed for proof of payment.

RECONCILING THE BANK STATEMENT You will receive a monthly bank statement that includes all banking activity for the month. When you receive this statement, you should balance your checkbook immediately and verify the accuracy of your banking activities.

BALANCING THE CHECKBOOK Balancing a checkbook is not difficult if you have entered all transactions. The process is listed in **Figure 20.9**.

Figure 20.9 **Steps for Balancing a Checkbook**

BALANCING ACT Many stores now accept debit cards that draw money directly from the customer's checking account. *How would these be treated when balancing a checkbook?*

Step 1 *Write the bank statement balance on the first line of the reconciliation form.*

Step 2 *List any outstanding deposits on the appropriate line and add them to the balance.* Outstanding deposits are those that have not yet been added to your account.

Step 3 *Compare the canceled checks or those checks listed on your statement with your check register or check stubs.* Check off all items that have been returned to you or listed as paid. These represent amounts that have been subtracted from your account.

Step 4 *List service charges and outstanding checks on the appropriate lines and subtract them from the balance.* Outstanding checks are checks you have written that do not yet show on your statement. They represent money you have paid that has not yet been removed from your account. The result of these calculations is the adjusted bank balance.

Step 5 *Compare the balance from your checkbook to the adjusted bank balance.* The two figures should be the same.

Step 6 *If there is a difference, go back and check your work.* Be sure that all your calculations are correct. Verify that all checks, deposits, and service charges have been accounted for in the reconciliation.

BALANCING AND REPLENISHING THE PETTY CASH FUND If your business uses a petty cash fund, this should be verified and replenished on a monthly basis. A petty cash fund is used to purchase items that are too inexpensive to pay by check. Every time money is withdrawn from the petty cash fund, a receipt or voucher should be prepared. Once a month, the amount left in cash plus the total receipts should equal the fund's fixed balance. A check should be written for the total receipts and the cash brought back up to its fixed amount.

Using Technology

Recording, summarizing, and reporting financial information can be an extremely time-consuming activity. Computers now offer small business owners the ability to automate all the accounting functions. Daily, weekly, monthly, and annual reports can be generated quickly and accurately. With software and hardware being very affordable, most small businesses use some form of automated accounting.

Section 20.2 After You Read

Key Concept Review

1. Why must all businesses produce the same two primary financial statements?

2. Why is the statement of cash flows important to the operation of a business?

3. What could happen if a business fails to pay its bills on time?

Critical Thinking

4. Can you keep too many financial records? Why?

Role Play

Situation Last year, Cyrena started selling custom T-shirts. Her business has been good, but she never kept records or paid taxes. Yesterday, the IRS informed her that it will close down her business if she does not pay back taxes.

Activity Assume the role of a tax consultant. Research more information about income tax regulations. Then pair up with a partner and take turns role-playing a conversation between the tax consultant and Cyrena.

Evaluation You will be evaluated on how well you address these issues:

- Counsel Cyrena on what she can do so she can pay her taxes and remain in business.

- Advise her on ways she can avoid these problems in the future.

Chapter Summary

Financial Record Keeping

In order for financial statements to be of value, all businesses must follow set principles and procedures to record and report financial information. Business owners and others must rely on this information in order to make sound business decisions. The absence of current, accurate financial data is often the sign of a failing business.

Section 20.2 **Preparing Financial Statements**

All businesses produce two primary financial statements. These are the income statement, which reports revenue, expenses, and net income, and the balance sheet, which gives the financial position of the business on a specific date. Another statement that provides important information is the statement of cash flows. For businesses to create accurate statements, several accounting functions take place weekly and monthly.

Key Terms Review

1. Write a one-page business letter to the loan officer at your local bank. In the letter you want to explain your knowledge of the accounting system. Use the following key terms from the chapter:

GAAP (p. 428)	debits (p. 432)
financial reports (p. 429)	credits (p. 432)
accounting period (p. 429)	cash basis (p. 432)
calendar year (p. 429)	accrual basis (p. 432)
fiscal year (p. 429)	journal (p. 432)
assets (p. 430)	journalizing (p. 432)
current assets (p. 430)	general journal (p. 432)
accounts receivable (p. 430)	posting (p. 433)
fixed assets (p. 430)	income statement (p. 437)
liabilities (p. 430)	balance sheet (p. 438)
accounts payable (p. 430)	cash flow (p. 440)
owner's equity (p. 430)	statement of cash flows (p. 440)
chart of accounts (p. 431)	

Chapter 20 | Review and Activities

Key Concepts Review

2. **Explain** the important role accounting plays in every business. (20.1)
3. **Explain** the accounting system for a small business. (20.1)
4. **Describe** the importance of daily sales and cash receipts reports. (20.1)
5. **Describe** the items of information included on each financial statement. (20.2)
6. **Identify** ongoing accounting activities. (20.2)
7. **Describe** how technology helps business owners with all the accounting functions. (20.2)

Critical Thinking

8. Explain what might occur if businesses were allowed to set up any accounting system they wanted.
9. Discuss what would happen if large corporations did not prepare financial statements.
10. What factors might cause a small business owner to neglect to keep accounting records up-to-date?
11. Explain how computerized accounting can help a small business.
12. Describe, other than those mentioned in this chapter, ongoing financial activities a small business should perform on a weekly or monthly basis.
13. Explain why in this era of technology accountants are still in demand.
14. Discuss what a small business might use as a basis for decision-making if there were no financial statements to analyze.

Write About It

15. Ask a small business owner to list the weekly and monthly accounting activities he or she performs. Write a report detailing the activities.
16. Write a report on the history of double-entry accounting.
17. Is one of the financial statements more important than the others? Explain your answer in a short paragraph.
18. In a one-page report, list the asset and liability accounts your proposed new business might have.
19. In a letter to your chamber of commerce, identify one or two types of small business operations that are not in your neighborhood and explain why they might be successful.
20. If your expenses reported on the income statement are increasing at a more rapid rate than your revenue, as a business owner, what could you do? Explain your answer in a memo to your staff.

Academic Skills

Math

21. Suppose that cash sales for the day were $1,825.00; customers paid you $381.00 they owed you from previous sales; you sold an office computer monitor to an employee for $35.00; and you received $100.00 in rent for a storage area. Complete the Cash Receipts section of the daily Summary of Sales and Cash Receipts.

Summary of Sales and Cash Receipts
May 21, 20—

Cash Receipts

Cash Sales   _____

Collections on account   _____

Miscellaneous receipts   _____

     Total Cash Receipts   _____

Language Arts

22. Your aunt has opened an insurance agency and is ready to hire her first employee— a bookkeeper. She has asked you to help her choose just the right employee. Write a paragraph detailing the skills and characteristics the new employee should have.

Entrepreneurship in Your Community

23. As a class select a local business. Working in teams, make a list of the assets and of the debts or liabilities you believe the business might have. As a class compare your lists.

24. Form teams that contain at least one classmate who has a job. Ask the job supervisor or manager about the financial statements that have proven to be most helpful in running the business. How often are these statements prepared? How are they helpful? If possible collect samples. Share your findings with the class.

Ethical Practices

Financial Report or Repair?

25. Your cousin, who owns an Internet café, has asked you to help with her bookkeeping. She desperately needs a bank loan and wants you to prepare the financial statements. After going over her accounting records, you do not believe a bank will give her a loan; but you notice that by leaving out an expense or two, your cousin's business could look more promising. After all, she does have some good ideas for improving the business. What should you do? Write a paragraph explaining your answer.

INTERNET *connection*

Research Technology

You have been keeping the books for your garden shop by hand since it opened three years ago. Your business has grown, and you think it is time to invest in software to help with this activity.

Connect

Use a Web directory or search engine to research software programs that will allow you to automate your accounting functions. Find out the following for two different software packages:

- Cost
- Basic functions the software performs
- Special features the software provides

Application

Compare the two software programs you researched in a chart. Based on your comparison, determine which software package is right for your business.

The Electronic Entrepreneur

E-Commerce Advertising Options

Developing and implementing a Web site is not enough to guarantee success—a company must then get consumers to visit it. A number of advertising options are available to help businesses generate traffic to their site.

Exchanges One of the most common—and least expensive—forms of online advertising involves exchanging advertising. Sites can trade online ads with one another, or they can agree to **banner swapping**, posting banner ads for each other. Exchanges only make sense between two sites that are not selling the same products. Another popular way to exchange advertising is link swapping, also called reciprocal linking. **Reciprocal linking** is an agreement between two Webmasters to place hyperlinks on their own Web sites leading to each other's Web site.

Viral Marketing In recent years, viral marketing, or "online word-of-mouth" has become a hot trend. **Viral marketing** is a marketing technique that uses customers to promote the product. The term *viral marketing* comes from biology and the notion of how a virus spreads. Companies can use viral marketing by encouraging individuals to spread the word about their online business.

Affiliate Programs Many e-commerce businesses share a portion of their profits with individuals who bring in traffic to the Web site. An **affiliate program** is an online marketing agreement in which member Web sites drive targeted traffic to an e-commerce merchant. If an affiliate program member places a link on his or her Web site that points to the e-commerce site, he or she is paid a 5 percent to 25 percent commission on the sales generated at the merchant site. Amazon.com offers an affiliate program that has over 400,000 members.

Going Offline You can advertise your Web site in the "real world" as well as the online world. Companies should be sure to include their site's URL on all printed material like business cards, brochures, and letterheads. They should also be listed in printed business directories, such as the yellow pages.

FACT AND IDEA REVIEW

1. What are two ways to exchange online advertising?
2. What is viral marketing?
3. How does an affiliate program work?
4. Why should a company include its URL on printed materials such as letterheads and brochures?

FOR DISCUSSION

5. Are there any advertising methods that you think are inappropriate for online businesses?

TechTerms

- banner swapping
- reciprocal linking
- viral marketing
- affiliate program

Financial Management

CHAPTER OBJECTIVES

When you have completed this chapter, you should be able to:

SECTION 21.1

- Describe the purpose of comparative financial statements.
- Describe how different ratios are calculated.
- Explain why financial statements are essential for decision making.

SECTION 21.2

- Describe why evaluating profit potential is a useful technique to plan for profits.
- Describe ways to help manage your cash flow.
- Explain the importance of controlling capital expenditures.
- Describe ways to control your taxes.
- Describe how you can manage credit offered to customers.

STANDARD & POOR'S
Money Talk

BUSINESS ACTIVITIES

Regardless of the type of business, there are four main functions involved in an organization's operation: production or procurement, marketing, management, and finance.

- Production is the process of creating, manufacturing, or improving on goods and services.

- Procurement involves buying and reselling goods that have already been produced.

- Marketing includes all of the activities that are taken from the time a product leaves the producer or manufacturer until it reaches the final consumer.

- Management is the process of achieving company goals by effective use of resources through planning, organizing, and controlling.

- Finance is a function of business that involves money management.

The success of business is dependent on how well these activities are coordinated, managed, and performed.

@ Go to **entrepreneurship.glencoe.com** to complete the Standard & Poor's Money Talk Financial Literacy Activity.

PREPARE TO READ

THINK ABOUT THESE QUESTIONS AS YOU READ.

What are comparative financial statements?

What information does ratio analysis provide a business owner?

Analyzing Your Finances

KEY TERMS
- comparative financial statement
- ratio analysis
- current ratio
- working capital
- debt ratio
- net profit on sales ratio
- operating ratio
- quick ratio

KEY CONCEPTS
- Using Financial Statements
- Ratio Analysis
- Management Decision Making

THE MAIN IDEA

By maintaining and analyzing financial records and reports, business owners and other interested parties have the information necessary to make sound business decisions.

READING ORGANIZER

Draw the reading organizer on a separate piece of paper. As you read about the different ratios, identify from which financial statement the information is reported.

INCOME STATEMENT	BALANCE SHEET
	current ratio

Using Financial Statements

In Chapter 20, you learned that businesses use several financial statements and documents to report their financial status. Every business prepares two primary financial statements. The first is the income statement, also called the *statement of operations and earnings,* which reports the revenue (income), expenses, and net income or loss for the period. The second is the balance sheet—which reports the assets, liabilities, and owner's equity accounts. It reports the financial position of the business on a specific date.

Comparative Financial Statements

When an income statement and balance sheet are prepared at the end of the month or fiscal period, these statements reflect the success or failure of

Advice on the Right Adviser

Managing a business often leaves little time for attending to personal finance. If you can't handle that chore, be very careful who does.

All businesses need sound financial advice—and not just at tax time. But be careful about the person you hire as a consultant or adviser. While most are competent professionals, there are also unethical and unqualified people hanging out their shingles in the hope of snagging harried entrepreneurs, who sometimes don't take the time they should to check credentials. That's the advice from the Council of Better Business Bureaus (BBB), which advises small-business owners to first seek counsel inside their own companies—a source many entrepreneurs tend to overlook. Your CPA is often in the best position to make recommendations about strategies regarding tax, investment, or retirement. You just have to ask.

If you have the time, you may want to try researching financial advice on the Web.

There is a wealth of great information online, but be aware of sites that offer plenty and deliver little to nothing—after getting you to pay an upfront fee. And of course, it goes without saying that you should always be cautious about unsolicited E-mail offering "get-rich-quick" investments.

SOURCE: *BusinessWeek*, JULY 15, 2003; BY KAREN E. KLEIN

APPLICATION

Interview a local financial consultant or adviser. Find out about the adviser's credentials, the types of services he or she provides, and the fees charged for the services. Make a slide show presentation of your findings to the class.

 Go to **entrepreneurship.glencoe.com** to complete the *BusinessWeek* Case Study Reading Guide Activity.

the business over that period of time. However, business owners realize that an important analysis tool is to examine the income statements and balance sheets for two consecutive periods. A financial statement with financial data from two accounting periods is called a **comparative financial statement**.

COMPARATIVE INCOME STATEMENT An example of a comparative income statement is shown in **Figure 21.1** on page 452. Notice that the amounts for each category are given for a two-year period. The amounts are then compared, and the differences are expressed in both dollars and percentages. This information allows the owner to compare the present amounts to the previous year's amounts and determine key indicators that affect the running of the business. Important items to examine are sales, cost of merchandise sold, gross profit, and operating expenses.

COMPARATIVE BALANCE SHEET A comparative balance sheet is illustrated in **Figure 21.2** on page 453. The amounts should be analyzed to determine why certain accounts increased or decreased during the last period.

Figure 21.1 **Comparative Income Statement**

Stratford Gift Shop
Comparative Income Statement
For the Year Ended December 31, 20—

	Previous Year	Current Year	Dollar Change	Percent Change
Revenue:				
Sales	284,180	291,203	+7,023	+ 2.5%
Cost of Merchandise Sold:	182,734	190,721	+7,987	+ 4.4%
Gross Profit on Sales:	101,446	100,482	− 964	− 1.0%
Operating Expenses:				
Advertising	5,830	5,318	− 512	− 8.8%
Insurance	2,617	2,695	+ 78	+ 3.0%
Maintenance	2,811	3,416	+ 605	+21.5%
Miscellaneous	1,862	1,907	+ 45	+ 2.4%
Salaries	17,902	18,523	+ 621	+ 3.5%
Rent	14,200	15,800	+1,600	+11.3%
Utilities	4,192	3,784	− 408	− 9.7%
Total Operating Expenses	49,414	51,443	+2,029	+ 4.1%
Net Income	52,032	49,039	−2,993	− 5.8%

TRACKING INCOME A comparative income statement lets you compare this year with last year. *What expense had the greatest percent increase?*

Ratio Analysis

Ratio analysis involves the comparison of two or more amounts on a financial statement and the evaluation of the relationship between these two amounts. Owners, lenders, and creditors use ratio analysis to determine the financial strength, activity, or bill-paying ability of the business. The amounts for the different ratios are taken from the "current year" columns of the comparative income statement and balance sheet.

While You Read

Predict How do businesses use financial statements?

Current Ratio

The **current ratio** compares current assets (cash or items that can be converted to cash quickly) and current liabilities (debts due within a year). These amounts are found on the balance sheet. The current ratio indicates the ability of a business to pay its bills. The ratio is calculated as follows:

$$\frac{\text{CURRENT ASSETS}}{\text{CURRENT LIABILITIES}} = \text{CURRENT RATIO}$$

Figure 21.2

Comparative Balance Sheet

Stratford Gift Shop
Comparative Balance Sheet
December 31, 20—

	Previous Year	Current Year	Dollar Change	Percent Change
Assets				
Cash in Bank	22,743	24,937	+2,194	+ 9.6%
Accounts Receivable	4,390	4,626	+ 236	+ 5.4%
Merchandise	82,297	79,271	−3,026	− 3.7%
Supplies	3,028	3,522	+ 494	+16.3%
Display Equipment	31,821	39,035	+7,214	+22.7%
Office Equipment	6,339	5,602	− 737	+11.6%
Total Assets	150,618	156,993	+6,375	+ 4.2%
Liabilities				
Accounts Payable	27,734	28,725	+ 991	+ 3.6%
Notes Payable	33,937	31,204	−2,733	− 8.1%
Total Liabilities	61,671	59,929	− 1,742	− 2.8%
Owner's Equity				
Torres, Capital	88,947	97,064	+8,117	+ 9.1%
Total Liabilities & Owner's Equity	150,618	156,993	+6,375	+ 4.2%

TRACKING WORTH Comparing changes in the worth of a business is very important.
Did this business increase or decrease in value?

Based on the balance sheet presented in **Figure 21.2,** the current assets and current liabilities for the Stratford Gift Shop for the current period are:

CURRENT ASSETS:		
CASH IN BANK	$24,937	
ACCOUNTS RECEIVABLE	4,626	
MERCHANDISE	79,271	
SUPPLIES	3,522	
TOTAL	112,356	
CURRENT LIABILITIES:		
ACCOUNTS PAYABLE	$28,725	

The current ratio is calculated using information from the "current year" balance sheet.

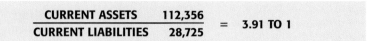

$$\frac{\text{CURRENT ASSETS} \quad 112{,}356}{\text{CURRENT LIABILITIES} \quad 28{,}725} = 3.91 \text{ TO } 1$$

Stratford Gift Shop has about $3.91 of current assets for every $1 in current liabilities. A ratio of 2:1 or higher is considered favorable by creditors and lenders.

While You Read

Connect How are financial statements similar to report cards?

Working Capital

Businesses use information from the "current year" balance sheet to determine working capital. **Working capital** shows the capital available to the business to carry out its daily operations. To determine the working capital, use the amounts from the current ratio calculation but subtract current liabilities from current assets.

CURRENT ASSETS	−	CURRENT LIABILITIES	=	WORKING CAPITAL
112,356	−	28,725	=	83,631

Stratford Gift Shop has a working capital of $83,631.

Debt Ratio

The **debt ratio** measures the percentage of total dollars in the business provided by creditors. The debt ratio is calculated using information from the "current year" income statement.

$$\frac{\text{TOTAL LIABILITIES}}{\text{TOTAL ASSETS}} = \text{DEBT RATIO}$$

$$\frac{59{,}929}{156{,}993} = 38.2\%$$

The debt ratio for the Stratford Gift Shop is 38.2%. This means that Stratford is in debt for 38.2% of its assets. If the debt ratio is high, this means that a large portion of the business operation is being financed by creditors.

Quick Math

If your business has assets that total $320,000, and liabilities that total $200,000, what is the debt ratio?

Net Profit on Sales Ratio

Net profit on sales ratio shows the number of cents left from each dollar of sales after expenses and income taxes are paid. The net profit on sales is calculated using amounts from the "current year" income statement.

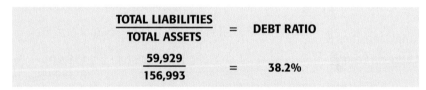

$$\frac{\text{NET INCOME}}{\text{SALES}} = \text{NET PROFIT ON SALES RATIO}$$

$$\frac{49{,}039}{291{,}203} = 16.8\%$$

It is best to calculate net profit on sales ratio and compare it to other similar businesses. If you find your net profit is below other similar businesses, your prices may be too low or your expenses too high.

While You Read

Question Where can you find information about average ratios in your industry?

Operating Ratio

The **operating ratio** shows the relationship between each expense and total sales as reported on the income statement. The formula is as follows:

$$\frac{\text{EXPENSE}}{\text{SALES}} = \text{OPERATING RATIO}$$

If sales for the year for the Stratford Gift Shop are $291,203 and rent expense was $15,800, the operating ratio would be 5.4%. This means that the rent represents 5.4% of sales.

$$\frac{\$15,800}{\$291,203} = 5.4\%$$

This analysis will also give you a sense of whether or not your expenses are in line with other similar businesses. The ratio should be calculated for each expense account. If an expense appears to be much higher than industry averages, which are often published in trade publications, it should be examined for better, more efficient operation. This type of analysis allows owners to identify possible problem areas quickly.

Issues in Entrepreneurship

SELECTING A FINANCIAL PROFESSIONAL

Accounting is not just adding and subtracting. An accountant handles a broad range of responsibilities, makes business decisions, and prepares and interprets financial reports. These are skills that successful businesses cannot do without.

Many accountants move up in their careers by becoming CPAs. CPA stands for certified public accountant. CPAs pass a national test and meet specified experience and education standards to become "certified" to practice accounting.

Think Critically

As a business owner, why might you need a CPA instead of a regular accountant?

@ Go to **entrepreneurship.glencoe.com** to complete the Issues in Entrepreneurship Research Activity.

Quick Ratio

A **quick ratio** is a measure of the relationship between short-term liquid assets and current liabilities. Short-term liquid assets include cash and accounts receivable. The quick ratio is calculated using amounts found on the balance sheet.

$$\frac{\text{CASH} + \text{ACCOUNTS RECEIVABLE}}{\text{CURRENT LIABILITIES}} = \text{QUICK RATIO}$$

$$\frac{29,563}{28,725} = 1.02$$

A ratio of 1.1 is considered satisfactory, and the higher the ratio, the better.

Management Decision Making

The financial statements and reports provide you with vital financial data. You must analyze this information, identify problem areas, and make decisions. At times, risks must be taken. With accurate financial data, you can make decisions with greater confidence. Constant examination and analysis of financial information of your business operation is essential to success.

Many entrepreneurs consider themselves more of a bookkeeper—the person who "keeps the books." Many feel they do not have the skills and knowledge to interpret and analyze accounting documents. In these cases, an accountant should be consulted. Accountants are trained professionals whose job it is to optimize profits and minimize risks. Their role is to assure that your financial records are kept according to accounting standards, all reports are completed and analyzed, and your taxes are calculated and paid.

Section 21.1 After You Read

Key Concept Review

1. Why is comparing financial information from the present period with the previous period a good way to analyze financial trends?

2. Why do businesses use different forms of ratio analysis to obtain indicators used in decision making?

3. When planning for the future, why is past and present financial information used?

Critical Thinking

4. Name some common types of business expenses that are difficult to lower.

Role Play

Situation You own a delivery service. Two of your employees drive company cars while the other ten drive their own cars. You feel your business is ready for more growth.

Activity Pair up with a classmate. Have your classmate assume the role of a local entrepreneur, who will offer advice and information. Role-play a question and answer session.

Evaluation You will be evaluated on how well you address these issues:

- Discuss the possible changes to the marketing mix that could increase sales.

- Identify cost-control adjustments that could be made.

- Describe ways to include employees in the decision-making process.

Managing Your Finances

GET READY TO READ

KEY TERMS
- variable expenses
- fixed expenses
- budget
- capital expenditures
- credit bureaus

KEY CONCEPTS
- Planning for Profits
- Managing Cash Flow
- Planning for Capital Expenditures
- Managing Taxes
- Managing Credit

THE MAIN IDEA

Careful management of your business finances is an essential element for running a successful business.

READING ORGANIZER

Draw the reading organizer on a separate piece of paper. As you read, list different variable expenses on the left and different fixed expenses on the right.

VARIABLE EXPENSES	FIXED EXPENSES
	Rent

Planning for Profits

The main goal of a business is to make money. However, profits do not just happen. The owners of businesses have to plan for them. Planning for profits includes forecasting sales, evaluating profit potential, controlling costs, and budgeting.

Forecasting Sales

Profit planning begins with forecasting sales. As an ongoing business, you can base your projections on sales records of previous periods. You can also use the current rate of sales growth in your field, geographic area, or the rate of growth of the gross national product. You also must adjust your forecast based on economic factors such as inflation or recession.

The Sweet Taste of Success

Childhood friends Eileen Spitalny and David Kravetz always wanted to start a business together, and in 1992 they decided to build a company based upon David's mother's recipe for homemade brownies. They had no baking or marketing experience when they started Fairytale Brownies Inc. That was not enough to deter them. For a year they borrowed kitchen space from a friend who owned a catering company before moving out on their own. Today, Fairytale ships brownies around the globe.

CRITICAL THINKING

Spitalny and Kravetz started slow, by not leasing their own space right away. How did this help them get established?

 Go to **entrepreneurship.glencoe.com** to complete the Success Stories Writing Activity.

Suppose that in the car accessory industry, sales have been up 5 percent per year for the last three years and inflation rates have been stable at 2 percent. If you sold $300,000 of automobile cup holders last year, this is how you could forecast sales:

5%	+	2%	=	7%	
.07	×	$300,000	=	$21,000	
$300,000	+	21,000	=	$321,000	

In order to keep up with inflation (2 percent) and the industry increase in sales (5 percent), you need a 7 percent increase over this year's sales. If this year's sales are $300,000, you would forecast a $21,000 increase in sales ($321,000) for the next year.

Evaluating Profit Potential

If you are satisfied with your forecast, you do not need to adjust your profit planning. However, you probably want to improve your profit picture. One way to increase sales revenue is by going after additional market share. You might add new products (such as sun visors), raise prices, or increase advertising.

Before you decide to invest in a change, you have to evaluate its profit potential. One way to evaluate profit potential is with break-even analysis. This shows how many units of product must be sold to make a profit based on the change:

$$\frac{\text{FIXED COST}}{\text{SELLING PRICE} - \text{VARIABLE COST}} = \text{BREAK-EVEN POINT}$$

Variable expenses are business expenses that change with each unit of product produced such as supplies, wages, and production materials. **Fixed expenses** are expenses that do not change with number of units produced. Examples include insurance and rent.

Suppose you read about a potential market in making portable backboards for basketball tournaments. The article predicts sales of 100 units in your region. You can sell each backboard for $250. The materials, labor, and other variable expenses will be about $150. Because you have to buy equipment, your fixed expenses will be $5,000. How many units would you have to sell to break even?

While You Read

Predict What is the difference between fixed expenses and variable expenses?

$$\frac{\$5,000}{\$250 - \$150} = \frac{\$5,000}{\$100} = \textbf{50 UNITS}$$

The break-even point is 50 units. For every unit over 50, you will have $100 ($250 – $150) going toward profit. However, if sales are fewer than 50, there would be no profit. If you had to spend more than $10,000 for fixed expenses, there would be no profit. You would have to sell more than 100 of the backboards, which would exceed the predicted sales.

You can use this type of analysis to evaluate any change in your marketing mix. The costs of launching a new advertising campaign, hiring salespeople, or changing location should also be considered.

Controlling Costs

In Section 21.1 you learned about operating ratios. If there is a big difference between your costs and the industry average, you should investigate all costs in your business and identify possible problems.

Assume your percentage for rent expense compared to sales was 10 percent. If the industry average is 5 percent, then you are paying a greater percent for rent than others. Perhaps your rented space is too large and a smaller, cheaper space should be considered. If the industry average is 15 percent, then you are paying a lesser percent than others.

In other instances, referring to your previous experience might give you another comparison. Let us say your shipping costs have doubled over the previous year. You may be able to increase your profit by finding a different trucking contractor or leasing your own trucks. **Figure 21.3** on page 460 identifies additional ways to control costs.

Budgeting

A **budget** is a formal, written statement of expected revenue and expenses for a future period of time. It is one of the most important financial tools for a business. Using financial data from previous periods, a projected income statement, also called a *pro forma income statement,* is prepared for the next fiscal period. This offers a financial glimpse into the future and provides a basis for business decisions.

To be of value, a budget should be compared periodically with actual income and expenses. If the actual amounts are not reasonably close to the budgeted figures, you will need to make adjustments.

Figure 21.3 **Ways to Control Costs**

COST CONTROL There are many ways for small businesses to control their costs. *Can you think of any other ways for a business to control its costs?*

Lease the Business Location
Instead of buying a building, lease one. If your facility costs are too high, consider relocating.

Lease the Equipment
You can save money by leasing equipment instead of buying it. If you want to buy equipment, you could consider buying used equipment.

Hire Part-Time Help
If you hire part-time workers, your labor costs will be lower.

Monitor and Control Utility Costs
Conservation is an excellent way to save money. Energy can be a big business expense, so do not use energy if you do not need to.

Managing Cash Flow

A goal of efficient financial management is to assure a constant flow of cash through the business. This is easy to say, but it is not always easy to do. Economic and financial conditions change. Sometimes sales are good and then drop off. Expenses are sometimes under control and then rapidly increase. A business can be growing and profitable and still run into serious problems. If sufficient cash is not available, merchandise cannot be replaced, bills cannot be paid, and funds for future growth cannot be invested.

Using a Cash Budget

In order to help monitor your business's cash flow, you can create a cash budget such as the one shown in **Figure 21.4** on page 462. It records estimated cash flow, actual cash flow, and the difference between the two amounts.

Businesses often prepare cash budgets for a three-month period. By recording and analyzing the line items each month, any significant changes from the budgeted amounts can be quickly identified and addressed.

Improving Your Cash Flow

Certain areas in a business operation have more room for improving cash flow than others. Some are described below:

- **Closely monitor your credit and collections.** If a customer is past due with a payment, take action.

- **Take advantage of credit terms.** Pay all bills on time but take all discounts and the time available to you.

- **Manage inventory carefully.** Excess inventory or the wrong items can tie up cash. If items do not sell, cut prices, sell them, and generate additional cash.

- **Offer cash discounts.** Offer discounts to customers for early payment.

- **Set up a cash reserve for uncollectible accounts.** Create a cash fund to offset the effect of unpaid receivables.

- **Monitor payroll expenses.** Examine the amount of hours employees need to work to run your business efficiently.

- **Put cash surpluses to work.** If you have excess cash on hand, invest it.

- **Reduce expenses.** Reduce expenses if they are not in line with the amount of business you are doing.

Remember, cash flowing through a business is like blood flowing through your body. A steady cash flow is essential for good business health. A healthy business must have a healthy cash flow.

Write About It

Use a spreadsheet application to create a cash budget to monitor your cash inflow for a three-month period. Estimate when and how much cash you will take in from allowances or wages you may earn from part-time jobs. Then record the actual amount you take in.

Figure 21.4 **Cash Budget**

For Quarter Ending _____

	MONTH 1			MONTH 2			MONTH 3		
	EST.	ACT.	DIF.	EST.	ACT.	DIF.	EST.	ACT.	DIF.
Projected Cash Receipts									
Cash sales									
Collections on accounts receivable									
Other income									
Total Receipts									
Projected Cash Disbursements									
Purchases (raw materials, merchandise)									
Advertising									
Dues, subscriptions, licenses									
Insurance									
Interest									
Legal and professional expenses									
Office supplies									
Payroll taxes									
Rent									
Salaries									
Sales taxes									
Telephone									
Travel and entertainment									
Utilities									
Notes payable									
Other _____									
_____									
_____									
_____									
_____									
Total Disbursements									
Net Cash Increase (Decrease)									

CASH BUDGET The cash budget form has three columns for each month.
What is the purpose of such a layout?

Planning for Capital Expenditures

Capital expenditures are long-term commitments of large sums of money to buy new equipment or replace old equipment. How do you plan for capital expenditures? First, determine if you can pay for the equipment. Then consider the revenue it will generate and how long it will take to pay for itself.

When you make a capital expenditure, you will probably have to pay for some of it yourself and borrow the rest. To borrow, you will have to make your debt ratio low and attractive for lenders. This means paying off some debts before incurring new ones.

Managing Taxes

We discussed your legal obligations to pay taxes in Chapter 8. However, there are some additional tax considerations:

- **Time income so that you can control when it is taxed.** Scheduling sales for the beginning of the upcoming year will defer taxes.

- **Time your deductions.** During high-income years, identify costs that can be deducted during that year.

- **Choose the depreciation method that is most beneficial.** Because new businesses often have more to write off than they have income, it is better for them to spread write-offs over time.

- **Write off uncollectible accounts.** If you are extending credit, you can write off accounts deemed uncollectible.

- **Claim research and development expenses.** You may not have many of these, but be aware that they are deductible.

- **Keep records of all expenses.** Any honest expense is deductible, but it is up to you to keep the records.

- **Keep up-to-date on tax laws.** You may need to consult with a financial advisor, an attorney, or the IRS for advice.

While You Read

Connect Make a list of the kinds of taxes your parents pay. Then make a list of the kinds of taxes business owners pay.

Managing Credit

The main advantage of offering credit to customers is increased sales volume. The main disadvantage is collection of the money owed in a timely manner. Other advantages and disadvantages of extending credit are presented in **Figure 21.5** on page 464.

TECHNOLOGY Today

Dynamic Planning Software

Financial planning, budgeting, and forecasting are crucial activities to companies of all sizes. However, many planners and financial officers do this important work using basic spreadsheet software, which is not only difficult and cumbersome but also could lead to inaccurate forecasts and overlooked information. Dynamic planning software is specifically tailored for handling these complex processes and makes it simpler to manage these enormous masses of data.

Cooperative Learning Activity

Why is it so important for executives to have accurate, up-to-date financial information and forecasts?

@ Go to **entrepreneurship.glencoe.com** to complete the Technology Today Vocabulary Practice Activity.

Figure 21.5 Advantages and Disadvantages of Extending Credit

CREDIT VALUE There are benefits and drawbacks to extending credit. *What some other advantages?*

ADVANTAGES

- You can build closer relationships with customers by making purchasing easier.

- Selling by telephone or mail is easier.

- Credit account records provide a useful marketing tool.

- Credit can increase and broaden sales.

DISADVANTAGES

- Slow-paying customers can affect cash flow.

- Dollars can be tied up in goods sold on credit.

- If you borrow money to extend credit, interest is added to the cost.

- You have the additional costs of credit checking, additional bookkeeping, billing, and collections.

Granting Credit

Credit management begins before credit is given to a customer. The process of granting credit to customers involves five steps.

1. **Obtaining information.** Have the customer submit information on employment, income, assets, liabilities, and credit references.

2. **Checking credit and background. Credit bureaus** are agencies that collect information on how promptly people and businesses pay their bills. These bureaus charge a fee to provide information to businesses who are considering loan or credit applications.

3. **Evaluating credit applications.** When a business extends credit to consumers, it takes for granted that some people will be unable or unwilling to pay their debts. Therefore, lenders establish policies for determining who will receive credit. First and foremost, a credit applicant must have a good credit history. Businesses that extend consumer credit consider the credit applicant's character, capacity, and capital. Bankers making large commercial loans also consider collateral and conditions.

4. **Making your decision.** You can extend a certain amount of credit to a customer or you may require a cosigner, collateral, a down payment, or different credit terms.

5. **Informing the customer.** Under the Truth in Lending Act, businesses must inform customers how the finance charges are calculated, when the charges begin, and when payment is due.

While You Read

Question What is the typical fee charged by a collection agency?

Collecting Accounts

A business can collect accounts internally or externally. The most effective internal collection procedures involve progressively forceful steps. Start with timely notification before the bill is due. Once an account is past due, send a reminder notice to the customer. If there is no response to numerous mailings, contact the customer by telephone. If you cannot collect an account yourself, you have to get help externally. One option is to hire a collection agency. The agency will charge a fee—usually 33 to 50 percent of the amount collected.

Section 21.2 After You Read

Key Concept Review

1. Explain why forecasting data for a future period provides a basis to make decisions regarding your business operation.

2. Why is cash flow a critical part of financial planning?

3. Explain why you should carefully examine your finances before entering long-term financial commitments.

Critical Thinking

4. Name some of the disadvantages a business would have if it did not prepare a budget.

Role Play

Situation Last year, you began offering credit to customers of your custom furniture business. One of your best customers has become delinquent in her payments.

Activity Pair up with a classmate and take turns role-playing one of these conversations with the customer.

Evaluation You will be evaluated on how well you address these issues:

- Select appropriate methods to respond to customer concerns.

- Demonstrate ways to collect the money owed.

- Make an effort to retain valued customers who are delinquent in their payments.

Chapter Summary

Section 21.1 **Analyzing Your Finances**

Financial statements provide the information owners and others need to make decisions. You can compare financial information from the present period to the previous period. You can also take information contained on the statements and analyze the data using ratio analysis. Without thoroughly analyzing your financial position, sound business decisions cannot be made.

Section 21.2 **Managing Your Finances**

Business owners must plan for profit by forecasting sales, evaluating profit potential, controlling costs, and budgeting. For a business to be successful, control of cash is essential. Cash flow is the life blood of the business. If it flows out faster than it flows in, your business dies. Monitoring your cash and taking steps to have a positive cash flow are critical aspects of good management. Business owners must also plan for capital expenditures, long-term commitments of large sums of money for buying new equipment and replacing old equipment. There are many legal obligations to consider when you own your own business. One of the most important is managing your taxes. It is important to keep up-to-date on tax laws and carefully track your expenses. The main advantage of extending credit to customers is increased sales volume. The main disadvantage is collection of the money owed in a timely manner.

Key Terms Review

1. Imagine you are the loan officer at the local bank. A customer asks you to explain what you look for in a small business operation that would justify a large investment loan. Use the following key terms from the chapter:

comparative financial statements (p. 451)

ratio analysis (p. 452)

current ratio (p. 452)

working capital (p. 454)

debt ratio (p. 454)

net profit on sales ratio (p. 454)

operating ratio (p. 455)

quick ratio (p. 456)

variable expenses (p. 459)

fixed expenses (p. 459)

budget (p. 459)

capital expenditures (p. 462)

credit bureaus (p. 464)

Key Concepts Review

2. **Describe** the purpose of comparative financial statements. (21.1)
3. **Describe** how the operating ratio is calculated. (21.1)
4. **Explain** why financial statements are essential for decision making. (21.1)
5. **Describe** why evaluating profit potential is a useful technique to plan for profits. (21.2)
6. **Describe** ways to help manage your cash flow. (21.2)
7. **Explain** the importance of controlling capital expenditures. (21.2)
8. **Describe** ways to control your taxes. (21.2)
9. **Describe** how you can manage credit offered to customers. (21.2)

Critical Thinking

10. Discuss which two ratios, presented in this chapter, you feel are important for analyzing a business's finances.
11. Explain how cash flow is related to credit management.
12. Describe the effect on your financial statements if some merchandise purchased for your store was not recorded.
13. Describe some possible reasons the sales for this year are 8 percent below what was budgeted.
14. Describe the value of preparing a budget for a business.
15. Describe why lenders want to see a low debt ratio when you are looking to borrow large amounts of money for capital improvements.

Write About It

16. Write a paragraph detailing the advantages of consulting an accountant concerning the operation of your business.
17. In a memo to your teacher, explain why having too much cash can be inefficient.
18. Write an e-mail to a friend explaining why is it important to keep your personal credit rating and your business's credit rating as high as possible.
19. What type of businesses in your area might have more current assets than fixed assets? Use the computer to compose your answer.
20. In a memo to your sales team, explain what actions to take if a few of your customers have been late with their payments.

Academic Skills

Math

21. Using the following graph of sales for the past three years, answer the following questions.

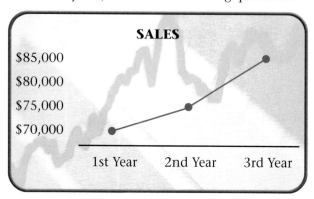

SALES

$85,000
$80,000
$75,000
$70,000

1st Year   2nd Year   3rd Year

What is the percent increase in sales from year one to year two?

What is the percent increase in sales from year one to year three?

Language Arts

22. Research a small business in your area that has recently expanded. Write a report on all the reasons you can think of that motivated the business owner to expand.

Entrepreneurship in Your Community

23. Locate a business in your area. Ask the owner if he or she could name the fixed expenses incurred by the business. Give an oral report to the class on the expenses named by the owner.

24. Interview a small business owner in your town. Ask the owner to describe some of the business activities that take place on a daily, weekly, monthly, quarterly, and yearly basis. Write a report detailing the business activities mentioned. In the report, categorize business activities as production, marketing, management, or finance. Describe the interdependence each business activity has with marketing.

Ethical Practices

Attitudes and Behaviors

25. Every business wants employees with positive work attitudes and behaviors. These attitudes and behaviors include honesty, compassion, respect, responsibility, fairness, and caring. Employees with these attitudes and behaviors are able to work cooperatively in any situation, and with any coworker. You recently hired an employee who exhibited an excellent attitude in her interview. However, since she has started her position, you have found out that she does not seem to tolerate diversity among the staff. How do you handle this situation?

INTERNET *connection*

Finance Facts

Rosa owns a greeting card and stationery store. You offer to show her some Internet sites that will provide her with financial information.

Connect

Use a search engine or Web directory to research sites offering this information:

- Free accounting software for financial statement preparation
- Financial advice for small businesses
- Tax advice for small businesses

Application

Use a spreadsheet application to present the results of your research in a table. In the first column list the names of the sites, along with their URLs. In the next column write a short description of information or services each site offers.

The Electronic Entrepreneur

Digital Signatures

Our society depends on the concept of a signed document—your signature on a contract or other piece of paper shows that you agree to what the document says and will stand by it. Without signatures, it would be nearly impossible for us to have personal property, bank accounts, houses, or cars. E-mail presents a new problem: How do you make sure an e-mail is actually coming from the person whose name appears on it, and how can you be sure it has not been modified?

Public Key Encryption One answer is digital signatures that uniquely identify each e-mail and the person who sent it. A **digital signature** is a method of authenticating digital information. The most common type of digital signature is **public key encryption**, a message encoding system that uses two digital keys.

Transaction Security For a secure e-mail transaction to take place, both sender and recipient must have public keys and private keys. The **public key** is a password that scrambles or encrypts the message so that if intercepted it will be unreadable. **Encryption** is the process of converting a text message into code. The **private key** is a password that unscrambles or decrypts the message. **Decryption** is the process of converting from code into readable text. Public keys are shared, but private keys are kept secret.

Digital Certificates People who take part in online transactions can also use a **digital certificate**, an e-commerce security feature that establishes the certificate holder's identity. Digital certificates prove that companies are who they say they are. Information from this certificate is encoded in each message.

FACT AND IDEA REVIEW

1. Why is it important to be able to validate documents and their source?
2. What is the most commonly used method of digitally signing an electronic communication?
3. Explain the difference between public and private keys.
4. What is the purpose of digital certificates?

FOR DISCUSSION

5. What are some of the electronic communications that you might want to protect using a digital signature and certificate?

TechTerms

- digital signature
- public key encryption
- public key
- encryption
- private key
- decryption
- digital certificate

UNIT 5 LAB **BUSINESS PLAN PROJECT**

Financial Plan

The Financial Plan section of a business plan presents past and current finances and financial forecasts and explains the assumptions made when calculating forecast figures. It includes the investment proposal and three key financial statements.

✓ STEP 1 EVALUATE START-UP COSTS AND EXPENSES

When starting a new business, there are many start-up and one-time expenses. Create a chart like the one below to document the amounts of money required for each of the start-up costs and expenses listed.

ITEM	AMOUNT	ITEM	AMOUNT
Lease		Business Cards	
Security Deposit		Salaries	
Utilities Deposit		Flyers and Brochures	
Remodeling		Signs	
Furniture		Office Supplies	
Fixtures		Fees	
Machinery		Licenses	
Equipment		Starting Inventory	

✓ STEP 2 WRITE AN INVESTMENT PROPOSAL

Write an investment proposal that describes why you are applying for financing, how much money you need, how you plan to raise the money, and the specific uses for the funding. Project when investors can expect to earn a profit.

Growth Plan

The Growth Plan looks at how the business will expand in the future. Investors and lenders like to know that a business has plans to deal with growth in a controlled way.

✓ STEP 1 DESCRIBE YOUR GROWTH STRATEGIES

Write a description of your proposed business's growth strategies. Address all of these issues in your description:

- How and when the business will grow
- Products or services the business will develop to achieve growth
- How growth strategies focus on the business's areas of expertise
- How market research will be used to support and justify growth
- What critical skills are needed to effectively manage growth
- How you will evaluate and initiate revisions to growth strategies

✓ STEP 2 CONSIDER THE EFFECTS OF GROWTH

Before growing a business, you must consider the effects of the growth. Write an explanation of how your planned growth will affect all of these areas:

EFFECTS OF GROWTH	
Business Location	Manufacturing Process and Costs
Warehousing and Storage Needs	Financial Control Procedures
Human Resource Expenses	Record Keeping Policies
Management and Staffing Needs	Legal and Insurance Issues
Company Goals and Objectives	Sales Team and Sales Process
The Business's Target Market	Promotional Goals and Messages
Technology and Equipment Needs	Marketing Mix Strategies

Use the **Business Plan Project Appendix** on pages 532–543 to explore the content requirements of a business plan in more detail.

▶ The **Financial Plan** section of a business plan presents past and current finances and financial forecasts and explains the assumptions made when calculating forecast figures.

▶ The **Growth Plan** looks at how the business will expand in the future.

BUSINESS PLAN PROJECT TEMPLATE

 Go to **entrepreneurship.glencoe.com** for a document template in which you can write your own business plan.

UNIT 6

GROWING YOUR BUSINESS

UNIT OVERVIEW

Introduction

The research, planning, and management skills it takes to start and protect your business will also allow it to survive, grow, and profit. Ethics are important. Treating employees, customers, and the community responsibly enhances your venture's reputation. Protecting your business, planning for growth, and practicing ethics will help your business prosper.

BUSINESS PLAN PROJECT PREVIEW

When you complete Unit 6, you will begin to explore these sections of the business plan:

▶ The **Contingency Plan** examines the assumptions in the business plan and the greatest risks to the business and suggests plans to minimize the risk.

▶ The **Executive Summary** recounts the key points in the business plan.

▶ The **Cover Page, Title Page, and Table of Contents** offer basic information about the company and the structure and contents of the plan.

▶ The **Supporting Documents** section of the business plan includes items, exhibits, and documentation relevant to the business.

473

Chapter 22

Risk Management

Section 22.1

Identifying Business Risks

Section 22.2

Dealing with Risk

CHAPTER OBJECTIVES

When you have completed this chapter, you should be able to:

SECTION 22.1

- Explain why risk is inevitable.
- Describe speculative risk.
- Describe three categories of pure risk.

SECTION 22.2

- List the four risk management strategies.
- Describe the steps involved in selecting an insurance agent.
- Discuss the procedures for deciding on security measures.
- Develop emergency response plans for potential crises.

STORM
WINDOWS
AND
SCREENS

UNDERSTANDING FINANCIAL RISKS

If you decide to ride your bicycle on a busy street, you are taking a risk that a car may hit you. When you make a financial decision, you also are taking certain risks. Some types of financial risks include:

- **Inflation risk.** If you wait to buy a car until next year, the price might increase.

- **Interest rate risk.** Interest rates go up or down, which may affect the cost of borrowing or the profits you earn when you save or invest.

- **Income risk.** You may lose your job due to unexpected health problems, family problems, an accident, or changes in your line of work.

- **Liquidity risk.** Some long-term investments, such as buying a house, affect your liquidity, the ability to quickly access your wealth as cash.

@ Go to **entrepreneurship.glencoe.com** to complete the Standard & Poor's Money Talk Financial Literacy Activity.

PREPARE TO READ

THINK ABOUT THESE QUESTIONS AS YOU READ.

What is risk?

How can risk management help businesses reduce and avoid risk?

Identifying Business Risks

KEY TERMS
- speculative risk
- pure risk
- burglary
- robbery
- electronic credit authorizer
- negligence

KEY CONCEPTS
- Risk Is Inevitable
- Speculative Risk
- Pure Risk

THE MAIN IDEA

Risk is a fact of life for entrepreneurs. To build a successful business and maximize profits, they must understand risk and make decisions to deal with it.

READING ORGANIZER

Draw the reading organizer on a separate piece of paper. As you read, fill in the chart with the three areas of pure risk.

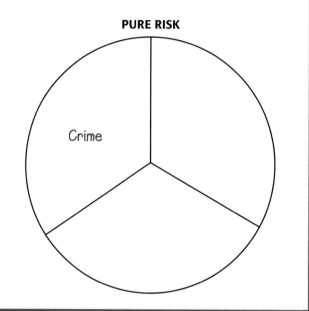

PURE RISK

Crime

Risk Is Inevitable

In its daily operations, every business faces risk—the possibility of loss or injury. For example, if you decide to extend credit, you run the risk that some customers will not pay. If you construct a building, you run the risk that it will be destroyed by fire. If you rely on a partner for sales, you risk sudden loss should something happen to the person.

These and other business risks fall into two general categories: speculative risk and pure risk.

Speculative Risk

Speculative risk is risk that is inherent to the business; it involves the chance of either profit or loss. Most business decisions, such as marketing a new product, involve speculative risks. If the product succeeds in the market, you realize a profit. If it does not, you have losses.

Pure Risk

Pure risk is the threat of a loss to your business without any possibility of gain. The threat of employee theft, burglary, and robbery are pure risks to your business, as are natural disasters (such as floods, earthquakes, and tornadoes) and accidents involving customers and employees.

Crime

Small businesses are 35 times more likely than large businesses to be victims of crime. Retail stores are most likely to experience crime because so many people pass through them in the course of a business day. As a result, the cost of crime is also highest for retail operations.

Suppose a music store loses a $15 CD every day for a year. As a result, the store loses $5,475 a year ($15 × 365 = $5,475). If the store operates at a 10 percent profit margin, it must sell $54,750 worth of merchandise to make up the loss ($5,475 ÷ 0.10 = $54,750)!

SHOPLIFTING Shoplifting is the most common retail crime. It accounts for about 3 percent of the price of any item. A shoplifter is anyone who takes an item from a store without paying for it. Shoplifting often takes place when stores are understaffed. Use these techniques to reduce your risk:

- Train employees to recognize shoplifters. Shoplifters may act nervous, browse a long time, carry large bags, or wear bulky clothing. When in groups, one or two may create a disturbance while others shoplift.

- Keep the store well lit and display cases low so you can see your entire operation at a glance.

- Employ two-way mirrors, peepholes, or closed-circuit TV.

- Use tamper-proof price tickets or electronic tags.

- Hire a uniformed security guard.

While You Read

Predict What type of businesses do you think are most likely to experience crime? Why?

TECHNOLOGY Today

Enterprise Asset Management

Smart entrepreneurs work to minimize risks whenever possible. Enterprise asset management (EAM) software is a set of specialized tools that keeps track of a company's resources, and schedules important tasks like maintenance, upgrades, and other important needs. It also keeps tabs on what resources are available and how to better utilize them. EAM can seem expensive at the front end, but it has the potential to save companies major dollars over the long term.

Critical Thinking

How can EAM software be practical and useful for a business?

Go to **entrepreneurship.glencoe.com** to complete the Technology Today Vocabulary Practice Activity.

If you spot a shoplifter, the safest approach is to alert a police officer. Let him or her confront the person. Usually, this is done outside the store to make the legal case against the shoplifter stronger.

Although the laws for apprehending a shoplifter vary from state to state, in general, the store owner must do the following:

- See the person take the merchandise.
- Identify the merchandise as belonging to the store.
- Confirm that the merchandise was taken with the intent to steal.
- Prove that the merchandise was not paid for.

Once a shoplifter is caught, you must decide whether to prosecute. By pressing charges, you are telling other would-be shoplifters that crime will not be tolerated in your store. As a result, you reduce your risk of becoming a shoplifting victim again.

EMPLOYEE THEFT The Department of Commerce reports that about 50 percent of all retail crime is employee theft. Businesses may lose as much as one-third of their profits due to employee theft. The cost to the consumer is about 15 percent of retail prices.

Business owners are sometimes careless about the way they handle cash. Money constantly coming in and going out can tempt workers, providing an opportunity for dishonesty. A large number of voided or no-sale transactions may signal that an employee is covering up theft. A good rule is not to let just one person control a transaction from beginning to end. Instead, have one person handle the funds and another record or account for them. **Figure 22.1** shows other ways to discourage employee theft.

To prevent employee theft, hire honest people. Use a thorough application process. Ask for and check character references. Aptitude and psychological tests can also be helpful. Certain types of businesses can require applicants to take a polygraph, or lie-detector test. (Check with your attorney to see if your business can conduct preemployment polygraph testing.)

BURGLARY The act of breaking into and entering a building with the intent to commit a felony is called **burglary**. (A felony is a serious crime, such as stealing.) The problem of burglary is growing, but there are ways to minimize your risk.

- **Site selection.** Select your business site carefully. Consider the level of crime in the area and select a secure building for your enterprise.
- **High-quality locks.** Install high-quality locks and control access to the keys.
- **Alarm systems.** With a supervised alarm system, all points of entry are constantly monitored from a central location. An alarm alerts police to trouble. A nonsupervised alarm is active only when the owner arms it. These alarms may also be set to alert the police.
- **Security guards.** Some businesses employ a security guard to patrol the premises during when the business is closed.
- **Proper lighting.** The use of lighting deters burglars. Many owners leave lights on in the building at night. Floodlights in parking lots and at rear entrances also make it difficult for someone to break in unnoticed.

While You Read

Connect Think of some steps a retail store could take to reduce the likelihood of employee theft.

Figure 22.1 **Reducing Employee Theft**

Establish Policies
Let employees know that employee theft is not tolerated. Policies should be communicated verbally and in writing.

REDUCE YOUR RISK
Businesses that do not establish policies, controls, security procedures, and penalties send a message. They tell their employees that people who steal are not likely to get caught. Certain procedures will help to discourage employee theft. *Will you be concerned about employee theft in your business? Why or why not?*

Lock Up
Lock all doors that do not need to be used for entry or exit.

Watch Your Trash
Dishonest employees sometimes hide stolen items in the trash to get them out of the building undetected.

Control Security
Control the distribution of keys and other security devices.

Question How can a business confirm that the credit cards they accept from customers are not stolen?

Quick Math

If a check written in California for $397.85 turns out to be bad, what may be the amount of the penalty?

ROBBERY Robbery involves the taking of property by force or threat. Most robberies involve a weapon. It is the business owner's responsibility to protect employees and customers. This means letting the robber take what he or she wants.

If you are robbed, try to get a description of the person(s) committing the crime. Note a robber's height, hair color, and distinguishing features or mannerisms. These details can help police identify the thief.

One security measure you can use is a safe. Using a safe minimizes the amount of cash you keep in the register (a robber's likely target). Surveillance cameras are another valuable measure. When placed where potential robbers can see them, they, too, serve as deterrence.

STOLEN CREDIT CARDS AND BAD CHECKS Using credit cards or checks to pay for purchases is a major convenience for consumers. To businesses, they can be a source of financial loss. Stolen credit cards are used to run up huge bills. Customers may write checks against insufficient funds or closed accounts.

There are ways to identify an invalid or stolen credit card. Many businesses use **electronic credit authorizer** machines that verify whether a credit card is good. They are linked to a central credit bureau that identifies stolen or invalid cards. Other companies call a central authorization phone number to check credit cards. This allows them to find out if a card is good before they complete a sale.

Bad checks represent another problem for businesses. As a deterrent, companies usually charge a service fee if a customer's check is returned from the bank. In addition, many states have passed laws making the writing of bad checks a crime, imposing stiff fees. In California, the penalty is three times the face value of the check. Many businesses place signs by their cash registers announcing these penalties.

▶ **PREVENTING SHOPLIFTING** Electronic tags on expensive items are one way to minimize losses as a result of shoplifting. *What are two ways they help?*

An Easy Antidote to Employee Theft

A leading security consultant is urging business owners to take a simple step that will make customers their first line of defense. For retailers large and small, the cash register is the center of the universe. It collects the bucks, measures success, and underwrites the future. Yet, the cash drawer often proves irresistible to light-fingered employees. According to the 2001 National Retail Security Survey conducted by the University of Florida, 46% of the $32 billion in total retail theft losses nationwide are due to employees helping themselves to the profits.

Security consultant Bruce Schneier believes he has a simple way to make customers the first line of defense against employee theft. His solution: retailers should hang signs on their registers saying, "Your purchase free if I fail to give a receipt." Not only will customers have an incentive to pay attention to the action on the other side of the counter, it will also motivate them to report store employees who fail to hand over proof of purchase when making change, says Schneier, a cryptography expert and publisher of the monthly Crypto-Gram security newsletter.

SOURCE: *BusinessWeek*, MAY 20, 2003; BY ALEX SALKEVER

APPLICATION

Use the Internet to research creative ways to prevent employee theft in a retail business. Try to identify methods that are different from those mentioned in the text.

 Go to **entrepreneurship.glencoe.com** to complete the *BusinessWeek* Case Study Reading Guide Activity.

Business owners can also reduce the number of bad checks with a check reader. This is similar to an electronic credit authorizer. It tells the business owner whether the account on which the check was written is open. It also identifies accounts with a history of bad checks.

In any case, you should write the driver's license number on the customer's check. This ensures that you can track down the individual if the check is bad. Always ask check writers for photo identification.

COMPUTER CRIME The threat of computer crime has grown rapidly as companies rely more on computers. Computer criminals have developed a variety of ways to access computers and steal or change information. Computer hackers penetrate the security of computer systems for mischievous purposes. Disgruntled employees erase thousands of hours' worth of work or install viruses. Some companies even engage in industrial espionage.

By taking simple precautions, a business owner can reduce his or her chances of becoming a victim of computer crime. These measures include securing important data by using passwords, encoding programs, and installing virus detectors. Physically secure disks and other data storage devices.

Natural Disasters

Crime is not the only risk a business faces. Many owners have lost everything due to natural disasters such as fires, earthquakes, tornadoes, and floods. Protecting your business from these risks is difficult. You can prevent damage by choosing a location that does not have a history of these natural disasters, but that may mean moving to another state!

You can protect your business against fire by installing smoke detectors and sprinkler systems. These help protect your staff. They can be used to extinguish fires before they grow too big. When choosing a safe for cash and important documents, you can buy one that is fireproof.

Accidents and Injury

Another risk that concerns businesses is accidents. Workers can hurt themselves and others on the job. Customers can slip and fall on the premises. Accidents like these can be financially devastating to a small business. For example, a company can be held responsible for an act of negligence. **Negligence** is the failure to exercise reasonable care. At the very least, a business would be required to pay the medical expenses of the person injured. The company might also have to pay amounts awarded by a jury in a lawsuit. Unfortunately for business owners, in recent years, the number of such lawsuits has been increasing, and so has the size of the awards.

Section 22.1 After You Read

Key Concept Review

1. What is the difference between speculative risk and pure risk?
2. What factors might cause employees to steal?
3. Describe how a natural disaster that occurs in your community affects businesses.

Critical Thinking

4. Create a three-column chart. Label it "Crime, Natural Disaster, and Accidents and Injury." Identify risks your proposed business would face in each category.

Role Play

Situation Your company has been hired by Jacque to do a complete risk analysis of his retail computer store. As background information, Jacque tells you that he has five employees, a computer inventory worth $1.5 million, and that he repairs an average of 30 computers per week.

Activity Team up with a classmate and prepare a presentation for Jacque.

Evaluation You will be evaluated on how well you address these issues:

- Recommend methods to prevent loss of merchandise.
- Recommend security measures.
- Develop an emergency response plan for Jacque and his employees in the event of a natural disaster.

Section 22.2

Dealing With Risk

GET READY TO READ

KEY TERMS
- premium
- business interruption insurance
- casualty insurance
- errors-and-omissions insurance
- product liability insurance
- fidelity bonds
- performance bonds
- workers' compensation
- independent insurance agent
- direct insurance writer

KEY CONCEPTS
- Risk Management Strategies
- Selecting an Insurance Agent
- Choosing Security Measures
- Planning for Emergencies

THE MAIN IDEA

It is impossible to completely protect your business from pure risks, but you can lessen their impact through risk management and planning.

READING ORGANIZER

Draw the reading organizer on a separate piece of paper. As you read, fill in the chart with the four risk management strategies.

RISK MANAGEMENT STRATEGIES

Risk avoidance	

Risk Management Strategies

Risk management is preventing or reducing business loss. It involves a three-stage process. The first stage is to identify the risks to which a company is exposed. The second stage is to estimate potential losses from those risks. The third stage is to determine the best way to deal with each risk.

Many people assume that insurance is the only way to deal with risk. While it is important, there are other options. In fact, in some situations, they may be less costly or more practical than insurance. This section will examine all four risk management strategies—avoidance, reduction, transfer, and retention. It will also provide examples of business risks that can be addressed with each strategy. In addition, this section will discuss decisions to consider when completing your risk management plans.

Risk Avoidance

When you locate your business in a safe area, you are using a risk avoidance strategy. You are attempting to avoid crime by shunning environments in which it is more likely to occur. Does your decision guarantee that you will not be the victim of burglary, robbery, or shoplifting? No, but it does reduce your chances.

While You Read

Predict Do you think that businesses can reduce their exposure to risks? How can they do this?

Risk Reduction

For risks that cannot be avoided, businesses adopt another strategy. They practice risk reduction.

Many of the procedures and practices mentioned in Section 21.1 are examples of this strategy. Suppose you own a retail store and are installing a sprinkler system. You are trying to prevent damage to your inventory or loss of your building. You may not be able to avoid a fire, but you can reduce the damage it does. When you place electronic tags on expensive merchandise, you are attempting to discourage theft. You may not be able to eliminate shoplifting, but you can reduce it. You can also reduce the value of the merchandise you lose. Business owners should take these steps to reduce risk:

- **Design work areas to lower the chances of accident or fire.** This includes offices, retail spaces, and manufacturing floors.
- **Hold meetings with employees to educate them about the safe use of equipment.** Make sure they know how to handle emergency situations.
- **Check and service safety equipment.** Test fire extinguishers and smoke detectors regularly. Do the same for security equipment, such as burglar alarms.
- **Test company products under the most extreme conditions in which they will be used.** Inform consumers about how to use your products safely. Provide instructions for correct use of products as well as warnings about possible hazards.

Risk Transfer

Suppose you have located your business in a relatively crime-free part of town (risk avoidance). You have also installed locks, burglar alarms, and sufficient lighting (risk reduction). Still, you may experience losses.

SAFETY MEASURES Just having safety equipment on hand is not enough. *What else must you do to ensure that the equipment actually reduces risk?*

What else can you do to protect your business against possible losses? Most likely you will use the third strategy—risk transfer. Usually, that means buying insurance to cover any losses. You pay a fee, called a *premium,* to transfer some of your risk to an insurance company. A **premium** is the price of insurance an insured person or business pays for a specified risk for a specified period of time.

If you want to purchase insurance, you must be able to demonstrate an insurable interest in property or life. That means you could suffer a loss, financial or otherwise, from a fire, an accident, a death, or a lawsuit.

As a new entrepreneur, you may be overwhelmed by all of your insurance options. Follow these steps to plan for insurance coverage that will meet your business's needs and goals:

• Set insurance goals and make a plan of action

• Research insurance costs and coverages

• Make decisions and implement your plan

• Review your results and make adjustments if needed

Four types of business insurance are needed: property insurance, casualty insurance, life insurance, and workers' compensation insurance.

PROPERTY INSURANCE Your business may own a wide range of physical property, including cash, inventory, vehicles, and buildings. This property is usually classified as real property or personal property. Real property includes buildings and things attached to them. Personal property is anything that is unattached, such as a vehicle. These distinctions are made for legal purposes and, consequently, carry over to insurance coverages. That is, each type of property must be insured separately. In addition, certain risks (such as floods and earthquakes) require separate policies.

A business's standard insurance policy might protect the premises against burglary, robbery, fire, and water damage. Coverage for the last risk, however, would be limited to damage from storms or broken water mains. It would not include flood damage. A fleet of delivery vans would be protected from all of these risks and more. However, the vans would be covered under a separate auto insurance policy.

Businesses can also take advantage of insurance that deals with the consequences of property damage. **Business interruption insurance** is insurance coverage against potential losses that result from having to close a business for insurable reasons. Business interruption insurance pays net profits and expenses while a business is shut down for repairs or rebuilding. The insurance makes up for lost income. Therefore, it allows a business owner to continue making rent, salary, and other important payments.

CASUALTY INSURANCE Suppose an accident occurs on your business premises. A customer trips and suffers a serious back injury. The result could be a lawsuit blaming your business for the accident. The lawsuit may demand payment for medical expenses, lost wages, legal fees, and pain and suffering. To protect your business, you would need casualty insurance. **Casualty insurance** is insurance coverage for loss or liability arising from a sudden, unexpected event such as an accident.

Write About It

Imagine that you and a partner own a pizza restaurant with several employees who deliver pizzas in company-owned vehicles. Write a summary of the types of insurance your company would need.

Casualty insurance also covers the cost of defending your business in court against claims of property damage. For example, suppose in your tree-trimming service, a tree limb falls through a roof. The home owner sues. Casualty insurance would pay for your defense and, if necessary, the claim.

There are many different types of casualty insurance. Companies that advertise can purchase errors-and-omissions insurance. This protects them from lawsuits for mistakes in advertising. **Errors and omissions insurance** is insurance coverage for any loss sustained because of an error or oversight on the business's part.

Manufacturing firms can purchase product liability insurance. **Product liability insurance** is insurance coverage that protects a business from injury claims that result from use of the business's products.

Bonding is another type of casualty insurance. **Fidelity bonds** are a form of insurance that protects a company in case of employee theft. **Performance bonds** is insurance coverage that protects a business if work or a contract is not finished on time or as agreed.

LIFE INSURANCE Imagine the loss a new business would incur if its creator and owner died unexpectedly. Financial loss would only be part of the tragedy. In the event of an insured person's death, the insurance company pays the face value of the policy. This money allows the business time to make a decision about replacing the key person. It offsets some of the losses that may occur during the transition.

WORKERS' COMPENSATION Business owners are required by law to make contributions to the state workers' compensation plan. **Workers' compensation insurance** is insurance that is required by the government and paid for by employers to provide medical and income benefits to employees injured on the job. Job-related illnesses, such as carpal tunnel syndrome, are also covered.

The amount of compensation a worker receives is based on a number of factors. It depends on the wages or salary of the employee. It also depends on how serious the injury is and whether the injury is permanent. To file for compensation, an injured or ill employee must submit a claim with the compensation board. The board decides how much money to pay out.

The program is designed to free businesses from the threat of employee lawsuits. Workers who accept benefits under the program are barred from suing their employers over their injuries. However, in some states, workers' compensation premiums are a major financial burden for businesses. Therefore, many people consider workers' compensation costs to be a key indicator of a state's attitude toward business.

Risk Retention

In some instances, a company can not transfer a business risk. Either the firm can not get insurance or it can not afford the policies that are offered. In these circumstances, the business must self-insure. In other words, the owner puts aside a certain amount of money every month to help cover the costs of a loss. The owner is keeping, or retaining, the risk.

Selecting an Insurance Agent

Before talking to an agent, you should define the risks your business faces and find out about the types of insurance required in your state.

There are two types of agents. An **independent insurance agent** is an insurance agent who represents multiple insurance companies. Independent

Issues in Entrepreneurship

MATCHING COVERAGE WITH THE SHIFTING JOB SITE

As noted in Chapter 18, workplace flexibility, in particular telecommuting, is becoming increasingly popular. Telecommuting allows employees to do all or part of their job away from the business. It often results in increased productivity and provides other benefits for the company.

At the same time, a business owner must make sure telecommuters have sufficient insurance coverage. There are special considerations when the workplace extends beyond the walls of the company.

Think Critically
What do you need to do to ensure that you and your telecommuters are protected?

@ Go to **entrepreneurship.glencoe.com** to complete the Issues in Entrepreneurship Research Activity.

agents are usually local. Having your agent in the community in which you do business may result in faster service. Typically, these agents offer competitive rates. In addition, some specialize in bonding and liability insurance for certain types of businesses, such as construction.

A **direct insurance writer** is an insurance agent who works for one particular insurance company. Business owners often buy life and automobile insurance through direct agents.

Choosing Security Measures

A wide variety of security options are available to small businesses. You can install secure doors and windows, burglar alarm systems, and panic buttons. You can use card-access systems and closed-circuit TV monitors. Fire alarms, smoke detectors, and sprinkler systems provide protection from fires. Some monitoring systems send out calls for fire, medical, and police assistance. Other options include guards, guard dogs, and patrol services. You can even get security for your computers.

How do you decide which security systems are right for your company? First, assess your security needs. Consider your type of business, its location, and the number of employees. Then list specific problem areas. Do you have exposed outdoor equipment? Is vandalism common in your neighborhood?

When you have completed your assessment, ask a professional security company to conduct a review. The company's representative should be able to spot weaknesses and areas of concern. He or she should also help you prioritize your security needs. Before contracting with a security company, research its background and check its references.

While You Read

Connect Visit a local business and make a list of all of the security measures you can see.

Figure 22.2 **Emergency Response Plan**

IN CASE OF EMERGENCY
Creating response plans can help you handle emergency situations more smoothly. *Why do you need more than one plan?*

1. Assess the damage or emergency.
2. Call 911 to report the disaster/emergency.
3. Call for evacuation.
4. Have designated persons collect priority items for removal.
5. Have designated persons secure premises to prevent people (such as looters) from entering.
6. Have designated persons move to gate or entry to provide direction to rescue people.
7. Have evacuated employees report to a central location.
8. Check presence of all employees. If someone is missing, direct rescue workers to the person's workstation.
9. Have those trained in first aid administer treatment to injured people or help rescue workers.
10. Depending on extent of damage, dismiss employees. Have management team wait for cleanup or repair people.

Planning for Emergencies

No matter how many preventive measures you take or how much insurance you buy, disasters do happen. When they occur, they can overwhelm a small business.

While You Read

Question What should an emergency response plan include?

Your risk management objective should be to have procedures in place before a crisis occurs. Emergency response planning will minimize your losses and get you back in business quickly. Although there will be similarities, you should draw up plans for each possibility. Each plan should include a list of priorities and actions to take. **Figure 22.2** on page 488 provides a sample plan.

To prepare for emergencies, you should compile emergency phone numbers and floor plans for rescue teams. You should have important records tagged for quick removal. Your employees should be familiar with your emergency plans. Provide and post copies. Carry out practice emergency drills on a regular basis.

Section 22.2 After You Read

Key Concept Review

1. List specific steps you can take to reduce risk.
2. Explain the value of casualty insurance.
3. How can you determine the proper amount of insurance coverage for your business?

Critical Thinking

4. Why do you think the government requires businesses to pay workers' compensation insurance?

Role Play

Situation Your proposed business is a computer skills training school. You originated the concept for the business, which includes a mobile training unit, and will manage the operation. Jill, one of your partners, has agreed to put up the seed money and will act as the receptionist. Tim, your other partner, has technical expertise and will be the primary instructor. Additional part-time instructors will be hired as needed. You will be operating out of leased office and classroom space as well as the mobile unit you plan to buy and outfit.

Activity Rough out a plan for your insurance needs. Give your rationale. In preparation for presenting the package to an insurance agent for feedback and a quote, role-play your presentation in front of the class. Ask one class member to act as the agent.

Evaluation You will be evaluated on how well you address the following:

- Your decision regarding the partner(s) who should be insured and your rationale
- Your identification of personal property that should be insured and your rationale
- Your identification of real property that should be insured and your rationale

Chapter Summary

Section 22.1 **Identifying Business Risks**

Every business faces risks. Most business decisions involve speculative risks. Speculative risk is risk that is inherent to the business, such as having losses rather than making profits. Businesses face many pure risks, including crimes, natural disasters, and accidents and injuries. Pure risk is the threat of a loss to your business without any possibility of gain. Businesses should establish policies, controls, procedures, and penalties to prevent both shoplifting and employee theft.

Section 22.2 **Dealing with Risk**

Businesses can use four strategies to deal with risks: risk avoidance, risk reduction, risk transfer, and risk retention. Entrepreneurs need insurance and should put security and emergency measures in place. Property, casualty, life, and workers' compensation insurance are the types of insurance entrepreneurs usually need. There are two types of insurance agents—the independent agent (who works for many insurance companies) and the direct insurance writer (who works for only one company).

Key Terms Review

1. Working in teams of three or four, create a vocabulary flash card game using these key terms. Make sure your definitions are short and clear. Exchange games with other teams in your class and play each other's games.

speculative risk (p. 476)	casualty insurance (p. 485)
pure risk (p. 477)	errors-and-omissions insurance (p. 486)
burglary (p. 478)	product liability insurance (p. 486)
robbery (p. 480)	fidelity bonds (p. 486)
electronic credit authorizer (p. 480)	performance bonds (p. 486)
negligence (p. 482)	workers' compensation insurance (p. 486)
premium (p. 485)	independent insurance agent (p. 487)
business interruption insurance (p. 485)	direct insurance writer (p. 488)

Key Concept Review

2. **Explain** why risk is inevitable. (22.1)
3. **Describe** speculative risk. (22.1)
4. **Describe** three categories of pure risk. (22.1)
5. **List** the four risk management strategies. (22.2)
6. **Describe** the steps involved in selecting an insurance agent. (22.2)
7. **Discuss** the procedures for deciding on security measures. (22.2)
8. **Develop** emergency response plans for potential crises. (22.2)

Critical Thinking

9. What is the difference between credit card theft and writing bad checks? How can a store owner deal with them?
10. Does insurance eliminate risk? Why or why not?
11. Suppose that a business owner says, "If I put the proper procedures in place to avoid risks, I do not need to purchase insurance." How would you respond to such a statement?
12. How can risk be transferred, other than to an insurance company?
13. Offer examples of business risks that can be categorized as human, natural, or economic; controllable and uncontrollable; and insurable and noninsurable.

Write About It

14. Write a one-page paper comparing all types of business in terms of their vulnerability to crime. Explain which type of business is most susceptible and why.
15. Imagine that you are part owner of a retail store. In a memo to your partner, describe ways you can reduce shoplifting.
16. Draw a Venn diagram and use it to compare and contrast burglary and robbery.
17. Outline a plan that you could use to prevent customers from writing bad checks.
18. In two paragraphs, describe and give examples of risks, besides crime, that business owners face.
19. Contact the agency responsible for administering workers' compensation in your state. Determine the responsibilities of employers. Write a one-page summary.
20. At a computer, compose two paragraphs describing how risk retention works. Include examples.

Academic Skills

Math

21. Preliminary calculations show that this year your business earned profits of $50,000. In past years, however, the company lost up to one-third of its profits to employee theft and 3 percent to shoplifting. Given those figures, how much do you think your profits actually were?

Language Arts

22. You have decided to install an alarm system in your retail business. Call several companies in your community and ask them to send you information about their systems. Evaluate the products and choose the one that best serves your needs.

Entrepreneurship in Your Community

23. Working in teams of three or four, select a business you are interested in owning. Consider the risks the business might face. Create a chart (use a spreadsheet program if possible) with the following headings:

- Potential Risks
- Ways to Avoid Risk
- Ways to Reduce Risk
- Types of Insurance Necessary
- Other Ways to Transfer Risk
- Risks That Must Be Retained

Compare your findings with the rest of the class.

24. Interview two insurance agents (one independent and one direct insurance writer) who specialize in business insurance. Ask them about:

- Insurance needs of your business
- Type of insurance they recommend
- Approximate cost of the policies

How do their recommendations differ?

Ethical Practices

Fake Figures

25. You own an automobile detailing business where you clean cars until they look like new. Last night your shop was burglarized, and all of your cleaning supplies were stolen. Your insurance company requested an itemized list of the stolen goods. When you told your in-house accountant, he offered to help you pad the numbers. Is this ethical? Why or why not? Suppose there was no way for the insurance company to find out that you padded the figures. Would you be tempted to accept payment for inventory you never had?

Stopping Shoplifting

You own a chain of gift boutiques that cater to teens. You have a policy in place to deal with shoplifting, but it is time to develop one for employee theft.

Connect

Use a search engine or Web directory to research these issues:

- Surveillance methods and equipment
- Screening of potential employees
- Ways to deter employees from stealing

Application

Use your word-processing program to write a report outlining your plan for preventing employee theft.

The Electronic Entrepreneur

Collecting Customer Data

The Internet makes it possible for customers to connect with companies at any time, from virtually anywhere. For the business, this can be more than just a gateway to a sale—it can be a valuable source of information about the existing customer base and can give clues about how to reach new customers. Online businesses gather information in a number of ways.

Cookies By placing a small file called a *cookie* on the user's computer, a Web site can keep track of what pages within the site that person viewed. For instance, an online bookstore might use cookies to log the books a customer has clicked on—then offer to show them other books by similar authors.

Surveys and Forms Sometimes, the best way to get information is simply to ask for it. Many sites use online surveys to gather information. An **online survey** is a form of market research that appears on Web sites in which users respond to questions or provide opinions. Most online surveys often use online forms. An **online form** is a Web page that accepts user input. At the bottom of an online form, you will usually see submit and reset buttons; these allow users to either "send in" the information or clear out the form and start over.

Data Mining With information, quantity does not necessarily mean quality. Information often needs to be sorted into a meaningful set of results. **Data mining tools** are software programs that statistically analyze data to identify patterns, trends, and relationships within data. It is used in e-commerce to gain a better understanding of consumer behavior. For instance, if a certain product is selling well to younger customers, similar products might be offered when subsequent young customers visit the site.

FACT AND IDEA REVIEW

1. What is a cookie?
2. How can cookies be used by an e-commerce site?
3. How is a survey useful to an e-commerce business?
4. What are data mining tools, and why are they useful?

FOR DISCUSSION

5. What are some ways data mining tools might produce useful results? Think of an e-commerce Web site that you visit, and see if you can think of ways that using data mining tools might increase the site's effectiveness.

TechTerms

- online survey
- online form
- data mining tools

Making Your Business Grow

CHAPTER OBJECTIVES

When you have completed this chapter, you should be able to:

SECTION 23.1

- Evaluate the three primary methods for growing your business.
- Describe intensive growth strategies that can be used to take advantage of opportunities within a current market.
- Discuss integrative growth strategies that can be used to expand a business within its industry.
- Explain diversification growth strategies that can be used to take advantage of business opportunities outside a business's market or industry.

SECTION 23.2

- Describe the challenges that come with growth.
- Explain what it takes to acquire growth capital.
- Discuss the types of growth funding.

STANDARD &POOR'S
Money Talk

PLANNING FOR RETIREMENT

Your retirement years may seem a long way off right now, but it is never too early to start planning. A good plan can help you deal with sudden changes that may occur, and give you a sense of control over your future.

Consider your long-range goals. What does retirement mean to you? What type of lifestyle would you like to have? With these future plans in mind, decide how much money you will need to live comfortably, and determine how much you will need to save every month to reach that goal.

For instance, if you want to have $1 million when you reach age 65, and you start saving at 25, you will need to invest $127 per month in investments that earn 11 percent each year. The sooner you start investing, the easier it will be to reach your goal.

 Go to **entrepreneurship.glencoe.com** to complete the Standard & Poor's Money Talk Financial Literacy Activity.

PREPARE TO READ

THINK ABOUT THESE QUESTIONS AS YOU READ.

How do I make my business grow?

What are the challenges of expanding a business?

Making Your Business Grow

GET READY TO READ

KEY TERMS
- intensive growth strategies
- market penetration
- market development
- integrative growth strategies
- vertical integration
- horizontal integration
- diversification growth strategies
- synergistic diversification
- horizontal diversification
- conglomerate diversification

KEY CONCEPTS
- Planning the Growth of Your Business
- Intensive Growth Strategies
- Integrative Growth Strategies
- Diversification Growth Strategies

THE MAIN IDEA
Growing a business requires research and planning. Three major strategies can be used to grow a business: intensive strategies, integrative strategies, and diversification strategies.

READING ORGANIZER
Draw the reading organizer on a separate piece of paper. As you read, categorize the different types of growth strategies.

GROWTH STRATEGIES

INTENSIVE	INTEGRATIVE	DIVERSIFICATION
1. market penetration	1. _____	1. _____
2. _____	2. _____	2. _____
3. _____		3. _____

Planning the Growth of Your Business

An entrepreneur puts together a good team and develops a practical concept. As a result, his or her new business probably will not stay small very long. Growth is the natural by-product of a successful start-up. It helps a business secure and maintain a competitive advantage. Some entrepreneurs fear growth because they do not want to lose control of the business. Their fear is understandable. The growth period of a new venture is both an exciting and risky time. **Figure 23.1** on page 497 illustrates some commonly used growth strategies.

Intensive Growth Strategies

Intensive growth strategies are growth strategies that take advantage of opportunities within a current market. A business that wants to increase sales to its target customers might use this approach. Intensive growth strategies include market penetration, market development, and product development.

Figure 23.1 **Growth Strategies**

Intensive Growth Strategies

Market penetration is an intensive growth strategy in which a business attempts to increase sales in its current market. Product development is an intensive growth strategy in which new or improved products are introduced. Market development is an intensive growth strategy in which a business expands its product to reach new locations. Franchising, a form of market development, is one of the most popular ways to expand a business.

GROWTH STRATEGIES
Intensive growth strategies exploit opportunities within a current market. Integrative growth strategies allow your company to expand within the industry by growing vertically or horizontally. Diversification growth strategies involve investing in products or businesses that are different from the products you sell or the businesses you own. *How can an entrepreneur decide which strategies to use to achieve growth?*

Integrative Growth Strategies

Horizontal integration entails growing your business by buying up competitors. With vertical integration, a company expands by acquiring the distributors, retailers, or dealers of your products. Levi Strauss has used vertical integration strategies by opening retail stores and selling at a discount to consumers.

Diversification Growth Strategies

One way to expand a business is to diversify. Synergistic diversification involves finding new products or businesses that are compatible with your business. Conglomerate diversification involves finding products or businesses that are unrelated to your product or business. Horizontal diversification involves adding a product that is technologically unrelated to the original business. Barnes & Noble has used horizontal diversification as a growth strategy by opening coffee shops within its bookstores.

Market Penetration

Market penetration is an attempt to increase sales in your current market. You can do this in a variety of ways:

- **Get your customers to use your product more often.** The makers of Arm & Hammer® Baking Soda increased sales by suggesting new ways to use it. Customers once purchased baking soda only for cooking. Now they use it to brush their teeth and to keep their refrigerators smelling fresh.
- **Attract your competitors' customers.** A retail store owner might locate near a competitor to encourage comparison shopping.
- **Go after people in your present market who are not using products like yours.** Marcel Ford found new customers for his silk plant cleaner by demonstrating the product in Costco outlets. People who would not have picked his product off the shelf readily saw and experienced its benefits.

Market Development

With **market development**, a business expands its product to reach new locations. A business can open a branch in another community. It can also go nationwide or expand internationally.

Franchising is one way to grow a business. California Pizza Kitchen, Chief Auto Parts, and automobile dealerships are examples of franchises. Franchisers sell the right to do business under a company's name. For a fee, the franchiser also provides training and other assistance. One of the biggest advantages of franchising is that you can expand the business with someone else's money.

Franchising also makes it easy for you to manage your growing organization. With franchising, you personally train your franchisees. They, in turn, hire and are responsible for the employees who work for them. You do not have to oversee the workers.

However, franchising has its challenges. It is like starting your business all over again. You must prepare training manuals, write operating instructions, and prepare market and competitor analyses. In addition, the costs of setting up the franchise structure add up. There may be legal, accounting, consulting, and training costs. Also, it may be a long time before a franchise turns a profit. One company in Memphis sold more than 70 franchises. However, it did not show a profit for a year. Waiting three to five years for a profit is not uncommon.

How do you know if your business is ideal for franchising? Ask yourself the questions shown in **Figure 23.2.** Franchising is a complicated process that requires help from experienced attorneys and accountants.

Do not limit your growth to the United States. U.S. franchises can be found throughout the Pacific Rim, Europe, and many other parts of the world. You can find a Hard Rock Cafe in Beijing and a Timberland shoe store in London. Businesses other than franchises form partnerships and enjoy tremendous success in global markets. Foreign businesspeople come to the United States looking for franchisers and partners. They want to take successful business concepts back to their countries.

Quick Math

As part of a franchise contract, a franchisee must pay 9 percent of its profits during the first year and 5.8 percent during the second year. If its profits were $88,765 for Year 1 and $92,627 for Year 2, how much royalty did it pay to the franchiser?

Figure 23.2 Ten Questions to Ask Before Franchising

1. Does your business have a tested business concept and successful track record?

2. Do you have a product with growth potential and an established and large market?

3. Will it be easy to take your product to other areas and other markets?

4. Can your business generate a high percentage of gross profit?

5. Can your business be systematized and duplicated?

6. Have you secured a trade name or trademark?

7. Do you have a patented design, process, or formula?

8. Do you have financial systems in place?

9. Do you have a marketing plan?

10. Can you take advantage of volume purchasing and advertising?

FRANCHISING TO ACHIEVE GROWTH Being a franchiser can be a mechanism for growth. If you decide to franchise your business to grow it, you must ask yourself some questions to prepare. *What is the primary advantage to the franchiser of franchising?*

Product Development

Product development is another way to increase sales to existing customers. This is the introduction of brand new or improved products to the marketplace. In most industries, companies must continually develop new products to keep customers interested. New products are those that did not exist previously. They are different from improved products, which are simply small improvements on existing products. You have probably noticed companies advertising "new and improved" versions of existing products.

While You Read

Predict To *integrate* means to join with something else. Knowing this, predict the meaning of "integrative" growth strategies.

Integrative Growth Strategies

Integrative growth strategies are growth strategies that allow your company to expand within the industry by growing vertically or horizontally.

Vertical Integration

Vertical integration is the merging of companies that are in the same distribution chain of a product. With vertical integration, a company expands in two ways. It acquires suppliers upstream in the distribution channel. It also acquires distribution outlets downstream in the channel.

If you use backward integration, you try to gain control of the supplies used to make your products. Suppose you are a manufacturer of plastic items. You could purchase one or more of the companies that supply your raw materials. This would help you better control the timing and quality of your supply. It is also a way to diversify your business.

A Career in the Bag

The square purse which today bears the Kate Spade label has become a staple of modern fashion, but just a few years ago it was only an idea on a drawing board. Kate Brosnahan was working as a fashion editor in 1992 when she designed her first purse out of construction paper. Today, along with her husband, Andy, Kate Spade lends not only her eye for design but also her name to a company that has become a fashion titan—the company Kate Spade is a $70 million firm producing everything from purses to fragrances to shoes.

CRITICAL THINKING

How did Kate Spade become identified with a certain style of purse—and how did that help the company?

 Go to **entrepreneurship.glencoe.com** to complete the Success Stories Writing Activity.

When you choose forward integration, you attempt to gain control of the distribution systems for your product. Generally, you can do this in two ways. First, you can eliminate intermediaries by selling directly to your customers. This allows you to reduce the price to the customer, and it saves your company money. Second, you can acquire the distributors, retailers, or dealers of your products. Many manufacturers, such as Nike and Mikasa, have opened retail stores, selling at a discount to consumers.

Horizontal Integration

Horizontal integration involves increasing your market share and expanding your business by buying up competitors. For example, you may decide to purchase a company that has a product and market compatible with yours. An example is a gas station that purchases an auto parts store. Both businesses serve the same general customer base. You might also buy a troubled company in a different area that already has buildings and distribution channels. This way, your product can move into a new market quickly. You do not have the expense of finding or constructing buildings or setting up distribution channels.

> **While You Read**
>
> **Connect** Think of an example of a business that has grown using a diversification growth strategy.

Diversification Growth Strategies

Diversification growth strategies are growth strategies that involve investing in products or businesses that are different from yours. Businesses often diversify when they have exhausted opportunities within their present industry or market. Unlike intensive or integrative strategies, this growth strategy takes advantage of opportunities outside a business market or industry by synergistic, horizontal, or conglomerate diversification.

Synergistic Diversification

Trying to find new products or businesses that are technologically compatible with yours is called **synergistic diversification**. You may, for example, buy the rights to a product manufactured similarly to yours, or you may buy a business that is technologically similar to yours but produces different products. For example, if you own a bakery, you may decide to buy a small gourmet restaurant. You can use it as a showcase for your baked goods.

Horizontal Diversification

To seek products that are technologically unrelated to yours is **horizontal diversification**. When you diversify in this manner, the new product or service must be salable to present customers. For example, Nike Sports, which manufactures athletic shoes, began selling sports clothing and accessories.

BusinessWeek Case Study

Your Ticket to a New Career?

Franchising can put your skills to work in your own business, but be sure to read the fine print before writing any checks.

Franchising is giving James Radebaugh a second chance. Three years ago, after he was laid off from his job as a human-resources executive at food-products company Bob Evans Farms, Radebaugh, now 55, found himself disillusioned with the corporate world. So, Radebaugh, based in Powell, Ohio, consulted for several software companies while he figured out what to do next. Then it dawned on him: Why not buy a franchise? That way, he could run his own business without having to start from scratch.

This month, he plans to open a Great Clips hair salon, which he discovered when he got a haircut at a unit of the franchise a year ago. With a $300,000 line of credit acquired by putting up his house as collateral, Radebaugh intends to open two more salons by the fall, and possibly three more after that. He says he expects each unit to earn about $60,000 on $300,000 in revenues within 18 months. "I wish I had done this a long time ago," he says.

If you're a corporate refugee like Radebaugh—or fear you might become one—franchising could be the answer for you, too. You'll have the advantage of starting a business with the resources, brand, and established system of the franchiser. What's more, franchisers these days are seeking out executives for their management skills and financial savvy.

SOURCE: *BUSINESSWEEK*, MAY 1, 2003; BY ANNE FIELD

APPLICATION

Select a franchise business. Research the requirements for starting the franchise. What qualifications must a franchise applicant have? What costs are involved? Are there any restrictions? Summarize your findings in a one-page report.

 Go to **entrepreneurship.glencoe.com** to complete the *BusinessWeek* Case Study Reading Guide Activity.

Conglomerate Diversification

Using **conglomerate diversification**, look for products or businesses that are totally unrelated to yours. Why would you want to do that? You may be looking for an enterprise that fills a gap in your business. For example, suppose your primary business requires employees to travel a great deal. You may purchase a travel agency to cut costs and provide convenience, or you may decide to buy the building in which your company is located. You could then lease the extra space to another business. This would bring your business added income.

While You Read

Question Under what circumstances should a business undertake diversification growth strategies?

QUESTIONS TO ASK Diversification can be profitable, but it also can be distracting, particularly at start-up or in the early years of a company. Before you choose to diversify, make sure your primary business is under control. It should be showing a profit and generating a positive cash flow. Then ask yourself these questions to decide whether the potential for growth outweighs the costs and risks:

- Am I knowledgeable about the new product or service?
- Can I manage the extra paperwork, finances, and decisions?
- Will the new venture require additional staff?
- Can the work space handle the new operations?
- How much will new material, staff, and equipment cost?

Section 23.1 After You Read

Key Concept Review

1. Describe the difference between market development and product development.
2. List drawbacks to franchising your business.
3. What are some strategies for expanding your business to another country?

Critical Thinking

4. Interview a franchisee—the owner of an individual franchise—to learn what was involved in purchasing the franchise and how the franchisee plans to grow the business. Write a summary of the interview. Evaluate if and why you agree with the owner's growth strategies.

Role Play

Situation You own a successful tutorial business called Reaching High. Your research shows a demand for this service in a city 20 miles away. To open a second location, you need to hire a manager for the current store so you can oversee the new one. You also need to secure a bank loan to cover start-up costs.

Activity Pair up with a classmate. Role-play a conversation between the entrepreneur and the banker. Discuss the company's growth strategy and the issues to consider before making a final decision.

Evaluation You will be evaluated on how well you address these issues:

- Describe your growth vision for Reaching High.
- Explain the steps you will follow to achieve your goals.
- Explain your marketing and operational plans for the new store.
- Discuss your strategy for raising money to open the second store.

Challenges of Expansion

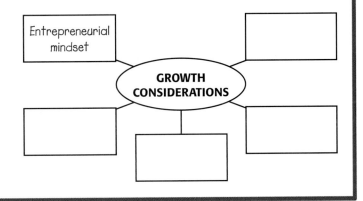
Challenges That Come With Growth

Business expansion is a natural outgrowth of a successful business. A business that expands and diversifies has the advantage. However, you must consider whether your business is suited for growth. Several factors affect the ability of a business to grow:

- **Target market characteristics.** If the niche you created is too small, your ability to grow will be limited. To grow further, you must expand outside the target market.

- **Industry innovativeness.** If your industry thrives on innovation, you must learn to do it better and faster.

- **Ability to delegate responsibility.** Many entrepreneurs are successful at recognizing opportunity and starting a business. However, they may not have the skills to manage. You may need to hire someone who does.

While You Read

Predict Imagine that you are the sole proprietor of a small restaurant. You have decided to open a new restaurant in a nearby town. What challenges might you face?

- **Entrepreneurial mindset.** Everyone in your company needs to think like an entrepreneur. They must share the same vision of growth and work to achieve it.

- **Systems and controls.** The appropriate systems and controls need to be in place. These involve such diverse areas as management, marketing, finances, and record keeping. This ensures that your business can deal with the demands of growth.

The Challenge of Multiple Sites

When you move from an owner-operated business to two or more additional sites, you can become distanced from your customers and employees. Consequently, it may not be easy to keep up with their needs. Also, you must decide whether to transfer your present business image to the new location. Perhaps you should establish a different image. An image that works in one community may not meet the needs of another community. This is particularly true in retail. Therefore, you will have to expand and change your marketing.

In management, you must decide whether your new store will operate independently, or perhaps it will be controlled by the main store. Sometimes the main store controls the marketing, accounting, finance, and purchasing functions. They tend to be common functions in all of the stores and are easily centralized. Another arrangement leaves the branch store to concentrate on its day-to-day operations. It sends detailed records to the main store on a regular basis.

Expansion requires additional managerial staff. It can be an expensive and difficult undertaking to find people who have the necessary skills and who can be trusted. You need to hire carefully. Look to hire people referred to you by business associates or current employees.

TECHNOLOGY Today

Technology and Growth

As the old business adage goes, "If you are not growing, you are shrinking." A competitive marketplace means that in order to stay in business, a company must always be on the lookout for new opportunities to generate revenue. Technological tools make it possible for savvy entrepreneurs to create new product offerings and improve existing ones. The demand for new technology causes a need for technology experts, which makes for excellent growth potential in the technology training and consulting fields.

Cooperative Learning Activity

Can you name some businesses that have used technology to create new products and services or improve existing ones?

@ Go to **entrepreneurship.glencoe.com** to complete the Technology Today Vocabulary Practice Activity.

The Effect on Record Keeping

With expansion, record-keeping requirements become more complicated. You need an accounting system that tracks key data at all locations. Fortunately, technology makes record keeping easy to accomplish. You should plan for the purchase of a computer network system before you grow the business.

The Problem With Success

Entrepreneurs cannot become complacent about success. They should watch the industry and the market for new trends and changes that can affect their business. With success comes a healthy cash flow, which is often a big trap for entrepreneurs. Many business owners, flush with success, take money out of the business or invest in expensive overhead. If the market changes and business slows, they may be saddled with payments they cannot make. When your business is growing, you should put extra cash back into the business to produce more revenues. Then the business will have created enough wealth for you to take money out when you need it.

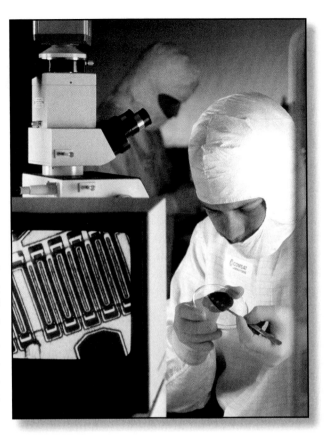

HIGH TECH Businesses that deal in technology may grow faster than others. *What are some reasons?*

What It Takes to Find Growth Capital

When financing the expansion of your business, try the same sources you used to start the business. These include personal savings, friends and family, private investors, and banks. Some of these options were described in Chapter 19. However, the amount required for expansion is often more than you needed at start-up.

The Process of Raising Money

Growth is costly. It takes money to raise money. As the entrepreneur, you pay all of the costs of raising the money before you receive it. It can put a strain on the limited resources of your business. However, by demonstrating that your business is successful, you can easily raise growth capital.

- **Raising money takes time.** Plan on several months to a year to find the money you need. Several more months may pass while the potential investor or lender checks out you and your business, and it may take up to six months to receive the money. So plan ahead and do not wait until you need the money to begin looking for it.

- **Your money deal may not work out.** After months of work, your investor or lender may decide not go through with the deal. To avoid being left with no alternatives, have a backup plan.

- **You may have to buy out your relatives.** Professional investors do not want to deal with your initial investors, often friends and family of the business owner. Investors have nothing to lose by demanding a buyout. Other deals are plentiful.

While You Read

Connect If you owned a successful business, would you invest your profits back into the business?

POORLY PLANNED GROWTH

Poorly planned growth is an obstacle that faces many small businesses. Some advantages of entrepreneurship can become disadvantages when the time comes for a small business to grow. For example, one of the greatest benefits of being an entrepreneur is being in control. However, growth often requires the business owner to give up some direct authority. Some entrepreneurs find it difficult to cede control.

Another growth trap is that, as small businesses succeed, their owners may begin to feel trapped. Instead of feeling on top of the world, they feel like prisoners of long hours and hard work.

Think Critically

What is the best way to avoid falling into the trap of poorly planned growth?

 Go to **entrepreneurship.glencoe.com** to complete the Issues in Entrepreneurship Research Activity.

Types of Growth Funding

Growing a business requires planning, but it is exciting. You finally get to see the rewards of your hard work. As more cash comes into the business and less cash leaves, you can use the excess to fund expansion. This is known as funding growth internally. If you have enough cash flow, this is the best source of expansion capital. It is inexpensive, and you control it. Moreover, you do not have to give up any equity in your business or take on any debt.

Unfortunately, most fast-growing businesses require more cash than they can generate and still maintain operations. Other sources of financing must be considered. A few alternatives follow. Some of these sources were discussed in Chapter 19.

Private Placement

Private placement is a way to raise money by selling investment interests in your business to private investors. You need to develop a type of business plan called a prospectus. A **prospectus** is a formal document that details the risks involved in the private offering. Its purpose is to give investors the information they need to make informed decisions. Get help from an attorney to do this correctly. You may have to register the private placement with the SEC.

Write About It

Interview a business owner whose business failed due to poorly planned growth. Write a summary of the interview.

Public Stock Offering

Only corporations can raise money by selling shares of stock, or making a **public stock offering** on a public stock exchange. To make a public stock offering, your corporation should show increasing revenues for several years. It should also have revenues of at least $10 million annually. The public offering process is regulated by the SEC to protect the public from illegal or poorly prepared offerings.

While You Read

Question What kind of company can raise funds through the sale of stock?

Employee Stock Option Plan

An **employee stock option plan (ESOP)** is a source of financing in which a company gives its employees the opportunity to buy a portion of the business. To raise money with an ESOP, you must have at least 25 employees and revenues of $5 million. An attorney can tell you whether you meet additional requirements. In an ESOP, a company takes existing stock or borrows money to buy stock. The stock is bought by the company's employees and placed in a trust fund. The company makes tax-deductible contributions to the trust fund to repay the bank debt. The stock serves as collateral for the bank note.

Section 23.2 After You Read

Key Concept Review

1. What are some challenges of operating multiple sites?
2. What are two types of growth funding available to the small business?
3. What is an employee stock option plan?

Critical Thinking

4. Visit a banker or someone you know who invests in businesses. Find out how much money it costs to raise capital through a bank loan or a private investment. Write a summary of your findings. Evaluate which method of raising capital you would select if you were attempting to grow a business.

Role Play

Situation Two years ago Felipe started a personal shopping service. His clients are busy professionals who work downtown and do not have time to run errands during the day. Felipe picks up dry cleaning, purchases gifts for family members, and even plans and purchases clients' wardrobes. His business is growing so fast, however, that his customer service is beginning to deteriorate. He also does not have time to take care of the books and keep the necessary records for his business. Felipe has no employees. There is no competition, but he is afraid that may change.

Activity Team up with a classmate and role-play a conversation in which you advise Felipe about his business decisions and what he needs to do to successfully expand his business.

Evaluation You will be evaluated on how well you address these issues:

- Describe the challenges Felipe is facing because of the success of his business.
- Explain what Felipe should do to improve the quality of his service.
- Evaluate how Felipe should respond if his business is threatened by new competition.

Chapter Summary

Section 23.1 **Making Your Business Grow**

An entrepreneur can take advantage of different strategies to grow his or her business. Intensive growth strategies provide opportunities for growth within a current market. These strategies include market penetration, market development, and product development. Integrative growth strategies give you the opportunity to grow within your industry either vertically or horizontally. Diversification growth strategies provide opportunities outside the market or industry in which your business normally operates. Three diversification growth strategies are synergistic, horizontal, and conglomerate. When considering expansion, entrepreneurs should consider the characteristics of their target markets, how innovative the industry is, their ability to delegate responsibility, and whether they can get everyone else in the company to think like an entrepreneur.

Section 23.2 **Challenges of Expansion**

Many challenges come with growing a company. Expansion often complicates business management, marketing, finances, and record keeping. Finding growth capital can be costly in terms of time and money. Three sources of funding for expansion are private placement, a public stock offering, and an ESOP.

Key Terms Review

1. Create a graphic that demonstrates the relationship among these terms:

intensive growth strategies (p. 496)

market penetration (p. 498)

market development (p. 498)

integrative growth strategies (p. 499)

vertical integration (p. 499)

horizontal integration (p. 500)

diversification growth strategies (p. 500)

synergistic diversification (p. 501)

horizontal diversification (p. 501)

conglomerate diversification (p. 502)

private placement (p. 506)

prospectus (p. 506)

public stock offering (p. 507)

employee stock option plan (ESOP) (p. 507)

Key Concept Review

2. **Evaluate** the three primary methods for growing a business. (23.1)
3. **Describe** intensive growth strategies that can be used to take advantage of opportunities within a current market. (23.1)
4. **Discuss** integrative growth strategies that can be used to expand a business within its industry. (23.1)
5. **Explain** diversification growth strategies that can be used to take advantage of business opportunities outside a business's market or industry. (23.1)
6. **Describe** the challenges that come with growth. (23.2)
7. **Explain** what it takes to acquire growth capital. (23.2)
8. **Discuss** the types of growth funding. (23.2)

Critical Thinking

9. Your product, a new kind of cereal, seems to have reached a plateau in the growth of market share. Which growth strategies could you use to increase its sales? Explain.
10. Choose a business with which you are familiar and identify ways to expand it using integrative growth strategies.
11. What problems are associated with conglomerate diversification?
12. What steps would you take to expand a business internationally?
13. What are the advantages of a private placement over a public offering for a growing business in need of expansion financing?
14. What are three factors that affect growth?

Write About It

15. Write a one-page report about a business on the Internet or use one in your community that is vertically or horizontally integrated.
16. Serena makes jewelry and sells it at local craft shows. In a letter to Serena, discuss how she can expand her business.
17. In a couple of paragraphs, describe how a restaurant can use diversification strategies to grow its business.
18. Identify a niche you could fill if you owned a small business and a nationally known chain was planning to open in your area. In a one-page paper, describe the niche.
19. In a one-page paper, describe long-term alternatives for a business to reach profitability.
20. Jade owns an Internet magazine in Albuquerque geared toward teens. In a letter to Jade, discuss how she can expand her business and what type of capital and other resources she needs.

Academic Skills

Math

21. Your business revenues in the first six months of operations were $2,500; $2,800; $3,050; $3,500; $4,200; and $4,900. By what percentage did your monthly revenues grow from month to month?

Language Arts

22. You are ready to expand your business and must hire a general manager. Your two best employees have applied for the position. Daphne is most qualified on paper, but Geri is more experienced in the field. You need to make the best decision for your business without alienating the other employee. Write a memo to the employee you do not select explaining why she did not get the job.

Entrepreneurship in Your Community

23. Interview an entrepreneur with a new business about his or her plans to grow the business. Identify the type of strategy being used. Is it appropriate for this business?

24. Imagine that your business has been very successful over the last five years. You have been thinking about expanding internationally. Prepare a written document justifying your expansion plans. Include the following:

- The international market(s) where you think expansion is appropriate for your type of business
- Growth strategy options given the type of business and the fact that it is young
- Method(s) for raising expansion capital

Ethical Practices

Bribes

25. You have secured an international partner and are about to take your business global. It is well known that paying cash to officials smooths the process of business transactions in the country to which you are expanding. You understand that paying bribes is illegal in the United States, the home base for your business. However, this contract will ensure that your company establishes a foothold in the country before your competitors do. What should you do?

INTERNET *connection*

Stock Options

Ian wants to expand his import/export business. He thinks an ESOP might be an excellent way to finance the expansion.

Connect

Use the Internet to research this information about ESOPs:

- The advantages and disadvantages of using the ESOP structure
- The requirements for raising money with an ESOP
- The process a company uses to start an ESOP

Application

Use your research to write a one-page report advising Ian on whether an ESOP is appropriate for his business.

The Electronic Entrepreneur

Electronic Communications

Paper memos and notes have become a thing of the past. Electronic communication has revolutionized business communications. **E-mail**, mail that is electronically transmitted by a computer, allows business people to send communications anywhere in the world, at any time, in an instant. **Newsgroups** are Web-based forums on specific topics where users can post messages and reply to other users. Similar to newsgroups, **bulletin board services (BBS)** allow users to leave and access messages and access other electronic files. No matter which form of online communication you use, netiquette should always be observed.

Be Polite Be polite in all electronic communications. Do not send **flames**, or rude e-mails. Do not type in all capital letters. All capitals means you are screaming. Avoid personal or sensitive issues. Use polite language. Never make insulting remarks, whether in e-mail or in person.

Be Considerate Always complete the subject line on an e-mail so the receiver can identify the subject quickly. When responding, state to what you are responding, or copy the original message into your e-mail. Never just say yes or no.

Be Concise and Precise Make your message specific and focused. You can make sure that it is free of errors by proofreading it and using a spell checker, a software application that checks for spelling and grammar errors, before sending the message. In business communications, it is also important to include a **confidentiality notice**, a statement that says that the message is intended only for the recipient.

FACT AND IDEA REVIEW

1. What are the advantages of using e-mail for business communications?
2. Why might a business owner use a BBS or a newsgroup?
3. What are flames?
4. List two things you can do to be considerate when sending e-mail.

FOR DISCUSSION

5. Should all business communications be done through e-mail? Explain the reasons for your answer.

TechTerms

- e-mail
- newsgroups
- bulletin board service (BBS)
- flames
- confidentiality notice

Social and Ethical Responsibility

CHAPTER OBJECTIVES

When you have completed this chapter, you should be able to:

SECTION 24.1

- Explain the relationship between entrepreneurs and social responsibility.
- Discuss how entrepreneurs can contribute to their communities.

SECTION 24.2

- Define *ethics* and *ethical behavior*.
- Explain how to develop a code of ethics.
- List special ethical problems that entrepreneurs face.

ESTATE PLANNING

Estate planning is the process of creating a detailed plan for managing your assets so that you can make the most of them while you are alive and ensure that they are distributed wisely after your death. It is an essential part of both financial and retirement planning.

An estate plan involves various legal documents, including a will. A will specifies how you want your property to be distributed after you die. There are a variety of types of wills, and the differences among them can affect how your estate will be taxed. Some types of wills are:

- Simple will

- Traditional marital share will

- Exemption trust will

- Stated dollar will

An estate plan can also contain a trust, a legal arrangement that helps manage the assets of your estate for the benefit of you or your beneficiaries.

@ Go to **entrepreneurship.glencoe.com** to complete the Standard & Poor's Money Talk Financial Literacy Activity.

PREPARE TO READ

THINK ABOUT THESE QUESTIONS AS YOU READ.

What are my social responsibilities as an entrepreneur?

What are my ethical responsibilities as an entrepreneur?

Social Responsibility

KEY TERMS
- philanthropy
- social responsibility
- Environmental Protection Agency (EPA)

KEY CONCEPTS
- Entrepreneurs and Social Responsibility
- Contributing to the Community

THE MAIN IDEA

Businesses must do more than provide jobs and make a profit. They also are expected to run their business responsibly.

READING ORGANIZER

Draw the reading organizer on a separate sheet of paper. As you read, write notes about how businesses can protect customers and the environment.

PROTECTING CUSTOMERS	PROTECTING ENVIRONMENT
make safe products	

Entrepreneurs and Social Responsibility

History is rich with stories of entrepreneurs such as J. P. Morgan, John D. Rockefeller, Andrew Carnegie, and Bill Gates. These entrepreneurs chose to make generous and enduring contributions to society. Morgan gave books and art to libraries and museums. Rockefeller gave more than a half-billion dollars to charity. His money fights hunger and disease even today. Carnegie set up more than 2,800 libraries. He also founded the Carnegie Institute for Science. Microsoft founder Bill Gates set up the largest charitable foundation in history, with a gift of $27 billion. The Bill and Melinda Gates Foundation provides funds to improve schools and promote health care around the world, especially in developing nations.

Being a responsible entrepreneur, however, involves more than **philanthropy**, or making charitable donations to improve the welfare of society. It means running your enterprise responsibly every day. For a business to survive, it must be socially responsible. **Social responsibility** is the principle that companies should contribute to the welfare of society and not be solely devoted to maximizing profits.

Success Stories

An Athletic Approach to Business

Michael Rubin has always loved sports, and he always found a way to take that love and make it profitable. At age 13, he opened a ski repair shop; by the time he graduated high school, it had grown to five retail locations. Then the Internet boom came along, and Rubin saw another great potential: he created Global Sports Interactive, an e-commerce company that helps other businesses run profitable online sports-related shopping sites. Some of his customers include The Athlete's Foot, FoxSports.com, and Kmart. His creative view of e-commerce, combined with his love for the product, has made him a success—in 2000, the company did over $42 million in business.

CRITICAL THINKING

What do you think were some of the factors that helped Rubin succeed?

 Go to **entrepreneurship.glencoe.com** to complete the Success Stories Writing Activity.

Social responsibility requires a business to acknowledge that it has a contract with society. That contract includes many duties. A business must make safe products. It must treat customers well and employees fairly. It should be run honestly. Being socially responsible can inspire loyalty in employees and customers. Many socially responsible businesses experience great success.

There is much evidence that social responsibility is associated with improved business performance. Many people will not buy from businesses that receive publicity about misconduct. Studies have found a direct relationship between social responsibility and profitability. Social responsibility is linked to employee commitment and customer loyalty. These are major concerns for any firm that is trying to increase profits.

Your Responsibility to Customers

Businesses must act responsibly toward their customers. Companies must not mislead customers about a product's quality, performance, or safety. Information must be given about proper use, and unsafe products must be labeled as such. The free market is the consumer's best protector. Businesses are free to compete with one another in satisfying consumer wants. As a result, they are motivated to offer the best quality products at the lowest prices.

Two other forces that protect customers are the consumers' rights organizations and government regulation. Institutions like the Consumers' Union has provided consumers with information about the quality, safety, and costs of competing products.

Laws also affect how business is run. The Truth-in-Lending Act requires businesses to fully inform their customers about purchases. The Fair Credit Billing Act requires businesses to respond quickly to consumer complaints. Businesses that break such laws can face fines and punishment.

Government regulations have led businesses to improve their service to customers. However, most successful businesses see customer service as a competitive advantage on its own. Some state and local governments also require businesses to post government ratings on how well they follow health and safety regulations.

Your Responsibility to the Environment

Have you noticed how many ads are environmentally oriented? Oil companies show how they protect rare birds. Chemical companies describe how they protect crops without poisoning the soil. Soap companies advertise recyclable boxes.

Companies want to show customers that they are environmentally responsible. To create and enforce environmental standards, in 1970, the U.S. government formed the Environmental Protection Agency (EPA). The **Environmental Protection Agency (EPA)** is an independent federal agency established to coordinate programs and enforce regulations aimed at reducing pollution and protecting the environment. For example, in 1978, the EPA banned the use of harmful fluorocarbons in aerosol products such as hairspray. It also makes sure businesses properly dispose of hazardous wastes. Business executives who do not follow the standards can be fined or even imprisoned.

Partly in response to federal laws and partly in response to consumer concerns, many businesses are taking responsibility for helping to improve the environment. Many large companies employ environmental affairs executives who help them to achieve their goals in an environmentally responsible manner. Environmental efforts may increase the company's costs, but they also may allow a company to charge higher prices, to increase market share, or both. For example, Ciba, a Swiss dye manufacturer, developed and patent-protected textile dyes that require less salt than traditional dyes. The result was cleaner waterways and lower water treatment costs for textile businesses. Ciba has also been able to gain market share and charge more for the low-salt dyes.

Many firms are working to eliminate wasteful practices and the emissions of pollutants and chemicals from their manufacturing processes. Other companies are seeking ways to improve products, like developing new products in more efficient ways. For example, many car makers have developed automobiles that run on alternative fuels.

Contributing to the Community

You do not need to be a big corporation to contribute to your community and to society. Many small businesses have found creative ways to be generous. Examples are shown in **Figure 24.1** on page 518.

TECHNOLOGY Today

Workplace Surveillance

While tools like e-mail and Web browsing have been a great boon to business, they have also brought with them some unique problems. Companies today are concerned about how much time is being wasted by employees checking personal e-mail or shopping online while at work. They also have to deal with legal issues if those employees use company resources to commit illegal activity. To fight these problems, many firms are turning to surveillance software, which can read private e-mail, track the Web sites an employee has visited, even log every keystroke made.

Critical Thinking

What are some things that employees might do on company computers that the company should be concerned with? What do you think are some ethical ways to handle this problem?

 Go to **entrepreneurship.glencoe.com** to complete the Technology Today Vocabulary Practice Activity.

Figure 24.1 **Making a Contribution**

GIVING BACK TO THE COMMUNITY These are ways a business can give back to the community. *How else can a business contribute?*

Donate Your Products and Services
Donating a portion of what you produce can mean a lot to those who receive it. The Panera Bread Company collects cash donations for community causes from customers in its bakery-cafés. Then it matches those donations with freshly baked bread to feed the hungry or cash distributed to local nonprofit organizations.

Get Your Employees Involved in Philanthropy
Encourage your employees to give something to the community. Offer them time off each month or a certain number of hours a year to do community service. Appoint a community service committee to generate ideas.

Join With Other Companies to Promote Social Responsibility
Organize a group of small businesses to work on a community project. Just Desserts, a San Francisco bakery, rallied 35 businesses to the cause of fixing up local elementary schools. Each business adopted an elementary school, doing such jobs as painting classrooms and planting trees on school property.

Being a Socially Responsible Employer

As a small business owner, you have a responsibility to treat your employees fairly. Additional benefits are up to you. The government encourages businesses to offer flextime, health care, and assistance to the physically challenged. Some businesses offer other perks, such as telecommuting options and on-site child care. These benefits may cost you money. However, happy, productive, and loyal workers often are the result.

Being a Socially Responsible Employee

Personal responsibility is the basis of socially responsible employees. Giving back to the community is meaningless if employees do not exhibit socially responsible behavior. Taking supplies or giving friends unauthorized discounts are not acceptable practices. Responsible employees should maintain high ethical standards when dealing with coworkers, management, and customers.

While You Read

Question What are some ways that businesses can be socially responsible to their employees?

Section 24.1 After You Read

Key Concept Review

1. What does it mean to be socially responsible?
2. What are two areas in which your business can become socially responsible?
3. What are two ways a business can contribute to its community?

Critical Thinking

4. Identify a business in your community that you believe is socially responsible. What contributions does it make to the community?

Role Play

Situation You work for a company that makes gift baskets for birthdays, anniversaries, and holidays. Your job is to purchase the baskets and the products that go into them. One of your suppliers called and offered you two free tickets to the sold-out basketball game Friday night. You have been trying for weeks to get tickets to that game.

Activity With a partner, take turns role-playing a discussion between you and the supplier.

Evaluation You will be evaluated on how well you address these issues in the role play:

- Discuss the ethical issues involved in accepting the tickets.
- Describe whether accepting the tickets will impact your decision about purchasing the supplier's products.

Ethical Responsibility

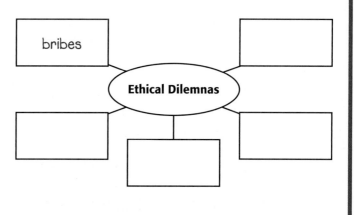
What Does It Mean to Be Ethical?

Ethics are guidelines for human behavior. They are the moral code by which people live and conduct business. **Ethical behavior** is conduct that adheres to this moral code. Ethics help people decide how to act in situations where moral issues are involved. They set the standards for moral, or ethical, behavior.

Understanding Your Values

Your values govern your actions in dealing with others. Your values are reflected in your reputation in the community. For example, the values of honesty, integrity, and responsibility may be the basis of your ethics. Your business will be shaped by your values.

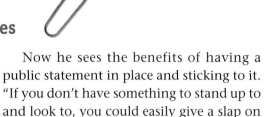
Putting Teeth in Corporate Ethics Codes

Feeling pressure on all sides, more CEOs are pushing to make sure these documents are detailed, understood—and enforced. Clark Consulting (CLK), a compensation and benefit consulting firm, has had a corporate code of ethics in place for years. But following the 2002 passage of the Sarbanes-Oxley law reforming corporate governance, Chief Executive Tom Wamberg revised it, redistributed it, and started referring to it in weekly newsletters distributed to all employees. It wasn't long before the code was put to the test.

Earlier this year, Wamberg learned that one of his senior consultants was bragging to other employees about how he had "fired" a particularly demanding client. Wamberg was outraged. Rule No. 1 of the code is that clients come first. "For us, that was a cardinal sin," says Wamberg, who dismissed that consultant, citing the code.

Now he sees the benefits of having a public statement in place and sticking to it. "If you don't have something to stand up to and look to, you could easily give a slap on the wrist and say, 'Don't do it again,'" says Wamberg.

SOURCE: *BUSINESSWEEK*, FEBRUARY 19, 2004; By AMEY STONE

APPLICATION Develop a one-page written code of ethics for your proposed business. How would you make sure this document was understood by your employees? How would you enforce the code if it were infringed? Share your responses with the class.

 Go to **entrepreneurship.glencoe.com** to complete the *BusinessWeek* Case Study Reading Guide Activity.

Here are some of the benefits of understanding your value system:

- You make better decisions when you do not consider actions that go against your values.
- When you are confident about your values, you are able to persuade others to agree with you.
- You usually do not regret decisions you make based on your value system.

While You Read

Predict Why should business owners develop written ethics policies?

What Are Business Ethics?

Business ethics is the study of behavior and morals in a business situation. Business ethics begin at the top. In other words, a business owner who does not act ethically can not expect his or her employees to act ethically.

The standards of ethical behavior within a business is in large part determined by the business owner's principles and values. Many problems and ethical conflicts can be avoided if business owners clearly communicate their ethical expectations to their employees.

Are Everyone's Ethics the Same?

People do not share the same ethical values. For example, many employees understand that workplace equipment is provided for them to use in completing their job. Others believe it is acceptable to steal from their employers. They may take pens and computer disks or use company e-mail or mail services for personal use.

Employers can be dishonest, too. They may try to avoid paying taxes by not reporting employee earnings. They may fail to report or remedy unsafe working conditions.

Because not everyone has high ethical standards, the entrepreneur needs to create a clear policy. He or she should clearly communicate what is and is not acceptable conduct in the business.

At Special Risk—Small Businesses

Because large businesses are in the public eye, they must be careful about how they conduct business. Small businesses are not watched as carefully. They may be more vulnerable to unethical practices for other reasons as well. Small companies are generally less structured and formal. The environment in which small businesses operate often propels them toward unethical conduct.

Developing a Code of Ethics

A **code of ethics** is a group of ethical behavior guidelines that govern the day-to-day activities of a profession or organization. Many entrepreneurs develop an explicit code of ethics that spells out appropriate conduct for their business. There is, however, a practical reason why entrepreneurs should have a code of ethics. It can be used to defend the company against a criminal action should an employee violate federal law.

While You Read

Connect Think of a situation you have been involved in that tested your ethical behavior. Did you make the ethical choice? How did your choice make you feel about yourself?

TOKENS OF APPRECIATION In some small businesses, salespeople are not allowed to accept gifts from clients. *Why might accepting a gift be unethical?*

Written Versus Unwritten Codes

Codes of ethics can be written or unwritten. Unwritten codes are simply norms, or ways of doing things that have come about over time. For example, in your business, it may be understood that salespeople do not accept gifts, including meals. This rule would not be written down. It would be passed on verbally from one salesperson to another.

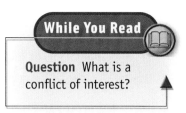
While You Read

Question What is a conflict of interest?

Formal, or written, codes usually grow out of unwritten ones. As a company's business and number of employees grow, so does the potential for misunderstandings. A large company also has more to lose by engaging in unethical practices. It can lose valuable relationships and goodwill. Once a company's reputation has been tarnished, it can be impossible to regain.

A written set of guidelines reduces the chance of unethical behavior. Follow these steps to create a code of ethics:

1. **Brainstorm ethical dilemmas.** Do this with your employees. Come up with potential ethical problems the business might face.

2. **Discuss potential solutions.** Have employees offer suggestions on how to handle these situations. This discussion will give you a sense of employees' values and help everyone reach a positive outcome.

3. **Write a set of general guidelines.** Base them on your discussions. The guidelines should offer a range of acceptable ways to deal with different situations.

4. **Improve your code.** When a new situation or solution occurs, discuss it. Then add it to your guidelines.

As part of its code of ethics, Cray Research, Inc., asks its employees to use the following question as a standard of conduct. How would I feel if my actions appeared on the front page of the newspaper for my family and friends to see? You may want to incorporate this standard into your personal ethical values—and into your business.

Special Problems for Entrepreneurs

Entrepreneurs, by definition, operate in dynamic environments under a great deal of pressure. In such situations, people may decide to put aside ethics to meet short-term obligations or make short-term gains. Some typical ethical problems include conflicts of interest, desperate measures, cultural differences, bribes, and patent or copyright infringement.

Conflict of Interest

A **conflict of interest** is a clash between a person's private interests and his or her responsibilities in a position of trust. Suppose a newly opened resort in Florida offered free stays to journalists and securities analysts. The amount of publicity and goodwill created by such a gesture would be immeasurable. However, the gesture would also create a conflict for the journalists and securities analysts. Why? They are supposed to have an objective point of view. How could they report anything negative about the resort after being treated so well? Their gratitude toward the resort and their responsibility to their readers would be in conflict.

Issues in Entrepreneurship

HANDLING ETHICAL DILEMMAS

The rise in corporate scandals of the past decade has created a demand for a new type of corporate officer: the ethics officer. What does an ethics officer do? An ethics officer typically oversees all aspects of ethics and compliance programs, including standard setting; communication of standards; dealing with exceptions or problems; and overseeing, monitoring, and ensuring the proper ethics programs. He or she also advises senior management on ethical decisions.

Critical Thinking

Why would a company choose to hire an ethics officer rather than handle ethical matters among other corporate officers?

 Go to **entrepreneurship.glencoe.com** to complete the Issues in Entrepreneurship Research Activity.

What should the journalists and analysts do? Many would say that they should turn down the trips. That would be a sacrifice to many of them, but it would be the right thing to do.

Desperate Measures

There is a saying that "you do what you have to, to survive." A store owner in debt may be tempted to circulate negative advertisements about a competitor. His or her aim would be to gain more business. It is important, however, to live by one's code of ethics in all situations, no matter how difficult that may be.

Cultural Differences

Dealing in international business presents challenging ethical dilemmas for Americans. In fact, some businesspeople avoid international markets because of such difficulties. When doing business in other countries, it is important to understand the ethical expectations of that country's culture.

Bribes

Bribes are payments made to secure special services for a business or special consideration for its products. In the United States, bribes are illegal. In many other parts of the world, they are an accepted part of doing business. They are seen as courtesies or gifts. Therefore, before doing business abroad, you must determine your company's policy on giving or accepting bribes.

Write About It

Select a foreign country, and research ethical standards in that country. Find out if the ethical standards in that country are different from the ethical standards in your home country. Write an e-mail to your teacher to report your findings.

Patent or Copyright Infringement

Some governments are not respectful of patents and copyrights held by people in other countries. They infringe on the rights of a foreigner, forcing the person to go to court to enforce the law. Other countries have a long patenting or copyrighting process that foreigners must go through. The delay gives local businesses time to familiarize themselves with the item. This allows them, if they so choose, to submit similar patents or copyrights first.

It may seem that businesses that put ethics aside gain the profits. In the short term, they may. However, you are in business for the long run. Your integrity and reputation are what keep customers coming back. Following an ethical code of behavior is the way to grow a thriving business.

Section 24.2   After You Read

Key Concept Review

1. Why is it important to understand your value system?

2. Why are small businesses at special risk for ethics violations?

3. What are some examples of ethical business practices?

Critical Thinking

4. Interview an entrepreneur to find out how he or she deals with ethical issues in business. Does the business have a formal code of ethics?

Role Play

Situation You are a small business owner who is committed to a values-led corporate concept. You believe in "linked prosperity," where both the company and the world can profit from the success of the business.

Activity Pair up with a classmate and conduct research on socially responsible businesses that have a values-led business concept. Role-play a conversation in which you discuss the influence that business has on society.

Evaluation You will be evaluated on how well you address these issues:

- Discuss to what degree businesses are responsible for social welfare.

- Discuss the role the entrepreneur has in promoting ethical business practices and relationships.

- Identify social responsibilities and legal issues involved in making ethical choices in business.

- Describe other companies that have a values-led philosophy.

- Offer examples of how this type of a values-led philosophy can permeate all aspects of the business.

- Address whether a values-led philosophy can actually hurt a business.

Chapter Summary

Section 24.1 Social Responsibility

Social responsibility is a business's contract with society to make safe products, treat customers and employees fairly, and conduct business honestly. A company has a duty to protect its customers from unsafe products and misinformation. The Environmental Protection Agency (EPA), the media, and the public all promote environmentalism among businesses. Entrepreneurs can contribute to the community by donating products or services, encouraging employees to participate in community service, and joining other companies to work on community projects.

Section 24.2 Ethical Responsibility

Ethics are the moral code by which people live and conduct business. An entrepreneur should develop a written code of ethics to reduce the chance of unethical behavior occurring in his or her business. Employees should be involved in developing the code of ethics. Businesses often face ethical problems when there are conflicts of interest, when their economic survival is threatened, and when doing business abroad (where ethical practices may differ).

Key Terms Review

1. Select a business in your community. Create a poster that promotes social and ethical responsibility in that company. Use the following key terms and be creative.

> philanthropy (p. 514)
>
> social responsibility (p. 514)
>
> Environmental Protection Agency (EPA) (p. 516)
>
> ethics (p. 520)
>
> ethical behavior (p. 520)
>
> business ethics (p. 521)
>
> code of ethics (p. 522)
>
> conflict of interest (p. 523)
>
> bribes (p. 524)

Key Concept Review

2. **Explain** the relationship between entrepreneurs and social responsibility. (24.1)
3. **Discuss** how entrepreneurs can contribute to their community. (24.1)
4. **Define** *ethics* and *ethical behavior.* (24.2)
5. **Explain** how to develop a code of ethics. (24.2)
6. **List** special ethical problems that entrepreneurs face. (24.2)

Critical Thinking

7. What is the difference between social responsibility and ethical responsibility?
8. Think of a company that has not acted responsibly toward consumers. Describe the company's behavior and the consequences.
9. How do socially responsible firms improve quality of life?
10. What is the value of developing a written code of ethics?
11. Should American businesses pay or accept bribes when operating in countries where bribes are the norm? Explain your answer.
12. Is there ever a time when desperate measures are the right thing to do; for example, when the business's very survival is at stake?
13. Compare unwritten codes with written codes of ethics.
14. Why is everyone's code of ethics not the same?

Write About It

15. In a one-page paper, describe a situation that called on you to make an ethical decision. What did you do and why?
16. Do you believe your code of ethics should remain firm in every situation? Why or why not? Answer in one paragraph.
17. In a one-page report, discuss two ways, beyond those presented in the chapter, a company can demonstrate its social responsibility.
18. Choose two companies in different industries. Interview someone in management about the company's code of ethics. In a one-page report, compare and contrast the two companies' codes.
19. In a diary or log entry, identify your personal and business ethics. Then discuss what you believe your responsibility is to customers. Are your beliefs based on what is required by law or by your own value system or both?
20. In a paragraph, discuss why it takes more than philanthropy to be a responsible entrepreneur.

Academic Skills

Math

21. The goal of a schoolwide project is to provide holiday baskets to 200 families. Each basket will contain at least ten cans of food. Sixteen groups of students are competing to see who can collect the most food.

- How many cans are needed to meet the school's goal?

- How many cans would each group need to collect to meet the school's goal?

- If each group collects 150 cans, what percentage of the goal did students collect?

Language Arts

22. Working with a partner, research a famous entrepreneur (past or present). Find out how this person demonstrated social and ethical responsibility. Report your findings to the class in an oral presentation.

Entrepreneurship in Your Community

23. With your classmates, create a formal code of ethics for the class. Include the following sections:

- Purpose of the code

- Social principles (general guidelines)

- Ethical principles (general guidelines)

- Potential ethical dilemmas and solutions

How is this code similar to or different from that of a business?

24. As a class, develop and implement a service project to promote the idea of social responsibility in your community. Organize into teams to complete the following assignments:

- Project selection

- Coordination of students

- Marketing and promotion of event

- Implementation of event

Ethical Practices

Cheating

25. The class is taking its final exam for the year. It is a difficult test, and you have studied for days in preparation. As you enter the classroom, you hear a classmate bragging about how he stored the answers to the test on his cell phone. Would you say something to this student? Would you tell the teacher what you heard? What would you do?

INTERNET *connection*

Clean Jeans

You own a company that manufactures blue jeans for several distributors worldwide. You have decided to become a more environmentally friendly company but need help to achieve this goal.

Connect

Conduct research on the Internet on the following issues related to your business:

- Measures for conserving resources

- Methods to reduce waste and pollution

- Recycling plans

- Promotion activities

Application

Use your research to develop a two-page proactive policy on the environment as it relates to your business.

 entrepreneurship.glencoe.com

The Electronic Entrepreneur

Accessibility for All

Web sites often include elements that can limit their usability for many people. For the success of your e-business, make sure that the site you create is accessible to all.

Different Needs Making a Web site **accessible** involves making sure that all types of people can access and use the site's content. Some users may have difficulty seeing, hearing, or understanding text, graphic, or audio elements. Web users with physical impairments may have difficulty using a mouse or keyboard.

Accessibility Guidelines Successful Web sites allow all visitors to get the information they want quickly and easily. The **World Wide Web Consortium (W3C)**—an organization that produces standards for the World Wide Web—and Section 508 of the United States Rehabilitation Act provide Web site accessibility guidelines.

Include Options Always provide text versions of graphics or audio, including navigation buttons. For example, if clicking a photo of chili displays a recipe, then the text version might read "Recipe for Making Chili." This is especially important for persons with visual impairments using **screen readers**—devices that read a site's content aloud. Use **cascading style sheets (CSS)**—a feature of HTML that gives users more control over how Web pages are displayed. Pages designed with CSS allow users to easily change settings.

Design for Multiple Technologies Some users may be using old technology or out-of-date software. Web sites should be accessible to individuals using any major browser as well as older technologies. Always check your pages to make sure users can understand them with graphics turned off. That way you can make sure that all users have a satisfying visit to your site.

FACT AND IDEA REVIEW

1. What are some of the different needs Web site visitors might have?
2. What is W3C?
3. Why is it important to provide text versions of graphics or audio on a Web page?
4. What is a cascading style sheet (CSS)? Why is it helpful to use them?

FOR DISCUSSION

5. Why would accessibility be important to the success of a business?

TechTerms

- accessible
- World Wide Web Consortium (W3C)
- screen readers
- cascading style sheets (CSS)

Contingency Plan

The Contingency Plan examines the assumptions in the business plan and the greatest risks to the business and suggests plans to minimize the risk.

✔ STEP 1 BRAINSTORM POTENTIAL PROBLEMS

Brainstorm a list of potential problems that could cause your business to fail. Describe how to deal with any of the situations should they arise.

✔ STEP 2 PLAN SOLUTIONS FOR POTENTIAL PROBLEMS

Describe how the company will respond to these changes:

SITUATION	
Demographic Shifts	Product Liability Lawsuits
Socioeconomic Trends	Lower-than-Projected Sales
Economic Events	Lower-than-Projected Revenue
Changes in Government Policies	Competitive Threats
Energy Costs	Price Cutting by Competitors
Cost Overruns	The Introduction of New Products by Competitors

Executive Summary

The Executive Summary recounts the key points in the business plan. It is written last because it summarizes the most important information from the business plan. Investors rely on it to decide if the business concept interests them.

✔ STEP 1 RECAP KEY ISSUES

In six paragraphs, describe your company's mission, goals, objectives, current stage of development, owners, and key management team members.

✔ STEP 2 RECOUNT THE ESSENTIALS

Describe the company, business model, legal structure, industry, product or service, target market, and the unique opportunity.

Cover Page, Title Page, Table of Contents, and Supporting Documents

Every business plan should have a cover page, title page, and table of contents. A good business plan also includes documentation relevant to the business.

✔ STEP 1 GATHER BASIC INFORMATION

Gather this basic information: company name; names, titles, and addresses of the owners; business address; phone number; Web site address; and e-mail address.

✓ STEP 2) COLLECT SUPPORTING DOCUMENTS

The Supporting Documents section of the business plan includes items, exhibits, and documentation relevant to the business. Gather as many of these items as you can:

the owners' resumes	specifications of machinery
the owners' tax returns	business location map
financial statements	copy of lease or purchase agreement
franchise contract	contracts and licenses
partnership agreement	other legal documents
articles of incorporation	purchase orders
photos of products	letters of intent from suppliers
blueprints of products	business cards
specifications of products	market research highlights
photos of facilities	marketing materials
blueprints of facilities	press releases
blueprints of equipment	organizational blueprint

Use the **Business Plan Project Appendix** on pages 532–543 to explore the content requirements of a business plan in more detail.

▶ The **Contingency Plan** examines the assumptions in the business plan and the greatest risks to the business and suggests plans to minimize the risk.

▶ The **Executive Summary** recounts the key points in the business plan.

▶ The **Cover Page, Title Page, and Table of Contents** offer basic information about the company and the structure and contents of the plan.

▶ The **Supporting Documents** section of the business plan includes items, exhibits, and documentation relevant to the business.

BUSINESS PLAN PROJECT TEMPLATE

@ Go to **entrepreneurship.glencoe.com** for a document template in which you can write your own business plan.

Business Plan Project

THE BUSINESS PLAN: YOUR ROAD MAP TO ENTREPRENEURIAL SUCCESS

Developing a good business plan can put you on the track to success in a small business. A business plan summarizes an entrepreneur's proposed business venture. It provides an organized report of a company's goals and how management intends to achieve those goals. A business plan is a continuing work in progress that should evolve as your business evolves. Developing a business plan is like outlining a strategy for turning your business idea into a reality.

What Is a Business Plan?

- A guide to the company's operations
- A document presenting your company's strategic vision
- A tool to persuade lenders and investors to finance your business
- A standard by which you can measure and improve business performance
- A plan to use as a basis for making sound business decisions

BUSINESS PLAN ELEMENTS

The Business Plan Project Appendix explains the content requirements for the essential elements of a business plan. For detailed instructions and worksheets to help you prepare your business plan, refer to the *Business Plan Project Workbook.*

BUSINESS PLAN PROJECT TEMPLATE

@ Go to **entrepreneurship.glencoe.com** for a document template in which you can write your own business plan.

ASSIGNMENT

Select a business that you are interested in starting. Then develop a business plan for the venture. When you are finished writing the business plan, package the business plan using the guidelines on page 109. Then present it and defend it in an oral presentation.

MANAGEMENT TEAM PLAN

In the Management Team section of the business plan, you will present your management team's qualifications for making the venture a success.

KEY MANAGEMENT

- Describe each management team member, including title, salary, abilities, duties, responsibilities, educational experience, previous industry and related work experience, and past successes. Describe the benefits that team members will provide to the company.
- Provide copies of the owners' tax returns, personal financial statements, and résumés.

ADVISORS AND PROFESSIONAL SERVICE PROVIDERS

- Describe the role, responsibilities, and members of the advisory board, if you have one.
- List the outside consultants the company will use. Include accountants, attorneys, bankers, insurance agents, technology advisors, Web developers, security contractors, and payroll specialists.

 ## COMPANY DESCRIPTION

The Company Description outlines the company's basic background information, business concept, and goals and objectives.

BUSINESS HISTORY AND DESCRIPTION

- Explain your reasons for starting a new business or expanding an existing business.
- Describe the entrepreneurial opportunity.
- Provide a history of the business with development milestones that have been completed to date and the current status of the business.
- Describe the legal structure of the business and why you chose it.
- Include details about prior funding, royalty, partnership, and joint venture agreements.

GOALS AND OBJECTIVES

- Establish the business's goals and objectives and relate them to the investment you seek.
- Explain why you think the venture will succeed.

 ## PRODUCT AND SERVICE PLAN

The Product and Service Plan describes the features and benefits of the business's products and services.

OVERVIEW OF PRODUCTS AND SERVICES

- Describe the product or service, including purpose, size, shape, colors, features, benefits, cost, functionality, design, quality, capabilities, technology, protections, and unique selling points.
- Describe competing and similar technology.
- Describe the need the product or service addresses in the market and how it benefits customers.
- Explain briefly how the products and/or services will be produced, the materials required, and the type of labor needed.

PRODUCT DEVELOPMENT STATUS

- Discuss the history and current status of product development.
- Provide projected dates for achieving other stages of development.

VISION AND MISSION STATEMENTS

The Vision and Mission Statements section of the business plan sets forth the guiding principles by which a company functions. These statements should be clear and concise. They communicate what the business stands for, what its founders believe in, and what the company intends to achieve.

VISION STATEMENT

- Write a vision statement that establishes the scope and purpose of your company and reflects its values and beliefs.
- Express the company's vision in broad terms so that it will stand the test of time.
- Convey the future of the company as its founders see it.
- Develop strategies for achieving the vision of the business.
- Establish criteria for monitoring achievement of the vision.

MISSION STATEMENT

- Write a mission statement that expresses the specific aspirations of a company, the major goals for which it will strive.
- Define the direction in which the company will move.
- Convey a challenging yet achievable mission that the organization will be dedicated to accomplishing.
- Develop strategies for achieving the mission of the business.
- Establish criteria for monitoring achievement of the mission.

 INDUSTRY OVERVIEW

Your business plan must address basic trends and growth within the industry. Think of your industry as those companies providing similar, complementary, or supplementary products and services.

INDUSTRY TRENDS AND GROWTH

- Describe the industry, including size by both revenue and number of firms.
- Describe how the industry functions, including a general explanation of the industry's distribution system.
- Describe the barriers of entry to the industry.
- Describe the positive and negative trends in the industry.
- Describe the past and future trends in the industry.
- Discuss growth trends and how many companies are expected to enter the industry in the future.
- Explain the factors that are influencing growth or decline in the industry.
- Include the failure rate in the industry.
- Describe the typical profitability in the industry.
- Describe the government regulations that affect the industry in general and your business in particular.
- Describe the local, national, or international industry standards with which your business will need to comply.
- Include current and historical industry employment data.
- Provide visualizations of industry data (charts, tables, graphs).

MARKET ANALYSIS

The Market Analysis section of the business plan is important because it presents your market research and features a customer demographic profile that defines the traits of the company's target market. Information about potential target markets should originate from primary and secondary research resources.

TARGET MARKET DEMOGRAPHIC PROFILE

- Write a demographic profile of the company's target market.
- Identify and explain market segments.
- Describe the market niche served.
- Describe the size of the target market.
- Explain if your market is domestic or international and describe the cultures and ethnicities within it.
- Describe the geographic statistics of your target market; where are your customers from and where do they live?
- Describe what members of the target market do for a living, their level of income, their social and economic status, and their level of education.
- Describe the ages, genders, family structures, lifestyle, and leisure activities of the target market.
- Explain what motivates the target market.
- Answer specific questions about your target market that are directly related to your products or services.
- If your product or service is marketed to businesses, describe the target market in terms of industry, product and/or service, geographic location, years in business, revenue, number of employees, and buying motivations.
- Describe how you analyzed your target market.
- Provide visualizations of demographic, geographic, and psychographic data (charts, graphs, tables).

TARGET MARKET PROJECTIONS

- Describe the proportion of the target market that has used a product or service like the company's product or service before.
- Project how much of the product or service the target market will buy (gross sales and/or unit sales).

MARKET TRENDS AND GROWTH

- Describe current trends and trends that have been forecast to occur within the target market.
- Describe the historical growth, current market size, and the growth potential of the market.
- Provide visualizations of market trend statistics (charts, graphs, tables).

CUSTOMER NEEDS ANALYSIS

- Conduct market research to uncover customers' wants and needs and to survey their impressions of the business and its promotions.
- Use the market research results to write a customer needs analysis that interprets and prioritizes the needs of the business's current and future customers.
- Prepare a visualization that presents highlights from the results of your customer needs analysis.
- Explain how the company will meet the target market's needs.

COMPETITIVE ANALYSIS

The Competitive Analysis section of the business plan should focus on demonstrating that the proposed business has an advantage over its competitors. You can gather information on competitors by viewing their Web sites; by talking to their customers, vendors, suppliers, and employees; by attending trade shows; and by searching newspaper and magazine databases.

COMPETITIVE OVERVIEW

- Identify, investigate, and analyze your top direct competitors, businesses that are offering identical or similar products or services as your business.
- Identify, investigate, and analyze your top indirect competitors, businesses that are offering products and services that are close substitutes.
- Identify, investigate, and analyze your top future competitors, existing companies that are not yet in the marketplace but could enter the marketplace at any time.
- Explain whether the business will have nonlocal competitors.
- State the locations of your top competitors.
- Describe how long your competitors have been in business.
- Describe the products and services your competitors sell and how much they sell (in units and sales dollars).
- Evaluate your competitors' product selection, product quality, and product availability.
- Describe the markets or market segments your competitors serve.
- Describe the benefits offered by the competition.
- Describe your competitors' images and their level of growth and success.
- Describe your competitors' advertising and promotion strategies and branding, packaging, and labeling strategies.
- Describe your competitors' pricing policies and pricing structures.
- Explain competitors' customer service and after sale service policies.
- Assess your competitors' financial condition and level of debt.
- Evaluate your competitors' equipment and production capacity.
- Outline the strengths and weaknesses of each of your competitors.
- Include charts or pie graphs showing the market share among your competitors as well as trends and changes over time.
- Prepare a grid or table that presents highlights from the results of your competitive analysis.

COMPETITIVE ADVANTAGE

- Describe the competitive advantage of your venture.
- Explain the key assets that your business has and its competitors do not have.
- Differentiate your company's products and services from your competitors' products and services.
- Describe how your business strategies and marketing mix strategies (product, place, price, promotion, and people decisions) will help you to attract and defend market share.
- Explain the percentage of the market the business intends to capture and how the business will achieve this market penetration.

MARKETING PLAN

A Marketing Plan describes a company's marketing mix strategies or how it plans to market, promote, and sell its products or services.

MARKETING MIX STRATEGIES

- Write a marketing plan, including an Internet marketing plan if appropriate, with product, place, price, promotion, and people strategies.
- Describe the marketing mix strategies and explain the message they are meant to convey.
- Describe the company's plan for finding the best market.
- Explain how the marketing mix strategies will be implemented and evaluated for effectiveness.

PRODUCT STRATEGY

- Describe your product, including how it functions, its design, image, appearance, packaging, labeling, warranties, service, and support.
- Describe the product's branding, including brand name(s), brand marks, trade names, trade characters, trademarks, logos, and corporate symbols.

PLACE STRATEGY

- Explain how your product will be made available to customers and where it will be sold.
- Describe channels of distribution and how they will help to foster market penetration.

PRICE STRATEGY

- State your company's pricing objectives and pricing strategy goals.
- Develop a pricing structure that takes into account fixed and variable costs, the competition, company objectives, proposed positioning strategies, the target market, and the consumer's willingness to pay.
- Describe the typical prices in the industry and how your business's prices compare.
- State whether you will accept checks, credit, debit cards, or other forms of payment.

PROMOTION STRATEGY

- Explain the company's promotional goals and promotional messages and how they will appeal to the target market.
- Develop a pre-opening promotional plan to establish a positive image and promote interest.
- Detail the promotions to be used, such as advertising, publicity and public relations, sales promotion, personal selling, direct mail, and e-mail.
- Describe the specific marketing mediums the company will use to deliver the promotional message to the target market. Include how often each will be used, what they will cost, why you chose them, and why they will appeal to the target market.
- Describe the marketing materials you will you need, who will design them, how much they will cost, and how they will be designed to appeal to the target market.
- Describe the sales team, the sales process, and the sales incentives the company will offer.
- Provide your media budget and detail the cost of marketing materials per prospect.
- Provide examples of marketing materials.
- Describe how you will evaluate the effectiveness of promotional strategies.

PEOPLE STRATEGY

- Explain how you will recruit, hire, and train the people and employees who will help you to achieve business success.

OPERATIONAL PLAN

The Operational Plan section of the business plan includes information about all the processes that take place in the business.

LOCATION
- Describe where your business will be located, the number of locations, the zoning, the square footage needed, the layout and type of space, and renovations needed.
- Explain why you chose the location.
- State the average traffic count in front of the outlet.
- Describe any factors that hinder or help accessibility to the business and visibility of the site.
- Describe the businesses near your business's site, including target markets.
- Describe any community sign laws and local parking laws.
- Identify tax rates and state how they compare to other sites you considered.
- Project costs associated with the location.
- Describe how much the business can expand before it will need to relocate.
- Provide a map of the business location and facility layout blueprints.

PROPERTY OWNERSHIP OR LEASE TERMS
- Detail the terms of the lease or purchase of the property.
- Provide a copy of the proposed lease or building space purchase agreement.

EQUIPMENT NEEDS
- Describe and provide blueprints and specifications for the machinery and equipment needed.
- Explain whether you will purchase or lease the equipment.

MANUFACTURING PROCESSES AND COSTS
- Describe the manufacturing process and the technology requirements.
- Assess the manufacturing process in terms of direct and indirect costs.

SUPPLIERS AND PURCHASING
- Outline your key suppliers and the purchasing process.
- Provide copies of purchase orders and letters of intent from suppliers.

STORAGE AND INVENTORY
- Analyze the inventory needed to open and operate the business.
- Describe storage needs, space required, and costs involved.
- Explain inventory control procedures, equipment, and technology.

CHANNELS OF DISTRIBUTION
- Describe the channels of distribution and the associated costs.
- Explain the degree of difficulty in gaining industry distribution access.

QUALITY MEASURES AND SAFETY
- Describe how quality will be measured, controlled, and improved.
- Explain security precautions and health and safety regulations.

ORGANIZATIONAL PLAN

The Organizational Plan offers information about the business's legal structure, methods of and responsibilities for record keeping, and legal and insurance issues. It also covers the people aspects of the business, including staffing and training of personnel, and the organizational structure of the planned business.

LEGAL STRUCTURE

- Describe your legal structure and why it is advantageous for your company.
- Describe any legal agreements governing how owners can exit the company, how the company can be dissolved, how profits will be distributed, and who will have financial responsibility for losses.
- Project future changes in the company's legal structure and how such changes would benefit the company.
- Provide a copy of your partnership agreement if you have formed a partnership.
- Provide a copy of the Articles of Incorporation if the company is formed as a corporation.
- Provide a copy of the franchise contract and supporting materials if the company is a franchise.

RECORD KEEPING

- Describe the accounting system that will be used and why it was chosen.
- Describe what record keeping will be done internally and who will be responsible for keeping internal records.
- Explain when the business will use an outside accountant, such as to finalize monthly/year-end statements.
- Describe who within the company has the expertise to read and analyze the financial statements provided by outside accountants.
- Describe how you will use your financial statements to implement changes to make your company more profitable.

LEGAL AND INSURANCE ISSUES

- Describe any legal considerations that will impact your business, such as legal liability issues, government regulations, environmental regulations, zoning matters, or licensing requirements.
- Identify the insurance company the business will use, the types of insurance the business will need, and the costs involved.

LABOR, STAFFING, AND TRAINING

- Outline human resource policies, including staffing and personnel management procedures.
- Diagram and describe the organizational structure of the business.
- Provide an organizational flowchart.
- Develop a job description for each position on the organizational flowchart, including skill sets needed and salaries offered.
- Describe how many employees the business will have and in what types of positions.
- Outline hours of operation, scheduling policies, and types of shifts worked by employees.
- Complete a work schedule for a typical work week.
- Develop charts or graphs that classify employees by function, skill set, hourly pay, and part-time or full-time status.
- Identify situations where outsourcing should be used for hiring needs.

FINANCIAL PLAN

The Financial Plan presents past and current finances and financial forecasts and explains the assumptions made when calculating forecast figures. It includes the investment proposal and three key financial statements: a cash flow statement, income statement, and balance sheet.

INVESTMENT PROPOSAL

- Describe why you are applying for financing and how you plan to raise and use the money.
- Describe various investment structures and project when investors can expect to earn a profit.
- Identify, categorize, and analyze the start-up costs and fixed and variable operating expenses.
- Project the total cash needed to start the business.
- Include details about revenue streams and prior funding agreements.

EXIT STRATEGY

- Outline the business life cycle and explain your long-term plans for the business.
- Explain how your investors can expect to recoup their investment and earn a sufficient return.
- Define how investors can cash out their investment and achieve liquidity.

CASH FLOW PROJECTION

- Plan a cash budget that forecasts cash inflow (cash revenue from sales) and outflow (cash disbursements) projections for the first year and quarterly or yearly projections for the second and third years.

PROJECTED THREE-YEAR INCOME STATEMENT (PROFIT AND LOSS STATEMENTS)

- Prepare a three-year income projection that includes monthly projections for revenues, expenses, and profits (Revenues – Expenses = Profit or Loss) for the first year and quarterly or yearly projections for the second and third years.

PROJECTED BALANCE SHEET

- Prepare a projected balance sheet (assets, liabilities, and net worth) with quarterly projections for the first year and yearly projections for the second and third years.

BREAK-EVEN ANALYSIS

- Prepare a break-even analysis detailing when the company's expenses will match the income.
- Present the data in a graph format with sales on the X-axis and units sold on the Y-axis.

HISTORICAL FINANCIALS

- Provide cash flow statements, income statements, and balance sheets from the last three years if the company is an existing business.

FINANCIAL ASSUMPTIONS

- State the assumptions on which the financial projections are based.
- Explain how you derived forecasts for sales, costs of goods sold, operating expenses, accounts receivable, collections, accounts payable, inventory, taxes, and other items.
- Disclose whether the financial statements have been audited by a certified public accountant.

FINANCIAL RATIOS

- Calculate liquidity ratios to measure creditworthiness.
- Calculate profitability ratios to show operational performance.
- Calculate turnover ratios to measure changes in certain assets and to expose nonincome-producing assets.

 GROWTH PLAN

Planned growth can be very rewarding, and unplanned growth can be chaotic. The Growth Plan looks at how the business will expand in the future. Investors and lenders like to know that a business has plans to deal with growth in a controlled way.

GROWTH STRATEGIES

- Describe how and when the business owners would like the business to grow.
- Describe the products or services the business will develop to achieve growth.
- Describe the planned growth cycle.
- Describe how the business's growth strategies focus on the business's areas of expertise.
- Describe whether market research will be used to support and justify growth strategy decisions.
- Identify the critical skills that are needed to effectively manage growth.
- Explain how you will evaluate and initiate revisions to growth strategies.

BUSINESS LOCATION ISSUES

- Assess the current business location and how it can accommodate growth.
- Explain if growing the business will mean having to relocate the business to a larger facility.
- Analyze the costs involved in expanding or upgrading current facilities and/or moving to new facilities.
- Evaluate whether the business's lease agreement allows for modifications to the building and facilities.
- Describe alternative affordable premises.
- Explain if and when warehousing and storage facilities will be expanded to accommodate growth.

EFFECTS OF GROWTH

- Explain how planned growth will affect human resource expenses and management and staffing needs.
- Describe how planned growth will affect company goals and objectives.
- Assess if the business's target market will be affected by the growth plan.
- Describe how planned growth will affect technology and equipment needs.
- Describe how planned growth will affect the manufacturing process and costs.
- Explain how planned growth will affect financial control procedures, record keeping policies, and legal and insurance issues.
- Evaluate how planned growth will affect the sales team and sales process.
- Describe how planned growth will affect promotional goals and messages and marketing mix strategies (product, place, price, promotion, and people decisions).

GROWTH FINANCING

- Examine how growth costs will affect the overall financial health of the business in the short term and the long term.
- Evaluate growth financing options and describe the best plan to finance growth.
- Provide visualizations of growth projections (charts, tables, graphs).

CONTINGENCY PLAN

The Contingency Plan examines the assumptions in the business plan and the greatest risks to the business and suggests plans to minimize the risk.

- List and examine the assumptions in the business plan.
- Examine risks that could cause the business to fail.
- Categorize business risks as human, natural, or economic; as speculative, controllable or uncontrollable; and as insurable or uninsurable.
- Identify the most significant risks that the new venture faces and describe plans the business owners have developed to deal with any of the situations should they arise.
- Describe how the company will respond to changes in market conditions caused by demographic shifts, socioeconomic trends, economic events, energy costs, and changes in government policies.
- Explain how the company will anticipate and respond to competitive threats from expected and unexpected sources, price cutting by competitors, and the introduction of new products by competitors.
- Explain how the company will handle cost overruns.
- Outline contingencies to meet staffing challenges and limit problems due to a dependence on key people.
- Describe how the company will respond if projected sales and revenue targets are not achieved.
- Describe the company's contingency plan in case of a major accident, event, or disaster that interrupts cash flow.
- Explain how the company will respond to product liability lawsuits.

EXECUTIVE SUMMARY

The Executive Summary recounts the key points in the business plan. It is written last because it summarizes the most important information from the business plan. Investors rely on it to decide if the business concept interests them. The executive summary should be just two pages long, and it should answer who, what, where, why, when, and how.

- Describe the company's mission, goals, objectives, current stage of development, owners, and key management team members.
- Describe the company, business model, legal structure, industry, product or service, target market, and the unique opportunity.
- Include evidence that justifies the soundness and future success of the opportunity.
- Describe the strategies the company will use to beat the competition.
- Include financial highlights such as:
  - The investment you are seeking
  - How much equity you would be willing to transfer
  - Collateral offered
  - How the funds will be used
  - How and when any loans will be repaid
  - Three-year projections of sales
  - Estimated annual after-tax profits

⚙ COVER PAGE

Every business plan should have a Cover Page. It is the first page the investor sees when he or she reads the business plan. Include this information:

* The company name, address, phone number, Web site address, e-mail address, and company logo

⚙ TITLE PAGE

The page following the cover page is the Title Page. It includes this basic information about the business and the business plan:

* The company name
* The names, titles, and addresses of the owners
* The date the business plan was issued
* The name of the person who prepared the business plan

⚙ TABLE OF CONTENTS

The Table of Contents details the components of the business plan and the page numbers where they can be found within the business plan. Include this information in the Table of Contents:

* The titles of the major sections and subsections of the business plan
* The page number where each section and subsection is located

⚙ SUPPORTING DOCUMENTS

The Supporting Documents section of the business plan includes items, exhibits, and documentation relevant to the business. Include these items:

* Copies of the owners' résumés, personal financial statements, and tax returns
* For franchised businesses, a copy of franchise contract
* For franchised businesses, all supporting documents provided by the franchisor
* For partnerships, a copy of the partnership agreement
* For corporations, a copy of the Articles of Incorporation
* Photos, blueprints, and detailed specifications of products
* An organizational blueprint
* Photos and blueprints of the layout of the business's facilities
* Photos, blueprints, and detailed specifications for all equipment and machinery
* A map of the business location
* Copy of proposed lease or purchase agreement for building space
* Copy of contracts, licenses, and other legal documents
* Copies of purchase orders and letters of intent from suppliers
* Business cards
* Market research highlights
* Marketing materials
* Press releases
* Visualizations of industry data, demographic data, and market trend statistics

MAKING CAREER CHOICES

A career differs from a job in that it is a series of progressively more responsible jobs in one field or a related field. You will need to learn some special skills to choose a career and to help you in your job search. Choosing a career and identifying career opportunities require careful thought and preparation. To aid you in making important career choices, follow these steps:

STEPS TO MAKING A CAREER DECISION

1. Conduct a self-assessment to determine your:
   - values
   - lifestyle goals
   - interests
   - skills and aptitudes
   - personality
   - work environment preferences
   - relationship preferences

2. Identify possible career choices based on your self-assessment.

3. Gather information on each choice, including future trends.

4. Evaluate your choices based on your self-assessment.

5. Make your decision.

After you make your decision, plan how you will reach your goal. It is best to have short-term, medium-term, and long-term goals. In making your choices, explore the future opportunities in this field or fields over the next several years. What impact will new technology and automation have on job opportunities in the next few years? Remember, if you plan, you make your own career opportunities.

PERSONAL CAREER PORTFOLIO

You will want to create and maintain a personal career portfolio. In it you will keep all the documents you create and receive in your job search:

- Contact list
- Résumé
- Letters of recommendation
- Employer evaluations
- Awards
- Evidence of participation in school, community, and volunteer activities
- Notes about your job search
- Notes made after your interviews

CAREER RESEARCH RESOURCES

In order to gather information on various career opportunities, there are a variety of sources to research.

- **Libraries.** Your school or public library offers good career information resources. Here you will find books, magazines, pamphlets, films, videos, and special reference material on careers. In particular, the U.S. Department of Labor publishes three reference books that are especially helpful: the *Dictionary of Occupational Titles (DOT),* which describes about 20,000 jobs and their relationships with data, people, and things; the *Occupational Outlook Handbook (OOH),* with information on more than 200 occupations; and the *Guide for Occupational Exploration (GOE),* a reference that organizes the world of work into 12 interest areas that are subdivided into work groups and subgroups.
- **The Internet.** The Internet is becoming a primary source of research on any topic. It is especially helpful in researching careers.
- **Career Consultations.** Career consultation, an informational interview with a professional who works in a career that interests you, provides an opportunity to learn about the day-to-day realities of a career.
- **On-the-Job Experience.** On-the-job experience can be valuable in learning firsthand about a job or career. You can find out if your school has a work-experience program, or look into a company or organization's internship opportunities. Interning gives you direct work experience and often allows you to make valuable contacts for future full-time employment.

THE JOB SEARCH

To aid you in your actual job search, there are various sources to explore. You should contact and research all the sources that might produce a job lead, information about a job. Keep a contact list as you proceed with your search. Some of these resources include:

- **Networking with family, friends, and acquaintances.** This means contacting people you know personally, including school counselors, former employers, and professional people.
- **Cooperative education and work-experience programs.** Many schools have such programs in which students work part-time on a job related to one of their classes. Many also offer work-experience programs that are not limited to just one career area, such as marketing.
- **Newspaper ads.** Reading the Help Wanted advertisements in your local papers will provide a source of job leads, as well as teaching you about the local job market.
- **Employment agencies.** Most cities have two types of employment agencies, public and private. These employment agencies match workers with jobs. Some private agencies may charge a fee, so be sure to know who is expected to pay the fee and what the fee is.
- **Company personnel offices.** Large and medium-sized companies have personnel offices to handle employment matters, including the hiring of new workers. You can check on job openings by contacting the office by telephone or by scheduling a personal visit.
- **Searching the Internet.** Cyberspace offers multiple opportunities in your job searching. Web sites, such as Hotjobs.com or Monster.com provide lists of companies offering employment. There are tens of thousands of career-related Web sites, so the challenge is finding those that have jobs that interest you and that are up-to-date in their listings. Companies that interest you may have a Web site, which will provide valuable information on their benefits and opportunities for employment.

APPLYING FOR A JOB

When you have contacted the sources of job leads and found some jobs that interest you, the next step is to apply for them. You will need to complete application forms, write letters of application, and prepare your own résumé. Before you apply for a job, you will need to have a work permit if you are under the age of 18 in most states. Some state and federal labor laws designate certain jobs as too dangerous for young workers. Laws also limit the number of hours of work allowed during a day, a week, or the school year. You will also need to have proper documentation, such as a green card if you are not a U.S. citizen.

JOB APPLICATION

You can obtain the job application form directly at the place of business, by requesting it in writing, or over the Internet. It is best if you can fill the form out at home, but some businesses require that you fill it out at the place of work.

Fill out the job application forms neatly and accurately, using standard English, the formal style of speaking and writing you learned in school. You must be truthful and pay attention to detail in filling out the form.

PERSONAL FACT SHEET

To be sure that the answers you write on a job application form are accurate, make a personal fact sheet before filling out the application.

- Your name, home address, and phone number
- Your Social Security number
- The job you are applying for
- The date you can begin work
- The days and hours you can work
- The pay you want
- Whether or not you have been convicted of a crime
- Your education
- Your previous work experience
- Your birth date
- Your driver's license number if you have one
- Your interests and hobbies, and awards you have won
- Your previous work experience, including dates
- Schools you have attended
- Places you have lived
- Accommodations you may need from the employer
- A list of references—people who will tell an employer that you will do a good job, such as relatives, students, former employers, and the like

LETTERS OF RECOMMENDATION

Letters of recommendation are helpful. You can request teachers, counselors, relatives, and other acquaintances who know you well to write these letters. They should be short, to the point, and give a brief overview of your assets. A brief description of any of your important accomplishments or projects should follow. The letter should end with a brief description of your character and work ethic.

LETTER OF APPLICATION

Some employees prefer a letter of application, rather than an application form. This letter is like writing a sales pitch about yourself. You need to tell why you are the best person for the job, what special qualifications you have, and include all the information usually found on an application form. Write the letter in standard English, making certain that it is neat, accurate, and correct.

RÉSUMÉ

The purpose of a résumé is to make an employer want to interview you. A résumé tells prospective employers what you are like and what you can do for them. A good résumé summarizes you at your best in a one- or two-page outline. It should include the following information:

1. **Identification.** Include your name, address, telephone number, and e-mail address.

2. **Objective.** Indicate the type of job you are looking for.

3. **Experience.** List experience related to the specific job for which you are applying. List also other work if you have not worked in a related field.

4. **Education.** Include schools attended from high school on, the dates of attendance, and diplomas or degrees earned. You may also include courses related to the job you are applying for.

5. **References.** Include up to three references or indicate that they are available. Always ask people ahead of time if they are willing to be listed as references for you.

A résumé that you put online or send by e-mail is called an *electronic résumé*. Some Web sites allow you to post them on their sites without charge. Employers access these sites to find new employees. Your electronic resume should follow the guidelines for a regular one. It needs to be accurate. Stress your skills and sell yourself to prospective employers.

COVER LETTER

If you are going to get the job you want, you need to write a great cover letter to accompany your résumé. Think of a cover letter as an introduction: a piece of paper that conveys a smile, a confident hello, and a nice, firm handshake. The cover letter is the first thing a potential employer sees, and it can make a powerful impression. The following are some tips for creating a cover letter that is professional and gets the attention you want.

- **Keep It Short.** Your cover letter should be one page, no more.
- **Make It Look Professional.** These days, you need to type your letter on a computer and print it on a laser printer. Do not use an inkjet printer unless it produces extremely crisp type. Use white or buff-colored paper; anything else will draw the wrong kind of attention. Type your name, address, phone number, and e-mail address at the top of the page.
- **Explain Why You Are Writing.** Start your letter with one sentence describing where you heard of the opening. "Joan Wright suggested I contact you regarding a position in your marketing department" Or, "I am writing to apply for the position you advertised in the Sun City Journal."
- **Introduce Yourself.** Give a short description of your professional abilities and background. Refer to your attached résumé: "As you will see in the attached résumé, I am an experienced editor with a background in newspapers, magazines, and textbooks." Then highlight one or two specific accomplishments.

- **Sell Yourself.** Your cover letter should leave the reader thinking, "This person is exactly what we are looking for." Focus on what you can do for the company. Relate your skills to the skills and responsibilities mentioned in the job listing. If the ad mentions solving problems, relate a problem you solved at school or work. If the ad mentions specific skills or knowledge required, mention your mastery of these in your letter. (Also be sure these skills are included on your résumé.)

- **Provide All Requested Information.** If the help wanted ad asked for "salary requirements" or "salary history," include this information in your cover letter. However, you do not have to give specific numbers. It is okay to say, "My wage is in the range of $10 to $15 per hour." If the employer does not ask for salary information, do not offer any.

- **Ask for an Interview.** You have sold yourself, now wrap it up. Be confident, but not pushy. "If you agree that I would be an asset to your company, please call me at [insert your phone number]. I am available for an interview at your convenience." Finally, thank the person. "Thank you for your consideration. I look forward to hearing from you soon." Always close with a "Sincerely," followed by your full name and signature.

- **Check for Errors.** Read and re-read your letter to make sure each sentence is correctly worded and there are no errors of spelling, punctuation, or grammar. Do not rely on your computer's spell checker or grammar checker. A spell check will not detect if you typed "tot he" instead of "to the." It is a good idea to have someone else read your letter, too. He or she might notice an error you overlooked.

INTERVIEW

Understanding how to best prepare for and follow up on interviews is critical to your career success. At different times in your life, you may interview with a teacher or professor, a prospective employer, a supervisor, or a promotion or tenure committee. Just as having an excellent résumé is vital for opening the door, interviewing skills are critical for putting your best foot forward and seizing the opportunity to clearly articulate why you are the best person for the job.

RESEARCH THE COMPANY

Your ability to convince an employer that you understand and are interested in the field you are interviewing to enter is important. Show that you have knowledge about the company and the industry. What products or services does the company offer? How is it doing? What is the competition? Use your research to demonstrate your understanding of the company.

PREPARE QUESTIONS FOR THE INTERVIEWER

Prepare interview questions to ask the interviewer. Some examples include:

- "What would my responsibilities be?"
- "Could you describe my work environment?"
- "What are the chances to move up in the company?"
- "Do you offer training?"
- "What can you tell me about the people who work here?"

DRESS APPROPRIATELY

You will never get a second chance to make a good first impression. Nonverbal communication is 90 percent of communication, so dressing appropriately is of the utmost importance. Every job is different, and you should wear clothing that is appropriate for the job for which you are applying. In most situations, you will be safe if you wear clean, pressed, conservative business clothes in neutral colors. Pay special attention to grooming. Keep makeup light and wear very little jewelry.

Make certain your nails and hair are clean, trimmed, and neat. Do not carry a large purse, backpack, books, or coat. Simply carry a pad of paper, a pen, and extra copies of your résumé and letters of reference in a small folder.

EXHIBIT GOOD BEHAVIOR

Conduct yourself properly during an interview. Go alone; be courteous and polite to everyone you meet. Relax and focus on your purpose: to make the best possible impression.

- Be on time.
- Be poised and relaxed.
- Avoid nervous habits.
- Avoid littering your speech with verbal clutter such as "you know," "um," and "like."
- Look your interviewer in the eye and speak with confidence.
- Use nonverbal techniques to reinforce your confidence, such as a firm handshake and poised demeanor.
- Convey maturity by exhibiting the ability to tolerate differences of opinion.
- Never call anyone by a first name unless you are asked to do so.
- Know the name, title, and the pronunciation of the interviewer's name.
- Do not sit down until the interviewer does.
- Do not talk too much about your personal life.
- Never bad-mouth your former employers.

BE PREPARED FOR COMMON INTERVIEW QUESTIONS

You can never be sure exactly what will happen at an interview, but you can be prepared for common interview questions. There are some interview questions that are illegal. Interviewers should not ask you about your age, gender, color, race, or religion. Employers should not ask whether you are married or pregnant or question your health or disabilities.

Take time to think about your answers now. You might even write them down to clarify your thinking. The key to all interview questions is to be honest, and to be positive. Focus your answers on skills and abilities that apply to the job you are seeking. Practice answering the following questions with a friend:

- "Tell me about yourself."
- "Why do you want to work at this company?"
- "What did you like/dislike about your last job?"
- "What is your biggest accomplishment?"
- "What is your greatest strength?"
- "What is your greatest weakness?"
- "Do you prefer to work with others or on your own?"
- "What are your career goals?" or "Where do you see yourself in five years?"
- "Tell me about a time that you had a lot of work to do in a short time. How did you manage the situation?"
- "Have you ever had to work closely with a person you didn't get along with? How did you handle the situation?"

Career Skills

AFTER THE INTERVIEW

Be sure to thank the interviewer after the interview for his or her time and effort. Do not forget to follow up after the interview. Ask, "What is the next step?" If you are told to call in a few days, wait two or three days before calling back.

If the interview went well, the employer may call you to offer you the job. Find out the terms of the job offer, including job title and pay. Decide whether you want the job. If you decide not to accept the job, write a letter of rejection. Be courteous and thank the person for the opportunity and the offer. You may wish to give a brief general reason for not accepting the job. Leave the door open for possible employment in the future.

FOLLOW UP WITH A LETTER

Write a thank-you letter as soon as the interview is over. This shows your good manners, interest, and enthusiasm for the job. It also shows that you are organized. Make the letter neat and courteous. Thank the interviewer. Sell yourself again.

ACCEPTING A NEW JOB

If you decide to take the job, write a letter of acceptance. The letter should include some words of appreciation for the opportunity, written acceptance of the job offer, the terms of employment (salary, hours, benefits), and the starting date. Make sure the letter is neat and correct.

STARTING A NEW JOB

Your first day of work will be busy. Determine what the dress code is and dress appropriately. Learn to do each task assigned properly. Ask for help when you need it. Learn the rules and regulations of the workplace.

You will do some paperwork on your first day. Bring your personal fact sheet with you. You will need to fill out some forms. Form W-4 tells your employer how much money to withhold for taxes. You may also need to fill out Form I-9. This shows that you are allowed to work in the United States. You will need your Social Security number and proof that you are allowed to work in the United States. You can bring your U.S. passport, your Certificate of Naturalization, or your Certificate of U.S. Citizenship. If you are not a permanent resident of the United States, bring your green card. If you are a resident of the United States, you will need to bring your work permit on your first day. If you are under the age of 16 in some states, you need a different kind of work permit.

You might be requested to take a drug test as a requirement for employment in some states. This could be for the safety of you and your coworkers, especially when working with machinery or other equipment.

IMPORTANT SKILLS AND QUALITIES

You will not work alone on a job. You will need to learn skills for getting along and being a team player. There are many good qualities necessary to get along in the workplace. They include being positive, showing sympathy, taking an interest in others, tolerating differences, laughing a little, and showing respect. Your employer may promote you or give you a raise if you show good employability skills.

There are several qualities necessary to be a good employee and get ahead in your job.

- being cooperative
- possessing good character
- being responsible
- finishing what you start
- working fast but doing a good job
- having a strong work ethic
- working well without supervision
- working well with others
- possessing initiative
- showing enthusiasm for what you do
- being on time
- making the best of your time
- obeying company laws and rules
- honesty
- loyalty
- exhibiting good health habits

LEAVING A JOB

If you are considering leaving your job or are being laid off, you are facing one of the most difficult aspects in your career. The first step in resigning is to prepare a short resignation letter to offer your supervisor at the conclusion of the meeting you set up with him or her. Keep the letter short and to the point. Express your appreciation for the opportunity you had with the company. Do not try to list all that was wrong with the job.

You want to leave on good terms. Do not forget to ask for a reference. Do not talk about your employer or any of your coworkers. Do not talk negatively about your employer when you apply for a new job.

If you are being laid off or face downsizing, it can make you feel angry or depressed. Try to view it as a career-change opportunity. If possible, negotiate a good severance package. Find out about any benefits you may be entitled to. Perhaps the company will offer job-search services or consultation for finding new employment.

TAKE ACTION!

It is time for action. Remember the networking and contact lists you created when you searched for this job. Reach out for support from friends, family, and other acquaintances. Consider joining a job-search club. Assess your skills. Upgrade them if necessary. Examine your attitude and your vocational choices. Decide the direction you wish to take and move on!

Glossary

A

accessible The capability of a Web site that allows all types of people to access and use the site's content. (p. 529)

accounting period A block of time, such as a month, a quarter, or a year, covered by an accounting report. (p. 429)

accounts payable The amount a business owes to creditors. (p. 430)

accounts receivable The amount customers owe a business. (p. 430)

accrual basis An accounting system in which income is recorded when it is earned, and expenses are recorded when they are paid. (p. 432)

achiever A person with a record of success. (p. 37)

advertising agency A company that acts as intermediary between a business and the media to communicate a message to the target market. (p. 269)

advertising The paid nonpersonal presentation of ideas, goods, or services directed at a mass audience by an identified sponsor by means of print and broadcast. (p. 258)

affiliate program An online marketing agreement in which member Web sites drive targeted traffic to an e-commerce merchant in return for a commission on the sales generated at the merchant site. (p. 447)

angel A private, nonprofessional investor, such as a friend, a relative, or a business associate, who funds start-up companies. (p. 409)

appointments The furniture, equipment, and accessories contained in a building. (p. 195)

approach A salesperson's first contact with a customer. (p. 284)

asset Anything of value that a business owns, such as cash, equipment, or a building. (p. 430)

automation The use of machines to do the work of people. (p. 353)

B

B2B community An electronic marketplace where companies can bid on products and services or offer their services up for bid. (p. 341)

B2B e-commerce Ventures that sell products and services to other businesses. (p. 67)

B2B exchanges Electronic forums where businesses trade goods and services. (p. 67)

B2C e-commerce Ventures where businesses sell directly to the consumer. (p. 67)

bait and switch A deceptive and illegal method of selling in which a customer, attracted to a store by an advertised sale, is told either that the advertised item is unavailable or is inferior to a higher-priced item that is available. (p. 169, 233)

balance sheet A report of the final balances of all asset, liability, and owner's equity accounts at the end of an accounting period. (p. 438)

banner swapping A form of exchanging online advertising in which sites post banner ads for each other. (p. 447)

barriers to entry A condition or circumstance that makes it difficult or costly for outside firms to enter a market to compete with established firm or firms. (p. 125)

benefits Any extra compensation that workers receive on a job, such as paid vacation and sick days, flextime, and child care. (p. 374)

benefit Something that promotes or enhances the value of a product or a service to the customer. (p. 95)

"best prospect" list A list compiled by the government of products that other countries are looking to purchase. (p. 79)

bootstrapping Operating a business as frugally as possible and cutting all unnecessary expenses, such as borrowing, leasing, and partnering to acquire resources. (p. 407)

brainstorm To think freely in order to generate ideas. (p. 51)

brand The name, symbol, or design used to identify a product. (p. 208)

brand loyalty The tendency to buy a particular brand of a product. (p. 125)

break-even point The point at which the gain from an economic activity equals the costs involved in pursuing it. (p. 241)

bribe A payment made to secure special services for a business or special consideration for its products; illegal in the United States, it is accepted in some other parts of the world as a part of doing business. (p. 524)

budget A formal, written statement of expected revenue and expenses for a future period of time. (p. 459)

bulletin board service (BBS) A Web-based service that allows users to leave and access messages and access other electronic files. (p. 511)

bundle pricing A pricing technique in which several complementary products are sold at a single price, which is lower than the price would be if each item was purchased separately. (p. 238)

burglary The act of breaking into and entering a building with the intent to commit a felony (a serious crime). (p. 478)

business broker Someone whose job it is to bring buyers and sellers of businesses together for a fee. (p. 61)

business concept A clear and concise description of a business opportunity. It contains four elements: the product or service, the customer, the benefit, and the distribution. (p. 94)

business cycle The general pattern of expansion and contraction that the economy goes through. (p. 15)

business ethics The study of behavior and morals in a business situation. (p. 521)

business failure A business that has stopped operating, with a loss to creditors, and one that no longer appears on the tax rolls. (p. 21)

business interruption insurance Insurance coverage against potential losses that result from having to close a business for insurable reasons; insurance pays net profits and expenses while a business is shut down for repairs or rebuilding. (p. 485)

business model A description of how entrepreneurs plan to make money with their business concepts. (p. 99)

business plan A document that describes a new business and a strategy to launch that business. (p. 100)

buying process A series of steps a customer goes through when making a purchase. (p. 283)

calendar year The accounting period of time from January 1 to December 31. (p. 429)

campaign A series of related promotional activities with a similar theme. (p. 256)

capacity A borrower's ability to repay a debt as judged by lenders. (p. 366, 416) The legal ability to enter into a binding agreement. (p. 159)

capital The buildings, equipment, tools, and other goods needed to produce a product or the money used to buy these items. (p. 31) The net worth of a business, the amount by which its assets exceed its liabilities. (p. 416) The overall assets of an individual or a business. (p. 366)

capital expenditure A long-term commitment of a large sum of money to buy new equipment or replace old equipment. (p. 462)

carrying capacity The ability of industry to support new growth. (p. 117)

cascading style sheets (CSS) A feature of HTML that gives users more control over how Web pages are displayed. (p. 529)

cash basis An accounting system in which income is recorded when it is received, and expenses are recorded when they are paid. (p. 432)

cash discount An amount deducted from the selling price for payment within a specified time period. (p. 327)

cash flow The amount of cash available to a business at any given time. (p. 440)

casualty insurance Insurance coverage for loss or liability arising from a sudden, unexpected event such as an accident and for the cost of defending a business in court against claims of property damage. (p. 485)

C-corporation An entity that pays taxes on earnings; its shareholders pay taxes as well. (p. 142)

census tract A small geographic area into which a state or country is divided for the purpose of gathering and reporting census data (p. 180)

channel of distribution The path a product takes from producer or manufacturer to final user or consumer. (p. 210)

character A borrower's reputation for fair and ethical practices, including business experience, dealings with other businesses, and reputation in the community. (p. 366, 416)

chart of accounts The list of accounts a business uses in its operation. (p. 431)

clicks and mortar A business that operates both a traditional physical storefront and an online store. (p. 67)

climate The prevailing atmosphere or attitude in a business. (p. 311)

Glossary

code of ethics A group of ethical behavior guidelines that govern the day-to-day activities of a profession or organization. (p. 522)

collateral Security in the form of assets that a company pledges to a lender. (p. 416)

commission A fee for services rendered based on a percentage of an amount sold; payment is based on sales alone. (p. 291) A means of compensation based on percentage of sales. (p. 374)

common carrier A firm that provides transportation services at uniform rates to the general public. (p. 354)

communication The process of exchanging information. (p. 312)

comparative financial statement A financial statement with financial data from two accounting periods used as an analysis tool by a business owner. (p. 451)

competition The rivalry among businesses for consumer dollars. (p. 30)

competitive advantage A feature that makes a product more desirable than its competitors. (p. 126)

competitive grid A tool for organizing important information about a business venture's competition. (p. 98)

complexity The number and diversity of contacts with which you must deal. In business, firms that operate in complex industries have more suppliers, customers, and competitors than firms in other industries. (p. 117)

conceptual skill A skill that enables a manager to understand concepts, ideas, and principles. (p. 316)

conditions The circumstances at the time of the loan request, including potential for growth, amount of competition, location, form of ownership, and insurance. (p. 416)

confidentiality notice A statement sent along with an electronic message that says that the message is only for the eyes of the intended recipient. (p. 511)

conflict of interest A clash between a person's private interests and his or her responsibilities in a position of trust. (p. 523)

conglomerate diversification A diversification growth strategy in which a business seeks products or businesses that are totally unrelated to its own products or business. (p. 502)

consideration What is exchanged for the promise to do something or refrain from doing something and causes a contract to be binding. (p. 159)

consumer pretest A procedure in which a panel of consumers evaluate an ad before its release. (p. 269)

content The text and graphic information contained in a Web site. (p. 175)

contingency fund An extra amount of money that is saved and used only when absolutely necessary, such as for unforeseen business expenses. (p. 421)

contract A binding legal agreement between two or more persons or parties. (p. 159)

contract carrier A shipping company that transports freight under contract with one or more shippers. (p. 354)

controlling The process of comparing expected results (objectives) with actual performance. (p. 310)

cookie A file sent to a Web browser by a Web server that is used to record and store information for later use. (p. 275)

cooperative advertising An arrangement in which advertising costs are divided between two or more parties. (p. 268)

copyright A legal device that protects original works of authors, including books, movies, musical compositions, and computer software, for the life of the author plus 70 years. (p. 156)

corporate venture A new venture started inside a larger corporation. (p. 49)

corporation A business that is registered by a state and operates apart from its owners. It issues shares of stock and lives on after the owners have sold their interest or passed away. Corporations can purchase goods and services, sue and be sued, and conduct all types of business transactions. (p. 142)

cost effective Economically worthwhile in terms of what is achieved for the amount of money spent. (p. 386)

country code top-level domain (ccTLD) The part of the TLD that indicates the country of the Internet address, such as .us for United States and .fr for France. (p. 133)

crawler A program used to compile information about Web sites. (p. 399)

credit An arrangement for deferred payment for goods and services; credit allows a business or individual to obtain products in exchange for a promise to pay later. (p. 364) An addition to the right side of an account that decreases the balance for all assets and expense accounts and increases the balance for all liability and revenue accounts. (p. 432)

credit bureau An agency that collects information for a fee on how promptly people and businesses pay their bills. (p. 464)

current asset Cash or any other item that can be converted to cash quickly and used by a business within a year. (p. 430)

current ratio The comparison of current assets (cash or other items that can be converted to cash quickly) and current liabilities (debts due within a year), used to indicate the ability of a business to pay its bills. (p. 452)

customer benefit An advantage of personal satisfaction that a customer will get from a product. (p. 282)

customer needs analysis A study that pinpoints the features and benefits of goods or services that customers value. (p. 128)

customer profile A complete picture of a venture's prospective customers, including geographic, demographic, and psychographic data. (p. 128)

cybermediary A business that acts as a broker or agent to facilitate transactions over the Internet. (p. 359)

data mining tools Software programs that statistically analyze data to identify patterns, trends, and relationships within data; used in e-commerce to understand consumer behavior. (p. 493)

debit An addition to the left side of an account that increases the balance of all assets and expense accounts and decreases the balance of all liability and revenue accounts. (p. 432)

debit card A card issued by a financial institution that can be used as an alternative to cash; purchase amounts on a debit card are withdrawn directly from the purchaser's checking or savings account. (p. 251)

debt capital Money raised by taking out loans, which must be repaid with interest. (p. 409)

debt ratio The measurement of the percentage of total dollars in a business that is provided by creditors. (p. 454)

decryption The process of converting from code into readable text. (p. 469)

demand The quantity of goods or services that consumers are willing and able to buy at various prices. (p. 11)

demographics Personal characteristics that describe a population by age, gender, income, ethnic background, education, and occupation, among others. (p. 52)

descriptive research The collection of information to determine the status of something, such as in developing a customer profile. The information may include age, gender, occupation, income, and buying habits and can be collected through questionnaires, interviews, or observations. (p. 120)

development activity An action, such as an industry conference, that prepares managers to lead the company into the future. (p. 385)

digital certificate An e-commerce security feature that establishes the certificate holder's identity and that proves companies are who they say they are. (p. 469)

digital signature A method of authenticating digital information. (p. 469)

diminishing marginal utility The effect or law that establishes that price alone does not determine demand, and other factors, such as income, taste, and the amount of product already owned, play a role as well. (p. 13)

direct channel The means of delivering a service or product directly to the customer, such as via a Web site. (p. 104)

direct insurance writer An insurance agent who works for one particular insurance company, such as life and automobile companies. (p. 488)

directing The process of guiding and supervising employees, often one-on-one, while they work. (p. 310)

Glossary

discontinuance A business that disappears from the tax rolls because it may be operating under a new name or because the owner has purposely discontinued in order to start a new business. (p. 21)

discount pricing A pricing technique that offers customers reductions from the regular price; some reductions are basic percentage-off discounts and others are specialized discounts. (p. 239)

disintermediation The removal of intermediaries, such as wholesalers or retailers, from business transactions between producers and consumers. (p. 359)

disposable income Money people have to spend after paying for necessary expenses. (p. 80)

distribution channel The means by which a product or service is delivered to the customer. (p. 104)

diversification The process of investing in products or businesses with which an existing business is not currently involved. (p. 223)

diversification growth strategy A growth strategy that involves investing in products or businesses that are different from a company's own products, using synergistic, horizontal, or conglomerate diversification. (p. 500)

domain name The name that identifies the numeric IP address. (p. 43)

domain name extension The letters contained in each URL that tells the user what type of organization uses the address, such as commercial (.com), education (.edu), or governmental (.gov). (p. 43)

double opt-in list An online opt-in mailing list with a two-step confirmation process; subscribers must confirm their registration by responding to an e-mail message. (p. 299)

due diligence The investigation and analysis a prudent investor does before making business decisions. (p. 417)

e-business A company that does business over an electronic network, such as making sales calls on the telephone or providing electronic bill payment services. (p. 25)

e-cash A legal form of electronic money transfer used in e-commerce and transacted via the Internet, such as Paypal. (p. 251)

e-commerce The act of selling products and services over the Internet. (p. 25)

economic base The major industries that provide employment in an area. (p. 179)

economics The study of how people allocate scarce resources to fulfill their unlimited wants. (p. 7)

economy of scale A situation where the cost of producing one unit of a good or service decreases as the volume of production increases; the decrease of production costs relative to the price of goods and services. (p. 125)

educational activity An action, such as a human relations workshop, that prepares employees for advancing in the organization. (p. 385)

elastic demand Situations in which a change in price creates a change in demand. (p. 13)

electronic credit authorizer A machine that verifies whether a credit card is good, that is, not stolen or invalid. (p. 480)

e-mail Mail that is electronically transmitted by a computer. (p. 511)

e-meeting A meeting that takes place online or via a telephone conference call. (p. 321)

emotional buying motive A feeling a buyer associates with a product, such as recognition or prestige. (p. 281)

employee complaint procedure A formal procedure for handling employee complaints, usually in writing and distributed to employees. (p. 387)

employee stock option plan (ESOP) A source of financing in which a company gives its employees the opportunity to buy a portion of the business; to raise money with an ESOP, a business must have at least 25 employees and revenues of $5 million. (p. 507)

encryption The process of converting a text message into code. (p. 469)

enterprise zones Specially designated areas of a community that provide tax benefits to new businesses locating there; communities may also provide grants for new product development. (p. 19)

entrepreneur An individual who undertakes the creation, organization, and ownership of a business. (p. 6)

entrepreneurial Acting like an entrepreneur or having an entrepreneurial mind-set. (p. 7)

entrepreneurship The process of recognizing an opportunity, testing it in the market, and gathering resources necessary to go into business. (p. 7)

Environmental Protection Agency (EPA) An independent federal agency established to coordinate programs and enforce regulations aimed at reducing pollution and protecting the environment. (p. 516)

e-procurement The business-to-business purchase and sale of supplies and services over the Internet. (p. 341)

Equal Employment Opportunity Commission (EEOC) The government agency charged with protecting the rights of employees; it ensures that employers do not discriminate against employees because of age, race, color or natural origin, religion, gender, or physical challenge. (p. 162)

equilibrium The point at which consumers buy all of a product that is supplied. At this point, there is neither a surplus nor a shortage. (p. 13)

equity An ownership in a business. (p. 408)

equity capital Cash raised for a business in exchange for an ownership stake in the business. (p. 408)

errors-and-omissions insurance Insurance coverage for any loss sustained because of an error or oversight on a business's part, such as a mistake in advertising. (p. 486)

e-tailing Selling on the Internet; the word is derived from the word *retailing.* (p. 67)

ethical behavior Conduct that adheres to the moral code by which people live and conduct business. (p. 520)

ethics Guidelines for human behavior; the moral code by which people live and conduct business. (p. 520)

e-wallet A software application used across a variety of Web sites that stores a customer's data, such as name, address, and credit card number, for easy retrieval during online purchases. (p. 251)

exchange rate The rate at which one currency is converted into another. (p. 87)

exclusive distribution Placement of a product where its number of sales outlets are limited to one per area. (p. 211)

executive summary A brief recounting of the key points contained in a business plan. (p. 102)

exploratory research The initial collection and analysis of information used when very little is known about a subject; it forms a foundation for later research. (p. 120)

export management company An organization that handles all the tasks related to exporting for a manufacturer. (p. 81)

exporting The selling and shipping of goods to other countries. (p. 70)

facade The face or front of a building. (p. 194)

factor An agent who handles an entrepreneur's accounts receivable for a fee. (p. 407)

factors of production The resources businesses use to produce the goods and services that people want. (p. 11)

family leave A policy that allows employees to take time off work to attend to significant personal events, such a births, deaths, and family illness, without fear of job loss. (p. 393)

feasibility analysis The process that tests a business concept; it allows the entrepreneur to decide whether a new business concept has potential. (p. 96)

feature A distinctive aspect, quality, or characteristic of a product or service. (p. 95)

FICA (Federal Insurance Contributions Act) A Social Security payroll tax, figured as a percentage of an employee's income; an employer is required to contribute an amount equal to the amount deducted from each employee's paycheck. (p. 169)

fidelity bond A form of insurance that protects a company in case of employee theft. (p. 486)

financial report A statement or document that summarizes the results of a business operation and provides a picture of its financial position. (p. 429)

financing cost The cost of interest paid to borrow money. (p. 330)

fiscal year The accounting period of time that begins and ends in months other than the calendar year. (p. 429)

Glossary

fixed Costs and expenses that are not subject to change depending on the number of units sold. (p. 230)

fixed asset Any item that will be held by a business for more than one year, such as equipment, a truck, or a building. (p. 430)

fixed expense A business expense that does not change with number of units produced, such as insurance and rent. (p. 459)

flame A nasty or insulting e-mail. (p. 511)

flextime A policy that allows employees to choose the work hours and days that are most effective for their personal lives. (p. 393)

focus group A group of people whose opinions are studied to determine the opinions that can be expected from a larger population. (p. 120)

foreign joint venture An alliance between an American small business and a company in another nation. (p. 81)

foundation skills The skills used in all jobs and when setting up and running a business. (p. 35)

franchise A legal agreement to begin a new business in the name of a recognized company. (p. 60)

franchisee The buyer of a franchise who is given the right to its product, process, or service. The buyer receives the way of operating a business and a product with name recognition. (p. 60)

franchisor The seller of a franchise who is giving the buyer its planning and management expertise. (p. 60)

free enterprise system An economic system in which people have important rights: to make economic choices of what products to buy, to own private property, and to choose to start a business and compete with other businesses. (p. 8)

Free on board (FOB) A delivery term that designates a shipment as delivered free of charge to a buyer. (p. 355)

freight forwarder A company that arranges shipments and prepares necessary exporting paperwork. (p. 81)

functionality The way a product or service works, such as a Web site's features. (p. 113)

GAAP Generally accepted accounting principles established to allow all businesses to use the same system of recording and reporting financial information. (p. 428)

Gantt chart A graphic schedule of a project's phases, activities, and tasks plotted against a time line. (p. 349)

general journal An all-purpose journal that records any business transaction. (p. 432)

general partner A participant in a partnership who has unlimited personal liability and takes full responsibility for managing the business; all partnerships must have at least one general partner. (p. 139)

generic top-level domain (gTLD) The part of a TLD that indicates the type of Web site on the Internet address, such as .com for commercial, .edu for educational, .org for organization, .gov for government, .mil for military, and .biz for business. (p. 133)

geographics The study of the market based on where customers live, including region, state, country, city, and/or area. (p. 118)

global economy The interconnected economies of the nations of the world. (p. 70)

goods Tangible (or physical) products of our economic system that satisfy consumers' wants and needs. (p. 11)

goodwill The favor and loyalty a business acquires by its good reputation. (p. 59)

graphic user interface The design, content, and navigation of a Web site. (p. 87)

Gross Domestic Product (GDP) The total market value of all goods and services produced by workers and capital within a nation during a given period. (p. 14, 72)

groupware Software designed to be used by more than one person at more than one location. (p. 321)

guarantee An assurance of the quality of a product. (p. 220)

historical research The study of the past to explain present circumstances and predict future trends. (p. 121)

horizontal diversification A diversification growth strategy that involves seeking products that are technologically unrelated to a company's own products or business. (p. 501)

horizontal integration Increasing a business's market share and expanding by buying up competitors. (p. 500)

hosted shopping cart A business that offers e-commerce services for a monthly fee; users can upload product information and have their business launched instantly. (p. 151)

hot spot A clickable hyperlink on a Web page; a division of an image map. (p. 379)

human relations The study of how people relate to each other. (p. 315)

human resource management The part of business concerned with recruiting and managing employees; the main goals are to facilitate performance and improve productivity. (p. 382)

human resources The people employed in a business, commonly referred to as *personnel*. (p. 382)

hygiene factor A factor that does not improve a situation, but keeps situations from getting worse. (p. 390)

hyperlink An electronic link that provides direct access from one place in a hypertext document to another place in the same or different hypertext document. (p. 43)

hypertext A system for writing and displaying text that can be linked to related documents. (p. 43)

Hypertext Markup Language (HTML) The code used to structure Web pages and set up hyperlinks between documents. (p. 43)

Hypertext Transfer Protocol (HTTP) A protocol used to request and transmit Web pages. (p. 43)

image map A graphic image on a Web page that is used for navigation. (p. 379)

image The impression people have of a company; a company's personality. (p. 255) The mental picture and feelings people have when thinking about a business or its products or services. (p. 311)

import regulations The rules that govern the types and amounts of products that can be sold, packing that can be used, and taxation. (p. 87)

importing The buying or bringing in goods from other countries to sell. (p. 70)

incentive A reward or advantage that helps businesses, including lower taxes, cheaper land, and employee training programs. (p. 179)

income statement A report of the revenue, expenses, and net income or loss for the accounting period. (p. 437)

incubator An enterprise that is set up to provide flexible and affordable leases, office space, equipment, management assistance, mentoring assistance, and access to financing for new businesses. (p. 186)

independent insurance agent An insurance agent, usually local, who represents multiple insurance companies. (p. 487)

indirect channel The means of delivering a service or product indirectly to the customer, such as through a wholesaler. (p. 105)

industrial market A group of customers who buy goods or services for business use. (p. 118)

industrial park An area set aside in a community for industrial use. (p. 182)

industry A collection of businesses with a common line of products or services. (p. 96, 116)

industry average The standard used to compare costs among companies; usually expressed as a percentage. (p. 266)

inelastic demand Situations in which a change in price has little or no effect on demand for products. (p. 13)

inference-based personalization A data analysis tool that is used to suggest products that are similar to the products a customer has viewed or purchased. (p. 275)

information age The era of history that began in the 1970s when computers became popular with the masses. (p. 25)

information technology (IT) Any technology that is used to communicate or exchange information. (p. 25)

initial public offering (IPO) The sale of stock in a company on a public stock exchange. (p. 418)

Glossary

innovation A new way of doing things; a new idea, method, or device. (p. 50)

instant messaging A software application that allows real-time communication between two or more people through a network. (p. 321)

insurance cost The cost associated with insuring inventory. (p. 331)

integrative growth strategies A growth strategy that allows a company to expand within the industry by growing vertically or horizontally. (p. 499)

intellectual property law The group of laws that regulate the ownership and use of creative works. (p. 154)

intensive distribution Placement of a product in all suitable sales outlets. (p. 211)

intensive growth strategy A growth strategy that takes advantage of an opportunity within a current market, using market penetration, market development, and product development. (p. 496)

intermediary A person or business that is involved in the process of moving a product from the manufacturer or producers to the final users, including wholesalers, retailers, distributors, and agents. (p. 210, 359)

International Business Exchange (IBEX) The electronic commerce system that allows businesses to sell products and services online anywhere in the world. (p. 79)

Internet A global computer network of computer networks that facilitates data transmission and exchange. (p. 43)

Internet Corporation for Assigned Names and Numbers (ICANN) A nonprofit regulatory body that oversees domain registration. (p. 133)

interpreter A person who translates one language into or from another. (p. 77)

intranet An electronic network used to communicate in-house with staff. (p. 25)

investment The amount of money a person puts into his or her business as capital. (p. 31)

invoice An itemized statement of money owed for goods shipped or services rendered. (p. 329)

IP address A unique numeric code that identifies a computer on the Internet. (p. 43)

job description A statement that describes the objectives of a job and its duties and responsibilities (p. 371)

job enlargement The act of increasing the tasks, responsibilities, and scope of a job. (p. 391)

job enrichment The act of making a job more rewarding and less monotonous for the worker by adding elements at a different or higher skill level. (p. 391)

job specification A document that details the abilities, skills, educational level, and experience needed by an employee to perform a job. (p. 371)

journal A financial diary of a business. (p. 432)

journalizing The process of recording business transactions, usually on a daily basis as they occur. (p. 432)

keyword A word or phrase you type in order to begin an online search that then gives you a list of results of the search. (p. 399)

label The part of the package used to present information about the product. (p. 208)

labor union An organization that represents workers in their dealings with employers. (p. 384)

launch The first date on which a business is put into operation, such as a Web site. (p. 113)

layout A floor plan or map that shows the interior and exterior arrangement of a business, including such items as display cases, lighting fixtures, traffic patterns, landscaping, and parking spaces. (p. 187)

lead time The gap in time between placing an order and receiving delivery. (p. 337)

liability A debt of a business. (p. 430)

liability protection Insurance against debt and actions of a business. (p. 137)

license A certificate that shows that the holder of the document has the necessary education and training to perform a job. (p. 159)

limited liability Partial responsibility of a corporate shareholder; he or she is responsible only up to the amount of the individual investment. (p 144)

limited liability company (LLC) A company whose owners and managers have limited liability and some tax benefits, but avoids some restrictions associated with Subchapter S corporations. (p. 145)

limited partner A partner in a business whose liability is limited to his or her investment; a limited partner cannot be actively involved in managing the business. (p. 140)

line of credit An arrangement whereby a lender agrees to lend up to a specific amount of money at a certain interest rate for a specific period of time. (p. 410)

line organization A form of business organization where managers are responsible for accomplishing the main objectives of the business and are in the direct chain of command. Top management makes the decisions that affect the entire company; middle management implements the decisions; supervisory, or first-line, management supervises the activities of employees; and employees carry out the plans made by top and middle management. (p. 370)

line-and-staff organization A form of business organization that incorporates staff into line organization. (p. 370)

logistics The planning, execution, and control of the movement and placement of people and/or goods, part of distribution management. (p.353)

management-by-objectives A management technique in which employees are involved in setting their own objectives and gauging their own progress. (p. 394)

manager A person who is responsible for directing and controlling the work and personnel of a business, or a particular department within a business. (p. 307)

markdown The amount of money taken off an original price. (p. 244)

market A group of people or companies who have a demand for a product or service and are willing and able to buy it. (p. 118)

market development An attempt by a business to reach new locations for its products. (p. 498)

market penetration An attempt to increase sales in a business's current market. (p. 498)

market positioning The act of identifying a specific market niche for a product. (p. 126)

market research The collection and analysis of information aimed at understanding the behavior of consumers in a certain market. (p. 119)

market segment Subgroup of buyers with similar characteristics, segmented by geographics, demographics, psychographics, and buying characteristics. (p. 118)

market segmentation The process of grouping a market into smaller subgroups defined by specific characteristics. (p. 118)

market share A portion of the total sales generated by all competing companies in a given market. (p. 126)

market structure The nature and degree of competition among businesses operating in the same industry; market structure affects market price. (p. 9)

marketing mix The five marketing strategies used to reach a market: product, place, price, promotion, and people. (p. 207)

marketing objective What a business wants to accomplish through its marketing efforts, such as market share, projected profitability, and pricing. (p. 207)

marketing plan A plan used by a business to guide its marketing process to a desired conclusion based on information obtained through market research and target market decisions. (p. 206)

marketing tactic An activity that needs to be taken to carry out a marketing plan; part of an action plan. (p. 215)

markup The amount added to the cost of an item to cover expenses and ensure a profit. (p. 242)

mass marketing The attempt to reach all customers with a single marketing plan. (p. 125)

merchant account A bank account that enables a business to receive the proceeds of credit card purchases. (p. 251)

meta tags Information coded within the HTML programming of a Web page. (p. 399)

metrics Methods used to measure activity and progress, such as those on a Web site; metrics software can measure number of visitors, time of day the site is most active, and which products receive the most hits. (p. 113)

mission statement A declaration of the specific aspirations of a company, the major goals for which it will strive. (p. 102)

model inventory A target inventory of what a business thinks it will need to keep in stock. (p. 325)

monopoly A market structure in which a particular commodity has only one seller. (p. 9)

morale A state of an individual psychological well-being based on a sense of confidence, usefulness, and purpose. (p. 294)

motivating factor A factor that motivates employees, such as achievement, recognition, responsibility, advancement, growth, and the reward from doing the work itself. (p. 390)

multiple-unit pricing A pricing technique in which items are priced in multiples, such as 3 items for 99 cents. (p. 238)

navigation The act of moving around a Web site by clicking on hypertext links. (p. 175)

need A basic requirement for survival. (p. 11)

negligence The failure to exercise reasonable care. (p. 482)

net profit on sales ratio The number of cents left from each dollar of sales after expenses and income taxes are paid. (p. 454)

netiquette The code of conduct that governs online behavior. (p. 299)

networking The process of building and maintaining informal relationships with people whose friendship could bring business opportunities. (p. 315)

newsgroup A Web-based forum on a specific topic where users can post messages and reply to other users. (p. 511)

new venture organization The infrastructure or foundation that supports all the products, processes, and services of a new business. (p. 20)

news release A brief newsworthy story that is sent to the media. (p. 261)

niche A small, specialized segment of the market based on customer needs discovered in market research. (p. 50, 126)

nonprofit corporation A legal entity that makes money for reasons other than the owner's profit. It can make a profit, but the profit must remain within the company and not be distributed to shareholders. (p. 145)

nonverbal communication Communication not involving words, transmitted through actions and behaviors, such as facial expressions, gestures, posture, and eye contact. (p. 315)

objection Any concern, hesitation, doubt, or other reason a customer has for not making a purchase. (p. 284)

obsolescence cost The cost associated with products or materials that become obsolete while in inventory. (p. 331)

odd/even pricing A pricing technique in which odd-numbered prices are used to suggest bargains, such as $19.99. (p. 238)

oligopoly A market structure in which there are just a few competing firms. (p. 9)

online auction An auction that takes place on a Web site such as eBay. (p. 151)

online business A company that conducts business by means of the Internet. (p. 47)

online customer service The service businesses provide to customers via the Internet. (p. 425)

online form A Web page that accepts user input. (p. 493)

online survey A form of market research that appears on Web sites in which users respond to questions or provide opinions. (p. 493)

open-source software Software applications that are distributed free of charge; a number of e-commerce shopping cart programs are available as open-source software. (p. 151)

operating capital Money a business uses to support its operations in the short term. (p. 410)

operating ratio The relationship between each expense and total sales as reported on the income statement. (p. 455)

operational plan A short-term objective that helps achieve a tactical plan, including policies, rules and regulations, and budgets for day-to-day operations. (p. 308)

opportunity An idea that has commercial value when consumers are ready and willing to buy that product. (p. 20)

opportunity cost The cost associated with giving up the use of money tied up in inventory. (p. 330)

opt-in list An online mailing list made up of subscribers who have given permission to be sent e-mail by the mailing list owner. (p. 299)

opt-out list An online mailing list to which recipients do not choose to subscribe; recipients must complete an online form or send an e-mail if they choose not to receive mailings. (p. 299)

order getting Seeking out buyers and giving them a well-organized presentation; sometimes referred to as "creative selling." (p. 279)

order taking The completion of a sale to a customer who has sought out a product. (p. 279)

organizing The grouping of resources in combinations that will help you reach your objectives. (p. 309)

outsourcing Hiring people and other companies to handle tasks a business can not do or chooses not to do itself. (p. 48, 345)

owner's equity The total amount of assets minus total liabilities; the worth of a business. (p. 430)

package The physical container or wrapper used to present information. (p. 208)

partnership An unincorporated business with two or more owners who share the decisions, assets, liabilities, and profits. (p. 139)

patent A document that grants to an inventor the right to exclude others from making, using, or selling an invention or other intellectual property during the term of the patent. (p. 155)

patent pending The status of an invention between the time a patent application has been filed and when it is issued or rejected. (p. 156)

payment gateway Software that automatically processes credit-card information so that it does not have to be manually typed in. (p. 199)

pay-per-click A search engine payment model in which companies only pay for clicks to the destination site through the search engine site based on a prearranged rate. (p. 399)

pay-per-performance A search engine payment model in which companies pay a fee to be listed at the top of the search results page. (p. 399)

penetration pricing A method used to build sales by charging a low initial price to keep unit costs to customers as low as possible. (p. 237)

performance bond Insurance coverage that protects a business if work or a contract is not finished on time or as agreed. (p. 486)

performance evaluation The process of judging how well an employee has performed the duties and responsibilities associated with a job. (p. 394)

permit A legal document giving official permission to run a business. (p. 159)

personal selling Selling conducted by direct communication with a prospective customer. (p. 278)

personalization The process of tailoring Web pages to individual users' characteristics. (p. 275)

PERT diagram A project schedule that is arranged in a diagram used for scheduling more-complex projects. (p. 350)

philanthropy The act of making charitable donations to improve the welfare of society. (p. 514)

piece rate A means of compensation based on an amount per unit produced. (p. 374)

planning The act of setting goals, developing strategies, and outlining tasks and timelines to meet those goals. (p. 308)

policy A statement of guiding principles and procedures that serves as a guideline for daily business operations and supports the company's goals and objectives. (p. 362)

position The place a search engine falls on the result list in a Web search. (p. 399)

posting The process of transferring amounts from the general journal to accounts in the general ledger. (p. 433)

preapproach The marketing activities that precede a salesperson's approach to a prospective customer that are intended to help achieve a successful sale. (p. 284)

Pregnancy Discrimination Act A federal law that requires that employers treat their pregnant employees like all other employees when determining benefits. (p. 387)

premium Any item of value that a customer receives in addition to the good or service purchased; designed to attract new customers or build loyalty among existing customers, they may include coupons and gifts. (p. 262) The price of insurance a person or business pays for a specified risk for a specified time. (p. 485)

preselling The act of influencing potential customers to buy before contact is actually made. (p. 256)

prestige pricing A pricing technique in which higher-than-average prices are used to suggest status and prestige to the customer. (p. 238)

price discrimination The charging of different prices for the same product or service in different markets or to different customers. (p. 165)

price fixing An illegal practice in which competing companies agree, formally or informally, to restrict prices within a specified range. (p. 232)

price gouging Pricing above the market when no other retailer is available. (p. 232)

price lining A pricing technique in which items in a certain category are priced the same. (p. 238)

price skimming The practice of charging a high price on a new product or service in order to recover costs and maximize profits as quickly as possible; the price is then dropped when the product or service is no longer unique. (p. 237)

primary data Information that is collected for the first time, is current, and relates directly to the collector's study. (p. 122)

privacy policy A statement on a Web site that explains how a company collects, uses, protects, and shares a customer's personal information. (p. 275)

private brand A brand that is owned and initiated by a wholesaler or retailer. (p. 220)

private carrier A business that operates vehicles primarily for the purpose of transporting its own products and materials. (p. 354)

private exchange An exchange that is operated for exclusive use of a single company, for example a company that sets up an exchange to deal with vendors for all the parts and services it uses each day. (p. 341)

private key A password that unscrambles or decrypts an electronic message; this key is kept secret. (p. 469)

private placement A private offering or sale of securities directly to a limited number of institutional investors who meet certain suitability standards; ownership interests are called *securities*. (p. 418, 506)

pro forma Proposed or estimated financial statements based on predictions of how the actual operations of the business will turn out. (p. 413)

product development The process of creating new or improved products, involving taking an idea for a product, designing it, building a model, and testing it. (p. 344)

product liability insurance Insurance coverage that protects a business from injury claims that result from use of the business's products. (p. 486)

product mix All the products a company makes or sells. (p. 209)

product positioning How consumers see a product in comparison to another product, achieved through quality, availability, pricing, and uses. (p. 209)

productivity A measure of how much a business produces in a given time, or the output of each worker per unit of time. (p. 352)

profile A set of characteristics or qualities that identifies a type or category of person. (p. 35)

profit Money that is left over after all expenses of running a business have been deducted from the income. (p. 8)

project organization A temporary organization brought together from different parts of a business for a special project. (p. 371)

promotional mix The combination of different promotional elements that a company uses to reach and influence potential customers. (p. 257)

promotional pricing A pricing technique in which lower prices are offered for a limited period of time to stimulate sales. (p. 238)

prospect A potential customer. (p. 278)

prospecting A systematic approach to developing new sales leads or customers, who are identified through referrals, public records, or surveys. (p. 284)

prospectus A formal document that details risks involving in the private offering; its purpose is to give investors the information they need to make informed decisions. (p. 506)

prototype A working model used by entrepreneurs to determine what it takes to develop their products or services. (p. 97, 346)

psychographics The study of consumers based on social and psychological characteristics, including personality, values, opinions, beliefs, motivations, attitudes, and lifestyle elements. (p. 118)

psychological pricing A pricing technique, most often used by retail businesses, that is based on the belief that customers' perceptions of a product are strongly influenced by price; it includes prestige pricing, odd/even pricing, price lining, promotional pricing, multiple-unit pricing, and bundle pricing. (p. 237)

public domain Intellectual property whose protection has expired; it belongs to the community at large and people can use any aspect of the property free of charge. (p. 155)

public exchange A business-to-business network open to any company that wants to take part; there is usually a fee to join the exchange. (p. 341)

public key A password that scrambles or encrypts an electronic message so that if it is intercepted it will be unreadable; this key is shared. (p. 469)

public key encryption A message-encoding system that uses two digital keys: public key and private key. (p. 469)

public relations Activities designed to create goodwill toward a business or control damage done by negative publicity. (p. 261)

public stock offering The sale of shares of stock on a public stock exchange. (p. 507)

publicity Placement in the media of newsworthy items about a company, product, or person. (p. 260)

purchasing Also known as procurement, the buying of all the materials needed by the organization. (p. 324)

pure risk The threat of a loss to a business without any possibility of gain, such as robbery or employee theft. (p. 477)

quality circle A small group of employees who do similar jobs and meet regularly to identify ways to improve the quality of what they do. (p. 351)

quality control The process of making sure the goods or services a business produces meet certain standards, such as appearance, performance, and consistency. (p. 350)

quality control program A set of measures built into the production process to make sure that products or services meet certain standards and performance requirements. (p. 310)

quantity discount A discount that a vendor gives to a buyer who places large orders. (p. 327)

quick ratio A measure of the relationship between short-term liquid assets, which include cash and accounts receivable, and current liabilities. (p. 456)

ratio analysis The comparison of two or more amounts on a financial statement and the evaluation of the relationship between these two amounts, used to determine the financial strength, activity, or bill-paying ability of a business. (p. 452)

rational buying motive A conscious, logical reason to make a purchase, such as convenience or comfort. (p. 281)

real time The actual time that something takes place. (p. 87)

real-time transaction A process that instantly transfers funds from buyer to seller. (p. 199)

rebate A return of part of the purchase price of a product used as an incentive for customers to purchase the product. (p. 263)

reciprocal linking An agreement between two Webmasters to place hyperlinks on their own Web sites leading to each other's Web site. (p. 447)

Glossary

recruit To bring in prospective employees; businesses use classified ads, employment agencies, and other placement offices to find potential employees. (p. 373)

registrar A company that manages lists of Web site domains and their owners. (p. 133)

resale price maintenance Price fixing imposed by a manufacturer on wholesale or retail resellers of its products to deter price-based competition. (p. 232)

résumé A summary of academic and work history, skills, and experience of a prospective employee. (p. 372)

return on investment (ROI) The amount earned as a result of an investment. (p. 234)

return policy A policy that establishes the conditions under which items that have been ordered, shipped, or delivered may be returned. (p. 367)

rework policy A policy that establishes conditions under which items will be reworked, that is doing something again because it was not done right the first time. (p. 367)

risk capital Money invested in companies where there is financial risk. (p. 408)

robbery The taking of property by force or threat, usually by means of a weapon. (p. 480)

role model A person with attitudes and achievements that others wish to emulate. (p. 33)

rule A standard set forth to guide behavior and actions; a rule tells employees exactly what they should and should not do. (p. 363)

rules-based personalization A data analysis tool that is used to recommend products that go with products a customer has viewed or purchased on a Web site. (p. 275)

safety stock A cushion of products or materials that prevents a business from running out of inventory while waiting for an order. (p. 337)

salary A fixed amount of pay an employee receives for each week, month, or year the employee works. (p. 291, 374)

sales call report An account of sales activities, including such items as number of calls made, orders obtained, and miles traveled. (p. 292)

sales check A written record of a sales transaction. (p. 287)

sales force A group of employees involved in the selling process. (p. 279)

sales force automation Tools that automate the business tasks of sales, such as order processing, contact management, lead tracking, and inventory control. (p. 425)

sales forecast An estimate of sales for a given period, such as the next quarter. (p. 288)

sales planning The process that involves determining the goals and timing of sales efforts. (p. 288)

sales quota A performance goal assigned to a salesperson for a specific period. (p. 290)

sales territory A geographical area in which existing and potential customers are grouped. (p. 289)

scarcity The difference between demand and supply; limited resources. (p. 11)

screen reader A device that reads a Web site's content aloud, especially important for persons with visual impairments. (p. 529)

search engine An online software application that creates indexes of Internet sites based on the titles of files, keywords, or the full text of files. (p. 399)

secondary data Information that been collected by someone else. (p. 121)

secured fund A form of guaranteed payment, such as a credit card, a cashier's check, a wire transfer, or cash. (p. 328)

security certificate A credential issued by a third-party company that assures the user that all transactions made on a Web site are private and safe. (p. 199)

selective distribution Placement of a product where its number of sales outlets are limited in an area. (p. 211)

selling price The actual or projected price per unit. (p. 241)

service mark A word, symbol, sign, or color that describes a service business. (p. 158)

services Intangible (nonphysical) products that satisfy consumers' wants and needs. (p. 11, 47)

shareholder An owner of shares of stock in a corporation. (p. 144)

shrinkage cost The cost associated with the loss of inventory items that are broken, damaged, spoiled, or stolen. (p. 331)

site layout The design of a Web site. (p. 175)

situational management The style of adapting the management approach to particular circumstances. (p. 313)

Small Business Administration (SBA) The federal agency that provides services to small businesses and new entrepreneurs, including counseling, publications, and financial aid. (p. 107)

smart card An electronic prepaid cash card that includes a computer chip that can store data; used to make purchases or financial transactions over the Internet. (p. 251)

social responsibility The principle that companies should contribute to the welfare of society and not be solely devoted to maximizing profits. (p. 514)

sole proprietorship A business that is owned and operated by one person. (p. 136)

spam Unsolicited commercial e-mail. (p. 299)

specialty item An advertising device that includes giveaways, such as pens, T-shirts, and caps, printed with a business name or logo that serve as a reminder of a business. (p. 260)

specialty magazine A periodical published for people with special interests, such as sports, camping, fashion, and a variety of other areas. (p. 55)

speculative risk Risk that is inherent to a business, involving the chance of either profit or loss. (p. 476)

staff The managers and others who provide support and advice to line managers, such as accounting, legal, and training activities. (p. 370)

Standard Industrial Trade Classification (SITC) codes A system that details the kinds of products that are traded in specific countries and how well certain products do in different marketplaces. (p. 79)

start-up resources The capital, skilled labor, management expertise, legal and financial advice, facility, equipment, and customers needed to start a business. (p. 20)

statement of cash flows A report of how much cash a business took in and where the cash went. (p. 440)

sticky content The information and features on a Web site that gives users a compelling reason to visit it. (p. 199)

stock A type of security that signifies ownership in a corporation and represents a claim on part of the corporation's assets and earnings. (p. 418)

storage cost The cost associated with renting or buying space needed to store inventory.(p. 330)

strategic alliance A partnership formed among two or more companies. (p. 49)

strategic plan A long-range objective based on long-term goals used to map out a business for three to five years. (p. 308)

Subchapter S corporation A corporation that is taxed like a partnership; profits are taxed only once at the shareholder's personal tax rate. These corporations can have only one class of stock. (p. 144)

suggestion selling Selling additional goods to a customer to go along with a product or products the customer purchases. (p. 284)

supply The amount of goods or services that producers are willing to provide. (p. 13)

sweepstakes A simple game of chance used by a business to get customers interested in what the company has to offer. (p. 263)

SWOT analysis A strategic planning technique that analyzes a company's strengths, weaknesses, opportunities and threats in the external sales environment. (p. 293)

synergistic diversification A diversification growth strategy that involves finding new products or businesses that are technologically compatible with a company's products or business. (p. 501)

table A data structure that is used to organize Web-page elements spatially, making it possible to easily create complex page layouts. (p. 379)

tactical plan A midrange objective that focuses on a period of one year or less, built on specific objectives with target dates. (p. 308)

target customer One most likely to buy a business's products and services. (p. 96)

target market A specific group of customers whom a business wishes to reach. (p. 118)

tariff A type of trade barrier imposed by a government as a tax on imported or exported goods. (p. 71)

team building The act of encouraging teamwork through activities designed to foster respect, trust, cooperation, camaraderie, and communication among employees. (p. 312)

technology infrastructure All the hardware and software used to support electronic communication, as well as satellites, fiber-optic networks, telephone wire, and so on. (p. 25)

telecommute To work outside an office on a computer linked to the workplace via a modem. (p. 321)

telecommuting The act of performing some or all of a job away from the business. (p. 393)

template A file that establishes the format and appearance of a Web page. (p. 227)

Theory X An assumption that states the belief that employees are basically lazy and need constant supervision. (p. 389)

Theory Y An assumption that states the belief that employees are responsible, like to work, and want intrinsic rewards. (p. 389)

time management The process of allocating time effectively. (p. 316)

top-level domain (TLD) The most general part of a domain name in an Internet address. (p. 133)

trade area The region or section of the community from which a business draws customers. (p. 181)

trade association An organization made up of individuals and businesses in a specific industry that works to promote that industry. (p. 108)

trade barrier A restriction on goods entering or leaving a country. (p. 71)

trade credit Credit one business grants to another business for the purchase of goods or services; a source of short-term financing provided by one business within another business's industry or trade. (p. 410)

trade discount A discount from the list price of an item allowed by a manufacturer or wholesaler to a merchant. (p. 327)

trade intermediary An agency that serves as a distributor in a foreign country. (p. 81)

trade magazine A periodical published for a specific type of business or industry. (p. 55)

trade mission An opportunity offered by the U.S. government and private agencies to small businesses to travel to other countries in order to meet and talk with foreign agents, distributors, or potential business partners. (p. 79)

trade show A gathering or exhibition where vendors and manufacturers introduce new items and promote established products and services. (p. 55)

trademark A word, symbol, design, or color that a business uses to identify itself or something it sells; it is followed by the registered trademark symbol ™. (p. 158)

translation The process of changing one written communication into a second language with the same meaning. (p. 87)

turnkey A preprogrammed and ready-to-operate e-commerce hosted site. (p. 227)

Uniform Commercial Code (UCC) A group of laws that regulates commercial business transactions. (p. 167)

uniform resource locator (URL) A series of letters and/or numbers specifying the precise location of a specific document on the Web. (p. 43)

unit pricing The pricing of goods on the basis of cost per unit of measure, such as a pound or an ounce, in addition to the price per item. (p. 232)

unlimited liability Full responsibility for all debts and actions of a business. (p. 138)

usage rate How quickly inventory will be used in a given period of time. (p. 337)

value chain The distribution channel through which a product or service flows from the producer to the customer. (p. 99)

values The beliefs and principles by which you choose to live that define who you are, shape your attitudes and choices, and help you identify your priorities. (p. 57)

variable Costs and expenses that are subject to change depending on the number of units sold. (p. 230)

variable expense A business expense that changes with each unit of product produced, such as supplies, wages, and production materials. (p. 459)

vendor A business that sells inventory to a merchant. (p. 325)

venture A new business undertaking that involves risk. (p. 6)

venture capital A source of equity financing for small businesses with exceptional growth potential and experienced senior management. (p. 409)

venture capitalist An individual investor or investment firm that invests venture capital professionally. (p. 409)

vertical integration The merging of companies that are in the same distribution chain of a product, either by acquiring suppliers upstream in the distribution channel or acquiring distribution outlets downstream in the channel. (p. 499)

viral marketing A marketing technique that uses customers to promote a product. (p. 447)

virtual store An online storefront that allows entrepreneurs to sell products they do not own. The Web site is maintained and provided by the distributor or manufacturer of the product. (p. 151)

vision statement A declaration of the scope and purpose of a company. (p. 102)

wages An amount of money an employee receives for every hour he or she works. (p. 374)

want Something that you do not have to have for survival, but would like to have. (p. 11)

warehousing The act of holding and handling goods in a warehouse. (p. 336)

warranty of merchantability A guarantee on the quality of goods or services purchased that is not written down or explicitly spoken. (p. 167)

Web affiliate A company that aims to drive targeted traffic to a Web site, usually an e-commerce merchant, usually for a commission for the sales they generate on the merchant site. (p. 359)

Web browser A software program used to view Web pages. (p. 43)

Web designer A person who plans the aesthetic and navigational aspects of a Web site. (p. 227)

Web developer A person who programs a Web site from a technical standpoint. (p. 227)

Web host A business that provides server space and file maintenance services for Web sites controlled by businesses that do not have their own Web servers. (p. 113)

Web server A computer that delivers Web pages. (p.113)

work team A group of employees assigned a task without direct supervision and with responsibility for their results. (p. 394)

workers' compensation insurance Insurance that is required by the government and paid for by employers to provide medical and income benefits to employees injured on the job, or for job-related illnesses. (p. 486)

working capital The amount of cash needed to carry out the daily operations of a business that ensures a positive cash flow after covering all operating expenses. (p. 419, 454)

workstation An area in a business with equipment for a single worker. (p. 190)

World Wide Web A vast collection of Web pages that can be read, viewed, and interacted with via computers. (p. 43)

World Wide Web Consortium (W3C) An organization that produces standards for the World Wide Web. (p. 529)

wrongful termination The right of an employee to sue his or her employer for damages if he or she is terminated for an unacceptable reason. (p. 163)

WYSIWYG An acronym that stands for "What You See Is What You Get;" the software used by Web authors that enables them to design their page visually, without having to learn HTML. (p. 379)

Index

Index

Credits

PHOTO CREDITS

Atlantide S.N.C./Age Fotostock **10**(bc); Paul Barton/CORBIS **TM7, TM40, x, 140, 204–205**; Peter Beavis/Getty Images **219**; Ed Bock/CORBIS **127**(c), **335**(cl), **365**(br); Leslye Borden/PhotoEdit **157**(t); Sky Borillo/PhotoEdit **262**(b); Tim Boyle/Getty Images **262**(t), **365**(tcl), **367**; Robert Brenner/PhotoEdit **484**; Rex Butcher/Getty Images **279**; Ken Chernus/Getty Images **512–513**, **xvii**; Mike Chew/CORBIS **168**; Steve Chenn/CORBIS **53**(b); Nick Clements/Getty Images **78**(c); Jim Craigmyle/CORBIS **415**; Jim Cummins/Getty Images **410**; Darama/CORBIS **393**(bl); Dex Images, Inc./CORBIS **365**(bcl); Lon C. Diehl/PhotoEdit **10**(t), **34, 246**(b); George Disario/CORBIS **vii**, **44–45**; Mark Douet/Getty Images **365**(tc); Jim Erickson/CORBIS **494–495**; Robert Essel NYC/CORBIS **80**; Susan Van Etten/PhotoEdit **192**(cl); Randy Faris/CORBIS **95**; Najlah Feanny/CORBIS SABA **252–253**; Jon Feingersh/CORBIS **402–403**; Jon Feingersh/Masterfile **TM38, 314**(t); Jay Freis/Getty Images **276–277**; Tony Freeman/PhotoEdit **354**(b), **480**; Rick Friedman/CORBIS **391**; Spencer Grant/PhotoEdit **331**; Garry Gay/Getty images **270**; Getty Images **74, 160, 188, 263**(t), **363**; Glencoe/McGraw-Hill **158**; Spencer Grant/PhotoEdit **120, 192**(t); Jeff Green/Reuters/CORBIS **61**; Jeff Greenberg/PhotoEdit **202–203, 263**(br), **263**(cl); Charles Gupton/CORBIS **2–3, 407**; George Hall/CORBIS **71**; Chris Hamilton/Corbis **TM41, 387**; Bruce Hands/Getty Images **354**(c); Ken Hawkins/CORBIS SYGMA **518**(tcl); John Henley/CORBIS **viii, 92–93**; Frank Herholdt/Getty Images **314**(b); Jack Hollingsworth/CORBIS **266**; J. M. Horrillo/Age Fotostock **460**(bl); Chase Jarvis/CORBIS **282**(t); Steven W. Jones/Getty Images **310**; Wolfgang Kaehler/CORBIS **238**; Bonnie Kamin/PhotoEdit **38**(t); Michael Keller/CORBIS **127**(b); Kim Kulish/CORBIS **351**; John Lamb/Getty Images **38**(b); Kevin Lamarque/Reuters/CORBIS **416**; Javier Larrea/Age Fotostock **114–115**; Lisette Le Bon/SuperStock **30**; David Lees/Getty Images **90–91**; George D. Lepp/CORBIS **184**; James Leynse/CORBIS **497**(cr); Yang Liu/CORBIS **106**(c); R. Ian Lloyd/Masterfile **192**(cr); Ed Malitsky/CORBIS **497**(bl); Lawrence Manning/CORBIS **68–69**; Don Mason/CORBIS **232**; Masterfile **4, 292**; David McNew/Getty Images **325**; Darren Modricker/CORBIS **307**; Gail Mooney/CORBIS **146**(cl); Warren Morgan/CORBIS **314**(c); Michael Newman/PhotoEdit **176–177, 479**(bc), **479**(tl), **518**(br); Steve Niedorf Photography/Getty Images **283**; Jonathan Nourok/PhotoEdit **282**(cl), **335**(tl); Scott Olson/Getty Images **208, 236**(t); Gabe Palmer/CORBIS **vi, 4–5, 505**; Lori Adamski Peek/Getty Images **146**(br); Jose L. Pelaez/CORBIS **xv, 78**(b), **404–405**; Eric Perlman/CORBIS **19**; Photomondo/Getty Images **393**(cr); PM Images/Getty Images **xi, 228–229**; Andreas Pollok/Getty Images **47**; Benelux Press/Getty Images **335**(br); Premier Snowskate **429**; Tom Prettyman/PhotoEdit **497**(t); Reuters/CORBIS **29, 516**; Mark Richards/PhotoEdit **38**(cl); John A. Rizzo/Age Fotostock **460**(cl); Royalty-free/Banana Stock/Age Fotostock **181**; Royalty-free/BananaStock/PictureQuest **380–381**; Royalty-free/Brand X Pictures/Getty Images **146**(t), **157**(b); Royalty-free/Comstock Images/Getty Images **393**(t); Royalty-free/CORBIS **TM38, TM48, xii, xiii, 38**(cr), **217**(b), **217**(t), **221, 282**(br), **290, 293, 304–305, 322–323, 342–343, 408, 420**(bcr), **426–427**; Royalty-free/Digital Vision/Getty Images **ix, 134–135, 522**; Royalty-free/Getty Images **384**; Royalty-free/Getty Images/Veer **26–27**; Royalty-free/Photodisc/Getty Images **xvi, 10**(bc), **106**(t), **236**(b), **448–449, 460**(cr), **479**(tc); Royalty-free/Pixtal/Age Fotostock **419, 420**(tcr), **518**(t); Royalty-free/Pixtal/SuperStock **10**(tc); Anders Ryman/CORBIS **53**(c); Dan Sams/Getty Images **479**(bc); Chuck Savage/CORBIS **TM58, xviii, 217**(c), **302–303**; Alan Schein Photography/CORBIS **354**(t); David Schmidt/Masterfile **53**(t), **374**; Clayton Sharrard/PhotoEdit **420**(tc); Juan Manuel Silva/Age Fotostock **106**(b); Ariel Skelley/CORBIS **152–153, 472–473**; Paul A. Souders/CORBIS **474–475**; Tom Stewart/CORBIS **127**(t), **256**; Strauss/Curtis/CORBIS **55**; LWA-Dann Tardif/CORBIS **328**; William Taufic/CORBIS **212**; Tom Wagner/CORBIS SABA **78**(t); LWA-Stephen Welstead/CORBIS **157**(c); Randy Wells/Getty Images **7**; David Young-Wolff/PhotoEdit **108, 192**(b), **243, 460**(tr); Keith Wood/CORBIS **335**(cr); Jeff Zaruba/CORBIS **xiv, 360–361**; Bo Zaunders/CORBIS **231**.

SCREEN CAPTURE CREDITS

Alienware Corporation **96**; Fairytale Brownies, Inc. **458**; GSI Commerce. Inc. **515**; Kate Spade, LLC **500**; Salesforce.com, Inc. **285**; Zappos.com, Inc. **145**